The Battle for the Catholic Mind

The Battle for the Catholic Mind

Catholic Faith and Catholic Intellect in the
Work of the Fellowship of Catholic Scholars
1978–95

Edited and introduced by
William E. May and Kenneth D. Whitehead

ST. AUGUSTINE'S PRESS
South Bend, Indiana
2001

published in association with
The Fellowship of Catholic Scholars

Library of Congress Cataloging in Publication Data
The battle for the Catholic mind : Catholic faith and Catholic intellect
in the work of the Fellowship of Catholic Scholars, 1978–95 / edited and
introduced by William E. May and Kenneth D. Whitehead.
          p.   cm.
          "Published in association with the Fellowship of Catholic Scholars."
          Includes bibliographical references.
          ISBN 1-890318-06-X (alk. paper)
          1. Catholic Church – Doctrines – Congresses. I. May, William E.,
          1928- II. Whitehead, K. D. III. Fellowship of Catholic Scholars.
     BX1751.2 .B29 2000
     230'.2 – dc21   00-008718

∞ *The paper used in this publication meets the minimum requirements of the
American National Standard for Information Sciences—Permanence of Paper for Printed Materials, ANSI Z39.48-1984.*

Contents

Introduction

William E. May and Kenneth D. Whitehead

Any collection of scholarly articles dedicated to the Catholic intellectual life in recent years cannot help reflecting the fact that the years since the Second Vatican Council have been, in many ways, as eventful for the Catholic life of the mind as perhaps any comparable period in the Church's history. There has been, first of all, the enormous spectacle which the world has afforded to the believing Christian during this period. This has included, for example, the gradual dissolution and collapse of the Communist empire, once thought to be the Catholic Church's greatest historical adversary, if not the anti-Christ *tout court*; and this decline of Communism has been paralleled by a precipitous and steady decline in belief and morality and active Christian practice in Europe and the Americas, the very regions which once constituted the core of historic Christendom and hence also constituted the Church's special provinces.

Today widespread cultural decadence and a stark decline in personal morality in the formerly Christian West have reached the point where the very moral foundations of a free society based on the rule of law appear to have been seriously undermined. Perhaps Communism was not the major enemy of the faith, after all; certainly it has not been the only enemy. Meanwhile, the usual "wars and rumors of wars" (Matthew 24:6; Mark 13:7) have gone on more or less unabated but, it would seem, with particular violence today owing both to the advance of modern military technology and to the intensity of modern ideological rivalry.

At the same time, for the Catholic, and especially for the Catholic scholar, there has been the epochal experience of the Second Vatican Council and its aftermath. By any standard, Vatican Council II was one of the most important religious events of the twentieth century. No less a personage than President Charles De Gaulle of France once remarked that it was the most important event of any kind in the twentieth century. The Council, the twenty-first ecumenical council in the long history of the Church, brought together more than 2,500 Catholic bishops from around the world at the end of each of the four successive years between 1962 and 1965 to deliberate and debate and decide about a host of issues important to the future of the Church and of the world. Once they were given their charge, they did debate and deliberate and decide, and in a very creative and even formidable way. The Church could never be the same again; the Church has not been the same since. As if to underline the great importance of the Council, each one of the three popes elected during or following the time of the Council, Pope Paul VI, Pope John Paul I, and Pope John Paul II, promptly and decisively declared as his first official act the dedication of his entire pontificate to the fulfillment of nothing else but the aims of the Second Vatican Council.

Pope John XXIII had originally called the Second Vatican Council in 1959 for four major purposes which he clearly set forth, both in his 1961 apostolic constitution *Humanae Salutis* convoking the Council, and in his famous 1962 Opening Speech to the Council. These purposes can be summarized in the following four points, which Pope Paul VI promptly re-iterated and re-affirmed in his inaugural address to the second session of the Council in 1963: the Council was convoked in order (1) to bring the Church up to date in a rapidly changing world (*"aggiornamento"*), *(2) to complete the Catholic process of self-understanding begun at the First Vatican Council nearly a century earlier in 1870, (3) to promote reunion with non-Catholic Christians in an increasingly secularized and unbelieving world,* and (4) to enable the Church to reach out more effectively to that same de-Christianized world with the perennial message of the Gospel.

Pope John XXIII thrilled the world with hope in his magnificent Opening Speech to the Council in October, 1962, when he declared: "To mankind, oppressed by so many difficulties, the Church says, as Peter said to the poor who begged alms from him: `I have neither gold nor silver, but what I have I give you; in the name of Jesus Christ of Nazareth, rise and walk' (Acts 3:6)."

In view of the way the Council later came to be misinterpreted, it is also worth recalling, along with the above four major purposes of the Council, what Pope John XXIII called in his Opening Speech "the greatest concern of the ecumenical Council." This greatest concern, he said, was that "the sacred deposit of Christian doctrine" confided to the Church "should be guarded and taught more efficaciously." Sacred Deposit? Doctrine? How in the world was "doctrine" supposed to help renew the Church and the world?

Quite simply, of course, the answer is that the Church believes that the doctrine which she teaches and which has been handed down in the Church from the time of the apostles, even as it has been developed and elaborated upon during those same centuries, represents nothing else but "saving truth... revealed for the salvation of all peoples," as Vatican II itself affirmed (*Dei Verbum* #7). Not just for Catholics, but for "all peoples." Since the Council, however, the world has witnessed many rather strenuous efforts, both theoretical and practical, and both inside and outside the Catholic Church, to downgrade the relevance of Catholic doctrine generally and, especially, to obscure or deny that what the Church's God-given Magisterium declares to be authentic Catholic doctrine is indeed such. It is therefore salutary to recall the centrality of Catholic doctrine and the Church's living Magisterium which authentically expounds it in the mind and discourse of the same Pope John XXIII who was inspired to convoke an ecumenical council in order to set the Catholic Church on the road to renewal.

In the same Opening Speech to the Council in which he disagreed with what he called the modern "prophets of doom" and affirmed that the Church better meet "the needs of the present day by demonstrating the validity of her teaching rather than by condemnations," this pontiff, so fondly remembered for his optimism and joviality, also affirmed that "in calling this vast assembly of bishops, the latest and humble successor to the Prince of the Apostles who is addressing you [has] intended to assert once again the Magisterium (teaching authority), which is unfailing and perdures until the end of time, in order that this Magisterium, taking into account the errors, the requirements, and the opportunities of our time, might be presented in exceptional form to all men throughout the world."

The presentation of the Church's Magisterium to all men throughout the world a main concern of the Council? That is indeed what the pope said. In its origins and intentions, then, Vatican II clearly represented no departure from the Catholic tradition; rather, it represented a strong reaffirmation of it. This also proved to be true of its results. Sixteen documents issued from the Council. These, along with a veritable flood of subsequent postconciliar implementing documents issued by the Holy See (including the entire revised 1983 Code of Canon Law), have collectively brought about one of the most thoroughgoing internal reforms in the Church's history. Her entire liturgy and her rites for the administration of the sacra-ments, for example, as well as many other reforms in Church practices and procedures, have all been systematically revised since the Council. The Church's course in all these areas has thus surely been set for many years to come – perhaps for many centuries to come – and in this sense the original conciliar aim of *aggiornamento*, bringing the Church's rites and practices up to date, can be said to have been substantially achieved.

With regard to the second conciliar aim of promoting the Church's in-creased self-understanding, this too can be said to have been substantially achieved in what was brought out in the Council's own sixteen documents on such topics as faith, revelation, morality, religious freedom, ecumenism, education, media, and, in general, in the way in which the Church must now approach the largely de-Christianized world in which she currently lives. For scholars in particular, the Council's documents have opened up a myr-iad of new lines to pursue. More than that, in the Council's own two great documents on the Church herself – the Dogmatic Constitution on the Church *Lumen Gentium* and the Pastoral Constitution on the Church in the Modern World *Gaudium et Spes* – the Church has succeeded in setting forth her most developed authoritative ecclesiology in her entire history; she has succeeded thereby in describing more fully and clearly than ever before who and what she really is. She is nothing else but "the kingdom of Christ now present in mystery" (*Lumen Gentium* #3), all of whose members "in any state or walk of life are called to the fullness of Christian life and to the perfection of love" (*LG* #40). The importance of this "universal call to holi-ness" of Vatican II, as it has aptly been called, is likely to loom larger and larger as the decades – and the centuries – progress. As Professor John Haas points out in his essay in these pages, the holy cannot really be separated from the good.

It was inevitable that the Church's developed new view of herself would find many echoes in the contemporary Catholic life of the mind as well. The references to *Lumen Gentium* (and to other conciliar documents as well) in the present collection of scholarly articles will be immediately noticed; they are no accident. In addition, one of the contributions, Father James T. O'Connor's "The Church of Christ and the Catholic Church," it-self represents a concise but model exposition of one important aspect of the Church's new self-understanding.

Then there is the second great Vatican II constitution on the Church, the "pastoral" document, *Gaudium et Spes*, of which most people too often seem to remember only the opening line to the effect that the followers of Christ share "the joy and hope, the grief and anguish, of the men of our time." Indeed they do.

However, *Gaudium et Spes* too represents considerably more than has sometimes been realized. It is, for example, the Vatican II document which teaches that because of sin, no less, "man finds that he is unable of himself to overcome the assaults of evil" (#13); grace is needed. "Deep within his conscience man discovers a law which he has not laid on himself, but which he must obey" (#16). "Those who willfully try to drive God from their heart and to avoid all questions about religion . . . are not free from blame" (#19). "Man is prone to evil" (#25). Thus, those who have sometimes invoked *Gaudium et Spes* as a charter for an uncritical new brand of liberalism in the Church have apparently not read the document either too carefully or in its entirety. It should also be noted, as *Lumen Gentium* declares, that "the Church of Christ, trusting in the design of the Creator and admitting that progress can contribute to man's true happiness, still feels called upon to echo the words of the apostle: 'Do not be conformed to this world' (Romans 12:2)" (*LG* #37).

With regard to the third conciliar purpose of reunion with other Christians, the Council's teaching and subsequent Church actions may be truly said to have removed to a great extent most of the former major obstacles to Christian unity on the Catholic side; but if the ultimate goal of ecumenism is unity of faith within one Church, then there can ultimately not be any true unity except on the basis of faith. In a 1993 talk on this subject, Cardinal Joseph Ratzinger, prefect of the Congregation for the Doctrine of the Faith in Rome, emphasized the truth that unity is ultimately a "gift of God because the Church belongs to him, not to us." He continued by saying that "any unity built by us alone in a political or intellectual way would only be capable of creating our kind of unity and our kind of Church. So it would not be the type of unity of the Church of God for which we strive."

One of the problems in seeking Church unity, the cardinal observed further, is that "ecumenism is often seen in terms of the political model and is believed to be negotiations between states. . . . It is thought that negotiations between the different Churches should gradually come up with compromises and by means of these compromises arrive at agreements on the different elements of division." This approach, he said, "is constructed with no consideration for the specific nature and reality that the Church is. The Church's radical dependence on God is relegated to a parenthesis, forgetting that the real agent in the Church is God. . . . If we are to have authentic ecumenism, then it is important to recognize the primacy of divine action. . . . Ecumenism demands patience; real ecumenical success does not consist in one new agreement after another, but in our perseverance to press on together with humble respect for each other, even when compatibility on the doctrine or order of the Church has still not been attained" (Address at the Waldensian Faculty of Theology in Rome on January 29, 1993; text in *30 Days* [February, 1993], pp. 66–67). Surely Cardinal Ratzinger's present understanding of ecumenism is not incompatible with the original goal of Pope John XXIII and the Council.

The final conciliar purpose of trying to make more effective the Church's communication of the Gospel to the world essentially remains to be carried out in the future (despite some tentative initiatives already taken). It is not at all the case that a sustained new initiative of evangelization has been tried and has failed; as Chesterton once remarked of Christianity generally, it has not yet been tried. Making the message of the Gospel more credible in the face of the shallow scientism and prejudice and *immoralisme* that reign at the present time in modern society at large must surely be one of the pre-eminent tasks of the current and coming generation of Catholic scholars. Some of the contributions to this volume, for example, those of Father Benedict Ashley and Dr. Stephen M. Barr, represent essays in precisely that direction.

In addition to the documents of Vatican II themselves, and the postconciliar implementing documents, the postconciliar period has also seen a whole series of outstanding papal encyclicals and apostolic exhortations; these too represent important grist for the Catholic scholar's mill; a number of them will be specially examined in the pages which follow, for example, in the contributions of Father Ronald Lawler, Dr. John Finnis, Fr. Thomas Weinandy, Dr. Alice Ramos, and Dr. J. Brian Benestad. There has been a perhaps equally outstanding series of other declarations, decrees, and instructions besides papal documents issuing from the Holy See during the same period, especially those which have emanated from the Congregation for the Doctrine of the Faith, not to speak of many significant pastoral letters and initiatives coming from some of the episcopal conferences.

Finally, what some have aptly called the "last" document of Vatican II – the new *Catechism of the Catholic Church*, the subject of the contribution to this book of His Eminence John Cardinal O'Connor – was promulgated by Pope John Paul II on December 8, 1992. The new *Catechism* is the first

Church-wide catechism issued since 1566; it resulted from a call for an authoritative modern statement of the whole faith of the Church from the 1985 Synod of Bishops (yet another Vatican II innovation which enables representatives of the world episcopate to gather periodically in Rome and by their deliberations to assist the Holy Father in his universal mission of teaching, ruling, and sanctifying in and over the whole Church).

Precisely because of the many rich documents issued by the Church's Magisterium during the conciliar and postconciliar periods and because of the extensive literature – some excellent, some frankly appalling – commenting on these documents, quite ample material has been provided for many lifetimes of Catholic scholarship – a rich vein of ore capable of being mined in accordance with what Dr. Patrick Lee in these pages has aptly styled "The Principles of Catholic Scholarship." Some of this work has already been undertaken, as this volume itself indicates; much, much more remains to be done. Of course, the Catholic intellect and Catholic scholarship should in no way ever be limited to expounding what the Church declares to be the faith. Rather, the contrary: Even though informed with authentic Catholic principles, the Catholic mind and Catholic scholarship should attempt to range as far as the human mind can range, and the farther the better. Indeed, one of the goals of Catholic scholarship should be to move beyond mere "churchy" issues and work much harder at developing Catholic solutions to the problems that beset mankind, as John XXIII wished, and as several of the contributors to this volume also suggest. There are certainly abundant opportunities to accomplish this today.

Nevertheless, since the Catholic Church is "the teacher of truth" (*Dignitatis Humanae* #14; *Sacrosantum Concilium* #15), and since the object of the intellect is truth, it follows that the Catholic intellect must be based on the Catholic faith if it is to remain truly Catholic. The Catholic intellect cannot be truly Catholic if it is divorced from the faith – i.e., if it separates itself from what the Magisterium of the Church declares to be the faith. This consideration raises an enormous question which is understandably one of the major preoccupations of the present volume, namely, what happens when a version of the Catholic intellect is presented which has decided that it *need not* necessarily be grounded in the Catholic faith?

For the fact is that, virtually since the end of the Council, there has been a pronounced split between the Catholic faith as the Magisterium has never ceased to declare and expound it, and the Catholic intellect – or what has continued to present itself as representative of the Catholic intellect – in many Catholic colleges and universities, in Catholic scholarly associations and publications, journals, conferences, religious orders, houses of study, and even seminaries. Father Richard Roach in his contribution to this volume has captured the atmosphere at some of the modern Catholic universities at the high tide of what has been too widely represented as the *aggiornamento* of the campuses; Fr. Robert Sokolowski, in the final chapter of the volume, has similarly described some of the unfortunately prevalent current features on the campuses of schools that nevertheless continue to describe themselves as Catholic.

Even before the proverbial ink was dry on the conciliar and post-conciliar documents, a concerted process of revisionism had begun among many Catholic academics and opinion makers; this process has continued with only minor interruptions up to the present day. Vatican II had manifestly inaugurated a period of officially sanctioned and specified change in the Church; in this generalized atmosphere of "change," however, it turned out that quite a few had their own ideas and agendas concerning what some of the changes should be, and these were not necessarily limited to the changes authorized by the Magisterium in its exercise of the mission confided to it. Indeed, close attention to the teaching set forth in the official conciliar and postconciliar documents has scarcely been the hallmark of the era. Rather, what came to be widely propagated as the supposed real legacy of the Council was something called "the spirit of Vatican II."

This "spirit of Vatican II" was the slogan under which many changes not only not prescribed by the Council Fathers but not even remotely imagined by them came to be introduced into the Catholic Church and into various Catholic milieus. It was not long, indeed, before the ideal of *aggiornamento* came to mean in some quarters not so much bringing the Church's rites and practices up to date in a way that would make it easier for them to influence and affect the world, but rather conforming the Church's practices to the world's. Very soon after the Council some came to understand the conciliar aim of greater Catholic self-understanding not as plumbing the authentic sources of the faith more profoundly but rather as an often uncritical embrace of many reigning modern secular ideas. For some reunion with non-Catholic Christians came to mean downgrading if not abandoning certain Catholic beliefs, practices, and traditions in order to reach a lowest common denominator. The notion of bringing the message of the Gospel to the world became transformed for some Catholics to mean importing the world's standards and views into the Church in place of the Gospel. How such a collapse of Catholic standards in the minds of so many erstwhile practitioners could happen so fast and so thoroughly still remains a mystery, although Professor Glenn Olsen's observation, in his contribution to this volume, that some people simply cannot imagine being anything but part of their own times, is surely pertinent here, as is the "historical perspective" provided by another historian-contributor to this volume, Father Marvin O'Connell. Anyone seriously schooled in and accepting of the authentic Catholic tradition – including especially the real Vatican II, not its "spirit" – could be pardoned for concluding about today's widespread abandonment of the Church for the world by Catholics that, quite simply, "an enemy has done this" (Matthew 13:28).

It was in such an atmosphere of growing confusion and increasing "private judgment" on the part of Catholics that occurred another epochal event in the life of the postconciliar Church; this event was the issuance of Pope Paul VI's 1968 encyclical *Humanae Vitae*, re-affirming the Church's constant teaching that "each and every marriage act must remain open to the transmission of life" (*HV* #11), in other words, re-affirming the Church's traditional teaching that contraception is intrinsically evil and can never be justified.

Humanae Vitae and the massive opposition it aroused, both inside and outside the Church, was a watershed event; the growing opposition to traditional morality which had been developing both in the secular culture at large, and also among many Catholics, suddenly became open and hostile when Paul VI courageously proclaimed the truth. In fact, the uninterrupted teaching of the Catholic Church that any deliberately willed attempt to break the bond uniting human love and human life is gravely wrong had been, until the early 1960s, very widely accepted and recognized as true by Catholics, especially educated Catholics, in their married lives.

Another thing that was largely forgotten by the 1960s, however, was the fact that the Catholic teaching on the subject represented the historical common Christian tradition, affirmed by virtually all Christians along with Catholics up until the year 1930, when the Anglican Church's Lambeth Conference in that year broke ranks and allowed the use of contraception in "hard cases." The effect of this was like removing the proverbial Dutchman's finger from the dike; the trickle quickly became a flood, which shortly afterwards broke up and washed away the dike itself; by the 1960s virtually every Christian denomination had joined modern secular society in holding that contraceptive use was not only morally licit, but even somehow constituted a positive and indeed an indispensable good. It also came to be nearly universally believed that it was only a matter of time until the Catholic Church too would be obliged to accept contraception – a viewpoint encouraged by not a few Catholic leaders, as Monsignor George A. Kelly amply documents in his contribution to this volume.

The modern world had come to see "nothing wrong" with contraception, and soon all too many Catholics had also come to share that same conviction. When Pope Paul VI defied the near-universal new view of world public opinion on the subject by issuing *Humanae Vitae*, therefore, the dissent was simply massive. Among Catholics in America, a group of 87 theologians issued a public statement against the pope's encyclical which was given widespread favorable publicity by the media over the message of the encyclical itself, and the statement very quickly came to be subscribed to by over 600 Catholic theologians, canonists, and scholars in related disciplines.[1]

Such public opposition on the part of Catholic academics against an authoritative papal teaching was unheard of; papal encyclicals had come to be the normal vehicle for authoritative teaching on the part of the supreme pastor of the Church, and Catholics simply did not dissent from papal encyclicals! Nevertheless, it soon became clear that the 600-plus dissenting Catholic academics, very many of them ordained priests, were rallying behind their leadership a disturbingly high percentage of the Catholic faithful, including especially "educated" Catholics. The dikes were thus perceived as having been broken up and washed away by many of these ordinary Catholics too.

This rejection of the truths so courageously proclaimed in *Humanae Vitae* proved to be a catastrophe both for the Church and for the world. Once the unitive meaning of the marital act became separable in people's minds from the procreative aspect, sexual satisfaction or pleasure or self-expresion quickly became legitimatized and self-justifying in and of itself, and soon the very idea that sexual activity even needed to be limited to marriage, for example, quickly went by that famous board. As George Gilder has shown so well, severing the bond leads to "sexual suicide." Thus, for example, nearly 30 percent of all the births in America in the 1990s were to

---

1 Among the signers of this reprehensible document were Father Richard Roach, a contributor to this volume, and one of its editors, Dr. William E. May. Both now deeply repent their deed.

unmarried mothers – a 25 percent jump over the preceding decade – and the number was more than double that for blacks. And this, of course, was the situation for the babies who managed to get *born*; the over 1.5 million legal abortions now being performed every year in America testify all too tragically to the even more serious consequences of the broken link between the use of the human sexual faculty and marriage and possible procreation than out-of-wedlock births – namely, the outright willed killing of a significant percentage of the next generation.

Moreover, the fact that, as this book goes to press, the United States is now debating the legitimacy of unnatural sexual relations, indeed marriage, between persons of the same sex testifies further to the massive modern loss of understanding of why it was that God "created them male and female" (Genesis 1:27). Even while many people continue to be repelled by homosexual acts, the "gay rights agenda" still goes forward because few can apparently any longer think of any *reason* why homosexual acts should not be legitimate, if that is what some people want or are "oriented" toward; this new acceptance by our society of what was formerly considered gravely immoral is not without consequences for Catholic institutions, as Professor Gerard V. Bradley, among others, points out in his contribution to this volume.

The same thing is also true of the new technologies of *in-vitro* fertilization, surrogate motherhood, and the like, which are increasingly practiced in our society; even when they are often uncomfortable with these things, people can no longer think of any *reason* why they should not be permitted; and so more and more once-unthinkable things have become routinely doable in our society.

The reason these things should not be done, of course, as the Congregation for the Doctrine of the Faith lucidly pointed out in its 1987 Instruction *Donum Vitae*, is that these technologies violate "the inseparable connection, established by God, which man on his own initiative may not break, between the unitive significance and the procreative significance which are both inherent in the marriage act" (*Humanae Vitae* #12). As the same Instruction likewise notes, these technologies treat new human life as if it were a product inferior to its producers and not as a person equal in dignity to it parents. They thus transform the beautiful act of *procreation*, in which human life is begotten, not made, into an act of *reproduction*, in which it is made, not begotten. They treat the child, in other words, as a thing, not as a human being possessing human dignity. Such have been only a few among the many far-reaching consequences of the rejection of the pope's encyclical.

Moreover, the logic of the dissent which *Humanae Vitae* elicited proved to be very insidious, as Monsignor William B. Smith demonstrated early on in his contribution included in this volume. If the Church could be wrong about her teaching on contraception, against which she had taught so firmly and so solemnly for so long, then surely she could be wrong about other teachings as well. This was a conclusion which many were not slow to reach, especially certain Catholic intellectuals and academics; and very soon there were very few Catholic beliefs and traditions of any kind which had not been publicly questioned and even belittled.

Meanwhile, the hierarchy, the bishops, the authoritative teachers and guardians of the faith, found themselves living in such a generalized condition of open dissent on the part of some that it was as if they were riding that proverbial Chinese tiger: They could not easily get off without the beast turning and rending them. Hence the stance of the hierarchy in practice, for more than the past quarter of a century, has been an uneasy kind of truce with dissent; there has been little open acknowledgment that dissent is really all that widespread; and there has been perhaps even less acknowledgment of the harm such dissent does not only to the faithful but also to the bishops' own authority.

Despite the seeming tolerance of dissent, however, at least in words, and in their pastoral letters and the like, the U.S. bishops have generally and sometimes strongly upheld authentic Church teachings, including unpopular ones, as often as not doing so with words of praise for the Holy Father's various stands. Nor have they in any way recognized today's common dissenting positions as being in any sense licit for the Church. At the same time, though, there are few known instances where any open dissenters have been publicly rebuked or corrected or removed in this country by a bishop for their dissenting opinions. By and large, dissenters in this country have been able to remain in place pretty much undisturbed, just as so many "Catholic" publications, from the scholarly ones found mostly in university libraries or circulating among specialists to the popular ones found in Church racks, continue to come off the presses regularly containing material sometimes in flat contradiction to what the Church's Magisterium continues to affirm is the Church's authentic faith.

Meanwhile, there also do remain many Catholic scholars, scientists, philosophers, theologians, exegetes, historians, moralists, social scientists, critics, writers, and intellectuals in general who are not only able, but sometimes even outstanding, in their fields, and who are also loyal on principle both to "the Catholic faith that comes to us from the apostles" and to the Catholic intellectual life as it has been traditionally lived and understood. After all, the Catholic intellectual life represents one of the oldest intellectual traditions in the world, just as the Catholic Church herself remains one of the world's oldest continuously existing institutions. As in the case of the Church herself, the demise of the Catholic intellectual life has been many times confidently predicted or pronounced, and this continues to be the case today; but even though many successive powers that be have often fondly imagined that they would be able to throw out the Church and her views "with a pitchfork," to alter slightly the famous line of Horace about nature – *ecclesiam expelles furca* – she nevertheless always keeps on coming back – *tamen usque recurret.*

For the eyes of faith there can be no mystery in the continuing vitality and fecundity of an authentic Catholic intellectual life, sometimes against all the odds, or at least against many of them; for again like the Church herself, when the Catholic intellectual life remains true to its authentic sources and inspiration, it is based on nothing else but the words of the One who declared that "heaven and earth will pass away but my words will not pass away" (Matthew 24:35; Mark 13:31; Luke 21:33).

In 1977, a group of such Catholic lovers of the life of the mind got together and formed the Fellowship of Catholic Scholars, an association mostly of Catholic academics explicitly and wholeheartedly dedicated, in the words of the Fellowship's Statement of Purpose, both to "the renewal of the Church of Christ undertaken by Pope John XXIII, shaped by Vatican II, and carried on by succeeding pontiffs" *and* to "the entire faith of the Catholic Church [embodied] not merely in solemn definitions but in the ordinary teaching of the pope and those bishops in union with him . . ."

The Fellowship of Catholic Scholars was not intended to supersede or take over from the regular societies and associations in most academic and scholarly disciplines. On the contrary, most of the members of the Fellowship already belong to appropriate associations, participate in appropriate conferences, and contribute to scholarly journals in their field. The Fellowship, however, has tried to be, precisely, a *fellowship*, in which scholars in all fields could come together not only as scholars but also as friends and fellow workers in the same vineyard and for mutual help on the basis of their Catholic faith held in common.

Moreover, there can be no doubt that the Fellowship has had its impact on the life of Catholic America. Among other things, each year since 1978 the Fellowship has held an annual convention, usually dedicated to a chosen theme, at which selected Catholic scholars have delivered papers on a great variety of the topics that have concerned the Church and the world during these past eventful years. The papers for each year's convention have regularly been gathered between the two covers of a paperback book in the form of "Proceedings" in the usual manner of scholarly organizations. (Not all speakers at Fellowship conventions have even necessarily been members of the organization, by the way, though obviously the non-members have not been uncomfortable about speaking under Fellowship sponsorship.)

As the years have gone by and the volumes of the "Proceedings" of the Fellowship have accumulated, it became more and more apparent to many of those who have followed the work of the Fellowship that many of the papers delivered at these annual conventions often really represented significant contributions to the Catholic intellectual life of the present turbulent period in the history of the Church in America. Accordingly, the Board of Directors of the Fellowship of Catholic Scholars asked the editors to compile the present volume containing some of the best and most representative addresses delivered at Fellowship conventions between 1978 and 1995.

In carrying out this task, the editors immediately found themselves confronted with an embarrassment of choices. Many other Fellowship papers prepared and delivered over the years could have been chosen and included here as readily as the ones which in fact have been chosen and included. Some of these choices have already been mentioned in passing in the course of this Introduction; all of them, the editors believe, should be of interest to anyone who has pondered the problems of maintaining the integrity of the Catholic intellect in a time of crisis of the Catholic faith. It is no easy task, as anyone who seriously tries it today will quickly discover. In some cases, especially those where the contribution dates back a number of years, contributors have added a few remarks from the standpoint of today.

In presenting this particular volume to the reading public, the editors are conscious that, without duplicating any of the topics or authors included here, at least another volume equal in length, seriousness, quality, and scholarship to the present one could easily have been compiled from the eighteen volumes of Fellowship "Proceedings" that have been published up to this time. At the same time, it is the hope of the editors that what the present volume does provide in the way of intellectual and spiritual nourishment will be seen to be a worthy contemporary response to the perennial New Testament injunction to "be prepared to make a defense to anyone who calls you to account for the hope that is in you" (I Peter 3:15).

1.
Catholic Faith and Intrinsically Evil Acts (1978)
Germain Grisez

The theology developed by Catholic moralists in the centuries between Trent and Vatican II had many virtues, but it also had some serious defects. Among its defects not least was the separation of moral reflection from the effort to understand the basic doctrines of faith. Taking for granted the principles of Christian living which had been received and taught in the Church for centuries, the moralists systematized these principles and worked from them by a casuistic method adapted from the method of law. This method preserved the received body of moral wisdom but did not conduce to its development except with respect to casuistic applications. Moreover, this method did nothing to clarify the moral-theoretical concepts implicit in substantive Christian moral wisdom.

Today everyone agrees that moral theology ought to be more closely integrated with reflection upon fundamental Christian doctrines, and many thinkers have been trying to articulate an adequate moral theory for Christian life. This paper is an essay in these tasks. Of course, a brief essay cannot deal with the whole of Christian doctrine and its implications for Christian life. I limit my reflection here to five points of Christian doctrine, and from these points I illustrate only one proposition relevant to Christian morality, namely, that certain kinds of acts are such that acts of these kinds always are objectively evil.

The first of the points of doctrine is the transcendence to morality of the vocation of humankind. Christ's mission was not to establish a new moral order, nor was his intent to inculcate morality conforming to the order of creation. Rather, his mission was to redeem sinful humankind, to call human persons, who were created in God's image, to share in divine life. This sharing in divine life is altogether disproportionate to human powers to achieve. Redemption and sanctification are wholly the work of grace.

Morality is concerned with the goods of human nature and the fruits of human work. If it were possible for a person to be morally perfect without being a Christian, this moral perfection would avail nothing toward salvation. A full and happy human life remains merely human, and infinitely inferior to the divine life to which humankind is called in Christ. For Christian life, then, morality never can be primary and architectonic. Moral goodness, no matter how important it might be, always remains a secondary and subordinate consideration. It is part of that whole world which it profits men and women nothing to gain if they do not share in the reign of God and his justification.

The second point to be considered is an aspect of the Christian understanding of human persons. The human person is not merely one kind of animal, specialized by the peculiar ability to reason. Rather, the human person is a subject who projects his or her own world. Human thinking is creative. Outward behavior is significant only insofar as it expresses one's subjectivity, executes the proposals one articulates by deliberation, and adopts by choice.

Thus Christian morality is a morality of the heart, of inner dispositions and attitudes. It is not to be confused with some legalistic list of rules designed to regulate outward behavior. Because of the essential inwardness of Christian morality, what is most important in it are the fundamental dispositions of faith, hope, and love. Without these formative principles, no human action can be of positive significance for the life of the Christian. With them, it matters little what one does.

The Christian view of the subjectivity of the person dictates that moral norms not be imposed arbitrarily. One is morally responsible only to the extent that one is aware of being morally responsible. And one is morally responsible for doing precisely what one believes with a sincere heart one must do. No moral requirement is in force for the Christian unless the requirement is understood and accepted as valid.

The third point to be considered is that the created world is not eternal and static. According to Christian faith, the world is created by God from nothing, and it is a historical process unfolding under the guiding hand of his providence. Moreover, creation is undergoing a radical and pervasive transformation in virtue of the incarnation and redemptive work of the divine Word.

Human persons are not mere passive parts of the created world. They are active participants in the work of creation and redemption. Made in

God's image, they share in his intelligence and freedom. Human persons dispose of their existence by their own free choices.

Human persons are set over the works of God's hands. By their actions, persons confer meaning and value; at God's direction they name things, transforming them into a world of human significance. Thus human persons are not called to conform to a static set of natural laws but are to take responsibility for the world, to shape it, to rule over it. It follows that the whole of the human world including human society itself is constantly unfolding new dimensions. In different times and places, under different social and cultural conditions, even those acts which come naturally, such as engaging in sexual intercourse, change their meanings.

Nor will it do to suppose that this process of transformation is only superficial, that it reaches no further than the accidental features of things. There is no positive, invariant core of human life, since the whole of existence is a living and integrated system of meanings. A change in any part of this system affects all its other parts. To deny this point, to assert a static human nature, will entail the denial either of the radical significance of sin or of the radical effect of grace.

This leads to the fourth point. According to Christian faith, the world is infected by sin. Although the redemptive work has begun, nowhere in the world is it completed. Nothing in the world is perfectly right, nothing untouched by corruption. The world is a broken world. The Church itself is a gathering of sinners. No institution, no structure possesses the holiness to which Christians are called. Only God is good, perfect, holy.

Universal sinfulness has obvious implications for morality. Any morality worth considering must be based upon a realistic acceptance of the truth about the way things are. A set of moral standards which would be appropriate in an ideal, sinless world would be simply irrelevant to this world in which Christian life must be lived. Moreover, it would be a gross mistake to suppose that moral perfection could be found in mere conformity to the Church as structure and institution because pure holiness is to be found only in heaven. In this life, holiness is commingled with sin. Mere conformity to the Church would mean identification with its sinfulness as well as with its holiness.

The fifth doctrinal point is that by virtue of the redemptive grace received in baptism, Christians enjoy by participation the liberty of God himself. The freedom of the children of God will find its expression in their lifestyles. There is no minute code of rules to which Christians must conform. Rather, Christians can develop their own personal and communal forms of life. The governing law is the inward grace of the Spirit, who works within the heart and conscience of each person.

It follows that Christian morality must be a morality of responsibility. Christians have only one vocation: to share in divine life. They have as many diverse missions as their varied abilities and the opportunities presented by their different situations suggest – suggest when prayerfully reflected upon in the inner light of the Spirit's gentle teaching. The responsibility of a Christian cannot be captured in universal rules. Responsibility is shaped by each unique context of life. Moreover, it is shaped by the Spirit to the gradual development of faith, hope, and love, which are the only constant factors running through all of every Christian's life.

The preceding doctrinal principles are acknowledged by everyone working today in the field of Catholic moral theology. Some might add various refinements and qualifications to these summary statements of doctrine. But nobody would deny any of these principles. All of them obviously are very near the most central tenets of Christian faith. It would be easy to illustrate each of them with texts from Scripture and other sources of theological reflection.

I am going to use these points of doctrine to clarify the proposition that certain kinds of actions are intrinsically evil. What is meant by the phrase "intrinsically evil acts"?

No one doubts that there are moral norms which admit of no exception, if these norms are formulated in morally significant terms. Unjust acts are always wrong. So if "murder" means unjust killing, murder is always wrong. But such moral norms are hardly instructive.

Sometimes the question about intrinsically evil acts is formulated as follows: Are there certain patterns of behavior which render actions in which they are included objectively evil so that the evil cannot be eliminated by any circumstance in which or intention with which the action is done? I do not accept this formulation of the issue, and it is important to make clear why not.

Human acts are not specified by outward patterns of behavior. Rather, one does what one thinks one is doing. Behavior has the character of human action only insofar as it executes a proposal which a person has adopted by choice, after having articulated the proposal through deliberation. Hence, kinds of acts must be distinguished by the kinds of proposals one adopts.

Proposals are excogitated as ways of realizing appealing possibilities. Possibilities are appealing either because their realization is seen as intrinsically good and satisfying (that is, seen as an end) or because their realization appears to be a step toward bringing about a state of affairs seen as intrinsically good and satisfying (that is, appears to be a means to an end).

If there were no necessity to choose, there would be no moral problem. If all appealing possibilities had only positive and no negative implications for goods considered as ends, there likewise would be no moral problem. The moral problem arises because all possibilities about which anyone deliberates have some negative aspects – at least the aspect of excluding other possibilities which are somehow appealing. In many cases, a proposed means to an end would result in preventing, damaging, harming, or destroying something else which is considered as an end.

In speaking of what is intrinsically good here, the word "good" is not used in a moral sense. All human acts, whether morally good or morally evil, aim at something which appeals to the one choosing as humanly and personally good. Anything else in which one can be interested ultimately reduces to some aspect of the fulfillment or flourishing of persons. Such aspects of the full-being of persons are ends; they are seen as intrinsically good and satisfying. I call them "basic human goods." Examples of basic human goods are human life and health, knowledge of the truth, peace, and friendship. It is worth noticing that these and other human goods are constantly acknowledged as proper, central human concerns in Scripture and Christian tradition.

Now, I understand "intrinsically evil act" as follows. If one's proposal to take a certain means to one's end includes a proposal to prevent, damage, harm, or destroy one of the basic human goods – whether in oneself, in another person, or in some multitude of persons – then the proposal defines a kind of action which is intrinsically wrong, no matter what other circumstances and intentions might be taken into consideration or even included within one's proposal.

It is important to notice that on the stated definition, a norm forbidding an intrinsically evil act is not formulated in terms which already signify moral goodness, for the word "good" used in reference to the basic human goods is not used in a moral sense, and intrinsically evil acts are specified by their relation to basic human goods.

It also is important to notice that according to the stated definition, an intrinsically evil act is specified by a proposal contrary to a basic human good, not merely by the fact that the execution of a proposal will have some negative consequences in respect to such a good. Thus, if it is an act intrinsically evil to propose that one kill oneself, to adopt this proposal by choice, and to execute it, still not every performance which causes one's own death is an act of that intrinsically evil kind. A performance which leads to one's own death might execute a proposal which includes no proposal that one kill oneself. For example, Jesus laid down his life in obedience to the Father's will, but he did not adopt a proposal to kill himself.

The next question is whether there are any intrinsically evil acts. I hold that there are, and that the five doctrinal points previously summarized can help clarify why there are. But some Roman Catholic moral theologians today deny that there are any intrinsically evil acts, and often they use one or more of these same points of doctrine in arguing theologically for their position. While I do not need for my present purpose to examine their theological reasoning at length, a brief, somewhat simplified summary of it will help to point up the significance of the explanations I am going to articulate.

First, it can be argued that since morality is secondary and subordinate in Christian life, since the true vocation of Christians altogether transcends the moral sphere, no kind of act is inherently absolutely incompatible with the Christian vocation, and so no kind of act is intrinsically evil. The Spirit blows where he wills and is not limited in the varieties of fruit he can produce. Christian life will be the overflow and outgrowth of reconciling and elevating grace. Grace does not specify a certain set of performances as its necessary expression. Nor could it, without making the vocation of Christians homogeneous with the finite, merely human goods which are the starting points of morality.

Second, it can be argued that since persons can be morally responsible only to the extent that they are aware of what they are doing, and since different persons have different conceptions of the significance of various patterns of behavior, no kind of act can be intrinsically evil. Since moral obligations are mediated by conscience and since Christians of sincere conscience do not universally agree in sensing any kind of act to be absolutely incompatible with faith, hope, and love, it also can be argued on this score that no kinds of acts are in fact always wrong.

Third, it can be argued that since all things human are subject to radical transformation and since actions are determined by human meaning giving, which varies according to times and places, no kind of act can be wrong always and everywhere. The apparent constancy of certain kinds of acts is only apparent; morally considered, they are transformed through and through in the course of history.

Fourth, it can be argued that since Christian morality must take realistic account of evil, kinds of acts which would be forbidden absolutely in an ideal world cannot be considered wholly inappropriate in the real world. In many difficult cases, one must have the courage to do the lesser evil. Moral compromises are necessary, it is argued, since one is required by charity to do good to others without any pharisaic nervousness about one's own moral purity.

Fifth, it can be argued that since Christian responsibility is individual and contextual, the real moral demand always is concrete and unique. General norms can be helpful as guidelines, but they must not be taken as legalistic absolutes. What is common to all people at all times and in all places is merely an abstract human nature; concretely, the responsible Christian will be responsive to the total situation and will not be absolutely bound by any single, abstracted aspect of it.

Now it is important to notice that those who advance some or all of these arguments, or arguments similar to them, do not hold that there are no acts which are almost always wrong. Indeed, most of them hold that there are moral norms which are practically or virtually exceptionless. Their position is that traditional Christian moral wisdom properly located certain kinds of acts which are very generally wrong, and perhaps under given cultural conditions were inevitably wrong because of their relationship to certain human goods. Even today, it is admitted, one can think of kinds of acts to the wrongness of which one cannot imagine any exception – for example, for an adult male to compel a six-year-old child to engage in sodomitic intercourse (where "sodomitic" is used in a merely descriptive sense). Those who hold that there are no intrinsically evil acts merely wish to say that it is a contingent – in no sense a necessary – truth that acts of certain kinds always are wrong. In principle, they could be right in some circumstances or if done with some intention. Perhaps, for example, if new psychological knowledge indicated that the only way to stop certain psychotic conditions developing in children was to rape them sodomitically, then in that situation the act would become virtuous.

Now, within the context of Roman Catholic faith, I think it must be held that there are intrinsically evil acts. Although this proposition has not been defined as a truth of faith, I think it has been infallibly held and handed down in the Church.

Vatican Council II, in its discussion of the teaching office of the bishops, explained how doctrine proposed by the ordinary magisterium can be taught infallibly:

> Although the bishops individually do not enjoy the prerogative of infallibility, they nevertheless proclaim the teaching of Christ infallibly, even when they are dispersed throughout the world, provided that they remain in communion with each other and with the Successor of Peter, and that in authoritatively teaching on a matter of faith and morals they agree in one judgment as that to be held definitively. (*Lumen gentium*, #25)

John C. Ford, S.J., and I wrote an article which appeared in *Theological Studies* (June 1978); in our article we present a careful exegesis of this passage from the teaching of Vatican II, and then go on to argue that the received Catholic teaching on the morality of contraception has been proposed in a way which meets the conditions for infallible teaching by the ordinary magisterium. We do not attempt to show that Vatican II's formulation of the conditions in this passage itself expresses a truth of faith, but I think it does and that this can be shown.

Assuming Vatican II's formulation as a premise, one can easily conclude that many points of traditional Catholic moral teaching have been proposed infallibly. Throughout the world during the centuries from Trent to Vatican II, the Catholic bishops in union with one another and the popes exercised their teaching office by establishing and closely supervising seminaries where their priests were trained. These priests passed on Catholic moral teaching both in the confessional and in other ways.

The vehicles for communicating moral teaching in the seminaries were the approved textbooks in moral theology. Much of the content of these books varied; most of it was not proposed as Christian teaching to be held definitively. However, in these books, various kinds of acts were characterized as intrinsically and gravely evil, and in most cases any kind of act thus characterized by one of the approved authors was similarly characterized by all of them.

This substantive moral teaching had been held and handed down as part of the Christian tradition for centuries before the reformation, both by the

Roman Catholic Church and by the Eastern Catholics, and it continued to be held and handed on by all Christians for centuries after the reformation. These teachings were clearly proposed as beyond doubt, as moral norms to be held definitively. In fact, many of them were backed by citations to Scripture. No matter what a modern exegete might think of the use to which Scripture was put in moral teaching, those who appealed to Scripture to back up moral teaching *thought* they were appealing to divine revelation, and the faithful understood the claim which was made. Obviously, if one claims that a certain point of teaching is divinely revealed, one calls for an assent of faith, and *a fortiori* proposes this point of teaching as one which is to be held definitively.

Thus, the substantive moral teaching common in the Catholic Church from Trent to Vatican II was proposed by the bishops in a way which meets the conditions articulated by Vatican II for teaching which is infallible, even though not solemnly defined. This body of moral teaching was proposed as unquestionable and absolutely binding, and the faithful accepted it as such. People considered themselves sinners if they did not live up to it.

Now, if the Catholic Church already has taught infallibly that certain kinds of acts are intrinsically and gravely evil, then the question whether there are intrinsically evil acts is settled in the affirmative so far as Catholic moral theology is concerned. But it is one thing to accept a fact, and it is another to try to understand it. The main point of the present paper is to try to clarify the fact that there are intrinsically evil acts, by considering this point of teaching in the light of more basic teachings of faith. In particular, I wish to show that the five points of doctrine previously summarized, far from implying that there are no intrinsically evil acts, rather imply that there are – or, at least, help make this fact intelligible. It is a matter of faith that fornication can bar one from the heavenly kingdom. The problem is to see why this barrier is not a merely arbitrary test, so that it could not as well have been the case that eating Jonathan apples would bar one from the kingdom but fornicating would not.

The transcendence of the Christian vocation implies that Christian morality is much less concerned with results – since the ultimate destiny of Christians is not proportionate to human action – than it is with the right disposition toward God. God is to be loved above all things for his own sake. God's goodness is identical with himself. In its infinite plenitude, divine goodness embraces in a superior way all of the goods of creatures. The various goods of creatures, including all of the basic human goods, are only various inadequate images of divine goodness.

But precisely as images of divine goodness, basic goods of persons deserve to be loved and revered just to the extent of their goodness. The exemplar is dishonored if the image is not duly revered. Moreover, the calling of human persons to share in divine life, far from nullifying the inherent value of proportionate goods, ennobles them. The basic human goods are intrinsic aspects of the full-being of persons called to share in divinity, and so these goods share in divine dignity.

The assumption of human nature and the human condition by the Word of God also implies that in him and in those united with him, an offense against human goods is an offense against God. Moreover, human goods have not been created to be annihilated. In the heavenly kingdom they too will have their place, for the divine life we are called to share will be shared by us as human persons, richly satisfied with all of the human goods for which we also hope. Seek first the kingdom of God and all else shall be added besides – not discarded as rubbish.

It follows that Christian morality is a morality of love of neighbor and of oneself for the love of God. How can one love God whom one does not see if one hates one's neighbor whom one does see? As long as one does something to the least of Jesus' siblings, one does it to him personally. In Jesus, God is our neighbor, and through him our other neighbors share in divinity. Their goods must be treated with due reverence.

The intrinsic goods of human persons are multiple. Each reflects God's perfect goodness inadequately and each catches a somewhat different aspect of it. The common denominator of all of these goods, the divine goodness itself, transcends human comprehension. Thus we have no way to estimate the ultimate significance of any one of these goods in terms of another. Insofar as these goods are possibilities to be realized or fragile realities to be protected, we are called upon by love of God to realize and to protect them. Yet human power is limited and human resources never adequate to the good which is to be done and pursued.

In this situation, however, an attitude which incarnates love of God can and must have one constant implication for one's action. The implication is that one's heart maintain reverence toward all the basic goods of human persons. Reverence does not demand a performance in every case, but it does forbid violation in each and every case.

Since human action is not merely external performance, but rather is a matter of inward disposition, one does not necessarily violate a basic human good whenever one does something which happens to harm it. But one does necessarily violate a human good if one adopts a proposal to prevent, harm, damage, or destroy it. In adopting such a proposal, one sets one's heart against the human good one chooses to violate. And in setting one's heart against a human good, one sets one's heart against God himself, since the human good is an image of God, an intrinsic aspect of a person called to share in divine life, an aspect of the flourishing of a sibling of the Word incarnate, and a secondary but real constituent of heavenly glory.

It follows that acts of kinds which include the adoption of a proposal to violate in some way one of the basic goods of a human person are always wrong. Such acts are necessarily incompatible with Christian love. For Christian love extends not only to the divine goodness in God himself, but also extends, just as God's own love extends, in due measure to this same divine goodness as it is participated in creatures. God is not jealous of human love of created goods, for he did not create them to be unloved, but so that in their very created otherness they might share in his own goodness. But God is jealous of that unique and irreplaceable aspect of his own infinite goodness which is found in each and every finite good which contributes to the flourishing of human persons. To treat such a good irreverently is to offend God.

This brings us to the second point of doctrine: the Christian conception of human persons as subjects.

Human subjectivity does imply that human action is no mere external pattern of behavior but rather is the enactment of a humanly given meaning. But it does not follow that human acts are endlessly plastic. Behavioral patterns are not acts except insofar as they execute proposals adopted by choice. Such proposals are human understandings articulated in deliberation. The human subject, by reinterpretation, can give new meaning to anything other than understandings themselves. But understandings are not subject to interpretation and so they are not plastic to reinterpretation. If one's proposal is to negate some intrinsic good of a human person, nothing else one thinks about the action can remove the interpretation which this very understanding imposes upon it.

It is true that what is most important about Christian existence is that it incarnates faith and love. For this very reason, the view that it is morally permissible and even necessary to use whatever means might be required to achieve some humanly good results or to avoid disastrous consequences is alien to Christian moral reflection. Consequences are not morally determinative. Ultimately, the outcome of any difficult situation must be left to providence. In this respect, hope is as essential a Christian disposition as is faith or love.

Furthermore, as I have explained already, a life which truly incarnates Christian love will be marked by reverence for every aspect of the intrinsic full-being of human persons. The affirmative demands of love are open-ended and indefinable. But the adoption of a proposal to negate a basic human good always is incompatible with love of God. That for the sake of which one would adopt such a proposal is treated as if it were superior to the divine goodness present by participation in the good which is violated. The end used to justify the means is an idol – a created good loved not insofar as it shares God's goodness, but beyond this, as if it were good of itself and apart from God. Had the end not been idolized, had it been loved only in due measure, the good which is violated would also have been loved in due measure – that is, to the extent of its own goodness – but then one could not have adopted a proposal to violate it.

Faith and love are real relationships. One does not have these dispositions of the heart merely by feeling in a certain way, merely by wishing for them, merely by using the right jargon. As real relationships, faith and love set real, interpersonal requirements. Real, interpersonal requirements must be understood and accepted for what they are. Thus Christian morality cannot be an arbitrary set of rules, imposed by fiat.

Neither the pope nor the Church, not even God himself, can make actions right or wrong by a mere act of will. Christian morality excludes all such authoritarianism. It is not a despotic morality; it is a morality of truth. The requirements of Christian existence are the true demands of the real, interpersonal relationships of faith and love. If despotic commands were given, servile obedience to them would be of no value. Even when real moral requirements are proposed, mere outward conformity which does not express the inward dispositions of faith and love is useless.

Precisely for this reason, the subjectivity of the person does not entail subjectivism. Subjectivism is mere individual arbitrariness, a denial of the morality of truth, an assertion that nothing will be immoral for oneself if one does not accept it as such. Against such individualistic self-assertion, the intrinsic demands of the interpersonal reality of faith and love make their appeal. This appeal always is intelligible to the Christian in the light of faith by virtue of the inward teaching of the Spirit.

A Christian is bound only by conscience. But the first duty of conscience is to seek to learn the moral truth and to be ready to accept and follow it. Because moral truth must be learned, an upright person with a sincere conscience can be mistaken in a particular matter. The Spirit is infallible, but one must listen closely to him, and not confuse one's own feelings with his promptings. Moreover, to the extent that we are not perfect Christians, our hearts are not pure. A divided heart inevitably deceives itself about some moral truths.

The historicity of humankind and the intimate participation of Christians in the work of creation and redemption do entail that human acts develop new meanings from age to age. People in diverse cultures who might seem outwardly to be doing the very same things are in reality doing very different things. Marital intercourse for Christians, for example, pertains to a sacrament, and so it has a far greater and richer significance than does an apparently similar act for pre-Christian or post-Christian pagans. And even within the Christian context, such an act can unfold new dimensions of meaning.

Some who have studied the history of Christian morality have brought to this study a set of suppositions appropriate to the study of the history of law, but not suited to the study of the history of Christian morality. The mistake is understandable because of the adoption by moral theology of a methodology adapted from law. The inappropriate suppositions brought to the study of the history of Christian morality include the following: that human acts are patterns of outward behavior, which can change their meaning in the course of history; that in different environments, human goods can be promoted and protected in different ways, and moral norms are merely rules devised to promote and protect human goods in a certain historical context; and that one can legitimately criticize and perhaps revise even those moral norms which derive directly from basic human goods by assuming as a standard the relative importance given to the various basic human goods in the lifestyle of a given society.

As I have explained already, the first of these suppositions is mistaken. Actions are not mere patterns of behavior; people do what they understand themselves to be doing. If people understand themselves to be doing something different, the result is not the same act with a different moral quality, but a different act. However, acts which are the same in kind insofar as they include a proposal to violate some basic human good can also be different in kind insofar as they include many other diverse elements. For example, acts the same in kind insofar as they include the proposal to kill a person can be different in kind insofar as they are suicide or homicide, executed by performance or by omission, done with beneficent feelings or with great cruelty, done to the Word Incarnate to the least of his unborn siblings. Through the course of history, people in different situations and cultures understand human life and its destruction rather differently; on this account, killings differ in kind. But insofar as a class or acts is specified by the proposal to violate human life by killing a person, acts of that class are the same in kind and always evil.

Human goods can be promoted and protected in different ways in different historical contexts. Many moral norms do express no more than a culturally conditioned understanding of ways in which human goods can be promoted and protected under given conditions. However, those fundamental requirements of Christian morality which demand reverence for the basic human goods are not merely instrumental. They express in a direct way the minimum demands of love in relation to these goods. As truths, not rules, such moral norms are immune to change.

To assume that one can criticize and perhaps revise such moral norms by taking as a standard the relative importance which is given the basic human goods in the lifestyle of a given society – for example, the lifestyle characteristic of the contemporary, economically developed, non-communist nations – is to lose one's historical consciousness. Historicity demands rather than excludes insight into the unity of the basic goods of human persons, a unity which cannot be located without arbitrariness in the contingent conditions of the here-and-now which happen to delimit one's own point of view. Only with insight into the unity of human goods can the various ages and conditions of humankind be understood as a history, as a continuous evolution, rather than as a disjoined succession of such arbitrarily absolutized points of view.

It is important to notice that those who think that historicity excludes intrinsically evil acts could not draw this conclusion without assuming, in addition to historicity, that basic human goods and various instances of them can be weighed and balanced against one another, so that in different times and circumstances, a different conclusion might be reached. At one time and place, for example, the goodness of procreation, the importance of the education of children, the sacredness of innocent life, the personal dignity of spouses, and the holiness of marital love might be weighed and balanced in such a way that they would be best protected by the moral wall of a rule forbidding contraception as evil. Under different conditions, the results of weighing and balancing, it is assumed, would be different so that perhaps the wall would be a prison rather than a bulwark and would have to be removed.

The assumption that the basic human goods and all instances of them can in some way be rationally weighed and balanced is common to almost all moral theologians who deny that there are any intrinsically evil acts. The practically or virtually exceptionless moral norms, according to them, are not absolute because in some cases there is a proportionate reason – a greater good to be gained or a greater evil avoided – for violating the basic human good which the moral norm otherwise protects.

Although the argument is too long to articulate here, it is worth noticing that one of the chief aspects of the Christian conception of the subjectivity of human persons excludes the weighing and balancing which is assumed possible by those who deny that there are intrinsically evil acts. According to Christian faith, human persons can make free choices. Nonbelievers can deny this, but Christians cannot, for it is an aspect of the Christian conception of the human person closely tied to the belief that we are made in the image of God who creates and redeems freely, and it is essential to the Christian conception of both sin and the act of faith.

Free choice excludes psychological determinism. Psychological determinism is the theory that one's choice is settled by that which appears to be the most desirable possibility under consideration. If those goods which are ends for human action were commensurable, so that one could tell which alternative contained in some univocal sense the greatest net good or the least evil, one possibility would appear most desirable. If this were so, then psychological determinism would be correct, for one chooses for the sake of the good, and could not adopt a proposal promising less good, if another proposal promised all of that good and more.

It follows that the Christian doctrine of free choice rules out the weighing and balancing which is assumed possible by most who deny that there are any intrinsically evil acts. As I say, this argument is subtle and needs to be articulated at greater length. I have attempted to do so in various other places, perhaps most clearly in a book, of which Joseph Boyle is co-author, entitled *Life and Death with Liberty and Justice: A Contribution to the Euthanasia Debate*, chapter 11, Sections C and D; but in more detail in an article, "Against Consequentialism," which appeared in the *American Journal of Jurisprudence* (1978).

I now move on to the fourth of the doctrinal points: the Christian appreciation of the brokenness of the world and the pervasiveness of sin.

Christian morality does take full account of the reality of evil. Thus, it never has proposed standards for living in an ideal world, a world free of sin and its effects. For this very reason, Christian morality, unlike many moral theories which begin by sounding far higher and more humane, never has tried to define moral obligation in terms of maximizing good and minimizing evil. The primary demand of Christian morality is a demand for sinners: Repent!

The supposition that a realistic awareness of evil requires that one make exceptions to moral norms as required to mitigate evil in difficult situations presupposes the possibility of weighing and balancing which I have just been criticizing. One cannot make compromises without measuring the violation one chooses against the evil one would have to accept if one refused to violate the good for which the norm to which one makes an exception claims one's reverence.

Other points already considered also tell against the supposed need for compromise. Since Christian morality is primarily a morality of inwardness, consequences are not determinative. A Christian heart, without abandoning faith and love, can tolerate and suffer much evil, and will do so when the alternative is to identify with the evil.

One cannot adopt a proposal to violate a basic human good without identifying oneself with evil. The act is not the outward performance, detachable from the self. To adopt a proposal to kill a person is to make oneself a murderer. One cannot adopt such a proposal, make oneself such a person, without constricting love of the human goods and violating the divine goodness in which they are participants.

To suppose of a Christian who refuses to do evil that good might follow therefrom is evading responsibility out of pharisaic concern with personal moral purity is to presuppose that human responsibility extends in one and the same way to everything to which human power could extend. This assumption would render null the Christian doctrine of trust in providence, for there would be no occasion to stop short of doing everything possible, and to rely on providence, if there were no limits to the methods one might use in trying to overcome evil.

For Christians, however, there are very definite limits. The necessary refusal to do what violates human goods inevitably leads to alienation between the sinful world and the Christian, just to the extent that the Christian is united with Christ. The alienation means that Christian virtue is its own punishment, for the faithful Christian is plunged into evil, not as a doer of it but, together with Jesus, as a sufferer.

The readiness to suffer evil as a function of refusing to cooperate in it and compromise with it is an essential, although currently unpopular, aspect of Christian life. It is the properly Christian way of struggling with evil and overcoming evil. This is the law of the cross, which requires of every Christian the readiness for martyrdom, the Christian act par excellence.

Christians do share in the very liberty of God. This is the fifth point of doctrine to be considered.

If Christians are guided by the Spirit, the law loses its hold. But the liberty of the children of God must not be misunderstood. It is freedom from sin, reconciliation with God. Like all goods of Christian life, this liberty must be understood according to the model exhibited in Jesus. Being one with God, in perfect liberty he emptied himself, was obedient, served humbly, suffered, and died. Jesus is the model of responsibility and no legalist, but he deals with evil by patient suffering, with reverence for every good, not by action which would violate and destroy – violate the good in order to destroy and so minimize evil.

Christian morality cannot be captured in universal norms, for each Christian's mission is different. This morality is one of individual responsibility, and the primary law of Christian life is the inward grace of the Spirit.

Nevertheless, if the people of God, carrying on the redemptive work of Jesus through the ages, shared no common good, they could not be united in the same project of salvation history. But in fact they do participate in this common project, and they do so not as puppets but as informed and willing cooperators. As revelation has unfolded, the meaning of the good to be hoped for also has unfolded. This good does transcend the proportionate goods of human persons, but does not exclude them, as I explained previously.

Throughout salvation history there have been certain constants: for example, that death, humankind's oldest enemy, is to be overcome. The subordinate, but essentially related practical insight that human life is a good, that it is sacred, that God is lord of it, and that its violation offends him has been equally constant. And so while there are no moral rules which tell Christians precisely what they ought to do, there are some kinds of proposals which will always be repugnant to a heart into which God's love is poured forth, a heart which hopes for the salvation he promises.

Legalism does indeed need to be excluded from Christian morality. But reverence for the basic goods of human persons is not legalism. The legalistic style would articulate itself into endless prescriptions to direct one to the good, to make sure that one did not miss it, and thus, unfortunately, would delimit the good to certain goals which could be anticipated. Christian morality does not attempt to delimit the good. Its affirmative prescriptions always are open-ended. Yet Christian moral teaching can make clear what must be avoided if one is to live in Christ – responsibly, freely, and through the grace of the Spirit.

This paper articulated, in a preliminary and very condensed way, ideas subsequently developed much more adequately in the author's *Way of the Lord Jesus*, Volume One, *Christian Moral Principles* (Chicago: Franciscan Herald Press, 1983). While the author still holds the positions asserted in the paper, he now would express them somewhat differently. In particular, rather than talking about the violation of basic human goods, he now talks about the violation of *instances* of such goods. For example, instead of saying that abortion violates the basic human good of life, he now says that each abortion violates an instance of the basic good of human life, namely, the life of the baby who is aborted.

2.
Catholic Theology, Catholic Morality, Catholic Conscience (1978)
Rev. Msgr. William B. Smith

In doing some research on the formation of conscience, I was struck by this curious convergence – in our pursuit and study of things divine most of the trouble seems to be with the "human." By that I mean that most of the flash points in current controversies about the formation of a Catholic conscience seem to involve the Latin word for human, *humanus*, as in:

> Pope Pius XII, *Humani Generis* (August 12, 1950);
> Vatican Council II, *Dignitatis Humanae* (December 7, 1965);
> Pope Paul VI, *Humanae Vitae* (July 25, 1968); and
> Congregation for the Doctrine of the Faith, *Persona Humana* (December 29, 1975).

This chronological listing is surely just a verbal listing, but I find that all of these authentic teachings are very much connected. It is my listening and reading experience that when a Catholic does not accept and/or believe one of these teachings, he or she inevitably has difficulty with these other teachings. For example, dissent form *Humanae Vitae* and *Persona Humana* normally involves a rejection of *Humani Generis* together with a distortion of *Dignitatis Humanae*.

Whether this must be the case is an interesting question; that it has been the case in our past decade of dissent (1968–78) seems to be beyond question. Nonetheless, my purpose here is not to re-examine in detail the nature and function of conscience in Catholic theology; rather, I would like to focus on certain connected elements that are much involved in the proper formation of conscience and most especially the so-called "right" to dissent within the perspective of Catholic theology, Catholic morality, and Catholic conscience.

If I am not mistaken, there are current explanations of dissent that almost preclude the possibility of forming a correct Catholic conscience because the presuppositions and methodology of this dissent do in fact change the nature of sacred theology and thus profoundly alter Catholic morality whatever be the application in question.

I. Nature and Function of Conscience

The conventional textbooks of Catholic moral theology explain the nature of conscience and its function at some length and in precise detail.[1] A reliable treatment of "Conscience in the Catholic Theological Tradition" is an article by that title authored by Joseph V. Dolan, S.J.[2] While the word "conscience" (Greek: *syneidesis*) appears some twenty-eight times in the singular and once in the plural in the New Testament (it does not appear in the O.T.), its use there is basically a reflective one. That is, man is understood to be so constituted by God that should he go beyond the moral limits of his nature, he will sense the pain of conscience.[3]

Quite frankly, the precise moral nature and function of conscience in contemporary moral theology is much more delimited than that. While fully aware of a broad psychological understanding of conscience – a remembering that is *retrospective* and *reflective* – the moral usage of the term "conscience" is and has been for centuries an act of *judging*, i.e., a *prospective* and *directive* act of judgment.

Many metaphors, in current coin, describe conscience as the "voice of God," an "inner voice," or as a "still small voice" within one's so-called

---

1 For textbooks: Aertnys-Damen-Visser, *Theologia Moralis*, Vol. 1 (ed. 18) (Rome: Marietti, 1967), nn. 138–59, pp. 189–218; Noldin-Schmitt-Heinzel, *Summa Theologiae Moralis*, Vol. 1 (ed. 33) (Innsbruck: Felizian Rauch, 1960), nn. 208–56, pp. 197–240; M. Zalba, *Theologiae Moralis Compendium*, I (Madrid: B.A.C., 1958), nn. 640–734, pp. 355–419; E. D'Arcy, *Conscience and Its Right to Freedom* (New York: Sheed & Ward, 1961); P. Delhaye, *The Christian Conscience*, (New York: Desclée Co., 1968); A. Fagothey, *Right & Reason* (ed. 6) (St. Louis: C. V. Mosby Co., 1976), pp. 39–49.

2 J. V. Dolan, S.J., "Conscience in the Catholic Theological Tradition," in W. C. Bier (ed.) *Conscience: Its Freedom & Limitations*, (New York: Fordham Univ. Press, 1971), pp. 9–19

3 J. C. Turro, "Conscience in the Bible," in Bier (ed.), *Conscience*, p. 6. (Readers might note that C. A. Pierce's *Conscience in the New Testament* [London: S.C.M. Press, 1955] is still considered the model work in this area.)

heart of hearts. Such expressions are useful only insofar as they are recognized and acknowledged as metaphors. Conscience is often described as a sense of guilt or of pangs; as a system of values, feelings, insights; conscience is said to blame, to sting, to accuse, prompt, or assuage. Moral theology knows these descriptions, but the precise nature and function of conscience in Catholic moral theology is that act of passing or making a personal judgment on the moral quality of a proposed and particular action.

It is this *prospective-directive* act of judgment – the technical name of which is antecedent conscience – that is the chief interest of the theologian and the moralist.[4] All properly moral questions involve this.

Properly speaking, conscience neither invents law nor does it create objective value. Its function is to apply either general or particular moral knowledge to any prospective and particular action. Throughout, there is an objective and subjective referent. Moral knowledge or wisdom is based on some objective consideration – some norm other than myself (e.g., God's revelation, the teaching of the Church, the teaching of Buddha, the teaching of Ghandi, etc.). But it is the personal subject (you or I or anyone) who applies that moral wisdom to concrete situations, and it is that concrete application that so concerns moral theology.

Indeed, moral law or moral wisdom would be rather useless, unless each person has the power and ability to apply them to specific situations. This focus on the "decision" or "judgment" of conscience is well established in our ancient and recent Catholic theological tradition. Vatican Council II presents and presumes this understanding (*Gaudium et Spes*, #16). The Canadian Catholic Conference underscored this point in their closely reasoned *Statement on the Formation of Conscience* (December 1, 1973) saying that conscience is that ultimate "judgment."[5] More recently still our National Conference of Catholic Bishops, in their moral pastoral, *To Live in Christ Jesus*, put it this way:[6]

> We still must decide how to realize and affirm them in the concrete circumstances of our lives. Such decisions are called *judgments of conscience* (emphasis added).

Since it is a judgment, two possibilities are always real – we can judge

---

4 J. V. Dolan, "Conscience in the Catholic Theological Tradition," p. 10.

5 Canadian Catholic Conference, *Statement On The Formation of Conscience* (Dec. 1, 1973), N.6 in *Crux Special* (January 4, 1974), p. 1.

6 N.C.C.B., *To Live in Christ Jesus* (November 11, 1976), #1, Introduction, "Conscience," (Washington, D.C.: USCC, 1976), p. 10.

correctly or incorrectly. At this point, two practical rules for action are recalled: 1) always obey a certain conscience; 2) never act on a doubtful one. To this point, most nod in agreement. But it is often here that slogans substitute for study. It is, for some, now common practice and almost common parlance to say, "follow your conscience!" and say no more. But, this is misleading and most incomplete. It is here that more must be said about forming and informing a correct conscience in the first place.

It is here, in the proper formation of a correct Catholic conscience, that the sources of sacred theology – and thus the sources of Catholic morality – will loom largest. These sacred sources will either be accorded primary place or reduced in status, by various arrangements, to be "privileged" or even "precious" in-put among many other sources of input of reference in the formation of conscience. The more one dissents from Catholic teaching, the less likely the sacred sources {"*loci theologici*") will be primary.

Indeed Vatican Council II has but one *ex professo* statement on the formation of conscience:

> In the formation of their conscience, the Christian faithful ought carefully to attend to the sacred and certain doctrine of the Church (*Dignitatis Humanae*, #14).

The official footnote of the Council Fathers (*DH*, #14, n. 35) cites the *locus classicus* on the formation of a Catholic conscience, the discourse of Pope Pius XII of March 23, 1952, "On the Correct Formation of a Christian Conscience."[7]

Factor for factor, no single element looms so large in the formation of a Catholic conscience as does the "sacred and certain doctrine" of the Catholic Church. Some see our Spirit-guided teaching as a heavy burden on already overburdened intellects. I prefer to see such Spirit-guided guidance as a blessing, indeed a necessary blessing, resting as it does on sacred sources.

In my judgment, it is now also pedagogically important to employ precise and accurate terminology in this area; e.g., "correct conscience," "erroneous conscience." I say that because expressions such as "sincere conscience" and "good conscience" seem to be very much in vogue. I would like to think that we can presume that all parties to all discussions are "sincere." If not, that is a different kind of problem, that would be a problem of "bad" or "insincere" faith.

II. Freedom of Conscience in Vatican II?

7 *A.A.S.* 44 (1952), pp. 270–78.

One other point here is a matter of some confusion. Let us not confuse "religious freedom" which Vatican II did teach (cf. *Dignitatis Humanae*, the Declaration on Religious Freedom) with so-called "freedom of conscience," which the same Council did not teach and, in fact, took some pains to avoid.

In the first place, we should not confuse "physical freedom" with "moral freedom" and then escalate this blend into the status of an alleged "right." *Physical* freedom is the *physical ability* to do something, to act or not act, as in the physical ability to throw yourself in front of a moving car. *Moral* freedom is the moral *right* to perform an act. One does have the *physical ability* to throw oneself before a car (presuming this is not a rescue at all), but no one has the *moral right* to do so suicidally.

In essence, no one has the "moral right" to do what is "morally wrong." Recall, that the religious freedom taught by the Council is a *freedom form coercion* – an external civil right in the civil order. On this, the Council document is explicit:[8]

> Religious freedom, in turn, which men demand as necessary to fulfill their duty to worship God, has to do with immunity from coercion in civil society. Therefore it leaves untouched traditional Catholic doctrine on the moral duty of men and societies toward the true religion and toward the one Church of Christ (*D.H.*, #1).

Religious freedom, here proclaimed, is then a freedom *from* coercion – a freedom *from*, *not* a freedom *for* doing whatever one wants. The required nuance and necessary precision about the meaning of this Declaration has been provided by John Courtney Murray, one of the contributors to the document, and one who took great pains that this teaching not be confused with a non-Catholic understanding of freedom of conscience.

Fr. Murray writes:[9]

> It is worth noting that the Declaration does not base the right to free exercise of religion on "freedom of conscience." Nowhere does this phrase occur. And the Declaration nowhere lends its authority to the theory for which the phrase frequently stands, namely, that I have a right to do what my conscience tells me to do, simply because my con-

---

8 W. M. Abbott, S.J. (ed.), *The Documents of Vatican II* (New York: Guild Press, 1966), p. 677.

9 *Ibid*, pp. 679 and 694–95.

science tells me to do it. This is a perilous theory. Its particular peril is subjectivism – the notion that, in the end, it is my conscience, and not the objective truth, which determines what is right or wrong, true or false.

Commenting later on #14 of the same Declaration, the same Fr. Murray writes:

> It might be noted here that the Council intended to make a clear distinction between religious freedom as a principle in the civil order and the Christian freedom which obtains even within the Church. These two freedoms are distinct in kind; and it would be perilous to confuse them. Nowhere does the Declaration touch the issue of freedom within the Church . . .

Thus, this Declaration and one of its best-informed commentators took great pains to prevent misunderstanding and to preclude moral confusion. After all, where I have a "moral right" to do good, and a "moral right" to do the opposite, I would then have a "moral right" to do anything and simply call that "moral." That would be moral nonsense.

Vatican Council II employs the word "conscience" some seventy-two times.[10] Only once does the term "freedom of conscience" ever appear in the texts of the Council (cf. *Declaration on Christian Education*, #8). That single use is in the above sense, that the Church has a right to be free from coercion, in the civil order, in establishing her schools. All other seventy-one mentions of the word are with the conventional qualifications in the accepted terminology mentioned above: correct conscience, rightly informed conscience, etc.

No doubt, this is a small point, but it is a necessary distinction, and one which Pope Paul VI saw fit to reemphasize.[11] This distinction between "religious freedom" and so-called "freedom of conscience" is one that careful scholars have examined at some length,[12] but which popular writers con-

---

10 *Cf.* X. Ochoa, *Index Verborum cum documentis Concilii Vaticani Segundi* (Roma: Commentarium Pro Religiosis, 1967), pp. 106–7.

11 Pope Paul VI, To College of Cardinals (Dec. 20, 1976) in *The Pope Speaks* 22 (1977), p. 20.

12 P. Pavan, "Declaration of Religious Freedom" in H. Vorgrimler (ed.), *Commentary on the Documents of Vatican II*, Vol 4. (New York: Herder & Herder, 1969), pp. 49–86; R. J. Regan, S.J., *Conflict and Consensus* (New York: Macmillan, 1967); R. J. Regan, S.J., "Conscience in Documents of Vatican II," in W. Bier, (ed.) *Conscience*, pp. 29–36; M. Carter, "Dignitatis

stantly confuse.[13] The non-Catholic understanding of "freedom of conscience" cannot be foisted upon nor located in the documents of Vatican II. Indeed, the Council itself made no small effort to avoid just that kind of confusion.

III. The Alleged "Moral Right to Dissent"

A similar post-Vatican-II revision has come about of late, again in the name of conscience. This alleged "development" is the so-called "moral right to dissent." Here too, the physical and at times moral duty to *withhold internal assent* has been converted and escalated into an alleged positive *moral right to dissent*. I take it that *withholding internal assent* is different from *positive expression of dissent*, but I see them everywhere lumped together, and some authors use the concepts interchangeably. Curiously, the advocates of the alleged right to dissent would have it that we, as faithful Catholics, not only have the moral right and moral duty to assent to Church Teaching (Vatican II, *Lumen Gentium*, #25; *Dei Verbum*, #10), but that we also have the "moral right" to dissent from it.

Fr. Charles E. Curran is, perhaps, the leading advocate of theological dissent in this country, as an article of his verifies.[14] As with several authors, Fr. Curran, passes rather easily from a possibility of dissent (i.e., *withholding internal assent*), to an alleged and explicit right of Catholics to dissent from Catholic teaching.[15]

We know from logic that the pass from the possible to the actual is a transfer more easily stated than verified. Now, it is Fr. Curran's particular claim that the Canadian Catholic Bishops – while they themselves did not dissent from *Humanae Vitae* – did in their post-*Humanae Vitae* Statement (September 27, 1968) about that encyclical, "acknowledge the explicit right of Catholics to dissent," according to Fr. Curran.[16]

Humanae – Declaration on Religious Freedom," *The Jurist* 36 (1976), pp. 338–52.

13 E.g., John Deedy, "Troubled Vatican," *New York Times* (October 13, 1972), p. 39; D. J. Thorman, "Views & Reviews," *National Catholic Reporter* 13 (October 21, 1977), p. 6.

14 C. E. Curran, "The Catholic Hospital and the Ethical & Religious Directives For Catholic Health Facilities," *Linacre Quarterly* 44 (Feb. 1977), pp. 18–36; in particular re: dissent, pp. 25–30.

15 *Ibid.*, p. 25.

16 *Ibid.*

Upon reading and rereading that Statement of the Canadian Hierarchy of September 27, 1968,[17] I can find no acknowledgment by them of any "explicit right to dissent." I do find in #17 and #25 of that Statement that:[18]

> In particular, the argumentation and rational foundation of the encyclical, which are only briefly indicated, have failed in some cases to win the *assent* of men of science, or indeed of some men of culture and education who share in the contemporary empirical and scientific mode of thought. . . .

> But they should remember that their good faith will be dependent upon a sincere self-examination to determine the true motives and grounds for such *suspension of assent* and on continued effort to understand and deepen their knowledge of the teaching of the Church. (#17).

> In the situation we described earlier in this statement (paragraph 17) the confessor or counsellor must show sympathetic understanding and reverence for the sincere good faith of those who *fail* in their effort to *accept* some point of the encyclical. (#25).

> Counsellors may meet others who, accepting the teaching of the Holy Father, find that because of particular circumstances, they are involved in what *seems* to them a clear conflict of duties . . . (#26) (emphasis added).

Now certainly, Fr. Curran is not among the latter, that is, among those who accept the teaching, because he has written elsewhere:[19]

> For the sake of the truth and the best interests of the Church and all mankind, I have concluded that it is necessary to take the more radical solution which maintains that the papal teaching on this point is in error.

Similarly, he is just as emphatic on what he considers his own refutation of Church teaching on direct sterilization[20] – a teaching also affirmed in

17 John Horgan (ed.) *Humanae Vitae & the Bishops: The Encyclical and the Statements of the National Hierarchies* (Shannon, Ire.: Irish Univ. Press, 1972) for the Canadian hierarchy, cf. pp. 76–83.
18 *Ibid.*, re: #17, p. 79; re: ##25–26, p. 81.
19 C. E. Curran (ed.) and his Introduction in *Contraception: Authority & Dissent* (New York: Herder & Herder, 1969), p. 14.
20 Cf. his "Sterilization: Exposition, Critique & Refutation of Past Teaching," in *New Perspectives in Moral Theology*, (Notre Dame, Ind.: Fides, 1972), pp. 194–211.

Humanae Vitae.[21] Nonetheless, granting the Canadian mention of actual and possible *lack of assent,* I find no explicit mention of any "explicit right to dissent" as Fr. Curran claims to find.

It is true that the Statement of the Canadian hierarchy of September 1968 received much attention and generated some amount of confusion. But it is also true that that Statement was not that hierarchy's last word on conscience formation. It approaches the disingenuous, for someone who reads widely in the field, not to mention the Canadian hierarchy's more recent and relevant Statement on the Formation of Conscience of December 1, 1973.[22] Surely this fuller and later Statement of the same episcopal conference must be considered an important part of their complete discussion of this matter.

A careful review of the statements of so many episcopal conferences reveals that the word "dissent" rarely, if ever, appears. Several do mention the possibility of persons coming to different conclusions or accepting only parts of the teaching or of withholding internal assent; but any alleged "right to dissent" cannot easily be grounded on these statements. Interestingly, the Belgian and Austrian hierarchies are often cited for this purpose. Yet, the Belgian statement (August 30, 1968) reads in part:[23]

> This disapproval by the supreme authority of the Church constitutes a rule of conduct for the Catholic conscience; and no one is authorized to dispute that its character is in itself obligatory. (#11)

And again:

> Someone, however, who is competent in the matter under consideration and capable of forming a personal and well-founded judgment – which necessarily presupposes a sufficient amount of knowledge – may, after a serious examination before God, come to other conclusions on certain points. In such a case he has the right to follow his con-
>
> viction provided that he remains sincerely disposed to continue his enquiry. (A similar doctrine, which we find also in St. Thomas Aqui-

---

21 Pope Paul VI, *Humanae Vitae* (July 25, 1968), #14; confer footnote #15 of same for the sources of past and present teaching.

22 C.C.C., *Statement on the Formation of Conscience* (Dec 1, 1973), nn. 1–56; in *Crux Special* (January 4, 1974) 4 pp.; also in *Catholic Mind* 72 (April 1974), pp. 40–51.

23 F.J. Horgan (ed.), *Humanae Vitae & the Bishops,* #1, p. 64; #2:4, pp. 65–66.

nas (I-II, q. 19, a. 5), inspires the conciliar Declaration on Religious Freedom, #2). (#2)

It may be of interest that the question referred to in the *Summa Theologiae* is "*utrum ratio errans obliget?*" – Is a mistaken conscience binding? (*ST*, I-II, q. 19, a. 5).

Also in the Austrian statement (September 21, 1968), prior to their comments on those who feel unable to accept the judgment of the Church, they make the following observation by way of preface: "It follows that there is freedom of conscience, but not freedom in the formation of conscience. (N. 2)"[24]

Claims about other statements of other hierarchies also deserve study and careful review, lest that curiosity entitled "geographical morality" go unquestioned.

By way of conclusion to this section, I would ask the reader not to equate uncritically a lack of internal assent with some alleged positive right to dissent. I would further suggest that those who insist that the alleged right to dissent is found in the statements of episcopal conferences after *Humanae Vitae* should document such explicitness; incantation will not supply where documentation is lacking.

IV. Dissent in Practice

In the past decade of dissent, the literature of dissent continues to grow – with varying degrees of nuance – but now apparently with unlimited applications.

Quite recently, Frs. Avery Dulles[25] and Richard McCormick[26] have, more or less, coalesced in a mutually agreeable "theology of dissent." Since both authors figure rather prominently in this country, in their respective fields, it seems to me worthwhile to review some of their latest statements

---

24 *Ibid.*, p. 60.

25 A. Dulles, *The Resilient Church* (New York: Doubleday, 1977), Chapter 5, "Doctrinal Authority for a Pilgrim Church," pp. 93–112; esp., pp. 107–12; also cf. his earlier "What is Magisterium?" in *Origins* 6 (1976), pp. 81–87.

26 R. A. McCormick, "Notes on Moral Theology," in *Theological Studies* 29 (1968), pp. 714–18; *TS* 30 (1969), pp. 644–48; his address in *Proceedings CTSA* (1969), pp. 239–54; "The Magisterium: A New Model," *America* 122 (June 27, 1970), p. 675; *TS* 38 (1977), pp. 84–100, (re: Dulles, pp. 96–97); "Conscience, Theologians & the Magisterium," *New Catholic World* 220 (Nov./Dec. 1977), 268–71; *TS* 39 (1978), pp. 76–79, 136–38.

and assess how their theology of dissent affects the sources of sacred theology and thus Catholic morality and the formation of conscience.

For Fr. Dulles, the phenomenon of dissent has intensified of late because of three general aspects that he considers worthy of special mention:

1) Our age is alleged by him to be "particularly sensitive to the values of freedom and authenticity, and to the dignity of conscience as the ultimate norm for moral choice";[27]

2) We live in a "pluralist situation" – and a pluralism "sanctioned by Vatican II";[28]

3) Secular sources remind us that officeholders are constantly tempted to employ power to bolster their position. "When popes and bishops insist very heavily on apostolic succession, divine right and the special graces attached to their office, they leave themselves open to the suspicion that ideology is at work."[29]

As to the above: (1) Just what our age is particularly sensitive to is largely debatable. For example, one might note the chilling silence of our age toward such sensitivities as: Soviet slave labor camps, slaughter in Uganda. harassment of the Kurdish people, and genocide in Cambodia.[30] More to our purpose here is what Dulles calls "the dignity of conscience as the ultimate norm for moral choice." This is surely something that requires qualification; it requires at least making clear the distinction between correct and erroneous conscience since it is the absence of the former and the presence of the latter that account for the atrocities just mentioned.

(2) As for "pluralism," this too requires some essential distinctions between its multiple secular forms and ecclesiastical expressions of the same. The formulations of the present pope, Paul VI, are both necessary and enlightening when considering "pluralism" within the Church.

Pope Paul VI recognizes a certain pluralism of research and thought which investigates and expounds dogma but without disintegrating its identical objective meaning. Indeed, there is a certain and welcomed *complementary* pluralism of concord and cohesion; but there is as well a certain *contradictory* pluralism of division and dissent. The former highlights and

---

27 F Dulles, *The Resilient Church*, p. 108.

28 *Ibid.*

29 *Ibid.*, p. 109.

30 Cf. W. Safire, "Silence is Guilt," *New York Times* (April 24, 1978), p. A23.

strengthens unity; the latter obscures and dissolves the sacramentality of the Church.[31]

(3) As to this third aspect, I would question the appropriateness of comparing popes and bishops with suspect political powers and the known abuses of same. To insist "very heavily" on apostolic succession, divine right and special graces of office does not lead me to suspect that ideology is at work; rather, I suspect and indeed believe that the Holy Spirit works through these gifts and graces.

Fr. Dulles then states that Vatican Council II did not "directly" challenge what he calls "the reigning neo-scholastic theory," which turns out to be not just "theory" but rather #25 of *Lumen Gentium*. Thus, he writes of the Council:[32]

> It affirms the obligation to assent to the ordinary non-infallible teaching of the Roman Pontiff without any explicit mention of the right to dissent.

This statement is only partially accurate. True, the Council did affirm the obligation to assent to ordinary non-infallible teaching, but it did so without any — implicit or explicit – mention of dissent, much less any alleged right to dissent.

Relying, as he states, on the McSorley and Komonchak studies,[33] Dulles argues further that several bishops (in fact, three bishops proposed modus #159 to #25 of *Lumen Gentium*) proposed some allowance be made for the case of "an educated person who for solid reasons finds himself un-

---

31 Pope Paul VI, *Paterna Cum Benevolentia* (Dec. 8, 1974) esp. ##3, 4, 5. For theological commentaries and exposition of this exhortation, confer the studies of many members of the International Theological Commission in *Problems of the Church Today* (Wash., D.C.: USCC, 1976), 106 pp.

32 Dulles, *The Resilient Church*, p. 109.
   Two other points could be added here:
   (i) One might, with profit, combine *L. G.*, #25 with *D.V.* #10, as did the CDF (Feb. 15, 1975) in pointing out an error of Prof. Kueng re: the Magisterium of the Church; cf. *AAS* 67 (1975) 203–4; (Eng.) *L'OR* e/e 10/362/75), p. 2.
   (ii) It should not be presumed throughout that everything that every author describes as non-infallible teaching is actually and properly described as such.

33 Dulles, p. 209, n. 26.

able to assent internally to such teaching."[34] All agree that the Council's Doctrinal Commission responded that the approved authors should be consulted for this.

Thus, Fr. Dulles is correct: the Council in its formal teaching did not advance the discussion of dissent; indeed, "dissent" is not mentioned at all; rather, the problem and possibility of a lack of internal assent is referred to where it was and is explained – in the approved authors.

Dulles then attempts to establish *indirectly* what is not *directly* taught by the Council, and he presents this through what he calls the "reversals" and "other revisions" of the Council. The latter are what he calls rehabilitated theologians who had met with pre-conciliar restrictions in their teaching and publishing efforts: John Courtney Murray, Pierre Teilhard de Chardin, Henri de Lubac, and Yves Congar.

That these scholars moved from under a "cloud of suspicion in the 1950s" to what Dulles calls being "surrounded with a bright halo of enthusiasm"[35] is true to the extent that three of these four scholars did serve as *periti* at the Council. (The exact brilliance and size of the Teilhardian "halo" is and will probably remain a subject of lively discussion.) De Lubac and Congar are scholars who have conceded that they improved several of their theological themes in light of *Humani Generis*. Curiously, Murray himself brings a great deal of precision and needed nuance to the very question under discussion. (Confer his commentary on *Dignitatis Humanae* in the Abbott edition of the *Documents of Vatican II*; especially notes 3, 5, and 58, pp. 676–77, 678–79, and 694–95.). I say "curiously" because so many of Fr. Murray's admirers seem not to admire or remember what Fr. Murray himself taught in this regard.

Also, I find in none of the above *periti* anything that could be accurately described as "contradictory pluralism." Thus, when Dulles concludes that the Council *in actual practice* "implicitly" taught the "legitimacy and even the value of dissent," and "in effect, the Council said that the ordinary magisterium of the Roman Pontiff had fallen into error and unjustly harmed the careers of loyal and able scholars,"[36] I find his conclusion unsupported and unpersuasive – It is largely one of inference, and it is a rather strained

---

34 *Ibid.*, p. 109.
35 *Ibid.*, p. 110.
36 *Ibid.*

construction, resting not on what the Council did teach, but more on who attended the Council and in what capacity.

In any case, Fr. Dulles concludes his chapter with the statement that dissent can be a source of confusion and discord, and, to alleviate this, he submits six recommendations re: dissent:[37]

> (1) All concerned should keep in touch;
> (2) Pastoral leaders should not speak unless there is a wide consensus; this is achieved when the "weight of responsible opinion decisively favors one side over the other";
> (3) When there is no consensus, acknowledge that good Christians disagree, which admission today is no scandal; what is a scandal is when "holders of pastoral power" suppress freedom of expression and debate, where there is, as yet, no agreed solution; (scandal, apparently, is a one-way street!)
> (4) When there is no consensus: popes and bishops "may clearly and candidly state their convictions" and "seek to win assent for their own positions," but they should do this without imposing "their views by juridical pressures";
> (5) When Church members are not able to give assent, Dulles cites Fr. McCormick in saying "non-infallible teaching does not bring with it an immediate obligation to assent." (This point is rather an odd one for Fr. Dulles, since two pages earlier he himself cites *Lumen Gentium* #25 to the contrary);
> (6) "Dissenters should not be silenced," and his reason for this is that in many cases, "those who dissent from Church teaching in one generation are preparing the official positions of the Church in the future." (This statement certainly lacks the historical perspective one has come to expect in an author of Fr. Dulles's stature. Surely, the opposite has more often been the case and most especially so in moral matters. Consider, e.g., the errors of Michael du Bay (*D.S.* 1901–80); Laxist errors (*D.S.* 2021–48, 2049–65, 2101–67); Molinos (*D.S.* 2201–69); Jansenists (*D.S.* 2301–32); Quesnel (*D.S.* 2400–2502). The sixteenth and seventeenth centuries are actually littered with dissenting moral positions – enjoying, as they did, varying degrees of academic consensus – which I am sure we all agree and even pray will not and cannot become "the official positions of the Church in the future."

Fr. Dulles concludes that his six recommendations – by page 111, they are "principles" – will be contested by some, and especially by those looking to the Church for "oracular responses" to all really important questionhs

---

37 *Ibid.*, pp. 110–12.

and those who regard dissent as tantamount to disloyalty. I, for one, do not look to the Church for "oracular responses." I do look to the Church for the authentic teaching of Jesus Christ, or, in the words of Vatican Council II, I, in the formation of my Second Vatican Council Catholic conscience, must carefully "attend to the sacred and certain doctrine of the Church" (*D.H.*, #14), and for the very reason stated by the same Council: "The Church is, by the will of Christ, the teacher of the truth" (*D.H.*, #14).

As a member of the Catholic Church – with or without degrees after my name – I owe this authentic teaching the religious assent of my soul (*Lumen Gentium*, #25; *Dei Verbum*, #10). If that is loyalty, I understand it. If withholding my religious assent or, to up the stakes, positively dissenting from the same authentic teaching is also loyalty, that I do not understand quite so well.

In my judgment, the magisterium of the Church is not an operative functionary of an ongoing consensus nor a mere referee of consensus building; it is rather one of the sacred sources of sacred theology, and, as Vatican II teaches, these sacred sources (Sacred Tradition, Sacred Scripture, and the Teaching Authority of the Church) "in accord with God's most wise design, are so linked and joined together that one cannot stand without the others. . ." (*Dei Verbum*, #10).

As above, I do not consider this a particularly itchy penchant for the "oracular" but a rather sober theological stance completely in agreement with an identical proposition of the International Theological Commission. After concluding a lengthy study of theological pluralism, the I. T. C. addressed the question of where does one locate the thread of Catholic unity in a plurality of moral opinions; their considered proposition is:[38]

> The unity of Christian morality is based on unchanging principles, contained in Sacred Scripture, clarified by Sacred Tradition, and presented in each age by the magisterium. (proposition, #14)

When Fr. Dulles cites Fr. McCormick, he cites as well McCormick's

---

38 International Theological Commission (Oct. 11, 1972) in *La Documentation Catholique* 70 (May 20, 1973), p. 460; (Eng. Trans. in London) *Tablet* 227 (July 7, 1973), p. 647.

rather full position on magisterium and dissent.[39] It is not my present purpose to comment on McCormick's "double magisteria" theory:[40]

> Unless and until this close interdependence is acknowledged and indicated both the hierarchical magisterium and the magisterium of theologians (the term is appropriate as indicating a true competence and authority not possessed by the hierarchy as such) are in trouble.

The explicitness of this most recent expression of McCormick may be somewhat novel, but as Dulles's citations of him indicate, the present position of McCormick has been gaining ground – largely by way of repetition – and almost entirely within this past decade of dissent.

In commenting unfavorably on Fr. McCormick, one must apparently risk the charge of collapsing "theological courtesy."[41] Of late, Fr. McCormick has become an avid expositor of Aristotelian logic; I say this because he accuses so many of *petitio principii* (begging the question): a charge he levels against the Congregation for the Doctrine of the Faith,[42] now also against Prof. May[43], and several other and lesser sources who do not read *Humanae Vitae* as he does.[44]

Further, no one can doubt that Fr. McCormick is a truly gifted verbal craftsman. Indeed, he has, in my judgment, a positive charisma for "grabbing the rhetorical middle." For instance, in proposing a "Save or Let Die" ethic for grossly or severely deformed infants,[45] he begins with vintage McCormick: let us avoid *dogmatism* (which prescinds from circumstances) and avoid *concretism* (which denies the usefulness of guidelines); let us avoid *medical vitalism* (life at any cost) and avoid *medical pessimism* (which kills when frustrating or useless). "Is there no middle way?" he asks. Surely there is an alternative to supporting mere physical life as long as possible by all means available. Indeed, there is a middle way and Fr. McCormick knows too much moral theology to hint or pretend otherwise – just as he knows better than most that his vitalism-pessimism bind is such

---

39 Confer note 26 above.

40 Cf. his "Conscience, Theologians & the Magisterium," *New Cath. World* 220 (Nov./Dec. 1977), pp. 268–71.

41 R. McCormick in *TS* 38 (1977), p. 85.

42 *TS* 37 (1976), pp. 474–75.

43 *TS* 39 (1978), pp. 96–97.

44 *TS* 37 (1976), p. 474.

45 In *America* 131 (July 13, 1974), pp. 6–10.

only by verbal arrangement. These are neither the only alternatives, nor are they especially illuminating as alternatives, if they are such at all.

But when you paint a little picture of one opinion out here to the right of me and another out here to the left of me – guess who has grabbed the rhetorical middle?

Of late, the same style is brought to bear on the formation of conscience. McCormick argues it is not a matter of forming one's conscience by following either *Persona Humana* of the Congregation for the Doctrine of the Faith or the *Human Sexuality* book of the Catholic Theological Society of America Committee of 5. He argues instead:[46]

> Such mutually exclusive alternatives seem to suppose and reinforce two questionable ideas:
>
> 1) that the formulations of the Congregation are accurate and unchangeable;
> 2) that theology has nothing to do with whatever modification or alteration might be regarded as appropriate.

There must be room for enlightened study, for reflection and conversation in the Church: "if we leave no room for doubt and questioning, we will have no room for the privilege of growth."[47] Apart from neatly defining himself in the rhetorical middle, does Fr. McCormick really believe that the alternatives are unchangeable formulations v. do-nothing theology?

I am taking the long way around here in order to locate Fr. McCormick's recent review of the difficulties theologians encounter. In this, he considers as "utterly persuasive"[48] a rather questionable dichotomy advanced by Fr. Walter Burghardt on the task and difficulties of theology.[49]

Burghardt distinguishes two different notions of theology: (1) justification (of magisterial statements) and (2) understanding. For McCormick, far too many see the first as the primary, and even unique, task of theology.

Now, apart from collapsing theological courtesy, is this a serious disjunction? The papal team of statement-justifiers (who care not for understanding), and the thoughtful team of learned, understanding, wise men (who care not for statements)? McCormick will close the same "Notes on

---

46 In *N. Cath. World* 220 (1977), p. 271.
47 *Ibid.*
48 *TS* 39 (1978), p. 77.
49 W. Burghardt, "'Stone the Theologians!' The Role of Theology in Today's Church," *Catholic Mind* 75 (Sept. 1977), pp. 42–50.

Moral Theology" with this droll statement of his own: "Doubt and questioning are peculiarly the onerous task of the theologian, a task assigned to him by the Church.[50] But, as almost any moralist knows, "doubt" is a sin against faith; and, just where would one look to find such a task "assigned" to anyone in the Church by the Church?

Fr. McCormick opens and closes his recent moral notes[51] with an almost rationalist caution similar to what Fr. Dulles took some pains to disavow.[52] McCormick, endorsing F. Böckle, proposes that neither revelation nor authoritative statement replace human insight and reasoning, and that "reasonable" means "not ultimately mysterious."[53]

In his view, the magisterium is a "precious vehicle of our shared experience and knowledge,"[54] with the further qualifications that the magisterium is pastoral in character, limited to more or less adequate formulations, and addressed to different cultural backgrounds with different value perceptions.[55] Church teaching for him is much more a "teaching-learning" process so that, with Dulles, the pope and bishops "should not formulate their teaching against a broad or even very significant theological consensus."[56]

As before, this is no insignificant methodological presupposition but rather a serious ecclesiological shift in which one would have not simply a double magisteria, *ex aequo*, but a pastoral magisterium (pope and bishops in union with him) whose teachings are not deemed adequate unless and until validated by a broad or even very significant consensus of the magisterium of theologians. Since all of the cautions mentioned by McCormick seem to circumscribe only the pastoral magisterium (pope and bishops), one wonders whether this arrangement is even *ex aequo*.

The proposed analysis surely departs from and is at variance with *Lumen Gentium* #25 and *Dei Verbum* #10 of Vatican II, and it is also at variance with *Paterna Cum Benevolentia* of Pope Paul VI. It also seems to depart especially from the Letter of Pope Paul VI to the Theologians of Louvain (September 13, 1975),[57] wherein theology, or, more accurately,

---

50 *TS* 39 (1978), p. 138.
51 *Ibid.*, pp. 77–79 and 138–39.
52 Dulles, *The Resilient Church*, pp. 93 and 106–7.
53 *TS* 39 (1978), p. 79.
54 *Ibid.*, p. 137.
55 *Ibid.*
56 *Ibid.*, p. 138.
57 In *L'Osservatore Romano* (Eng. ed) 41/393 (Oct. 9, 1975), p. 8.

sacred theology, is not a private nor is it an autonomous effort but one *in* and *for* the Church within the *communio ecclesiae*. The temptation is and has been to substitute a secular notion of academic freedom – drawn from the profane sciences – and transfer same into sacred theology, much to the detriment of the principles peculiar to sacred theology (i.e., the articles of faith; and the special medium of knowledge – divine revelation).

Thus, a Catholic theologian must be faithful to Christ, to the Church, and to those who, by the express will of Christ, are the true interpreters of this Word of God in the Church. Theology cannot be conceived as an independent authority in the Church nor as an alternative to the magisterium, without changing the specifically sacred sources of sacred theology (Sacred Scripture, Sacred Tradition, Magisterium).

Ultimately, all the Catholic faithful are obliged to give religious assent of soul to these sacred sources; for we do affirm – not unreasonably but reasonably – that there is more than human wisdom here; i.e., Sacred Scripture is revealed by God, Sacred Tradition is guided by the Holy Spirit, and that there is an office in the Church, willed by Christ, to teach in His name.

This does not, I think, amount to a flight into mystery; but rather, it is consonant with the classic task of theology – *fides quaerens intellectum*. To reverse and/or dislocate that axiom is no small adjustment for the formation of a Catholic conscience; rather, it is to change the nature of Catholic theology, and in turn, Catholic morality because the sources of sacred theology have been significantly changed.

The decade of dissent first fueled by the rejection of *Humanae Vitae* could not be contained or limited to dissent on abortion, sterilization, and artificial contraception (*HV.* #14) because much of the logic of this dissent does not rest on difficulty with these specific teachings, but rather the logic involves an ecclesiological shift and a revision of the very nature of sacred theology.

When the magisterium of the Church is made the functional equivalent of theological consensus or the operational errand-boy of consensus making, this is no small thing. Quite often, those who make this transfer (which, although not found in the teaching of Vatican Council II, will be said to be "developments" of post-Vatican II ecclesiology) also transfer the object of belief. This translates into a very different science: I will believe and accept from the Church what I find intellectually compelling and rationally persuasive. This amounts to an act of faith in one's own I.Q. or that of others – which posture cannot be limited to non-infallible teaching but extends to infallible teaching as well, be that ordinarily or extraordinarily so taught.

Indeed, where "reasonable" means not ultimately mysterious, the mysterious realities that are in fact the sources of sacred theology are likely to be seriously revised. I do not suggest that Fr. McCormick has arrived at that point. I would, however, submit that there is a logic to the past decade of dissent that is not limited by the language in which it is expressed. Much recent theological traffic seems to be going only in one direction, and that is not in the direction of the *Theos* in theology. Carried to the ultimate this will operatively transform the proposition of Alexander of Hales: *theologia* will be replaced by *anthropologia* and be in revised form: *humanum docet, a humano docetur, ad humanum ducit.*

This all-too-human tendency affects not only the formation of a correct Catholic conscience but changes Catholic theology and Catholic morality as well. Vis-à-vis the magisterium, the learned Cardinal Newman, in explaining the absolute necessity for a Spirit-guided magisterium, foresaw the same kind of tendency. I would certainly share Cardinal Newman's belief that unaided human reason – when left unaided – tends toward simple unbelief in matters of religion.[58] And so the learned Cardinal considers Church teaching to be a most wise and necessary provision, by a merciful Creator, not only to preserve religion in the world, but also to rescue unaided human intellect from its own suicidal excesses.[59]

I began with a play on words – varied forms of *humanus*. The coincidence of the different titles is just that – coincidence; but the connections, in my judgment, are no coincidence. *Dei Verbum*, #10 of Vatican II specifically cites *Humani Generis* (cf. *D.V.*, n. 9; in Abbott (ed.), n. 25, p. 118) which, when rejected, sets the basis for dissenting from *Humanae Vitae* – often enough in the name of an alleged moral autonomy said to be found in *Dignitatis Humanae* of Vatican II, with the inevitable result that *Persona Humana*, the CDF Declaration on Certain Questions concerning Sexual Ethics, is neither accepted nor believed.[60]

Allow me to close with the Council's *ex professo* statement on the for-

---

58 John Henry Cardinal Newman, *Apologia Pro Vita Sua,* (ed. M. J. Svaglic (Oxford: Clarendon Press, 1967), p. 218.
59 *Ibid.*, p. 220.
60 Consider McCormick's evaluation in *New Cath. World* 220 (1977), p. 270.

mation of conscience. In my judgment, it sums up in three sentences what I have been trying to say in these several pages:

> In the formation of their consciences, the Christian faithful ought carefully to attend to the sacred and certain doctrine of the Church. The Church is, by the will of Christ, the teacher of truth. It is her duty to give utterance to, and authoritatively to teach, that Truth which is Christ Himself, and also to declare and confirm by her authority those principles of the moral order which have their origin in human nature itself. (*Dignitatis Humanae*, #14).

It may interest the reader, as it does the author, that the basic thesis of this paper was confirmed and affirmed in the later and formal teaching of the Congregation for the Doctrine of the Faith, namely, in "The Instruction on the Ecclesial Vocation of the Theologian" (May 24, 1990, in *AAS* 82 (1990), pp. 1550–70). Of special interest in that Instruction is Part IV, B, "The Problem of Dissent" (##32–41), particularly the denial of any alleged "right" to public dissent, which applies extensively the Apostolic Exhortation of Pope Paul VI, *Paterna cum Benevolentia* (December 8, 1974), as did the above paper.

3.
The Bitter Pill the Catholic Community Swallowed (1978)
Rev. Msgr. George A. Kelly

I. The Background

The pill was contraception.

How the Catholic Church lost the support of its people over this matter is a story still to be told with finality. But lose many of its people to contraception the Church did in a very few years.

Fr. Andrew Greeley announced with ferocious certainty in 1976 that the deterioration in American Catholicism was due to the encyclical *Humanae Vitae* which in 1968 upheld the Church's ban on contraception. Greeley has a chapter in his book *Catholic Schools in a Declining Church* which "proves" by mathematical formula that what he had been saying since 1968 is true: A continued ban on contraception was a disaster for the American Church (p. 316).

That book itself deserves comment later, but for the purposes of this article, it is sufficient to say that the Greeley thesis can be maintained as a working hypothesis only if "the contraceptive issue" is seen – not as a single item – but as a "mixed bag" of many Catholic issues which were the subject of fierce attack before, during, and after Vatican Council II. Although the direct confrontations seemed at first to center on steroid pills such as Enovid and Ortho-Novum, and later on condoms and diaphragms, the basic controversy was always over more basic questions: What is the law of God? What is the will of Christ? Who says so and with what authority?

Those priests and married couples who after World War II organized what was the most successful family life apostolate in the history of the American Church saw their work crumble within the space of a few years. The Cana and Pre-Cana Conferences, the Christian Family Movement, the Cana Clubs and the Holy Family Guilds, the marriage preparation courses, family consultation centers, marriage counseling, training of priests, regular attention to Catholic family life by all Catholic magazines, especially *Sign* and *America*, under the respective editorships of Fr. Ralph Gorman, C.P. and Fr. Thurston Davis, S.J., were the crests of rock-like Catholic family formations which supported the Catholic family-value system, by then a lonely isle in an all-embracing surrounding sea of broken homes, one-two children families, rising rates of illegitimacy, divorce, and abortion. Sociologist John L. Thomas, S.J., wrote a pioneer book, *The Catholic Family*, which laid out the ingredients necessary to protect the identity and future of the Catholic family system as a viable sub-culture when the power of secularized culture was overwhelming. Continuing education, mechanisms of motivation, and regular support systems were the instruments by which the Church kept Catholic family life intact and guaranteed its future.

Looking backward from the time when the American bishops created the Family Life Bureau in the National Catholic Welfare Conference (1931) to the eve of the Second Vatican Council (1961), the rise and rapid growth of the family-life apostolate was phenomenal. In fact, this apostolate seemed to take off all by itself (sometimes without bishops knowing what was going on), as if parish priests (most of the early organizers were priests) and married couples were driven by a compulsive need to survive as a Catholic body. In view of the bitterness later demonstrated by Catholic contraceptionists, a flashback to those days only reveals enthusiasm, love of the Church, and outpourings of energy on behalf of *the Word.*

And *the Word* was what the Church said it was (including the rejection of contraception). Not only were the private discussions and the nationwide network of Cana, Pre-Cana, and CFM meetings positive in their exploration and appreciation of Catholic family values, but the literature was also formative and enthusiastic. John Delaney, editor for Doubleday, published a book in 1958 designed to show that Catholic family values were not "the imposition of the will of a few cranky clerics on the Catholic populace" and to show further that "there is nothing arbitrary about the Church's stand" on marriage matters. The book was John L. Thomas's *The Catholic Viewpoint on Marriage and the Family.* Rereading Fr. Thomas's exposition of "the Catholic problem" offers *prima facie* evidence of how secure Catholic scholars then were interpreting not only the mind of the Church but the mood and needs of the Catholic people. What was the source of the Catholic problem in 1958? Fr. Thomas listed a few: (1) the sixteenth-century denial of the sacramental bond of marriage; (2) the gradual rejection of the influence of religious doctrine on the formation of marriage and family values;

(3) the tendency of social scientists to look upon the human person as nothing more than a complex combination of basic urges, conditioned reflexes, and acquired habits; (4) the American habit of being "practical" in judgment without necessary reference to principle or doctrine (pp. 25–27).

In the face of the practical options being offered at that time to marrieds and about-to-be marrieds in America, on what did the special Catholic family system depend? According to Thomas: on its clearly defined but distinctive set of ideals, standards, and patterns of conduct related to sex and marriage. Said Thomas in 1958: "If you want to know why people judge certain family practices to be right or wrong, you must find out how they define the nature and purpose of marriage. If you want to understand why they define marriage as they do, you must discover their view of human nature. In the final analysis, therefore, all definitions of human values are ultimately derived from some view of man, the human agent. If people hold different views concerning the origin, nature and destiny of man they will logically define the purposes of marriage differently and will develop different patterns of conduct in relationship to marriage" (p. 23). For almost two hundred pages, Fr. Thomas proceeds to explain why Catholics do not agree with other Americans on the essential purposes of marriage, the moral laws regulating marital relations, and the use of sex outside of marriage.

In those halcyon days it was clear that the marital issue separating Catholics from non-Catholics was not the condom or the diaphragm but a cluster of issues having to do with the sacred elements of human nature and the Church's understanding of God's revelation. Popes Pius XI and XII frequently used terms like "divine institution," "divine design," and "divinely established order" when speaking of many subject areas of religious thought. Contraception was only one of them. As seculars first, and then, more and more, Protestants and Jews, moved away from these notions, behavioral patterns changed with the changed concepts. The Catholic world view, on the other hand, retained the "wholeness" which underpinned its family life. However, when tampering began either with a practice (contraception) or with an idea (divine design), it was inevitable that changed behavior would also call for changed ideas, and vice versa. Even if the average Catholic did not always understand the connection between mind and conduct, Fr. Thomas saw it quite clearly.

However, assertions about the coherence of the Catholic family value system or the Church's struggle to make it operative in the lives of people led to the following practical questions: Did the Church's labors succeed? Did Catholics actually live by the Church's book?

Almost all priests who heard confessions or were effective parochial pastors of souls in the past half century would agree that the answers to both questions were yes. Family-life directors of any major diocese, also, where sexual aberrations among the faithful were always higher, can bear witness that the best Catholic family apostolates in the nation were precisely in the large metropolitan centers where the pressures on couples, old and young, were most severe.

But there is still a better witness to what was going on in American Catholic family life prior to 1962.

He is Andrew Greeley.

In the spring of 1963, Fr. Greeley wrote an article for *Chicago Studies* entitled "Family Planning among American Catholics." He was not yet ten years a priest and was still a curate at Christ the King parish in Chicago. The *Chicago Studies* article based its conclusions on two secular studies – one a 1959 Michigan Study and the other a 1961 Princeton Study – through which Greeley hoped to demolish some favorite myths about Catholic family planning. He reported as follows:

> 1. Concerning the myth that most Catholic families really do not accept the Church's teaching on birth control, Greeley says: "The Michigan Study shows the contrary to be true: *Catholics accept the Church's teaching with a vengeance*" (italics added).

> Only 32% of Catholics gave unqualified approval to birth control, compared to 72% of Protestants and 88% of Jews.

> Greeley concludes that on the subject of family limitation that "some Catholic respondents were more Catholic than the Church."

> 2. Concerning the myth that family-limiting-Catholics use methods condemned by the Church, Greeley reports that only 30% used contraceptives.

> Only 22% of regular Mass-goers used contraception.

> 3. Greeley concludes: "Religious affiliation is a very powerful determinant of behavior in this area – the success of Church efforts to induce the younger generation of Catholic couples to adopt approved methods [contradicts] assertions occasionally made that Catholics are increasingly adopting appliance methods."

> 4. Concerning the myth that upper class Catholics are more likely to

adopt contraception, Greeley concludes: ". . . the more education, the more income, the higher the occupational category, the more likely Catholics are to keep the Church's law and the more likely they are to have or to want larger families."

5. Concerning the myth that periodic continence is an inefficient method of family limitation, Greeley estimates: "The rhythm method is not drastically less efficient than the others."

Greeley also warns the reader that "such studies do not merit the same kind of acceptance as would, let us say, mathematical demonstrations or experiments in the physical or biological sciences." In defending the professional integrity of sociologists, he chides those who think "that demographers do not understand the consistency of the Church's teaching on sex and procreation, that they do not have a respect for the Catholic conscience, that they expect the Church to change its position, or that they expect Catholics to violate their moral principles." Greeley's article may have demolished myths, but it underlined the existence of Catholic moral principles on contraception, a Catholic conscience on the subject, and a Church firmly committed to its principles.

From this high plateau of adherence and practical observance, there followed a precipitous decline among Catholics within the ten-year period following 1963. Obviously, something more was at work than a new Catholic desire to use a condom, a diaphragm, or a pill. The Catholic people earlier under equally adverse social pressures – the Great Depression and the Great Wars – continued to recognize contraception as a sinful use of marriage. Something else must have happened after 1961.

II. The Catholic People Are Indoctrinated

Many things were going on in the Catholic community relative to contraception from the time the post-war baby boom began to alarm population experts. In 1944, government statistician Oliver E. Baker was declaring demography to be the most exact of the social sciences. He also predicted (on the basis of statistical computations) the leveling off of population growth in the United States. But people changed the numbers by placing high value on parenthood. Whereas in 1936 1,000 women aged 15–44 bore 76 children, a similar cohort of women bore 121 children in 1956. Later demographers coined words such as "the population explosion," "the population bomb," and "standing room only" to make their point that planned parenthood (soon to be more euphemistically retitled "responsible parenthood") was now as much a requirement for Americans, as it was for Third World peasants.

The tools of persuasion would become more sophisticated, but the motivation was similar to that made into a crusade years earlier by Margaret Sanger. During the depth of the Depression, when almost one quarter of all women of childbearing age had no children at all, the founder of the birth-control movement wrote an article for *The American Weekly* (May 27, 1934) in which she proposed an "American Baby Code." The essential ingredients of her philosophy are found in the following articles:

Article 3. A marriage shall in itself give husband and wife only the rights to a common household and not the right to parenthood.

Article 4. No woman shall have the legal right to bear a child and no man shall have the right to become a father without a permit for parenthood

Article 6. No permit shall be valid for more than one birth.

These embarrassing statements are now buried in library stacks, but Mrs. Sanger's haunting fears of unwanted and unneeded babies have worked their way into the psyche of American intellectuals and through them into the souls of mothers and prospective mothers. But technical advances, which provided the power by which unmarried and married adults alike separate sexual activity from parenthood, did not automatically mean social approval of contraception or widespread dissemination of devices, as long as there was popular consensus that contraception was evil. In fact, the "Protestant ethic" about contraception was frequently enforced by written and unwritten laws. Contraceptives could not be sent through the mails; they could not be advertised (although obtainable at the back of drugstores); they could not be sold to minors or the unmarried; nor could birth control advice be given in public hospitals. Those restrictions lasted as long as the religious consensus lasted – that is, up until the late 1950s.

The birth-control crusaders, however, were not without determination. They had begun as early as 1908 working to persuade the Church of England to give at least limited endorsement of the use of contraceptive by Christians. Successively they were turned down by the Lambeth Conferences of 1908 and 1920, but they finally gained sympathetic hearing from some Anglican bishops for exceptional use of contraception "in abnormal cases." This was the view which prevailed at Lambeth in 1930 when for the first time a prominent Christian body, while still insisting that "the primary and obvious method is complete abstinence (as far as may be necessary) in a life of discipline and self-control lived in the power of the Holy Spirit," gave permission for contraceptive use in abnormal cases. Contraception, hereafter, for Anglicans was a tolerated practice, though still without approval. Once this breakthrough was accomplished, further dispensations from standard Anglican behavior were readily granted. The Lambeth Conference of 1958 favored "a positive acceptance of the use of contraceptives within Christian marriage and family life." This was the first time contraception was seen as enriching married life, and that the term "responsible parenthood" was introduced into the ecclesial vocabulary, and, finally, that family planning was raised to the status of noble duty. The revolution within Protestantism was complete. Five years later a booklet entitled *Toward a Quaker View of Sex* would reject the traditional approach of organized Christianity to sexual morality, specifically its judgments about fornication, adultery, and homosexuality.

It is not without significance that in the late fifties an organized effort was made – successfully, as it turned out – to put the medical profession in the forefront of a birth control campaign to break down all written or unwritten resistance to contraceptive advice or clinical assistance for clients. The effort was first made in New York in 1956, then in Denver, Maryland, Chicago. By 1959 the American Public Health Association was on record in favor of birth control services. The White House Conference on Children and Youth followed this lead in 1960. By 1961 John D. Rockefeller III was in favor of government supported birth control programs. Simultaneously, but less spectacularly, was the success in making the social workers, employed by the network of bureaus of public assistance, agents of contraceptive advice. The public relations stress was on freedom for the client, but the welfare recipient was not unmindful of the social worker's position.

These political efforts were accompanied by widespread public relations programs and intensive lobbying. Planned Parenthood still encountered some resistance in high places. One of its setbacks came when General William H. Draper, an investment banker and Planned Parenthood activist, heading up a government committee, released a report on July 24, 1959, calling for government financed and managed population programs. Draper avoided the words "birth control" and stressed the word "request," but it was clear that the International Planned Parenthood Federation wanted the United States Government to endorse and underwrite its worldwide efforts to "sell" contraception. While Catholic politicians such as John

F. Kennedy and Edmund G. Brown walked a tightrope on the subject, President Dwight D. Eisenhower buried the Draper Report, banned all government family planning assistance for the duration of his term, with the comment that nothing was more improper for government than activity of this type.

But if Eisenhower was firmer on the subject of contraception than other politicians, Planned Parenthood came to recognize the vulnerability of public officeholders on this issue, particularly Catholics. Though the U.S. Catholic Bishops immediately (1959) warned the public that Catholics would not support assistance programs which promote artificial birth prevention, Planned Parenthood stepped up their campaign to change public opinion. They held a World Population Emergency Conference in 1960, took out full page ads soliciting $1,120,000 to promote the plans of the Draper Committee, brought Margaret Sanger out of retirement (June 14, 1960) as a fund-raiser, and induced the National Council of Churches in the USA to take positions favorable not only to contraception, but to sterilization as well (*New York Times*, February 24, 1961, p. 16). The NCC statement justified its endorsements on the basis of "the general Protestant conviction that the motives rather than the methods form the primary moral issue." The editorial comment of *America* (March 11, 1961) on the NCC statement reads: "At stake in these matters is not merely the integrity of marriage; but the very nature of morality. Christian morality is increasingly penetrated by the tendency to scuttle all objective norms of conduct and rationalize the flight from the absolute by appeals to the spirit of the gospel."

Planned Parenthood also realized the importance of enlisting for their campaign important public figures. By 1962 they had former Secretary of State Christian Herter taking up their cause. As an Episcopalian gentleman of some standing, he came to Planned Parenthood's annual conference in New York to be a bridge to the Catholic community. Herter told his audience that it was no longer correct to think that discussion of the population crisis was offensive to Catholics. He counted on the new ecumenical atmosphere which Pope John XXIII had encouraged to help because the Vatican was well aware, according to him, that the issue of birth control was one of the most important bars to a reunion of Catholics and Protestants (*New York Herald Tribune*, October 28, 1962).

The Planned Parenthood leadership also made a significant gesture toward its only formidable opponent – the Catholic Church. The key through the door of the Church was to be "dialogue." At first, Planned Parenthood's leaders did not expect to have any radical effect on the Catholic doctrinal positions, hoping merely to debilitate whatever political force was left in the anti-contraception movement. They took advantage of the fact that Catholic jurisprudence allowed greater leeway in public law for moral evil than Comstock legislators did. The distinction between the propriety of public policy in a pluralistic society and the moral positions of its citizens was well known. Catholic experts like John Courtney Murray and Gustave Weigel, Jesuit professors from Woodstock, and bishops like Belgian Cardinal Suenens, were quoted liberally, as if they blessed the political aspirations of Planned Parenthood.

Another Catholic distinction also came into play, namely, the distinction between responsible parenthood and contraception. Catholics were comfortable with the differences. Stress came to be laid on research to develop morally acceptable methods of family limitation. This was a soothing proposal in 1962, even though comparatively little money or results have since been realized from it.

In the dialogues between Planned Parenthood and Catholic family-life leaders after 1958, the following subjects were *never* discussed: the virtues of the unplanned family, the positive values of motherhood, and the rejection of contraceptive use by teenagers. Ten years later, the Planned Parenthood Federation launched a $4 million two-year program to have available in New York City contraceptive counseling and services to every teenager. In the early stages of the dialogue, subjects like sterilization and abortion were soft-pedaled. Planned Parenthood officials did not say publicly what some would admit privately, namely, that there was then (even more than now) greater reliability for family limitation through natural family planning than for at least half the contraceptives on the market. Probably the most troubling part of the one-sided dialogue in 1962 was Planned Parenthood's down-grading of the risks of "the pill." Most doctors, when asked, rejected the notion of giving "the pill" to their wives or daughters. The British Medical Society was already facing up to its harmful effects on women who took them. But Dr. Alan F. Guttmacher was dismissing this evidence, arguing that potential risks such as heart attacks, embolism, and cancer had to be balanced against the risks of child bearing. Twenty years later, as "the pill" diminished in popularity (because of its proven dangers to women's health and longevity), Planned Parenthood came under criticism for this neglect.

Yet, at one point of dialogue, "the pill" was the putative "savior" of interfaith cooperation on birth control. The "pill" was the thing which might provide the "natural family planning" acceptable to Catholics. Not a few Catholics swallowed this pill.

Planned Parenthood had quietly been working on selected Catholics for some time prior to 1962. "Leading Catholic members" of the American Public Health Association were credited with helping draft a pro-birth-control resolution as early as 1959. During 1960, the Federation polled 166 Catholic educators, lawyers, editors, and public officials seeking a sense of Catholic lay opinion. They found more than half of their interviewees (while continuing to assert Catholic orthodoxy on the subject) ready to accept a tolerant public policy, if that is what non-Catholics wanted. The news media, naturally, made much of this release, as they had earlier of the Draper Report. Panel discussions and interviews with disgruntled welfare clients who (allegedly) could not obtain birth-control information became quite common, with the Catholic Church always pictured as the ogre interfering with freedom.

By 1962, Planned Parenthood extended their forays deep into Catholic territory. The Reverend William Genner of the National Council of Churches and Naomi Gray of the Planned Parenthood staff appeared at the National Catholic Family Life Convention in Saint Louis. Other representatives sought meetings with leading Catholic family-life directors throughout the country or made trips to Europe seeking dialogue and understanding from leading Catholics in the ancient citadels of Christendom. One internal memorandum of Planned Parenthood, not intended for public consumption, recapped each visit with a paragraph on how "Father X" or "Monsignor Y" looked at the problem. It was obvious that Planned Parenthood expected support for its objectives from people inside the Catholic University of Louvain (Belgium) and within the Vatican itself. In the cited memorandum was described a visit to (a poorly concealed) Msgr. Luigi Ligutti in Rome (Ligutti then being a leading rural life expert); it was interpreted as indicating how sympathetic prelates could be in the Holy City itself. Cass Canfield, chairman of the Editorial Board of Harper and Brothers and one of the most sophisticated promoters of Planned Parenthood's cause, was so encouraged by his conversations with officials at the Vatican that in a letter dated July 5, 1962, he extended an invitation to Msgr. John C. Knott, the American bishops' National Director of Family Life, to become one of four Catholics who would dialogue with eight non-Catholics, in part to show that the area of differences between Catholics and non-Catholics was smaller than is popularly supposed.

Canfield's procedures, designed to attract leading Catholics, met with modest success – at first with Catholic journalists in the East, and later with some Catholic family-life leaders in the Midwest. But Catholic resistance to contraception in 1962 had not yet crumbled. Practically all Catholic spokesman, including scholars, were still calling contraception a moral evil.

Cass Canfield was not revealing all his approaches to the Catholic community. In production (1962) was a volume which would to be a Planned Parenthood *coup de grâce*. Dr. John Rock was the author, and Christian Herter the endorser, of a book (released in 1963) which was to stir up real controversy *within the Catholic Church*. The book was skillfully conceived. Its title: *The Time Has Come: A Catholic Doctor's Proposal to End the Battle over Birth Control*. Herter called Rock's contribution to religious discussion on birth control only slightly less important than his scientific contribution to the discovery of the pill. The publisher, Alfred A. Knopf, praised the special qualifications of John Rock for this role, proposing him "as a dedicated Roman Catholic." Rock was, in fact, by virtue of thirty years direct service a dedicated Planned Parenthood Federationist and a distinguished Harvard Professor of gynecology; but his Catholic qualifications were not recognized in any edition of the *American Catholic's Who's Who* for any of the ten years prior to the publication of *The Time Has Come*. Rock's familiarity with things Catholic became evident, too, when asked at a press conference why the book, if it was Catholic, lacked an imprimatur; Rock replied that he was unaware of this requirement. Dr. Herbert Ratner, then Commissioner of Public Health in Oak Park, Illinois, raised serious questions at that late date in Rock's life about the propriety of appending the word "Catholic" to the author's qualifications. Rock's statements justifying abortion (e.g., "embryos have the same responsibility to the preservation of the human race as soldiers") and his predictions about the ultimate acceptability of abortion also, according to Ratner, made the use of the word "Catholic" a misleading promotional aspect for the sale of this book (*Commonweal*, July 5, 1963). When Rock co-authored *Voluntary Parenthood* in 1947 with the Public Information Director of Planned Parenthood, there was no reference to his Catholicity. The reasons for introducing the religious identification in 1963, however, were compelling from the Federation's public relations perspective.

But Catholic complaints to the contrary, Planned Parenthood's ploy proved to be successful. Rock's book was widely discussed in Catholic circles. While some Catholic critics looked upon it as a piece of Planned Parenthood propaganda, a careful compilation of half-truths about Catholic doctrine, a literary pill to lull unsuspecting Catholics into the reasonableness of the contraceptive cause, Catholics read the book and discussed it. The editors of *Commonweal* (May 17, 1963), though admitting Rock had distorted important facts of Catholic life (most Catholic theologians opposed Rock's view on the morality of the pill and opposed his effort to downgrade the Papal doctrine as an "authoritative position binding on Catholics"), thought that the time had come for Catholic theologians to confront the issues Rock raised.

This was precisely what Planned Parenthood had hoped would happen. And the new affluent and well-educated middle-class Catholics apparently were ready.

III. The Issues Facing the Catholic Church

The issues which by 1960 began to surface for the Catholic Church were the same issues which had faced the Church of England in 1930.

The question uppermost in the minds of many was: Is contraception really intrinsically immoral?

All other matters in the discussion about contraception were side issues.

The debate frequently raged on those side issues, but the core questions about contraception always remained: Was there something in the very nature of the marriage act – a "given" from God – which precluded the moral right of human beings directly and effectively to exclude his purposes while pursuing their own? Was there by divine intent a necessary connection between sexual loving in marriage and God-loving, too, at least to the extent that every sexual union must be open to a child, if it be His will?

The Catholic Church had always said yes.

But in 1960 old questions were raised anew. Catholics who wanted the condemnation lifted would be required to demonstrate that contraception was not intrinsically immoral and that contraceptive use in marriage could be positively virtuous.

This moral-theological controversy over contraception factually was only a small argument within a much larger debate exploring more radical ground: Has God commanded anything absolutely? Is there really a divinely established moral order? Are we talking about a Real God or man's own primitive myths about "God"? Has God revealed himself in nature as he has in Jesus Christ? Who says He has and who decides what He has revealed, if He has?

For purposes of separating the later arguments, it is well to understand what the issues were *not*:

> Condemnation of contraception did not necessarily imply a denigration of sex itself or sexual loving by husband and wife. Loving is an integral part of married life, even when childbearing is unlikely or impossible.
>
> Hardship in childbearing or social difficulties in raising a family have nothing to do with the morality or the immorality of a contraceptive marital act.
>
> The intrinsic morality or immorality of any human act is not decided by popular vote. (Obviously the Catholic vote in 1950 was different from what is reported for 1970.)
>
> The conscience of the individual person does not decide the goodness or badness of contraception. At best a person's conscience – if it is a good conscience – declares him sinless or guiltless. He does not judge rightness or wrongness except for himself.
>
> The "pill" is not the issue. Standard Catholic moral doctrine permits therapy, even chemical therapy, for all kinds of disorders. Steroids were discovered as therapy for disorders before it was realized they also sterilized fertile women while they were being taken. The morality of chemical contraceptives must be decided on the same basis as mechanical devices.
>
> The formal note "infallibility" used or not used in connection with pronouncements of the Church on moral matters is not a central issue to the evaluation of contraception as immoral. The Church teaches many things without fear of error, i.e., with certainty, without explicitly calling a doctrine "infallible." Infallibility is a technical term rarely used and used for special reasons to make clear to the faithful the special solemnity of a particular pronouncement. In other words, if a doctrine is not pronounced "infallible," this does not mean, in popular English terminology, that it is "fallible" – i.e. likely to be wrong.
>
> The right of dissent is not an issue in determining the morality of contraception, if by that is meant that dissenters represent another rule of faith apart from the teaching Church. Catholics may as individuals disagree, deny, disobey (and in that sense "dissent" from) a Church teaching or ruling, but the fact that dissenting voices exist does not mean that they exist by right, especially if dissenting views have been condemned by the teaching Church.

The subsequent encyclical *Humanae Vitae* addressed itself to all these side issues, but it centered attention first and foremost on the central issue of contraception's intrinsic immorality and in a way that many Catholics did not.

IV. Catholic Contraception Prior to 1965

Almost until 1963 no one conceived that the Catholic Church would ever accept artificial contraception as an approved method of birth control.

From the early days of Christian history, the bishops of the Catholic Church all over the world and from different cultural settings, together with many popes, had taught consistently that contraception was wrong and had insisted that the Catholic people take that rejection as part of God's law. It is also true that the Catholic people understood and accepted the Church's doctrine, even when they departed from its norm, as many frequently did.

But contraception was said to be wrong; it was taught to be wrong everywhere in the Church; and the issue appeared to be closed forever. John T. Noonan's review of the doctrine's history concluded:

> The teachers of the Church have taught without hesitation or variation that certain acts preventing procreation are gravely sinful. No Catholic theologian has ever taught, "contraception is a good act." The teaching on contraception is clear and apparently fixed forever (*Contraception*, p. 6).

Though at the end of his volume Noonan goes on to question this fixity, the former Notre Dame Law professor was able to make that positive judgment in 1965.

A report prepared for the American bishops in the same year in response to a query from the Holy See concerning the birth control tendencies among American Catholics summarized the state of the question as follows:

> American theologians and moralists have not defended in published articles a departure from traditional teaching on birth control. They have unanimously condemned contraception, whether by means of interference with the marriage act or by means of sterilizing operations. Even with regard to the "pill," American theologians have disapproved its use to prevent conception, apparently, *with practical unanimity* (italics added). Nor is there any tendency in their published writings to defend the idea that the Church will or can change her substantial teaching on birth control.

This paragraph was written during the period in which the professional theologian assigned himself an active but modest role in the teaching

Church. In 1962, retiring president Fr. Aloysius McDonough, C.P., reminded the 17th Annual Convention of Catholic Theological Society of America (CTSA) that, while the professional theologian made influential and invaluable contributions to the Church, "in relation to the hierarchy, the position of the theologian in the economy of the teaching Church is auxiliary, subsidiary." Even journalist John Cogley admitted to a *New York Times Magazine* audience that those in the Church who rejected the Catholic doctrine, as of June 20, 1965, were only a small group.

All American Catholic scholars upheld Catholic doctrine with remarkable unity, so the faithful experienced no deviance between abstract teaching and Catholic practice, either in the pulpit or the confessional – at least until the latter months of 1964.

In 1960, John L. Thomas, S.J. (*Theological Studies*, Volume 20) had specified contraception's particular evil to be the prevention of the marital act from fulfilling its "primary natural purpose." In the December 1961 issue of *Theological Studies*, Joseph J. Farraher, S.J., had clearly taught the same. In 1962, Fr. Enda McDonagh of Maynooth in Ireland said: "The two ends [of marriage] are not separable. They are not even completely distinct" (*Irish Theological Quarterly*, 1962, p. 283). In 1963, Gerald Kelly, S.J., explained to the 18th annual convention of the CTSA why contraception was evil. With his colleague, John C. Ford, S.J., in the same year, he told why the Church's teaching on birth control would not change (*Catholic World*, November 1963), a conclusion their colleague D. O'Callaghan would reassert with conviction a year later in *The Irish Ecclesiastical Record* (November 1964). Felix F. Cardegna, S.J., in 1964, while expressing the hope that "the Church will again and more strongly condemn all forms of contraception," predicted, too, that "all Catholics are ready to accept the judgment of the Holy See in this matter" (*Theological Studies*, December 1964). On June 15, 1965, Fr. Richard A. McCormick, S.J., informed the Catholic Physicians Guild of Chicago that the Catholic norms on contraception, even for using the pill, were still in force.

One statement of the Catholic case was made in 1963 by Jesuit Moralist Joseph Fuchs, in his little book on the relationship of chastity and sexuality (*De Castitatate et Ordine Sexual*, p. 45).

> The Creator so arranged the sexual act that it is simultaneously both per se generative and per se expressive of intimate oblative love. He has so arranged it that procreation would take place from an act intimately expressive of conjugal love and that this act expressive of con-

jugal love would tend toward procreation. Therefore, an act which *of itself* is not apt for procreation is by this very fact shown to be one which does not conform to the intentions of the Creator. The same thing should be said about an act which *of itself* is not apt for the expression of oblative love. Indeed, an act which is not apt for procreation is by this very fact shown to be one which is of itself not apt for the expression of conjugal love; for the sexual act is one.

Fuchs says here that within Christian understanding what God has joined together (the procreative and loving elements of sexual relations in marriage), no man may put asunder. Anything which destroys the essential God-given purpose of life giving or spouse loving is wrong. Contraception offends the procreative meaning, but other practices – such as artificial insemination, condemned by Pius XII – are also intrinsically evil, although conducive to procreation, because such behavior radically denies the essential love element required for natural, morally good, sexual relations between husband and wife.

Pope Paul VI five years later was to say the same thing in other words, but by then Fr. Fuchs was himself ready to accept contraception.

V. What Went Wrong?

Although family-life movements in the United States were flourishing, even in 1950 Europe (where an obscure auxiliary bishop in Belgium, named Leon Joseph Suenens, began a book, *Love and Control*, with the assumption that contraception was taboo for Catholics), pressures were being brought to bear on Church authorities and on the Catholic faithful which were designed to soften the Catholic climate considerably.

First, there was the subtle shift within Catholic circles in the stress from having children to responsible parenthood, to restricting family size.

Secondly, the deliberations of the Second Vatican Council itself contributed to a new mood.

The pressure for smaller and smaller Catholic families was considerable. A book like the present writer's *The Catholic Marriage Manual* sold 250,000 copies from 1958 onward in part because of its positive approach to multi-child families. When a sequel followed in 1963, entitled *Birth Control and Catholics*, reviewer Fr. John A. O'Brien of Notre Dame observed: "A serious defect [of the latter book] is the overemphasis placed upon the large family" (*Ave Maria*, November 30, 1963). O'Brien also objected to tying family planning to contraception and sterilization.

Fr. O'Brien became an early advocate of "responsible parenthood" among Catholics. While not yet endorsing contraception, this erstwhile Catholic apologist calls for responsible parenthood were avidly greeted, not only by Notre Dame's *Ave Maria*, but by such Protestant publications as *Christian Century* and the slick weekly *Look*. On November 21, 1961, Fr. O'Brien joined such Planned Parenthood advocates as Philip Hauser, William Vogt, and William Draper in a symposium of opinion for *Look*, entitled "America's Population Crisis." Hauser was concerned about what population growth was doing to parking and driving in New York City. Vogt asked (in 1961): "Do you think your children have a right to offspring beyond perhaps the second one?" Draper praised post-war Japan for radically cutting its birthrate "by drastic measures such as legalized abortion" which, Draper added, "we would not approve."

This was the rising climate in the immediate pre-Vatican-II period for those Catholics discussing birth control publicly. Panelists on TV – usually three or four to one in favor of contraception, sterilization, and abortion – always made it appear that the orthodox Catholic was an oddity in American Society. In the *Look* piece, Fr. O'Brien followed the Planned Parenthood agenda. His article, entitled "A Priest's View: Let's Take Birth Control Out of Politics," suggested to Catholics that they cease fighting public policy on contraceptive measures. In spite of many state laws, said O'Brien, "the Roman Catholic Church sanctions a much more liberal policy on family planning." Since the Catholic Church had nothing to do with the birth-control laws then on the state law-books, Catholics who fought to retain them were compared by O'Brien to prohibitionists. His final suggestion, namely, that Catholics carry their fight about contraception into theological circles, but not into the political arena, seems naive in hindsight. The politics of contraception in 1961 became its theology in 1965. Later, permissive politics on abortion would lead to a theological shift on that subject also.

Two years later Fr. O'Brien simultaneously published in *Ave Maria* and in *Christian Century* an article entitled "Family Planning in an Exploding Population." A development in O'Brien's thinking had occurred. There is now something intrinsically good about a regulated family. While Winfield Best, Executive Vice President of the Planned Parenthood, praised the article, Msgr. John C. Knott of the Family Life Bureau of the National Catholic Welfare Conference chided O'Brien for the things he did not say about Catholic family planning:

> I am afraid he leaves in the minds of both Catholic and Protestant readers that these things (about the legitimacy of regulating births) are all

that the Church says. And this is not so. The very authorities he cites go on to insist in the next breath that the Church does not and will not accept the contraceptive view of married life, which the birth-control ideology takes for granted (*America*, September 7, 1963).

If one Catholic mood countenanced political silence about the spread of contraception, a different temper of popular writing and television appearances dictated attacks by Catholics on the Church doctrine. In *Jubilee* (December 1963), a man and woman expressed doubts about the Catholic position. Later on, in the *Saturday Evening Post* (April 10, 1964), the same woman pleaded more explicitly for a reversal of the traditional doctrine, claiming that the Church "places married Catholics in an impossible position." The crescendo of dissenting Catholics wending their way to television studios became so intense that when the American Broadcasting System wished to balance a series of one-sided pro-contraceptive presentations by televising a panel of religious leaders who opposed contraception, one distinguished Orthodox Jewish Scholar refused to participate because he doubted the determination of the Catholic Church to defend the essentials of the Judaeo-Christian tradition on contraception.

What made ABC concerned about having an "orthodox" presentation of the issue is symptomatic of how the Church was treated in general by the media. During a dispute in New York City over whether social workers should have authority to dispense birth control counsel to the poor, a Catholic leader was kinescoped in the afternoon saying no one in New York over sixteen was unknowledgeable about where to purchase a contraceptive. When the presentation was made on the evening news, the ABC reporter had in the meantime found a Spanish lady (provided by Planned Parenthood) to say that *she* did not know and that her priest would not tell her. The reporter later was discharged, but the anti-Catholic bias evident in such news stories remained a factor in moving the Catholic community toward acceptance of contraception.

Other ancillary factors also helped loosen Catholic loyalties to traditional doctrine. Books like *Contraception and Holiness, Contraception and Catholics, Catholics and Birth Control, Population: Moral and Theological Considerations, The Experience of Marriage*, and *Contraception Versus Tradition* began to receive favorable comment in Catholic magazines. *The National Catholic Reporter*, freed of its Kansas City foundation, became under the editorship of Robert Hoyt a widely read newspaper for priests and religious. NCR devoted space and featured views favorable to contraception. Even a bishop-financed "Catholic Hour" was programmed for four nationally televised panel discussions on birth control, written by *Commonweal* editor John Leo and narrated by former *Commonweal* editor Philip Sharper, both contraceptionists. *Time* (January 18, 1968) indicated surprise at the program's recall, but the real wonder is that these programs reached the point of production and distribution with money supplied by the Catholic bishops.

The educational machinery of the federal government was another element in popularizing family planning, or at least in muting opposition to government involvement in such activity. The Catholic bishops in 1959 had said that they would not support publicly financed programs of this kind, but four years later 53 percent of American Catholics were reported by the Gallup Poll as favoring governmental dispensation of information about birth control. By 1965, when 78 percent of Catholics had moved to the affirmative side of the question, federal involvement in birth-control programs was on the upswing. The first grant of federal funds had already been made by the Office of Economic Opportunity to Corpus Christi, Texas, for a community birth-control program. Through the Public Health Service, many similar projects related to birth control were already under way.

On January 4, 1965, in a carefully worded sentence, the newly re-elected President Lyndon B. Johnson, told Congress in his State of the Union message: "I will seek new ways to use our knowledge to help deal with the explosion in world population and the growing scarcity in world resources." This was the first time in the nation's history that a president gave official sanction to government efforts in this area.

Congress was not idle either. Senator Ernest F. Gruening of Alaska, a long-time advocate of Planned Parenthood, introduced a family planning-bill into the Senate. Feeling that his greatest contribution to the cause would be to turn Senate hearings into a public platform, Gruening first called those witnesses who could glamorize the principles of his bill. When Gruening questioned John Rock, he raised the question of possible changes in Catholic teaching and spoke about the "immorality" of the social conditions which grew out of the absence of birth control. *The New York Times* and the *Washington Post* gave extensive coverage to these hearings, as did the Huntley-Brinkley report on NBC TV. In the meantime, National Educational Television, financed in part by government money, prepared a series of six films on the population crisis in Brazil, Europe, Japan, India, and the United States. Filming took place in every part of the world, and a panel of demographers contributed to this production. The last film dealt with the medical aspects of family planning.

The full impact on Catholics of all this contraceptive promotion during 1963–65 was not yet measurable. Catholic partisans of contraception usually shied away from endorsing the wrong methods publicly. But they talked repeatedly about liberal public policy, about civil freedom for the non-Catholic conscience, and about responsible parenthood by Catholics. Later, the effect of this quiet approach became noticeable. Fr. John A. O'Brien, for example, who had never previously endorsed contraception, published almost simultaneously with *Humanae Vitae* a new book, *Family Planning in an Exploding Population*, with three distinctive features: (1) The book was dedicated to President Lyndon B. Johnson, John D. Rockefeller III, and Senator Ernest F. Gruening; (2) it contained an insert citing the Catholic University professors who had publicly dissented from *Humanae Vitae*; and (3) the last two paragraphs in the book pleaded with the pope to let Catholics use contraceptives.

VI. The Second Vatican Council

Many people blame the Council itself for the ultimate confusion of the Catholic faithful. Others trace dissent from Catholic doctrine to false allegations about what the Council said about marriage and family life.

Before recalling the dynamic confrontations between the Council Fathers over Vatican II's final document (*Gaudium et Spes*, the Pastoral Constitution on the Church in the Modern World), it is important to summarize the Council's final decisions on this controverted subject:

1. God himself is the author of marriage and has endowed it with various benefits and with various ends in view (#48).

2. By their very nature the institution of marriage and married love are ordered to the procreation and education of the offspring (#48).

3. It is imperative to give suitable and timely instruction to young people – about the dignity of married love (#49).

4. Without intending to underestimate the other ends of marriage, it must be said that the true married love and the whole structure of family life which results from it is directed to disposing the spouses to cooperate valiantly with the Love of the Creator and Savior, who through them will increase and enrich his family from day to day (#50).

5. It is the married couples themselves who must in the last analysis arrive at these judgments before God (#50).

6. Among the married couples who thus fulfill the God-given message, special mention should be made of those who after prudent reflection and common decision courageously undertake the proper upbringing of a large number of children (#50).

7. When it is a question of harmonizing married love with the responsible transmission of life, it is not enough to take only the good intentions and the evaluation of motives into account; objective criteria must be used, criteria drawn from the nature of the human person and his acts, criteria which respect the total meaning of mutual self-giving and human procreation in the context of true love (#51).

8. In questions of birth regulation, the sons of the Church, faithful to these principles, are forbidden to use methods disapproved of by the teaching authority of the Church in its interpretation of the divine law (#51). (There follows here the famous footnote 14 which refers to statements of Pius XI, Pius XII, Paul VI, upholding the ban on contraception, with a reminder also that Paul VI had reserved certain birth control questions to himself. The last line of this footnote has been used to "prove" the Council's intended ambiguity. It reads: "With the doctrine of the magisterium in this state, this Holy Synod does not intend to propose immediately concrete solutions.")

Gaudium et Spes thus attempted to reconcile the personalist values symbolized in the expression "married love," without downgrading its relationship to child-bearing, even the bearing of many children. This positive endorsement of private judgment in matters of birth regulation is balanced by the reminder that objective as well as subjective norms of morality govern decision making, and with the special reminder that "methods disapproved of by the teaching authority of the Church were forbidden." All this seems clear in the final texts.

But all was not so crystal clear in the conciliar debates and in the jockeying over the terminology to be used, especially as the disagreements were related to the general public by media representatives already committed to the proposition that the Catholic Church must change, will change.

First, the jockeying over terminology. The preliminary text of the section on marriage (May 16, 1965) was vague on contraception, and a second schema (November 16, 1965) was drafted to include a reference to objective moral criteria and contraception. Omitted at that time, however, was any reference to previous papal statements on the subject. Some parties to the drafting process preferred that the document remain as it was: others sought to limit the possibility of a loose interpretation of the Council's meaning *after* the bishops went home by having contraception specifically mentioned. The fear that silence in the text would be taken to suggest a Church backing away from its historical condemnation of contraception was not small. Prior to submission for final approval, the Council Fathers tightened the proposed schema.

On November 23, 1965, the pope instructed the Secretary of State to inform the Council's Theological Commission that he wanted the final text to contain clear and open references to Pius XI's encyclical *Casti Connubii* (1930) and Pius XII's *Allocution to Midwives* (1951), both of which condemned contraception. The Commission added these references and also Pope Paul's own statement of June 23, 1964 ("They [the norms given by Pius XII] should, therefore, be regarded as valid, at least as long as we do not consider ourselves obliged in conscience to modify them."), with its advisory that the pope was reserving certain questions to himself. This turned out to be one of the strongest interventions of Pope Paul during the Council, but it also proved to be only partially effective.

The intervention was looked upon by contraception-minded *periti* as a blow to their efforts to place the Church behind a doctrinal statement which effectively granted couples the right to choose conjugal love over children (without regard to the means of birth control). The pope's intervention, though private, made front page news in next morning's Roman papers, implying in its text that a showdown of conciliar forces was in the making. The move to strengthen the text against contraception was interpreted as a strike at the independence of the Council. Bishops were quoted as resenting being "bulldozed" by the pope. But the pope responded that, while not choosy about *how* the Council took up his demands (with his permission some accommodations on the actual formulations were reached), he wanted no tampering with Catholic doctrine in the Council text (Xavier Rynne, *The Fourth Session* pp. 211–24). Whether the pope was as firm as he has been reported is a matter of dispute.

Prior to the vote, the Council Fathers heard it explained that the text submitted was intended in #47 to condemn "illicit practices against generation," called "unlawful contraceptive practices" in the Flannery translation. (Some use this explanation to suggest that the Council was implying that there were "lawful" contraceptive practices.) It was amid this confusion that the schema was brought to a vote on December 4, 1965, and passed. (A strange thing occurred two days before the vote. The printed text given to the bishops *lacked* the exact page reference to *Casti Connubii*'s specific condemnation. The Holy Father himself had this omission called to public attention and the page reference re-inserted in the promulgated document.)

Footnote #14 later was to be used to "prove" that all questions on contraception were still open, and that the pope had allowed the footnote to say so. (See John L. Thomas, S.J., *America*, February 2, 1966, and the response of John C. Ford, S.J., *America*, April 16, 1966). However, the publication of *Humanae Vitae* illegitimizes such an interpretation. The only open question on June 23, 1964, was the relation of the "pill" to Catholic doctrine, not the doctrine itself. Those who read otherwise tried to establish a linguistic case, but clearly they did not read Pope Paul's mind correctly. (They claim, however, the correctness of their reading of the Council's mind. But there was no single conciliar mind to which anyone can refer on this matter – because the accepted formulas are ambiguous.)

During the same pre-*Humanae Vitae* period, another justification of contraception appeared in Catholic journals, namely, that single marriage acts need not be procreative, if the entire marriage was. This defense of contraception was based on the allegation that the Council equated marital love with intercourse, that married love without intercourse is not a love of husband and wife in the conciliar sense, and that contraceptive intercourse can be a real marital act. The Council did not say so, but Catholic readers were told it did. (See Fr. Theodore Mackin's article "Vatican II, Contraception, and Christian Marriage," *America*, July 15, 1967). Following 1965, the pro-contraceptive Catholic literature became voluminous.

Regarding the conciliar debates themselves, certain bishops were clearly counted among the pro-contraceptionists. Bernard Cardinal Alfrink, representing the Dutch hierarchy, made the method of choice a matter of conflict of duties and made private conscience supreme. Cardinal Leger of Canada and Cardinal Suenens of Belgium were quoted at length on the need for doctrinal re-examination and re-formulation. Bishop Reuss of Mainz, without equivocation, was a contraceptionist (and a member of the papal Birth Control Commission). All these prelates were quoted at length in the press and in articles, while outside of official documents, there was little extended or sympathetic treatment of the traditional view held by Cardinals Ottaviani, Ruffini, and Browne. John Cardinal Heenan for the British bishops tried to end the debate in England (as he said "once and for all" by declaring that for the Council Fathers "contraception is not an open question.") Heenan was contradicted by moral theologian Fr. Bernard Haring, C.S.S.R., who thought that "the British bishops erred" (*Newsweek*, May 25, 1964). Haring, also a member of the Birth Control Commission, in advance of any decision by pope or council, was pushing the "pill." During lulls in council deliberations, he conducted workshops in the United States, mostly in the Midwest, where with the help of Fr. John A. O'Brien of Notre Dame and Fr. Walter Imbiorski, director of Chicago's Cana Conference activity, he insinuated the advisability of married couples making up their own minds on the matter. The year was 1964, and Pope Paul had already said that the Catholic norms were still in force, but he said it in such a gentle way that insinuating future change did not seem unreasonable. Haring in an interview with Fr. O'Brien, first passed around in mimeographed form and later published in the *Homiletic and Pastoral Review* (July 1964), stressed this possibility of doctrinal reformulation; he thought the Church could change on parenthood as it had on usury (this was not true even in 1964), and he belabored the catastrophe of four children in four years, categorizing as rigorism any position "which forbids almost all tenderness to those couples who do not wish a new pregnancy [and which] is responsible for many broken homes and broken hearts." He left the final impression that sexual sins need not be looked upon as mortal, i.e., serious.

While Haring was more discreet in his 1964 formulations than later, his "message" of tolerance of methods of birth regulation other than periodic continence encouraged partisans of contraception in South Bend and Chicago. At the 29th National Catholic Family Life Convention in Washington, D.C. (June 25, 1964) – whose theme was "The Rights of Children" – the pressure was strong on delegates to open up the convention to a discussion of contraception, though this effort did not succeed.

Following the close of the Council, the pressures increased. Pope Paul tried to stem the tide by repudiating the idea that the Church was in doubt about contraception (October 29, 1966). But another publicly noticed shift came (*Theological Studies*, December 1966) when Richard McCormick, S.J., concluded his treatment of contraception by indicating how easy it was to sympathize with the view that "one might still be tempted to wonder, notwithstanding contrary opinions, whether the existing laws on contraception are the object of a purely theoretical doubt, which is admitted by all, or whether a practical doubt – ultimately freeing conscience – may legitimately be posited." In June 1967, his confrere Robert H. Springer, S.J., writing in the same journal, said the traditional Catholic teaching already had been modified by Vatican II, thus making future realignment necessary. The *Dutch Catechism* (published also in 1967), representing the Dutch hierarchy, declared (p. 403) that in spite of Vatican II's cautionary language against immoral methods, "the last word lies with conscience," not with doctor or confessor. *America* magazine, which under the editorship of Thurston Davis had valiantly fought contraceptionists, on (September 30, 1967) came under the direction of sociologist Donald Campion, S.J., and immediately called upon the first Synod of Bishops meeting in Rome to sanction "the use of contraception for the achievement of a truly Christian marriage." When Richard McCormick decided (*Theological Studies*, June 1967, pp. 799–800) that Pope Paul's earlier repudiation of doubt (October 29, 1966) was not enough ("Only an authentic teaching statement is capable of dissipating genuine doctrinal doubt."), the tide had already turned. The authentic teaching statement was to come a year later, but by then the doubters were not inclined to listen.

VII. The Papal Birth Control Commission

The Papal Birth Control Commission, if it was planned only as a "pill commission," certainly ended up accomplishing little good for the Church. The Commission began as a study of steroids that, in view of the final decision of *Humanae Vitae*, served the practical purpose of sowing division within the Church over issues other than contraception. In hindsight, it would have been better to let the bishops argue about contraception on the Council floor, thus finishing the matter once and for all, than it was to allow an ever-expanding group of experts to feed doubts into local arenas throughout the Catholic world, issuing insulting statements about the rectitude of the traditional Catholic position. *Humanae Vitae* has ratified the Catholic teaching on contraception as a matter of God-given moral law. A century from now – when natural family planning may be commonly used as the means of regulating family size – intellectuals, presently enamored of chemical and surgical warfare on the human body – may take note of the Church's courage in sticking to its principles under heavy fire. But in 1964–65, Pope Paul, who through the National Catholic Welfare Conference canvassed the bishops of the world on contraception (as Pius XII did prior to declaring Mary's Assumption), knew precisely where bishops stood on this doctrine. Of the American bishops responding to the questionnaire distributed through the National Catholic Welfare Conference, only one or two favored modification of the doctrine. Characteristically, Pope Paul VI, cautious administrator of the Church that he was, inclined to the belief that public discussion of this emotionally packed issue by the bishops might prove scandalous and upsetting to the Catholic faithful; so he reserved this matter to himself. Yet critics still downgrade *Humanae Vitae* because it was not the collegial decision of the council, but rather that of the Pope *solo cum solo*. The truth is, however, that short of an outright public vote, the birth-control encyclical followed more discussion with bishops (and their private vote locally) than any other similar papal decision in the history of the Church. The trouble for the Church originated with the four-year delay between consultation and decision. The pope took a powder keg off the floor of the Aula and stored it in the basement of the Vatican with a long fuse, then seemingly forgot that fuses can be ignited unintentionally. During the period of study, the pope afforded contraceptionists the time they needed to raise questions about artificial devices, and questions, too, about whether the Church's understanding of marriage was correct; whether God had anything much to say about marriage at all, and especially about having or not having babies; whether it was within the province of the Church to bind consciences on such personal matters; whether the Church could give more than advice; and whether the papacy itself had not become an outdated autocracy which should be tailored to proper, if not primitive, size.

The creation and management of the Papal Birth Control Commission was an example of how not to organize a scientific study group. The questions to be studied were never defined. The members were not instructed in the procedures to be used in doing their work. Had the questions been precise and the members required to submit briefs in support of specific answers, votes would have been as unimportant as the number of lawyers pleading before a court. Only arguments would count. The meetings of the Commission did not provide for genuine debate and cross-examination, so preponderance of people, rather than argument, became the major factor in determining "rightness." High Church authorities were interested in answers to questions, but the method they chose to get them was hardly rigorous. They did not even appreciate the role the media would play, or how the media would be used by Commission members, in disseminating pro-contraceptive views to the faithful. As well-known priests (and bishops) began to disagree with each other, the laity followed priests of their choice. As months of study passed into years, the opinion was circulated that the pope was looking for a face-saving device before altering the Catholic position. Expectancy of change became practical doubt for many Catholics.

The historical record shows, of course, that the guessers were wrong and that the members of the conservative minority, which said that the Church would not change its doctrinal position, were right. Both in the record of the Council and thereafter there was evidence that the pope's only uncertainty concerned the morality of the pill. Was it capable really of regulating women's monthly cycles so that natural family planning would become more secure? Were Enovid and Ortho-Novum sterilizing agents or abortifacients, rather than contraceptives? What were the long-range medical effects of fooling with a woman's pituitary gland? Dr. John Rock and Planned Parenthood had huckstered the pill as a soporific to Catholic family planners. Indeed, advertisements suggested that pill-taking was just another form of natural family planning. European theologians like Fr. Louis Janssens and Fr. Bernard Haring swallowed the pill as an antidote to the Catholic birth control problem. The first Papal Birth Control Commission did not agree on the pill, and the second expanded Commission quickly began to understand (what is even clearer in 1978 than in 1965) that the pill was medically dangerous for long-term use. Theologians continued to argue about the conditions under which the pill could be morally acceptable, as the pope's medical advisers were writing it off as the universal answer to the birth-control problem.

About the time this conclusion was reached, the focus of attention was turning to any and all kinds of contraception, and to the Church's basic and historic position. This change was also unanticipated by Church authority. While morning vision is always clearer, a commission composed of sociologists, economists, biologists, theologians, parish priests, married couples, statisticians – fifty seven in all – would tend to be empirical rather than doctrinal, and would be divided in the opinions of its members. A social scientist could only say that contraception works or does not, that people want this method or that, or none. Once the world of doctrine was left behind, no scientist, no married couple, no individual priest could demonstrate with certitude a moral position on any subject. Apart from doctrine, a private reading, a common reading, or an official Church reading would prevail at the same time for different audiences. Using the tools of science or sophisticated logic cannot guarantee conviction that contraception (or abortion, or divorce, etc.) is right, wrong, always or sometimes. A private reading satisfies many religionists and humanists; a common reading is helpful to the determination of public policy in a democratic society; but a Catholic-Church reading was bound to be based on the 2,000-year-old teaching as an interpretation of God's law.

There are other questions which can be raised about the Commission. Granted that it represented an honest effort to explore new scientific developments, why was not membership confined to scientists who knew about such things and theologians who were professionally qualified to evaluate new discoveries against the Church's insistence that their use be governed by the *objective* requirements of the moral law? The Commission then would have been "scientific," less moved by subjective feelings, factual states, or by political forces. (Subjective feelings and factual states were worth knowing; population statistics and the extent of resistance was found mostly in the better economically situated Catholics of the Western world). But these data contributed nothing to determining the morality of contraception. Rome had known this from the time the secretary of the second Birth Control Commission began to propose members and to determine the Commission's agenda. Fr. Henry de Reidmatten, O.P., the son of a diplomatic European family, has been variously criticized since for the make-up of the Commission and its agenda; yet he was Rome's choice for secretary. If, at the final session of the pope's Commission, Reidmatten was observed standing, clapping, and cheering the vote which put the majority on the side of contraception, the question earlier might have been asked: Will he balance the interests of the Holy See against his own preferences and/or political pressure? On March 9, 1965, immediately prior to the first Roman meeting, Reidmatten was forwarding to commission members the work of John T. Noonan (American) and Canon de Locht (Belgian), both of whom were pro-contraceptionists. The first formal session of the theological section of the Commission began with an exposition by Noonan, whose chief thrust suggested that the Church's condemnation of contraception was a historically conditioned response to protect the value of infant life itself. If that value could be protected nowadays in other ways, the continued condemnation of contraception might not be necessary. De Locht, while no fan of contraception, had argued a year earlier that for many people contraception was better than nothing.

Almost from the start, therefore, the trend of the commission's labor was toward opening up the entire issue. Noonan, for example, set one framework for the debate by asserting that the Church's ancient doctrine on contraception was merely an ancient response to attacks on sexuality, marriage, and childbearing from Stoics, Gnostics, Manicheans, and the like. The one-time Notre Dame scholar gave little emphasis to the fact that early Christian thinkers more likely reflected their Jewish ethical background (which in orthodox circles was always critical of most circumstances surrounding contraception), rather than the need to answer pagans or heretics. The Christian heritage of anti-contraception was not, therefore, an accident of time and place, but derived from a common understanding of the relationship of marriage to parenthood which went back to the Jewish patriarchs and was consistently restated by Church Fathers. Even the repeated use of Onan's sin (Genesis 39:9–10) as a scriptural base for the Catholic doctrine (in spite of modern research which makes his sin merely the refusal to have children by his brother's wife, not spilling his seed) correctly tells what the Church was teaching about contraceptive intercourse. The fact that Orthodox Jews and Protestant Christians factually held to this interpretation until very recent times only confirms the traditional reading of Genesis 38, regardless of its acceptance by modern scholars. No one, however, should concede infallibility to the newer interpretation, which possibly may have grown out of a modern scholarly attempt to undercut the anti-contraceptive interpretation of Onan's sin.

Another dubious device of Noonan's (which has been used by other pro-contraceptive debaters, notably Fr. Haring) was the argument that, since the Church after consistently and solemnly condemning usury for centuries, later found ways to justify interest taking, so the Church can also find ways to justify contraception. But factually, the teaching of the Church on usury (taking money on a loan without some extrinsic title) has not changed. Usury in that sense is still condemned. Furthermore, the Church's teaching on usury was never proclaimed as long, as consistently, as universally, or as solemnly as the Church's teaching on contraception, as reflected in Pope Pius XI's encyclical *Casti Connubii*. The proper comparison to the usury case would be the development of approval for "periodic continence," once science had discovered the existence of fertile and infertile periods in women.

Once, however, relativism entered the Commission's deliberations, it should have been seen, as a foregone conclusion, that absolute principles could not be maintained. Without an absolute anchor, moral judgments necessarily follow subjective determination. As early as December 1962, the Hugh Moore Foundation (a Planned-Parenthood sponsored organization) distributed "An Appeal to the Vatican" by Dr. Suzanne LeSoeur Chapelle, a French mother of five and a gynecologist, which spoke of "the immense cry of distress from innumerable homes, torn between their faith and parental duties." She considered it "impossible that the paternal goodness of the Holy Father will not be able to bring a solution to this destructive problem." Not only did an official of the Holy Office (M. Leclerq) assure her that "the decision of the [forthcoming] Council will certainly be sought," but after her visit to Archbishop Jean Levillain, he expressed his sincere wishes "that the problem [birth regulation] might be reconsidered from top to bottom."

Soliciting these opinions became a function of the Birth Control Commission. Reidmatten, prior to the 1965 Roman meeting, had sent questionnaires around the world seeking to discover, among other things, the acceptability among Catholics of the various methods of regulation and the methods also which ran "the greatest risk of hindering the couple's emotional maturity." In the United States, the Christian Family Movement became the instrument of distribution. As might be expected, the "horror stories" justifying contraception were many. One of the better and early accounts of what went on in the pope's Birth Control Commission was published in the *Lady's Home Journal* for March 1966. The opening paragraphs contain the following poignant lines:

> Emotionally and psychologically, the rhythm method has been harmful to our marriage. Our love, which is continually deepening in Christ and in each other, must, of its nature, seek union. This union is almost continually denied, and the frustration is great . . .

> Ten children in twelve years – it hardly seems as if it works. After a complete nervous breakdown and an attempted suicide, we have nothing left to do but abstain.

Quoting the summary of responses to the Holy See, the article continues:

> They represent so much anguish and suffering. When there is this much widespread unhappiness, this much that is destructive of the very ideals of marriage the Church wants to preserve, something is wrong.

Drawing on what could only be inside information (intended to deprecate the traditional Catholic view of marriage), Lois R. Chevalier, the author, made this reference to what only could have been the presentation to the Commission by Dr. and Madame Rendu, France's equivalent of America's CFM: "The French are wild. They have a full-blown mystique about sex and love. Their expositions were poetry and prose: absolutely incomprehensible to an Anglo-Saxon." The Rendus talked with Commission members about sex within the context of Christian married love and the beauty of marital chastity for perfecting true married love.

John and Eileen Farrell, formerly of Chicago's Cana Conference, were dubious from beginning about what the Commission's questionnaire might elicit beyond the pressing urgency of contraception for aggrieved couples. Questionnaires, like prophecies, often contribute to their fulfillment. The Farrells raised the central question which the questionnaire raised in their minds.

> It is hoped that the questionnaire does not represent the mentality of the [Birth Control] Commission but is somehow intended to stimulate discussion leading to a clearer understanding of the Church's consistent teaching. There seems to be no other explanation for initiating an inquiry about contraceptive methods with no mention of the basic issue which is the natural and supernatural value of children.

On reading the questionnaire from Rome closely, the Farrell's found it also inconceivable that in the Papal Commission's list of subject matters "no mention is made of continence or mortification." Neither did they like the questionnaire's assumption of an ongoing high rate of "fertility which does not exist," nor "the tone of many questions [which] suggests that family planning is a foregone conclusion." In providing their view of the world to come, the Farrells prophesied (January 1965) that "sterilization is the family planning method of tomorrow," and suggested at the same time (what would later be a concern of Pope Paul) that a close look should be taken at the correlation of contraception and sexual promiscuity among the young.

These views, however, did not compete on equal terms with the humanistic concerns of the growing majority, nor with the natural sympathy for the burdens sometimes placed on fertile married couples, advancing in age and already fruitful. The Dutch representative offered existentialist arguments, and several German spokesmen also leaned in that direction. World War II cruelty had radically touched both Dutch and German intellectuals. Dutch Catholicism in particular, which once was rigid and separatist (bishops there frequently told politicians how to vote, and Catholics and Protestants were highly ghettoized), in the post-war era developed a passionate desire to break down barriers with other religionists. One professor from the Catholic University of Nijmegen explained: "When you share bunkers and churches with fellow countrymen of all persuasions under a cascade of bombs sent by an unbelieving madman, religious differences do not seem to count for much."

African and Indian commission members viewed birth control differently. Africans respected large families. One of the best defenders of natural family planning came from India. For those who were interested, a highly successful government plan of natural family planning on the African coastline island *Mauritius* (mostly non-Catholic) was brought to the attention of the delegates.

In the end, however, the influence of the mid-European intellectuals prevailed, with some solid help from the American delegation whose majority had gone contraceptionist. The Americans were encouraged also by what was going on at home, such as the statement prepared by thirty-seven Catholic academicians meeting in conference at Notre Dame. The Notre Dame group concluded that old Catholic norms are no longer operative because they do not reflect "the complexity and the inherent value of sexuality in human life."

Sharp division among commission members was taken by some to mean that the "Church's mind" was not settled on the subject. Michael Novak thought the obstacle to Catholic acceptance of contraception was "emotional, not theological" (*Newsweek*, April 12, 1965). Charles Davis, writing later in the *Clergy Review* (December 1966), asserted that "the Church is in danger of losing its soul to save its face." All the while the pope kept studying the question. John Noonan sympathized with the pope: "In a matter of such great importance to millions of persons, born and to be born, he believes he cannot discharge his office by accepting the report of experts. He, himself, must know and judge personally. This is the decision not of a callous but a conscientious man. Its honesty requires respect" (*Commonweal*, February 17, 1967).

But someone soon decided that the pope's conscientiousness and honesty needed nudging, so they leaked the drafts of both majority and minority conclusions of the Papal Birth Control Commission to the *National Catholic Reporter*. The story made front page news everywhere on April 17, 1967. The squeeze on the pope was real.

Commonweal editorialists told its readership (April 28, 1967) what the commission drafts meant to them:

> For better or worse, the debate over birth control in the Church has served as a focal point for all manner of issues far more basic than the

morality of contraception. Among these have been the nature of marriage, the man-woman relationship, the role and value of the Church's teaching authority, the place of the free conscience in the Church, the validity of natural law, the nature of morality and the Church's witness to the world.

These certainly were the fundamental issues which would continue to be argued in the press, and in the classrooms and parish halls of the Church throughout the ensuing fifteen months, while changemakers had the Catholic faithful primed for the Church's acceptance of contraception. Apparently at the highest level of the Church, no one at all gave consideration to counter-efforts of education to prepare Mass-goers for the encyclical *Humanae Vitae*. This proved to be a disastrous error in judgment.

VIII. The Encyclical Humanae Vitae

On July 25, 1968, Pope Paul VI issued his now much abused encyclical *Humanae Vitae*. Though dealing with the transmission of human life, as its title indicated, the United States Catholic Conference published its contents under the title "The Regulation of Birth." This is what interested the Western World, even if that was not what the encyclical was *all* about!

No papal pronouncement was ever greeted with such hostility from its own. Up to the moment of publication, the Catholic converts to contraception thought their fight was ended. A special eleven-page report for *U.S. Catholic* magazine on the status of the birth-control question, issued one month before (June 1968), concluded that the traditional Catholic law was in doubt and no longer applied. On the secular front, *Time* magazine began on June 21st to publish what would be the first of six articles in three months on Catholic birth control. One week before July 25, family-life pioneer John L. Thomas, S.J., predicted for an Omaha audience Catholic-Church approval of medically acceptable birth control methods, other than sterilization (*NCR* July 24, 1968).

And then the pope dropped a population bomb of his own. Important sentences (#11–12) of *Humanae Vitae* read as follows:

> The Church, calling men back to the observance of the norms of the natural law, as interpreted by her constant doctrine, teaches that each and every marriage act must remain open to the transmission of life. That teaching, often set forth by the magisterium, is founded upon the inseparable connection, willed by God and unlawful for man to break

on his own initiative, between the two meanings of the conjugal act:
The unitive meaning and the procreative meaning.

In #14 the pope went on to outline the Catholic doctrine on "illicit ways of regulating birth," saying, "We must once again declare that the direct interruption of the generative process already begun, and, above all, directly willed and procured abortion, even if for therapeutic reasons, are to be absolutely excluded as licit means of regulating birth." The pope warned (#17) about the grave consequences of desacralizing marriage in this manner and the social consequences of contraception.

These specific references to contraception, and its rejection by the pope, do not stand alone. They must be seen within the context of his entire teaching, which can be summarized as follows:

1. On Human Life

The encyclical *Humanae Vitae* is a sharp reminder that human life is unique. Every human being who comes into existence is a person, the exact like of whom the world has never seen before, and will never see again, someone whom God Himself wants to exist with Him for all eternity, an individual with a capacity to reach out beyond himself and help build new worlds and transform this one. Because of this, the act that brings him into existence involves cooperation by two human beings with the creative power of God, who alone can bring this immortal person into existence – and this act of procreation acquires a sacredness which may never be denied.

This is why the Church has always been so concerned with human life, why she has opposed abortion and euthanasia, why she has taken care even of infants born so malformed that they will never reach full mental maturity in this life. It is why her social doctrine has been so concerned, over the past century, to help men live in the conditions that are worthy of their human dignity. It is why she is concerned with peace at a time when modern weapons of war can wipe out human lives on a scale undreamed of in the past.

Humanae Vitae recalls men to a deeper recognition of the importance of human life and ways that God has provided for human beings to share in bestowing it on others.

2. On Sex

The encyclical *Humanae Vitae* is a sharp reminder that sex is sacred in God's eyes – something that may not be cut off from its proper relationship to the origin of human life. This does not mean that sex has no other important roles to play – as a concrete expression of the marriage bond's unity, as something joyful and enjoyable, as a celebration of human life itself. But it does mean that sex loses its truest and most profound meaning in God's plan if it is separated from its necessary relationship to the origins of life. The evidence of where this kind of separation leads is all around: a flood of pornography that would have been inconceivable thirty years ago, a commercialization of sex in stage and film productions that leaves nothing sacred, a casual acceptance of promiscuity in varying degrees, a so-called sexual revolution in the matter of pre-marital relationships, and a tendency to disregard any moral implication in homosexuality.

Humanae Vitae recalls us to a deeper acknowledgment of the sacredness and the beauty of sex because God created sex to enable men to cooperate with Him in the greatest of all natural acts and powers – bringing a new person into the world.

3. On Absolute Principles

The encyclical *Humanae Vitae* is a sharp reminder that, in a world of shifting values, there are still principles that hold now as in the past – in all places and circumstances – and that will still hold true on the day when God calls the whole of the human race to be happy with Him forever. Many things which were once worthwhile no longer are so. The modern world encourages use and comfort and enjoyment of the good life, and holds out promise of greater goods to come – and in this sense has positive value. But good values can be dismissed along with worn-out customs. Ease and comfort can lead men to give up what they believe in. The promise of a better life can lead us to forget moral responsibilities in the present.

Humanae Vitae reminds men that God wants the law of the Lord obeyed, that what seems to be easiest is not always best, that God's grace enables us to live up to his norms even when it requires great effort.

4. On the Supernatural

The encyclical *Humanae Vitae* is also a reminder that the Holy Spirit is real in the life of a Christian and at work in our own day. In asking for acceptance of what the Church had always taught in this matter, the Holy Father appealed to the promise of assistance from the Holy Spirit made to Peter and the Apostles and through them to popes and bishops. Pope Paul knew that if the arguments were so clear in either direction as to exclude all doubt, there would never have been a wait of four years for a final answer. But he also knew that the Holy Spirit, who had been with the Church in harder days than these, would not fail to provide the direction that was needed.

Also, the pontiff knew that Catholics, whose lives are built on faith in things that are not fully seen, would realize that God's plan was at work even in those cases where contraception would seem from a human point of view to offer a simpler solution. Someone looking at a consecrated host without the eyes of faith misses the true reality that is there; someone speaking to Jesus as He walked the street of Nazareth would never, on his own, recognize that this man was God; someone beholding an infant fresh from the baptismal font does not see the life of God within him; those who looked at a man suffering on a cross 2,000 years ago did not see redemption. But the eyes of faith, and the virtues of trust, and our love of God, who loves us more than we love Him, even when He asks hard things of us, shows us that God's ways are the best ways, in this as in all other things.

Humanae Vitae reminds men to look beyond the surface view of things to the divine truth beneath.

5. On Involvement with others

The encyclical *Humanae Vitae* is a sharp reminder that every Christian must be concerned with the problems of every other human being. The teaching of the encyclical makes hard demands on some people. It is not enough for bishops, priests, or laity to consider this someone else's problem. If there is something that Catholics can do – to solve problems or relieve them, with better medical information or economic aid, with spiritual guidance and support of the sacraments, with sympathy and concern in cases where there is no simple answer – this must be done.

Humanae Vitae reminds men of the obligation imposed by Christian love.

IX. Immediate Response to Humanae Vitae

Probably the most harmful response to *Humanae Vitae* came in Rome itself from the man entrusted by the Holy See to release the encyclical to the world's press, Msgr. Fernando Lambruschini, a professor at the Lateran University and a member of the Birth Control Commission, who, in the end, voted with the majority. The rationale for selecting this particular man to be press secretary for the pope on this subject defies understanding.

Lambruschini in the press conference literally undercut any possibility that *Humanae Vitae* would tip the scale back toward Catholic doctrine by telling the press – not once, but twice – that the encyclical was *not an infallible pronouncement* (*Catholic Mind*, September 1968). Not only was this an invitation for continuing debate on an issue the pope thought he was closing, it was to suggest to Richard McCormick seven years later that the very ongoing debate about contraception, not the pope's words, were the clearest sign of God's will (*The Tablet* [London], February 7, 1975). That was precisely the assumption pro-contraceptionists wished to use as justification for their vigorous dissent.

That public acceptance of the encyclical did not follow should surprise no one. Fr. Charles Curran and fifty-one Washington priests gained notoriety over their rejection of the encyclical. But all over the United States priests and theologians followed Lambruschini's lead. Five days after issuance (July 30, 1968), Fordham University sponsored a panel discussion for 2,000 ready listeners and reporters for the *New York Times*, *Newsweek*, *Time*, and the Religious News Service as well. The panel was staffed against the pope. The one priest of five, cast in the role of "pope's man," was quoted as giving only a "qualified defense" of the encyclical (*America*, August 17, 1968). *America* itself, in the same issue, justified continued dissent in the Church and the use of contraceptives by Catholics, noting that Msgr. Lambruschini, "as official spokesman in Rome for the encyclical," hinted at a possible future and radical change. Fr. James T. Burtchaell, at that time chairman of Notre Dame's Theology Department, called for "conscientious resistance," based in part on the principle that the pope's responsibility must be recalled "to more conscionable limits," and in part on the fact that "practically the only spokesmen to support the encyclical vocally are men whose careers depend on ecclesiastical preferment" (*Commonweal*, November 15, 1968). Journalist John Cogley asked: "Why not say that the Anglican and Protestant Churches were more correct in their ecclesiology, their moral teachings, and their faithfulness to the spirit of the gospel than the Church of Rome, which for so long made the kind of claim its own best theologians are now rejecting? If, for example, the Anglicans were right about contraception all along and the Romans were wrong, who are the surer moral teachers?" (*Commonweal*, October 11, 1968). Bishop James Shannon of St. Paul told the Holy Father (September 23, 1968) that his "rigid teaching is simply impossible of observance" (*NCR*, June 6, 1968).

And so the dissent continued down to the low levels of the Church, prompting the *Christian Science Monitor* to editorialize (October 11, 1968): "Birth Control Wins!" The Protestant newspaper, citing a Notre Dame Study showing that 95 percent of assistant pastors under 30 favored contraception, predicted that "nothing on the face of the earth can stem or reverse" the rejection.

The pope appeared very much like a defeated man.

X. Catholic War on the Potomac

While dissenters worldwide began to follow identical patterns of resistance, the pope, facing this opposition, built a few defenses of his own. Within a month of his pronouncement on birth control, Pope Paul VI was on his way to Bogota, Colombia, for the Latin American Bishops' Conference. He decided once more to confront his critics with a reminder of who they were and who he is.

Among his remarks – which received scant attention in the United States – were the following:

> Unfortunately among us some theologians are not on the right path...
>
> Some have recourse to ambiguous doctrinal expression and others arrogate to themselves the permission to proclaim their own personal opinions on which they confer that authority by which they more or less covertly question him who by divine right possesses such a protected and awesome charisma. And they even consent that each one in the Church may think and believe what he wants . . .
>
> [*Humanae Vitae*] is, ultimately, a defense of life, the gift of God, the glory of the family, the strength of the people. God grant also that the lively discussion which our encyclical has aroused may lead to a better knowledge of the will of God (*NC* [Foreign] *News*, August 24, 1968).

When this visit was ended, he had his Secretary of State, Amleto Cardinal Cigognani, tell papal representatives all over the world that, in view of the "bitterness" which *Humanae Vitae* had caused, "all priests, secular and religious, and especially those with responsibility as general and provincial superiors of religious orders . . . [had] to put forward to Christians this delicate point of Church doctrine, explain it, and vindicate the profound reasons behind it. The Pope counts on them and on their devotion to the Chair of Peter, their love for the Church, and their care for the true good of souls" (*NC News*, September 6, 1968).

As far as fifty-one priests in the Archdiocese of Washington were concerned, however, the Pope could count on nothing of the kind. These priests were ready for public battle over contraception, even before the encyclical was in the offing.

The international notoriety of these fifty-one priests (later to be scaled down to the "Washington Nineteen"), in their contest with Patrick Cardinal O'Boyle, had its beginning in Baltimore, not Washington. Lawrence Cardinal Sheehan of Baltimore saw a need in 1967 for a set of *Guidelines for the Teaching of Religion*. Because part of the Washington archdiocese overlapped the state of Maryland, he persuaded Patrick Cardinal O'Boyle in Washington to make the project a common enterprise. Such collaboration made sense. The early draft of these *Guidelines* caught the attention of diocesan education officers in far away places because two years after the Council's close, strange things were going on in the religion classrooms of the nation. On the advice of some priests, a section was added to the *Guidelines* on contraception which instructed the teacher that "he may not permit or condone contraceptive practices." A year later when the *Guidelines* were to be ratified by the two cardinals for use in both dioceses (*Catholic Standard* [Washington], June 27, 1968), the Washington Archdiocesan Council of High School teachers called the *Guidelines* "triumphal as well as negative in content," objectionable too because they were drafted without prior consultation with the Council. Though no one knew at the time, *Humanae Vitae* was only four weeks away.

At this moment, Fr. John E. Corrigan, chairman of the executive committee of the Association of Washington Priests, intervened. The Association, which had begun as a Vatican II Study Club, followed the pattern set by Msgr. John Egan of Chicago, who had developed there a priest's association distinct from the Priest's Senate (The Priest's Senate is the only organization recommended by Vatican II). A priest's association, because it voluntary, usually represents only a minority of priests, whereas the Priest's Senate collaborates with the bishop of each diocese in representing the interests of all priests. The Washington Association sounded the second protest against the *Guidelines*, releasing a "statement of conscience" for 142 of the 1,200 priests in Washington D.C. Calling some magisterial and doctrinal tenets "mere theological tenets," Corrigan stated that "the bishops issuing the *Guidelines*, in and of themselves, do not constitute the authentic magisterium." Because Corrigan's group favored the approach of the *Dutch Catechism*, the *Guidelines* of Cardinals Sheehan and O'Boyle were accused of adding to confusion in the Church.

Then, on July 29, 1968 (as if anticipating the momentary release of the pope's long-awaited decision – the press had advance copies), Fr. Charles E. Curran of the Catholic University of America in Washington was quoted in the *Washington Star*:

> I believe the majority of contemporary theologians and Catholics today believe Catholic couples are free in conscience to use contraception in the responsible exercise of their marital relationship, I believe the bishops as well as all the people of the Church should speak out to prevent the pope from making a statement that would merely reaffirm the former teaching of the hierarchical magisterium. . . . It seems incredible that the pope should be thinking of such a statement. . . . It would be disastrous.

Diocesan priest Corrigan had arranged a press conference for July 30, 1968, in the Mayflower Hotel to protest the *Guidelines* of the two cardinals. Fr. Curran took over that room for his own protest against *Humanae Vitae*, leading some to conclude that Corrigan, who participated in Curran's July 28th meeting, was an active participator in Curran's well-planned strategy to mount an all-out campaign against any encyclical forthcoming from Rome. In return, Corrigan received support from Curran's group in his confrontation with Cardinal O'Boyle. Without the tactical assistance of professors at the Catholic University of America, the celebrated "War on the Potomac" might have failed quickly.

On July 31, 1968, the American bishops called upon "priests and people to receive with sincerity what he [the pope] has taught, to study it carefully and to form their consciences in its light" (*NC News*).

On August 1, 1968, Cardinal O'Boyle told his priests that they must follow *Humanae Vitae*. He issued a pastoral letter (August 2, 1968) which said in part:

> The Church can do without the dissent of those gentlemen who forget that in the Catholic Church even the most expert theologian must accept the teaching authority of the Church – that authority which resides in the bishops, and especially in the successor of Peter. Pope Paul listened to the theologians and to the rest of the Church, in fact to the whole world – for five long years. Now it is our turn to listen to him.

For the fifty-one Washington priest-dissenters, conscience was the independent judge of moral doctrine and the opinion of dissenting theologians an alternative to the Church's authentic teaching.

On August 4, 1968, Fr. T. Joseph O'Donoghue – the priest who after his later defection from the priesthood headed up the short-lived National Council of the Laity – was suspended.

The confrontation was on.

O'Donoghue later told a rally, which included Protestants:

> You are saying what our brethren of other faiths have long been waiting for you to say, something we have not clearly said since the Reformation. Namely, that Catholics are men and women of faith who in conscience listen to the word and in conscience decide (*Washington Post*, September 16, 1968).

On August 10, 1968, Cardinal O'Boyle wrote to each of the dissenters a ten-page letter explaining the historical background of the problem and the present status of doctrine and dissent, concluding with the following official policy for his priests:

> Since I am the bishop of Washington, you recognize me as a successor of the Apostles sent by Christ. I have commissioned you to teach and preach Catholic doctrine, and to exercise your pastoral ministry both in confession and out of it in strict accordance with the authentic teaching of the Catholic Church. To present this teaching merely as one alternative is not in accordance with it. I cannot allow you to diverge from this teaching, because I can only authorize you to do what I am authorized to do myself.

Not only was this a customary statement from a Catholic bishop, but a standard response from a chief executor of any enterprise which expects discipline among officials.

The *New York Times* editorialized (October 1, 1968) that O'Boyle's mistake was refusing to accept dissent, in view of the Catholic trend to use contraceptives anyway. The *Washington Evening Star* lamented (October 3, 1968) the "tragic escalation" as a result of O'Boyle's stand: "Despite Pope Paul's refusal to move the Church off its present stand on birth control, such a move will come soon. No organization, spiritual or temporal, can long disregard the overwhelming sentiments of its members."

Some Catholic statements were more unsympathetic. John B. Mannion, former executive secretary of the Liturgical Conference, thought Cardinal O'Boyle had "blown his cool." Defending the dissenters, Mannion said their most deeply felt fear was "the prospect of not being a priest." (At least twenty five of the fifty one ultimately left the priesthood.) Mannion concluded:

> We see at work in the birth-control issue the celibacy debate, the germinal drive for divorce and remarriage, the frequency of intercommu-

nication, and a number of other doctrines such as purgatory, hell, transubstantiation, Mary as co-redemptrix, and so on. What a decade it is going to be for the O'Boyles of this world (*Commonweal*, October 18, 1968).

In his delineation of the issues Mannion was perfectly correct.

On the other side of the dispute, few people at the time took notice that two days after *Humanae Vitae* (August 1, 1968), the *Washington Star* polled 315 priests to discover that 203 supported the pope. Notice had been given to the thirteen Jesuits at Georgetown University who opposed Cardinal O'Boyle, but not much attention to the seventeen Jesuits there who supported him. No significance at all was seen in Catholic University's Fr. Robert L. Faricy's immediate withdrawal from dissent when it was clear that Curran and company were turning the differences on birth control into an authority fight. Less public comment was made later when Jesuit Faricy's contract at Catholic University was not renewed. During the weeks following the publication of *Humanae Vitae*, Cardinal O'Boyle was a busy man. Forced to discipline a minority of diocesan priests, he found more testy opponents among the priests at the Catholic University of America, of which he was Chancellor. (In any Pontifical Catholic University established under a papal charter, the Chancellor is the man assigned by the Holy see as the guarantor of orthodoxy.) After listening to what CUA dissenters had to say, O'Boyle was prompted to make a poignant observation: "I wonder whether theology is not being perverted from its high office in the service of the Catholic faith into an instrument for destroying the faith we have received and replacing it with a new set of man-made ideas" (*NC News*, August 22, 1968).

O'Boyle, of course, was not without resources – and supports of his own. A flight to Rome on August 10, 1968, brought assurance from Pope Paul VI that the pope intended *Humanae Vitae* to be taken as a full affirmation of the Catholic teaching. Returning to his see, the Cardinal insisted (August 31, 1968) that dissenters accept the authentic teaching of the Church, especially in their classroom activity, confessional practice, and counseling, at the same time terminating public dissent. The dissenting priests answer was continued insistence on the superiority of conscience. When the cardinal announced his decision in the pulpit of St. Matthew's Cathedral, the mass-attenders cheered. All during this protracted dispute, his personal mail ran heavily in his favor.

For enforcing the encyclical at a time when the entire American culture was going through its worst anti-authority days, the cardinal archbishop of Washington paid a price. He was picketed at the Church of the Sacred Heart on the occasion of the Labor Day Mass (September 2, 1968). The following day at the Cathedral Latin School he was greeted with obvious hostility by the media representatives. That night on national television, the edited version of the press conference made the hearty and friendly cardinal look unbending and grimacing.

On October 9, 1968, Cardinal O'Boyle instructed his priests further: "I do not accept an opinion concerning conscience that reduces the Church of Christ to the role of just one more advisor among many."

This was and still is the key issue in the dispute. The contest with his priests continued for two years, until September 1, 1970. Thirty-eight priests still remained under discipline. During this period Cardinal O'Boyle expended from diocesan monies more than $100,000 toward the maintenance of these priests – over and above what they received from their pastors or former pastors.

Pope Paul VI encouraged Cardinal (May 15, 1969) with this assurance: "Not only did you give immediate acceptance of the teaching of the magisterium, but you also strove, with exemplary and apostolic concern, that all priests and laity should give the same acceptance." By this time O'Boyle had initiated scores of interviews, individually and in groups, with the priests who were giving him trouble. With encouragement from the pope, the archbishop of Washington returned to these men (June 27, 1969), on the first anniversary of *Humanae Vitae*, seeking agreement with the following statement:

> Having considered the message addressed to us by the Holy Father, I respond by declaring that I accept the teaching of *Humanae Vitae* as the authentic teaching of the Church with regard to contraception and shall follow it without reservation in my teaching, preaching, counselling and hearing confessions.

A few of the dissenting priests accepted O'Boyle's offer at this juncture. Fr. Corrigan celebrated the anniversary of *Humanae Vitae* (August 3, 1969) with an irregular liturgical ceremony in a Protestant Church.

The remaining "Washington Nineteen" priests took their case to Rome in 1970, although by this time no one knew for sure the exact number of priests still under discipline. On April 26, 1971, the Congregation for the Clergy issued a verdict which prompted the *New York Times* (April 30, 1971) headline: "Vatican Rules Against Priests Who Disagreed on an Encyclical!" Not only did the Vatican find that Cardinal O'Boyle had followed canonical procedures, but it found that his theology was also soundly Catholic. The document reads:

> The ordinary magisterium, i.e., the pope and the bishops in their local churches, has the duty and responsibility to teach on matters pertaining to faith and morals . . .

> Those who receive the canonical faculties of a diocese are assumed to communicate this teaching, according to the traditional norms of the Church, to those under their care.

However, the priests who were still functioning were not required to withdraw their public rejection of *Humanae Vitae*.

Ten years earlier priests would not have publicly contested their bishop on a matter of doctrine, agitated the Catholic faithful, or divided their loyalties. The ongoing dialogue over three years did not seem to have solved anything, since the confrontation had been politically motivated.

Cardinal O'Boyle stood up for the Catholic principle of Church organization and was vindicated in the end. But he did seem to stand alone.

XI. What About the Other Bishops?

Cardinal Lawrence Sheehan criticized the Washington dissenters several months after *Humanae Vitae* (*Washington Post*, November 13, 1968), but earlier, when seventy two of his Baltimore priests had signed a statement similar to Washington's, he made no effort to force a change in their position (*Washington Post*, September 16, 1968). Twenty-six Newark priests led by CUA's Robert Hunt, seventy six others in Minneapolis, sixty four in Oklahoma City following the lead of Bernard Cooke, also challenged the Pope without penalty. Some Canadian bishops are cited as expressing "horror" at the sanctions Cardinal O'Boyle imposed (*Commonweal*, October 18, 1968).

The pastoral problems – after as well as before the encyclical – were many. The bishops as a body may not have been as permissive as they appeared because the dissident priests were comparatively few, and these few in most cases issued only one press release and were heard from no more in public. Had CUA clubs existed in other dioceses with the same determination to establish ongoing dissidence against local bishops as the Curran-Corrigan group did, there probably would have been more suspended priests. There is a limit to the insubordination that even the most indulgent bishop will tolerate, if he exercises the responsibility of his office at all.

Even without Washington-type confrontations, however, bishops were required to deal with pastoral confusion. During the length of the controversy contraceptives had been blessed in some confessionals, but not in others. The use of contraceptives by married couples was a grave matter and a serious sin, if all other conditions for serious sin were present. What would Church authority do about dissent in the bedroom? Historically, the Church has been strict with its people only when the people themselves are disciplined in the practices of Catholic life – stricter in the early Church than later, in Ireland and Poland more than in France or Italy, in small towns more than in big cities. Whatever the reason, the "power of loosing" rather than the "power of binding" was to be a matter of silent policy during the post–*Humanae-Vitae* turbulence. Some looked upon this as a retreat from the high standards of observance to which the American Church had become accustomed. In a sense it was. But most American priests, even after *Casti Connubii* (1930), preached a firm Gospel in the pulpit, while practicing mercy in the confessional. Absolution was rarely denied to Catholics practicing "birth control," unless arrogance or defiance appeared in the penitent. Customarily, the promise "to try" to cure contraceptive habits, as would be sought for other sexual sins, was sufficient to gain penitents absolution.

The difference in recent pastoral practice is a new phenomenon of priests sanctioning contraception and sexual sins of all kinds. The new approach is alleged to be a reaction to the puritanical attitudes of the nineteenth-century Church. Factually, however, sexual sins were always major objects of the Church's penitential discipline precisely because their privacy and their power made self-control by the individual or social control by the Church (or society) rather difficult. The Church intervened in these matters where few others dared – in the consciences of her faithful.

The pastoral problem now – after as before the encyclical – would be to raise the sights of Catholic people so that they understood where virtue lay, to move (even prod) them to make themselves virtuous as the Church understood that term.

It is in this area of the formation of conscience that Church authorities recently have created some of their own problems. Rome prompted national hierarchies to respond to the encyclical and they did, most of them reaffirming the papal ban without equivocation. The Holy See apparently did not expect that some hierarchies might blur the teaching, however. Pastoral practice (binding or loosing) always varies from nation to nation. African bishops had no problem with *Humanae Vitae* because Africans – an unsophisticated people – were not contraceptionists. Nor did the Philippine bishops. These statements were ignored by the American press because they were strict (*NC News*, November 7, 1968). The Australian bishops told their people: "Every member of the Church must be considered bound to accept the decision given by the pope. To refuse to do so would be a grave act of disobedience" (*NC News*, August 10, 1968). The Australian bishops recently felt compelled to restate that the Church ban on contraception binds all "without ambiguity," as reported in the *Tablet* (Brooklyn), of February 17, 1977. The Mexican bishops said: "It is never licit to accept the opinions of theologians against the constant teaching of the Church" (*NC News*, August 13, 1968). The bishops of England and Wales took note of conscience, but stressed the necessity of a conscience formed by doctrine (*NC News*, October 4, 1968).

The secular press and the dissenting theologians, however, were not interested in affirmation and reaffirmation. They wanted confirmation of the right to have two contrary doctrinal positions and still be "loyally Catholic." Here the French, Dutch, Canadian, German, Austrian, and Scandinavian hierarchies provided statements which gave the press the seeming loopholes they sought. They have been exploiting these loopholes ever since.

The Dutch statements were the most damaging chiefly because the secular press had come to realize how newsworthy Holland's hierarchy was from the moment in March 1963 when Bishop W. Bekkers made it clear on television that people must make up their own minds on contraception (*Herder Correspondence*, October 1963). *Humanae Vitae* was no sooner made public than the Dutch hierarchy was being cited as leaving the matter to conscience, regardless of what the pope said. The first Sunday after publication (August 4, 1968), sermons throughout Holland told churchgoers that the final decision must be made by them (*NC Foreign News*, August 9, 1968). Msgr. H. J. Roygers, vicar general of the Breda diocese, declared: "A papal encyclical has no other authority than the force of the arguments used. The pope is not infallible, only the Church is infallible, i.e., the pope together with his bishops and priests" (*NC Foreign News*, July 30, 1968). The American-born bishop of Stockholm, John E. Taylor, O.M.I., pointed out that the encyclical "does not have to be regarded as infallible" and "no one should act against the conscience" (*NC Foreign News*, August 5, 1968).

The French bishops took a different tack but ended up going in the same direction. Conceding that "contraception can never be a good," they leave the decision with couples, if they face a conflict of duties between their service to each other and to Church teaching.

Closer to home, the Canadian bishops made a statement which some now regret. But in 1968, these bishops, while asserting solidarity with the pope, refrained from endorsing his reaffirmation of the immorality of contraception. They did not encourage dissenters, but consoled the faithful, and talked about a conflict of duties. Their remarks were interpreted by Canadian reporter Douglas J. Roche as (1) upholding the prohibition of contraception as an ideal; (2) permitting those in good conscience to receive holy communion without going to confession first (*Commonweal*, October 18, 1968). Bishop Alexander Carter, president of the Canadian Catholic Conference, was quoted (*Washington Post*, September 25, 1968) as saying:

> We know there are going to be days and times when they are not going to know how to live up this ideal. . . . If the time comes from them to make a decision on contraception and if they are convinced they are doing their best, they should not feel they are violating God's word.

The American bishops, on the other hand, were more consistent in their response to Paul VI but found difficulty anyway. Part of their problem originated with their soft first response which had merely asked people "to receive it [the encyclical] with sincerity, to study it carefully, and to form consciences in its light." Several dissenting theologians leaped on that sentence to argue this is what they had been saying. Bishop Joseph Bernardin, then general secretary of the National Conference of Bishops, immediately denied this, insisting (what dissenting theologians do not insist) that the consciences had to be formed correctly.

The American bishops' collective pastoral, *Human Life in our Day* (November 15, 1968), repeated standard Catholic theology:

1. Contraception is objectively evil.

2. Circumstances reduce guilt.

3. Sinners should use the sacrament of Penance and the Eucharist.

4. Disagreeing theologians have to follow the Church's rules on such matters.

However, because words like "conscience," "reduced moral guilt," "licit theological dissent" – all technical theological concepts – appeared in a statement intended to be read in lay language, the media were able to distort the tenor of its content. One New York radio station on Friday night said "the American bishops have approved a limited use of contraceptives for Catholic couples." The *New York Times* headlined the story for Saturday (November 16th): "Bishops Temper Curbs on Birth Control." The *Washington Evening Star* on the same day had this lead-in: "Bishops Back Birth Edict: Note Roles of Conscience: Prelates Assert Church Shouldn't Deny Sacraments." The *New York Times* on Sunday in its "Review of the Week" reported that no matter what the thrust of the pastoral, a "loophole" had been provided for a Catholic to practice contraception.

Loopholes were sought or invented. Fr. John B. Sheerin, C.S.P., in a foreword to the Paulist Press edition of the bishops' pastoral, himself invented a loophole which is not in the text. Quoting the bishops, who asked those "who have resorted to artificial contraception never to lose heart but to continue to take advantage of the strength which comes from the sacrament of Penance" (p. 7), Sheerin then added his own *obiter dictum*, "without saying they must go to confession." The bishops could not have meant this because the sacrament of Penance involves confession. Unquestionably, some priests and couples found the same loophole – the bishops not seeming to anticipate how the sentence would be interpreted. Sheerin also raised in his foreword (p. 11) what he called "unanswered questions" about the encyclical: Why was it not the decision of the Council rather than the pope alone? Why did the pope keep the matter off the bishops' 1967 Synod agenda in Rome? Will papal authority be irretrievably damaged by dissent? Such questions raised about the encyclical in a publication of the bishops' own pastoral letter did not help the literal credence of the pastoral itself.

On the other hand, Kenneth Woodward, religion editor of *Newsweek*, an active proponent of contraception himself, saw the exact meaning of what the American bishops had said. *Newsweek* (November 25, 1968) reported: "Unlike the liberal Dutch and French bishops, the Americans showed scant respect for the supremacy of conscience – particularly in the face of debatable teaching. They were chiefly concerned with defending the teaching authority of the Church."

This review of the various bishops' reactions to *Humanae Vitae* prompts the question first raised by St. Paul in the early Church: "If the bugle call is uncertain, who will get ready for battle?" (I Corinthians 14:18). Pope Paul's bugle call was clear enough. But some generals in the field sounded a different tune. Bishop John Wright of Pittsburgh placed a finger on the problem (*NC News*, August 2, 1968) when, after denying that the pope had consigned to Gehenna Catholics trapped in contraception, he gave stern warning to those who foster, counsel, or impose what is wrong, especially if they are spiritual directors. Fr. John C. Ford, S.J., also took *America* magazine to task for seeming to suggest that Cardinal O'Boyle should restore his dissenting priests in a spirit of reconciliation (April 25, 1970), while accusing O'Boyle of being unfair, inequitable, and unjust.

Fr. Ford made two important rejoinders to this editorial (May 30, 1970):

1. No group of priests has the right of public, scandalous dissidence from their own bishop on a point of doctrine that he is teaching with the explicit support of the Holy Father.

2. When priests publicly and persistently refuse to do so, their bishop is bound in conscience to withdraw their authorization to teach.

The view of reconciliation of *America* magazine editor Donald Campion, S.J., was later rejected by the Holy See in 1971, but his reply to Fr. Ford at the time, in 1970, rejected the Ford reading. He denied Ford's "talent for interpreting papal letters," saying that it was one "not granted to the hierarchies of several nations" (*America*, May 30, 1970).

Pope Paul VI never expressed a word of approval for the hierarchical statements of Holland, France, Sweden, or Canada, as he praised Cardinal O'Boyle's stand on *Humanae Vitae* many times; but as long as bishops themselves were counted as dissidents, and remained unreproved, the suspicion circulated that Rome might settle the problem fraudulently by holding to its anti-contraceptive terminology, while countenancing "exceptions." This would make the encyclical in time a dead letter. Some scholars say this now.

XII. The Alleged Right to Dissent

Probably there is no more serious question to be faced by the officers of the Catholic Church than the alleged right to dissent claimed by contemporary theologians. It makes no difference what the Church says about anything if theologians – eminent or pedestrian – can set themselves up as rival teachers of the Gospel. It makes little difference whether the questioned teaching is infallible because dissenters, who once resisted noninfallible statements (the Mosaic authorship of the Pentateuch, religious freedom in civil society, the primary and secondary purposes of marriage, etc.), now argue over admittedly infallible positions of the Church (on Christ's nature, Mary's role in redemption, the primacy and infallibility of the pope, etc.).

Other Christian churches do not have this difficulty. They define themselves differently, usually as congregations or assemblies of believing Christians with a common fellowship in their faith, who celebrate this faith through common prayer, and share a common understanding of what Christ wants. But evangelical churches never claim to *stand as mediators between* Christ and the believer.

The Catholic Church makes this claim. The Catholic Church claims to speak with the authority that Christ gave, asserts its right to bind and loose, not only conduct but minds. The assumption of Catholic faith is that the believer is willing to make that submission. If he does not, he cannot remain a Catholic, at least not for long.

Therefore, in the Catholic Church two voices of Christ, if it means the Church formally teaches two different things as Christ's mind, cannot co-exist. Two voices saying that Christ did/did not rise from the dead; Mary is/is not a virgin; the Church is/is not divinely established; bishops are/are not the successors of the apostles, cannot be simultaneously true. A great deal of speculation can go into explaining how these "mysteries" of Catholic faith are true, but not that they might be false. That is speculation reserved for unbelievers. Dissent as defined by contemporary theologians means two rival teaching voices in theory, and two different churches in practice.

The fact that the Jewish and Protestant religious traditions provide living space within the same body for contradictory Orthodox, Conservative, Reform styles of believing and behaving is no reason for the Catholic Church to consider these as acceptable models. Factually, the genius of the Church is its ability to tolerate high, middle, and low behavior patterns in her people, *while insisting on one creed, one code, one cult.* Decisions about Catholic truth are made authoritatively, not as the result of consensus among theologians. Church authority permits theologians, as special experts in God's word, to counsel the faithful authoritatively. But when the Church clearly states doctrine it denies permission – explicitly or equivalently – to anyone to teach or preach other than what was authentically pronounced as coming from Christ. The modern dissenting theologian denies the Church this authority, placing himself between the pastors of souls and the faithful as an alternative voice of Christ, considering it his right and duty to teach directly, over the heads of the pastors, thus opposing what they authentically teach.

In two millennia, ground rules have been developed for expressing theological opinions, ground rules which permitted development, while preventing wild speculation or irresponsible behavior from weakening the faith of Catholic people or compromising high Church standards. Five basic rules have come to govern theological speculation which contravened existing Catholic formulas.

1. Believing Catholics may not openly dissent from their faith.

2. Pastors of souls may not accept dissenting views as norms in parochial ministry.

3. The faithful may not follow the opinions of dissenting theologians in practice.

4. Theologians may research Church questions freely, but if they doubt the validity of any teaching, they must bring their doubts and evidence discretely and privately to the attention of Church authority.

5. Catholics in doubt about a noninfallible teaching may suspend or withhold their assent, while they take every opportunity to resolve their difficulty through study, consultation, or prayer.

The mature understanding of the theologians who developed these principles is pertinent. A few typical citations reveal the flavor of their thinking.

> [the pope] must not be publicly contradicted, nor may an opposing doctrine be publicly defended, unless he himself permits the matter to be debated by Catholics so that truth may more clearly be revealed or to provide a period of study leading to solemn definition, or for some other reason (D. Palmieri, *Tractatus De Romano Pontifice*, 1931, p. 551).

> Noninfallible doctrinal pronouncements from the Pope or from the Roman Congregations are universally obligatory . . . [this] does not prevent anyone from raising questions and respectfully proposing to legitimate authority arguments . . . [then] it is permissible for him to suspend internal assent . . . [but] he must maintain external respect for the decree as long as it remains in force (J. M. Hervé, *Manuale Theologicae Dogmaticae*, Volume I, 1935, pp. 551 ff.).

G. Van Noort calls *magisterium* "a practically certain expert'" so that even when assent may legitimately be suspended, the posture is still one of reverence (*Dogmatic Theology*, 1961, p. 275).

The only author cited by Charles Curran (*Dissent in and for the Church*, p. 12) who can be said to offer him a handle for his own dissidence is Otto Karrer, who writes:

"These personal [i.e., of the pope] and curial pronouncements demand reverential assent *salva conscientia*, that is, with the right of conscience respected" (*Handbuch Theologischer Grundegriffe*, Volume 2, 1967, p. 274).

In summary, dissidence within the Church came to be exercised according to these norms.

- Noninfallible teaching requires assent from all Catholics.
- Outward disobedience is always excluded.
- Noninfallible teaching can be refined by further study.
- The presumption of truth is on the side of the magisterium.
- Magisterial officers are in control of the findings from research.

Thus, traditional doctrine did not really sanction dissent at all. It permitted withholding assent during private research. A rival teaching office to the magisterium by the nature of things was excluded. This policy resulted in the adoption of Canon 2317 of the *Code of Canon Law* (1918), which, referring specifically to noninfallible teachings, reads:

All who obstinately teach or either publicly or in private defend a doctrine that has been condemned by the Apostolic See or by an ecumenical council, but not as a formal heresy, are to be excluded from the ministry of preaching the Word of God or hearing confessions, and from the office of teaching. This in addition to the penalties which the sentence of the Ordinary, after a due warning, may consider necessary to repair the scandal given.

After the Council's close, the First Synod of Bishops in 1967 took up the relationship of theologians to the authentic magisterium, and while bishops were encouraged to seek the advice of theologians and encourage their investigations, they – the bishops – were to protect the magisterium by repeated proclamation of its content (*NC News*, September 5, 1968). This position favors the rights of church authority. The burden of proof always remains on change-makers. The bishops and Rome did not invoke traditional sanctions against dissenters. But neither did they accept the rationale justifying dissent.

what was called an uncreative hierarchy. One argument alleges that
(1) bishops and pope have erred in the past because theologians were not
consulted and another (2) that doctrinal development is due to inventive
theologians working outside teaching formulas. However, the function of
Catholic theologians to propose new propositions does not imply that their
function to invent incorporates the right to determine the orthodoxy of their
inventions.

The more fundamental and substantial arguments for dissent can be
summarized under four headings,

> First, the effort of dissenters to reinterpret the decrees of the Second
> Vatican Council.
>
> Secondly, the effort to redefine Catholic theology.
>
> Thirdly, the effort to create a second magisterium in the Church.
>
> Fourthly, the effort to redefine the Catholic Church.

While many theologians can be cited to defend one or all of these arguments, this presentation will confine itself to the writings of moralists
Charles Curran and Richard McCormick.

1. Reinterpretation of Vatican II

Fr. Charles Curran and his co-authors in *Dissent In and For the Church*
(pp. 100–101) speak as follows:

> With all reverence, theologians recognize that the documents of Vati-
> can II were "dated" on the first day after solemn promulgation . . .

> The spirit of Vatican II might be ignored in favor of the letter and limi-
> tations of officially promulgated formulations; reference in the future
> to the letter of the pronouncements of Vatican II as the final norm for
> evaluating data would bring Roman Catholic ecclesiological progress
> to a halt. This is not because Vatican II formulations are unsuitable;
> rather, it is because they are intrinsically limited to what the Council
> Fathers intended them to be – formulations which express, for the most
> part, the maximum capacity of that time, but which do not preclude fu-
> ture, on-going developments beyond the categories of Vatican II itself.

If that statement had been made in 1998, thirty-three years after Vatican II, after the Church had evaluated the practical effect of the 1965 decrees, the pluses and minuses, and the new needs of the Church as seen by

magisterium, the previous paragraphs might be reasonable statements for reforming an ongoing status quo. But these lines were penned in 1965, before the pope's signature on the conciliar documents was even dry, before anyone knew what Vatican II meant, and before the Holy See itself had organized its implementing decrees.

The practical import of the Curran thesis is that documents – any documents, including the most sacred – have no real binding power in what they say. For dissenters, they are at best useful tools for subjectively interpreting what they really mean. If, for example, the Council rejected, as it did, the move of *periti* to separate the *unitive* from the *procreative* purposes of marriage, or the *collegiality* of bishops from the *primatial* power of the pope, then, argues Curran, those restrictive documents must not be allowed to inhibit immediate moves to complete the job he thinks should have been done. Within this ideology, it is impossible to have dissent because it is impossible to have orthodoxy.

2. Redefinition of Catholic Theology

Process theology is an invitation to religious skepticism. As the argument is developed: revelation comes from study, not from God; it is a process, never an offer of final truth; statements by the Church as to what revelation is, says, teaches, requires must always be subject to personal reinterpretation; if at any given time statements of the Church are taken simply as truth itself, without scrutiny, reexamination, or retesting, "new truths" will never be discovered and the Church will stand still. Presumably, the best interpreters of Church statements are theologians, the suppliers of "new truths."

There is enough plausibility in this position to gain it a superficial hearing. Development of doctrine comes about because the Church gains new insights into unchangeable truths when it applies the Gospel principles to situations which are different form one century to the next. The challenge of atomic war or genetic engineering were not the things Peter and Paul faced. However, there are also constants in Christianity – Jesus is God, Mary is a Virgin, there is a heaven, adultery is wrong. All the ratiocination does not alter the basic reality of their simple meaning given by revelation itself.

Even the simple truth that the magisterium decides when "the process" comes to a halt, when the presumed man of faith accepts or does not accept (assents to or dissents from) the "truth" of faith, when "the faithful" are called to say *"credo"* is a *constant*. The reason why so many theologians did not like Pope Paul's 1968 "Credo of the People of God" was because it laid stress on the constants of Christianity.

A theology which is "in process" indefinitely is not Catholic theology. A theology which no longer finds certitude in what the Church defines as absolutely certain is not Catholic theology. A theology which does not recognize that it is at the service of magisterium – and is not the magisterium itself – is not Catholic theology.

Once Charles Curran led his eighty-seven dissenters in a public revolt against *Humanae Vitae*, the Committee on Doctrine for the Catholic Bishops was forced to say that contemporary theologians were insensitive to the pastoral care of the faithful and had minimized the importance of the magisterium. To correct and alleviate the scandal caused, Bishop Joseph Bernardin arranged a meeting in the Statler Hotel, in New York City on August 18–19, 1968, between four American bishops, six dissenters, and four auditors. These included Bishops Joseph Bernardin, Philip Hannan, John Wright, and Alexander Zaleski, dissenters Charles Curran, John F. Hunt, Daniel Maguire, Walter Burghardt, Bernard Haring, James McGivern, John P. Whelan (acting rector of Catholic University), and three nondissenters, Carl Peter, Paul McKeever, and Austin Vaughan. Bernardin at the outset had hopes the dissenters would move toward a position more acceptable to the bishops. But that never materialized. Some of the dissenters admitted that they wanted to create a crisis. Besides elevating their own role in the Church, they reduced the pope's role radically. Some even wanted the bishops to disagree with the pope. The capstone of the entire meeting was the threat by one scientific theologian that, if the bishops used penalties against them, as many as 20,000 people, including nuns, would leave the Church!

3. A New Status for Theologians

The claim that there is a second magisterium in the Church – staffed by theologians – has brought this response from Jesuit Joseph F. Costanzo, who, while at Fordham University, evaluated this claim:

> The insistence [of dissenters] that theologians are intrinsic to the ecclesial magisterium is the most rootless of all protestations. There is no warrant for it in the mandate of Christ, neither explicitly, implicitly, or by any manner of prolonged inferential ratiocination. There is no evidence of such a role for theologians in the writings of the Fathers of the Church, papal or conciliar. And for all the dissidents' facile rhetori-

cal references to Vatican II, the Council Fathers never graced them with a distinct classification or separate consideration, as they did with the Roman Pontiff, the Bishops, the Religious, laity, and priests. Indeed, the word itself "theologians" appears *only once* among the 103,014 words of the sixteen official texts promulgated by the Ecumenical Council. Considering the centrality of the dissidents' concept of the role of theologians as "an intrinsic element in the total magisterial function of the Church" to their ecclesiology, it seems that they have been slighted by a Council celebrated for its formulation of the collegiality of bishops and by those very bishops who were accompanied by *periti* (*Thomist*, October 1970).

4. The Redefinition of the Catholic Church

Richard McCormick, S.J., rightly concludes that concepts about the binding force of Church teaching and the right to dissent are closely tied into what one thinks about the Catholic Church. He writes:

> If a heavily juridical notion of the Church prevails, is it not inevitable that a heavily juridical notion of the magisterium will accompany this? This means that the teaching office of the Church could easily be confused, to some extent or other, with the administrative (or disciplinary) office . . .

> The Second Vatican Council enlarged our notion of the Church by moving away somewhat from the juridical model. The dominant description of the Church became the People of God. If this notion of the Church is weighed carefully, would it not affect the notion of the Church as teacher? Just one of the effects would be a clearer separation of teaching and administration (discipline). In the light of this separation magisterial teachings would not be viewed as "imposed, commanded, demanding submission, and obedience," for these terms suggest disciplinary jurisdiction, not teaching authority. Rather, noninfallible Church teachings would be seen as offered to the faithful. Obviously, such teaching must still be viewed as authoritative, but the term "authoritative" would shed many of its juridical, and sometimes almost military connotations. The proportionate response to authoritative teaching might not *immediately* be religious assent, even though such acceptance would generally follow (*Theological Studies*, December 1968, pp. 714–15).

Apart from the fact that general acceptance of Church teaching does not seem to follow after the dissenting teachers have done their work, these two paragraphs lay the groundwork for McCormick's own reversal on contraception, and for other theologians' dissent on more fundamental Catholic issues. Their underlying assumptions call for some scrutiny.

First, the dominant description of the Church in Vatican II is not "the People of God." That concept is merely one of seven used. It is an additional emphasis provided, but not an entirely new one. "The People of God" described in *Lumen Gentium* are not a mass of flattened bodies and souls scattered across the plains of the Church, but a community of believers varying in their faith-needs, faith-responses, faith-roles, and all shepherded by leaders called priests, bishops, and pope. Priests, bishops, and pope are very much part of the people of God and are the divinely instituted leaders of those people.

However, if dissenting scholars succeed in flattening the Church into an amorphous mass, then it is easier to make a case for a leadership other than hierarchy.

Secondly, the notion of the Church as a law-making body is central to the teaching of *Lumen Gentium*. Teaching with authority is teaching within the context of discipline. A teacher with knowledge is not on the same footing as the learner. The Church does not merely give friendly advice to believers about Christ and the requirements of salvation. The classroom teacher does not place the formula that $2 + 2 = 4$ on that basis either. The authoritative teacher insists on his teaching – if he knows it to be true. He gives failing grades to the student who insists on writing $2 + 2 = 5$, or to the alleged believer who says Jesus Christ is not God.

If proposed as a pedagogical device for reaching unbelievers, McCormick's approach is useful. John Dewey was not the first teacher to decide that indirect discourse or the parable may be more effective tools for educating the retarded, the culturally deprived, and skeptics. But this is not the way Christ dealt with his believing disciples, nor the way the catechisms of the Church, from Augustine to Trent, taught the faithful. In these source books, authoritative teachings of the Church did not merely enjoy a presumption of truth waiting for endorsement by theologians prior to intellectual commitment. The obligation of acceptance was stated unambiguously by the Church, and became incumbent on the believer, the theologian as well, to give assent. Any other principle of operation would have rendered the Church superfluous.

One thing worth noting is that, although McCormick and others reject the juridical conception of magisterium, they keep a juridical or legalistic conception of obedience. They say that authority is not legalistic but then proceed to give legalistic reasons why one is at liberty to think or do as one wishes.

But a faithful person does not look at a magisterial document and ask: "Do I *have* to accept this?" Or: "How much of this may I deny before I run afoul of some legal-moral obligation?" The faithful person instead regards the magisterium within its sphere with confidence and trust, and takes its judgments as *inherently* authoritative, very much – although for different reasons – as the average person trusts a judge or a surgeon within their respective competencies.

McCormick and the other theologians do not reject this concept of authoritative competency, as if they thought it had *no* application in the domain of religious truth. Rather, *they displace this sort of authority to themselves – to scholars. They do this because they think of religious truth as if it were to be gained primarily by scholarly inquiry, not as a personal truth about man's relation to God received from him by personal communication.*

Cardinal O'Boyle had already met the McCormick position head on (August 21, 1968) when he confronted CUA's theologians:

> What they are saying is either that human judgment stands above the law of God or that the Catholic Church is lying when it claims divine authority for its moral teaching" (*NC News*, September 5, 1968).

Historic Church limitations on public dissent by theologians were acknowledged by the U.S. bishops in *Human Life in Our Day* (November 15, 1968). One sentence, however, written under the title "norms of licit dissent," leaves the bishops open to the charge of conceding what the Holy See might not concede: "The expression of theological dissent from the magisterium is in order only if the reasons are serious and well-founded, if the manner of the dissent does not question or impugn the teaching authority of the Church and is such as not to give scandal." It should have been clear by November 15, 1968, when this was written, that the dissent going on, however serious the intent, was not well-founded in Church tradition, *did* impugn the teaching authority of the Church, and did give scandal, if by that is meant obstacles were deliberately placed in the way of observance by the people for whom *Humanae Vitae* was intended.

Why did the American bishops make the above concession?

There are those who say that the bishops were intimidated by the sheer volume of the opposing voices, amplified no doubt by sympathetic mass media. By then, the U.S. bishops were also aware of what other hierarchies, notably the Canadians, had said. Some of them also believed (mistakenly) that this was a tempest which quickly would pass over so that the ship of the Church would move readily into the peaceful waters to which they were accustomed.

What is not fully documented at this time is the extent to which a few bishop-advocates of contraception kept the document from taking a stronger line. The American pastoral does support *Humanae Vitae* and says nothing erroneous on the doctrinal aspects of the question. But dissenters were saying and advertising widely that spouses could responsibly make birth control decisions for themselves (ignoring *Humanae Vitae*, if need be). The bishops had an opportunity to condemn that opinion and did not. By withdrawing from that particular contest, they provided the basis for the theologians to reaffirm their counsel to Catholic married couples.

Another aspect of the bishops' retreat was their failure to harness scholarly and popular support for the Church's position. At that point (November 15, 1968), Catholics had not been alienated as they would be later. There was also a large body of Catholic scholarship, perhaps a majority, still faithful to the magisterium. Solid Catholic scholars, with very few exceptions, remained silent in public. The general feeling among some was that their academic reputations or careers might be hurt by vigorously confronting dissenting peers; or they felt the problem was so acute that only the hierarchy could or should handle it. In any event, the bishops did not attempt to harness the scholarly opinion which did support *Humanae Vitae*.

XIII. The Aftermath of Humanae Vitae

In the ten years after Pope Paul VI ended the period of ambiguity and speculation about the Church's position on birth control, five different trends are observable in and out of the Church.

1. The dramatic rise in the use of contraceptives by Catholics.

2. Growing concern about contraception in non-Catholic circles.

3. Grand silence about contraception by Church authorities.

4. The continuance of contradictory counsel to the Catholic faithful.

5. The rise of new support for the papal position.

1. Catholic contraception

Charles Westoff and Larry Bumpass, both reputable demographers, drew the contemporary Catholic picture in one short article (*Science*, January 5, 1973). Their conclusions can be summarized as follows:

1. The use of contraceptives by Catholic women increased as follows:
1955 – 30 percent
1965 – 51 percent
1970 – 68 percent

2. In 1970, the use according to age was:
20–24 – 73 percent
25–30 – 74 percent
30–34 – 68 percent
35–39 – 50 percent

3. Whereas formerly the less educated Catholic practiced birth control against Church norms, by 1970 this trend was reversed. Educated Catholic women more frequently now resorted to contraception.

4. Whereas formerly the less pious Catholics used contraception, now the committed Catholics who go to communion at least monthly were violating Catholic norms.

5. In 1965, only 35 percent of monthly communion goers, compared to 53 percent in 1970, used contraceptives. More remarkable 67 percent of this group under-30 now use contraceptives.

6. The Westoff-Bumpass study takes note of two trends going on among Catholics – attrition from the Church and rejection of the Catholic teaching on contraception. The authors do not relate one to the other.

These data certainly lend basis to the opinion that the Catholic Church in America has lost the battle for contraception among its own faithful. The losses certainly are serious. But considering what has gone on in the Church, the remarkable data may be the percentage under-30 who *do not* use contraceptives. Andrew Greeley makes much of the argument that *Humanae Vitae* caused the leakage. The situation is more complex. As the review of the years 1961–68 has made clear, the dissenting scholars (often merely to justify their own views on contraception) felt compelled to undermine confidence in the Church itself. Once people were placed into "the conscience box" for this major issue, there was only one exit permitted, if they wanted escape – rejection of the Church on many fronts, perhaps the Church itself. If one considers that the under-30 group of Catholics likely reject many doctrines – and so are nominally Catholic only – then the percent *not* using contraceptives can be called impressive. Many of them are the Catholics associated both with the pro-life and natural family planning movements.

2. Non-Catholic Contraception

Those who once were called Catholic alarmists about contraception are now being vindicated by the growing concerns about what is happening to women, children, men, and the family because of contraception. Demographer Charles F. Westoff believes that the United States is coming closer and closer to the perfect contraceptive population – i.e., a nation with no unwanted births. In one recent study, he discovered that only 14 percent of all births were unwanted (*Science*, January 9, 1977). As body counts go, this statistic is impressive. This birth–no birth calculus, beyond demonstrating a victory for scientific sex, also has raised once more the long since sidetracked matters of human values, to say nothing of religious values, in sexual activity, natural (God-given) processes, marital stability, human health, family health, and social well-being. As Americans become more technological about sex (sterilization is rapidly replacing the pill as the preferred method of child-prevention), the serious questions once raised by Catholics alone are now to the front and center of public discussion. The 1 million-plus annual abortions in the U.S. say something about the American value placed on life. (Planned Parenthood used this same 1 million figure in 1957 concerning alleged "back-alley" abortions, but it was a figure used for propaganda purposes, without basis in fact.)

Dr. Robert Kistner of the Harvard Medical School, who helped develop the pill (with Pincus and Rock), recently remarked (*Cincinnati Inquirer*, April 14, 1977): "For years I felt the pill would not lead to promiscuity. But I have changed my mind. I think it probably has – and so has the IUD."

In 1976 there were 1 million teenage pregnancies.

The use of the pill, which Dr. Herbert Ratner calls "chemical warfare on women," is no longer the panacea it once was thought to be. While statisticians have established various correlations between the pill and its perils – its relation to cancer, thrombosis, gall-bladder disease, erosion of cells of the cervix, heart disease, blood-vessel disease, and death itself – it is still important in birth control procedures because its use is fostered by drug companies with assistance from government domestic and foreign aid agencies. In 1970 the Food and Drug Administration published a booklet called "What You Should Know about the Pill" for distribution in every packet of oral contraceptives. The booklet ended up not in pharmacies but in doctors' offices, where most pill users never see it. Another FDA warning of IUD dangers (43 deaths in recent years) also has not found its way to the users.

Contraception has always been big American business. Profits in pills are larger than ever. Vested interests protect those profits. Dr. Gordon Duncan, associate director of a population study center, says: "There is also very little fundamental biological research being done that would support innovative developments." The perfection of a natural family planning method does not attract large grants because successful research in this area has no profitable return. More money is earned in condoms than in continence. Dr. Allan Barnes, a Vice President at the Rockefeller Foundation, adds a further indictment: "It is entirely possible that if the ideal contraceptive were developed today, it would never be introduced in the United States" (*New York Times*, March 5, 1975). There is not enough profit in a creative discovery of this kind.

Meanwhile another zero point has been reached – what Kenneth Keniston of the Massachusetts Institute of Technology calls "the emptying family." The "latchkey" child and possibly his one other sibling grow up with no care at all, awash in skateboards and stereos, while emancipated mothers work to fulfill themselves. Not only have parents disappeared from many children's lives (two out of five now live in a single-parent family) but grandparents, aunts, and uncles have gone as well. Since over 1 million children are propelled by divorce into single-parent families annually the problem will get worse before it gets better.

3. The Grand Catholic Silence

Fr. Richard McCormick coined the expression, "The Silence since *Humanae Vitae*," when he surveyed the Catholic scene on the fifth anniversary of the encyclical (*America*, July 7 and October 20, 1973). The "silence" he inferred was, of course, the seeming willingness of the hierarchy to let the matter of contraception in the Church rest without further confrontation. McCormick suggested that, this time, a new commission be established this time to discover what God's will on this subject really is.

Silence certainly represents a vacuum within the Church which has been permitted to grow in Catholic catechesis on matrimony. McCormick himself claims that contraception is not necessarily evil, and may occasionally be used. The magisterium, on the other hand, says contraception is always evil, that it is a grave evil, and may never be used by a Catholic.

Furthermore, a "little contraception" exists nowhere in the world. Contraception, once accepted, becomes a way of life. It logically follows, therefore, that Catholic leadership would normally follow through with counter-measures.

But articulation of the Church's position has all but disappeared from Cana and Pre-Cana Conferences, and never really became an essential part of the Marriage Encounter program. Catechetical magazines, seminars, and worship for religious educators, continuing education courses for priests and religious, almost never deal with the subject. Sex education courses continue to increase in Catholic schools, but they are aimed at training the young to "become persons," rather than to form them to use sexuality within a Catholic context. During 1974, the United Nations designated "Population Year" (initiating a series of international conferences on the subject), and *Theological Studies* (March issue) assembled an accumulated rejection of Catholic doctrine. The Catholic Archbishop of Durban, South Africa, Denis E. Hurley, O.M.I., on behalf of the Church, made the following contribution to the population question:

> To keep the Catholic conscience bound to the official view on birth control would, in the circumstances today, require superhuman insistence on the part of the magisterium. This insistence is not manifest. Rather there is a tendency to avoid the topic or to treat it with tolerance or benign interpretation. So by default a major change is occurring in the moral teaching of the Church – which hardly enhances the image of the magisterium (p. 163).

Since the credibility of the magisterium is clearly at stake, the question has been raised by more than Archbishop Hurley about why Catholic leadership has not been boldly effective in helping people live Catholic married life in conformity with the principles of *Humanae Vitae*. In small countries like New Zealand, bishops have natural family planning centers almost in every parish and/or town. In the United States, no nationally successful effort by the Church has yet proved its effectiveness in forming the attitudes, supplying the knowledge and training, or providing the support necessary to make natural family planning work, especially among the poor. Motivating Catholics to accept the unwanted baby (the essential meaning of being "open" to life), which the contraceptionists customarily destroys, has not been dramatically noticeable in Catholic circles in recent years.

In 1969 Cardinal O'Boyle secured an initial grant of $800,000 from the American bishops to establish the Human Life Foundation, which was to organize research in natural family life procedures and educational programs. The U.S. has invested $1 million in research since then, and WHO has research projects going in twenty countries. Up until 1975 no serious effort was made to bring natural family programs into the dioceses of the country. John Kippley's Couple to Couple League in Cincinnati and Fr. Paul Marx's Human Life Center in Collegeville, Minnesota, were localized efforts to effectuate *Humanae Vitae* principles in Catholic lives. The Human Life Foundation of America now promises to nationalize the effort, although it has a long way to go, with only single training centers in most dioceses. The trend is changing. At the present time $4 is being invested in Foundation programs by government for every $1 contributed by the American bishops. As natural family planning takes its place with contraception as a technique of birth regulation endorsed by government, the programs of the Human Life Foundation, which transcend technique, continue to grow. But the Church has yet to bring natural family planning to the parish level, where it will do the most good.

Leo Cardinal Suenen's *Love and Control* in 1964 provided an educational blueprint necessary to make Catholic principles of marital chastity work. As the International Planned Parenthood Federation organizes multiple fortunes and worldwide programs to influence citizens of the world toward contraception and abortion, the Catholic Church is only beginning to marshall its forces for a belated effort to back *Humanae Vitae* with programs of comparable proportions and public acceptability.

4. Contradictory Catholic Counsel

Catholic priests, nuns, magazines, even diocesan newspapers frequently do not reinforce Catholic doctrine as proclaimed by bishops and pope; this has encouraged the secular press to continue its habit of reporting an imminent official Catholic change. *Newsweek* (July 30, 1973, pp. 40–41), never reconciled to *Humanae Vitae*, celebrated the encyclical's fifth anniversary by "uncovering" an alleged statement being secretly edited for Columbian bishops which would have supported all forms of contraception, except sterilization and abortion. The story also placed those bishops in support of government family-planning centers at which birth control pills are dispensed. A year later, the *New York Times* (January 23, 1974) published another report of a confidential Vatican circular to bishops, allegedly easing Catholic opposition to birth control.

If the secular organs continue to make repeated references to Catholic contraception, so do Church spokesmen. Parishioners have become accustomed to parish discussions where competing priests argue for and against the pope (*Tablet* [Brooklyn], February 24, 1972). The clearest example of what the current pastoral picture is was given by the issues of the *Brooklyn Tablet*, following a presentation made (January 9, 1975), when Msgr. Francis B. Donnelly, Brooklyn pastor and former chief judge of the diocese, wrote an article calling for Catholic obedience to the pope's encyclical, asserting that "the teaching of theologians or of individual priests, however intelligent or persuasive, may not be preferred to the Church's official teaching." For the nine months following, the readers were treated to a newspaper debate between editor, priests, subscribers, and other columnists over how much attention must be paid to the pope. Msgr. Donnelly was not lacking in supporters, but the *Tablet* editor thought the Brooklyn pastor was interfering with Vatican-II-guaranteed "freedom of conscience" and *Tablet* columnist Mary Carson accused Donnelly (January 9, 1975) of not understanding Church teaching on parenthood. A young Brooklyn College seminary professor nine months later (September 23, 1976) told *Tablet* readers that "in reality most Catholics don't come to a moral judgment to practice birth control by plowing through statements from magisterium. . . . Being good, conscientious people, they know in their hearts what they must do; what Catholics who decide to practice birth control usually say is: `I believe in my heart what I'm doing is right.'" And then the young seminary professor added, as an afterthought: "Understand here that it is not that birth control is right. It can never be a good."

On the other hand, in the neighboring diocese of Rockville Center, New York, the editor of the *Long Island Catholic* provided his counsel (October 7, 1976):

> Are we obligated then to accept the constant teaching of the Church on artificial contraception – as affirmed by the pope and the bishops prior to *Humanae Vitae*, as affirmed by the pope in *Humanae Vitae*, as affirmed by the pope and the bishops today? Yes.

5. New Support for the Pope

The Church has supported "lost causes" at other times in history, even when its defense of those causes was timid. A moral position, to be moral, need not have effective technological guarantees. A moral view may be correct and, if adopted, involve personal or social risk. This is evident in issues of social justice, and of war and peace. The Church, for example, may state a principle on race relations without necessarily committing itself to a particular affirmative action program of government. Or the Church may receive abuse for proposing a specific program for enforcement. Similarly, the Church can be correct on contraception without having the ability to make practical decisions of the faithful easy or palatable. Government has that same problem. Obliteration bombing can effectively terminate a war; it may be the only way to win a war; and yet it can still receive condemnation on moral grounds. Gaining a good can be highly immoral if achieved wrongly. Contrariwise, a saint like St. Francis of Assisi can be holy and, by human standards, inefficient too.

Pope Paul VI waited so long to speak that in 1968 he appeared like a lonely defender of the Church's position. Ten years later, few perceived as clearly as he did that sexual activity may not be separated from its procreative purpose without dire consequences for individuals, for society, for sex, and for the moral order itself. The American bishops, however, in issuing their "Catholic Hospital Directives" with their condemnation of contraceptive or sterilizing practices in Catholic hospitals (1971), reaffirmed the necessity of these links.

Lawrence Cardinal Sheehan, who in 1966 had approved the majority report of the Papal Birth Control Commission, said the following five years later (*Homiletic and Pastoral Review*, November 1973):

> The dissenters will insist that it has not been proved that contraception is intrinsically evil. That may be true if one disallows the norms drawn from human nature by Paul VI, and the norms drawn from the nature and dignity of the human person as presented by Vatican II; and if one rules out the light shed by divine revelation, particularly by Paul's Epistle to the Romans, taken in conjunction with the constant tradition of the Church, i.e., if one approaches the problem of contraception from the purely rationalistic and not from the Christian point of view. But the whole point is that we are Christians and we have to approach the problem of contraception and family limitation and birth regulation from the Christian point of view.

Peter Riga, who was an early dissenter, changed his mind when in October 1973, he wrote for *Triumph* ("I wrote it for *Triumph* – no one else would take it."):

> Acts which seek directly to separate sexuality from procreation have no future, and therefore are doubly sterile. They enter into no transcendent endeavor, which is precisely what the family is about. Marriage

and its necessary consequence, the family, is a transcendent relationship in which two persons engage themselves and seek to perfect themselves in a common endeavor that reaches outside of the relationship, to new life, to the future of the human race, to God's glory. There is no more important or vital work than this.

Dr. Hanna Klaus, otherwise known as Sr. Miriam Paul, SCMM, is a gynecologist. After seven years as a medical missioner among the Pakistanis, she returned by way of Europe convinced that *Humanae Vitae* was more of an ideal than a norm. Theologians whom she had met on her way home through Europe impressed her with this. Once face to face with abortion in the affluent contraceptive culture of her own country, however, she was forced to rethink the relationship between womanhood and contraception. Her final conclusion was that for the "feminine woman" every coitus contains within it the psychic germs of a child, that *Humanae Vitae* speaks of `the integral vision of humanity' beyond partial perspectives: what it proposes is not optional for human nature but completes it" (*Homiletic and Pastoral Review*, October 1973).

The work of Dr. John Billings of Melbourne, Australia, promoter of natural family planning, is perhaps a harbinger of Pope Paul's ultimate vindication. In the nineteenth century, the Church, by taking a strong stand against craniotomy, helped encourage the perfection of the Caesarean section. The hand of science, again as a result of the Church's condemnation of direct interference with life and the process of giving life, may contribute toward new developments in the science of reproduction.

XIV. The Ford-Grisez Thesis

Fr. John C. Ford, S.J., and Dr. Germain Grisez focus on the common teaching of the Church on contraception, of which *Humanae Vitae* is only the latest handing on of authentic teaching. On the tenth anniversary of *Humanae Vitae*, in a lengthy article for *Theological Studies* (June 1978), they took up the ancient origin of the teaching, the universal scope of the teaching, and the certainty with which it had been proposed as an imperative determinant in the behavior of married Catholics.

From 1963 on, however, theologians seeking to justify contraception, after observing (correctly) that the teaching had not been formally defined, proceeded to infer (erroneously) that the doctrine had not been infallibly taught. This "dethroning" of the Church teaching enabled them (so they argued) to attack more forcibly the certainty and truth of the traditional position.

Ford-Grisez believe in the light of the way the teaching on contraception has been proposed through the centuries that the "infallibility" claim of the teaching is very much alive, that the received Catholic teaching is still being proposed infallibly by the ordinary and universal magisterium. The conditions under which the ordinary magisterium of the bishops dispersed throughout the world can proclaim the teaching of Christ infallibly have been articulated by the Second Vatican Council. Ford-Grisez argue that *Humanae Vitae* meets those criteria, thus making the Church doctrine a divinely guaranteed teaching.

They make an important point. Frequently, dissenters start with the assumption that teachings not formally defined are not infallible. This is not true. Many Catholic teachings are de facto infallibly taught even though not formally defined. *Lumen Gentium* (#25) reads:

> Although the bishops individually do not enjoy the prerogative of infallibility, they nevertheless proclaim the teaching of Christ infallibly, even when they are dispersed throughout the world, provided that they remain in communion with each other and with the Successor of Peter and that in authoritatively teaching on a matter of faith and morals they agree in one judgment that is to be held definitively.

The Declaration, as the Council debates indicated, extends ordinary infallibility in the Church not only to matters formally revealed (e.g., Divinity of Christ), but to things virtually revealed (e.g., Mary's Immaculate Conception), to what is necessarily connected with revelation (e.g. the existence of a natural moral law), to things which are to be believed, *and* to things which are to be done.

The four conditions of *Lumen Gentium* under which bishops, dispersed throughout the world, proclaim the doctrine of Christ infallibly, are summarized by Ford-Grisez as follows:

1. The bishops remain in communion with one another and teach with the pope.

2. They teach authoritatively on a matter of faith or morals.

3. They agree on one judgment.

4. They propose this judgment as one to be held definitively.

Just as the divinity of Christ was taught by the ordinary and universal magisterium of the Church prior to its definition by the Council of Nicea in 325, so the teaching on contraception has been proposed by the Church as a teaching to be held definitively by believers. Factually, while many Arian bishops denied the doctrine of Christ's divinity before and after the definition, no more than a handful of Catholic bishops during or after Vatican II denied the teaching on contraception as *the taught and believed Catholic doctrine*.

Indeed, as John T. Noonan abundantly documented, no Catholic theologian up until 1963 ever taught that contraception was good. What is clear also is that in spite of internal opposition, Catholic teaching was and still is proposed as the *constant doctrine of the Church*. Even when scholars – outside the Church, later within – questioned the doctrine's scriptural base or the validity of some rational arguments in its favor, the pope and the bishops continued to reaffirm the Catholic norm.

Pope Paul, while not using the term "infallible" (Pius XII did not use the term in proclaiming Mary's Assumption), does speak in solemn language. He is not speaking as another theologian, nor as one intervening in a theological dispute. The pope is explicitly teaching a doctrine to which, by divine patrimony, he avers that the Catholic Church is unalterably committed. He reaffirms the Church's certainty on the subject. He rejects the possibility of altering its substance.

In essence, Ford-Grisez say: If the Catholic tradition on contraception is not infallible teaching, what can be called infallible?

Even an affirmative answer to this question will not settle the argument for dissenters. But it does put the argument back in context. Michael Novak, for example, only recently has come to recognize (in the debate over the ordination of women) what he did not accept in the earlier argument over contraception: "For centuries the Church has had an unbroken tradition, so unchallenged that reasons for it have not been articulated. Obscurely, many persons sense some weight in those reasons" (*Commonweal*, September 2, 1977).

Christ did not win all his public debates over what he was *revealing*. The Church has also learned that the validity or certainty of a teaching does not depend for acceptance on its plausibility, or on the solemnity of the preaching. Faith in the *given* teacher usually settles the argument for the believer. This does not terminate intellectual discussion because the Church, with its intellectual tradition, encourages research and investigation. Eventually formal pronouncements by the Church's teaching authority set parameters for theological exploration. Ford-Grisez know that scholars are tempted to read history backward and now find practices, attitudes, and institutions incompatible with the law of Christ, which once were accepted or tolerated by Christians, and even by the magisterium, e.g., slavery. This becomes the basis for proposing contraception as a new Christian insight comparable to the Church's late acceptance of political equality. However, what the Church accepts and tolerates is quite distinct from what it teaches. Insight into the unstable mentality of modern culture enables the Church to realize why certain marriages today can be declared null and void, which formerly would not have been so understood. It does not follow, however, that the Church's teaching on the indissolubility of a sacramental marriage itself changes.

The contraception teaching must be judged in this light. An infallibly taught doctrine continues to be taught without formal definition because factual questions keep recurring. For example, what is a contraceptive? When the pope and the Council undertook a second study of the pill they were dealing with factual questions. If the pill could be judged noncontraceptive, at least under certain circumstances, it would not fall under the Church's general ban. The magisterium, never in doubt about the immorality of contraception itself, was in momentary doubt about the absolute immorality of the pill. Since *Humanae Vitae*, the Church is no longer uncertain even about that.

A major management problem remains, however. This is the dissonance between doctrine and practice. The issue is no longer contraception but the ability of the Church to make its doctrine live in the lives of the faithful.

4.

God as Prisoner of Our Own Choosing:
Critical-historical Study of the Bible (1979)

Rev. Dennis J. McCarthy

I.

"Criticism," Edgar Krenz writes in *The Historical-Critical Method*, "sets the Bible squarely in our history and makes the 'full brightness and impact of Christian ideas' shine out."

Enthusiastic praise this, but not a startling expression of an eccentric position. On the contrary, too much of the world of biblical scholarship concerns itself with the recovery of the *Urtext* and its *Ursitz*, since the essential task of such scholarship is seen to be reconstruction by recognized techniques of "origin," of the words and situation lying behind, often far behind, our present biblical text. That is, explanation, or interpretation, *is* the reconstruction of the (hypothetical) historical form and locus of a text. Thus, what is important in Colossians 1:12–20 is not Paul's words but the Christian hymn lying behind them; or, in the Old Testament, a ninth-century Israelite story urging a polemic against fertility cults and their symbolic snakes and trees of life is the real stuff of Genesis 2–3 (not to mention other, independent strains which may be sifted out of the narrative); and all this business about an *Ursünde* is mere secondary accretion and, worse, later interpretation.

My examples are deliberately sharpened to make a point: the overwhelming preoccupation with history in exegesis, the concern for the "original," the source, and its external factual referent. "The historian," Krenz says, "interrogates documents to determine their precise significance," and so learn the *truth*. And it is but a step from this excessive focus on a particular kind of historical truth (that is, factual reference) to the paean of historical criticism as *the* royal road to find and feel Biblical truths with which we began.

One might wonder what bright light a precise location of the land of Uz and a dating of the visit of Eliphaz, Bildad, and Zophar would throw on the overwhelming poetry describing basic religious experience in Job. Or whether, if we really could gain a knowledge of what inspired whom to utter the basic structure of the tremendous hymn to Christ Jesus in Philippians 2:5–11, it would shine brighter. To be sure, being able to place the utterance in some dramatic historical or polemical situation might throw light on the meaning of the present text. However, experience warns us not to expect too much from this direction. For example, a reading of Bandello's *Romeo and Juliet*, Shakespeare's attested source, far from revealing the true significance and beauty of the story or at least throwing real light on Shakespeare's meaning, simply makes us marvel at his originating genius.

These examples raise basic questions which somehow never seem to affect the central thrust of modern exegesis. One searches for the milieu which produced the speeches in our texts or even produced the persons made to speak in them (as the milieu of Hellenism and persecution, not necessarily the milieu of Hellenist persecution, produced the personage of Judith as well as her words). When one has found the milieu to his satisfaction, he explains the words and the persons in its light – with particular attention to the antecedents in that milieu which led up to the particular form of words and the conception of the persons as they are found in our texts. This *is* interpretation, exegesis. In the course of this process, the historicity of the texts (i.e., their reference to real external events) may well come into doubt. The texts are the result of a process in which a community responds to various discernible external or internal pressures, expresses known psychological needs, uses the words and images certain situations evoke from certain people in definable historical and sociological contexts, and so on. This is by no means always erroneous. To return to Judith: the book *is* the product of a brilliant Hellenic-Jewish short-story writer reacting to a persecution problem.

For the moment, however, I do not want to dwell on this aspect of the problem, that is, on any tendency there is for historical exegesis to minimize historical content. There is a deeper problem: the fascination with historical critical study as though it were the philosopher's stone that would turn all interpretative dross to exegetical gold so that "Christian ideas" could "shine out." Historical interpretation of a text, the attempt to reconstruct the actual world of events to which the text refers, is just one possible kind of interpretation. Why must we always ask: "What is the factual reference of this text?" Why not: "What does this text mean?" Apart from other things, a great deal of the Bible is poetry and doctrinal discussion, and our first question with regard to these kinds of texts in other contexts in not "to what events do they refer?" but "what do they mean?" Why is the Biblist, in other words, trapped within historical questions, patient so often only with hypothetical, probable responses, and therefore always open to new hypothetical, probable objections so that he gets locked into an academic squirrel cage returning on itself, ever renewing the same essential problems and answers?

The answer goes back surely to the famous *crise de conscience européenne*, which we can for convenience locate around the beginning of the eighteenth century. Almost two centuries of religious quarrels had tired men of theology. A full century had been trumpeting the claim that reason with the right method – that "right method" being a matter of dispute – could solve all problems. *We* may have our doubts these days, but, in fact, the seventeenth century with its emphasis on quantification, on experiments, on accumulation of data had produced magnificent results with its (apparently) all encompassing Newtonian synthesis in physics. Other fields had, perhaps, not moved as fast, but if we try to imagine how it looked to a man of middle age in 1700, fantastic changes had occurred. Timepieces had become accurate. There were thermometers, barometers, microscopes, and a thousand practical improvements from mining techniques to navigational equipment. Remember, as an impressive example to a world that had lived with the plague, endemic and often epidemic for centuries, that the disease disappeared from Europe after a last flair-up in Marseilles in 1720–21. It was as though one were to give our age a "cure" for the atom bomb. And the introduction of the humble turnip was about to end the leaving of one-third of the land fallow every year. It could be grown in an otherwise fallow field, and the field still brought rich grain the next year. A trivial example? Hardly, when it showed the experimental method pushing further away the specter of famine that had literally always been at the door.

Reason, observation, collection had had a long run of good press, and they had given results. The "knowledge explosion" was well under way. People of any education knew so much more, and not just in the physical sciences. The "moral sciences" were flooded with knowledge of an earth that was gradually being filled in with the outlines of new lands and with inhabitants of diverse cultures. No more could one picture Dante's empty southern hemisphere as real, however glorious its symbolism remained. Nor were the outlanders the fantastic creatures met in tales. One traded with the Chinese for tea and porcelain and, for the men of the age, trade gave a very real consistency, a three-dimensional density, to their feeling of the reality of these others.

For one reason or another, then, the age faced and wanted to face a host of new facts. Missionaries from China reported a race whose chronology antedated that of the Hebrews. The immensity of the earth now was not just known but realized – felt by everyone who touched tea or tobacco, coffee or china; it suddenly became hard to visualize a global flood. And such a diversity of races! Their differences and their chronological spread made it hard to fit them into the genealogies of Genesis 10.

The situation was simple enough. A vast accumulation of knowledge had become too large to fit into the "six ages of history" which had been part of the habitual mental equipment of the European mind since Augustine. The situation was the historical and sociological analogue to the Ptolemaic world view of physics. It had simply become too crowded, and it burst its boundaries.

Surely, this need not have created a problem. The Bible is not a universal history; nor is it a textbook in geology. If it had been so used for ages in Europe, it was because there was nothing else at hand to cover these areas. Neither was much ever *noticed* which interfered with the data thus delivered. The pre-modern man could, as *man*, delight in the lovely balance of a world map centered on Jerusalem with all the parts centered around it, and, as a sailor, be very aware of the unbalanced nature of winds and headlands off Brittany and Finisterre. But now things were very much noticed, and instead of fitting his historical world view into the biblical picture, man now had to fit his picture of the biblical world into the larger frame of a new world view – and this not long after Archbishop Ussher had nailed the date of creation down tightly at 4004 B.C.!

Now this change in the ordering of a commonly held historical view may have been shock enough. Change of habit is usually difficult. However, it was really no more than a re-categorizing of general knowledge. It did not affect the *theological* vision of history, which was the common possession of the Western mind from the spread of Christianity until after Shakespeare: the scheme of the fall of the angels, creation, temptation-fall, and the incarnation, redemption, and rebirth in Christ. This had been everyone's view and still was the view of the vast majority, whatever some intellectuals said more or less on the quiet. This scheme was no catalogue for ordering knowledge like the six ages scheme with its Adam to Noah, Noah to Abraham, Abraham to David, and the rest. This was the heart of Christian doctrine. Christianity could survive the shock to slovenly intellectual habits by the substitution of a new cataloguing scheme forced by the accumulation of new facts. The history of sin and redemption was something else again. It *is* Christianity. And yet, how was one to make distinctions? On an external, even frivolous level, our summary of redemption has six stages as Augustine's history had six stages. This comparison has not been deliberately created *ad hoc* – the six stages are not mine but E. M. W. Tillyard's in his survey of the Elizabethan world picture – and it is easy enough to move imaginatively from the loss of the six historical ages to the loss of the six doctrinal stages. I do not know if something like this ever happened, but it illustrates the problem. New content burst the boundaries of a purely historical scheme that had been primarily biblical. What next? Could other biblical meanings remain true, or were they too "out of date"?

The problem was worse because the theological story of sin and redemption does touch history. It is historical, sinful man who is redeemed by an event. This is a serious problem, but I wish to touch on only one aspect of it for a moment, that is, on the way this theology came to the European of the *crise de conscience*. It was tied to all kinds of stories, foretellings in the Old Testament, and assertions in the New and post–New Testament miracles. All this was emphatically tied to the six-age view of world history: Christianity was the age of maturity. None of this interweaving in detail is necessary in logic or doctrine, but it is in fact open to easy confusion and is big with consequences at the beginning of the modern age.

There was this passion for exact measurement, for facts. This was the era that equated truth with reference to external things and ruled out imagination and symbol. The former were the proper province of man, of reason. The latter supplied "decorations" to doll up the truth or to while away idleness. There was also the Protestant principle of *sola scriptura* as the unique source of saving truth along with its corollary idea that the believing reader would find the truth for himself. Among other things, such principles ruled out other sources of theological knowledge, such as tradition and traditional development. Most important for us, it ruled out all interpretation of Scripture except the literalist. Indeed, many contemporary proponents of the historical-critical method proudly proclaim that its ruthless search for truth, i.e., demonstrable fact, in Scripture, is the proper development of the Protestant principle. It may be, but not that part of it which, supposedly, gave the Bible into the hands of the people. It has finally given it rather into the hands of a very limited band of professors!

But the "Protestant principle" was not a single-minded ally of criticism. Indeed, Protestant doctrine of literal interpretation as the dictation of God was a serious impediment. Could God have dictated untruths? Scarcely! Eventually, inspiration so understood had to go, and since in the minds of modern theologians inspiration tends to be identified with this old Protestant dictation view, when it went, inspiration as such went as well. There is available a far more nuanced view in Catholic theology, leaving the human instrument free and emphasizing the role of the community from which the Scriptures arose, to which they are addressed, and which finally received them. So far I see little done to exploit this treasure which we can offer the Christian community. It would be a service to ecumenism. It would be an even greater service to exegesis if theologians would give us an adequate, supple presentation of the doctrine of inspiration and revelation. Without it we tend to accept without question the negative results of the old Protestant idea. But we must return to the problems of our time of crises.

In 1700 the covert enemies of Christianity, the Bayles and later the Voltaires, who believed that the religious wars had proved religion a dubious blessing or who felt that it was a curb on free investigation (not to mention free exercise of faculties and urges generally held to be less noble), could make use of the insistence on fact to foster doubt. If all in the Bible was supposed to be literally true – and it was so often urged that it was – what then? What of the genocide commanded in God's name in Deuteronomy? And so it goes. The snipers agreed with the pious that God's word must be true to fact (truth here to be judged by one's own common-sense standards, for the Bible was open to all!). Then they seized on some choice "fact" and turned the argument: Could this enormity be from God? Later Tom Paine's *Age of Reason* summarized this often crude argument, and his work had a long run: It was still the source book for the working-class skeptics in Mrs. Humphry Ward's *Robert Elsmere* a century later. A passion for narrow fact, an insistence on literalness, the overthrow of an accidental but time-honored historical scheme, plus positive attacks on the believability, and even the morality, of certain events recounted in the Bible – all this was indeed a blow at the foundations.

It remains a real problem. The ordinary man in the street lives by intuitions and symbols – some, we hope, given by natural insight and sound tradition, others we fear, by TV and the advertising industry. But when he reflects he does not see it so. He thinks he lives by "facts," and it is dangerous to give what he has taken as a fact in a simple, straightforward reading of the Bible another value. Tell him that the story of Cain and Abel is a tale reflecting pastoral and agricultural rivalry used to illustrate the sin pervasive in human history, and he is bothered. If Cain and Abel are not historical persons, then who, in Scripture, is? So the common feeling, and it must be reckoned with. This is not an easy thing to do, and we can sympathize to some extent with those who chose to meet the enemy on his own ground centuries ago.

Hence the rush to supply evidences to establish the facticity of biblical narrative. It must be so. "Dogma" said this was God's word in the most literal sense. It also said that the word was immediately available to the man in the street. He took it as truth, and truth is reference to external fact. Thus the hunt for the necessary external facts began. It was well under way in the eighteenth century, and a later age gave us Edmund Gosse's father asserting that God put fish fossils on Alpine peaks to humble the learning of the wise. In our own day there has been the claim to the finding of Noah's Ark right on Mt. Ararat, unfortunately too much iced in to be clearly identified, let alone approached. And so it goes.

One can respect the sincerity of this extreme literalism with its equation of truth with an external factual reference, but the end result is to convince no one but the converted – to the sacrifice of much of religion's credibility. Yet the hopeless effort continues in some quarters. What we really need is what was probably impossible in the eighteenth century but not now, namely, an epistemology and a consequent apologetic that distinguishes the various kinds of truth (separating the truth of factual reference from the truth of general meaning, for starters).

But again to our time of crisis. There were those who saw that a last ditch defense of a literalist reading was not the only hope, nor even the best hope. One way out was to avoid the embarrassing historical problems entirely. One could turn to Nature. This was the central word for most of the eighteenth century. As Basil Willey has pointed out, it covered an unperceived diversity of meanings, a fact which did not really conduce to clear or profound thought; but it did allow the *philosophes* to talk without end. Pope could express the central vision in his *Essay on Man*: a perfectly ordered world with "a place for everything, and everything in its place." In the early eighteenth century this ordered vision was widely spread among the pacesetters of society who took such a theism to be the deliverance from untrammeled reason supported by that solid argument, universal consent. Churchmen, imbued with this vision, showed that Christianity paralleled the religion of nature, teaching one God and inculcating the highest morals. True, one had to put up with many crudities in Christianity's Bible. It had its oddities, but *at least* it provided the means of bringing the common man, who was, perhaps, incapable of the deeper reasonings of the philosopher, to worship God and respect his fellows. Deism became the religion of the elite, the educated, and even of the Churchmen (Archbishop Tillotson).

The religious spirit soon took its revenge with the much deplored "enthusiasm of Wesleyanism, the Great Awakening, Pietism." It seems as though it might be safer to ignore religion than feed it empty platitudes. It might die of sheer neglect, inanition; but as long as it is kept alive, it will out, and that usually in ways that affront the genteel.

The religion of nature of the eighteenth century looks somewhat crude and simple to us today. Why dwell on it? Well, it represents an early and clear example of what becomes, under many guises, one of the regular attempts at dealing with the historical problems of the Bible: the claim that historicity does not matter. It is not fact of the biblical story of sin and redemption, but the general idea that counts: the idea of God and ethics, the "something not ourselves that makes for morality." It is not long before this stance produces the question: "Why such emphasis on Christianity if it is on a natural level with other cultures?" Buddhism or Confucianism can teach high moral standards, and their cultures, if not the doctrines themselves, offer divinity. For that matter, even voodooism provides a satisfying religious, sociological, and emotional integration. "Nature" (i.e., a catalogue of historical human traits) produces these many religions that work in satisfying human needs. Why choose one rather than another? The eighteenth century, living on its unconscious Christian presuppositions, could make its choice without reflecting on the base of the presuppositions.

But other generations are not so naïve. They do not equate Christianity with a universal religion "given by nature" – which is really a sort of ersatz Christianity created all unknown for its partisans by a particular historical conjunction really dependent on Christendom. One tries to break loose from the relativist realm of history into some sort of absolute. So Christianity becomes the positive existential commitment to be. Or it is the laying hold of true selfhood. Or it is seeing Jesus as the paradigm of the true self. Or it is the encounter with the Person of Christ. In the end it is all just more philosophy made to refer to a particular person's attitude or self-understanding. But if Jesus is not as extraordinary as the biblical canon claims or, at least, is not knowable as such, why does He call me to commitment or imitation any more than Theudas or Judas (Acts 5:36–37) or another? Why is the doctrine attached to Him better or more demanding than Confucius' or the Gautama's? And if one passes quickly over all but a few details of His life as historically difficult, what person does one encounter? How can it compare with the impact of a personality I am so much in contact with now, or even with a sharply defined historical personage? The best one can say is that He is the paradigm my particular bit of Western culture presents me with, as another culture would offer another paradigm. We are back to relativism again. It looks as though we must face history after all.

Nor was the century of crisis at all unwilling to do this. We have seen it as a time of both skepticism and belief and of great confidence in human ability to attain truth. The skeptics looked for ammunition, the believers looked to their defenses, and it was widely believed that the truth would come out through a diligent approach and a proper methodology. This, after all, was the age that laid the bases for the four-source theory of Pentateuch, discovered the synoptic problem, invented the "science" of Introduction (the search for the real dates and authors of the biblical books, their historical interrelations, the history of the development of the canon), and biblical theology – this latter as an effort to get away from the crusty formulations of tradition to the real meat that lay in the underlying formulations of the texts read as history. It was also the heyday of the "canon within the canon." The opportunity was obvious. When the critic had decided what was oldest, or most original, authentic, or reasonable (analogous to everyday experience) he had his measure, his canon. It might be doctrinal: ethics culled from the Sermon on the Mount for nineteenth-century liberal theologians, a fanatic eschatology for Schweitzer, or the idea that sequential and purposive, not meaningless and cyclic, history was peculiar to Judaism. It might be historical or literary: ancient "J" has special value, or Micah 4:9–12 is from Micah himself, while 6:1–5 is probably not and so is of secondary value. And so forth. Whatever the critic selected could and did become a criterion for judging what was normative. Things not in accord with it might have a passing historical interest but they were not religiously or morally exigent.

We have been living amid all this ever since, and I do not want to offer another history of critical scholarship. I would simply emphasize certain of its effects. Ultimately it took the Bible out of the pew into the library; and not the public library either, but the professor's seminar room. A later nineteenth-century Anglican parson was reported to have kept two large Bibles. A conscientious professional man, he kept up with his studies and noted the developing vagaries of critical scholarship in the margins of one. A conscientious pastor, he put material helpful for preaching in the other. Inevitably the split became a gap and then a chasm. And then the question had to be put: Can one preach what is shown to be factually untrue (or at least unlikely)? A conscientious man could only give one answer: No. An epoch fired by the search for truth (it had, after all, among other things proved profitable in commerce, manufacturing, agriculture), and which tended to equate truth with fact, could hardly have done otherwise. It was bound to test truth claims by its criteria, and that meant treating facts as facts even if, all unknown to it, seeming narrative facts were quite something else. Inevitably there was a narrowing of the religious message of such religious "facts" as the Bible might be forced to deliver.

II.

The Romantic Movement grew out of this era of rationalism. Not as a mere reaction; rationalist insistence on *politesse* helped produce the man of taste who easily became the man of feeling. The attempt of the associanist David Hartley to construct a "calculus of pleasure," to provide a basis for morals as quantitative calculus had for physics, had also worked to emphasize feelings, Jane Austen's "sensibility." Whatever its origins, Romanticism had a mighty impact on biblical study.

One very weighty factor was a kind of primitivism. This was the age when Percy collected his *Reliques*, Scott his *Border Ballads*, the Grimms their fairy tales, the Lonnrot the Finnish *Kalevala*. It was fooled by the Ossian forgeries because it wanted to be. Herder and Vico had seen that an early stage of human development naturally expresses itself in heroic poetry, fantastic tales, and the like. The idea was not so new, but the evaluation was. These early forms were seen, not as mere crude probings toward later scientific statement, but as valuable things, unspoiled, though at times lurid – insights into the heart of things without which mere reason was sapless and fruitless. The Grimms did not seek out their fairy tales because they were quaint but because they were an unsullied fountain of truth. The application to Scripture leaps to the eye. Here is the origin of that fascination with the *Urtext*, with the primitive community, and so on. Here in the pure beginnings lay shining truth. And still today, many a professor who has long lost any romantic illusions about the primitive unconsciously values his *Urtext* for these reasons. The force of the romantic idea is still powerful, all the more so because it is now unexpressed and unspecified.

Then there were the great evolutionary systems of Romantic philosophy. Their effect can hardly be overestimated. History was assuredly guided by immanent laws which might be the working out of the Absolute Spirit, the development of the ethical spirit, progress from the material to the divine, the unfolding of matter. The exact description of the immanent laws at work varied from philosopher to philosopher, but the conviction that there were such laws varied not at all! This was particularly fateful for New Testament study, where the immanent dialectical laws of Hegelianism were set to work. The Christianity of Peter and Matthew was the thesis, the Christianity of Paul, the antithesis, and early Catholicism the synthesis (*Fruhkatholocismus* is still very much with us!). The scheme is F. C. Baur's, and it is redolent of the spirit of its time: Rational laws governed history. The Hegelian scheme had already been imposed on Christianity by D. F. Strauss of *Life of Jesus* fame, younger than Baur but an earlier bloomer. Baur's contribution lay in his "finding" the scheme reflected especially in biblical literature. Indeed, Baur insisted on the need to evaluate the sources both for their date and for their determining purpose (a polemic tells the story rather differently from a mere chronicle, and the difference must be allowed for) and thus for their original core and *Tendenz*. In this way, he put Christianity squarely within the compass of secular history. It was subject to history's inner laws as well as to its critical methods. For Baur the laws were Hegel's. Others would posit other laws, but whatever happened, Christianity had become the object of profane historical study, entwined in a chain of laws, necessarily profane laws.

This was radically new. The changes in the eighteenth-century *crise de conscience* had demanded a new cataloguing system. So many new facts had been found that the traditional Christian scheme of world ages could no longer contain them all. Biblical facts, taken as such and left in their specialness, could fit into a new scheme which contained much else that was strange. There was no change of the laws of thought to which facts had to conform. Facts were accepted. An ill-advised effort to defend all these facts carried the seeds of much later trouble, but the major conflict was avoided, for the moment, by prescinding from the facts and proclaiming a "higher truth," namely, the correspondence between Christianity and general natural religion – at what cost we have seen.

Now the very workings out of history, the workings of Spirit, or Ethics, or Progress (whatever you choose to name it) in history, became the central source of the highest knowledge. Particulars were checked against this. If they conformed, they were true; if not, false. And Biblical religion was seen as simply one phase of this great mechanism. It conformed or it was rejected. Baur and Hegel thought it conformed; others were less sure, but in either case it did not matter. What mattered was that the biblical narrative was made to be a mere part of the workings of the great world historical scheme. That was all, and that was tremendous. There was now no way to fit the essential historical and unique sin, incarnation, redemption, and eschaton scheme of classic Christianity into this. The essential theology had to go. The biblical story was subordinate to the secular scheme of a philosophy of history.

This philosophy is now pretty well dead, but it has left a legacy important for our topic. The eighteenth century believed in unending progress in history, while the nineteenth tried to codify the laws of this progress. Our age is less confident of history. Apart from Marxists, it does not expect to discover the laws controlling history, and it is unsure that the on-rolling will be an advance. What comes brings future shock as much as progress. However, the old views still have a powerful effect when combined with theories of method drawn from the uses of natural science. The truth *is* not; it may simply *come to be*. More likely, it is *approached but never attained*. Thus the chronicler of traditional historical study, Douglas Knight, can still call the latest hypothesis the "truth," with which one must work until a new hypothesis replaces it.

In any event, this view of reality as becoming and not being challenges more than the factual reference of the biblical narrative. The eighteenth century had already done that. Now it goes on to reject its central theological meaning. Search for the truth of fact, search for the historical original, the application of the philosophy of history to the biblical narrative – all these things culminated in a wave that now threatens to swamp biblical religion.

We must pause to observe much irony here. This notion of an unbroken causal chain has taken firm hold on biblical studies through the constant and triumphant use of the historical method. This nineteenth-century theology is not its first appearance. "The Chain of Being" was already there in Pope's *Essay on Man*. But it was a chain of historical causes, and we find it gaining its first hold through the application of causal categories derived from history by Romantic philosophy. The categories would mostly be rejected now, but the causal chain they brought with them still retains its hold. In any case, it has been a standard objection to historical studies from Aristotle to Lessing that they deliver only isolated facts, not the universal laws sought by reason. From almost the contrary position, the historicist point of view developed in the later nineteenth century – which was given its classic theoretical statement by Frederick Meinecke – gloried in the very individualism of the historical. It saw the object of historical study as some sort of organic individual social unit or factor largely closed within itself, and only open to the influence of its unique and accidental time and place. This unit was comprehensible and so amenable to judgment only in relativist terms, the special terms of its unique growth. Just because it was individualist, it denied that history exhibited any general natural laws as much as the philosophers interested in the universal did!

However such warnings did not halt the *Zeitgeist*, which was so full of the "laws" of history. There must be truth there, and if critics tried to use it to reduce Christianity to the level of all other history or, with Feuerbach, to reduce everything to the finite and material, perhaps it could be the other way around. Perhaps history might be made to ground religion – even the specific religion of the Bible. Thus, for example, instead of being a problem to the rationalist critic, the so-called prophecies of Christ from the remote past became a positive plus. History is the history of redemption, *Heilsgeschichte* – a real development in which any particular event, even an apparent prophecy, can only be understood as a part of the whole.

The process unfolded the meaning. The coming of Christ made clear in part the earlier accounts (even the Gentile developments), and in part it is not yet even intelligible anyway. That can come only with the completion of history. There the Erlangen school led by J. C. K. von Hoffman introduced an idea and a word which we must still reckon with.

This use of causality can be used with great skill and appear to give comfort to what seems to be a relatively conservative interpretation of the Bible. Indeed, if the revealed word is seen in terms of tradition, an ongoing struggle to see the truths of religion in the light of new problems, new needs, and new ideas, it may have much to offer. However, there are problems. If one insists overmuch on the historical process, one soon meets the fact that events are dumb. Only interpretative words show their sense, as recent theology rightly insists. But whose or what word? Hardly the prophetic, which, read precisely as interpretative word, is misleading, if at the same time it is read for itself and according to the canons proper to reading all literature. It must wait on further events and on further interpretation; but then this new link in the chain needs *its* interpretation in turn and so on down the line, literally, on this hypothesis, until the end of the world.

A great scholar and theologian of our own time, Gerhard von Rad, has attacked the problem by emphasizing the immanent laws of history and not the dialectical process. He begins with the thesis that only those who make history can write history. One wonders, if as he wrote this, he realized his debt to that wonderful old Neapolitan papist, G. B. Vico, who, early in the eighteenth century, launched the fertile idea that only the maker really understands a product because he alone knows what or why anything went into it. So only God can really understand the world in depth, for He made it; we can only use it in part. Vico saw that man does make something on his own, namely, society and history, and so these are the things he can and should try to understand. Well, if Vico indeed stood behind the German's assertion, he stands unacknowledged. Von Rad goes on to show how true history writing develops. For this, there are no inspired figures (charismatics), no miracles. Events unwind according to their inner laws. The divine is there only in the *concursus divinus*, the Providence of God, which for the theist covers all history. Well enough, but then what is special about biblical history? What does it reveal that the history of England or Europe does not?

Walter Scott and Macaulay saw Providence clearly in the English "Glorious Revolution" of 1688 putting down Catholicism; Father Broderick saw Providence in the wealth of America arriving just in time for Spain to stem the Protestant tide, and so on. The *concursus divinus* is everywhere, and we seem dangerously close to making the Bible deliver up one of those undifferentiated natural religions which, we have seen, have been the bane of one line of apologetics.

This discussion involving the great nineteenth-century German philosophies, general theories of history, and much else can hardly conclude without a remark on a phenomenon which characterizes contemporary biblical studies: Compartmentalization. Whatever else they were, the critics of the eighteenth and nineteenth centuries were people who shared the general culture of their world. They knew the classics. Indeed, Pentateuchal source criticism went hand in hand with the Homeric question. They had read history. They knew a philosophical tradition. Now, however, more and more biblists are specialists, not particularly versed in even their own vernacular literature or at all well read in history. I have actually heard it argued that form-criticism is a method necessarily unique to the Bible because it is special (though not necessarily supernatural). But, in fact, the proper use of form-criticism should treat biblical literature as it is – closely related to literature in general, and aimed at relating biblical pericopes to their general class and, thereby, elucidating them in the light of what literary history, ethnology, sociology, and psychology can tell us about the place where such classes are at home in the human spirit or human culture. This turnabout, this isolation of biblical literature by later scholars, came about because terms and techniques have become fossilized in manuals of biblical introduction and are no longer *au courant* with advanced knowledge.

So also with von Rad. He thought and wrote under old influences, old ideas of history, at the very moment when the new quantified history was beginning to feel its oats. We have a new classic, Pautrell on the sixteenth-century Mediterranean, a mass of often fascinating facts cutting across all familiar historical lines. Or the Burckhardt of our age, Peter Burke, who "explains" *Tradition and Change in Renaissance Italy* with the aid of birth registers, inventories, etc., plus the inevitable computer. Historical research and writing is rapidly looking away from narrative; and yet without a story how can we see the Absolute, or Revelation, or whatever unwind itself before our eyes? What serious scholars call history is rapidly changing, and the biblical-critical fascination with "history" may well find itself without an object recognizable except to itself. It will catch up, of course, though how much "history" based on computer calculation of quantitative data the Bible, and all that can be brought to bear on it, will reveal is surely an open question. In any event, new trends will leave behind a sad debris of lost causes, forlorn hopes, theologies built on a view of history which is now as strange as King Tut. Which, of course, is the basic problem: Can theology, let alone religion, be based on the ever-shifting ground of what is momentarily taken as history? As biblists get further away from what goes on in academic history work and the rest – the problems become more acute.

One can, of course, avoid the problem of trying to see supreme meaning in the mere sequence of events by turning to the interpreters. The specific way this is done is to make the prophet the true voice of God because the prophet really has heard God. This is clear from the call stories of Hosea or an Isaiah. So Bernhard Stade tries to insert a unique divine element in the immanent evolutionary world of Wellhausen's reconstruction of Israelite history and religion in the light of the documentary hypothesis. This is an interesting idea, but it has its weaknesses. One has to take the call reports (e.g., Hosea 1–3; Isaiah 6; Ezekiel 1–3) seriously. Still they are often put together from different sources. Is every one of the disparate bits authentic? And even though they be sincere reports of experience, how do we know them to be *true* and not the delusions of an over-excited mind? The whole idea depends on accepting the validity of mystical experience, a phenomenon common enough to humanity, and so subject to some sort of check. However, it is a phenomenon which makes the rationalist just that very least bit uncomfortable until he can get it where he can measure it. Then we get ectoplasm and statistics on long-distance card tickets which make the whole phenomenon look silly.

We must return to this, but first let us notice the real difficulties the idea has run into on its home ground of biblical scholarship. Let us grant for the sake of argument the divine origin of the authentic prophet. Grant he was a true seer. How do we know what his inspired interpretations were? Here we come up against all the problems of discerning the true words of a Hosea or an Isaiah. For Hosea, in fact, the problem is not so difficult. Most of the book is accepted as reflecting the original prophet. The trouble is understanding him; the text is, with Job, the worst preserved in the Bible! But Isaiah! Scholars fight tooth and nail – and wouldn't you know it – the passages in doubt are your favorites, the poems of the Prince of Peace in chapters 9 and 11 and at least the place and meaning of the Emmanuel prophecy. But words which are not from the prophet, whose revelations are emphasized in his reported call, cannot be accepted without cavil as divine, let alone as true.

The case is positively pathetic with Deutero-Isaiah. Isaiah 50–55 are not guaranteed by Isaiah 6. They are the words of another man. One can scrape together a sort of call report in 40:1–11, but it does not really conform to the formal call report. It leaves the prophet with something like the incomplete fragments of a driver's license. Try the validity of that on your nearest friendly policeman! But with Deutero-Isaiah, it is the beauty and power of the message which is really felt to validate. There may be something in this, but it is no longer the criterion of the official call.

But let us grasp the nettle and accept Deutero-Isaiah without his fully authenticated call. We remain ill at ease, for amid the many wonders of Deutero-Isaiah the Servant Songs, especially 52:18 and 53:12, shine with special brilliance. But these all-important texts are often asserted to be secondary increments to an otherwise almost entirely homogeneous book. The very fates work against the critic, even the believing one: the moment he has elaborated a theory which allows some special value to the text, the text is torn from his grasp.

Of course, a theory of inspiration which looks to the text as it is and not to (largely hypothetical) reconstructions of divisions within the text, could be of use here; but as we have seen, such a theory has not been available to much of modern exegesis, even Catholic; for that exegesis is the conscious or unconscious progeny of "the Protestant principle," with its theory of dictational inspiration, which was abandoned as soon as it became clear that the ordinary man took the word of God as referring to facts when the critic knew it did not. God was equivalently lying to the people to whom He gave the Book! That would never do, and since there was no theory of inspiration to put in its place, the whole problem was dropped. One must wonder about the silent effects of this on Catholic scholars who quite properly learn and apply the technical means of biblical study, which are largely the work of Protestant scholars; learn and apply, that is, without investigating the theoretical aura which unnecessarily but *de facto* surround these techniques.

Indeed, a knowledge of spiritual theology would enable us to accept the visions of anonymous authors who added their bits to the work of an Isaiah or Jeremiah. We know that God speaks to the simple and the obscure. There is no need to restrict the possibility of revelation to a literary genius (Isaiah) or an extraordinary personality (Ezekiel). The insights, the thoughts, the words of an unknown disciple can be as much inspired as the revelations of a great master. As with inspiration, the failure to bring the rich Catholic tradition of mysticism and the theological critique of mysticism is a failure in ecumenism – failure to offer the insight and experience we possess to the enrichment of theology as a whole. The result of this failure is a drive to put prophecy on familiar, comfortable ground. The call report is a (properly) recognized form, a claim to office which can be read as analogous to other validating formulae used for kings or for creating officials and the like. It is freed of any eerie contact with the supernatural. The prophet is seen as a functionary paralleled in the ancient world, from second-millennium Syria to classical Greece. Some Hebrew prophets just happened to be geniuses. Thus a bold (for the critical world) attempt to get the supernatural into at least a bit of the Bible has been rendered innocuous.

We seem to be at an impasse. We find critical-historical study of Scripture constantly winding up at one of two dead ends: the general philosophical or the fundamentalist fideistic. The latter takes the Bible pretty much as a lump: It is all fact with little variety in the truths it has to tell. One winds up explaining the inexplicable and misses great masses of deepest truth in a desperate defense of universal facticity. The former regularly reduces it to some ongoing philosophical system, natural religion, historical dialectic, existentialism, personalism – you name it! To all of which the question keeps coming back: Why is the Bible our model of theism? Why are its heroes – and especially its Hero – our stimulus to commitment and growth? Because, to be frank, they are what "just happens to be lying around" in the West, to use Chesterton's phrase about uncritical habit.

Of course, one can claim a special place for the Bible to defend the external reference of its realistic statements. The Bible is indeed special, and from this I can build a logical case for factual reference: God could *always* make exceptions to the ordinary way of things to insure that His word pointed to external fact. But this is a logical house of cards, not really supportable, even from its own weight. Anyway, what would be the point? The argument convinces and converts no one, and it can cause the Bible to be subject to ridicule.

III.

We cannot abandon criticism. It is part of the fabric of the modern world, part of the whole picture of temporal sequence and material objects and theories and ways of doing things which make the frame into which we consciously or unconsciously fit our lives and thoughts; it is the frame which three centuries ago replaced the "ages of the world" and the Ptolemaic universe. Like it or not, we can no more escape it than the air (which nowadays we often do not like!). One could try a sort of isolation-ward technique, but that is the way of the Amish and the like – admirable testimony in its way to fidelity and firmness but hardly the Church militant marching like an army with banners of truth. We must allow critical history the freedom of the Church, the stronghold of truth, for the Church is strong and the method deals with truth.

More, we cannot grow prissy and stop it when it seems to be doing messy things to texts we love. With all the failures and weaknesses of its practitioners, it is trying to add to our fund of knowledge about Israel, about Jesus, about the nascent Church. It has its successes by which we gain more of the truth – which is convertible with the good. And can any man, any Christian, turn away from the true and the good? Hardly, for this is specifically Christian: "I am the Truth . . ." The only real question is how to use criticism properly. Surely after three hundred years of struggling with it, we should be able to move some distance in the right direction.

It is certainly time that we begin doing so, and one necessary approach is reflection on the ancient question of the division of the sciences, defined here both in terms of the object studied and the possibilities of the human instrument of study. It is encouraging that one hears from England, France, even Germany, murmurs of dissatisfaction with the limited historical methods and objects so far dominant. Another significant sign is the decline of "biblical archeology" aiming to affirm or deny historicity. Interest is no longer in "validating" the Bible, but in the culture of history of Syria-Palestine for its own sake, as it should be. Even the use of the Bible for strictly historical purposes should have this aim: learning more about the past for its own sake. That is what history is all about, not defending non-historical ideas. However, the movement is quite new and still tentative. One cannot plot its directions as though describing actual activities; one is trying to chart future developments. This can be difficult and unclear. Still, those three hundred years of experience should help to indicate some definite need one hopes will be met.

In any case, the quasi-identification of exegesis with historical research must end. Historical investigation has done great service: disabusing us of simple-minded errors, filling in a background in history for the things said in the Bible (the sort of background the understanding of any literature demands), and supplying a general picture of the stages within biblical literature. To be sure, work on history should continue, but it should be recognized for what it is – strictly historical research which uses the Bible as one of many documents that can help reconstruct the ancient milieu from which our culture comes. It is an honorable occupation, one to be encouraged – but let it do its own thing. To insist now on more history, and history primarily as the panacea for bringing biblical religious ideas to the light where they can "shine forth," is too narrowing. In practice it confines the scholar to those small and often unclear bits of the Bible which seem to have reference to external fact. Since the bits and their supposed referents keep changing as hypotheses change, the scholar finds his historical ground constantly shifting as he tries to use it as a platform for affirmations beyond the historical. He never *knows* what is historical! Within a few decades we have seen the patriarch and the structure of Israel in the era of Judges doubted by criticism; then affirmed with often surprising detail; and now pushed back again into the gloom of doubt and beyond. In the New Testament, honest historical criticism has gone from John as the best witness of historical fact and sequence in the New Testament (Schleiermacher and the succeeding generation) to a confidence in Mark (all those Lives of Jesus!) to a fairly confident affirmation that at least the crucifixion happened! Biblical theology based on last year's historical hypothesis must be this year's remainder in such a situation. How can history produce anything else, especially when we are dealing with a remote and poorly documented period, as we are in biblical history?

The first necessity, then, is to affirm the obvious. The Bible contains much besides history. The first task of scientific division is to discern the kind of text at hand. There is nothing esoteric about it.

It, of course, is full of poetry, and not just in the "poetical books." Images, symbols, the fanciful, the visionary, and even the fantastic are scattered everywhere. It must be read in this light. What are we to do with Leviathan who is variously made to sport in free joy in the depths (Psalms 104:26), be the captive pet of the Lord (Job 41:4), and to be crushed to provide food for the beasts (Psalms 74:14)? One can provide an imaginary history here: Leviathan is the symbol of evil (he is in the sea, always an enemy of order in the Bible); he is left free for its appointed time until the Messiah restrains him to be a show at his triumph and later the meal at the Messianic banquet. We can smile, perhaps, but the equation of truth with factual reference is really being carried out logically here within the real scheme of sin and redemption. The trouble is the narrow definition of truth which demands that the most real, the most meaningful scheme in the world be given its exact temporal (historical, factual) referent which then, incidentally, provides a neat time frame for poor old Leviathan's career.

Of course, what is going on is the use of an image taken from Canaanite mythology. In the various passages, the great fish shows forth the joy of sheer living; illustrates the power of the God who bends so mighty a creature to His will; and, finally, is seen as the symbol of chaos which the Creator keeps in order. Leviathan is, in sum, a mythological symbol with real meaning – but with no more factual reality than Venus and Adonis had for Shakespeare. This example may seem obvious, but it was not always so. The historicizing outlined really occurred and held place for long epochs. And there are many things in the Bible which are not so obviously "poetry" and yet they are. A commentary on Judith which concentrated on its literary excellence and its message would be much preferable to the discussion of its open shortcomings as a historical report and guesses about its historical origins.

The Bible also contains realistic narrative. It is important not to confuse it with history. For one thing, such confusion is open to debunking and subsequent ridicule. More positively, recognizing the "made" character of the narrative makes us focus on the meaning which is important when the facts often are not. In other words, what does the narrative *teach*? For instance, there is the tale of David and Bathsheba and the murder of her husband, Uriah, the Hittite. Personally, I think its historicity can be defended. But if it were not so, what a picture and what a lesson! David let himself be idle and so easily tempted. Here is a man of immense energy and talent made "technologically redundant" – a king too valuable to risk in the field – at the height of his powers. And Bathsheba: it took a Rembrandt to perceive and express the tensions, the psychological conflict she felt while deciding her reply to the king's urging. One could go on and on. With or without factual reference, this realistic narrative is a revelation of poignant human conditions and the causes of sin. Reflecting on the general truth found in realistic narrative, it is sobering to note that modern biblical study grew up in Germany, a nation which did not develop a realistic narrative literature until Thomas Mann's *Buddenbrooks* at the beginning of this century, a hundred years after England and France had developed the literary form to the point where Jane Austen or Stendhal could use it with the mastery of familiarity, and a hundred and fifty years after its sturdy beginnings with Richardson and Fielding. It was not just insularity that kept criticism in a corner for long years in the nineteenth-century England. There was the concrete experience that "there are more things (and more ways of expressing truth of meaning) than are dreamt of in your philosophies" – an experience largely unavailable to, because not a part of, German culture.

In short, exegesis and historical research, the search for factual backgrounds, sources and the rest, are not identical. They can and should be separated. Not that history is to be ignored. To ascribe a meaning attested to only in the fourth century to a word in an eighth century text is simple error. But as we said, historical investigation has done its job, and we have a reasonable background to enable us to understand our biblical literature without too many gross historical solecisms.

In short, we should feel free to do something besides historical research on the Bible. And no matter what we do, certain elementary statements of the purpose of the work we are doing should be clarified. When we have determined the kind of text before us, we must make clear what we are doing with it. If we are using it as a mine of historical information, well and good; but let us say so. If we are doing something else, we must say this clearly and justify it. There is no intrinsic reason for this – kinds of interpretation other than the historical are surely legitimate – but given the habitual identification of history and exegesis, the professional reader will find it hard enough to understand what we are doing if it is not history, unless we explain ourselves clearly – and often perhaps not even then!

This, of course, implies a clear division within biblical studies. One is surely history. Surely enough has been said about this by now. There is no danger of forgetting what it offers, and we may even add some information about stages of oral transmission and traditional development prior to the textual record. There is geography. The Bible and other documents can help us feel the climate, the plants and animals, the shape and contours of the land which formed the texts to which they refer. There is sociology, the study of the human structures which held Israel and the early Church together, the classes and their interaction within and outside the structures, as well as all the manifold societal aspects the Bible and other documents can reveal to us. There is comparative religion, the study of rite and of the shrine functionary, of doctrine and moral demands. All this is knowledge, perhaps only of men and environment and not specifically theological, but knowledge and as such good.

One could easily go on dividing the various forms of knowledge to which the Bible could contribute. But we must go on to the most obvious thing of all. The Bible is a book. It is the literary heritage of a nation and of a vital religious community. It can certainly be studied as such. We have already pointed out how historical study has given us the framework which enables us to study it diachronically without too many gross errors. And all the other sciences mentioned can do their part in interpretation. A knowledge of the community structure gives a word like "sojourner" (*gèr*), for example, real substance, not just a sound. Comparative religion helps understand the sacrificial rites and the prayer forms of the psalms. And geography will enable us to distinguish and understand desert, steppe, farm land, and pasture land.

But the primary object of literary study is the text, its primary tools a knowledge of words and phrases and a feel for their use. A first call then: Let us read the text for what it is with all the wit and skill we can bring to it.

This sounds very simple, but it is not. Normally, the biblist does not read the text. He breaks it up and reads parts. He tears out its sources. He does not explain the significance of the so-called "plague stories" in Exodus. He merely explains what the Yahwist writer or the Priestly writer thought about plagues. But it is the narrative as it stands which interests the Church or the men of culture concerned with the world's classics. This also should be the biblist's interest insofar as he is concerned with explaining the Bible.

A further proposal is even more revolutionary. The Bible is a whole, a single book with a unity. This is not simply a theological claim. It is a fact of history. The Bible was composed by the refinement of traditional elements and their collection and collocation by choice by the organs of that tradition (synagogues, rabbis, churches, bishops), not a mere compilation of all that happened to be lying around. Therefore, its parts, though they can be read intelligently as individual chapters, have full meaning when read as integral parts of a meaningful whole.

We must go even farther. The Bible is the community's book, and the community's use of it is an element in its total meaning. This is not the ongoing clarification of ever obscure events by more events of *Heilsgeschichte*. It is simply the recognition that the Bible has acquired even more meaning through an ongoing interpretation which can be found in the Bible itself and continued in the post-biblical Church. No one today has the training or methodology for such total interpretation. But the ideal remains over against the fragmentation present, and it must be kept alive as a hope.

I have not even touched on many basic problems, nor can I. However, one must be faced. We have seen that one "answer" to the problems raised by historical criticism is to rise above the particular to some general theological or philosophic theme. The trouble is that it is not real necessity but cultural conditioning which leads us to tie the general theme to Christianity. Have I not done just the same: called for interpretation of a basic text of Western culture just because it is there? It may only be interesting, but what further claim does it have on me?

Biblical religions are, in fact, special because they are not religions of general ideas and eternal truths; but they are historical. They claim that the divine, the Eternal Truth, has been at work in a special way in the world's events. We can discard the six twenty-four-hour days of creation and the six ages of the world as accidental, as outmoded cataloguing schemes, but not the theological vision of *history*, i.e., of the sequence of facts of sin, incarnation, redemption, and rebirth. This is Eternal Truth concretely at work in the world, and if it is "concrete," in the world, it is historical. I cannot just ignore this and leave history to the historian (who *will* ignore it).

However, this is not exactly an *exegetical* problem, a problem of interpretation. Such problems concern meanings. The problem of fact belongs to the historian and, in theology, the apologete, for whom the exegete as such is a mere auxiliary. Part of the confusion is biblical study in the past three centuries comes from the confusion over this distinction, the urge to make exegesis apologetics (or, in some cases, anti-apologetics). I, as a Christian interpreter, assume the reasonableness of accepting the historicity of the cardinal points of my theological vision of history (not, of course, the natural proof of the point of certitude – I want to keep the faith!). Then I go on to interpret as fully as I can the literature which conveys and expands that vision. In other words, I rely on the apologete whose methods and expertise are not mine (acquaintance with and understanding of current and ever changing problems and methods in epistemology, for instance).

With this, of course, we move from the problem of exegesis as such to looking at a larger prospect worth further consideration. Where are the apologetics for the modern world? Not, I mean, the eloquence which will bring back the faith. The loss of religion in the modern world is a matter of *Zeitgeist*, an attitude toward the world and a habit of mind which has been long developing. No, I am not appealing for persuasion looking to conversion, but for a solid intellectual basis which I can know is there though I have not worked it out myself. Knowing that it is there, I can go on with my work of interpretation with a good intellectual conscience. Perhaps good interpretation which delivers the biblical message in its rich beauty will be the converting eloquence mentioned. Still that does not obviate the need for scientific apologetics; and looking at theology as an exegete, I seem to find that apologetes are very thin on the ground these days. And oh how we need them!

As an exegete, perhaps I can help with some leading questions derived for the philosopher-apologete from these Troeltschian canons of historical criticism: (1) autonomy – the scholar must make up his own mind in light of the evidence he sees; (2) analogy – a past event is understandable and believable only if it is similar to our own experience; (3) the causal chain – events follow one another as an unbroken series of immanent causes and effects. Why cannot one assert that God intervenes in the causal chain without becoming a mere part in it, and remain intellectually respectable? Why can I not appeal to a theist philosophy and, though I, as a non-professional, cannot expound it, be sure I can refer to a respected philosophical community that can? As for analogy, it is simply a new way of proposing Hume's old saw about what we expect. Well, as a theist, I *can* expect the miracles which analogy supposedly forbids. A hundred years ago that entirely admirable exponent of honest doubt, Matthew Arnold, said there is no reason why the god of theist philosophy cannot work miracles; it just happens that he does not. Where is the vigorous religious philosophy which supports my belief that He can and does?

There is more epistemology. What of the validity of the insight over mere accumulation of knowledge? Why am I satisfied that Burckhardt's insight still tells me more about Renaissance art and history than all the birth-lists or inventories and account books that computers can absorb? At another level, what of insight as delivering first principles? Modern philosophy, as felt in biblical studies, has regularly denied this – with one significant "almost" exception. "Almost" because Coleridge is not usually treated as a philosopher, since he never succeeded in formulating his ideas very clearly. Nevertheless, the "sage of Highgate" did mighty battle for *reason* (and imagination) as opposed to *understanding* (and fancy). The latter was in the Lockean tradition, concerned with quantities and external relations. The former somehow saw deeper: Its "activity" gave life to the abstractions of understanding. One may be reminded of Kant and the mind imposing order on the *Dinge-an-Sich*, but there is more to it than this. Coleridge maintains that to this activity "mysteriously, their [external things] own life is revealed. Things to it are . . . symbols characterized by a translucence of the general in the particular."

This comes close to a doctrine of a real abstraction of universals from the particular – if it never becomes very clear. Still, it convinced many in nineteenth-century England that a human faculty could perceive things in the moral realm which were closed to the calculating powers directed to the merely quantitative and factual. It helped theologians as diverse as Newman, F. D. Maurice, and the Cambridge trio, "Westcott, Lightfoot, and Hort" (great biblical critics and orthodox believers). Presumably with it they could defend a solid theism and so a solid conviction in matters of doctrine and biblical interpretation, allowing Scripture to say the things it really says – all its truths including even those it is the virtue of criticism to reveal.

However, there is peril here when this idea is interpreted in terms of a moral faculty separate from intellect, as Kant is often interpreted. One should not, I believe, take Coleridge in this direction, although one is easily led to doing so by his tortuous efforts to express his idea of a unitary power of imagination and intellectual insight. Perhaps the English were protected from going too far by the supposed national tendency not to drive any principle too far in its conclusions. In any event, not everyone is like that, and danger arises when the idea is used to lift a personal religious stance above attack, which, by definition, can come only from those who lack or do not use the faculty. It leaves things other than the moral and religious life, things like the Bible, open to the never-ending work of the intellect with its canons of criticism. The religious stance becomes isolated, individual, almost a feeling, not a reasoned conviction. So the perennial problem: Why should the stance be especially Christian? This, especially, when remorseless historical criticism is "showing" that the basic Christian document is not really very reliable. Ritschl's theology, which many in the last part of the nineteenth century greeted as salvation for supplying a sound basis for Christian conviction through criticism, succumbed to just this combination of problems, if I read it aright. It would seem that only an integrated view of the person, able to see, formulate, and defend a full metaphysics – not just a few moral insights – will do.

Coleridge is especially important here because he puts an emphasis on the imagination not usual in the *philosophia perennis*; for we must confront the fact that we face a new epistemological situation. We *have* to accept the knowledge that comparative religion, literature, and folklore have given us. In cultures, it simply is true that great people and great events attract stories to themselves. Thus, the great come and go in an extraordinary way: Moses in the bulrushes is paralleled very closely by the birth legend of Sargon of Akkad; the first "world conqueror" – Hercules – strangles snakes in his cradle; there are heavenly portents when great Caesar dies; and so on. The great man has preternatural insight into other minds; he heals; he curses effectively. There is no need to expand. We know the argument, and it is a strong one. We must face it: If there were no extraordinary stories about David, let alone Jesus, the popular mind would have supplied them, and if this is the case, how do we know which stories it did not invent?

Theoretically one might just compare the legends. Hennecke's *New Testament Apocrypha* and Ginsburg's *Legends of the Jews* and massive folklore collections are at hand. Of course, few actually do this. It is assumed that it has been done and the religious "legends" disproved. How else could Frazer's *Golden Bough* be a pillar of our intelligentsia, its unexamined conclusions the basis for further speculation and literary criticism? It is the odd fellow who reads it who finds out how inaccurate is much of its information, how tendentious its reasoning. For comparative legends in general, just read the Infancy Narratives along with a mass of birth legends, and it is wild diversity, not similarity, which leaps to the eye. For an even more striking case, one can turn to accounts of resurrection.

However, the problem thus attacked remains unsolved. Many really cannot see the differences I say leap to the eye. Besides, popular culture's producing the occasional masterpiece does not make what that work says true to fact. "Sir Patrick Spens" does not become detailed historical narrative by being great poetry. So how can I rely on a piece of poetry, though it be splendid, to tell me the truth, especially when I know that an extraordinary individual would occasion fancies about him in a popular, oral culture in any case? That the fancies reach poetic heights may well be merely the accident of a genius's presence to tell the tale, not a sign of its truth – so my case of "Sir Patrick Spens." The accident of its being recorded in the version of a singer of great talent does not make it history!

However, the parallel is not perfect. It is quite accurate that "the hopes and fears of all the years" met in Bethlehem that night. There would seem to be a difference between those images and stories which occur everywhere and express universal longing for purity, for a savior and healer, for life, and popular poesie on lesser subjects. Do the great biblical images express the truth of what humanity has sought and expressed so often, sometimes haltingly, sometimes tellingly? I believe they do, but we need an epistemology which can confidently show that they do. Cannot students of literature, psychologists, philosophers help us here? Can we not press on beyond the lines drawn in Ricoeur's *The Symbolism of Evil*? He stops short at "the human condition" and the final step must show how that condition is tied not to *imaginative* but to *historical* paradigms. We are still at the stage when Langdon Gilkey can gently tap Karl Rahner's wrist for insisting that our sinful condition goes back to a *historic* fall. We need to show that such things must be, though the historic event be delivered to us decorated with poetic symbols (which, properly seen, elucidate the event, but now are adduced to bring it into question). Jung, of course, went some way in this direction with his idea of primordial experiences imprinted on the mind of the race, but so far his work is too occasional, intuitive, and unorganized to serve our purpose. Still, the hints are there. Can we not follow them to a conclusion which will satisfy the modern, who is doing plenty of seeking, that the Bible opens the way to his historical home?

I think some such an epistemology would be richer and more satisfying than the alternative which occurs to me. That is, to develop the earlier suggestion. Create a vital tract *de Deo uno*, the implications of revelation, of inspiration. One can answer most of the problems (probably not all) of the Infancy Narratives within this framework. The stories and poems reflect a Jewish milieu. What else? Should they reflect twentieth-century Chicago? They are attested by only one witness, not three or four, as in so much of the Gospel. Of course, they are about private matters, not the public life. But if there was such a stir, how were they forgotten and not adduced in evidence? What stir? "All the hill country of Judaea" would not be as large as many a Kansas township nor more densely populated. And any newsman knows that last week's stir is a dead issue. The stir of thirty years ago is simply nothing. What is a Shmoo? Who is Sparkle Plenty? Well, they were the stir of a whole nation thirty years ago! Still, I must admit that, as a historian, this thirty- or sixty-year submergence of the stories is a real stumbling block.

One can get around it, though the phrase "get around it," already raises bad implications of avoiding and not overcoming difficulties. But let it be: We accept a bad press if we must. What is the evidence for the truth as history of the events told and the poetic interpretation which is offered, as history always offers interpretation, though it is not usually such magnificent writing? No more and no less than the revelation and inspiration granted by God to those who told, developed, and finally wrote them. This is what God wanted us to know *e basta*! This is so, but to use it confidently in the intellectual marketplace, I need the support of philosophy and theology which convince. They must show that the God of theism can intervene among the causes immanent in this world. They must give an account of revelation and inspiration which frees it of a simplistic concept of inerrancy that respects neither psychological nor historical nor literary realities. And it must mark out the central theological citadel so that I can concentrate on it and not be dealing with a succession of outposts.

Most of all, it must respect knowledge acquired, be it from philology, literature, history, archeology, or wherever, and leave the biblist free to use all this and all the new stocks that will come. A confident theistic philosophy and consequent theology should have no problem doing this. Certainly, it will be a surprise to see how much this will show that non-historical elements in the Bible, poetry tales, comments, much that seems secondary, throw light on and enrich understanding of the central theological block that I have asked be emphasized.

It really comes down to one thing after all. Classic philosophy and theology must be reinvigorated and filled with confidence, so that an exegete who is neither a philosopher nor a theologian can look to and refer to them with confidence when he wants backing. One vital element in such a reinvigoration would have to be an epistemology that takes symbols seriously and demonstrates their real (not ideal or wish-fulfillment) relation to history. For this, classic methods need not be abandoned. The potential is there. In any case, we need not fear the "old," for truth has no age. Think how little has been done with Thomas's work on the integration of sense, imagination, and intellect, and how much this would help develop Coleridge's insight into the unitary imagination and reason and so on into the importance of symbol. Let work like this go on so that theology, active, interesting, and growing itself, will help and be helped by real exegesis. It certainly will be in no danger of giving way to an "exegesis" which absorbs it, as in many places it has – which has, in fact, become theology *tout court*.

5.
Transcendental Truth and Cultural Relativism: A Historian's View (1979)
Glenn W. Olsen

Back in 1951 that marvelous venture in cross-cultural study, *Eranos*, devoted its 1951 meeting to the theme "Man and Time."[1] When the papers given at this meeting were translated and published in English, they were introduced by a short essay, "The Time of Eranos," by Henry Corbin.[2] In a few pages Corbin launched a frontal assault on some of the most cherished assumptions of the history profession – indeed on the very idea of "explanation" as it occurs across the sciences today. His analysis seems to me so correct, and freighted with such significance, that I would like to devote this essay to explaining, defending, and enlarging on his views.

When asked what I do, I sometimes identify myself as an historian of ideas. This usually conveys the idea that I analyze intellectual themes and figures in terms of the schools to which they belong, the currents of ideas which influence them, the "causes" of these ideas, and the later influence or "migrations of themes."[3] (That is, the term "intellectual history" conveys the idea of a scientific method applied to the data of the past.) I have no quarrel with any of this. But, as Corbin points out, if this is all that scientific method does, it has "all the virtues, except the primary virtue that would have consisted in establishing its object by recognizing the way it gives its object to itself."[4] To elaborate, explanation for most modern scholars tends to mean tracing an object to all its causes. If this has been done, the object has been understood. For Corbin, the heart of understanding lies in the op-

---

1 Joseph Campbell, "Editor's Foreword," *Man and Time: Papers From the Eranos Yearbooks*, Bollinger Series XXX, 3, Princeton: 1957, pp. XI–XX.
2 *Ibid.*, pp. XIII–XX.
3 *Ibid.*, p. XIII.
4 *Ibid.*

posite direction, not in how an elaborate system of causes explains an object, but in what an object itself implies or explains.

We are all familiar with analyses that reduce the object under analysis to some formative influence. Clement of Alexandria's ethics become merely Stoic, and Origen is thought to be sufficiently described by tracing his cosmology back to Plato. We all, hopefully, have been exasperated by that kind of analysis of dynamic communities which traces significant changes in their patterns of life back to some primary cause. Think of all the changes in the life of the Church that Andrew Greeley has been able to explain as a result of *Humanae Vitae*! I suppose that the sociologists here are even greater sinners than the historians, for much of the claims made for their research would crumble if we really insisted that any living person or community is much more than whatever the biologists, sociologists, and historians can think to say about it in terms of causal chains exterior to the thing itself. Any person, any community, is so dominated by tension, paradox, and the pains of change that there is no way to understand what he, she, or it is except by attending to what the person or community is trying to say of itself.

I do not want to be misunderstood. I am not attacking the search for causes. I merely want to place this search in a proper perspective. Let me take as an example the problem of the post-Vatican-II decline in priestly and religious vocations. We have all read explanations of this decline written by progressives which account for the decline by the failure of the Church to implement a certain reading of the documents of Vatican II. We have also read traditionalist explanations which account for the decline by saying that the liberalization of the Church, the growing doubt of many public figures about the value of such things as celibacy, and a certain attempt to adapt the Church to contemporary mores have all led many young men to see no point in taking on a form of life considered outmoded. I think it is quite proper to go on looking for explanations for this decline in the quarters both progressive and traditionalist have sought out. But their explanations fail to convince that the problem has been understood. We are here at the heart of the question of "reductionism." It is not that the explanations offered are simply wrong, as that they are so inadequate. Both points of view have something to be said for them, but neither comes close to accounting for this change in the life of the Church. Naturally it helps to expand the number of factors taken into account, so that a wise scholar would push back his research in time, studying, for instance, how clergy and seminarians prayed before the Council, and how they were educated. The mature scholar would extend the sweep of his view to consider the tensions which exist between any form of ascetic life and a bourgeois culture. Yet, no matter how many explanatory factors are considered, they all, in some way, would be means of averting our eyes from the total complexity of what the object of our study was trying to explain about itself to us. For in all such explanations, we would be considering the object in terms of something other than itself.

Understanding, of course, cannot proceed at all without comparison and some form of reductionism. Reductionism is often understood to mean the explanation of objects of a given degree of complexity or structure by causes belonging to a less complex or less structured level of being. A classic example would be to say that religion is caused by, that is, is explained by, the dreams of the unconscious; another example would be to consider thought as caused by the brain. Here the life of the mind or of the spirit is reduced to some kind of material explanation. This kind of reductionism, though very widespread, has been under serious attack for its obvious inadequacies, and I do not want to linger over it.[5] Although it can offer factors to be considered in some fuller explanation of an object, it never comes to terms with the question of what precisely differentiates a claimed order of explanation from the higher degree of complexity found in the object it claims to be explaining.

I would rather use the term "reductionism" in a more general sense to mean the explanation of an object by objects of another order; I would like to include a theological explanation of an object, for instance, as also one way of explaining an object in terms other than its own order. Thus, in addition to a reduction "downward," so to speak, I would also like to speak of a reduction "upward." The life of a religious community might be explained both by reference "downward" to the economic factors which influence it, but also "upward," for instance to a certain internal logic of spiritual development which the community may embody. If one chooses to flee the world, certain things follow as to how one will try to organize the economic basis of one's life. Both "downward" and "upward" explanations are, of

---

5 Arthur Koestler and J. R. Smythies, editors, *Beyond Reductionism: New Perspectives In the Life Sciences*, New York: 1969; Guilford Dudley, *Religion on Trial: Mircea Eliade and His Critics*, Philadelphia: 1977, pp. 127–135.

course, ways of imaging aspects of reality found in the object itself that one is trying to explain.

My point then is that no explanation is possible without some form of reductionism. There are as many levels of possible explanation as there are separate sciences discoverable by the human mind. We may try to explain any order of objects by reference to any other order of objects. The biologist, physicist, sociologist, and theologian may all have their day in court, saying what the object looks like in terms of the perspective of their discipline. It seems to me that all this can be valuable, as long as we realize that each of these scientists is only giving an account in terms of his own discipline and that no such account can explain the object under study in itself. Thus, if by cultural relativism we mean that there is no such thing as truth which transcends culture, and that all ideas of good, true, etc., are simply in content the expressions of culture, we can see the obvious inadequacy of such a notion. This is merely one of the cruder forms of reductionism, which sees idea as caused by the configuration of material circumstances. It is true insofar as the very meanings of words are determined by the life-history of a person or a people, but false as a claim to reduce one kind of being to another. To drive home its falsity, we need merely turn to the mathematician or the ethicist, that is, to someone from a discipline which habitually deals with transcultural truths. To restrict ourselves to purely natural examples, the mathematician or logician can refer us to the principle of contradiction as something always true, granted that its terms are understood, and the ethicist can refer us to the general principle that one ought "do good and avoid evil" as an example of a proposition which can be understood to be true across all cultures, again granted that its terms are understood.

I need not belabor the point. The conclusion is that a proper relativism claims to explain only what can be understood in terms of a particular point of view and a particular science. Reductionism does not need to falsify; it merely accounts for something from a particular point of view. Only when *hubris* arises, when a particular point of view is taken to offer a comprehensive understanding of an object, does misjudgment necessarily enter.

A problem remains. I made the claim above that even a proper reductionism still explains an object in terms of something other than itself. The question remains whether the sum of human understanding is the sum of the possible perspectives on an object, understood in some proper internal order to one another, or whether there is some way of addressing an object more directly than through the chains of causal relations exterior to itself. Here we return to the thought of Corbin. Above all, he warns of explaining things "by their times."[6] To tell Corbin that something is "very much of its time" is not to advance a compliment. What he wishes is that people "be their times," that is, that they realize their own meaning and not be simply another example of conformity to an age. The best people are usually untimely, not receiving their meaning from things but giving meaning to things.

Let me illustrate. Today we scientifically – at least so we think – study everything. Although the good scientist knows that the calculation of what percent of the people are doing what should not become normative, on scientific grounds, for what percent of the people do what in the future, nevertheless, we are so enchained by cultural relativism that this is almost always the path we take. If the scientists can show that such and such a percent of the population is found to be performing such and such an unnatural act, we have a new minority to be tolerated and for whom we must make appropriate legislation to dignify their behavior. Implicitly we vote time and again for such a culturally determined truth. People see no alternative to being of one's own time. Although we should know that no science has the power to generate norms, outside of ethics, politics, and revealed theology itself, we rarely behave this way. I write these words a day after having been told by a priest that the sense of the faithful means that if the majority of Catholics refuse to accept the teachings of a papal document like *Humanae Vitae*, the teaching of the document will eventually have to be changed. Why the norm for teaching should be the sentiments of a bourgeois, materialist, anti-ascetic culture rather than those truths about man which transcend time and place is, of course, never explained. This priest – actually the catechist of my children – rather takes as his truth that of a particular culture, and prefers this to either the norm of a rational analysis of human nature or to the Church's magisterium. I in my naivete had assumed that it would be as difficult for a nation of rich men to find the kingdom of God as for that one rich man of whom Christ spoke. But no, if the egotism of enough rich men is multiplied, it becomes the sense of the faithful.

Why we should see no alternative to being of our times is not very clear, but in the first instance it seems to me that, having lost the sense of how mysterious life is, we want to reduce it to false clarities. I recently received a questionnaire produced for the National Conference of Catholic Bishops in-

---

6 *Art. Cit.*, pp. XIII–XIV.

tended to solicit my opinions on the question of the missions. Like every other questionnaire I have received, this one drove me to distraction. Somehow I was supposed to provide yes/no answers to what I thought were extremely complicated questions so that the surveyor could find out if I was "liberal" or "conservative," for or against liberation theology. I knew it would do no good to tell the surveyor that, as a Catholic, I could not be classified within the accidental framework of what liberal and conservative happened to mean within an American, or indeed any other, framework. So I did what I habitually do with such surveys, and gave it a gentle push in the direction of non-being.

This lack of a sense of mystery is a very serious thing. It not only leads to the persistent attempt to quantify that which cannot be quantified but also to the reduction of the uniqueness of the human person in the direction of a materialist grid of matter in motion. More perversely, it repeats the sin of Adam. It seems to me that the more important a thing is, the less likely it is to be a subject of what we call scientific (quantified) precision. We must remain vague, imprecise, and in a profound sense unscientific about the most important things in life because the most important things deserve all those adjectives. Or, if you prefer, we must recover notions of science that existed before the equation of the real with the quantifiable. Historians write very glibly about human motivation, but who knows even his own heart? I recall that one of the few really insightful things that Arthur Schlesinger, Jr., ever said, after having spent some time at least close to the inner workings of the American presidency, was that the real history of presidential decision cannot be written because the few scraps of evidence left after the fact, that is, the documents of history, give only the barest notion of the actual processes by which a decision was made. As a historian, I can live with this, but then I have a pretty lively sense of the effects of original sin.

So it is that, when a society loses its sense of mystery, the seven devils enter. Having lost our sense of the complexity of life, of the uniqueness of each person, we sweep everything bare, calling for openness and honesty in every quarter. The light of a certain notion of science must clarify and shine everywhere, reducing mystery to statistics. It seems to me that in this we demean each other. This is perhaps not the place to give an argument for the values of dissimulation, but the constant demand for bringing everything out in the open is but a form of not realizing the complexity of being. I am tempted to say that we need to identify with Michael in *The Godfather* at the moment he lies to his wife. This lie has a kind of ontological status as a symbol of what sometimes must be done to preserve truths about being so complex that only the most discriminating mind can sense even their complexity. There are truths that "the times" can only misjudge.

In our common speech we distinguish between persons and facts. For Corbin the great fact is the human person, without whom there is no event: "Hence we must reverse the perspectives of the usual optics, substitute the hermeneutics of the human individual for the pseudodialectic of facts, which today is accepted, everywhere and by everyone, as objective evidence."[7] We must retrace those awful and arrogant steps by which a certain idea of science, above all to be laid at the door of Descartes, has made impossible any steady view of reality. Beginning with the arbitrary decision to identify mind with the subjective and body with the objective, proceeding through the equally arbitrary decision to consider that which can be quantified as the most real, as factual, and concluding with the philosophic distinction between primary and secondary qualities, this view of science constructs an "objective" world of facts, of matter in motion, following its own autonomous causality, to which the human subject must submit. The position of course is circular, obtaining its "explanation" by submitting the human observer to causal chains which can only be maintained by the arbitrary identification of reality with the quantifiable.[8]

Against this view, Corbin insists that explanation is not the same as understanding. The critical principle here is *individuum est ineffabile* – the individual is unique and "can be neither deduced nor explained."[9] We all know that Aristotle (*Poetics*, chap. 9) saw history as a *narratio singularum*, and it seems to me that the specific mission of the historian will always center on the preservation of all the uniqueness of each historical object. Above all, the historian should have the disposition to respond to Corbin's insistence on the necessity not so much to explain objects as to understand what they imply. Let me take an example. It seems to me that, beyond the transcendentals that every man encounters, the truths of mathematics, morals, and revelation, the historian is particularly aware of having to come to terms with what is commonly called "human nature." The problem is that the historian never encounters human nature directly, merely humans. As he describes them in all their particularity, he nevertheless observes certain

---

7 *Ibid.*, p. XIV.
8 *Ibid.*, pp. XIV–XV.
9 *Ibid.*, p. XIV.

forms of analogous behavior. Thucydides (*History of the Peloponnesian War*, Book I, chap. I) already noted this when he made his famous statement that although historical circumstances are always changing, human nature remains the same. Hence the possibility of the study of history becoming a handbook of politics.

I would suggest that precisely in being attentive to what historical figures do, the historian comes up against a kind of transcendent, namely, human nature. That is, the actions of each figure imply something, much as, when we first meet a new person, we try to deduce from his actions what his motives are, and what his intentions toward us might be. We never directly encounter some fixed quality called human nature, but when we have observed a great diversity of figures in a variety of cultures we note that there are a number of common things that persons with the most varying histories seem to be seeking. Aristotle, Vico, and Georgio del Vecchio all observed this in their own days. These things are, in many ways, the great banalities of classical thought: education, prosperity, peace, love, etc. People in the most diverse cultural circumstances tend to order their lives, for instance, in such a way as to obtain peace. This is what Johan Huizinga meant when he said that what the cultural historian does is to study how human nature is stylized in a particular culture. Note that the various components of human nature, some of them not as benign as those I have mentioned, are not taken as exemplified by individual men; rather, that a collection of qualities which we may denote human is deduced from studying individuals. The collection is met in ever-differing combinations in concrete individuals, so that we can never know how a given individual will act by the mere fact of knowing that he is human. Nevertheless we can deduce in perfect loyalty to the individual in all his particularity that he embodies certain human qualities which transcend time and place.

This, I think, is what Corbin meant when he wrote that we must concern ourselves with what objects imply. As far as men are concerned, "What concretely exists are wills and relations between . . . willing subjects."[10] Events "are likewise the attributes of acting subjects; they are not beings but ways of being."[11] What happened in the Cartesian revolution was that, instead of persons giving reality to events, the order of relations was reversed so that facts came to be considered to be real in themselves. There followed

10 *Ibid.*, p. XV.
11 *Ibid.*, p. XVI.

from this the deep resentments of modern thought against the past, as it became more clearly realized that this inversion of reality chained man to facts and laws outside himself, and to an ineluctable causal determinism which B. F. Skinner, in his curious manner, has recently charted. If reality is matter in motion, that is, the quantifiable, then surely we are held in an absolute determinism. Illogically, we will turn to "the illusions of progressivism" as a way of escaping this past which we have laid upon ourselves.[12] If a Frenchman was one of the first to proclaim this idea of reality, it is the British who have developed it with a vengeance, and I do not take it as accidental that, until very recently, British philosophy has been built on the most superficial notions of what science is, omitting from discussion central hermeneutic questions, such as the role of memory in making facts possible. Forgetting the point which Augustine made so well, that without memory the observer lives in a perpetual present of which by definition he cannot even be conscious, these philosophers have forgotten that the only place a fact can exist is in the human memory. It is only memory that preserves my sense of identity, the sense of this sentence which I have begun but not yet finished, and the continuity of my perceptions of objects other than myself. Without memory there would only be perception taking place in the present, a kind of blind seeing. That I am able to speak of facts at all, that is, of the continued existence of anything, is because of memory. Knowledge is not the simple result of a present perception of an objective world different from the perceiver, but the result of a very complicated process of perception, deduction, and judgment centered in the memory of a person. Without the person, there are no facts.

In sum, understanding is "'interpreting' the *signs*, explaining not material facts but ways of being."[13] The place of history, therefore, is always the present, and the past is only understood when it is placed in the present: Its signs only imply to an individual living in his present. "The only 'historical causality' is the relations of will between acting subjects. 'Facts' are on each occasion a *new creation*; there is discontinuity between them. Hence to perceive their connections is neither to formulate laws nor to deduce causes, but to understand a *meaning*, interpret *signs*, a composite structure... To perceive a causality in 'facts' by detaching them from persons is

---

12 *Ibid.*, p. XV.
13 *Ibid.,* pp. XVI–XVII.

doubtless to make a philosophy of history on which our contemporaries have built up a whole mythology."[14]

Modern thought about the philosophy of history has a kind of schizoid quality about it. On the one hand, there is a persistent tendency toward secularization, in which real time, the time of the human subject, is reduced to "abstract physical time, to the essentially *quantitative* time which is that of the objectivity of mundane calendars from which the *signs* that gave a sacred qualification to every present have disappeared."[15] One would have assumed that on logical grounds this would have left man without any philosophy of history at all, for mere matter in motion can have no meaning. But no, it is precisely in the modern period that the great philosophies of history have appeared, trying to give a meaning to the whole. Dogmatically, as a kind of surrogate theology – indeed as a kind of stepson of the Christian theology of history – which never claimed to be grounded on anything but revelation, the philosophies of history, whether idealist or materialist, claim to have found in the historical process itself a meaning. Certainly Karl Löwith was right in rejecting all such notions of "universal history." We can sympathize with the modern attempt to find meaning in history, but must note that, granted the ideas of causation and explanation which have predominated in the modern period, this attempt is doomed to all but a cry of anguish. If history in general has a meaning, it will either be found in the subjects who construct history or outside the causal chains of abstract physical time altogether, as imposed from without, that is, as revelation. I do not, of course, mean by this that people and events may not be the bearers of revelation. I merely mean that this would never be perceived as science in terms of what that term has come to mean in the modern period.

The idea of historical objectivity, as it has generally been understood in the past two centuries, must also be abandoned, for it is but a version of the idea that there is a network of causal relations exterior to an object which can explain the object in terms of understanding it. Here we return to the question of a proper relativism. Corbin proposes: "It is impossible to compete with and against a scientific, materialistic, and atheistic socialization by a conformism of well-meaning people who can find no justification for being except in their social activity nor any foundation for their knowledge except in social sciences."[16]

14 *Ibid.*, p. XVIII.
15 *Ibid.*
16 *Ibid.*

Our choices narrow. Either we return to a mythological view of the world, fleeing from the idea of history altogether, or we find a meaning for time that is generally different from the objective time and space of the physical scientists. Mircea Eliade has been a passionate advocate of the former alternative. In spite of my great admiration for his work, and my belief that his attempt to recover a sacral world order is superior to the cosmos provided us in the modern secularized West, his proposal has an immense flaw. What is wrong about the worldview of the modern West is not that it is scientific, but that the legitimate advances, indeed the invaluable contributions, that can come from a quantification of nature have led to totalitarian claims on the behalf of a particular method and approach to understanding reality. We do not want to reject Newton in the mindless way his age rejected Aristotle. Therefore any new general view of the world must include, rather than reject, what quantification can tell us about the world.

A general view something like that of Bernard Lonergan is necessary, whereby the world to be understood can be understood at all kinds of levels. Let me pass from the world of human history to the world of nature for a moment. A proper understanding of a table should include physical description of the table at all levels and by all the instruments by which that is possible. But understanding is increased if in addition to the physical scientist, also the biologist, the political scientist, the sociologist, the ethicist, the theologian, etc., can each have a say about the table. In a sense, each level of comment, each perspective, leaves an empirical residue for another level of analysis to consider. Although at the level of physical description, a pursuit of final causation is not necessary, this is not true of a number of the other levels of study. This seems to me a proper relativism, with no level of analysis having claimed to have said everything that can be said about the table.

To turn then to our second alternative, that of finding a meaning for time and history which is generically different from the objectivities of the modern period. Given the Christian revelation, it seems to me a failure of the intellect not to embrace the possibilities offered by the distinctive understanding of time found in Christianity. Here the horizontal causal relationships of objective time, the time of nature if you will, are crossed by the vertical relationships of God with man, the time of persons. At the intersections of these two lines lie those events which are both a part of nature and which carry, or rather incarnate, the meaning by which history is interpreted. The message of the meaning of history is given by events that are both in nature, and which as symbols point forward to that which is still to come in history, as well as to that which is altogether beyond history. Type points to antitype, the paschal lamb to the Savior. History moves from shadow to image to reality. In such a view, time and history really do have a meaning. All flows to and from the Cross, that Event of events by which old prophecies are fulfilled and new realities break in, an Event at once historical and the measure of history.

Here meaning is not obtained by some kind of circular examination of history to find the meaning of the whole, but rather by the acceptance of a revelation which tells us that, although some things about the world can be understood without revelation, time and history only yield up their meanings to those who take God at his Word, as the Creator of nature and history and thus as the source of the final meaning of both. It is in history that man is being saved, that Meaning has become incarnate, that the New Mankind has begun to appear, that a Bride has been chosen. The meaning of history is found, not in the perpetual dance of matter, nor in the time-fleeing mythologies of the archaic peoples, but in the perseverance in time, reform to the better, sanctification, and rest at the end of time. It is in this sense that Christianity explains more about the world than do either the sciences or the mythologies. Christian revelation, centered on the inestimable worth of the individual person, becomes the supernatural compliment of a history of the human individual understood not as determined by exterior data, but as that present sign which always points to a meaning both within and beyond itself.

6.
Christian Moral Values and Dominant Psychological Theories: The Case of Kohlberg (1980)

Paul C. Vitz

I. Kohlberg's Theory

Since the late 1950s, Lawrence Kohlberg of Harvard University has developed a theory of stages of moral growth which, within education and child psychology, and within American schools, has been of great influence.[1] This theory is based on the philosophy of John Dewey and the work of the Swiss psychologist Jean Piaget; but, in many of its concepts, methods, and applications, Kohlberg has gone substantially beyond Dewey and Piaget to produce his own model of how moral reasoning develops in the child.[2] The basic research strategy has been to present moral dilemmas to children and young people and then to observe the reasons given why one course of action should be followed rather than another. Kohlberg claims to have observed that the patterns of reasoning which people use are quite distinct and few in number. Specifically, he maintains that there are six types

---

1   It is assumed that the reader is aware of the widespread influence in the United States of Kohlberg's model, not only in secular education but in religious education as well. My guess is what Values Clarification has been more of an influence with Protestant schools and Kohlberg relatively more influential in Catholic education.

2   Kohlberg frequently acknowledges his debt to Piaget (see, for example, Lawrence Kohlberge, "Stage and Sequence: Cognitive-Developmental Approach to Socialization," In D. Goslin (Ed.). *Handbook of Socialization: Theory Research*, New York: Rand, McNally, 1969); he is also quite clear about the seminal importance of Dewey's philosophy (see "A Cognitive-Developmental Approach to Moral Education," by Lawrence Kohlberg, in *The Humanist*, November/December 1972, 13–16).

or patterns of moral reasoning. Although recently he has qualified this number, Kohlberg's basic point that there are few patterns of moral reasoning remains intact.

Primarily, Kohlberg is interested in the person's dominant pattern of moral reasoning, not in the person's particular answer. He is concerned with the form and process of thought, not in the content or actual moral outcome. Thus, two people may disagree about what is to be done but use the same kind of reasoning, or they may come to the same conclusion for very different reasons. Like so many modern thinkers, he is concerned with structure and changes in structure (process) but not in content itself.[3]

Kohlberg comes to far-reaching conclusions about the set of patterns of moral thought he has observed. What he (like Piaget) claims to have discovered is that, when a person is studied over a number of years, the evidence shows that he goes through a developmental series of moral patterns.[4] Each pattern of moral reasoning in the sequence is a qualitatively distinct "stage" in the person's life. Further, Kohlberg claims that the sequence of stages is the same for all people, although some may never get to the higher stages. Since he claims there are six stages, everyone develops morally by starting at stage 1 and over time proceeds by moving up in order from 2 to 6, unless growth stops at an intermediate stage. According to Kohlberg, nobody ever skips a stage, nor regresses to an earlier stage. He admits, however, that a person can show a mixture of two adjacent stages, that is, one can be in a transition between two stages. Kohlberg's stages, very briefly, are as follows:

> Stage One: Punishment-Obedience Orientation
> Stage Two: Instrumental-Exchange Orientation
> Stage Three: Good Boy-Nice Girl Orientation
> Stage Four: System-Maintaining (or Law and Order) Orientation
> Stage Five: Social-Contract Orientation
> Stage Six: Universal Ethical-Principles Orientation

In more detail, the six stages are defined by Kohlberg and are classified at three different levels in the following manner:

---

3   The belief that content and structure can be effectively conceptualized and studied as separate categories underlies much contemporary thought and deserves a thorough analysis and critique.

4   For Jean Piaget's position, see *The Moral Judgment of the Child*, New York: Harcourt Brace, 1932.

1. Preconventional Level: At this level, the child is responsive to cultural rules and labels of good and bad, right or wrong, but interprets these labels in terms of either the physical or the hedonistic consequences of action (punishment, reward, exchange of favors) or in terms of the physical power of those who enunciate the rules and labels. This level comprises the following two stages:

Stage 1 – *Punishment and Obedience Orientation* – the physical consequences of an action determine its goodness or badness regardless of the human meaning or value of these consequences. Avoidance of punishment and unquestioning deference to power are valued in their own right, not in terms of respect for an underlying moral order supported by punishment and authority (the latter being Stage 4).

Stage 2 – *Instrumental Relativist Orientation* – right action consists of that which instrumentally satisfies one's own needs and occasionally the needs of others. Human relations are viewed in terms similar to those of the market place. Elements of fairness, of reciprocity, and of equal sharing are present, but they are always interpreted in a physical, pragmatic way. Reciprocity is a matter of "you scratch my back and I'll scratch yours," not of loyalty, gratitude, or justice.

2. Conventional Level: At this level, maintaining the expectations of the individual's family, group, or nation is perceived as valuable in its own right, regardless of immediate and obvious consequences. The attitude is one not only of *conformity* to personal expectations and social order, but of loyalty to it, of actively *maintaining*, supporting, and justifying the order and of identifying with the persons or group involved in it. This level comprises the following two stages:

Stage 3 – *Interpersonal Concordance or "Good Boy-Nice Girl" Orientation* – good behavior is that which pleases or helps others and is approved by them. There is much conformity to stereotypical images of what is majority or "natural" behavior. Behavior is frequently judged by intention: "He means well" becomes important for the first time. One earns approval by being "nice."

Stage 4 – *"Law and Order" Orientation* – there is orientation toward authority, fixed rules, and the maintenance of the social order. Right behavior consists of doing one's duty, showing respect for authority, and maintaining the given social order for its own sake.

3. Post-Conventional, Autonomous, or Principled Level: At this level, there is a clear effort to define moral values and principles that have validity and application apart from the authority of the groups or persons holding these principles and apart from the individual's own identification with these groups. This level again has two stages:

> Stage 5 – *Social-Contract Legalistic Orientation* – generally, this stage has utilitarian overtones. Right action tends to be defined in terms of general individual rights and in terms of standards that have been critically examined and agreed upon by the whole society. There is a clear awareness of the relativism of personal values and opinions and a corresponding emphasis on procedural rules for reaching consensus. Aside from what is constitutionally and democratically agreed upon, the right is a matter of personal "values" and "opinion." The result is an emphasis upon the "legal point of view," but with an emphasis upon the possibility of changing law in terms of rational considerations of social utility (rather than freezing it in terms of Stage 4, "law and order"). Outside the legal realm, free agreement, and contract, is the binding element of obligation. This is the "official" morality of the United States government and constitution.
>
> Stage 6 – *Universal Ethical-Principle Orientation* – right is defined by the decision of conscience in accord with self-chosen ethical principles appealing to logical comprehensiveness, universality, and consistency. These principles are abstract and ethical (the Golden Rule, the categorical imperative); they are not concrete moral rules like the Ten Commandments. At heart, these are universal principles of justice, of the reciprocity and equality of human rights, and of respect for the dignity of human beings as individual persons.[5],[6]

Before beginning the critique of this theory of Kohlberg, it is necessary to give a rather extensive example of how Kohlberg scores responses to moral dilemmas. It is the only way to make his scoring system clear, especially the way in which the assumptions determine the scoring. Kohlberg writes:

> As a single example of our findings of stage sequence, take the progress of two boys on the aspect "the value of human life." The first boy, Tommy, is asked "Is it better to save the life of one important person or a lot of unimportant people?" At age ten, he answers "All the people that aren't important because one man just has one house, maybe a lot

---

5   Found in many of Kohlberg's writings – this is taken from "Moral Thinking – Can It Be Taught?" by Howard Munson, *Psychology Today*, February 1979, 48–68.

6   Lawrence Kohlberg, "Stages of Moral Development as a Basis for Moral Education," in *Moral Education: Interdisciplinary Approaches*, Toronto: University of Toronto Press, 1971, pp. 86–87.

of furniture, but a whole bunch of people have an awful lot of furniture and some of these poor people have an awful lot of furniture and some of these poor people might have a lot of money and it doesn't look it." Clearly Tommy is Stage 1: he confuses the value of a human being with the value of the property he possesses. Three years later (at age thirteen) Tommy's conceptions of life's value are most clearly elicited by the question, "Should the doctor 'mercy kill' a fatally ill woman requesting death because of her pain?" He answers, "Maybe it would be good to put her out of her pain, she'd be better off that way. But the husband wouldn't want it. It's not like an animal. If a pet dies, you can get along without it – it isn't something you really need. Well, you can get a new wife, but it's not really the same." Here his answer is Stage 2: the value of the woman's life is partly contingent on its hedonistic value to the wife herself but even more contingent on its instrumental value to her husband, who can't replace her as easily as he can a pet. Three years later (age sixteen) Tommy's conception of life's values is elicited by the same question, to which he replies: "It might be best for her, but her husband – it's a human life – not like an animal; it just doesn't have the same relationship that a human being does to a family. You can become attached to a dog, but nothing like a human you know." Now Tommy has moved from a Stage 2 instrumental view based on the husband's distinctly human empathy and love for someone in his family. Equally clearly, it lacks any basis for a universal human value of the woman's life, which would hold if she had no husband or if her husband didn't love her. Tommy, though bright (IQ 120), is a slow developer in moral judgment.

Let us take another boy, Richard, to show us sequential movement through the remaining three steps. At age thirteen, Richard said about the mercy killing, "If she requests it, it's really up to her. She is in such terrible pain, just the same as people are always putting animals out of their pain," and in general showed a mixture of Stage 2 and Stage 3 responses concerning the value of life. At sixteen, he said, "I don't know. In one way, it's murder. It's not a right or a privilege of man to decide who should live and who should die. God put life into everybody on earth and you're taking away something from that person that came directly from God and it's almost destroying a part of God when you kill a person. There's something of God in everyone." Here Richard clearly displays a Stage 4 concept of life as sacred in terms of its place in a moral or religious order. The value of human life is universal; it is true for all humans. It is still, however, dependent on something else, upon respect for God and God's authority; it is not an autonomous human value. Presumably if God told Richard to murder, as God commanded Abraham to murder Isaac, he would do so.

Kohlberg's bias against religion is especially clear here. He simply assumes that the principle of "an autonomous human value" is higher. Thus his scoring system expresses and exposes his ideology. This central problem, i.e., the way his philosophic and ideological assumptions underlie his scoring system, should always be kept in mind.

Furthermore, it is not at all clear how this last answer is a standard Stage 4 answer. That is, it is not obviously directed at system-maintaining or law-and-order. Apparently, the sacredness of life and obedience to God is to Kohlberg the same thing as Archie Bunker's defense of Law and Order. Kohlberg continues:

> At age twenty, Richard said to the same question, "There are more and more people in the medical profession who think it is a hardship on everyone, the person, the family, when you know they are going to die. When a person is kept alive by an artificial lung or kidney, it's more like being a vegetable than being a human. If it's her own choice, I think there are certain rights and privileges that go along with being a human being. I am a human being and have certain desires for life and I think everybody else does too. You have a world of which you are the center, and everybody else does too and in that sense we're all equal." Richard's response is clearly Stage 5, in that the value of life is defined in terms of equal and universal human rights in a context of relativity ("You have a world of which you are the center and in that sense we're all equal"), and of concern for utility or welfare consequences.

> At twenty-four, Richard says: "A human life takes precedence over any other moral or legal value, whoever it is. A human life has inherent value whether or not it is valued by a particular individual. The worth of the individual human being is central where the principles of justice and love are normative for all human relationships." This young man is at Stage 6 in seeing the value of human life as absolute in representing a universal and equal respect for the human as an individual. He has moved step by step through a sequence culminating in a definition of human life as centrally valuable rather than derived from or dependent on social or divine authority.[7,8]

7   The scoring example is in Lawrence Kohlberg, "The Child as a Moral Philosopher," *Readings in Developmental Psychology Today*, Del Mar, Calif: CRM Books 1970.

8   Kohlberg has also speculated about a Seventh Stage with religious overtones where life is valued as a reflection of the "unity of the cosmos." Beyond his initial suggestion about such a stage 7, there is no further literature on this subject.

II. The Empirical Critique

Perhaps the first question to ask is whether the extensive research using and investigating Kohlberg's theory has generally supported the theory's main assumptions: first, the existence of the six stages and, second, the tendency over time to move from a lower to a higher stage and not to regress to a lower, earlier stage. This is not the place to go into a detailed summary of the very extensive research literature; instead, I will present the main conclusions of a thorough recent review of this issue published in 1974. More recent evidence bearing on this issue will also be included.

Kurtines and Greif in their review of the evidence bearing on Kohlberg's theory reach the following conclusions after discussing the first fifteen years of relevant studies.[9] (1) The six stages as described are arbitrary and unclear; (2) The scale which consists of a set of moral dilemmas (Moral Judgment Scale) has not been standardized, i.e., the actual dilemmas used in the scale have not been fixed in number nor kind. Similarly, the scoring procedure has been frequently revised, changed, and is often ambiguous. This has resulted in rather frequent use of scoring categories like "ambiguous," "transitional," etc. In one large study, 46 percent of the responses could not be placed in a stage.[10] The scale's revisions make earlier experiments no longer interpretable; the scoring manual has not been published and is available only by writing Kohlberg. (3) As of 1974, there were no published data on the reliability of the scale and evidence suggests that scores fluctuate greatly even over short periods of time. (4) There is no evidence that scores on the Moral Development Scale can predict any kind of moral action. (Indeed, one study reports that activist students at Berkeley were predominantly either at Stage 6 or at Stage 2.[11] These two very different levels of reasoning led to identical behavior.) In other words, there is no evidence that Kohlberg's stages have any practical bearing on conduct. There is, in particular, no evidence suggesting that the final three stages have any predictive significance. The authors suggest that a scale that divided subjects into two categories such as mature-immature would account for whatever predictive significance Kohlberg's scale of stages has demon-

---

9   William Kurtines and Esther Blank Greif, "The Development of Moral Thought: Review and Evaluation of Kohlberg's Approach," *Psychological Bulletin*, 81, 1974, 453–70.

10   *Ibid.*, p. 459.

11   *Ibid.*, p. 459.

strated. (5) Examination of types of evidence offered in support of the invariant sequence of stages revealed no clear support, and the cross-cultural
data on early development provide no support for qualitative differences
between stages or for their fixed order. Elizabeth Leonie Simpson in a review (1974) addressed just to the issue of cross-cultural evidence for
Kohlberg's stages concludes: "the definitions of stages and the assumptions
underlying them, including the view that the scheme is universally applicable, are ethnocentric and culturally biased."[12] This is perhaps too blanket a
claim as there is some cross-cultural support, but the ideological character
of Kohlberg's system would certainly support Simpson's general point.
Kurtines and Grief note studies which provide considerable coun-
ter-evidence to Kohlberg's assumption that moral development is basically
a form of natural intellectual maturation. These studies show moral judgment can be affected by social influence, such as modeling an adult figure.
From this, Kurtines and Greif concluded the following:

> The possibility remains that the stages do reflect actual development
> and that the general lack of evidence reflects the inadequacy of the
> measuring device used to assess the stages of moral reasoning. How-
> ever, without additional information on the scale or an alternative way
> to assess stages of reasoning, we cannot know whether it is the scale,
> the model, or both that is problematic. Thus, we can only conclude that
> the value of the model remains to be demonstrated.[13]

Although Kurtines and Greif's criticisms have not gone unchallenged,
most of their criticism has been accepted by many psychologists and even in
crucial ways by Kohlberg himself.[14] Kohlberg, for example, has acknowl-

---

12   Elizabeth Leonie Simpson, "Moral Development Research: A Case Study
     of Scientific Bias," *Human Development, 17*, 1974, 81–106.
13   Kurtines and Greif, *op. cit.*, pp. 466–67.
14   The response to Kurtines and Greif is by James Broughton, "Dialectics and
     Moral Development Ideology" in *Readings in Moral Education*, Peter
     Schard (ed.), Minneapolis: Winston Press, 1978, pp. 298–307, and by
     Peter Scharf, "Evaluating the Development of Moral Education: A
     Response to The Critiques of Flowers, Sullivan and Franenkel," *Ibid.* pp.
     288–97. Both responses are short. Although there is some new supporting,
     empirical evidence published after Kurtines and Greif (also new negative
     evidence, not noted), they are no effective rebuttals. Scharf takes for
     granted that all "all systems of oral education make critical assumptions of
     fact and value" (p. 294). One wonders why it took so long for this to be
     acknowledged. Presumably, if it had been understood from the start,

edged that the scale of moral development has never been standardized and has constantly been changed as a result of new problems with the earlier dilemmas. He also acknowledges that the scale's reliability and validity are not really known and that the scale is still only available through his laboratory where it is consistently under revision. He is now trying to remedy this weakness and to make a standard scale generally available.[15]

Kohlberg does, however, defend the empirical existence of the different stages and his developmental order.[16] He claims recent evidence supports his sequence of stages, although he now admits that stage regression may occur. Pointing out that none of his longitudinal subjects had achieved Stage 6 by 1976, Kohlberg lamented at a recent symposium: "Perhaps all the sixth-stage persons of the 1960s had been wiped out, perhaps they had regressed, or maybe it was all my imagination in the first place."[17]

Kohlberg has made a still more important change: He has dropped Stage 6, the highest stage, because; in a recent longitudinal study in America and Turkey, Stage 6 did not show up. He describes this recent major concession in the following manner:

> This result (i.e., the failure to find Stage 6) indicated that my sixth stage was mainly a theoretical construction suggested by the writings of "elite" figures like Martin Luther King, not an empirically confirmed developmental construct. . . . We now think the safest interpretation would be to view the construct of a sixth stage as representing an elaboration of the B (or advanced) substage of Stage 5.[18]

In spite of Kohlberg's attempt to defend the very existence of his stages, many psychologists are quite dubious. Professor Robert Hogan (Johns Hopkins), an especially lucid critic of Kohlberg, quite flatly states that there is no evidence that Kohlberg's stages exist.[19] Of course, different

---

Kohlberg would have made his critical assumptions clear. Scharf also comments rather lamely that Kohlberg's system "is by far the worst pedagogical system in terms of empirical and philosophical morasses, *except for all the others*" (his emphasis), p. 294.

15 He mentions (see Howard Munson, *op. cit.*, p. 57) the recent construction of a standardized scale but as of Fall, 1979, it had not appeared.

16 Lawrence Kohlberg, "Revisions in the Theory and Practice of Moral Development," *New Directions for Child Development*, 2, 1978, 83–87.

17 Howard Munson, *op. cit.*, p. 57.

18 Lawrence Kohlberg, *New Directions for Child Development*, 1978, *op. cit.*, p. 86.

patterns of moral reasoning or explanation exist, but the evidence for stage sequence, especially with respect to the higher stages, does not exist, according to Hogan. Hogan bases his position partly on the fact that Kohlberg's scale for measuring stages has not met the necessary standards of reliability and validity to justify any conclusions about stage existence, much less the order of supposed natural development.[20] Hogan also bases his criticism on evidence from his own research that strongly suggests that the difference between Stage 5 and Stage 6 individuals is a difference in personality type.[21] To claim a difference in a level of moral maturity is, Hogan argues, simply an unacceptable expression of Kohlberg's political beliefs.[22]

In conclusion, the empirical support for Kohlberg's model is tenuous at best and, although the issue is still an active one, the system is beleaguered and quite possibly already fading away. One prominent researcher, Joseph Adelson of the University of Michigan, commented: "I suspect the system [of Kohlberg] is beginning to fall apart."[23] Kohlberg himself describes his model as a "leaky boat" requiring much patching and which may sink.[24]

Putting aside the question of empirical support, we now turn to other types of criticisms, which have been steadily increasing in recent years.

III. The Rational Critique

The central philosophic or rational difficulty in Kohlberg's model is his assumption that moral development can be characterized as a development in morally neutral, rational competence without regard to the actual moral decision or to moral content. Kohlberg emphatically rejects moral relativism and he believes his approach avoids the errors of relativism. He writes:

> The cognitive-developmental or progressive view . . . claims that, at heart, morality represents a set of *rational principles* of *judgement and decision* valid for every culture. . . . Our research into the stages in the development of moral reasoning, then, provides the key to a new approach to moral education as the stimulation of children's moral judgement to the next stage of development.[25]

19 Personal communication, December 1979.
20 *Ibid.*
21 See Robert T. Hogan, "A Dimension of Moral Judgment," *Journal of Consulting and Clinical Psychology*, 35, 1970, 205–12.
22 Personal communication, December 1979.
23 Howard Munson, *op. cit.*, p. 51.
24 *Ibid.*, p. 57.

When psychologists such as Piaget talk about stages of intellectual development, they not only speak of the development of greater cognitive flexibility and differentiation but also show that the higher level leads to correct or more nearly correct answers. They show how the child has a better understanding of an agreed-upon external truth, for example, a truth of logic or mathematics or a truth about perceptual reality. But with morality the idea of reality testing, of being right, is rejected by Kohlberg since he claims there is no such possibility. This focus on mental structure and its development without an absolute standard ultimately leads to the very moral relativity Kohlberg supposedly rejects. I would again like to acknowledge my debt to Wolterstorff, – whose analysis I will often follow in my remarks below.[26]

Why and how does a person move from a lower to a higher stage? The Kohlbergian rationale goes something like this. A person at a lower stage discovers that moral questions become too complex and too conflicting in terms of the concepts which he is currently using. The pressure for cognitive integration and equilibrium leads him to formulate a new set of principles in order to handle moral issues more adequately. At each new and higher stage the person is cognitively more differentiated (complex) and more cognitively integrated in a way that has resolved the cognitive dissonance experienced at the prior stage. A crucial kind of experience which facilitates this growth, according to Kohlberg, is role taking. (Role taking for Kohlberg means the "tendency to react to others as like the self, and to react to the self's behavior from the other's point of view.")[27] Kohlberg posits that the impulse to take the role of others is natural, and that this leads to a natural concern for fairness and justice. It is this role taking in increasingly more varied and complex moral situations that is central to moral education.

Kohlberg's general strategy requires that his concept of cognitive adequacy be value-neutral. He is not claiming that the role-taking impulse and the pattern of reasoning it sets in motion are "good." These are simply natural facts, like any other form of natural growth and development. In spite of this claim, Kohlberg is frequently ambivalent on this matter. He says, for example: "At every stage, children perceive basic values like the value of human life, and are able to empathize and take the roles of other persons."[28]

---

25 Lawrence Kohlberg, in *The Humanist*, 1972, *op. cit.*, p. 14.
26 Nicholas Wolterstorff, *Education for Responsible Action*, Grand Rapids, Mich.: Eudmans, 1980, p. 94.
27 *Ibid.*, p. 102 from Kohlberg, *in Beck, op. cit.*

This is not entirely a descriptive comment for it suggests that people at all stages recognize life as good, and that it is, in fact, good. His tendency to move from neutral descriptions of morality to implicitly valuing such things as life, role-taking abilities, development per se, and finally the justice principle, is a source of chronic confusion in Kohlberg's system.

Perhaps the most controversial stages of Kohlberg have been 5 and 6, which he regards as the most morally advanced, and which are called "the *principled* stages." Thus, the principle of justice is the culminating stage in Kohlberg's moral development system. Now Kohlberg believes this principle, which involves fairness and social welfare, is naturally expressed when moral development proceeds to the highest level. But, as we saw earlier, Kohlberg has recently dropped Stage 6 because the evidence did not support its existence. This fact makes clear what many recent critics of Kohlberg have claimed: namely, that his system has been developed to exemplify his personal concept of morality as embodied in Stage 6, and *not* because the data required it.

Let us look in some detail at Kohlberg's system in terms of the Wolterstorffian analysis.[29] Kohlberg says he does not believe "that moral judgments describe states of the world in somewhat the same way as scientific judgments describe states of the world."[30] Instead, moral judgments and norms are ultimately to be understood as universal mental constructions which regulate social interaction. Kohlberg writes: "A higher conception of the value of love or a higher conception of moral emotion . . . is not directly truer than a lower conception."[31] He goes on in a most peculiar passage to say:

> Our claim that stage 6 is a more moral mode of thought than lower stages is not the claim that we can or should grade individuals as more or less moral. We argue elsewhere that there is no valid or final meaning to judging or grading persons as morally good or bad or judgements of praise and blame are not justified by the existence of universal moral principles as such. At the highest stage, the principle of justice (or the principle of maximizing human welfare) prescribes an obligation to act justly or to blame the unjust or give us rules for meting out blame to the unjust. Although there are some rational

---

28   Kohlberg in Beck, *et. al., op. cit.*, p. 52.
29   Wolterstorff, *Op. Cit.*, p. 104 ef.
30   *Ibid.*, p. 104; from Kohlberg, in Beck *et. al., op. cit.*
31   *Ibid.*, p. 105; from Kohlberg, in Beck, *et. al., op. cit.*, p. 48.

grounds for punishment, there are no ultimately rational or moral grounds for blaming other people. From a moral point of view, the moral worth of all persons is ultimately the same: it is equal.[32]

What has he said? Wolterstorff struggles nobly with this confused passage by first observing that Kohlberg's basic point is that it is never right, as such, or wrong, as such, to do something.[33] Instead, actions are only right or wrong relative to a certain principle. Relative to the justice principle, an action might be wrong. But relative to the utility principle, the same action might be right. And, Kohlberg seems to be arguing, there is no way to determine whether any principle is more right or wrong than another. It is not possible to choose an incorrect principle, as Wolterstorff concludes: "All one can do is apply correctly or incorrectly whatever principle one has chosen."[34]

If Wolterstorff's interpretation is correct, and I can see no alternate interpretation, then Kohlberg holds a special kind of antinomian position. Wolterstorff suggests the name "principle-relative-antinomianism."[35] In any case, Kohlberg considers there to be no absolute moral basis for making a moral judgement about principles of morality. This is the position he shares with Jean-Paul Sartre, R. M. Hare, and others. Consequently, despite his frequent denials of the validity of moral relativism, he ends up with this position himself.

Kohlberg defends his principle of justice because he claims it has the following three properties: first, it is *universal* in that it applies to all persons and all actions; second, it is *prescriptive* in that it states what should or ought to be done; and third, it is *autonomous* for it makes no appeal to what anyone else holds on moral matters – there is no appeal to moral "authority."[36]

Now if Kohlberg means only that these criteria describe the nature of a principle at the highest level of natural development, he has a problem. There are other possible principles which would fill the same requirements besides justice. Wolterstorff points out that the negation of justice meets all the same formal requirements.[37] Evil can be just as rationalized as good.

---

32 *Ibid.*, p. 105; from Kohlberg, in Beck, *et. al.*, *op. cit.*, p. 54
33 See *Ibid.*, p. 105.
34 *Ibid.*, p. 105.
35 This quote is from an earlier draft of the Wolterstorff p. 66.
36 *Ibid.*, pp. 105–107.
37 *Ibid.*, early draft, pp. 70–71.

Similarly, other possible principles such as those based on utility, mercy, and above all, a principle of love, cannot be ignored. Furthermore, there are times when Kohlberg seems to imply that his criteria for a principle are themselves intrinsically good. It is clear, for example, that Kohlberg believes autonomy, i.e., independence from any authority, is a desirable quality. When he slips into this mode of expression, he has, of course, violated his assumption of neutrality. For it is often very clear that Kohlberg regards Stage 6, based on universality, prescriptiveness, and autonomy, to be the *best* pattern of moral reasoning and not just the last natural stage. In doing this, he has taken an ideological stance.

Apparently, it is not just Kohlberg's critics who have been disturbed by his tendency to mix values with the supposed neutral processes of moral steps. Kohlberg himself – after twenty years of insisting on neutrality in moral education – has finally reversed his position:

> Although the moral stage concept is valuable for research purposes, however, it is not a sufficient guide to the moral educator, who deals with concrete morality in a school world in which value content, as well as structure, behavior and reasoning must be dealt with. In this context, the educator must be a socializer, teaching value content and behavior, not merely a Socratic facilitator of development. In becoming a socializer and advocate, the teacher moves into "indoctrination," a step that I originally believed to be invalid both philosophically and psychologically. I thought indoctrination invalid philosophically because the value content taught was culturally and personally relative, and because teaching value content was a violation of the child's rights. I thought indoctrination invalid psychologically because it could not lead to a meaningful structural change. I no longer hold these negative views of indoctrinative moral education, and I now believe that the concepts guiding moral education must be partly indoctrinative.[38]

This dramatic about-face by Kohlberg retroactively changes the meaning of his previous work a great deal. And until he integrates this new position with it, the present critique stands. At a minimum, he would have to make explicit the particular values in his indoctrination. In any case, the supposed moral neutrality of Kohlberg's present system can be rejected on straight rational or philosophical grounds.

IV. The Ideological Critique

38 Lawrence Kohlberg, *New Directions for Child Development, op. cit.*, p. 84.; See also Kohlberg, in *The Humanist*, Nov.-Dec., 1978, pp. 13–15.

The most recent and powerful attacks on Kohlberg, all from secular social scientists, have focused on the political and ideological assumptions embedded in his position. The most important of these have been the critiques by Sullivan and by Hogan and Emler.[39] I will present their analysis in some detail, leaning primarily on the work of the latter two psychologists. This critique is extremely important because it is not just leveled against Kohlberg, but against social psychology as a whole, and, indeed, against all social science. It is part of the now rapidly growing awareness within social science that there is no neutral or objective theory, nor is such a theory in principle even possible. This collapse of the implicit assumption of objectivity amongst social scientists has profound and encouraging implications for the use of Christian models of human nature within what has been called impartial social "science."

Hogan and Emler very generally see Kohlberg's theory as an expression of liberal ideology.[40] Specifically, they charge it with containing four major assumptions which Kohlberg has not examined nor even made explicit – assumptions of an intrinsically ideological kind.

The first assumption is that of *rationalism*. For Kohlberg, moral development is an entirely cognitive process. He is only concerned with setting up abstract moral problems or dilemmas which pit various abstract principles against each other. His intent is to focus reasoning on a choice between two different moral principles in such a way that the person's criteria for the choice are revealed. The entire concern is with getting rational arguments from the subject – arguments or reasons that defend his choice. Kohlberg's position totally ignores moral action. (In particular, I might add, there is no concern at all with the will). Equally obvious is Kohlberg's neglect of the profound emotional and interpersonal elements involved in all natural moral dilemmas. For Kohlberg, "I think, therefore I am" is clearly his fundamental approach to understanding the human moral situation. Kohlberg's use of highly abstract and often contrived moral dilemmas is one expression of his extreme rationalism. Apparently, Kohlberg is also now backing away from this property of his prior work, for he has recently spoken disparag-

---

39 E. V. Sullivan, "A Study of Kohlberg's Structural Theory of Moral Development: A Critique of Liberal Social Science Ideology," *Human Development*, 20 (1977), pp. 352–76, and Robert T. Hogan and Nicholas Emler, "The Biases in Contemporary Social Psychology," *Social Research*, 45, 978, 478–534.

40 Hogan and Emler, *op. cit.*, p. 518 ef.

ingly of his hypothetical, rational examples as "science fiction" dilemmas.[41]

Kohlberg also assumes that the natural direction of moral development supports and implies *individualism*. That is, he assumes that morality develops toward internalized moral controls in which the individual is socially and morally autonomous. Each individual is presumed to be able to ultimately discover for himself or herself a natural morality that owes nothing to cultural or historical heritage. The belief in the isolated autonomous individual is, of course, a fiction, since it is itself an expression, a creature, produced by our particular contemporary secular humanist culture. Kohlberg simply assumes, without discussion, that obedience to the self is superior to obedience to God. The nature of this self is not presented by Kohlberg, but he appears to assume it is entirely intrinsically good (why else make it the highest court?). If this is so, then the criticism of this psychological position in the case of Values Clarification holds with equal force for Kohlberg.

The assumption of individualism, as Hogan and Emler note, is smuggled into Kohlberg's theory by the use of moral issues which involve primarily individualistic values such as property, civil rights, the value of human life, and individual conscience.[42] Thus his examples implicitly assert the moral conclusion that "an individual's rights to life and control over his or her own affairs are the paramount values in life."[43]

Another basic assumption of Kohlberg's is that of *liberalism*. Hogan and Emler identify Stage 6, with its concern with the concept of justice, as an expression of Kohlberg's personal philosophy.[44] This stage, now dropped as previously mentioned, had been given great emphasis as the highest form of moral reasoning. Hogan and Emler identify the moral philosophies of Kant, Hare and especially John Rawls as influencing Kohlberg here.[45] It seems inappropriate for present purposes to go into a detailed treatment of liberal moral philosophy. Suffice it to say, whatever moral philosophy one takes, liberal or otherwise, it is seriously misleading to neglect discussing this issue and then to imply that one's theory is a pure expression of how human nature naturally develops when it grows to the highest state, as verified by objective evidence.

---

41   Howard Munson, *op. cit.*, p. 51.
42   Hogan and Emler, *op. cit.*, pp. 524–25.
43   *Ibid.*, p. 525.
44   *Ibid.*, pp. 525–26.
45   *Ibid.*, p. 527.

A further criticism of Kohlberg is that his theory is *androcentric*, that is, it expresses a "characteristically masculine view of morality." Carol Gilligan, a colleague of Kohlberg, has made this point rather well.[46] She points out that the initial 1958 study, which is still the core of empirical support, was run exclusively on young male subjects, from which Kohlberg generalized to everyone. Gilligan also claims that the preoccupation with male values – such as rationalism, individualism, and liberalism – is responsible for the fact that adult females are found, according to Kohlberg, to be disproportionately in Stage 3. Males tended to be "more morally advanced," and located at Stage 4. (Stage 3 is "good boy, nice girl," or conventional morality; Stage 4 is "system-maintaining morality," e.g., law and order). Kohlberg has responded to this criticism by deciding he made a mistake in how he scored Stage 4. He has subsequently claimed that many males who had been scored at Stage 4 were really giving answers at Stage 2.[47] That such an error could have been made for so many years strikingly underlines the ideological biases present in the scoring system and further reduces confidence in it. Gilligan succinctly summarizes the quite different approach to moral problems taken by women. Consider the well-known Kohlberg dilemma of Heinz. Heinz must steal a drug from a village druggist since it costs much more than he can pay – or let his wife die. Gilligan writes:

> Here in the light of its probable outcome – his wife dead, or Heinz in jail, brutalized by the violence of the experience and his life compromised by a record of felony – the dilemma itself changes. Its resolution has less to do with the relative weights of life and property in an abstract moral conception than with the collision it has produced between two lives, formerly conjoined but now in opposition, where the continuation of one life can now occur only at the expense of the other. Given this construction, it becomes clear why consideration (for women) revolves around the issue of sacrifice and why guilt becomes the inevitable concomitant of either resolution.[48]

She continues:

> The proclivity of women to reconstruct hypothetical dilemmas in terms of the real, to request or supply the information missing about

---

46 Carol Gilligan, "In a Different Voice: Women's Conception of the Self and of Morality," *Harvard Educational Review*, 47, 1077, pp. 481–517.

47 Howard Munson, *op. cit.*, p. 57.

48 Gilligan, *Op. Cit.*, p. 512.

the nature of people and the places where they live, shifts their judgement away from the hierarchical ordering of principles and the formal procedures of decision-making that are critical for scoring at Kohlberg's highest stages. Given the constraints of Kohlberg's system and the biases in his research sample, this different orientation can only be construed as a failure in development. While several of the women in the research sample clearly articulated what Kohlberg regarded as a postconventional meta-ethical position, none of them were considered by Kohlberg to be principled in their normative moral judgments. Instead, the women's judgements pointed toward an identification of the violence inherent in the dilemma itself which was seen to compromise the justice of any of its possible resolutions. This construction of the dilemma led the women to recast the moral judgement from a consideration of the good to a choice between evils.[49]

Gilligan quite correctly proposes that in giving exclusive moral weight to the principle of justice, Kohlberg underestimates the moral worth of other principles especially mercy. Hogan and Emler, as does Gilligan, describe this by citing Shakespeare: Thus the female virtue of mercy becomes a stage 3 conception. But, as Portia reminds Shylock, mercy qualifies justice, "though justice be thy plea, consider this, that in the course of justice, none of us should see salvation. We do pray for mercy."[50]

Gilligan sees Kohlberg's absence of concern for interpersonal and emotional issues in moral problems as androcentrism. A Christian would simply point out that the principle of love as a synthesis of mercy and justice is, in fact, a higher principle than justice.

One final ideological bias in Kohlberg, not mentioned by Hogan and Emler, is his *atheism*. This assumption lies behind Kohlberg's favoring individual autonomy and explains his placing answers giving a religious rationale as Stage 4. As mentioned, he assumes, among other things, that any reasoning based on accepting authority, human or divine, derives from rules – not from principles. Christian love, however, is a principle in the Kohlberg sense.

Two important concluding points: first, throughout Kohlberg's writings, I can find no treatment of man's capacity for evil – for exploiting others, for hatred and aggression, etc. By assuming that an individual with a reasonably favorable environment is naturally capable of developing to the highest level of moral reasoning, Kohlberg is making the same assumptions

---

49   *Ibid.*
50   Hogan and Emler, *op. cit.*, p. 529.

about the innate goodness of the self that are made by so many contemporary secular humanists – e.g., the Values Clarification theorists. As a result, all of the earlier criticism of this assumption bears directly on Kohlberg and provides another strong reason for rejecting his position. (See *Psychology as Religion: The Cult of Self Worship*, by Paul C. Vitz, Eerdmans, Grand Rapids, Mich., 1977). Second, when Kohlberg's system is introduced into schools, Christian parents are made to think they are at a lower moral level than the Stage-Six secular-humanist goal of the program. Since the parents are not in a position to see through Kohlberg, such Christians are "put down" very heavily and most unjustly by educationists, who present the Kohlberg system as the latest in impartial science.

Summing up: Although Kohlberg's model is of considerable interest to those doing research on moral development, his theory's empirical, rational, ideological, and Christian weaknesses are so great that one is hard put to find any reason for its widespread use in Christian moral education.

7.

Toward a Hermeneutic of Sexuality (1980)

Rev. Donald J. Keefe, S.J.

I.

In this most pagan and pragmatic age, it is difficult to speak of fundamental moral issues without an immediate confusion over the meaning of the terms employed. Particularly is this the case in those discussions which bear upon human sexuality. The contemporary parlance has lent to the vocabulary of sex a primarily empirical denotation; associated with this is a welter of elusive connotations whose vagaries tangle any discussion in a jungle of tangential issues which must somehow be cleared away if anything at all is to be communicated. This is a most ungrateful task: The day is past when even the hierarchy could rule upon the meaning of words. Language belongs to the community which uses it, and its vitality is its usage, its historicity.

But the democracy of language warrants and legitimates every contribution to the reworking of its verbal symbols, its structure of meaning. That structure is nothing else than the living consensus of the linguistic community, the community whose reality is the presupposition and the object of all teaching, all preaching, all communication of the truth. Part of the Church's mission, and not the least important part, is the upholding of the integrity of the symbols which, in their organic totality, constitute the faith-consensus of the people of God, their utterance into history of their unity in Christ, and their invitation to all who would share that unity. This utterance is integral to the pluralism of the whole linguistic community; like all other elements of that totality, the Catholic community is entitled to teach its faith, to enter vitally into the vitality of the common exchange of symbolic meaning, of the common struggle for the fullness of the truth of our common humanity. The price of doing so is the conflict and controversy which mark our fallen history, but the price of abstention is higher: the abdication of our historical reality, of the historical mission of the Church, and a surrender of the truth of Christ to the secular verities of contemporary humanism.

Such a surrender need not be deliberate. A little effort is required to resist the symbolic devaluation implicit in the pragmatic least-common-denominator solution to the problem of meaning as that problem is encountered in a technologically advanced civilization. Technology tends to an impatience with all language which resists reduction to the univocity of merely mathematical symbols.

Such univocity must eliminate all the qualitative differentiation of human life which we signify by such words as "dignity," "freedom," "morality," and the like, for univocal symbols deal solely with the measurable, the calculable, and the fungible integers of statistics. When our sexual symbols are submitted to this reduction, even by inadvertence, their qualitative significance is evacuated, dismissed from the recognition and reinforcement which they have traditionally received from the language of the Church's worship within the linguistic community.

All this is a prelude to the theological assertion that the proper and true meaning and significance of our sexuality is its sacramentality. As male or female, we are existential symbols of the holy; more, this symbolism is intrinsic to the truth of the revelation – Christ in his Church. Its truth is mystery, as Paul has insisted, the mystery of the New Creation, the New Adam, and the New Eve. So deeply rooted is the truth of our sexuality in the truth of the Catholic faith that any neglect of the former, any dilution of its splendor, imports some failure in the latter. This is a failure on the level of our sacramental worship, not to be remedied by further education or a higher level of sophistication, whether secular or theological. In short, we have here to do with sin, with "the mystery of iniquity," the "impossible possibility" of rejecting our own imaging of God. This possibility is always before us: that refusal to be which is the dark side of our dignity, a refusal of the light which enlightens all men.

The recognition that our humanity is sacramental, and that all true statements about it must respect this sacramentality, must then govern our discussion of sexual morality. We are forbidden a simple-minded reliance upon the results of scientific inquiry for the understanding of the language bearing upon sexuality, sexual activity, and masculinity and femininity; for no empirical science is interested or can be interested in the sacramentality of humanity. To recognize this is not to dismiss the value of the empirical sciences. It is only to remember that there is only one source of truth adequate to our needs – Christ in his Church, which no scientific methodology may be permitted to supplant. The various sciences may well provide indispensable questions, but even this they cannot do apart from their prior sub-ordination to a transcendent truth which is beyond the range of any methodology. By this subordination, the sciences become theologies; lacking it, they can only continue to refuse to interest themselves in the sacramental truth of our humanity.

II.

Sacramentality is not an easy concept to grasp, as the history of theology amply demonstrates. It is founded upon a worldview which finds the significance of historical creation in its complex relation to the Kingdom of God, to the Parousia, to the Second Coming of the Christ. From this viewpoint – which is particularly clear in the Pauline epistles and in the Gospel according to St. John – it is only in the fullness of creation, in the end-time of the Parousia, that the actual splendor of creation can appear; until then, the Fall continues at once to sully the beauty of our world and ourselves, and to dim our eyes and spirit to the real beauty it still possesses, and to darken our mind to its full truth and significance. Only by faith is the true worth of things given to us. By faith, we can know that the world is "very good," holy, charged with the splendor of God, and signed with his love; minimally, we can know that there is more here than meets the eye – we stand on holy ground, and we must be alert to the possibility of its profanation.

From all this has arisen the concern with tabu and uncleanliness which the comparative study of religions has made so familiar. From the earliest sources which can be identified as human, there is evident a continuing preoccupation with the numinous, with the *mysterium fascinosum et tremendum* which indefinably undergirds our world, and which is experienced most immediately and profoundly in the sexual relation.

The history of religions is the history of the obdurancy of the sexual symbolism, of its indispensability and of its irreducibility to any other more plastic, less adamantine reality. All attempts to eliminate its mystery, usurp its primacy, exorcise its presence, or deflect its dynamism have failed. It has defeated all attempts at its rationalization, whether by the subordination of one of its bi-polar elements to the other, by their merger into a simple univocal and unipolar symbol, or by their dissociation into two clear and distinct ideas with no intrinsic reference to each other. Man remains man, woman remains woman: Each is indispensable to the other; neither is prior to nor reducible to the other. Equal in their truth, neither masculinity nor femininity has its proper truth except as totally referred to the other; each discovers its own symbolic content by no narcissistic self-scrutiny, but by a self-donation to the polar other whose qualitatively different symbolic content is the warrant for and the indispensable support of that discovery of the significance of personal and human existence.

The truth of human sexuality, of the actual relationship between man and woman, has continued to be the fundamental structure of our existence and a humanly unfathomable enigma. We can neither ignore it nor comprehend it without being false to ourselves: It is our own mystery, a basic symbol, even the basic symbol of our ultimate meaning. That meaning is beyond us while remaining most intimately within us: truly our own. Its enigma, intrinsic to our own subjectivity, is our continuing and profoundly personal hunger for a union and a self-forgetfulness beyond anything we can conceive or utter; of this transcendent fulfillment all the great religions have spoken; and common to all their speaking, whether we are talking about pagan, Jewish, or Christian religions, is a sexual imagery, a sexual symbolism − for the structure of sexual existence, marked by ecstatic self-donation to a qualitatively other, actually provides the ultimate symbol of our union with God. So intimately linked are these things that any deformation of the truth of one corresponds to a deformation of the other; our attitude toward the sexual symbol, our approach to our own mystery, is continuous with our understanding of our final union with God. Where the relation between the sexes is taken to be ambivalent, and is characterized by an antagonism in which each seeks to eliminate the value of the other, because threatened by it, ambivalence also characterizes the understanding of salvation, which becomes equally contested, oscillating between a pantheistic obliteration of man and a radical denial of God. This is the path of the great Eastern religions outside the Judaeo-Christian tradition: It is also that of the ideological competitors with the Judaeo-Christian religious tradition such as the gnostic systems of the second century and the utopian systems which have appeared sporadically in the Christian West from the twelfth century onwards. The existential experience of reality, both within and without, as ambivalent, riddled with contradiction, and absurd, is the denial of all significance to historical humanity: It can find in the sexual relation only the hallmark of human futility. Salvation is seen as deliverance from this despair, a deliverance achieved by the elimination of the polarities experienced as ambivalent. But this is the elimination of the *mysterium fascinosum et tremendum,* of the encounter with the holy, whose primary symbol is that of human sexuality. Salvation in this despairing guise is the devaluation of the sexual polarity, its reduction to a merely pragmatic significance. Sexuality is then simply a fact to be understood in terms of its subordination to whatever secular salvation scheme may be in view. In our own day, men tend to look to technology as the agent of salvation; implicit in this tendency is the usurpation of any revelatory function by the scientific method. It is this methodology which now is increasingly understood to bestow meaning upon man and his world, and to do so by reducing all qualitative differences to differences in quantity. The attempt to reduce truth to number and number to unity is coeval with the earliest expressions of philosophical reason; underlying it is a far older religious stratum which would find salvation by a flight from all the enigmatic hazards of existence, from the experience of ambivalent temporal existence. Particularly obnoxious to this pagan mentality is the religious value placed in the qualitative distinction between the masculine and the feminine by Catholic sacramental worship. The sanctity of this intrinsic sexual qualification of human existence is inseparable from Catholic worship, and from the morality which is its outgrowth, but the assertion of that holiness, as in the sacrament of marriage, is heard with an increasing uneasiness in our society, acclimated as it is increasingly to another faith than that preached in the Church.

It is, therefore, not possible to set out the meaning of sexuality and its cognates without taking a position in an ongoing controversy, which is not simply one between Christian and non-Christian, Protestant and Catholic, but is a controversy that is also dividing Catholics. This should not be wondered at, if the sexual symbolism is of the fundamental importance defended here. In fact, it would be difficult to find a serious controversy in the history of Christianity which did not have some impact on this symbolism. If we would discover a firm basis for a Catholic discussion of sexuality, the meanings assigned the bipolar elements of the sexual symbol must be those drawn from the experience of the people of God where that experience is most concrete and most authentic: in the worship of the Church. That worship is now nearly two thousand years old. It rests upon a tradition of worship whose patriarchal roots are nearly as old again. During these four millennia of the worship of the Lord of History, the pessimism of the pagan experience of existence has been continually rejected, to be replaced by the experience which Gerhard von Rad and Eric Voegelin have described as the experience of order in history under God as the Lord of History. This experience, this faith, includes the conviction that the world is created good, that its history is the medium of our salvation because God is present and active within it, making it to be holy.

Prominent in the revelation to which this faith has responded is the use of sexual imagery, of a sexual symbolism; the culmination of this use is to be found in the culmination of the presence of God in history, in the finality of Revelation which is the incarnation of our Lord through the immaculate sexuality of our Lady, who is the symbol, and the glory, of the good creation. Thereby she is also the antetype of the Church; and in the Pauline captivity epistles the relation between Christ and his Body the Church is seen to be the basis, the ground, for the Christian truth of marriage, in which the real, historical, and therefore salvific truth of the sexual symbol is concretely expressed in sacramental worship.

This truth, which is normative for the hermeneutic of sexuality, is thus to be found, not by abstract considerations drawn from the sciences or from philosophy or law, but from the worship which is the continual appropriation of the Revelation by the Church in which the Revelation is continually present. This appropriation is most evident, most explicit, and most clearly witnessed to and uttered when and where the worship is most sharply challenged by practices or doctrines encountered as false, as profanations of the good creation and as rejections of its Lord. Thus, the magisterial *moral* teaching is for the most part defensive; it forbids that conduct which is incompatible with and contradictory to the sacramental existence and historical worship of the Church and its members. The *doctrinal* tradition also may be defensive, as in the upholding of the sacramentality of marriage; but its richer part has to do with the sacramental symbol itself as it is made historically concrete in the relation of the Christ to his Mother, of Christ to the Church. The Church's liturgical, moral, and doctrinal tradition is, then, the historical *a priori* upon which all Catholic consideration of sexual morality must find its ground. The meaning of our sexuality has been and will continue to be a mystery, our mystery, a truth beyond all manipulation by theory or technology. It is discovered, gradually and with difficulty, by the people of God, who engage in that worship with the cares, questions, and problems which mark the Church's existence in history. This communal discovery process is by now an ancient one: Its achievements are real and true, and not to be gainsaid, for their ground is the presence in history, in the community, of the Lord of History, of Him Who is our Truth.

The knowledge thus gained is knowledge of a mystery; any attempt to enclose it within any pragmatic, non-mysterious symbolism can only deprive it of its mystery and deform it. This means that we can give it only a negative verbal expression. This limitation should not disturb us. It is, after all, quite comparable to that which prevented the framers of our federal constitution from providing any positive definition of the constitutive freedom of man which that document is intended to protect. This fundamental human truth is expressed by pointing out in the Bill of Rights, and forbidding, certain kinds of governmental action which would be fundamentally in contradiction to it and therefore violations, profanations, of it. If we are to understand the mystery of sexuality, the truth of the sexual symbolism which is as constitutive of our humanity as is the freedom which the Bill of Rights would protect, we must also approach this truth by a common recognition of the conduct which stands in contradiction to it. This recognition is a continual and communal affair, as is the worship which grounds it: It is a consciousness of the reality of sin, and is inseparable from an awareness of the presence of Christ in the Church.

III.

Our contemporary moral quandary owes its emergence to an unprecedented achievement: the near-universal recognition that moral freedom is indispensable to a truly human existence. Until very recently – the First World War is perhaps the watershed dividing the old epoch from the new – morality was a matter of the customary observance of norms little reflected upon and consequently inadequately internalized. The norms themselves were a mix of moral doctrine, overly simplified canon law, theological casuistry, and conventional notions of social propriety, largely obediential, and all placed upon much the same level of importance. Christian virtue was in practice reduced to conformity to these norms, and the norms were understood in juridical terms as obligations imposed by unassailable authority. The consequence was a static morality which forgot nothing and learned very little. For as long as societies themselves underwent internal change at a glacial pace, such a view of morality, however inadequate, was not generally encountered as oppressive; where new questions do not arise out of new conflicts and tensions, the old answers tend to suffice. But some novelty is inescapable, and over the centuries the commonplace obediential morality, with its too easy identification of sin with crime and vice versa, began slowly to accumulate tensions, and this because of the dynamics of Christianity itself. The severities of the public penitential practice gave way to private confession and private penance; the identification of Church and state inherited from the Roman empire by way of Constantine gave way to an uneasy correlation between the new nation states and the universal Church. The early supposition that only a barter economy could be just gave way to the perceived justice of interest charges in the novel circumstances of a money economy. All of these movements were officially resisted: All prevailed. Parallel to them, contemporaneous with them, were other movements, also resisted, which did not prevail: Arianism, Nestorianism, Monophysitism; the new morality preached severally by the Montanists, the Docetists, the Priscillians, the Albigensians, the Spiritual Franciscans, the Jansenists, and the Protestant Reformers. These failures were marked by a single common denominator: a pessimistic view of the relation between God and man in history. It is by this that they each were found incompatible with the radical optimism of Catholic worship. But within that worship a ferment has been at work which in less embattled circumstances might have been welcomed; that it was not, that it has been resisted continually, has something to do with our fallen inability to accept the fullness of the Christian revelation of the union, and, therefore, the compatibility, of God and man in Christ. It is by this revelation that we know that human freedom is "very good," that it is not erosive of law and morality. And yet, only in the last half of the twentieth century, more than nineteen centuries after the Resurrection, has it been officially proclaimed that human freedom is essential to, prerequisite to, Catholic worship. It is a great tragedy that the advocacy of freedom took place in precincts so remote from Catholicism that its meaning became associated, within the Church as well as outside it, with opposition or at best indifference to the Catholic doctrinal and moral tradition. And yet the enfranchisement of all humanity is as essential to that tradition as it is to the sacramental worship which has nourished it. In such circumstances, the Church took a more and more authoritarian posture in its externals of cult and institution, while within a pressure built, a demand for institutional recognition of the mature free responsibility of the Catholic people. When this recognition finally came, the consequences were explosive: The real antagonism between Christian freedom and the authoritarianism of the pre-Conciliar governance of the Church, so suddenly revealed and acknowledged, seemed to undercut the very possibility of institutional religion as such, and so to relativize moral and doctrinal tradition. Contributing to and accelerating this disruption was the release of a long pent-up resentment, manifested in a multitude of ways – all of them scandalous to the pre-Conciliar mentality and destructive of the obediential conventions of the recent past. The aftermath of this explosion is, of course, chaotic, and this is particularly true in the realm of morality and in moral theology – which are by no means to be identified, by the way.

Christian morality, Catholic morality, is the quality of individual and communal existence *in Christo* which alone is consistent with the worship of the Church. As has been remarked, this is communal and consensual, a matter of free communal discovery in a discovery process which is sustained only by the continuity in worship of the people of God. Only in free responsibility can one contribute to the moral consensus of the Church; however, freedom is not a matter of black or white, of yes or no; none of us are ever entirely free in this life, and there are none who are entirely without freedom, either. Nevertheless, the official attitude toward freedom in the Church was so fearful and inhibited – and not entirely without reason – that little contribution to the moral consensus could be made by the average person in areas in which a contribution was essential. This has been particularly true of marriage itself, in which the celibate clergy is only secondarily concerned. While it is obviously true that all participation in the sacrament of matrimony is a concrete affirmation of the holiness of sexuality and, thereby, a real and effective contribution to the moral consensus, it is also true that the lived experience of this sacramental worship was permitted little voice in the academic discussion of moral questions, apart from the incalculable interchange within the confessional. Such matters were the province of the moralist, and the moralists presented a united and static front: The categories of nature and of law dominated their discussions, and left little room for freedom, even for the freedom essential to worship itself. The artificial academic consensus shaped by this notion of morality disintegrated as soon as catholic freedom was institutionalized at Vatican II, and no *theological* consensus on the major issues of sexual morality has come to replace the synthetic unanimity which has now vanished.

But this is not at all to say that no consensus exists within Catholicism with regard to sexual morality. The Catholic worship *is* the consensus. The problem before us is not the reality of the moral consensus but its articulation, an articulation at once ecclesial and free, authentic and responsible. Such an expression is at heart liturgical; it is never a theology, for it rests on ground more firm than human learning. It is never a system of law, for it is at one with the grace-sustained spontaneity of the worship of the Church. It provides the soil out of which all theology, all law, emerge, and furnishes the norm by which they are continually judged and reformed. This articulation of the consensus is then not technical in any sense, nor does it respond to any technological analysis. Its historicity and concreteness are that of a sacramental sign, given irrevocably, present and effective in the Church: a continuing community in communion with the risen Christ in his Kingdom. This *koinonia* is obviously Eucharistic; it is also baptismal (credal), penitential (moral), and marital (sexual). The maturation and the decline of its members are signed by confirmation and anointing; their unity across the centuries and across the diversity of the world of men is that of the apostles, whose successors continue to be radically responsible for the central and Eucharistic worship of the apostolic Church, and thus also for its holiness, its unity, and its catholicity. The nature of this responsibility has been clarified as its weight has been borne – and shirked – since the first Pentecost, a responsibility which is liturgical. An integral element of this responsibility is doctrinal, magisterial – for the worship of the Church must be a worship in truth, a liturgical and communal response to the perennial question of "Who do you say that I am?"

The Petrine reply continues to be our own, and it is not dissociable from that of Paul, who saw in the Christ the Bridegroom of the Church and found in that marital union the truth, the liturgical significance, and the actual and historical meaning of our sacramental sexuality, which has no other meaning or value than that which the Church celebrates in her liturgy. The depth of truth will never be exhausted by our inquiry; but it cannot be approached unless that inquiry is assimilated to the liturgy. Secular questions are simply beside the point; they are not directed at the reality; and if their interest prevails, the reality can only be dismissed.

We are not accustomed to thinking in the terms which are necessary today. In the recent past, matrimony was a matter for canonists rather than for theologians: The notion that sexuality may have something more to say than is detailed in *Casti Connubii* and the Allocution of Pius XII to the Midwives is even now heard with a considerable misgivings. To suggest that an adequate understanding of the meaning of human sexuality – adequate, that is, to the contemporary needs of the Roman Catholic community – is not possible without a recognition of the liturgical unity of matrimony, priestly celibacy, vowed chastity, the restriction of orders to men, and the "one flesh" of the Eucharistic celebration is to be seen to indulge in extravagance. It may be doubted, nonetheless, that a less extensive enterprise will serve. The Catholic and liturgical hermeneutic of sexuality is under general attack on a multiplicity of fronts, and it must be said here that not the least remorseless enemy of that sacramentality is the practice of the canonists staffing the Church's diocesan marriage tribunals in this country. A particularistic defense will not serve to meet these challenges, whether as a reply to their increasingly explicit pagan symbolism or as the basis for a competent Catholic moral theology. Only when some intimation of the splendor of sexual existence is an integrating part of what may be called a Catholic consciousness will the real degradation, the profanation of that splendor by the deformation of its symbolism be understood for what it is: nothing else but a radical and ultimately pagan denial of the Lord of History.

8.
Freedom, Christian Values, and Secular Values (1980)
Joseph M. Boyle

In considering the values involved in contemporary ideologies and social movements, one can hardly fail to notice some common themes – for example, the suspicion of or even disregard for traditionally established norms and authorities. Another, related example is an emphasis by many people today on freedom. Certainly, if one considers the rhetoric of most post-Christian social movements and ideologies, freedom and its cognates can be seen to play an essential role. The therapeutic value system of the post-industrial West is almost defined by its emphasis on a certain kind of freedom – the freedom from binding commitments which can cause pain and frustration and can even lead to fanaticism. The imperial self is unintelligible without the right to choose, to pursue any option, to find any kind of fulfillment.[1]

Moreover, this Western bourgeois conception of freedom is not the only freedom esteemed by those who have split with the Christian understanding of human life. The liberation movements of Marxist orientation are also based upon the judgment that people must be freed from the oppression of a capitalist social order which prevents the proper development of human potentiality.

This post-Christian emphasis on freedom – even when propounded by agents of Christian churches – often includes a scornful evaluation of the traditional Christian understanding of human life. The Christian emphasis on obedience to the will of God seems outrageous from the perspective of contemporary secularized Pelagianism.

Yet Christianity itself has always cherished freedom. The freedom of

---

1 For a fuller discussion of "the imperial self" see James Hitchcock, *Catholicsim and Modernity: Confrontation or Capitulation?* New York: 1979, pp. 31–37.

the children of God was emphasized by St. Paul and has been articulated by the great theologians. The notion of free choice was first developed in the Old Testament and has become a distinctive feature of Christian anthropology and morality.

It seems appropriate, therefore, to focus on freedom – a notion which is very central in the post-Christian scheme of things, but which is also very central to the Christian understanding of man and human values.

It is not my purpose here to argue in an extended way on any of the perplexing and controversial questions about freedom. Rather, my effort is to clarify the idea of freedom and to exhibit the distinctions and oppositions which must be kept in mind if there is to be clear-headed argumentation about freedom and the related questions of values. To put some order into my presentation, I will divide my presentation into a discussion of each of the following theses: (1) "Freedom" has a number of related meanings; these must be kept distinct if there is to be any clear, critical discussion of freedom and related concepts. (2) One "kind" of freedom, namely, free choice, is almost universally denied by post-Christian ideology, but is an essential part of the Christian view of human life; this opposition has far-reaching implications of both a practical and theoretical nature – implications that have direct bearing on one's evaluation of other kinds of freedom. (3) The Christian view of freedom – emphasizing the free choice of men and the freedom of the children of God together with an unqualified demand that Christians gratefully obey God in all things – is not incoherent, and is objectionable only if one assumes questionable propositions about freedom which are inconsistent with Christian faith.

I. The Sense of "Freedom"

My first point is that the word "freedom" is used to designate a number of distinct things which do not have a common definition.[2] This is also true of words like "responsible," which include freedom in their definition. Thus, the various meanings of freedom are not species of a common genus. Rather, the term is used in a number of analogous or systematically equivo-

---

2 The different senses of freedom have been clarified at great length by Mortimer Adler in *The Idea of Freedom*, vol. 2, Garden City, NY, 1961; a briefer analysis which is somewhat different from Adler's is in Joseph M. Boyle, Jr., Germain Grisez, and Olaf Tollefsen, *Free Choice: A Self-Referential Argument*, Notre Dame: 1976, pp. 8–10; the analysis presented in the following paragraphs is directly based on this latter work.

cal ways. The different meanings of the word do involve common elements, but these elements themselves shift in meaning in the different senses of "free."

It will, I trust, become clear enough that the different things called "freedom" do not fall into the same category. My own conviction on this matter is based on my experience in working on free will and determinism. The shifts of the meaning of "free" are clear after very little reading and discus- sion on this subject. The undergraduate objection – "I didn't have a free choice because my father commanded me to do it" – is one example. The sophism at the base of the compatibilist position known as "soft determinism" is another: "Free" is not opposed to "determined" but only to "coerced."

When a person acts freely in any of the various senses of freedom, the action involves the following two elements: that the person is acting or behaving, and that there is something which in some sense could be, but is not actually, in opposition to the activity. Thus, we can further distinguish the person or agent, the activity, and the potentially but not actually opposing or inhibiting factor. If this factor actually did inhibit or oppose the person's activity, the activity would not be free.

A consideration of the various kinds of activities persons can perform and the various ways in which these activities might and might not be opposed or inhibited generates a list of the various sorts of freedom. In what follows, I will try to generate such a list – focusing on the senses of freedom that are widely used today.

In one sense a person is said to act freely when the person acts without external constraint or restraint. Animals and even non-living things can be said to be free in this sense – as the phrases "born free" and "freely falling bodies" suggest. The agent in this kind of freedom need not be human; the activity involved is behavior that is natural or spontaneous but is not necessarily voluntary; the potentially opposing factor is external restraint of some sort – the bars of a cage or playpen, for example. For want of a better phrase, I will call freedom of this kind "physical freedom."

One might say that a person who is free in this sense is free to do as he or she pleases. The behavior the person wishes to do is not limited by external factors. However, there is another sense of "free to do as one pleases" which refers not to the lack of physical restraint but to the character of the basis for the behavior. An adolescent, for example, is not free to do as he pleases if what he wants to do is forbidden by his parents, even if there is no lack of physical freedom involved. The lack of freedom arises because of the conflict between the adolescent's desires and the parents' commands. Furthermore, the lack of freedom is not removed by doing the forbidden action; the adolescent is free in this way only when his desires no longer conflict with his parents' commands, or when his parents' commands cease to have any force. Freedom to do as one pleases, therefore (as distinct from the freedom to carry out one's desire), refers to the basis of one's actions. One's activity is free in this sense if there is no command which one feels to be binding and which opposes one's desire to do the activity in question. It is tempting to call this kind of freedom "autonomy." But "autonomy," like the other terms related to freedom, has several meanings. Certainly, it is this kind of freedom that adolescents frequently want,tha that slaves are essentially denied, that those who object to oppressive institutions are concerned with.

Freedom is also used, but less commonly, to refer to what can be called "ideal freedom" – namely, the freedom one has if one is not prevented from acting in accord with an ideal. The ideal in question can be known by the agent or the agent can be ignorant of it. This ignorance can itself be one of the opposing factors which make the person unfree. Similarly, the ideal can be consistent or inconsistent with the agent's desires, and, if inconsistent, these desires can be factors opposing the freedom in question. Thus, freedom to do as one pleases, or, for that matter, physical freedom, can be part of what makes a person unfree on most conceptions of ideal freedom – a point well understood by Plato, Aristotle, and the Stoics. Of course, there are different conceptions of ideal freedom, depending upon different views of the ideal life for man. The Stoics, for example, regarded freedom from desire – apathy – as an essential part of a human life lived in accord with reason. Similarly, Freud considered the neurotic not to be free, and the cured patient – freed from neurosis – to be free to act in accord with the psychological ideal. The freedom of the children of God is also a kind of ideal freedom: The sinner is unfree – blocked by sin from the ideal of a full human life and active incorporation into the mystical body. The person in the state of grace is liberated by Christ from the bondage of sin.

In another sense, "freedom" refers to creativity, that is, to a person's independence of prior accomplishments and standard ways of procedure. A creative person has the capacity to act in ways that were not previously articulated; such a person is free from established patterns of thought and is not locked into the possibilities expressed in standard procedures. The factors which oppose this kind of freedom are those which tend towards repetition. They can be intellectual, psychological, or cultural. Thus, since one's desires can be quite predictable and standardized, they can be factors which inhibit creativity. This kind of freedom is clearly exhibited in the work of creative scientists and artists. It is articulated and developed in the work of existentialist thinkers like Nietzsche.

Finally, there is "political freedom." This phrase can refer to the freedom of one nation vis-à-vis others. In this sense, it is a kind of freedom to do as one pleases possessed by a nation and not by an individual. Political freedom also refers to the various freedoms of individuals within a society. In this sense, it refers to the social analogues of the types of freedom we have been distinguishing – the freedom to move around, the freedom to set one's own goals, to live according to one's ideals, to be creative in various ways. The opposing factors in these social analogues of the various freedoms are the power of the state, of public opinion, and of established mores. Thus, various liberation movements oppose societal limitations upon people's doing as they please and the established patterns which inhibit creative life styles. Christians and some others oppose laws and customs which inhibit the living of the ideal life as they see it.

Freedom in any of the senses distinguished so far is among the things about which normative judgments are made. It is part of the subject matter of such normative disciplines as moral philosophy and theology and political philosophy. Freedom in each of these senses is a thing which people may or may not have. If they have it, they frequently seek to protect it or get more of it; if they do not have it, they will work and often fight to get it. In this sense, the freedoms we have been discussing so far are values. Of course, whether the value judgments made about these sorts of freedom are true is something that remains to be seen. Certainly, the Christian's value judgments on each of these matters will be quite different and frequently opposed to the judgments of contemporary post-Christians.

At the root of these differing value judgments there is a difference between Christians and post-Christian secularists on the correct understanding of human nature. This difference centers on a different sense of freedom – namely, free choice. The claim that human beings have the capacity to make free choices is not a practical judgment about what is to be done but a theoretical truth about what human beings are – that is, about human nature. So this question of fact about the reality of free choice is fundamental to the various value questions associated with freedom.

II. The Importance of Free Choice

Before trying to establish the claim about the *importance* of accepting or rejecting free choice, I will offer a brief account of what it is and of the Judaeo-Christian acceptance and modern secular denials of its reality.

A person makes a choice when he or she selects one of a set of practical options – that is, a person chooses when faced with alternatives for action. One sees that one could do this or that one could do that but not both, and consequently one selects one or the other. A choice is free, in the relevant sense, when the person's own choosing determines which of the available options is selected. In other words, all the factors determining the outcome of the act of choosing other than the agent's very choosing itself are insufficient to determine the selection that is made. In short, a free choice occurs when a person could select this or that, and the person himself determines which he will select.[3]

Free choice thus understood is an act of the will. The selection of one of a set of options is the person's determination to realize that option. Thus, the preference involved in choosing is not a matter of finding or rating one option as more attractive than the others. Choice is not an approving or disapproving of an object or a projected course of action, but is a person's commitment to *do* the act. Thus, one's own doing is necessarily a part of what it is that one chooses.[4]

This brief account of free choice will be developed as we proceed; at this point it is necessary to turn from considerations about what free choice is to the question of whether human beings can make free choices. Modern non-believers answer this question with a resounding and often scornful "No!" The doctrine of determinism is a received truth in the contemporary secular orthodoxy. For believing Jews and Christians, however, there is no doubt that free choice is real.

The reality of free choice is explicitly affirmed in Scripture: "It was he who created man in the beginning and he left him in the power of his own inclination. If you will you can keep the commandments, and to act faithfully is a matter of your own choice. He has placed before you fire and wa-

---

3 See *Free Choice*, pp. 11–20, for a fuller discussion of the definition of free choice.

4 See Joseph M. Boyle Jr., "Freedom The Human Person, and Human Action," in William May, Editor, *Principles of Catholic Moral Life*, Chicago: 1980, pp. 242–49.

ter: stretch out your hand for whichever you wish. Before a man are life and death, and whichever he chooses will be given him" (Sirach 15:14–17).

The author of Sirach echoes Deuteronomy: "I set before you life or death, blessing or curse. Choose life . . ." (Deuteronomy 30:19). Moreover, the Church has solemnly defined that human beings can make free choices:[5] and the magisterium of the Church has affirmed the reality of free choice down through the centuries.[6] Moreover, what Scripture and the Church teach about free choice is consistent with common human experience: most people have the experience of facing options – that is, the experience of situations where spontaneous action based on desire, habit, or the judgment that something is worth doing is blocked by the fact that several things suggest themselves as worth doing. Most people are aware that in some situations it is within their power to carry out either of the alternative courses of action which present themselves in deliberation and that there is no experienced factor which determines them to do one or the other. Furthermore, many people would judge reflectively that when one of the options was selected, it was they themselves by their own choices who selected the option.

The secular orthodoxy concerning free choice is, as I have already noted, quite opposed to the Judaeo-Christian affirmation of it. Modern determinists seek to explain away the common experience of free choice as illusory or as based on a failure to consider all of the determining factors of human actions – factors which are often outside of the introspective awareness of the person making the choice. Moreover, determinists are frequently convinced on *a priori* grounds that free choice is impossible. For them, the reality of free choice appears to be inconsistent with the causal determination of physical systems; it is inconsistent with the requirement of the principle of sufficient reason; it reduces human action to mere chance occurrence. For all these reasons, the reality of free choice makes the scientific study of man to be impossible. From this "scientific" perspective, the notion of free choice is part of a set of concepts that have had their use in the evolution of society, but are now outmoded and positively harmful. The guilt induced by the conviction of people that they act freely is a form of social oppression which must be set aside in favor of more positive reinforcers.[7]

---

5 See The Council of Trent, Session IV, Decree on Justification; DS #1521.
6 See Karl Rahner S.J., "Freedom – III, Theological," *Sacramentum Mundi*, vol. 2, pp. 361–62, for a discussion and reference to the relevant teaching.
7 The deterministic arguments suggested here are laid out more fully and the relevant literature is cited in *Free Choice*, pp. 48–103.

If these *a priori* reasons for the rejection of free choice have a question-begging sound to them, this should not be surprising. My point, however, is not to enter into the free will/determinism controversy but to indicate the opposition between the Judaeo-Christian affirmation of free choice and the many-faceted contemporary denial of it. There is, however, one feature of determinists' arguments which should be noted here – namely, that they make use of other senses of "free" to account for some of the facts for which free choice has been used to account. Nietzsche, for example, a strict determinist, has much to say about freedom; but the freedom to which he refers is not free choice but creative freedom. Determinists within the empiricist tradition, following the lead of Hobbes and Hume, insist that man can act freely and that the freedom they affirm is sufficient to account for moral responsibility. This freedom, of course, is not free choice, but freedom from coercion – a version of physical freedom. Hume proposed, as a novel insight that would "dissolve" the free will controversy, a position already thoroughly refuted by Suarez and condemned by the Church in the writings of Michel du Bay – namely, that the morally relevant type of freedom was not the freedom opposed to causal determination but rather the freedom opposed to coercion.[8] So Hume and his empiricist descendants, with increasing technical sophistication, have been developing the argument that the defenders of free choice are simply confused in their insistence on free choice when another sense of freedom will do. Of course, it will not do if one believes that man truly determines himself in choosing.[9]

The point I am making here is of some practical importance, and it can be stated as a general point: It does not follow from the fact that a person affirms one type of freedom or another that the person – whether existentialist or humanistic psychologist or anti-behaviorist social scientist – accepts the proposition that human beings can make free choices. The history of philosophy from the time of Hobbes and Spinoza to the present is full of determinists who sing the praises of freedom.

The disagreement between those who affirm, and those who deny, free choice seems to many people to be one of those insoluble metaphysical disputes that have little practical importance. I was told recently by a political scientist at a conference on behavior control that the dispute about free choice was a frivolous one, unworthy of serious attention, since human behavior was, after all, predictable. I think his judgment about the relevance of

---

8   See *Denzinger-Schönmetzer* (DS) #1939, #1941, #1966.
9   See *Free Choice*, pp. 105–10.

the dispute is false. The affirmation or denial of free choice makes a fundamental difference in how one understands moral responsibility, in how one understands morality itself and the role of moral norms, and, finally, in how one evaluates the various types of freedom which are valued in today's society.

Free choice is understood by those who affirm it as that act by which the person most fully self-determines himself: It is in making free choices that a person determines himself to be the sort of person he or she is. If choice is free, then the person in choosing is not determined by something other than himself – or even by determining features within his own nature – to be a certain kind of person; rather, the person in choosing freely determines himself or herself. This aspect of free choice has been understood by the Church as a way in which mankind is made in the image of God. As *Gaudium et Spes* states: "But that which is truly freedom is an exceptional sign of the image of God in man. For God willed that man should 'be left in the hand of his own counsel' so that he might of his own accord seek his creator and freely attain his full and blessed perfection by cleaving to him." (*GS* #17)

This self-determining character of man is an essential part of the Christian notion of moral responsibility. In fact, the connection between free choice and moral responsibility is often used as an argument for free choice: If free choice is denied, then people are not morally responsible because some factor other than the person's own commitment determined the action. By contrast, a self-initiated action is surely one for which one is responsible. And where the self-initiation in question is a free choice, the person is radically responsible for the act – it is one's own in the fullest sense. Furthermore, it is only if one is responsible in the sense involving free choice that the radical accountability involved in the Christian notion of judgment makes sense. "Before the judgment seat of God an account of his own life will be rendered to each one according as he has done either good or evil" (*GS* #17). This kind of accountability presupposes free choice.

The standard determinist response to this kind of argument is simply to deny that human beings are responsible or accountable in this radical way. In fact, denying this kind of responsibility is one of the basic motives of modern determinism. In place of this kind of responsibility, many modern determinists propose a weaker kind of responsibility and the role of morality in human life. According to this view, one is morally responsible when one knows what one is doing and when one is not coerced in acting. In other words, one is morally responsible if one is physically and psychologically unconstrained in acting.

One embarrassing consequence of this view is that there is no *essential* difference between the responsibility of a small child for his or her voluntary behavior and the responsibility of an adult for his or her choices. It is clear, therefore, as some determinists admit, that moral responsibility is not *accounted for* by this understanding of responsibility but *redefined*, and the Christian notion of moral responsibility is simply rejected. Bertrand Russell is very plain about this. He admits that "... the conception of 'sin' is only rational on the assumption of free will."[10] And he goes on to develop an alternative notion of the function of morality and moral responsibility.

> Praise and blame, rewards and punishments, and the whole apparatus of the criminal law, are rational on the deterministic hypothesis, but not on the hypothesis of free will, for they are all mechanisms designed to cause volitions that are in harmony with the interests of the community, or what are believed to be its interests.[11]

Russell's quote brings me to the second implication of the denial of free choice – namely, that it forces a radical shift not only in one's understanding of moral responsibility, but also in one's understanding of the nature of morality and the function of moral norms. If one accepts the proposition that human beings can make free choices, then moral norms have an obvious function – they direct free choices. There are choices to be made, and rational guidance is required if they are to be properly oriented. Thus moral norms are not, as such, opposed to free choice; but they guide and direct free choices to what is truly good. In other words, the fact that a person morally ought to do one of the things presented as options does not mean that his free choice is limited or compromised. Choices would have no decisive guidance if there were no moral norms.

Of course, this is not to say that moral norms present no opposing factor to the freedom to do as one pleases, if one's desire is to do what is contrary to the norm. Likewise, moral norms can oppose the pursuit of certain creative options if these are excluded by the norm. This opposition is, however, not fundamental because one's desires can be brought into conformity with the norm – even if not perfectly for fallen man – and choices in accord with

---

10 Bertrand Russell, *Human Society in Ethics and Politics,* New York: 1955, p. 80.

11 *Ibid.,* pp. 79–80

moral norms need not be mere repetitions of established practice. Moreover, to the extent that these types of freedom are compromised or opposed by moral norms, they can by definition have no normative status: they cannot be morally legitimate freedoms and cannot be truly justifiable values since they are contrary to legitimate moral norms. Such freedoms cannot be part of what ideally frees man because ideal freedom must include the proper use of man's capacities including free choice.

For the determinist, however, morality cannot be a matter of directing and organizing one's life insofar as that life is within one's own power to live it. Moral norms cannot be directives or guidelines for free choices since there are no free choices to guide. Moral language, therefore, must have some such function as Russell suggests – that is, to control behavior, to organize society and individuals' lives in order to get what people want. In this conception, moral norms are not directions for choice but factors which *determine* people to act in certain ways.

In this deterministic view of morality, it is very likely that freedom to do as one pleases will be regarded as a very basic value. Moral norms *are* literally coercive factors for anyone whose desires are not in accord with the norms.

Given this deterministic understanding, it is not surprising that the basic moral questions of classical liberalism – and of modern society generally – have to do with the extent to which society can legitimately impose upon the liberty of individuals. The first question of students in an introductory ethics class is not "how should I live" but "by what right does anyone tell me how to live." Since there is no free choice, the question is whose desires will be determinative – those of the individual or those of society. Given the subjectivism and individualism of modern Western thought, it is not surprising that the nod goes to individual preference. In short, moral norms are seen as determining factors in the secular view of morality. They are understood as a form of social or psychological constraint having no genuine normative status. Therefore, it is not surprising that modern people wish to be free of moral norms. So we get the paradoxical result that it is the denial of free choice that – among other things – leads to what *Gaudium et Spes* calls an improper cherishing of freedom – "as if it gave them [modern men] leave to do anything they like even when it is evil." (*GS* #17)

One other implication of the opposition between secular determinism and the Judaeo-Christian affirmation of free choice should be noted here. The various ideals of the good human life which form the core of the differing conceptions of ideal freedom necessarily involve some understanding of human nature. The reason for this is that the ideal involves some conception of what perfects or is good for man. Thus, it is not surprising that those who deny free choice will have a very different view of the good life than those who affirm it. For the latter but not the former the proper exercise of free choice is part of the ideal.

The good life has been understood by the Christian tradition essentially to include activity in accord with the moral virtues. A non-virtuous person cannot live a humanly good or genuinely happy life. The moral virtues involve directly or indirectly a perfection of the will – an integration of the self around morally good choices. So the ideal life on this conception involves the proper use of free choice.

By contrast, a determinist view of the good life need not involve the virtues as an essential part. For most modern thinkers, happiness does not include virtue but is frequently understood as opposition to virtue. So the prudence characteristic of the modern imperial self is intelligent efficiency in getting what one wants. It often includes the judgment that serious commitments must be avoided because they bring pain and disorder into a life which by the therapeutic ideal must be content and self-satisfied. Fidelity to commitments, far from being a part of the virtue of courage, is simply imprudent and irrational. Our fundamental self is not the moral self established by commitments; rather the true self is a natural, evolving person which need not be the same today as yesterday, and to which, therefore, reasonable adjustment must be made. Fidelity is irrational.

III. The Coherence of the Christian View of Freedom

Time does not allow the development of this theme in the detail I would like. Since the premises for what I have to say here have for the most part already been established in the prior section, I will use this section as a way of summing up my main points and bringing them to a focus.

Many modern people both inside and outside the Church are offended by the Biblical emphasis on the necessity of obedience. This emphasis on obedience is thought to be servile, childish, and unworthy of adult Christians who live with the freedom of the children of God. This line of argument can be used either to show that Christianity is inherently contradictory or, by "up-to-date" Christians, to show that we need to downplay the emphasis on obedience.

The distinctions I have been making show rather clearly, however, that the Christian understanding of freedom is not incoherent. There is no compromise of free choice by the presence of a moral norm; the obligation to obey God is surely no constraint on free choice. God's commands are surely moral norms – and moral norms proposed by One who is perfectly free in Himself and wills what is best for us. The act of faith, for example, involves a free human act, but it is not optional; the free act is an act of obedience to God.[12]

Of course, moral norms can be in opposition to a person's freedom to do as one pleases. It is true, therefore, that obedience to God's will may require what is opposed to what we may happen to want. However, this kind of freedom – freedom to do as one pleases in opposition to moral norms – has no ultimate normative status within the perspective of a morality based on free choice and the conviction that there are true moral norms.

I hesitate to bring up the complex subject of the freedom of the children of God. But it is important to note that this freedom does not mean that we are not obliged to obey God: In part, it means that by obeying God, we are freed from the bondage of sin; in part, it means that because of grace we can obey God's commands; and, in part, it means that if we obey God's will, our desires will be rectified so that, ideally, we desire only what God wills. To quote *Gaudium et Spes* once again: "Man's dignity therefore requires him to act out of conscious and free choice, as moved and drawn in a personal way from within, and not by blind impulses in himself or by mere external constraint. Man gains such dignity when, ridding himself of all slavery to the passions, he presses forward towards his goal by freely choosing what is good, and, by his diligence and skill effectively secures for himself the means suited to this end. Since human freedom has been weakened by sin, it is only by the help of God's grace that man can give his actions their full and proper relationship to God" (*GS* #17).

Thus, Christian freedom is not incoherent: It is consistent and firmly based on a recognition of man's nature and destiny. It is rather the modern views of freedom, based on a deterministic value system, that are rationally indefensible.

---

12 See Vatical Council I, Constitution concerning the Catholic Faith, Chapter #3; DS 3010.

9.

Freedom and the Catholic University (1981)

Rev. Richard R. Roach

I.

When I happily accepted the task of speaking to you about freedom and the Catholic University, I still took it for granted that "freedom" in some acceptable sense prevailed in our North American societies, and I also took for granted that it was meaningful to refer to institutions such as my own as "Catholic Universities." No less a figure than David Riesman, however, has challenged my second assumption – namely, that it was still meaningful to speak of institutions such as my own as "Catholic"[1] – and a still more important figure, Malcolm Muggeridge, has deepened my doubts that an authentic notion of freedom[2] a holds minimal sway in our societies.[3] The upshot of all this is that I no longer believe I have a topic *in the sense* I so believed when I accepted this honor. So it is incumbent upon me to justify my presence by defining my topic anew. That re-definition will make up a large part of my talk.

First, let us briefly turn to the notion of freedom. Muggeridge reminds us that for some, perhaps for very many, "freedom consists in being allowed and provided with the means to do whatever anyone has a mind to, and that a free society is one in which this is possible and the means readily available, the supreme example of such a society being, of course, the United States."[4] Muggeridge contrasts this unfortunate notion with one he claims Alexander Solzhenitsyn holds and which he offended us with when he de-

---

1   *Change*, Vol. 13, number 1 (January-February 1981), p. 20.

2   By "an authentic notion of freedom," I mean what the Church calls *vera libertas*, cf., *Gaudium et Spes*, The Pastoral Constitution on the Church in the Modern World, esp. #17.

3   Malcolm Muggeridge, "Solzhenitsyn Reconsidered – Part I," The *American Spectator*, Vol. 13, number 12 (December 1980) p. 12.

4   *Ibid.*

livered his famous Harvard address. Muggeridge rightly says that Solzhenitsyn's notion is derived from the New Testament. That notion, I believe, is substantially the one that also underlies *Gaudium et Spes, Dignitatis Humanae*, and other documents of the Second Vatican Council. For example in #17 of *Gaudium et Spes* we read:

> Only in freedom can man direct himself toward goodness. Our contemporaries make much of this freedom and pursue it eagerly: and rightly to be sure. Often however, they foster it perversely as a license for doing whatever pleases them, even if it is evil. For its part, authentic freedom is an exceptional sign of the divine image within man. For God has willed that man remain "under the control of his own decisions," so that he can seek his Creator spontaneously, and come freely to utter and blissful perfection through loyalty to Him. Hence man's dignity demands that he act according to a knowing and free choice that is personally motivated and prompted from within, not under blind internal impulse nor by mere external pressure. Man achieves such dignity when, emancipating himself from all captivity to passion, he pursues his goal in a spontaneous choice of what is good, and procures for himself, through effective and skillful action, apt helps to that end. Since man's freedom has been damaged by sin, only by the aid of God's grace can he bring such a relationship with God into full flower. Before the judgment seat of God each man must render an account of his own life, whether he has done good or evil.

I shall risk summarizing what I believe is implicit in this and other passages as follows: We are free in order to discover the truth and to do it in love. We are meant to be free from certain constraints which would compromise our embracing the truth and doing it in love. Lacking a proper freedom from constraint, these acts might seem compelled by external forces rather than impelled by internal conviction. So a measure of freedom from constraint must exist in order to protect the true nature of acts of faith, hope, and charity in which freedom from constraint, authentic freedom for the truth may be fulfilled.

Using this notion of freedom, which I believe is at least part of an authentic notion of freedom, our Holy Father has circled the globe crying out for religious liberty. He has known first hand for most of his life forces that constrain the free acts of faith, hope, and charity in order to divert those energies into demonic channels, dug by such agents as the Nazis and the Communists. I wish to suggest, however, that his message regarding religious liberty has a different meaning for us in the so-called free world. Among us, i.e., the affluent and thought-to-be free, there is a different way in which religion is persecuted. It comes in part from within the Church. There, it is the failure to teach what the Church actually teaches. This failure constrains through external force the free acts of faith, hope, and charity as much as, and in some instances, more effectively than the machinations of Communists and Nazis. No wonder the Russians envy us so. What they need a Gulag Archipelago to do, we achieve more efficiently through fashionable dissent, ideological education, and the media.

My suggestion that the difficulty with religious liberty in the United States and other affluent Western countries comes from within is not yet complete. I must first show that what is labeled Catholic ought actually to be Catholic, and so we turn to the "Catholic University." I believe two closely related things in this regard: first, that what the Church under the guidance of the Holy Spirit has taught is true really is true, and that it is not subject to change. Our understanding may develop, but that does not change the truth. Secondly, I believe that the Church has taught a large body of truth both about the way things are and about what we ought (not) to do (faith and morals).

There is nothing in the work of the Second Vatican Council or in any other source of Catholic truth which authorizes any Catholic to cast doubt upon what has been taught as true. The Catholic faith is not up for grabs; it can be set forth today with greater clarity than at any other time in history. That is to say, doctrine has developed to a point that we may give authoritative answers and more exact answers to more questions today than ever before in history. The faith and morals of the Church are not in doubt; they have, in fact, never been clearer. Those who would try to make us think otherwise are serving a master other than the Lord Jesus.

If freedom is a freedom for the truth, and if the Catholic Church is God's own instrument for imparting the fullness of his truth, then freedom and the Catholic University mean at least that a Catholic University must be a place where one is free from constraint and able to learn readily the truth of the Catholic faith. I say "readily" because I suppose that under tyranny one can, if lucky, ferret out the truth of the Catholic faith, say, by working in a research library and surreptitiously reading some of the collection maintained for antiquarian purposes. The works of St. Thomas or the Councils of the Church may be in the library of the University of Moscow. But this does not make it a Catholic University. The truths are not readily available. By the way, I consider this a minimalist definition of a Catholic University set up in order to bring out an irony, namely, the situation in many so-called Catholic institutions where forces instead exist to constrain persons to be anti-Catholic.

Before a sympathetic audience, I have thus far tried to evoke fresh images of what we all know in one degree or another is the case. I would now like to make two closely related points that I believe show exactly why, in the name of freedom for the truth of the Catholic faith, the present situation must be ended immediately; and I shall conclude with a proposal suggesting how to end it. I shall now ask you to explore with me an analogy which I trust will set out matters in a provocative way. I assume in this analogy that a Catholic University, in order to qualify as Catholic, must at least teach authentically Catholic theology, so, from here on, I will speak about Catholic theology rather than the Catholic University.

Analogy and metaphor can serve well the cause of understanding. In the hope that they will thus serve again, I shall now liken my topic to a paper on astronomy entitled, "Freedom and the Astronomer," written by a man who wants to be an honest astronomer. He had been troubled about the presence of astrologers at meetings of astronomical learned societies, but he had half accepted explanations such as the following: "Astrology has a rich history and contains a scientific psychological meaning which we have lost: These folk are re-discovering that meaning and exploring it." Or: "This is an age of pluralism; we must defeat the claims of astrologers in the free market place of ideas; it is harmful to the cause of astronomy to expel these folks in an 'authoritarian' manner; of course, anyone of importance among us astronomers knows that these astrological folk are outside the fold; however, do not be a 'nervous Nelly'; let them have their platforms and good sense will eventually laugh them away." With his head filled with such ideas, our astronomer even went along with the appointment of an astrologer to his department; and he also failed to check on the credentials of a number of other candidates, who after being hired, turned out to be sympathetic to astrology as well, and even covert practitioners of it.

The scenario is now one that is clear, though perhaps belabored; certainly it is familiar to this audience. We all woke up one morning and discovered that many, maybe most, of the well-known astronomers (read, Catholic theologians) were actually astrologers, that is, theologians of some kind other than Catholic. Now if astronomical societies have become predominantly astrological societies, then calling them astronomical societies is obscurantism. It is not justified, in my opinion, even if there are a few real astronomers left around – tenured folk who will soon die off.

Permit me to continue with the analogy. Let us follow our astronomer on the day he woke up to what was going on. After he had screamed and torn his hair, he began in every way available to him to resist this confounding of astronomy and astrology. He then met a somewhat new and sophisticated defense of the confusion, namely, the new doctrine of freedom. He was told that all astronomical societies had accepted the notion that man ought to be free. This acceptance entailed the recognition of the rights of astrology to its place in the academy. Since it contradicted that older teaching whereby an astrologer was rejected as unscientific, the new doctrine of freedom abrogated the judgment against astrology and therefore expelled it from the academy. That teaching was now set aside in the name of freedom. The new doctrine now known as the doctrine of astronomical freedom was not only a reversal of the dark past, but a herald of all sorts of other new developments in astronomy.

Our astronomer was then informed what he might and might not do according to the new rules of debate: He might state his conviction that astrological views are unscientific, but only as a private opinion. Invoking authority makes people nervous and was thus contrary to the "new" spirit of liberty. He also had to watch the tone of his comments whenever he referred to astrologers. They could attack him with the full panoply of rhetorical put-down, but he must always be deferential. The reason for this was that all astrologers are honestly questioning seekers, seeking the truth even when they made some mistakes but, in general, engaged in a noble occupations; since, however, he still believed in the old "authoritarian" claim to the effect that the official teaching of astronomy is that astrology is superstition rather than science, it behooved him always to advance his criticisms of astrology deferentially.

In conclusion, the new doctrine of freedom he found insisted that if his colleagues found astrology more "satisfying" than "astronomy," then they had a right to that endeavor as unrestricted as his right to astronomy. Heavy charges, such as calling astrology superstitious or unscientific, could have the effect of impeding the new astrologers in the exercise of this right of theirs, and, therefore, such charges against astrology must be curtailed. Our imaginary astronomer knew by then that some astronomical societies were controlled by astrologers who had silenced or otherwise punished their members still defending astronomy or who had spoken out against astrology. He was afraid, not least because he did not accept the "new" notion of freedom. He still believed that scientific freedom is a freedom from constraint sufficient to enable the scientific to seek and *find* the truth. He could not accept the idea that "freedom" meant using the history, prestige, and symbols of science in order to do whatever one wished. He realized that this notion of freedom was now regarded as heresy and so punished.

II.

I trust the above analogy has served its purpose. I would like now to make explicit certain of the morals of this story and then apply the whole to the topic, "Freedom and the Catholic University," with which I started out.

The most salient feature whereby we distinguish between astronomy and astrology, if I rightly understand the difference, lies in the claim rejected by astronomy and affirmed by astrology that the position of the heavenly bodies directly affects human behavior so that counsel may be given about human affairs from reading the stars and even predictions made about the future. Such a difference is sufficient to separate the two into two different worlds of discourse, even though they talk about the same stars and agree, at least roughly, in charting their positions. A logician, if interested, could lay out this separation quite clearly.

But this is precisely the point where our analogy breaks down. The logical differences that separate astronomy and astrology are not as great as those that divide differing orientations in what is today being called Catholic theology. The reason why the differences between theologies present greater difficulties than the difference between astronomy and astrology is simple: We can see the stars but we cannot see God. The logical problem of reference, therefore, is more easily solved when speaking about the stars than when speaking about God.

The problem of reference, when using a general term to refer to something, consists essentially in determining what description is sufficient in order to make the term refer. Names (i.e., what I was taught as a child to call "proper" names) refer without further ado, but the term "god" is not a name. It is the general term in our language for the deity. If I could see deity, I could use the term "god" to refer to reality even if I thought a lot of nonsense about it. An astrologer can refer to the stars that make up the Big Dipper even though he may say a lot of nonsense about them. They are visible, specific, nameable stars. The grammatical subject of the sentence, "The Big

Dipper is now causing high blood pressure," does not fail of reference; rather, its sense fails of truth. However, the sentence, "Occasionally God considers the practice of contraception, sodomy, fornication, or adultery well-ordered human behavior," may make specious sense to some while failing to refer to the God who actually exists. If it fails to refer, and I believe it does, then forming judgments of what objectively is right or wrong in the light of what the spurious 'god' of this sentence thinks would violate the First Commandment.

We are all aware that there are now persons who call themselves Catholic theologians who hold that the use of contraceptives to regulate human fertility at least in marriage is not disordered human behavior. They also, at least occasionally, find reasonably well ordered such human behavior as homosexual activity, some *in vitro* fertilization of human life with consequent destruction, some directly procured abortion under certain circumstances variously described, some fornication (more usually called pre-marital sex when excused), and even some adultery. It is not a case of saying, I think rightly, that some engage in these behaviors without committing deadly sin because of their lack of knowledge or freedom. Rather, the theological claim at issue is that such behavior is in certain circumstances objectively the right thing to do. The one, holy – Roman – Catholic, and apostolic Church, however, says that God considers such behavior always disordered. I submit that the dissident theologians and the Church are not referring to the same 'god' here; I further submit that there is but one divine nature that actually exists; therefore, only one description of deity refers to the divine nature that actually exists. This is to say that divine nature must be adequately described – i.e., what it is like and what it wills and commands adequately stated – if the term for deity in general is to refer to that nature. Obeying what contradicts, or worshipping what is not, this divine nature is a most grievous sin. Nor will the use of the term 'god' obviate the sin.

In his seminal work, "On Worshipping the Right God,"[5] from which my reflection on these matters took their rise, Peter Geach says that he does not know where to draw the line that separates a description of deity which, although faulty, still refers to the divine nature and a description that refers to nothing, or something less than the divine nature, such as the devil. From what has preceded, it may sound as if I have no such difficulty, that, for ex-

---

5 Peter T. Geach, "On Worshipping the Right God," in *God and the Soul* (1969; rpt., London: Routledge and Kegan Paul, 1978), pp. 100–116.

ample, I could tell Geach where to draw the line. I do not mean to give that impression and in order to correct it, permit me to explain the difficulty as I see it more fully.

Let us say that theologian X teaches correctly that God is the Creator of all else. A correct description of God as Creator does make the term "god" refer to the divine nature that actually exists. Let us then say that the same theologian maintains that 'god' approves of pre-marital sex. Does his correct description of God as Creator save his use of the term "god" when claiming that 'god' approves of pre-marital sex? If the more benign interpretation is taken, then the theologian's use of the term "god" refers in both instances but fails of sense in the second: That is, he is right about God in the first instance, which makes the term refer, and he is simply wrong about 'god' in the second instance. He thus combines in himself both the astronomer and the astrologer. They both referred to the Big Dipper, after all – but one talked nonsense about it.

I doubt that this benign interpretation, although, seemingly, it is more charitable, is correct. I suspect that the truth lies in the sinful practices of the Chosen People described in such detail in the Old Testament: namely, that the theologian in question, like our forefathers in faith, is simultaneously worshiping (referring to) Yahweh *and* Baal, or Molech (Moloch), or Astarte, or what have you. In other words, some worship of the right God, some reference to the divine nature that actually does exist, but it nevertheless does not save one from committing the sin of idolatry in the very next breath. The deviant theologian who may worship the right God at Mass in the morning is not thereby prevented from worshipping the devil as 'god' in his class on moral theology in the afternoon. It is a possibility worth pondering. In short, I believe that one and the same divine nature simply cannot be the source for the following contradictory moral directions: Yes, directly contracepting an otherwise virtuous conjugal act always is disordered human behavior; No, directly contracepting an otherwise virtuous conjugal act may be well-ordered human behavior, even necessary to maintain the virtuous character of the conjugal act. Or, Yes, for Bill and Mary to engage in sexual intercourse before they are married to each other is always disordered human behavior; or, No, it is not always disordered behavior. Or, Yes, it always is disordered human behavior for Sue and Alice to engage in cunnilingus in order to express their affection for each other; No, it sometimes is a well-ordered activity for them. You may multiply these kinds of examples for yourself. I believe that the 'god' who considers that directly sterilizing conjugal love well-ordered human behavior or that cunnilingus between two women is well-ordered human behavior is not divine but demonic. Teaching this 'god's' counsels as if they were Catholic doctrine or even acceptable within the parameters of the Catholic faith is to direct the believer and potential worshipper to the devil and not to the God and Father of Our Lord Jesus Christ.

I believe that there is an even subtler but less explicit rejection of the true God now abroad in theological circles. This rejection has to do with a specious development of doctrine, which as William Marshner has pointed out, actually is a metalinguistic heresy.[6] It is simple to illustrate. On the one hand, we have the clear declarations of both the First and Second Vatican Councils regarding doctrine. The First Vatican Council said: "If anyone says that as science progresses, it is sometimes possible for dogmas that have been proposed by the Church to receive a different meaning from the one which the Church understood and understands: let him be anathema."[7] I believe the substance of this anathema was reaffirmed at the Second Vatican Council in #62 of *Gaudium et Spes* and the footnote to the passage I have in mind refers to the allocution which Pope John XXIII gave at the opening of the Council where he said: "The Church should never depart from the sacred patrimony of truth received from the Fathers."

On the other hand, we have a specious development of doctrine proposed which goes like this: In 1854 the Church solemnly defined the dogma of the Immaculate Conception. The core of that definition reads: ". . . the Most Blessed Virgin Mary, in the first instant of her conception . . . was preserved free from all stain of original sin."[8] To simplify my example I will omit the temporal phrase "in the first instant of her conception" and reduce the sentence to this: the Most Blessed Virgin Mary was preserved free from all stain of original sin.

There are theologians today who propose that we can maintain the integrity and continuity of Catholic faith only if we maintain the linguistic form given here – that is, we can keep on repeating the sentence, but we must change the referent and adjust the sense. In the dogma, Mary is a name. The name refers to a Jewish maiden who conceived God's only Son

---

6 William H. Marshner, "The Defense of Dogma," in *Reasons for Hope*; ed. Jeffrey A. Mirus, Christendom College Press, 1978, p. 163.
7 *The Church Teaches*, no. 83 (D 1818, DS 3043; cf. D 1800, DS 3020).
8 *The Church Teaches*, no. 510 (D 1641, DS 2803).

by the power of the Holy Spirit.[9] The revisionist theologians would have the name refer to the *Church* and deny that it necessarily refers to the Jewish maiden because, among other reasons, they object to the doctrine that original sin is handed on by human generation.

This objection leads to tampering with other doctrines, viz., doctrines dealing with Our Lady's virginity as well as with the Incarnation. Briefly, they deny that Our Lord was conceived without a man (a male of the human species) as father by the sole action of the Holy Spirit. This denial involves the same kind of logical moves: References are changed and the sense adjusted. All that remains is the linguistic form. I think it is time to cry foul. Either Our Lady was a virgin at the birth of Christ, or she was not ("or" in the sense of *aut*, not *vel*); either Our Lady was a virgin all her life, or she was not; either she was immaculately conceived, or she was not. For the sake of my own integrity and the sensitivity of pious ears, permit me to affirm again that I believe that Our Lady was immaculately conceived and a virgin all her life, and my affirmation has lurking behind it *no* foul play with reference and sense!

From the above, I will be accused of failing to appreciate or failing to understand evolution (which in this matter is not the case), so I must say something about my alleged failure. The revisionists claim that the differences discussed above are not on the side of God, but in us. God once forbade sodomy because we did not understand sex as well then as we do today. God once allowed us to believe that He actually brought about the human conception of His Son without using a male and his seed as an instrument because we once did not understand the nature of religious truths, Biblical writings, and so forth. This is the deepest heresy. It makes it out that God is a deceiver and a liar, which is *the* absolute impossibility. God is truth; it is that other lesser spirit who is a liar and the father of lies. I ask you, in the Church in the United States today, which spirit are people being invited to obey and even worship by some of the Church's supposed teachers?

I must now draw these reflections to a quick and abrupt conclusion. In order to respect freedom for the truth and in order that any institution be "Catholic," particularly a university, Catholic doctrine must be labeled as such and must be readily available; non-Catholic or anti-Catholic teaching must be labeled as such and tolerated only insofar as freedom from constraint requires. Therefore, I propose an ecclesial "fair labeling law." Ordinarily in the U.S. it is not possible to take a cheaper white fish, pack it

---

9 Marshner, *op. cit.*, pp. 163–73. My argument is a summary of his work.

tightly, and sell it as tuna. The product must be properly labeled. The Church has the wherewithal to label her products, i.e., what She actually teaches about faith and morals. All institutions, particularly Catholic Universities, must put those labels on the right goods or the religious freedom of all involved will continue to be violated. Let us speak up for religious liberty.

I would like to add a postscript by way of an exhortation. I believe that if we demand religious liberty in all Catholic Universities we will be doing the truth Our Lord taught when he exposed the heresy of Pharisaism. We read in St. Mark as follows:

> ". . . You put aside the commandment of God to cling to human tradition." And he said to them, "How ingeniously you get round the commandment of God in order to preserve your own tradition. For Moses said: Do your duty to your father and your mother, and, Anyone who curses father or mother must be put to death. But you say, 'If a man says to his father or mother: Anything I have that I might have used to help you is Corban (that is, dedicated to God), then he is forbidden from that moment to do anything for his father or mother.' In this way you make God's word null and void for the sake of your tradition which you have handed down. And you do many other things like this" (Mark 7:7b–13 JB).

If the teachings of the one, holy – Roman – Catholic, and apostolic Church are the word of God, then those who set them aside do nullify that word. This is the heart of what I have had to say to you today. Notice that St. Mark presents Our Lord's authoritative teaching in a context in which Our Lord has already distinguished between "the commands of God" and "the traditions of men." I believe that a University could once again be Catholic and free if it would label "the commands of God," make them readily available, and distinguish them clearly from the "traditions of men." Surely, that task is not beyond us.

Author's Later Note: When I delivered this talk in 1981, the Cold War still raged, and within the Catholic Church in the United States, defenders of a so-called 'magisterium' parallel to, but differing from, the Magisterium of the Church, proudly distinguished themselves from the followers of the official teaching. In such an atmosphere a certain acerbic and polemical tone seemed appropriate in theological debate. The Cold War has ended and within the Church the irenic and dialogic policy which the Holy Fathers have followed since the Second Vatican Council seems to have born fruit.

Dissent has not disappeared, but no one can help but know it for what it is. People may choose to follow the authentic voice of the Church or a different voice, for they know the difference. I think the present task is no longer to bother trying to expose the "other voice," but to make the authentic voice of the Church as understandable and attractive as possible. So, I would today say the same thing I said in 1981, but I would say it differently. It may be of interest to some to know that the idea and passage from sacred Scripture with which I ended this talk in 1981 has served as the "thesis" of a book-length manuscript which I have completed, but have not as yet succeeded in publishing.

10.
Personalism in the Thought of John Paul II
(1982)
Rev. Ronald Lawler, OFM Cap.

When John Paul II arrived in Boston in 1979 to begin his visit to America, he told the huge crowd that greeted him how his own concerns focused on each distinctive person. He would desire ". . . to enter each home, to greet personally each man and woman, to caress every child."[1] The form of John Paul II's scholarly work, the dominant concern of his pastoral life, the chief interest of his personal life are all centered on the mysterious richness of the person. Because the person is so threatened in our day, the central thrust of all John Paul II's work is the defense of the transcendent worth of each person.[2]

At the White House, speaking before the Supreme Court justices who had affirmed the suitability of abortion, and before the legislative, executive, and military leaders of the strongest nation in the world, he declared: "I want to assure you that my esteem and affection go out to every man, woman and child without distinction."[3] Writing to Kurt Waldheim, then secretary general of the United Nations – in response to the question, "What basis can we offer as the soil in which individual and social rights may grow?" – he gave this brief answer: "Unquestionably that basis is the dig-

---

1 John Paul II, *Pilgrim of Peace* (U.S.C.C.) Edition of Addresses Give by John Paul II in His 1979 Visit to the United States). Washington D.C.: Publications Office U.S.C.C., 1979, p. 3.

2 His major philosophical work is *The Acting Person*, Vol. 10, Analecta Husserliana. *The Yearbook of Phenomenological Research*, Boston: Reidel, 1979. This is a study of the way the nature of human action, and human nature, is revealed to phenomenological analysis. That all his work is penetrated with the defense of the transcendent dignity of each person is a major theme of this paper.

3 *Pilgrim of Peace*, p. 113.

nity of the human person."[4] Most people who have studied his work, or who have frequently caught sight of him, even on television, with small children, or young people, or the aged, have felt they could *see* the utter sincerity of his passionate concern for each of the many images of God he encounters.

Yet it is only too clear that many other people have come to suspect the authenticity of his personal concern and the consistency of his personalism.

Kati Marton, in an article in *Atlantic Monthly* ("The Paradoxical Pope"),[5] summarizes the objections of many. The charge is that the pope has personal charm, but he exploits it to defend an authoritarian and fundamentally anti-personalistic stance. Marton writes: "There is a growing feeling that the pope's personal warmth belies his rigid doctrine, that there is in fact a deep contradiction between John Paul II's announcements on human rights and his treatment of bothersome theologians."[6] John Paul II, according to Marton, describes as proper to a person in society a conscientious stance of "opposition," but he apparently will not tolerate that opposition in the Church; he proclaims the worth of all persons, but he stifles the profoundly felt personal aspirations of Christian feminists; he fights for the liberties of believers before tyrants, but he rejects pleas for the toleration of certain apparently vital new ideas in the Church. Sister Ann Carr expresses a similar complaint: "In matters of internal search, he does not seem very sensitive to the difficulties people experience. He's just not open to new currents."[7]

This paper will have three major parts: A. First, we shall point out some of the meanings of personalism today, and some distinctive notes of John Paul's personalism. B. Next we shall reflect on certain relationships between faith and personalism. C. Finally, we shall inquire into the doubts expressed about John Paul's personalism. In doing this, we shall reflect especially on the relations between personal freedom and the requirements inseparable from personal Christian faith.

I. The Meanings of Personalism

"Personalism" is a moderately popular word today. But it is used in so

---

4 "Papal Message in Human Rights to the United Nations." *Pope John Paul II Center Newsletter*, vol. 1, # 1., Jan.-Feb. 1979, p. 7.
5 K. Marton, "The Paradoxical Pope," *Atlantic Monthly*, May 1980, pp. 41–49.
6 *Art. cit.*, pp. 41–42.
7 *Pilgrim of Peace*, p. 44.

many senses that it is necessary to explore several central senses of the word with some care. "Personalism" can be used to characterize any philosophy that insists upon the distinctive reality and worth of the person. In Enlightenment days there were many materialistic philosophies that tended to undermine entirely any intellectual defenses of the worth of the human person and the importance of his freedom and dignity. Against these, there arose philosophies like those of Immanuel Kant. His philosophy can be called personalistic to the extent that, against Enlightenment determinism, he did care earnestly to defend the freedom of man (in his noumenal reality), and to make the notion of person central in his ethics ("Always treat each person as an end, and never as a means").[8] After Hegelian thought threatened to submerge the transcendence and distinctive identity of the person in a monistic idealism, making man appear too much as a mere part of a total system, the existentialism of Kierkegaard was a personalist outcry. Many twentieth-century thinkers are known as personalists: One would include here Renouvier, Blondel, and Mounier. Christian existentialists like Marcel and Berdiaev also touch many personalistic themes. Even an atheistic existentialist like Sartre is concerned with saving the authenticity of a personal life in at least some of its aspects, however much his atheism may interfere with a fuller personalism. The earlier American personalists, like B. P. Bowne and E. S. Brightman, could hardly be said to have influenced John Paul II, but in their concern with insisting that God is a person, that moral and ethical truths flow from the absolute value of the person, and that person is a central category of thought, they have constructed philosophies that are in important ways congenial with that of John Paul II.

Personalism Penetrated by Relativism. There is one kind of personalism that John Paul has always rejected. Perhaps it is for this reason that thinkers affected by such personalisms deny the authenticity of the pope's personalism. But the fact is that John Paul II rejects every radically relativistic form of personalism. He denies that each person is the measure of truth and goodness for himself, whenever this is interpreted as declaring that the human person cannot, in any way, lay hold with certainty of the decisive truths in matters of greatest importance: that is, in questions of values, and where the meaning or purpose of life is concerned. He rejects every claim that there is no interpersonally valid truth that could bind together a multitude in love and rightly require their loyalty.[9]

8   I. Kant, *Foundation of the Metaphysics of Morals*, Section 1.
9   See "The Difference Between Subjectivity and Subjectivism," in *The Acting*

For such subjectivistic personalisms John Paul II has no affection. Faith cannot be proclaimed with confident firmness in an atmosphere of this kind of pseudo-personalism. The person is far too important to be sacrificed to such relativistic stances. John Paul II constantly points out that the great contemporary problems of the person, the problems of freedom, solidarity, protection of the common good, and so on, cannot be resolved without the energy to lay hold of what is simply true. He points out how the Gospel defense of personal dignity is firmly rooted in intense love of the truth. In his first encyclical, John Paul II reminded us: "When Jesus Christ Himself appeared as a prisoner before Pilate's tribunal and was interrogated by him about the accusation made against Him by the representative of the Sanhedrin, did He not answer: 'For this was I born, and for this I have come into the world, to bear witness to the truth'? It was as if, with these words spoken before the judge at the decisive moment, He was once more confirming what He had said earlier: 'You will know the truth, and the truth will make you free.'"[10] John Paul is a personalist profoundly concerned with liberating truth.

John Paul's Personalism. John Paul's own personalism is complex. It is rooted in the classical Christian tradition that received its magisterial expression in the work of St. Thomas Aquinas. He is indebted in a special way to the creative work of Maritain, and to others in the more existential branch of the Thomistic family, such as Yves Simon.[11] Through these John Paul learned to approach contemporary philosophy with a gracious openness; and he is happy not only to express his brand of personalism with a phenomenological approach, but also to learn from modern and contemporary thinkers to stress earnestly those elements of personalistic thinking that did not need so much stress in medieval philosophy and theology (perhaps because the dangers to personal dignity were not so towering), but need to be overwhelmingly defended today. He is profoundly interested in the subjective (by which he never means subjectivistic, or only relatively true): i.e., in the intrapersonal depths of the subject's thought and action, in those di-

---

Person, pp. 58–59.

10 John Paul II, *Encyclical Letter, Redemptor Huminis* (March 4, 1979), Washington, D.C.: U.S.C.C., 1979, p. 37.

11 For a discussion of the roots of John Paul's personalism, see A. Woznicki, "The Christian Humanism of Cardinal Karol Wojtyla," *Proceedings of the American Catholic Philosophical Association* (1979 meeting), Washington, D.C.: Catholic University, 1979, pp. 28–35.

mensions of the knowing and caring and acting subject who is the person.[12] He is happy to use the resources of phenomenologists who express with great care those experiential elements of personal action that reveal the distinctive traits of personality, and provide the opening for defenses of the person.

But John Paul II wishes to proceed far beyond the insights which phenomenological description provides, and to reach (through the casual analysis proper to realistic philosophizing, and through the realistic methods of faith) to the very nature of the human person.[13] In *The Acting Person*, Wojtyla reveals an intelligent dissatisfaction with the classical definition of "person" given by Boethius: "A person is an individual subsisting in a rational nature."[14] He finds far more satisfactory other accounts of Aquinas. "Person," says St. Thomas Aquinas, "signifies that which is most perfect in all nature."[15] It is a truism in Christian thought that each person is in a real sense a totality and is worth more than all the material universe. Each one is called to possess, by knowledge and love, everything that is, and to possess it in a distinctive way. In a way, "person" is a Christian idea. The word developed its central metaphysical meaning in the course of Christian reflection on the central mysteries of the Trinity and the Incarnation, and on Christian anthropology with its reflection on the meaning of man and the worth of a being destined to possess God entirely. Christianity professes to believe startling things about man, in fact. It portrays God as saying to men: "I no longer call you servants but friends."[16] If each human person can rightly say that He who is God died for me, then the individual is of a worth beyond eloquence. Aristotle insisted that there could be no friendship between God and man. Man and God are too un-alike, too radically different. Friendship, however, must find or make persons equals. Christian faith is not afraid of this challenge: It insists that God does in a way make us His equals when He calls us to friendship. His grace divinizes us; it makes us gods; it causes us to share in His very nature. Each undesirable refugee from Cuba or Haiti, the unwanted child, the senile and dying person – is of more worth than the sun and all the stars. To say this is not to speak poetry, but to

---

12 Cf. *The Acting Person*, pp. 56–57.

13 Cf. *The Acting Person*, p. 186.

14 Boethius' definition can be found in his *De persona et duabus naturis*, ch. 3 (PL 64:1345). Wojtyla criticizes this in *The Acting Person*, pp. 73–74.

15 *Summa Theologiae*, I, 29, 3, c.

16 *John* 15:15.

declare sober truth. And it makes an important difference if one believes and knows that it is literally true. We may think of man in ways that do or do not acknowledge his full worth.

If we think of man in models that mock his dignity, and do not correct these models in firm judgments about what the person essentially is, we easily drift into the kinds of inhuman conduct that has marked our age at its agonizing worst. Throughout his analysis of man, Wojtyla shows that he is familiar with those ways of thinking of man that, while useful and bearers of some truth, are not providing adequate expressions of man's meaning and worth. Behavioral sciences can serve man well. But, with these, we need a philosophy and a theology of man that is faithful to all the riches of the subjectivity and the completeness of the person.

Some of the notions that Wojtyla treats with care in *The Acting Person* need, at least, passing mention here. These notions reveal, in part, his concern also for the social nature of man. I wish to touch chiefly on the notions of solidarity and opposition.

Solidarity. The attitude of *solidarity* is an authentic, a properly human attitude.[17] It is necessary for human persons because we need to live and act together to achieve what every person needs. Solidarity is the attitude of community. Wojtyla writes: "Solidarity involves a constant readiness to accept and realize one's (role) in the community. . . . Man does what he is supposed to do not only because of his membership in the group, but because he has the 'benefit of the whole' in view: he does it for the 'common good.'"[18] St. Paul was constantly calling the early Christians to solidarity when he urged them to be of the same mind: not to press for singular and separate stances of a kind that wounds love, but to come to shared visions and labors so that the entirely indispensable common good of he community could be reached.

The very nature of community requires the generosity of solidarity. A person cannot be fulfilled in isolation. To be authentically oneself, a person needs to share in goods that can be brought about only by shared action, by persons caring not only for their isolated advantage, but for the common good that binds them together. If the person is concerned only with himself, he will never fulfill himself, for he is fulfilled authentically largely by common goods that can be had only by the humility of solidarity.

Opposition that Guards Solidarity. Solidarity does not mean always

---

17 *The Acting Person*, pp. 283–87.
18 *Op. cit.*, p. 285.

going along with others, so that there will be "peace" in pursuing the common good. Authentic, too, is the attitude of "opposition."[19] To live under authorities and with associates who have radically different intellectual and moral convictions requires a nuanced attitude. There must yet be a shared concern for the common good that is honest and real. But a good person must sometimes oppose the means, even authoritatively proposed, for achieving such common goods. Wojtyla writes: "The one who voices his opposition to the general or particular rules or regulation of the community does not thereby reject his membership; he does not withdraw his readiness to act, to work, for the common good."[20] He further notes that there can be many different kinds of opposition, and that some opposition is grounded in lack of concern for the common good. But the opposition he praises as authentic is "essentially an attitude of solidarity; far from rejecting the common good with a needed participation, it consists on the contrary in their confirmation. This opposition aims then at a more adequate understanding, and, to an even greater degree, the means employed to achieve the common good, especially from the point of view of the possibility of participation."[21] He gives as an example the case of parents who in conscience must disagree with the means that an educational system is using. The attitude of opposition is a nuanced one. It does not storm away and lose concern for sharing in the common good. But it is rather a service to the community, pressing for a reformulation of the end of shared tasks in such a way that the consciences of all may be honored, in order that the energies of all may more forcefully promote the desired common good.

One might note that critics of John Paul II have often underlined his treatment of opposition. They ask why he praises the attitude of opposition in the state, but does not seem to advocate much opposition in the ecclesial community. Cannot the dissenter be in solidarity with the magisterium, even while he rejects certain expressions of doctrine or policies upon which the magisterium firmly insists? Of this question we must speak more.

John Paul II has labored intensely to shape a challenging new form of Christian anthropology precisely because so many academic visions of man truly leave no room for the sublime dignity of the person. Philosophies that do not adequately respect the person have penetrated all our cultural forms and institutions, and they conspire to "take away all transcendent meaning

---

19 *Op. cit.*, p. 186.
20 *Ibid.*
21 *Ibid.*

from man's life." They need freshly thought-out responses. We cannot be silent when man's life is reduced "to the rank of a useless passion, a cosmic error, an absurd pilgrimage of nothingness in an unknown and mocking universe. All these (despairing attitudes) have caused many people to lose sight of the meaning of life, and have driven the weakest and most sensitive to fatal and tragic forms of escapism. Man has a profound need to know if it is worth being born, living, struggling, suffering, and dying; if it is important to commit himself to some ideal, superior to material and contingent interests; and if, in a word, there is a reason that justifies his earthly existence. This, then, remains the essential question: to give a *meaning* to man, to his choices, his life, his history."[22]

II. Faith and the Personalism of John Paul

As a young student in theology, John Paul wrote his dissertation on the meaning of faith in the work of St. John of the Cross.[23] St. John of the Cross was a mystic whose whole life and work were rooted in the personal depths of a lived faith. From St. John, from St. Thomas Aquinas, and from his own life of faith, John Paul II has grasped the importance of rooting a Christian personalism in the experienced realities of a life of faith. He is indeed determined to make the best possible use of all available philosophical and theological tools to clarify the distinctive principles of an authentic personalism. But it is not in philosophical analysis that his personalism is primarily grounded.

Faith as the Foundation of his Personalism. John Paul's own faith, discovered and lived in the Church, is the foundation of his vision of man. In speaking of his Christian personalism, it is essential to give a central place to his account of the meaning, and the foundational role of faith. His own faith appears to be at once so profound and simple that those who do not understand the inner nature of Catholic faith are likely to see it as a bit dangerous. A critic of John Paul quotes with evident concern Cardinal Wyszynski's words about him: "Wojtyla is a man for whom prayer is a full-hearted manifestation of an almost childlike purity of faith."[24] How

---

22 John Paul II, "Only Jesus, the Bread of Life, Gives Meaning to Human Existence," *L'Osservatore Romano*, August 20, 1979, p. 3.

23 This has appeared in English as *Faith According to St. John of the Cross*, San Francisco: Ignatius Press, 1981.

24 Cited by K. Marton, "The Paradoxical Pope," p. 42.

dangerous it is, she suggests, to have a mighty Church ruled by one whose spiritual core is so childlike!

John Paul II, however, recognizes that all his work must be built on such faith, i.e., a faith childlike in its simplicity, but far from childish in its profound personal roots. He knows that his principal task in the world is no longer that of the professor of theology or philosophy. Now it is his task above all to serve the persons entrusted to his care as witness to faith. This was the theme of his talk to the European Bishops' symposium in Rome in October 1975. "Bishops must first believe whole-heartedly in Christ in order to be able to serve the faith of the Church, the people of God. They must not only believe, like all Christians, in the faith of the Church, but must define their mission as bishops at its very foundation in faith."[25] "Faith is above all a mystery, the outcome of the work of the Holy Spirit. Such is the faith of the Apostles. Such is the faith of every person who confesses Christ. There can be no exceptions. It is the mystery of the person, the mystery of the inner life of man, even if it continues to 'happen' in the community of the people of God. In these two dimensions faith constitutes a mysterious sharing in divine life, in divine knowledge – a knowledge permeated by love."[26]

Autonomy of Faith. Whenever he speaks of faith with his fellow bishops and fellow believers, he appeals to something we know together. To be a Christian is to have received a gift and to participate in a life which transcends everything purely natural. If we have not yet mastered our faith and not yet taken free personal possession of it, it may be to a great extent a puzzle and a mystery to us. But there still remains the obscure awareness that God has touched our lives, and that we must listen to Him come to life. One who has reflected on faith more earnestly and profoundly realizes more and more the autonomy of faith. It is true that one can come to faith in many ways, by intelligence, and by hope for and love of what is good, through the prayers of others, and through a multitude of other ways in which God leads us to hunger for knowledge of truth and fullness of life. Still, we do not believe because we have by some naturalistic means calculated and created for ourselves the stance of faith. In faith, God does something to the person He calls to Himself, giving him faith which has a great simplicity and a great depth. By faith, we have a certainty and a joy that are grounded di-

---

25 K. Wojtyla, "Bishop as Servants of the Faith," *Irish Theological Quarterly* *43* (1976), p. 263.
26 *Ibid.*

rectly in God, not founded essentially on any human reasons or on merely human hopes. The simplicity that some find so puzzling in John Paul's faith is essential to the very nature of faith. The "I believe" of faith is always utterly simple and direct. Faith is literally believing God, a personal God who has helped us decisively in coming to recognize Himself and his saving word. Personal faith is intelligent, but it cannot be built on mere arguments. It is true that intelligence can guide one to faith, and that God made us thinking beings permeated with all the restlessness of rationality. But God is also able to find a remedy to the weakness of reason in our fallen state. God has the power to reveal Himself, and to do this successfully. He is able to make us say with integrity of mind and heart: I believe in you. He makes it possible to give in that act of faith all the intense commitment that can be justified only because God has enabled the believer to realize that it is the Lord who has touched his life.

Personal Faith and the Authority of Christ. John Paul's defenses of the teaching office of the Church are defenses of the personal nature of faith, not defenses of authoritarianism. He is very aware of the personal and mystery dimensions of faith. He knows well the joyful wonder of Paul at how the Thessalonians came to believe in Christ: "When you received the word of God, which we proclaimed to you, you received it not as the word of man, but as it really is, the word of God."[27] It is a spoken word that stirs up faith; faith comes by hearing – an interpersonal encounter. Hearing a message is not discovering a text or some other bit of evidence to be tussled with, and to which each hearer may assign his own meaning, which each age (misled by its own false prophets) may interpret in radically new ways. No: the word proclaimed in the family of faith is meaningful, enduring, and speaks what really is.

John Paul II is a sophisticated modern thinker. He knows very well that there are different conceptual frameworks in which the same truths can be frequently expressed. There is in him no unlettered integralism. He knows very well that "the substance of the faith is one thing; the formulations that express it are another."[28] He himself has sought to express faith in contemporary idioms far different from those of the past. Yet, as with every truly creative Catholic theologian, John Paul is especially concerned that his fresh expressions of faith are true to the mystery. He knows that not every

27 *I Thessalonians* 2:13.
28 Pope John XXIII, Allocution at the Opening of the Second Vatican Council, October 11, 1962.

reformulation of doctrine will point successfully and truthfully to the very realities in which the act of faith terminates. Too often revisionists have said that they are speaking the faith in a new language, when they are really speaking something other than faith in a language of some excessively narrow philosophies. John Paul knows that elementary love of the person must exclude a relativism masked as pluralism; for every such retreat weakens supports for the sublime vision of man that authentic Catholicism always sustains, and that the human spirit needs.

Some have felt that openness of spirit or a generous ecumenism should incline us to profess with less certainty those teachings of faith that other sincerely religious people reject. Perhaps, some have suggested, we should in personal humility be willing to acknowledge that we could be wrong, and so, in order to serve fellowship or unity, be prepared to put aside some matters we have held as points of faith. But John Paul points out how unsuitable this approach is. It is not a question of our ability to be wrong, which we know all too well. It is a question of fully and humbly acknowledging the power Christ shows in the mystery of faith, once he has enabled us, who are unworthy of it, to share personally the light of his word. John Paul concludes: "True ecumenical activity means openness, drawing closer, availability for dialogue, and sense. But, in no way, does it or can it mean giving up or in any way diminishing the treasures of divine truth that the Church has continually confessed and taught."[29]

III. Freedom and Christian Personalism

Pope John Paul II has often been charged with inconsistency in his attitude toward religious freedom. On the one hand, his life has been a cry for religious freedom: first for the people of his native Poland, and later for the peoples of the entire world. Out of his philosophy, his faith, and his deeply lived convictions, he is certain that no one should be coerced in religious matters. Every human act, and especially the profoundly important religious act of faith, must be free, if it is to have real value.

On the other hand, he regularly argues that teachers of the faith have no right to present as Catholic any teaching that contradicts what the family of faith has consistently handed down as the saving truth of Christ. He speaks of the obligation of scholars and preachers to offer the faithful the teachings of Christ as the Magisterium presents it.[30] By no means are scholars to as-

---

29 *Redemptor Hominis*, III, 13; p. 39
30 *Pilgrim of Peace*, 166–67.

sume the freedom to teach in ways opposed to that (though they are free to teach that same meaningful truth in fresh ways). In the case of Hans Küng and others, John Paul II has shown an insistent firmness, not unlike that of the pastoral epistles. He declares that teachers of the faith have no right to recede from the word of Christ as the Church has understood and understands it. In view of this fact, let us discuss John Paul's profound conviction that religious freedom is an essential right of each person and what he understands religious freedom to be.

Faith and Freedom. Faith must be free, for every authentic human action must be free.[31] To make an act of faith is to do something. To believe is to perform a most important action of one's inner life. And every act of a person, especially such a personal, spiritual act, should bear the values of freedom. In *The Acting Person*, John Paul speaks of the basic importance of what he calls the "personalistic value" of the action.[32] It is good for the actions of men and women to be truly personal, that is, to be acts which are free, acts which – rather than being coerced by circumstances or any force whatever – are actions in which the agents guide themselves by their own choices. There can be no moral value whatever to actions unless they are free. Hence the "personalistic value" precedes by nature the moral value of ethical goodness or badness in the action. No action can be morally good if it is forced; we must make room for freedom so that there can be good actions. To force (even toward goodness) is to take away the possibility of the best sort of goodness: the free and willing goodness of the authentic and right human act. Even if an act is not morally good, there is a certain basic value in an act's being personal and free. It is not enough for a good human act that it be free; but it is essential for human acts to be free. Only in such freedom can anything important or great flourish. As John Paul II writes: "Obviously any moral value, whether good or bad, presupposes the performance of the action, indeed full-fledged performance. If action fails to be actually performed, or if it betrays in some respects the authenticity of self-determination, then its moral value loses its foundation . . ."[33]

In his proclamation of the Gospel, John Paul recalls that Christ respected fully the dignity of the human person. He honored fully the freedom with which man is to fulfill his duty of belief in the word of God. God calls men to serve him, and he enables us to know our duty to do so. But he does

---

31 Cf. *The Acting Person*, pp. 264–67.
32 *Ibid.*
33 *Op. cit.*, p. 265.

not force us. John Paul writes: "It is one of the major tenets of Catholic doctrine that man's response to God in faith must be free. Therefore, no one is to be forced to embrace the Christian faith against his own will. This doctrine is contained in the word of God and it was constantly proclaimed by the Fathers of the Church. The act of faith is of its very nature a free act. Man, redeemed by Christ the Savior and through Christ Jesus called to be God's adopted son, cannot give his adherence to God revealing himself unless the Father draw him to offer to God the reasonable and free submission of faith."[34]

It is because we know with certainty the truth of man's dignity, and because Christ has revealed the splendor of human freedom, that we must so strongly insist on religious freedom. The Catholic vision of religious freedom, and of other freedoms like that of academic freedom, are different from and richer than agnostic interpretations of freedom. With regard to the latter, philosophical problems have led many to be convinced that the human mind cannot come to the certain and enduring knowledge of anything whatever. They base their demands for human freedom on the contention that no one can possibly be sure that the position he wishes to defend is entirely true; and, therefore, each has a duty to allow others to express and defend their views on every matter with full vigor. History reveals that this agnostic defense of freedom has disturbing limitations. If we have no certainty, then we have no certainty about our possession of the right to this freedom either; and oppressive societies can and do claim that the common good (often very corruptly understood) demands the sacrifice of dubious individualistic claims.

Christian defenses of academic and other freedoms have, rather, been based on the claim that those who pursue truth with insistent good will can come to know with certainty the basic dignity of the person. Christian freedom is not a freedom based on assurances of universal ignorance, but on assurance of the truth: "You will know the truth, and the truth will make you free."[35] In Christian faith, regard for truth is a condition for authentic freedom.

Duties to the Truth. On the other hand, John Paul recalls the Vatican II teaching that men have many duties toward the truth. It is possible to fulfill these duties only freely, and they are grave responsibilities.[36] He writes:

---

34 *Dignitatis Humanae*, n. 10.
35 *John 8:32.*
36 The Second Vatican Council, Declaration on Religious Liberty (*Dignitatis*

"While the religious freedom which men demand in fulfilling their obligation to worship God has to do with freedom from coercion in civil society, it leaves intact the traditional Catholic teaching on the moral duty of individuals and societies toward the true religion and the one Church of Christ."[37]

John Paul II sought to illumine these duties and this freedom in his 1979 address to theologians at the Catholic University of America: "True theological scholarship, and by the same token theological teaching, cannot exist and be fruitful without seeking its inspiration and its source in the word of God as contained in Sacred Scripture and in the Sacred Tradition of the Church, as interpreted by the authentic Magisterium throughout history. True academic freedom must be seen in relation to the finality of the academic enterprise, which looks to the total truth of the human person."[38] He quotes the words of his immediate predecessor John Paul I on the day of his death: "Among the rights of the faithful, one of the greatest is their right to receive God's word in all its entirety and purity."[39] And he adds: "It behooves the theologian to be free, but with the freedom that is openness to the truth and the light that comes from faith and fidelity to the Church."[40]

The obligation of the theologian to be faithful to the Church would make no sense unless he were (as every true theologian is) himself a believer. The believing theologian is one who in the mystery of faith has come to recognize, in a light more sure than all scholarship, the most precious truth a scholar can possess. He has duties to this truth not because of the interfering will of some extrinsic authority. Rather, this duty has personal and interpersonal roots.

Still, there are painful problems. What is a bishop, responsible for guarding the faith, to do when some teacher of faith denies some point definitively taught in the faith, or refuses to acknowledge some of the faith's most central truths? Pope John Paul II has shown himself to be a model of strength and gentleness in this matter. In dealing with Father Hans Küng, he sought earnestly to find ways to lead him to share the faith of the Church in

---

Humanae), # 1.

37 *Dignitatis Humanae*, # 10.

38 In his Address at Catholic University, "To Presidents of Catholic Universities and Colleges" (October 7, 1979); in *Pilgrim of Peace*, pp. 166–67.

39 John Paul II is here quoting the September 28, 1978, remarks of John Paul I; in *Pilgrim of Peace*, p. 167.

40 *Loc. cit.*

that gift of infallibility that has been firmly defined by Councils, and to affirm directly the divinity of Christ in the sense it has been asserted by Councils and the ordinary faith of the Church. When Küng expressed unwillingness to accede and a desire to teach others (as a Catholic theologian) that they should share his dissent instead, a difficult decision had to be made.[41]

There was no willingness to take away Küng's freedom in any of the senses in which faith affirms that freedom. John Paul did not judge the inner state of the person. He expressed no desire to compel Küng to hold any positions. But to guard the rights of others, John Paul insisted that no one who cannot conscientiously believe and teach what faith holds may be set forward as a teacher of Catholic faith. It is part of our faith as believed that we are certain of the truth Christ proclaims through his Church. We profess by our living faith that God is able to reveal to us his saving truth, and we have a duty to make this accessible to others. When problems of the kind we are considering here arise, it is possible to reach solutions that violate no one's rights. If a dissenting teacher cannot believe a point of faith that the Church is certain of, no one should seek to make him assert what he does not freely believe.

But, as the guardians of precious realities, bishops must act also to honor the faith of all believers. Were a bishop to present to the family of faith some theologian or preacher who cannot believe what Catholic faith must guard as the word of God as a teacher of our faith, he would be acting dishonestly. As we noted earlier, the faithful have a basic right to have the authentic teaching of the faith given to them. Bishops have no vocation to require belief in those who cannot or will not believe. But they do have a duty to attend to the rights and needs of the people and to insist that no one present himself as a teacher of Catholic truth if he does not freely believe the tenets of Catholicism.

In a letter to the German bishops, John Paul spoke of the difficulties of the Hans Küng case. He spoke of the theologian as his brother, and of his real desire that they might again share a common witnessing to the whole mystery of faith, as the Church has firmly proclaimed it. But he wished to remind us that while we respect and honor the freedom of those who reject essential elements of faith, we must show love for all men by remaining wit-

---

41 Cf. John Paul II, Letter to the German Episcopal Conference, May 15, 1980, *L'Osservatore Romano*, June 30, 1980, pp. 8–9.

nesses to the truth God has graciously made accessible to us.[42] For the sake of those who wish to believe, and for the sake of those who for any reason do not, we must remain faithful to the truth that is the healing of all. Personal faith requires that we be faithful always to the word of Christ for the sake of every person, that at length all may, as we hope, come to his truth, and believe it gladly.

42 *Op. cit.*

11.
The Fundamental Themes of John Paul II's
Laborem Exercens (1982)
John M. Finnis

The encyclical identifies with precision its own "guiding thread": "the mystery of creation" (para. 12; see also para. 4). The concept of Creation provides the basis for the two leading ideas:

A. All forms of property are ultimately for the good of all human beings, because all are either natural resources, i.e. a sheer gift from the Creator, or are (or are at least radically dependent upon) the product(s) of other men's creative activity, and are thus a kind of inheritance into which I enter (i.e., a quasi-gift);

B. By work, the human person fulfills, develops or realizes himself, i.e., we share in God's creation of us, even when the work is humble in its "objective character."

Throughout the encyclical there is a conceptual distinction between "work in the objective sense" and "work in the subjective sense." This distinction has nothing whatever to do with the distinction between objective truth and (mere) subjective opinion. Rather, it reflects the fact that work has two aspects, two dimensions, two *rationes*. In one aspect, work is (i) directed toward an external object, e.g., some part of the world's natural resources, and (ii) transforms that external object with another external object, e.g., some machine created by someone else's work in the past, and (iii) results in another external object, the finished product. All this is the objective aspect of work.

Even when (as the encyclical intends) work is taken in the more generic sense as including all forms of chosen activity, including even (I think) contemplation, there is an objective aspect: the chosen behavior as an observable phenomenon in time and space.

The objective aspect of work is introduced in the middle of para. 4, as follows:

> Work understood as a "transitive" activity, that is to say, an activity beginning in the human subject and directed towards an external object, presupposes a specific dominion by man over "the earth," and, in its turn, it confirms and develops this dominion.

Now the word "transitive" suggests its opposite: "intransitive." But the pope, not wishing to impose his own philosophical vocabulary on the Church, abstains from using the term "intransitive," even though it is the key to his own philosophical explanation of what in the encyclical he calls the subjective aspect of work. To see this, let us first look at the encyclical's own explanation of the subjective *ratio* of work, in para. 6:

> Man has to subdue the earth and dominate it, because, as the "image of God" he is a person, that is to say, a subjective being capable of acting in a planned and rational way, capable of deciding about himself [*deliberandum de se*] and with a tendency to self-realization [*eoque contendens ut se ipsius perficiat*]. *As a person, man is therefore the subject of work.* As a person, he works [*opus facit*]. He performs various actions [*actiones*] belonging to the work process. Independently of their objective content, these actions must all serve to realize his humanity, to fulfill the calling to be a person that is his by reason of his very humanity [*vocationi, ex qua est persona quaeque vi ipsius humanitatis eius est propria*] (*LE* #6).

So, he continues, the "truth which in a sense constitutes the fundamental and perennial heart of Christian teaching on human work," is the "fact that the one who carries it out is a person, a conscious and free subject, that is to say, a subject that decides about himself [*de se ipso deliberans*]" (#6). This is made clear in the explanation of the good of work, in para. 9:

> It is not only good in the sense that it is useful [*bonum utile*] or something to enjoy [*bonum fruendum*]; it is also good as being something worthy [*dignum*], that is to say, something good [*bonum*] that corresponds to man's dignity, that expresses this dignity and increases it . . . a good thing for man [*bonum hominis*] – a good thing for his humanity [*bonum humanitatis*] – because through work man *not only transforms nature*, adapting it to his own needs, but he also *achieves fulfillment* as a human being [*se ipsum ut hominem perficit*] and indeed, in a sense, becomes "more a human being" (*LE* #9)

This "perfecting, realizing, developing of oneself" [*se ipsum perficere*] is, of course, a theme of the treatment of work in *Gaudium et Spes* #35, quoted in para. 26 of *Laborem Exercens*:

> Just as human activity proceeds from man, so it is ordered towards
> man. For when a man works he not only alters things and society, he
> develops himself as well [*se ipsum perficit*]. He learns much, he culti-
> vates his resources, he goes outside of himself and beyond himself [*ex-
> tra se et supra se*]. Rightly understood, this kind of growth is of greater
> value than any external riches which can be garnered . . ." (*GS* #35).

Much of *Laborem Exercens* is a commentary on those sentences from the
Council. But so, too, is much of Karol Wojtyla's philosophical work on human personality and action. The central chapter of his book *The Acting Person* begins with the assertion that "the performance of an action brings
fulfillment" and with the comment:

> All the essential problems considered in this study seem to be focused
> and condensed in the simple assertion of fulfillment in an action (*The
> Acting Person*, p. 149).

And, at the same time, the author invites us to notice the bearing of "fulfillment in an action" upon "our previous discussion of the person's *transcendence* in the doing of an action." What is this transcendence which sounds
so reminiscent of Vatican II's assertion that in activity man goes *extra se*
and *supra se*? Is this all mere poetry and metaphor? Not at all.

The transcendence that Wojtyla regularly speaks of is what he calls
"vertical transcendence." His distinction between horizontal transcendence
and vertical transcendence corresponds to his distinction between (i) the objective and the subjective *rationes* of work, and (ii) the transitive and intransitive aspects of action. (And my whole discussion at present is directed,
you will remember, to offering an explanation of the intransitivity of action.
All in good time.)

Horizontal transcendence, then, is the fact that we can get outside ourselves by perceiving and knowing objects, and by intending and willing objects (including events and states of affairs) outside, beyond ourselves.
Vertical transcendence, on the other hand, is the fruit of self-determination;
the person transcends his structural boundaries through the capacity to exercise freedom (*The Acting Person*, p. 119). It is "associated with self-governance and self-possession" (p. 131). It is the person's "ascendancy over his
own dynamism" (p. 138), over all the natural dynamisms of body and mind
(*soma* and *psyche*) (p. 197), all those dynamisms of emotion and desire and
aversion that are in themselves merely things that *happen* in or happen to
oneself (i.e., that take place in me) and are not *me acting* – though they belong to me just as much as the dynamism of action itself belongs to me

(p. 80), and when I do act, they are integrated into that superior type of dynamism and receive from it a new meaning and a new quality that is properly personal (p. 197). (There is no dualism in Wojtyla's thought.)

Let me explain in my own words what I understand Karol Wojtyla to be referring to when he speaks of vertical transcendence in this context. Free choice is more, much more, than freedom from compulsion and freedom to do as one pleases. That is what the ancients understood by choice, and that is what the post-Christian moderns understand by freedom. But it is not what is presupposed by Deuteronomy 30:19 – "I set before you life or death, blessing or curse. Choose life" – or by Sirach 15:14 – "When God, in the beginning, created man, he made him subject to his own free choice. If you choose, you can keep the commandments." The sort of free choice which is presupposed in those passages and in the whole challenge of the Gospel, and which Wojtyla always has in mind when he speaks of freedom, is the choice between open alternatives *such that there is no factor but the choosing itself which settles which alternative is chosen* – no factor, whether it be a system of desires or preferences (as the typical Anglo-American philosopher would have it), or selfish genes, or any other "sufficient reason." So free choices, precisely because they are not merely the product of what was already "there" (one's existing wants, preferences, habits . . . and other such "dynamisms"), *create*. This creativity of choice is the essence of "transcendence."

And as we understand this creativity, so we also understand what Wojtyla calls the intransitivity of action. Again, I shall use first my own words. Free choices establish, create, one's own identity or character. One's choice is not only transitive toward the chosen behavior and the further results and products of that behavior. It also is intransitive, an act by which, willy nilly, I who am choosing constitute myself as the person I will henceforth be, as the person I will remain unless and until I repent of that choice, either formally by contrition and resolve to amend my ways, or informally by making a new choice incompatible with the former one. And here we have reached another distinctive theme of Wojtyla's analysis of action: what he calls the *persistence* of actions.

> In the inner dimension of the person, human action is at once both transitory and relatively lasting, inasmuch as its effects, which are to be viewed in relation to efficacy and self-determination, that is to say, to the person's engagement in freedom, last longer than the action itself. The engagement in freedom is objectified . . . in the person and not only in the action, which is the transitive effect. Human actions once

performed do not vanish without trace: they leave their moral value, which constitutes an objective reality intrinsically cohesive with the person, and thus a reality also profoundly subjective. . .

It is in the modality of morality that this objectification becomes clearly apparent, when through an action that is either morally good or morally bad, man, as the person, himself becomes either morally good or morally bad. In this way, we begin to glimpse the meaning of the assertion that "to perform the action brings fulfillment." Implied in the intentionality of willing and acting, in man's reacting outside of himself toward objects that he is presented with as various goods – and thus values – there is his simultaneous moving back into his ego, the closest and most essential object of self-determination. Because of self-determination, an action reaches and penetrates into the subject, into the ego, which is its primary and principal object (*The Acting Person*, pp. 150–51).

Thus Wojtyla's explanation of what *Laborem Exercens* calls the subjective *ratio* of action, and what his philosophical writings call the intransitive aspect of action, is an explanation of the subject, the chooser and doer, as in a sense the object, the intransitive object, of choice and action. This corresponds to the sense in which, as the encyclical repeatedly says, man decides about himself, *deliberat de se ipso*:

the person is, owing to self-determination, an object for himself, in a peculiar way the immanent target upon which man's exercise of all his powers concentrates, insofar as it is he whose determination is at stake. He is, in this sense, the primary object or the nearest object of his action. Every actual act of self-determination makes real the subjectiveness of self-governance and self-possession; in each of these [intra]personal structural relations there is given to the person as the subject – as he who governs and possesses – the person as object – as he who is governed and possessed. This objectiveness . . . seems to bring out in a specific manner subjectiveness itself.

And later he says that the subject is not only the primary and nearest object of his or her action but is also the basic, most direct, and innermost object.

Now here you may have a misgiving. Is Karol Wojtyla lending his support to the theory that man disposes of himself by a "fundamental option" which is not the choice to do this or that particular act but is somehow a radical choice for self or for God, a total disposal of self in the depths of the self where (so they say) the self is totally present to itself . . . so that no particular choice or act can be said to be of itself a mortal sin, since only the fundamental option, which is not an option to do anything in particular, could be mortally sinful or salvific? Might there not be evidence that John Paul II supports that theory in the fact that *Laborem Exercens* repeats that phrase *deliberans de se ipso*, the phrase which we find just once in the entire corpus of St. Thomas, in *ST* I-II, q. 89, a. 6c, in that famous passage about the seven-year-old pagan whose first act of free will is either a mortal sin or an act of conversion *ad debitum finem* and *ad Deum* – this being the Thomistic passage to which supporters of the fundamental option theory have appealed? (To be fair to St. Thomas, I add immediately that when he comes to describe that act of conversion *ad Deum*, there is no question of the fundamental option imagined by some of our contemporaries. Instead there is the down-to-earth reality of a free choice to "consent" to two particulars, *faith in God and detestation of sin: ST* I-II, q. 113, a. 7 ad 1; aa. 4 & 5.)

And Karol Wojtyla's theory of the intransitive object of action is, I think, radically opposed to that theory of fundamental option. For, in the very midst of his insistence on the directness and immediacy of that intransitive object, and on the ego as that innermost object, he makes the essential caveat:

> Nevertheless, the objectification of the subject does not have an intentional character in the sense in which intentionality is to be found in every human willing. When I will, I always desire something. Willing indicates a turn toward an object, and this turn determines its intentional nature. In order to turn intentionally to an object we put the object, as it were, in front of us (or we accept its presence). But this kind of intentionality does not properly appertain to self-determination. The objectification that is essential for self-determination takes place together with the intentionality of particular acts of the will. When I will anything, then I am also determined by myself. . . . The ego is not an intentional object of willing. (*The Acting Person*, p. 109; see also p. 309, last sentence of #40).

And the implication of the encyclical's references to deliberating or deciding *de se ipso* is similar: This deliberating is not some mysterious act of self-disposal in which the very objective intended is total self-disposal before God. No, the deliberating *de se ipso* is the very same deliberating that precedes any free choice, for example, the choice to engage in this specific work or project, and to do it well, for this or that purpose. The deliberating *de se ipso* is an implication of *any* serious choice; for any serious choice, however specific its topic, is willy nilly a self-disposal, a formation of character, a (partial) creation (or reinforcement, or destruction) of the character which lasts beyond the time of the action, and which, being a spiritual reality, can last into eternity. So the whole paragraph on the subjective *ratio* or work (*LE* #6) ends thus:

> ... in the final analysis it is always man who is the purpose of the work, whatever work ... even work which is merely a matter of "service," or lacking in all variety in the ordinary way of thinking, or work which puts one on the margins of society.

(Here I offer my own translation, since the English speaks quite misleadingly of "alienating" work; the Italian, from which the English was prepared, is better: *"emarginante"*; and the Latin is clear enough: *agatur de opere ... in societatis partes secundarias potissimum detrudente*. The use of the word "alienating" at this point of *Laborem Exercens* #6 is seriously misleading because the whole burden of the pope's analysis is that work in which man expresses his self-determination, self-governance, and self-possession is not alienating.)

> Nineteenth and twentieth-century philosophy has rightly interpreted alienation as draining or sifting man from his very own humanness, that is, as depriving him of the value that we have here defined as "personalistic" (*The Acting Person*, p. 297).

And "personalistic value" is explained thus:

> ... we must look back at the whole of the previous analysis to see the strictly personal content of the action. We will then notice that the performance itself of an action by the person is a fundamental value, which we may call the *personalistic* – or personal – value of the action (*ibid.*, p. 264).

The pope's point in *Laborem Exercens* is precisely that the conventional ranking of sorts of work as menial or insignificant or even servile, while it is not a necessarily pointless ranking from certain points of view or for special purposes, is not the true ranking of work, which rather is to be judged "above all by the measure of the dignity of the subject of work, i.e., the individual who carries it out" – where "dignity," as we know, stands for that whole complex of inner freedom, responsibility, and love of true good.

Now if even service, or monotonous and marginalizing work, can be humanizing, the question arises how work can be degrading, oppressive, and exploitative, as *Laborem Exercens* acknowledges in several places (see *LE* #5, concerning technology becoming man's enemy, and *LE* #9 in the footnote recalling *Quadragesimo Anno* #135, and *LE* #8 and #11 tracing the conflict between labor and capital to the justified reaction of workers to their degradation as the subject of work). Part of the answer lies in the "accompanying exploitation" which consists of inadequate wages, bad working conditions, lack of social security, unemployment, and so on (on which there are specific directives in Part IV, paras. 16–23, built around the notion of the duties of the direct and indirect employer [paras. 16–18]). But these do not constitute the degradation of the worker as such. That degradation must be found, rather, in the "taking away 'of all personal satisfaction and the incentive to creativity and responsibility" (*LE* #5). Above all, degradation is to be found in the lack of what is described in *Laborem Exercens* #15 ("The personalist argument"): awareness that one is working "for oneself," i.e., *in re propria*.

Thus we return to the question of *ownership*, which I said is controlled by the first theme of the encyclical: creation as gift. *Laborem Exercens* affirms the right to private property, even of the means of production (*LE* #14), partly because working *in re propria* improves the production process as an economic process (see *LE* #15 [mis]citing *ST* I–II, q. 66 [not 65], a. 2), and partly because working *in re propria* is necessary for attaining or realizing the "subjective" good of work. But the right of private property is subject to the "fundamental principle of the moral order in this sphere, viz., the principle of the common use of goods" (*LE* #18).

Again and again, the encyclical insists upon this "first principle of the whole ethical and social order, namely the principle of the common use of goods" (*LE* #19); or, more fully, "the universal destination of goods and the right to common use of them" (*LE* #14); or, more fully still, "the right common to all human beings to use the goods of the whole of creation: the right to private property [being] subordinated to the right to common use, to the fact that goods are meant for everyone (*destinationique bonorum universali*)" (*LE* #14; see also *LE* #18).

This principle, being fundamental to the whole tradition of Christian social thought, is *used*, not explicitly argued for, in the encyclical. But I want to suggest that the context provided by John Paul II's thought, in the encyclical and elsewhere, affords great assistance in grasping the principle with fresh conviction. For the two essential features of that context are: creation, as a gift and an ordering, and the personality of each and every as intrinsically capable of participation in creation by virtue of his absolutely non-metaphorical self-determination in the free choices which are his as the image of God (*LE* #1, #4, #6, #9, #25).

The encyclical's discussion of the priority of labor introduces immediately its discussion of the question of property (*LE* #12). And there the pope identifies what he calls "the guiding thread of this document": the affirmation that at "the beginning of man's work is the mystery of creation." And that affirmation is offered as the summary of the preceding sentences:

> In every phase of the development of his work, man comes up against the leading role of *the gift made* by nature, that is to say, in the final analysis, *by the Creator*. [For] . . . everything that comes from man throughout the whole process of economic production presupposes . . . the riches and resources of the visible world, riches and resources that *man finds* and does not create.

This might almost be written as a reply to Robert Nozick's argument that principles of distributive justice *would* apply to property *if* objects had appeared from nowhere, out of nothing, whereas in fact, as Nozick thinks, "things come into the world already attached to people having entitlements over them" (Nozick, *Anarchy, State and Utopia*, p. 160; cf. Finnis, *Natural Law and Natural Rights* [Oxford University Press, 1980], p. 187n).

Let me say a word or two about the role of the concept of God's Creation in *Laborem Exercens* as establishing the framework of dependence which Christian truthfulness humbly accepts even when asserting the transcendence of man. Let me return to the end of the paragraph (*LE* #4) about "work understood as a 'transitive' activity," i.e., work in its objective dimension. The final part of that paragraph begins:

> While people sometimes speak of periods of 'acceleration' [*accelerantur*] . . . none of these phenomena of acceleration exceeds the essential content of what was said in [the first chapter of Genesis]. As man, through his work, becomes more and more the master [*dominus*] of the earth, he nevertheless remains in every case and at every phase of this process [*progressionis*] within the creator's original ordering [*ordinatio*]. And this *ordinatio* remains necessarily and indissolubly linked with the fact that man was created, as male and female "in the image of God." This *ordo rerum* [the Italian, English, etc., questionably, have "process" here] is at the same time universal: it embraces all human beings, every generation, every phase of economic and cultural development, and, at the same time, it is an *ordo efficitur* [again, mysteriously, "process takes place"] within each human being, in each conscious human subject. Each and every human individual is embraced by it [*hoc ordine*] [and] . . . takes part in the *immens[us] ord[o]* whereby man "subdues the earth" through his work (*LE* #4)

This passage must remind us of the relation between paragraphs ##5 and 10 of *Gaudium et Spes. GS* #5 says:

> History itself is accelerating [*acceleratur*] on so rapid a course that individuals can scarcely keep pace with it . . . . And so the human race is passing from a relatively static conception of the *ordo rerum* to a more dynamic and evolutionary conception . . .

Para 10 confronts naïve evolutionary and process theologies with the following:

> The Church believes that in her Lord and Master are to be found the key, the center and the goal of the whole history of mankind [words adopted by John Paul II for the opening sentence of his first encyclical, *Redemptor Hominis*]. And the Church affirms, too, that underlying all changes there are many things that do not change, and that have their ultimate foundation in Christ who is the same yesterday, today, and forever. So it is in the light of Christ, the image of the unseen God, and the firstborn of every creature, that the Council is setting out to speak to everyone, to clarify the mystery of man and to cooperate in finding a solution to the principal problems of our time.

As John Paul II says at the beginning of *Laborem Exercens* #4: "Relating herself to man, [the Church] seeks to express the eternal designs and transcendent [*naturam transcendentem*] destiny which the living God, the Creator and Redeemer, has linked with him." In other words, what is good for man, what is the *bonum hominis*, fundamentally does not change.

With that clarification, I revert to the significance of the concept of gift as the basis for the affirmation that goods are for common use. In *Laborem Exercens* #13, the concept of gift is expanded to include that of inheritance:

> Working at any work-bench [*sedis operis*], whether a relatively primitive or an ultra modern one, a man can easily see that *through his work he enters into two inheritances*: the inheritance of what is given to the whole of humanity in the resources of nature, and the inheritance of what others have already developed on the basis of those resources, primarily by developing technology, that is to say, by producing a whole collection of increasingly perfect instruments for work. In working, therefore, man simultaneously "enters into the labor of others" (John 4:38) (*LE* #13).

I should like to read the whole of the rest of that section of the paragraph, but already it should be clear how the argument undermines any conception of

an absolute right of private property in any thing. No one can say that the
gift has been made simply to him, unconditionally and without regard to
any of the other human persons who like him have been created to have dominion over the earth. And this consideration is reinforced by the *density*
which is lent to the notion of human personality, in each and every human
being, by the understanding summed up by Karol Wojtyla as "transcendence":

> We can speak of socialization of property [*collatio in commune*] only
> when the subjective [not "subject"!] character of society is ensured,
> that is to say, when on the basis of his work each person is fully entitled
> to consider himself a part-owner [*compossessor*] of the great
> work-bench at which he is working with everyone else. (*LE* #14)

For:

> When man works, he wishes the fruit of this work to be available for
> himself and others, and he wishes to be able to take part in the very
> work process as a sharer in responsibility [*Particeps onerum
> munerumque*] and creativity [*socius rerum auctor*] at the work-bench
> to which he applies himself so that he can know that in his work, even
> on something that is owned in common [*in domino quodam commune*]
> he is working "for himself" [*in re propria*] . . . [as] a true subject of
> work with an initiative of his own (*LE* #15).

And this securing of the subjective character of society is not achieved
by a prior elimination of private ownership [*possessionis*] of the means of
production, which remains a norm [*principium*] upheld today as before by
the Church (*LE* #14) – not an exceptionless norm (*LE* #15), but a norm sufficiently rooted in "the personalist argument" (*LE* #16) to require
"well-founded reasons [*certas gravesque causas*]" for any exceptions.

As to communism, the message of *Laborem Exercens* is that it is just
another form of capitalism, the fundamental characteristic of capitalism being a denial of the priority of labor over capital. This proper priority results
from the fact that labor is in certain respects an end or good in itself, being
the self-determination and self-realization of a free and self-governing and
responsible person, whereas capital is all the natural resources and other instruments of production. So *Laborem Exercens* #7 says:

> The error of early capitalism can be repeated wherever man is in any
> way treated on the same level as the whole complex of material means
> of production, as an instrument and not . . . as subject and maker and,

for this very reason, as the true purpose of the whole process of production.

And dialectical materialism shares just that error in another form, since:

> In dialectical materialism too, man is not first and foremost the subject of work but continues to be understood and treated, in dependence on what is material, as a kind of "resultant" of the [economic] relations of production. (*LE* #13).

The encyclical gives a label to both "capitalism" and "socialism": "economism." This term refers to what the encyclical identifies as a "fundamental error of thought":

> It is an error of materialism, in that economism directly or indirectly includes a conviction of the primacy and superiority of the material, and directly or indirectly places the *spiritual* and the personal (man's activity, moral values [*bona moralia*] and such matters) in a position of subordination to material reality. This is still not theoretical materialism in the full sense of the term, but is certainly a practical materialism, a materialism judged capable of satisfying man's needs on the grounds of a particular method of evaluation, i.e., on the grounds of a certain hierarchy of goods [*ordo bonorum*] based on the greater immediate attractiveness of what is material. (*LE* #13).

When the pope speaks of "the spiritual and the personal," he is not using mere vague and well-sounding phrases. He has in mind a series of well-considered truths about human freedom, i.e., self-governance, self-possession, self-determination, responsibility in free choices of every kind. As he says, man's "spiritual nature reveals itself as the transcendence of the person in his acting" and only by comprehending that transcendence can we comprehend in what man's spiritual being consists (*The Acting Person*, p. 182).

The pope makes it very clear that the materialism and economism which he has in mind are by no means restricted to philosophical materialism or Marxism, but extend to all those ideas and attitudes, philosophical or practical, which found expression in "the philosophy and economic theories of the eighteenth century," as well as in "the whole of the economic and social practice of that time," a time of "primitive capitalism" and "primitive liberalism."

Thus, in the encyclical, we find a critique not only of certain forms of socialism and communism, but also of what I (not the encyclical) shall label "right-wing liberalism" and "left-wing liberalism." Right-wing liberalism sees man as a locus of satisfactions. It sees all his activities and his relations with other men and women as means of securing those satisfactions. Liberty (not the liberty of free choice, but the liberty of freedom from constraint) is seen as a necessary means for securing wealth and satisfactions. Left-wing liberalism is more concerned about equality than about liberty (freedom from constraint). But it too has no conception of genuine self-determination by free choices and is concerned about equality of satisfaction, not about the genuine spiritual goods attainable only by self-determination.

A word, finally, about the deepest meaning of work, in which participation in creation becomes also, by virtue of the Cross and Resurrection, a participation in the Redemption *peracta* (accomplished) by Christ (*LE* #2: not "in Christ"), the *opus salutis* (*LE* #24).

In *Laborem Exercens*, the guiding principle of the priority of labor is introduced under the shadow of a reminder of "the prospect [*timore*] of worldwide catastrophe in the case of nuclear war with a power of destruction virtually unimaginable" (*LE* #12). Again, still more forcefully: "the prospect of the extinction by which the human race would rub itself out [*extinctionis qua genus humanum se deleat ipsum*]." In fact, each of the pope's encyclicals contains at least one of these reminders, and *Dives in Misericordia* formulates the possibility that "in the world evil [may] prevail over good, [and] contemporary humanity [may] deserve a new 'flood' on account of its sins" (*DiM* #15; also *DiM* #11; *Redemptor Hominis* #8 and #15). All the transitive effects of our work may be brought to nothing.

It is in the light of this that we must understand the concluding paragraphs of *Laborem Exercens*:

> In work, thanks to the light that penetrates to us from the Resurrection of Christ, we always find a glimmer of new life, of the new good [*bonorum novorum*], as if it were an announcement of "the new heavens and the new earth" in which man and the world participate precisely through the toil [of] work. . . . Is not this new good – the fruit of human work – already [*iam*] a small part of that "new earth" where justice dwells? (*LE* #27)

The grand themes of the opening paragraphs of *Redemptor Hominis* were, as you recall, not only *truth*, but also *eternal life* – the already but not yet. John Paul II's profound understanding of the creative and "persisting" significance of human actions as constitutive of the spiritual reality of each one of us can help us understand the Christian teaching which (as the last paragraph of *Laborem Exercens* stresses) insists upon both the intrinsic links and the intrinsic distinction between earthly progress and the building up of the Kingdom of God.

12.
Americanism: The "Phantom Heresy" Revisited (1983)
James Hitchcock

In January of 1899, Pope Leo XIII addressed a letter to the American bishops, in the person of Cardinal James Gibbons of Baltimore, which he titled *Testem Benevolentiae* ("Witness of Good Will"), and which warned against certain errors designated under the general title of "Americanism."

At that time, and for many years afterward, the letter was seen as a rebuke to the "Americanist" or "liberal" wing of the United States hierarchy, of whom the acknowledged leader was Archbishop John Ireland of St. Paul. (Cardinal Gibbons was generally, although often timidly, supportive of the Ireland faction.) Later generations of American Catholics were commonly taught that Americanism was a "phantom heresy," deriving from a series of misunderstandings between Rome and the United States, and describing a phenomenon which in reality did not exist.

The brunt of the papal warning, which was interlaced with expressions of solicitude and praise for American Catholicism and with assurances that the Vatican did not think that the American bishops themselves professed heterodox ideas, was a defense of the "supernatural" virtues and the principles of traditional Catholic spirituality, as against a tendency to exalt what was purely human and to deny the applicability of traditional ideas to the modern American situation. The pope cautioned against the tendency to view the American experience as unique.[1]

Disentangling the Americanist crisis is not possible apart from an examination of the personalities of its principal actors—especially Archbishop Ireland; Bishop John J. Keane, first rector of the Catholic University of America; Msgr. Denis J. O'Connell, rector of the North American Col-

---

1 English translation in Thomas T. McAvoy, C.S.C., *The Great Crisis in American Catholic History, 1895–1900,* Chicago: H. Regnery Co., 1957, pp. 379–92.

lege in Rome; and Bishop John Lancaster Spalding of Peoria—who formed the nucleus of the Americanist group within the hierarchy. In time, their chief antagonists came to be Archbishop Michael A. Corrigan of New York; Bishop Bernard J. McQuaid of Rochester; and, to a somewhat lesser degree, Archbishop Patrick J. Ryan of Philadelphia.[2]

The very names of the episcopal antagonists reveal that, while ethnic divisions played some role in the controversy, they were not crucial—most of the participants were of Irish birth or extraction. Ironically, the most ardent Americanizers, with the exception of Spalding, who was from an old Kentucky family, had been born in Ireland, while Corrigan, their chief opponent, was a native of New Jersey.

In time, the division between "liberals" and "conservatives" came to be regarded as a split between proponents of a quasi-independent "American Church" and a Church fully loyal to Rome. In the beginning, however, there was no such neat division. Corrigan and McQuaid, more than a decade before the Americanist crisis, were among probably the majority of American bishops who were resistant to Roman influence in the United States; they thought Rome misunderstood the American situation, and suggested that Canon Law was not properly adapted to American needs.[3] They were among the bishops opposing the idea of a permanent Apostolic Delegation in the early 1890s, at a time when, initially, some of the liberals favored it.[4]

Indeed, for a while the first permanent apostolic delegate sent to America, Archbishop Francesco Satolli, showed himself more friendly to the liberals than to the Corrigan faction, a tendency which only began to reverse itself around 1895, when Rome finally became suspicious of certain trends in the United States.[5]

Americanism can be called a phantom heresy because so much of its ideology proved to be pure rhetorical smoke—extravagant hymns of praise to the American experience by men who rarely indicated what exactly they meant. Thus, in 1898, O'Connell, who was the agent of the American hier-

---

2 See McAvoy, *Crisis;* Robert D. Cross, *The Emergence of Liberal Catholicism in American,* Chicago: Quadrangle Books, 1958.

3 Robert Emmett Curran, s.j., *Michael Augustine Corrigan and the Shaping of Conservative Catholicism, 1878–1902,* New York: Arno Press, 1978, pp. 15, 16, 20; Frederuck J. Zwierlein, *The Life and Letters of Bishop McQuaid,* Rome: Desclee and Co. 1926, II, pp. 54, 171–84.

4 Curran, *Corrigan,* p. 16; Zwierlein, *McQuaid,* II, p. 171.

5 Curran, *Corrigan,* pp. 361, 363–34, 373, 395, 396, 399, 420, 423.

archy in Rome, wrote to Ireland that ". . . `for this you were born, for this
came into the world': to realize the dreams of your youth for America, and
to be the instrument in the hands of Providence for spreading the benefits of
a new civilization over the world."[6]

Although some of its antagonists were American-born prelates of Irish
extraction, Americanism, at least as exemplified by John Ireland, was at a
minimum an antagonism towards all "foreign" (particularly German) elements in American Catholicism. In private, and sometimes in public, Ireland was vehement in his opinion that bishops should not be appointed for
their ability to speak the immigrants' languages, and he bitterly opposed the
promotion of Frederick Katzer to be archbishop of Milwaukee in 1891.
Over and over again, Ireland and his friends talked about the unique and
providential nature of the American experience and of the willful wickedness of those who insisted on retaining their Old World ties.[7]

Although such attitudes might be explained as the opinions of Irishmen
who considered themselves assimilated in an English-speaking society,
something deeper appears to have been involved—a desire to prove to
American Protestants that the Catholic Church carried all the social and intellectual respectability of the Reformation bodies, a proof of which many
of the immigrants were a standing refutation. In 1889, Ireland, in apparent
exasperation, actually wished that nine-tenths of the membership of the
Church in the U.S. would disappear: "In Archbishop Carroll's time the
Church was truly American. Later the flood of foreign immigration over-
powered us, and made the Church foreign in heart and in act. Thank God we
are recovering from that misfortune."[8]

The Americanist bishops seem, consciously or unconsciously, to have
taken Protestant America as their touchstone, and to have interpreted their
own faith primarily in terms which Protestant America would find acceptable. Thus, John J. Keane once gave an address at Harvard under a foundation which had been specifically established to expose the "errors" of
Roman Catholicism, and, although his very invitation to speak might have

---

6 Gerald P. Fogarty, S.J., *The Vatican and the Americanist Crisis: Denis J.
   O'Conneel, American Agent in Rome, 1885–1903,* Rome: Universita
   Gregorian Editrice, 1974, p. 279.
7 Colman Barry, O.S.B., *The Catholic Church and the German Americans,*
   Milwaukee: Bruce Publishing Co., 1953, pp. 45–50.
8 James H. Moynihan, *The Life of Archbishop John Ireland,* New York:
   Harper and Row, 1953, p. 413.

been evidence of a budding ecumenism at America's premier university, it was also noted by Keane's critics that he spoke vaguely and ironically, avoiding substantive theological issues. There were similar criticisms following his appearance at the World Parliament of Religions in Chicago in 1893.[9] The curious and mysterious group of New York priests called the *Accademia*, which met regularly from the late 1860s on, and which thought of itself as planning the American Church of the future, was rife with expressions of embarrassment about the "backwardness" of Catholic liturgy and piety, sometimes contrasting it unfavorably with that of the Episcopal Church.[10]

Already by the 1880s there was apparent a pattern (repeated since the Second Vatican Council) whereby secular media more or less openly hostile to the Church praised particular bishops who allegedly represented "progressive" currents. Thus the president of Bowdoin College contrasted "bigoted" Catholics of a traditional stripe with the new "liberals."[11] *The New York Times*, often virulently anti-Catholic, lauded the "progressive" faction of the bishops.[12] When Keane was removed as rector of the Catholic University in 1896, he was publicly lauded by Protestants, who simultaneously attacked the Church as a whole.[13] Of Spalding, a Unitarian minister told his own flock, "If he is a Roman Catholic, then it is a Roman Catholic which I wish to make you."[14]

In general the Americanists found it necessary to minimize whatever anti-Catholicism existed in the United States, although the Vatican undoubtedly retained memories of how a previous apostolic delegate had been mobbed on his visit to the country. Thus when a priest raised the question of anti-Catholicism among the Republicans, Ireland deplored the introduction of "sectarian issues" into politics. In 1900, he opposed a plan to establish a

---

9 Cross, *Emergence*, p. 44.

10 Curran, Corrigan, p. 171; Richard L. Burtsell, *The Diary of Richard L. Burtsell, Priest of New York*, ed. Nelson J. Callahan, New York: Arno Press, 1978. The latter volume includes numerous reports of *Accademia* meetings, by a participant.

11 Cross, *Emergence*, p. 44.

12 *Ibid.*, p. 92; Curran, *Corrigan*, p. 247; Barry, *German Americans*, p. 214.

13 Patrick Henry Ahern, *The Life of John J. Keane, Educator and Archbishop, 1839–1918*, Milwaukee: Bruce Publishing Co. 1955, p. 186.

14 David Francis Sweeney, O.F.M., *The Life of John Lancaster Spalding, First Bishop of Peoria, 1840–1916*, New York: Herder and Herder, 1965, p. 282.

federation of American Catholic societies for the purpose of resisting religious bigotry, an opposition in which Gibbons joined.[15]

From the Civil War until the Great Depression, the Republican Party was the dominant political organization in America at the national level, and arguably also the apt vehicle for the expression of the values and beliefs of a self-consciously growing and expanding country. Not surprisingly, therefore, Ireland in particular gave his support to the Republicans with unstinting, though sometimes unrequited enthusiasm. His conviction, seemingly shared somewhat less emphatically by his fellow Americanists, was that the Democratic Party was the party of the immigrant, and was thus an embarrassment to a Church determined to prove its American character.[16]

Such partisan loyalty inevitably led to embarrassments of a different kind. Archbishop Ireland, for example, enthusiastically supported the American cause in the Spanish-American War, despite having been asked by the Vatican to intervene with the American government to help avert it. After the war, although some Catholics thought the Church was being treated unjustly with respect to property and other rights, Ireland was consistently willing to understand the position of the Roosevelt administration.[17]

Complaints from Catholics about prejudice in the federal government (which, except for the years 1885–89 and 1893–97, meant prejudice chiefly among Republicans) were consistently brushed aside by Ireland. He and Gibbons tended to discourage all public complaints about anti-Catholicism, by intimating that their close ties to prominent Republican politicians would effectively achieve the desired results.

In particular their trust reposed in Theodore Roosevelt, quintessential representative of the "WASP" establishment. Roosevelt, however, seems in private to have retained a genial contempt for Catholics, on one occasion referring to the liberal bishops as "Mick ecclesiastics,"[18] a wounding epithet, had its targets known about it, given their anxious desire to be thought of as

---

15 Moynihan, *Ireland,* p. 28.
16 John Tracy Ellis, *The Life of James Cardinal Gibbons, Archbishop of Baltimore, 1834–1921*, Milwaukee: Bruce Publishing Co., 1952, II, p. 524; Curran, *Corrigan,* p. 453.
17 Ahern, *The Catholic University of America, 1887–1896. The Rectorship of John J. Keane,* Washington: Catholic University of America Press, 1948, p. 162; Ellis, *Gibbons,* II, p. 96.
18 Ahern, *Life of Keane,* p. 114.

pure Americans. The Notre Dame University priest-scientist, John Zahm, a leading intellectual figure in the Americanist movement, traveled with Roosevelt in South America and established an ostensibly warm relationship with the former president. But this did not prevent Roosevelt from calling Zahm, in a letter, "a funny little Catholic priest."[19]

Anti-Catholicism had played a major role in the defeat of Republican presidential hopes in 1884, when a member of the G.O.P. candidate's entourage, a Protestant minister, uttered the famous remark denouncing "Rum, Romanism, and Rebellion" within the hearing of reporters. The candidate, James G. Blaine, claimed not to have heard the remark, and Ireland, Gibbons, and other Republican-leaning prelates did not hold him or his party accountable for it, although hundreds of thousands of Catholic voters seem to have been won to the Democrats as a result. Ireland in particular continued to have close political relations with Blaine.[20]

It is hardly surprising, therefore, that the Vatican eventually concluded that it was being misled about American realities by the most enthusiastic American bishops, since, while on the one hand they minimized all incidents of anti-Catholicism and insisted that the United States provided uniquely fertile soil for producing strong Catholics, on the other they strategically raised the specter even of a *Kulturkampf* when it suited their purposes, in order to frighten Rome away from firm action which would be "misunderstood" in the American context. O'Connell, in 1897, advised Ireland that the Americanists stood little chance in Rome of getting their way unless they threatened possible action by the American government against the freedoms of the Church.[21]

Most of the time, however, the Americanists carried high the banner of church-state separation as found in the United States, arguing that it was a system uniquely suited to allow true religion to grow unhampered. Thus, in the minds of many, the whole Americanist crisis came in retrospect to be seen as a defense of modern principles of religious liberty.

Although Ireland in particular often talked as though his principal concern was to defend the American political experiment against uncomprehending foreigners, in fact it is difficult to find anyone at the time who was

---

19 Ralph E. Weber, *Notre Dame's John Zahm, American Catholic Apologist and Educator,* Notre Dame, Ind.,: University of Notre Dame Press, 1961, p. 186.

20 Fogarty, *O'Connell,* p. 86.

21 *Ibid.,* pp. 197, 211.

attacking that experiment. Leo XIII certainly did not, although he warned against a tendency to absolutize that system.[22] Ireland's principal intellectual adversary, Msgr. Joseph Schroeder of Catholic University, strongly defended republicanism as the best form of government for the United States, merely opposing the tendency to insist that it be made universal.[23] But it was precisely such an insistence, couched in characteristically passionate and sweeping language, which was made by Bishop Spalding in an address at Catholic University shortly after its opening in 1888.[24]

If Archbishop Ireland was the most enthusiastic verbal defender of the principle of church-state separation, he was in practice also one of its chief violators, for he shamelessly and ceaselessly intrigued in secular politics—persuading a Minnesota senator to denounce the German Catholic movement called Cahenslyism on the Senate floor, enlisting the aid of President Benjamin Harrison for the same purpose, entering a New York state election in support of a priest expressly opposed by Bishop McQuaid, and, finally, enlisting Roosevelt and other leading Republican politicians in maneuvers designed to gain himself a cardinal's hat. It was richly symbolic that, when Archbishop Satolli first arrived in the port of New York in 1892, Ireland and his allies commandeered a Coast Guard cutter to take him off ship in the harbor, so he would not be formally welcomed by Archbishop Corrigan.[25]

Arguably it was necessary for American bishops, at some point, to test the limits of American institutions with respect to their own faith, and Ireland was uniquely qualified to do that. However, as in his blind loyalty to the Republican Party, and in his tendency to minimize American anti-Catholicism, his assessment of those institutions proved defective. The key controversy was the Faribault School Plan of 1893, whereby he achieved an agreement with a Minnesota school district in effect to permit the teaching of Catholic catechism in the public schools. The plan was strongly opposed by some bishops, who saw it as undermining the parochial school system mandated by the Fourth Provincial Council of Baltimore (1884) and reflecting an unfortunate willingness to compromise with forces hostile to the Church. At first Satolli gave limited support to the Faribault

---

22 McAvoy, *Crisis*, p. 381.
23 Barry, *German Americans*, p. 123.
24 Sweeney, *Spalding*, p. 143.
25 Moynihan, *Ireland*, p. 349; Ahern, *Life of Keane*, p. 377; Ellis, *Gibbons*, II, p. 682; Curran, Corrigan, p. 368.

plan, but Ireland was subsequently embarrassed when the public school district itself reversed the agreement.[26]

The Faribault controversy gave rise to a good deal of debate within American Catholicism about the respective rights of parents, church, and state in the education of children. With bitter memories of anti-Catholic legislation in Europe, many immigrants could not share Ireland's optimistic attitude about the public schools (an apprehension which seems abundantly justified by later developments), and some of the intellectual defenders of Ireland's plan showed a certain naïve complacency about the rights of the state in education.[27]

The Americanists—Ireland in particular—also often represented themselves as champions of intellectual freedom, deriving from the American Way, in contrast to Old World authoritarianism. Yet their control of the Catholic University board enabled them to purge those professors not in sympathy with their goals, notably Joseph Schroeder. Denis O'Connell, when he became rector of the university after the turn of the century, actually showed himself rather conservative in matters of doctrine and even arranged the ouster of a professor suspected of modernist tendencies in Scripture studies.[28] Contrary to common impressions, the Americanist prelates were not particularly learned men (certainly less so than was Schroeder, for example), and an early lay professor at Catholic University quipped that Keane had no vision of what the university should be other than "the Stars and Stripes sprinkled with a little holy water."[29] In the early years of the twentieth century the way was already being prepared, at prestigious secular institutions like Harvard, for a revival of medieval studies. Ironically, the reflexive embarrassment over all things "medieval" which

---

26 Moynihan, *Ireland,* pp. 84, 101.

27 Ellis, *Gibbons,* I, 656, 664, 667, The chief presentation of the "liberal" position was Thomas Boquillon, *Education: to Whom Does It Belong?* Baltimore, 1891.

28 Ahern, *C.U.A., 1887–1896,* p. 138; Ahern, *Life of Keane,* pp. 238, 434; Ellis, *Gibbons,* II, p. 434, p. 172; Fogarty *O'Connell,* p. 304; Peter E. Hogan, S.S.J., *The Catholic University of American, 1896–1902. The Rectorship of Thomas J. Conaty,* Washington: Catholic University of American Press, 1949, pp. 149–56.

29 Maurice Francis Eagan, *Recollections of a Happy Life,* New York: Geroge H. Doran and Co., 1924, p. 189

characterized the leading Americanists prevented them from finding a distinctive identity for their newly created university.

The best known and bitterest chapter of American Catholic history in the Americanist era was the case of Father Edward McGlynn, a New York priest suspended by Archbishop Corrigan for his increasingly fanatical and radical involvement in secular politics, especially Henry George's "single tax" crusade. The McGlynn case does not fit easily into the Americanist story, since men like Ireland were leading proponents of *laissez-faire* economic philosophy and hardly sympathized with George. In addition, most of the bishops (like Corrigan) who opposed a permanent Apostolic Delegation in America did so because they thought Rome was too willing to listen to priests disciplined by their bishops. (Satolli in fact did arrange for McGlynn's reinstatement, under terms which many people considered too lenient.)[30]

However, McGlynn's cause was espoused by some Americanists, who saw it as a test case for the American ideal of freedom of expression, and who were willing to use it as a wedge against Corrigan. Even some bishops supported McGlynn, notably John Moore of St. Augustine. McGlynn was accused by Corrigan of leading a scandalous personal life as well as being disobedient with respect to his political activities, and McGlynn seems to have been almost pathologically rebellious towards Church authority, on one occasion predicting that Catholics themselves would soon join in singing the Orangemen's song, "To Hell with the Pope."[31]

As noted, those prelates who would later come to be regarded as the leading conservatives in the hierarchy were themselves distinctly unenthusiastic about Roman authority, and, although some of the liberals at first welcomed the apostolic delegate because they believed they could persuade him to their point of view (for a while they succeeded), anti-Roman attitudes pervaded the Americanist wing of the bishops. Keane, for example, regarded the Vatican as hopelessly backward and urged the fledgling Paulist Fathers not to submit their rule to the Vatican for approval.[32] O'Connell, the American bishops' agent at the Curia, wrote Ireland in 1898, "For hundreds of years the *Curia Romana* has been in constant conflict with the Church . . ."[33] He was also highly critical of Canon Law.[34] Spalding

---

30 Curran, *Corrigan*, pp. 176, 258, 285, 295.

31 Stephan Bell, *Rebel Priest and Prophet, a Biography of Dr. Edward McGlynn*, New York: Devin-Adair Co., 1937, p. 219.

32 Ahern, *Life of Keane*, pp. 238, 256; Moynihan, *Ireland*, p. 238.

wrote that, while Americans accepted doctrine from the hands of the pope, "as for the rest, they ask him to interfere as little as may be."[35] *Testem Benevolentiae* was viewed by the leading Americanists as an unwarranted and offensive interference in American affairs.[36]

The decade following the Americanist crisis saw the breaking of the storm of Modernism in Europe, culminating in Pius X's condemnation of it in 1907. There were some rather tenuous connections between Americanism and Modernism, especially in the tendency of some of the Americanists, as early as the 1890s, to reach out in a friendly manner to controversial European thinkers like Alfred Loisy, George Tyrrell, and the English scientist St. George Mivart. The latter's name had been proposed for the faculty of Catholic University,[37] for example, and Ireland sent Mass stipends to Loisy.[38] Archbishop Patrick Riordan of San Francisco tried to obtain Tyrrell for his diocese even after the latter had been expelled from the Jesuits.[39] O'Connell was also attracted to Loisy.[40]

Yet when Loisy met Ireland and Spalding in 1902, he was disappointed. They seemed, he thought, to have opinions on no religious issues except those which touched politics.[41]

The most curious case was that of Edward Hanna, a professor at the Rochester diocesan seminary, who had been anonymously delated by a fellow professor for heresy, mainly pertaining to the question of Jesus' self-knowledge. Despite the controversy surrounding Hanna's writings, Riordan pushed hard to get him as his successor and coadjutor, and eventually succeeded. McQuaid, the stormy petrel of the conservative bishops, supported Hanna, because he regarded criticism of his seminary as criticism of himself.[42] In the Hanna case the tendency of even the "conservative" hierarchy was to ignore substantive issues of theology.

---

33 Ahern, *Life of Keane*, p. 189.

34 Fogarty, *O'Connell*, p. 189.

35 Sweeney, *Spalding*, p. 213.

36 Ellis, *Gibbons*, II, p. 67.

37 Ellis, *The Formative Years of the Catholic University of America*, Washington: American Catholic Historical Association, 1946, p. 354.

38 Moynihan, *Ireland*, p. 340.

39 James P. Gaffey, *Citizen of No Mean City: Archbishop Patrick Riordan of San Francisco (1814–1914)*, New York: Consortium Books, 1976, p. 392.

40 Fogarty, *O'Connell*, p. 257.

41 Sweeney, *Spalding*, p. 282.

Loisy had implied as much in his expression of disappointment at Ireland and Spalding, and it is thus finally true that Americanism was not a heresy in any formal or definable sense, and indeed Leo XIII never said that it was. The Americanists seem to have taken doctrine for granted, and at the same time to have regarded it as unimportant. In their minds everything significant in the Church took place on the level of social and cultural adaptation, and they seemed to share a naïve belief that the shape of the faith could be endlessly remolded without damage. On the other hand, Leo XIII correctly sensed that, for example, Ireland's opposition to traditional religious orders implied certain theological attitudes of which the archbishop himself might have been unaware.

Testem Benevolentiae was immediately provoked by a French translation of a biography of Isaac Hecker, the founder of the Paulists; it was written by one of his early disciples, Walter Elliott. It was an enthusiastic essay accompanying the French translation which alarmed the Vatican about the long-term significance of American Catholicism.[43]

Hecker, who died some years before the Americanist crisis broke, is not an easy figure to evaluate. Like the other Americanists, he was emphatic in insisting that everything pertaining to the core of faith was to be accepted without reservation. He was also an unusual combination of mystic and American pragmatist. Significantly, he visualized the community he founded as helping to effect the wholesale conversion of Americans to the Catholic Church, and he identified Catholic optimism about human nature, in contrast to the pessimistic Augustinianism of classical Protestantism, as the key to the Church's American appeal.[44] Certainly he was no heretic, but just as certainly his ideas about Catholicism and about America were muddled and wishful.

The Paulist order, contrary to his expectations, never grew very large, nor did the Church in America experience massive conversions. The Americanists of 1900 might have argued that it was the Roman mentality, as embodied in *Testem Benevolentiae*, which destroyed this opportunity,

---

42 Gaffey, *Citizen*, pp. 282–300.

43 Elliott, *Le Pére Hecker*, Paris, 1897. For an account of the controversy see McAvoy, *Americanist Crisis*, pp. 128–36.

44 Vincent F. Holden, C.S.P. *The Yankee Paul: Isaac Thomas Hecker*, Milwaukee: Bruce, 1958; John Farina, *An American Experience of God: The Spirituality of Isaac Hecker*, New York: Paulist Press, 1982. Elliot, *Life*.

and that such a mentality doomed the Church in the United States to perpetual status as an outpost of the Old World in the New.

Yet that expectation was not borne out by history, since in the period 1900–1965 American Catholicism enjoyed unprecedented numerical growth as well as impressive signs of spiritual vitality, such as an abundance of religious vocations (including those to the contemplative life, which men like John Ireland had dismissed as an irrelevancy).

Shortly after 1900, the Vatican began to appoint a new kind of bishop in the United States, best represented by William H. O'Connell (no relation to Denis), who became bishop of Portland (Maine) in 1901, archbishop of Boston in 1907, and cardinal in 1910. William O'Connell was chosen precisely for his loyalty to the Holy See, and his rise was opposed by some of the older hierarchy, including Ireland.[45] Most intelligent and informed observers in 1900 would probably have said that the Catholic Church's key to success in American society lay not in William O'Connell's direction but in John Ireland's. But, not for the first time, history had its surprises in store.

---

45 Ellis, *Gibbons,* II, p. 422.

13.

The Church of Christ and the Catholic Church (1983)

Rev. James T. O'Connor

With the support of numerous statements of the magisterium, it was customary for Catholics prior to the Second Vatican Council to defend the thesis that they belonged to "the one, true Church" founded by Jesus Christ himself. For them, the Nicene confession of faith, "We believe in one, holy, Catholic, and apostolic Church" referred unambiguously to that Christian community which was united in faith and obedience with the bishop of Rome, the successor of St. Peter.

Since the celebration of the last Council, this sense of Catholic self-identity has been challenged and even denied. It is asserted that the Church of Christ and Catholic Church are not the same reality. The Council, which used both expressions, namely, "Church of Christ" and "Catholic Church," is claimed to have drawn a distinction between the two, thereby indicating that they are not one and the same. In speaking of the society founded by Jesus himself, the Council referred to the "Church of Christ" and confessed that this "is the only Church of Christ, which we profess in the Creed to be one, holy, Catholic, and apostolic."[1] It is, however, nowhere stated that this unique Church of Christ *is* the Roman Catholic Church, nor is it affirmed that Jesus founded the historical reality which we know as the Catholic Church – at least so it is claimed. While teaching, indeed, that the Church of Christ *subsists* in the Catholic Church, the Council explicitly recognized the right of other Christian bodies to be called "Churches," thus giving authoritative confirmation to a use of language which was long-standing and consistent, at least in respect to the separated Churches of the East, i.e., Eastern Orthodoxy.

The bishops of Vatican II, furthermore, formally admitted that the Christian Churches and Communities separated from the Catholic Church

---

1 *Lumen Gentium*, #8.

have been and are being used by the Holy Spirit as "means of salvation"[2] for those who belong to them.

Now it must be admitted that we are faced with three facts concerning the teaching of Vatican II about the Church of Christ and the Catholic Church: first, the assertion that the Church of Christ subsists in the Catholic Church; second, the admission that at least some Communities not in union with the Catholic Church are truly Churches; third, the recognition that such Churches and even other ecclesial Communities serve as "means of salvation" in the effectuation of God's redemptive plan in Christ. Since Vatican II did not give us an elaborate ecclesiology, theological reflection is left to give an integrated picture of its teaching, keeping in mind the three facts just mentioned.

That theological picture has developed in some authors in the following way: The one Church of Christ, founded by him, now perdures or subsists in various forms or manifestations, each of which retains – to a greater or lesser degree – the essential ecclesial characteristics willed by the Lord. No one of the various forms can claim exclusive identity with the Church of Christ – which now exists like some kind of Platonic form which variously informs different communities. De facto, the unique Church founded by Christ now exists in different and separate bodies, although not necessarily in equal degrees.

The consequences of such a view are manifold. Among the more important may be cited the diminishment in appreciation of the Church's unique role as means and sacrament of salvation and the necessity of the sacraments and of sacramental grace. Questions have been raised about the true ecumenicity of those councils held since the division ut the Council of Trent and Vatican Council I. The missionary activity of the Church has likewise suffered, being reduced at times in theory and in practice to no more than efforts to better the temporal social, political, and economic situation of peoples. Efforts for conversion among non-Christians and for the bringing of non-Catholic Christians as individuals into full communion with the Catholic Church have been adversely affected.

I. I wish to address this claim

In response to such a state of affairs, the Congregation for the Doctrine of the Faith issued in 1973 the Declaration *Mysterium Ecclesiae* which said in part:

---

2 *Unitatis Redintegratio*, #3.

... Catholics are bound to profess that through the gift of God's mercy they belong to that Church which Christ founded and which is governed by the successors of Peter and the other Apostles, who are the depositories of the original apostolic tradition, living and intact, which is the permanent heritage of doctrine and holiness of that same Church.

The followers of Christ are therefore not permitted to imagine that the Church of Christ is nothing more than a collection – divided, but still possessing a certain unity – of Churches and ecclesial Communities. Nor are they free to hold that Christ's Church does not really exist anywhere today and that it is to be considered only as an end which all Churches and ecclesial Communities must strive to reach.[3]

These conclusions of *Mysterium Ecclesiae* were not new. In an article published after the Council and before the Declaration of Congregation for the Doctrine of the Faith, Karl Rahner had anticipated much of the thought and even the verbal expression of the Congregation's statement. He wrote:

The Catholic Church cannot think of herself as one among many historical manifestations in which the same God-man Jesus Christ is made present, which are offered by God to man for him to choose whichever he likes. On the contrary, she must necessarily think of herself as the one and total presence in history of the one God-man in his truth and grace, and as such as having a fundamental relationship to all men. . . . For this reason the Catholic Church cannot simply think of herself as one among many Christian Churches and communities on equal footing with her. . . . And the Church cannot accept that this unity is something which must be achieved only in the future and through a process of unification between Christian Churches, so that until this point is reached it simply would not exist.[4]

Unfortunately, *Mysterium Ecclesiae* did not have the desired effect. Appeal was made from it to the teaching of the Council itself, with the claim that *Mysterium Ecclesiae* was a restrictive reading of the conciliar texts which, supposedly, differentiated between the Church of Christ and the Catholic Church.

It is this claimed lack of harmony between the conciliar documents and the Declaration *Mysterium Ecclesiae* which I wish to address directly in this paper. With the publication of the final volumes, including the Index, of the

---

3 *Mysterium Ecclesiae*, #1. Trans. *The Pope Speaks*, vol. 18, number 2, pp. 146–47.

4 K. Rahner, "Church, Churches and Religions," *Theological Investigations X*, Herder and Herder, New York, 1973, pp. 40–41.

Acta Synodalia of Vatican II, the tools for such a study are now at hand. My purpose, therefore, is not to give an overall ecclesiology, nor to show the coherence between the doctrine of the last Council with previous teaching. Nor is my purpose to engage in theological polemic. (For that reason, I have not attributed the "alternative" ecclesiology sketched above to any individual theologian or theologians, although such could readily be done). Rather, I should hope to determine the clear meaning of the sections of *Lumen Gentium* and *Unitatis Redintegratio* pertinent to the question at hand, using the *Acta* to establish, when possible, the precise intention of the wording found in the final conciliar Constitution and Decree.

II. The *"relationes"* contain the key

Perhaps a preliminary word on the *Acta Synodalia* is pertinent. They comprise twenty-five volumes, containing all the Council's documents in their various stages of development, as well as the written and oral expressions of all the participants of the Council in respect to all of the Council's work. Each of the final documents of the Council went through various drafts. These drafts or *schemata* were written by special commissions appointed for the purpose. When a commission had completed its work, the draft or *schema* was then presented to the Council fathers by one of the bishops responsible for its preparation. This presentation is technically called the *relatio* and its purpose was to introduce the document, and to explain to the bishops its purpose and meaning as a whole, as well as the purpose and meaning of its parts. Therefore, the various presentations or *relationes* are the key to the correct interpretation of a given document. Without the *relatio* one could be "left in the dark" as to the precise intention of some of the Council's statements.

Nevertheless, the *relatio* alone is not sufficient. The document once presented had to be accepted by the bishops as the working document for discussion. This done, each section of the document in question was then discussed by the bishops with a view to final approval. Frequently, suggestions would be made to emend wording or even various parts of the working document. These suggestions, called *modi*, were then taken by the commission responsible for drafting the document, and either incorporated or rejected. The document was then resubmitted to the bishops as a whole, together with an official explanation concerning the incorporation or rejection of the various *modi*. It is these explanations, together with the original or subsequent *relationes*, which must be used in determining the final intention of the text. Fortunately, the final documents are normally clear enough as to their meaning and intent. Recourse to the *modi* or suggested emendations is not necessary for an the wording of the final documents is subject to various interpretations, one must recur to the *relationes* and the official explanations concerning the emendations or corrections.

III. Disputed phrase is "subsists in"

We may now look first at the Dogmatic Constitution on the Church, *Lumen Gentium*, and particularly at #8 (Chapter 1) of that document, in which the disputed phrase "subsists in" is found.

The original draft of schema for the Constitution on the Church was submitted to the Council in 1962. This draft stated that the Roman Catholic Church and the Mystical Body of Christ were identical and that only the Roman Catholic Church could be called *sola iure* Church.[5] As to who belonged to this Church, the Relator Cardinal Franic admitted that membership in an improper or analogous sense was a freely disputed question.[6]

This first draft was not acceptable to the bishops as a working document. It was considered too restrictive, too scholastic, and lacking an ecumenical spirit. Nevertheless, even Bishop Christopher Butler, who spoke against the draft, could ask rhetorically: "Who of those [who wish this draft rejected] would deny that the Church in communion with the vicar of Christ, the successor of Peter, is that Church which Christ founded?"[7]

A second schema or draft was submitted to the bishops in 1963. This draft was accepted for discussion as the working document, and, after emendations, became the Dogmatic Constitution *Lumen Gentium*. Number seven (Chapter 1) of this working document read as follows:

> This holy Synod teaches and solemnly professes that there is only one Church of Jesus Christ . . . which the Savior after His Resurrection handed over to Peter and the Apostles and to their successors. . . . Therefore this Church . . . is the Catholic Church, governed by the Roman Pontiff and the bishops in communion with him.[8]

---

5 *Acta Synodalia Sacrosancti Concilii Oecumenici Vaticani II*, Typis Polyglotis Vaticanis, Rome, vol. I, pt. 4, p. 15.

6 *Idem.*, p. 122.

7 *Idem.*, p. 389.

8 *Idem.*, vol. 2, pt. 1, pp. 219–220. "Docet autem Sacra Synodus et sollenniter profitetur non esse nisi unicam Jesu Christi Ecclesiam... Salvator post

Notice that the Church of Christ and the Catholic Church are identified: "Therefore this Church . . . *is* the Catholic Church." Along with much else in the working draft, this sentence was to be changed in the emended draft. That draft was presented to the bishops at the 80th General Assembly of the Council on September 15, 1964. This emended draft was accompanied by a written *relatio* for each section or number of the document. What had been section or number seven in the working document had here become section or number eight, where it still remains in the final Constitution *Lumen Gentium*. It read (and reads, since it was not further emended):

> This is only (*unica*) Church of Christ which we profess in the Creed to be one, holy, Catholic, and apostolic, and which Our Savior after His Resurrection handed over to Peter to be shepherded. . . . This Church, established and ordained as a society in this world, subsists in the Catholic Church, governed by the successor of Peter and the bishops in communion with him, although outside her bodily structure there are found many elements of sanctification and truth which, as gifts proper to the Church of Christ, impel toward Catholic unity.[9]

Notice that, along with minor changes not pertinent to our theme, the "subsists in" has been substituted for "is." What, then, is the significance of this substitution and how is one to understand the entire number or section eight? The written *relatio* or explanation on the section reads as follows as found in the *Acta*:

> From the great number of observations and objections which were brought forth by the bishops in respect to this paragraph (as it appeared in the working draft), it is evident that the intention and context of this section were not clear to all.

---

resurrectionem suam Petro et Apostolis eorumque successoribus tradiit.... Haec igitur Ecclesia... est Ecclesia Catholica, a Romano Pontifice et Episcopis in eius communione directa....

9 *Idem.*, vol. 3, pt. 1, pp. 167–168. "Haec est unica Christi Ecclesia, quam in Symbolo unam, sanctam, catholicam et apostolicam profitemur, quam Salvator noster, post resurrectionem suam Petro pascendam tradidit, eique ac ceteris Apostolis diffundendam et regendam commisit.... Haec Ecclesia, in hoc mundo ut societas constituta et ordinata, subsistit in Ecclesia catholica, a successore Petri et Episcopis in eius communione gubernata, licet extra eius compaginem elementa plura sanctificationis et veritatis inveniantur, quae ut dona Ecclesia Christi propria, ad unitatem catholicam impellunt."

Now, the *intention* is to show that the Church, whose deep and hidden nature is described and which is perpetually united with Christ and His work, is concretely found here on earth in the Catholic Church. This visible Church reveals a mystery – not without shadows until it is brought to full light, just as the Lord Himself through His "emptying out" came to glory. Thus there is to be avoided the impression that the description which the Council sets forth of the Church is merely idealistic and unreal.

Therefore, a clearer subdivision is set forth, in which the following points are successively treated:

a) The mystery of the Church is present in and manifested in a concrete society. The visible assembly and the spiritual element are *not two realities*, but one complex reality, embracing the divine and human, the means of salvation and the fruit of salvation. This is illustrated by an analogy with the Word Incarnate.

b) The Church is one only (*unica*), and here on earth is present in the Catholic Church, although outside of her there are found ecclesial elements.[10]

I do not think the statement could be clearer. Number eight of *Lumen Gentium*, according to official explanation, intends to teach that there is only one Church of Christ and that this Church is found concretely in the

---

10 *Idem.*, p. 176. "Ex magno numero observationum et obiectionum,quae de hac paragrapho a Patribus prolatae sunt, patet, intentionem et contextum huisu articuli non omnibus fuisse perspicua.

"*Intentio* autem est ostendere, Ecclesiam, cuius descripta est intima et arcana natura, qua cum Christo Eiusque opere in perpetuum unitur, his in terris concrete inveniri in Ecclesia catholica. Haec autem Ecclesia empirica mysterium revelat, sed non sine umbris, donec ad plenum lumen adducatur, sicut etiam Christus Dominus per exinanitionem ad gloriam pervenit. Ita praecavetur impressio ac si descriptio, quam Concilium de Ecclesia proponit, esset mere idealistica et irrealis.

"Ideo magis dilucida *subdivisio* proponitur, in qua successive agitur de sequentibus:

"a) Mysterium Ecclesiae adest et manifestatur *in concreta societate. Coetus autem visibilis et elementum spiritutale non sunt duae res*, sed una realitas complexa, complectens divina et humana, media salutis et fructus salutis. Quod per analogiam cum Verbo incarnato illustratur.

"b) Ecclesia est *unica*, et his in terris adest in Ecclesia catholica, licet extra eam inveniantur elementa ecclesialia."

Catholic Church. Every Platonic type of thinking is excluded. The concrete society and its spiritual element are not two realities but rather one complex reality, the spiritual reality being both revealed and hidden by the concrete society, just as the humanity of Christ both revealed and hid the divinity of the Word.

The oral *relatio* on the whole of chapter one of *Lumen Gentium* makes the same points succinctly:

> The mystery of the Church is not an idealistic or unreal creation, but rather exists in the concrete Catholic society itself, under the leadership of the successor of Peter and the bishops in communion with him. There are not two churches, but only one . . .[11]

In the face of such unequivocal declarations concerning the Church of Christ-Catholic Church, what is to be said of the substitution of "subsists in" for "is"? The written *relatio* gives the official explanation:

> Certain words have been changed: in place of "is," "subsists in" is used so that the expression may be in better harmony with the affirmation about ecclesial elements which *are present elsewhere.*[12]

The reason for the change from "is" to "subsists in" is, therefore, *technical precision.* The Council did not wish to appear to deny in one sentence what it would affirm in the next, namely, that ecclesial elements of sanctification and truth are present outside the visible society of the Catholic Church. We must now examine the nature of this technical precision more closely.

The phrase "subsists in" or "subsisting" is not peculiar to our text in *Lumen Gentium* #8. It occurs five other times in the final documents of Vatican II, and it is informative to see how the popular Abbott translation of the Conciliar texts translates these other appearances of the term or its variants.[13]

---

11 *Idem.*, p. 180. "Mysterium Eccleiae tamen non est figmentum idealisticum aut irreale, sed existit in ipsa societate concreta catholica, sub ductu successoris Petri et Episcoporum in eius communicone. Non duae sunt ecclesia, sed una tantum...."

12 *Idem.*, p. 177. "Quaedam verba mutantur: loco 'est' dicitur 'subsistit in' ut expressio melius concordet cum affirmatione de elementis ecclesialibus quae *alibi* adsunt."

13 *Documents of Vatican II*, Walter M. Abbott, S.J., America Press, New York, 1966.

1. In the Decree on Ecumenism #4, we find the sentence:

> This unity we believe, dwells in the Catholic Church as something she can never lose. . . .[14] (The Latin reads: "*in Ecclesia catholica subsistere credimus*."

2. The Declaration on Religious Freedom #1 reads:

> First, this sacred Synod professes its belief that God Himself has made known to mankind the way in which men are to serve Him, and thus be saved by Christ. . . . We believe that this one true religion subsists in the catholic and apostolic Church.[15]

3. The Declaration on the Relationship of the Church to Non-Christian Religions #13 reads:

> Upon the Moslems, too, the Church looks with esteem. They adore one God, living and enduring. (Latin "*viventem et subsistentum*.")[16]

4. *Gaudium et Spes* #10, reads:

> What is this sense of sorrow, of evil, of death, which continues to exist despite so much progress? (Latin "*Quinam est sensus doloris, mali, mortis quae . . . subsistere pergunt?*")[17]

The fifth instance I shall leave for consideration below. Looking at the above usages, it can be seen that the word "subsistere" is variously translated as "to dwell in," "to exist," "to endure," as well as the literal "to subsist in." Depending on which translation one chooses, one gets a slightly different understanding of *Lumen Gentium* #8. It would read:

> This Church [of Christ] . . . dwells in the Catholic Church, governed by the successor of Peter.
> This Church [of Christ] . . . exists in the Catholic Church, governed by the successor of Peter.
> This Church [of Christ] . . . endures in the Catholic Church, governed by the successor of Peter.
> This Church [of Christ] . . . subsists in the Catholic Church, governed by the successor of Peter.

IV. The rejections are significant

The question is: Which of the above translations best preserves the

14 *Idem.*, p. 348.
15 *Idem.*, p. 676–77.
16 *Idem.*, p. 663.
17 *Idem.*, p. 208.

stated intention of *Lumen Gentium* #8 which is to assert that the Church of Christ is "concretely found here on earth in the Catholic Church"? The importance of the question is highlighted when one realizes that the Council, in its Decree on the Catholic Oriental Churches (promulgated on the same day as *Lumen Gentium*), did not say that the Mystical Body of Christ subsists in the Catholic Church, but rather that the Catholic Church *is* the Mystical Body of Christ. We read in *Orientalium Ecclesiarum* #2: "The holy and Catholic Church, which is the Mystical Body of Christ . . ."[18]

An accurate answer to the question about the meaning and translation of "subsists in" can only be given if one examines the Council's teaching concerning the relationship between the Catholic Church and the "ecclesial elements" present outside her visible boundaries, for, by official explanation, it is because of these ecclesial elements that "subsists in" was introduced into the text. We must, therefore, look briefly at the Decree on Ecumenism, *Unitatis Redintegratio*, and particularly at #3 of that document. That number reads in part:

> In this one and only Church of God certain schisms arose even from the very beginning . . . ; in later ages wider dissensions were born, and large Communities were separated from full communion with the Catholic Church, and sometimes not without the fault of men on both sides. Those who are now born into these Communities and are imbued with the faith of Christ are not to be convicted of the sin of separation, and the Catholic Church embraces them with fraternal reverence and love. For those who believe in Christ and are properly baptized are established in a certain, although imperfect, communion with the Catholic Church. . . .

> Furthermore, of the elements or goods, which taken together build up and vivify the Church herself, certain and even many outstanding ones are able to exist (the Latin is *exstare possunt*, not *existere possunt*) outside the visible bounds of the Catholic Church; . . . all these, which come from Christ and lead to Him, belong *by right* to the only Church of Christ (Lat. "*haec ominia quae a Christo proveniunt et ad Ipsum conducant, ad unicam Christi Ecclesiam* iure *pertinent.*").

> It follows that these separated Churches and Communities, although we believe they suffer from the cited defects, have not at all been deprived of significance and importance in the mystery of salvation. The Spirit of Christ has not refused to use them as means of salvation, the efficacy of which is derived from the very fullness of grace and truth

---

18 "Sancta et catholica Ecclesia, quae est Corpus Christi Mysticum..."

entrusted to the Catholic Church. (Lat. *"quorum virtus derivatur ab
ipsa plenitudine gratiae et veritatis quae Ecclesiae catholicae
concredita est"*).[19]

Before the final votes, this entire section had been the subject of much
discussion, and many suggested changes. Most of the suggestions were rejected by the commission responsible for drafting the document, but the
reasons given for the rejections are significant for understanding the text itself.

It was suggested, for example, that to the sentence "all these [elements
and gifts] . . . belong by right to the only Church of Christ," there be added
the phrase "and through her are derived to all those who err in good faith."
This was rejected on the grounds that these gifts are derived from Christ
himself and that "the validity and efficacy of the many sacraments and other
means of salvation are not able to be impeded by the Church since they depend not on the will and jurisdiction of the Church but on the salvific will of
Christ."[20]

V. The understanding is confirmed

Such a response would seem to indicate that the separated Churches

---

19 Some of the words in this text have a history of their own. They were not
present in the penultimate draft of the text, nor in the accepted emendations
which the bishops voted upon chapter by chapter. On the 19th of November,
1964, the Secretary General of the Council, Pericle Felici, announced that,
on the following day, the vote on the final text as a whole would take place.
In the preparation for the vote, a printed version of the final text as a whole
would take place. In preparation for that vote, a printed version of the final
text was circulated. It included 19 emendations "inserted by the Secretariat
for Christian Unity, which in the way accepted suggestions of good-will
which had been authoritatively expressed" (*Acta*, vol. 3, p. 8, p. 422). Felici
then listed the emendations. These corrections, in fact, had been proposed by
Pope Paul VI and accepted by the Secretariat for Christian Unity which was
responsible for drafting the Decree on Ecumenism. They were approved by
the bishops in the final vote, held on Nov. 20 (cf. *Idem*, p. 553 and 636–37.)

Felici referred to these last minute additions as "clarifications" and
such in fact they were. They clarify in the final text itself what might not
otherwise have been clear, apart from a close reading of the *Acta*.

20 *Acta*, vol. 34, pt. 7, p. 33. "...Bona enumerata ab ipso Christo in fratres
separatos derivantur;... validitas et efficacia plurium sacramentorum et
aliorum mediorum salutis ab Ecclesia impediri nequent, cum non a voluntate
et iurisdictione Ecclesiae, sed a voluntate salvifica Christi pendeant."

and Communities function as means of salvation by or of themselves, directly dependent on Christ. That such is not the meaning, however, is immediately clarified by two subsequent responses. It is said that

> Without doubt God uses the separated Communities, not indeed as separated, but as informed by the aforesaid ecclesial elements . . .[21]

and that

> The necessity of communion with the Catholic Church to obtain the grace of Christ and salvation is sufficiently indicated in the whole context [of the document].[22]

From these responses, found in the *Acta*, it can be deduced that the ecclesial elements and the means of sanctification which are present in the separated Churches and Communities are present there to the extent of their union with the Catholic Church. This truth is, in fact, affirmed by both *Lumen Gentium* and by *Unitatis Redintegratio*. *Lumen Gentium* #8 says that these elements are "gifts proper to the Church of Christ and impel toward Catholic unity." Even more clearly, the Decree on Ecumenism #3 states that the efficacy of these elements and means of sanctification "is derived from the very fullness of grace and truth entrusted to the Catholic Church." The insertion of "Catholic" is the clarifying point, avoiding efforts to invent the false distinction between "Church of Christ" and "Catholic Church." The present tense of the verbs in both sentences is also important. The Council is not speaking about *vestigia Ecclesiae*, "traces of the Church," which the separated Churches and Communities retain and now hold as their own because they once were in full communion with the Catholic Church. Rather, the elements are operative here and now because they belong by right to the Church and *presently* derive their efficacy from the plenitude of grace entrusted to the Catholic Church. In other words, the ecclesial elements are elements of the Catholic Church presently operative in the separated Churches and Communities because of their real, although imperfect, unity with the Catholic Church.

This understanding of the nature of the ecclesial elements and their relation to the Catholic Church is confirmed in the Decree on Ecumenism in

---

21 *Idem.*, p. 35. "Deus procul dubio utitur ipsis Communitatibus seiunctis, non quidem qua seiunctis, sed qua informatis praedictis elementis ecclesialibus, ad conferendamcredentibus gratiam salutarem."

22 *Idem.*, p. 35. "Necessitas communionis cum Ecclesia catholica ad gratiam Christi et salutem obtinendam sufficienter indicatur in toto contextu."

that fifth use of the word "subsists in" which we postponed mentioning above. In #13 of the Decree, we read:

> [At the time of the Reformation], many national or confessional Communions were separated from the Roman See. Among these, in which Catholic traditions and structures continue to subsist in part (Lat. "*in quibus traditiones et structurae catholicae ex parte subsistere pergunt*") is the Anglican Communion.

Thus, not only does the Church of Christ subsist in the Catholic Church, but elements of the Catholic Church subsist in the separated Churches and Communities. To that extent, and for that very reason, they function as means of salvation, drawing their efficacy from the fullness of grace and truth in the Catholic Church. For this reason it would seem to be true to say that, if it were possible that the Catholic Church disappear, the Catholic elements in the separated Churches and Communities would be deprived of their efficacy, having lost the source from which they draw here and now. It is also for that reason, I think, that Bishop Charue, giving the *relatio* for #14 of *Lumen Gentium*, could say that the Roman Catholic Church is necessary for salvation.[23]

VI. These conclusions follow

It is true, indeed, that the ecclesial elements in the separated Churches and Communities do not function because of a permissive act of jurisdiction of the Catholic Church. But this, as a general rule, is true within the visible bounds of the Church herself. Even a suspended archbishop can serve the Lord, but does so – like the separated Churches and Communities – not inasmuch as separation exists, but only because of the incomplete communion preserved with the Catholic Church.

Any student of St. Augustine's works will recognize that the teaching of Vatican Council II on the ecclesial elements present outside the visible bounds of the Catholic Church, as I have just attempted to outline it, is similar to Augustine's position on the matter taken during his controversy with the Donatists. He wrote in his tract *On Baptism*:

> . . . there is one church which alone is called Catholic; and whenever it
> has anything of its own in these communions of different bodies which

---

23 *Acta*, vol. 3, pt. 1, p. 202. He later stated that the relatio retaine its value and repeated the cited remark (*Idem.*, p. 467).

are separate from itself, it is most certainly in virtue of this which is its own in each of them that she, not they, has the power of generation.[24]

If I may now summarize the conclusions of this study and draw it to a close:

1. The official *relatio* on #8 of *Lumen Gentium* states that the intention of the paragraph was to show that the Church of Christ is concretely found here on earth in the Catholic Church.

    A response of the Commission to a suggested change in #3 of the Decree on Ecumenism states that the Decree "clearly affirms that only the Catholic Church is the true Church of Christ."[25]

    The bishops voted on the final drafts of *Lumen Gentium* and *Unitatis Redintegratio* in the context of these and many other like explanations. And the final documents, apart from an arbitrary reading or one done out of context, testify to a clear affirmation that the Church of Christ and the Catholic Church are not two realities but one only.

2. It is affirmed that the Lord himself is the founder of this one Church.

3. The statement of *Mysterium Ecclesiae* that "Catholics are bound to profess that by the gift of God's mercy they belong to that Church which Christ founded . . ." is a fully accurate and concise restatement of the intention and teaching of the Church in Council at Vatican II.

4. Elements of this one Church are present outside her visible boundaries and are operative as means of salvation within the separated Churches and Communities. These elements belong to the Church by right, derive their efficacy from the Catholic Church, and are forces which impel to full communion with the Church.

5. The presence of these Catholic elements outside the visible bounds has occasioned a new terminology – not a new fact since the fact was seen already by Augustine. Thatholic Church subsisting in the separated Christian Churches and Communities.

---

24 St. Augustine, "On Baptism," *An Augustine Reader*, ed. By John J. O'Meara, Doubleday, Image, Garden City, N.Y., 1973, p. 220. The theme is frequent in Augustine. On the fact that the "ecclesial elements" belong by right to the Catholic Church, cf. *In Johannem*, VI, 15–16.

25 *Acta*, vol. 3, pt. 2, p. 12. "Postea clare affirmatur solam Ecclesiam catholicam esse veram Ecclesiam Christi."

6. The separated Churches and Communities, despite the presence of Catholic elements, are structurally deficient. This structural deficiency admits of greater and lesser degrees, depending on the nature and extent of their imperfect communion with the Catholic Church. The extent of that imperfect communion also determines their ability to be greater or lesser partial realizations of the one Catholic Church.[26]

7. The presence of Catholic elements outside the visible boundaries of the Church cannot be understood in such a way as to imply a diminishment of these elements within the Church herself.

When a man is ordained a bishop, the element of apostolicity is not increased in the Church. Rather, there is extended to him a participation in what the Church herself fully possesses. Likewise, when he dies, the Church on earth is not diminished in respect to apostolicity.

So it is with the Catholic elements in the separated Churches and Communities. These elements are not like pieces of pie which have been carried away to exist elsewhere. The Catholic Church of Christ remains fully one even when the separated Churches share imperfectly in that unity. The diminishment occurs in what has been separated – and to the extent to which it is separated. To imagine otherwise would be to understand the ecclesial elements as material not spiritual realities. The number of those united to the Church may increase or decrease; the unity of the Church herself does not increase or decrease. And so with the other ecclesial elements.

---

26 It is in this sense that the following statement must be understood. "In his coetibus unica Christi Ecclesia, quasi tamquam in Ecclesiis particularibus, quamvis imperfecte, praesens et mediantibus elementis ecclesiasticis aliquo modo actuosa est." (*Acta*, vol. 3, pt. 2, p. 335)

"On March 11, 1985, the Congregation for the Doctrine of the Faith, in criticizing Leonardo Boff's work, *Church, Charisma and Power*, made the following statement on the unicity of the Church: 'From the Council's famous expression *Haec Ecclesia (scl. Unica Christi Ecclesia)... subsistit in Ecclesia Catholica*, he [Boff] extracts a thesis exactly contrary to the authentic meaning of the Council text, when he asserts "in fact it (the one Church of Christ) can also subsist in other Christian Churches" (p. 131). The Council, on the contrary, chose the word subsistit precisely to make clear that there is only on "subsistence" of the true Church, while outside her visible framework there exists only "*elementa Ecclesia*" which – being elements of the same Church – tend and lead towards the Catholic Church.'" (*L'Osservatore Romano*, Eng. ed., 4/9/85, p. 11).

VII. Much more could be said

An analogy with the mystery of the Eucharist is appropriate. The number of consecrated Hosts in a ciborium has nothing to do with the fullness of the Lord's Presence. He is as fully present in one as he is in a hundred. So with the Church. Her unity does not grow; it is extended for others to share in.

There is much more that could and should be said. I am aware that there are many "loose ends." Something should be said about what makes some of the separated Communities Churches and others not. Something should be said about how the ecclesial elements present in the separated Churches and Communities manifest themselves in a richness of form and spirituality which would serve to enrich the Catholic Church herself. Much should be said on the whole notion of the Church as communion. Much more should be said about Our Lady as Mother of Unity. Enough could never be said on the role of the Eucharist. But, for now, the purpose of this article has, I hope, been achieved. According to the teachings of Vatican Council II, the Church of Christ and the Roman Catholic Church are one and the same complex reality.

14.

Existentialism on Trial: Albert Camus's *The Fall* (1984)

Maura A. Daly

In Camus's novel, *The Fall*, published in 1956, four years before the Nobel Prize winner's sudden death, modern society and, even more, modern man is on trial – the man about whom Camus sardonically comments in *The Fall*: "He fornicated and he read newspapers."[1] If one looks beneath the surface of this novel, it becomes clear that atheistic existentialism, the variety that has taken many of the major philosophers and writers of the twentieth century by storm and a philosophy to which Camus himself seemed to be an uncritical adherent in his earlier career, is called to account. In order to understand how Camus conducts this trial, however, it is necessary to review the novel itself, to define the variety of existentialism with which we are dealing, and to show how Camus's novel is a *mise en abîme*, an accusation within an accusation, and, ultimately, an indictment of an existentialism that admits no absolutes.

In *The Fall* we meet Jean-Baptiste Clamence, a self-styled judge-penitent and formerly successful Parisian lawyer who has taken refuge in the bar district of Amsterdam. Through his monologue with an unnamed visitor to the city, Clamence tells his life story. He recounts his ever-increasing fame as a lawyer who, despite his renown, defends widows and orphans for nothing. Moreover, according to Clamence, his was a charmed life: he was respected by his colleagues, admired and feted by his friends, and sought after by hordes of women. Clamence believes himself invincible until, finally, late one night as he is returning home he hears the cry of a young woman drowning in the Seine and does nothing to help her. Several years after the drowning when he is crossing a bridge over the Seine, he hears, for the first

---

1 Albert Camus, La Chute, Paris: Gallimard, 1956, p. 11. All references to La Chute will be to this edition and page numbers will be indicated in the text. The translation of all quotations is mine unless indicated otherwise.

time, a laugh that seems to come from nowhere. Henceforth, this laugh never completely leaves him.

There are many possible interpretations of this laughter. But its primary purpose is to reveal the duplicity of Clamence's life and the facticity of his conception of himself. This laugh shows him that he is not invincible, that his friends do not all like him, that he is not universally respected by his colleagues, and that some of his past mistresses denigrate him to their friends. Most of all, Clamence realizes that what he had believed to be his good nature is rooted in nothing but blind egotism. As he tells his anonymous listener in the novel: "Thus, I went along on the surface of life, more or less in words, never in reality" (56). The most shattering revelation of the laughter, however, is that of Clamence's guilt concerning the drowning, and in a godless world the impossibility of eradicating or of expiating it. Consequently, his solution is to become a "judge-penitent," to confess all of his sins so that no one else can judge him. Clamence explains: "Since one could not condemn the others without at the same time judging oneself, it was necessary to accuse oneself in order to have the right to judge the others" (146). By confessing first, Clamence feels that he can judge everyone else. He must remain superior at all costs. The personal and career "one-up-man-ship" that he had practiced in Parisian Society is transformed into a curiously would-be moral superiority in a system devoid of morals. At one juncture, Clamence explains to his companion that pardoning someone is the only way to put oneself above him (135).

Via the personage of Clamence, Camus indicts all the precepts of an atheistic existentialism that denies the existence of all concrete moral values, and he shows the *claustration* and ultimately the suffocation of a belief that inextricably locks man into his finitude. In its own way, *The Fall* is as much a vision of Hell as Sartre's *No Exit*. The crucial difference is that Camus's vision of Hell is even more circumscribed. Whereas Sartre's oft-quoted play proclaims that "hell is other,"[2] Camus's *The Fall* shows that the others are not even necessary, that the individual himself suffices.

If the individual himself is indeed sufficient to create an Inferno, it must be because of the *a priori* beliefs that undergird his life. In *The Fall*, because of the relentless focus on one individual, the nature of these beliefs becomes clear. Through the character of Clamence, Camus tries an existentialist system that admits no absolutes, and finds it guilty.

At this juncture, we must define the variety of existentialism with

---

2 Jean-Paul Sartre, *Huis clos*, Paris: Gallimard, 1947, p. 75.

which we are dealing precisely because so many contradictory definitions have been put forth. In his famous article, "Existentialism is a Humanism," Jean-Paul Sartre, describing atheistic existentialism, writes:

> Nowhere is it written that the Good exists, that we must be honest, that we must not lie; because the fact is we are on a plane where there are only men. Dostoevsky said, "If God did not exist, everything would be possible." That is the very starting point of existentialism. Indeed, everything is permissible if God does not exist, and, as a result, man is forlorn, because neither within him nor without does he find anything to cling to. He cannot start making excuses for himself.
>
> If existence really does precede essence, there is no explaining things away by reference to a fixed and given human nature. In other words, there is no determinism; man is free; man is freedom. On the other hand, if God does not exist, we find no values or commands to turn to which legitimize our conduct. So, in the bright realm of values, we have no excuses behind us nor justification before us. We are alone with no excuses.[3]

What Sartre neglects to say in his definition of existentialism is that often in the place of the traditional God deified modern man ensconces himself – replete with his accompanying court of would-be absolutes – in materialism, sensuality, and meaningless but frenetic action.

Jean-Baptiste Clamence, in accusing himself and his past, simultaneously condemns the moral vacuum inherent in this school of existentialism. Although Clamence's self-condemnation could be envisioned as a condemnation of a complacent bourgeois unaware of the essential *angst* of existence and, as such, guilty of what the existentialists deride as "bad faith," such an interpretation discounts Clamence's feelings of guilt and remorse. Moreover, in his major philosophical work, *The Rebel*, Camus criticizes the anomaly of any philosophy that totally discounts moral values. He observes trenchantly:

> If one does not believe in anything, if nothing has meaning and if we cannot affirm any value, everything is possible and nothing has any importance. There is no for or against; the assassin is neither right nor wrong. One can stoke the fires of the crematoria just as one can devote

---

3 Jean-Paul Satre, *Existentialism*, trans. Bernard Frechtman, New York: Philosophical Library, 1947, reprinted in William V. Spanos' *Casebook on Existentialism 2*, New York: Harper & Row, 1976, p. 393. This article originally appeared under the title "Existentialism Is a Humanis."

oneself to caring for lepers. Malice and virtue are only chance and whimsy.[4]

If such a doctrine were possible, Clamence, who has no family, no ethics and no concern besides his personal convenience and comfort, should have no regrets. Instead, however, he is tortured by both guilt and remorse. What is particularly interesting in *The Fall* is that the hero has advanced from one stage of existentialism to another, and it is from the vantage point of the second stage that the protagonist indicts the first. Indeed, it seems that in *The Fall* a definite progression is taking place. Neither the title with its explicitly religious connotations, nor the name of the protagonist with his allusions to Amsterdam as analogous to Dante's Hell, nor the obsessional themes of guilt, innocence, judgment, and redemption are accidental. They implicitly represent the alternative to the *Weltanschauung* that Clamence with his Luciferian pride is, as yet, unable to abandon. By virtue of his suffering, he rather dreams of the possibility of forgiveness, reconciliation, and a second chance.

Clamence, because of his guilt, is aware of the inherent lie in the assumption that there are no moral absolutes, but, paradoxically, although he suffers from guilt that would imply a transcendent scale of values, he is unwilling to accept the authenticity of any such system. Instead, he chooses an intermediary position that neither silences his conscience nor absolves it. Since he can no longer be happy himself, he wants to make everyone else suffer too – to convince them of their guilt. In this respect, Clamence seems to epitomize the strange twentieth-century mutant ideologies that simultaneously discount all absolutes, proclaim that the end justifies the means, and, in the height of contradiction, invoke a so-called higher principle to justify the carnage and genocide required to arrive at their desired end. These ideologies, although morally culpable, proclaim themselves innocent by virtue of historical necessity, economic practicality, the need for *Lebensraum*, or the creation of a superman. Clamence, on a human scale, personifies the beliefs of such self-contradictory mutant ideologies. Describing this phenomenon in *The Rebel*, Camus states: "Crime puts on the trappings of innocence by a curious reversal that is peculiar to our time."[5] This assessment seems applicable to the conduct of the two-faced judge-penitent depicted in *The Fall*, as does Camus's observation that,

---

4 Albert Camus, *L'Homme révolté*, Paris: Gallimard, 1951, p. 15.
5 *Ibid.*, p. 14.

"philosophy can be used for everything, even to change murderers into judges."[6]

The proverbial "fly in the ointment" for Clamence, however, is the elusive laughter that refuses to allow him to establish or to believe in his innocence. Explaining this realization to his anonymous listener, Clamence recounts:

> One day, however, during a voyage on which I had invited a female friend, without telling her that I was doing it to celebrate my cure, I found myself aboard an ocean liner, on the top bridge, naturally. Suddenly, I perceived on the horizon a black speck. . . . Immediately I looked away, my heart beginning to beat. When I forced myself to look at the black speck it had disappeared. I was going to yell stupidly, to call for help, when I saw it again. It was some of the flotsam that ships leave behind them. Yet, I had not been able to look at it. I had thought immediately of a drowned person. I understood, then, with acceptance, as one resigns oneself to an idea whose truth one has known for a long time, that that cry which years before had rung out on the Seine behind me had not ceased. Carried by the river towards the waters of the Channel to make its way in the world across the vast space of the ocean, it had waited for me until this day when I met it again. I understood also that it would continue to wait for me on the seas and on the rivers – everywhere where might be found the bitter water of my baptism. Even here, tell me, are we not on the water? (114–15)

This allusion to baptism is an important one because the symbolic value of water in *The Fall* is manifold: On the most literal level, the water of the Seine signifies the choice between life and death – both for the young woman who drowns and for Clamence who would have jeopardized his life had he attempted to save her. On a figurative level, what is at stake is the death of Clamence's cherished view of himself and the beginning of a new life in which he is confronted with the corrosive influence of self truth that works like sand paper on his formerly impervious conscience. Moreover, his refusal to help the victim corresponds metaphorically to his very real inability to submerge his ego for anyone or anything. Clamence refused the baptism of the river – the true giving of self for another. Spiritually, his refusal corresponds to the refusal to accept authentic suffering in any guise. By his resistance to suffering he attempts to deny the validity of the transcendent or spiritual elements in life.

Ironically, the baptism that Clamence refuses – literally, figuratively,

---

6 *Ibid.,* p. 13.

and spiritually – is one which he continues to undergo against his will. Paradoxically, Clamence suffers terribly because of his very refusal to suffer or to admit the authenticity or the meaning of his suffering. Just as Clamence had refused to submerge himself in the waters of the Seine, so too he refuses to accept the possibility of grace and redemption and the transcendence that they imply. Were he to accept the existence of absolutes, he would allow his ego to be resubmerged by them. This is something he will not do. Like Lucifer, he feels that it is better to reign, as it were, in Amsterdam than to serve: "What intoxication to feel oneself to be God the Father and to distribute definitive certificates of bad life and habits. I am enthroned among my evil angels, at the summit of the Dutch sky, watching the multitude of the Last Judgment coming up towards me, emerging from the fog and water" (151).

Despite Clamence's self-proclaimed euphoria, guilt has him in a stranglehold. Although the novel does not end optimistically, Clamence, in his last conversation with his faithful listener, says: "Pronounce yourself the words that for years have never stopped echoing in my nights, and that I will say through your mouth: 'Oh, young woman, throw yourself into the water again so that I will have a second chance to save both of us'" (155). Even though Clamence immediately qualifies his statement by calling himself imprudent, he says: "But let us reassure ourselves! It is too late, now, it will always be too late. Luckily!" (156). The paradox of *The Fall* is that although Clamence, by virtue of his guilt, obviously rejects an existential system that discounts all moral values, he simultaneously refuses to believe in a system that espouses them.

In this discussion of *The Fall*, we have seen that, within the context of multiple inversions and reversals, the protagonist, who is ostensibly accusing others, is himself being tried. Moreover, through him, the philosophy that he refuses to desert, of an existentialism that declares itself free from all values, is likewise being indicted. With *The Fall*, Camus's philosophical position shifts from the stance he had maintained earlier in his career – that man was the innocent victim of absurdity – to a new position – that man is the guilty perpetrator of evil. This transition has a decidedly Christian character about it. It seems that in *The Fall* Camus is working his way towards a rapprochement with Christianity. Conor Cruise O'Brien, one of Camus's most important critics, maintains that this is indeed the case:

> Under its surface of irony and occasional blasphemy, *La Chute* is profoundly Christian in its confessional form, in its imagery, and above all in its pervasive message that it is only through the full recognition of

our sinful nature that we can hope for grace. Grace does not, it is true, arrive, and the novel ends on what is apparently a pessimistic note. Yet the name of the narrator – that of the forerunner – hints teasingly, at the possibility of a sequel.[7]

Moreover, O'Brien goes on to say that when he wrote a review of *The Fall*, stressing its Christian character, Camus wrote to his English publishers confirming that O'Brien's approach was sound.[8]

In *The Fall*, Camus examines a philosophy that excludes all absolutes and finds it guilty of self-contradiction and self-deception. The verdict on Clamence, however, is still out, and it will remain so. Nonetheless, if one does believe in absolutes, and one of them is mercy, the outcome of Clamence's trial, in both meanings of the word, could be quite different from what we, or from what he, for that matter, might have expected. If, indeed, "The quality of mercy is not strained . . . [and] droppeth as the gentle rain from heaven,"[9] then Clamence's fall is a prelude to his redemption. Perhaps the watery canals of Amsterdam and the city's perpetual drizzle have the salvific force of the baptism that he once refused to undergo in the Seine, but has spent his life regretting and expiating.

---

7 Conor Cruise O'Brien, *Albert Camus of Europe and Africa,* New York: the Viking Press, 1970, p. 100.

8 *Ibid.*

9 William Shakespeare, "The Merchant of Venice," in *The Complete Plays and Poems of William Shakespeare*, eds. William Allan Neilson and Charles Jarvis Hill, New York: Houghton Mifflin Company, 1970, Act IV, Scene I, lines 184–85.

15.
Derrida or Deity?
Deconstruction in the Presence of the Word
(1985)
R. V. Young

I.

Recently I was teaching a course in the "Classical Backgrounds of English Literature." During one class I was attempting to explain how Virgil had established in the Dido episode of the *Aeneid* a thematic complex which had reverberated throughout the development of Western literature in a series of binary oppositions of which one term was always the focus of moral superiority: honor v. love, duty v. pleasure, public office v. private inclination. As I pointed out how Aeneas' epic heroism was virtually defined by his self-denying role in the fulfillment of destiny, one of my students objected. A very shrewd young lady, she argued that the *Aeneid* could be read in precisely the opposite fashion, that – given Aeneas' unrelenting anguish, his reluctance to struggle or inflict pain, only gradually overcome as he hardens into the ruthless butcher of Turnus at the close of the poem – given these features, Virgil could be seen as a covert sympathizer with Dido, pacifism, and the rejection of the imperial destiny associated with the Olympian gods. "It sounds like you're trying to do a deconstructive reading," I remarked, and immediately regretted it. But it was too late; the word had already slipped out. "I've heard so much about *deconstruction* lately," another student said. "Could you *deconstruct* the *Aeneid* for us?"

I looked at my watch and demurred; I did not think the job could be managed in the fifteen minutes remaining in that class. Still, now that deconstruction has become of concern even to undergraduates, and seems even to have filtered into their view of literary works, it will not be amiss for us to take stock of its relationship to Catholic intellectual life. At the heart of the controversy in this country stands the English department of Yale University, or, at least, its "Hermeneutical Mafia," comprising Harold Bloom,

Geoffrey Hartman, J. Hillis Miller, and the late Paul de Man. These four
stand accused of subverting objective standards of literary interpretation, of
blurring the distinction between criticism and imaginative literature, of dep-
recating the author and authorial intention for the sake of the imaginative
gambits of the critical interpreter, and of engaging in a generally
self-indulgent, irresponsible style of writing, which undercuts the scholarly
and educational aims of academic discourse. The evidence for these indict-
ments was not gathered by FBI wiretap; it is readily available in published
sources. "Criticism is . . . continuous with the language of literature," writes
J. Hillis Miller, one of the more vociferous of the *mafiosi*. And he continues
in this vein:

> The poem [Shelley's *Triumph of Life*], like all texts, is "unreadable," if
> by "readable" one means a single, definitive interpretation. In fact, nei-
> ther the "obvious" reading nor the "deconstructionist" reading is
> "univocal." Each contains, necessarily, its enemy within itself, is itself
> both host and parasite. The deconstructionist reading contains the ob-
> vious one and vice versa. Nihilism is an unalienable alien presence
> within Occidental metaphysics, both in poems and in the criticism of
> poems.[1]

It is apparent that more is involved here than an altercation among English teachers over passing literary fashion. Critical theory is necessarily inscribed within metaphysics, and, as the quotation from Hillis Miller makes
explicit, the deconstructionists are especially aggressive in collapsing the
partitions, not only between literature and criticism, but among all forms of
discourse. There is more at stake in deconstruction than a new reading of
Bleak House or William Blake. Not only the possibility of meaning, but the
status of being itself is put in question. This is not surprising, since lurking
behind the attack on conventional literary interpretation mounted by Yale's
"Gang of Four" is the somewhat sinister figure of the French philosopher,
Jacques Derrida.

It is Derrida who seems to have coined the term "deconstruction," by
which he means not only a method of radical textual analysis, but a whole
new way of thinking about the human experience of reality. What is, finally,
to be deconstructed is the whole "logocentric" tradition of Western metaphysics, or "ontotheology" as Derrida often calls it. From a Derridean perspective, reality itself – or at least mankind's apprehension of it – is a kind

---

1   "The Critic as Host," in Harold Bloom *et al, Deconstruction and Criticism*,
    New York: Seabury, 1979, pp. 223, 226.

of writing; and deconstruction seizes on the loose linguistic threads to unravel the textuality of the world. Derrida thus threatens the intellectual norms of Western culture. Yet deconstruction is not wholly a cause for alarm. It is a corrosive solvent to the utopian pieties of secular humanism and Marxism, but the Catholic faith remains basically untouched, although it is the ultimate "ontotheology" or "philosophy of presence." While the Derridean abyss opens sickeningly at the feet of contemporary humanism, it offers little terror to Catholics, whose saints have plumbed its depths in centuries past. The crucial "innovations" of deconstruction have been already perceived and assimilated by the doctors of the Church.

Born of Sephardic Jewish parents in Algiers in 1930, Jacques Derrida is professor of philosophy at the l'école Normale Supérieure in Paris, a position he has held for more than a decade, balanced with regular visiting professorships in the United States, first at Johns Hopkins and now at Yale. He drew broad attention in this country in 1966 with a paper delivered at an international symposium at Johns Hopkins. Derrida's paper, entitled "Structure, Sign, and Play in the Discourse of the Human Sciences," was basically a critique of the structuralism of Claude Lévi-Strauss just when structuralism was at its highest prestige. The following year saw the publication of no fewer than three books by Derrida: *Speech and Phenomena*, a critique of Husserl's theory of signs; *Writing and Difference*, a collection of essays; and *Of Grammatology*, a critique of the Western world's traditional privileging of actual speech over writing. In 1972, three more volumes from Derrida appeared: *Disseminations*, *Margins*, and *Positions*, the last a collection of interviews. Although at least three more volumes have appeared since, these are certainly the most influential and important.[2]

---

2   Although the dates of the original French editions are mentioned in the text, the titles are those of the English translations, which have appeared later: *Speech and Phenomena and Other Essays on Husserl's Theory of Signs*, trans. David B. Allison, Evanston, IL: Northwestern Univ. Press, 1973; *Writing and Difference*, trans. Alan Bass, Chicago: Univ. of Chicago Press, 1978; *Of Grammatology*, trans. Gayatri Chkravorty Spivak, Baltimore: Johns Hopkins Univ. Press, 1976; *Dissemination*, trans. Barbara Johnson, Chicago: Univ. of Chicago Press, 1981; *Margins of Philosophy*, trans. Alan Bass, Chicago: Univ. of Chicago Press, 1982; and *Postitions*, trans. Alan Bass, Chicago: Univ. of Chicago Press, 1981. "Structure, Sign, and Play" has been reprinted as the tenth chapter of *Writing and Difference* and, in a translation by Richard Macksey, in *The Structuralist Controversy*, ed. Richard Macksey and Eugenio Donato, Baltimore: Johns Hopkins Univ.

A useful perspective on deconstruction is secured by approaching it as the ingrate stepchild of Parisian structuralism, an academic movement which sought to place the human sciences on the same epistemological footing as the physical sciences. The principal intellectual inspiration for structuralism lies in the work of Marx and Freud, who both sought to analyze human behavior in terms of objectively conceived economic or psychological structures without worrying about the messy, unscientific business of the conscious individual will. The methodological model for structuralism, however, came from linguistics, most notably the *Course in General Linguistics*, posthumously compiled from lecture notes by students of Ferdinand de Saussure. Hence leading structuralists are usually linguists (like Roman Jacobson), or those who apply the structural model of linguistics to other disciplines such as psychology (like Jacques Lacan) or anthropology (like Claude Lévi-Strauss).

It has been widely noted that Derrida's great perception is that the basic principle of Saussurian structural linguistics – "That no intrinsic relationship obtains between the two parts of the sign, signifier, and signified" – undercuts even the structuralist enterprise itself. A signifier or sound-image, Saussure maintains, is arbitrarily linked to a signified, or concept; that is, since the sounds of words, or signifiers, are unmotivated conventions, a sign is a structure of difference: "The important thing in the word is not the sound alone but the phonic differences that make it possible to distinguish this word from all others, for differences carry signification."[3] This means that *all* discourse is subject to the same leakage of meaning precisely in order to mean at all. The very act of meaning – that is, of signifying – implies the absence of the signified which, therefore, can be grasped not in itself but only by means of the substituted signifier. Hence we confront not merely the gap between *res* and *verbum*, but a gap, or *aporia*, within the sign itself, which, in Saussure's terminology, is the complex of signifier and signified. Hence, the structuralist himself can never stand outside the structures he posits; he, too, is an inmate of the "prison house of language."[4]

Press, 1972, pp. 247–65

3 *Course in General Linguistics,* trans. Wade Baskin, 1959; rpt. New York: McGraw Hill, 1966, p. 118.

4 Cf. Hillis Miller, "The Critic as Host," P. 230: "We have no other language. The language of criticism is subject to exactly the same limitations and blind alleys as the works it reads. The most heroic effort to escape from the prisonhouse of language only builds the walls higher."

Now for Derrida this principle of linguistics and semiotics has important metaphysical – I should say *anti-metaphysical* – implications. Since man inhabits a universe of discourse, he is entangled in a chain of signifiers referring to absent signifieds: The world is thus one great circular definition. Every human term or concept is marked by what Derrida calls the *trace* of its incompletion and undecidability, and this applies with full force to subjective consciousness. In his earliest published works he attacks the notion of the self-possessed intentional subject of Husserlian phenomenology. There is no prelinguistic thought, Derrida maintains, fully present to the transcendental consciousness: "As soon as we admit this continuity of the now and the not-now, perception and non-perception, in the zone of primordiality common to primordial impression and primordial retention, we admit the other into the self-identity of the *Augenblick*; nonpresence and nonevidence are admitted into the *blink of an instant*. There is duration to the blink, and it closes the eye."[5] This means that our knowledge, deployed in temporarily extended signifiers, cannot all be simultaneously present. We know only in memory or in expectation; hence we know only what is not here and now, not present.

Our world of consciousness is not, then, inhabited by the presentation of its intentional objects, but by *re-presentation* implicated with *différance*. This neologism, spelled with an "a" rather than an "e" in the last syllable, is derived from the French verb *différer*, which, like its Latin cognate, *differre*, means both to defer in time or postpone, and to differ or be spatially distinct. The word "child," for example, is a "sound-image" which signifies a complex, equivocal notion: offspring, non-adult, immature person, innocent or inexperienced person, and so on. But then all of these terms, these "signifieds," also turn out to be signifiers which likewise ramify into another set of signifieds which spawn more signifiers. There can be no end to this process, no final, central concept or signified which can logically or fully account for the meanings which float freely around the arbitrary sound-image "child." *A fortiori* no particular visual image in the mind or in actual reality (i.e., a specific, individual child) can exhaust the implications of the term. "Child" has meaning *only* because it is distinguishable from other sound-images ("man," "adult," "baby," "parent"), *not* because it is rooted in a stable signification. Derrida thus seems to have gone a step beyond nominalism; he seems to suggest that substance occurs in a matrix of accidents, and he calls the latter *différance*.

---

5 *Speech and Phenomena*, p. 65.

Différance is, then, the defect or incompletion inscribed not only in every human utterance, but also in every human experience; the *trace* is the token, silent and invisible – literally nonexistent – of this interval or gap in being. Because writing is so plainly representational, a supplement for speech, it manifests the "textuality" of human experience. Hence, it is characteristically repressed in favor of the spoken word, with its illusion of unmediated presence by the Western metaphysical tradition which ceaselessly strives to occupy the vacancy in human experience, to fill the hole in being:

> The subordination of the trace to the full presence summed up in the logos, the humbling of writing beneath a speech by an onto-theology determining the archeological and eschatological meaning of being as presence, as parousia, as life without *différance*: another name for death, historical metonymy where God's name holds death in check. That is why, if this movement begins its era in the form of Platonism, it ends in infinitist metaphysics. Only infinite being can reduce the difference in presence. In that sense, the name of God, at least as it is pronounced within classical rationalism, is the name of indifference itself.[6]

For all the evident radicalism and anti-theism of such comments, Derrida's deconstruction of Western metaphysics has increasingly proven a source of unease to Marxist critics in recent years. Hence Edward W. Said, Columbia University's resident Palestinian anti-imperialist, is dubious about Derrida's ideological commitment:

> If everything in a text is always open equally to suspicion and to affirmation, then the differences between one class interest and another, between oppressor and oppressed, one discourse and another, one ideology and another, are virtual in – but never crucial to making decisions about – the finally reconciling element of textuality.[7]

The explicit charge here is that Derrida is unwilling to get his hands dirty in history and radical politics. Frank Lentricchia, another literary-critic fellow traveler, complains: "Derrida's deconstructive project is formalist through and through."[8] It is hard to conceive a more damning term

---

6 *Of Grammatology,* p. 71.

7 *The World, The Text, and the Critic,*Cambridge: Harvard Univ. Press, 1983, p. 214.

8 *After the New Criticism,* Chicago: Univ. Of Chicago Press, 1980, p. 177. Cf. The nagging questions of Guy Scarpetta and Jean-Louis Houdebine in *Positions* (pp. 56, 60–62, 67–68, 79–81, 88–89) in which the two interviewers,

in the current critical lexicon than "formalist." But the real worry is that Marx is quite as vulnerable to deconstruction – really more so – than Plato or Hegel. "A speech dreaming its plenitude" is a perfect description of the discourse of the radical left, with its binary oppositions of class conflict and its "eschatological" project of full human "presence" in a classless society devoid of repression. Deconstructed Marxism turns out to be secularized millenarianism, a self-deceived, materialist logocentrism. In this sense, the logic of Derrida's deconstruction is reminiscent of Jacques Monod, who quite openly dismissed Marxism as simply the last in a long line of "animist" myths seeking a center of originary meaning inscribed in the meaninglessness of the physical universe.[9]

II.

But what, then, of Christianity and the deconstructive project? Most of Derrida's impact – his shock value – arises from his demonstration that supposedly "critical" philosophies, exemplars of post-Enlightenment thought, are covertly logocentric; That is, that they are founded on the absolutizing of human reason or consciousness even as they claim to liberate us from divine absolutes. As the force of God's presence is diminished, the autonomous human subject becomes the "transcendental signified" of its own signification. But Christianity has always been explicitly "logocentric"; paradoxically, its confrontation with God – the radically other for which every sign is inadequate – forced Christian theology to deal with the issues Derrida raises, although in different terms, from the first. In this connection, it is interesting that Derrida, so far as I know, has not discussed St. Augustine and St. Thomas Aquinas. He would have to acknowledge that in their work the human condition had already been radically "deconstructed." And

---

especially the latter, try unsuccessfully to elicit from Derrida an affirmation of Marxist dialectic and its exemption from the deconstructive process.

9 Jacques Monod, *Chance and Necessity,* trans. Austryn Wainhouse, New York: Knopf, 1971, p. 172: "It is perfectly true that science outrages values... it subverts every one of the mythical or philosophical ontogenies upon which the animist tradition, from the Australian aborigines to the dialectical materialists, has made all ethics rest: values, duties, rights, prohibitions." Monod tries to save the situation by resorting to "an ethic of knowledge" which man "*prescribes... to himself*" (pp. 176–77, emphasis in the original). Derrida is not so naïve.

what is a man, any man," Augustine questions, "when only a man?"[10]

In the *Confessions* Augustine's preoccupation with time and memory anticipates Derrida's notion of *différance*. Augustine recognizes that even as we cannot grasp the present moment in our temporal existence in the physical world, even so our speech is never wholly and immediately present. But Augustine also maintains that these limitations are also the conditions of being, action, and knowledge. In order for discrete substances – beings distinct from necessary Being – to exist at all, they must suffer displacement in time, and the same temporal displacement is requisite for the differential process of speech:

> So much you gave to these things, because they are parts of a whole, which do not all exist at the same time, but all function in the universe, of which they are parts, succeeding one another and then giving way. Notice how our speech operates in the same way by means of signifying sounds. For an utterance is not complete, if one word does not give way, when its syllables have sounded, so that another can succeed it.[11]

Augustine perceives that in its very temporal progression, speech lacks complete reality, and, in this, it faithfully mirrors the incompleteness of human – indeed, of all temporal existence. But the discontinuities of spatio-temporal existence are not an insufficiency of being as such. The very incompleteness of being as it unfolds in time and space entails an absolute Being as its ground; the stream of our words into the abyss of oblivion – of signifiers pursuing elusive signifieds – entails the being of the immutable Word of God:

> And what was being spoken is not ended, and something else spoken, so that everything might be said, but everything is said at the same time and eternally; otherwise there would be time and change, and no true eternity or immortality.[12]

---

10 *Confessions,* IV.1: "Et quis homo est, quilibet homo, cum sit homo?"

11 *Ibid.,* IV.10: Tantum dedisti eis, quia partes sunt rerum, quae non sunt omnes simul, sed decdendo ac succedendo agunt omnes universum, cuius partes sunt. Ecce sic peragitur et sermo noster per signa sonatia. Non enim erit totus sermo, si unum verba non decedat, cum sonuerit partes suas, ut succedat aliud."

12 *Ibid.,* XI.7: "Neque enim finitur, quod dicebatur, et dicitur aliud, ut possint dici onmia, sed simul ac sempiterne omnia; alioquin iam tempus et mutatio et non vera aeternitas nec vera immortalitas."

Différance, Derrida maintains, inhabits the existential gaps of time: "nonpresence and nonevidence are admitted into the *blink of an instant*," the blink which "closes the eye."[13] But this is merely a human perspective. St. Augustine might reply that God does not blink; His eye never closes.

Derrida, of course, demurs; he dismisses even "the most negative order of negative theology" as dependent upon the prior trace of *différance*, which "has neither existence nor essence," which "belongs to no category of being, present or absent." Like the lines which define plane surfaces in geometry while having no breadth themselves, *différance* is the negative prerequisite of any apprehension of being:

> Not only is *différance* irreducible to every ontological or theological – onto-theological – reappropriation, but it opens up the very space in which onto-theology – philosophy – produces its system and its history. It thus encompasses and irrevocably surpasses onto-theology or philosophy.[14]

But if *différance* is the all-encompassing ground of being, then this ground is a hole, an abyss, and being itself becomes problematic, endlessly "deferred":

> "Older" than Being itself, our language has no name for such a *différance*. But we "already know" that if it is unnamable, this is not simply provisional; it is not because our language has still not found or received this *name*, or because we would have to look for it in another language, outside the finite system of our language. It is because there is no *name* for this, not even essence or Being – not even the name "difference," which is not a name, which is not a pure nominal unity, and continually breaks up in a chain of different substitutions.[15]

"What is unnamable," Derrida continues, "is not some ineffable being" – God, for instance – but "the play that brings about nominal effects." Hence there is no "unique word," no "master name," nothing "kerygmatic" about the "word" with a lower case "w."[16]

Now Derrida's reduction of metaphysics to a *Mise en Abîme* rests in his perception of the spatio-temporal dislocation of human perception and signification. Our saying and knowing are attenuated and fragmented in time and space, which in Derridean deconstruction, as in Einsteinian relativity,

---

13 See above n. 5.
14 *Speech and Phenomena*, pp. 134–35.
15 *Ibid.*, p. 159.
16 *Ibid.*

tend to converge. *To be in time*, Derrida urges, is a contradiction because movement in time entails continuous loss of presence: "The present alone is and ever will be. Being is presence or the modification of presence."[17] Hence even the assertion of the contrary deconstructs itself as it unfolds as temporal speech:

> The *I am*, being experienced only as an *I am present*, itself presupposes the relationship with presence in general, with being as presence. The appearing of the *I* to itself in the *I am* is thus originally a relation with its own possible disappearance. Therefore, *I am* originally means *I am mortal. I am immortal* is an impossible proposition. We can even go further: as a linguistic statement "I am he who am" is the admission of a mortal.[18]

Derrida's appraisal of the paradox of temporal being is by no means novel; St. Augustine grapples with it at great length in the *Confessions* and reaches virtually the same impasse regarding being in time:

> How therefore do *two* of these times, past and present, exist, when the past already is not, and the future is not yet? As for the present, if it were always present and did not move into the past, it would not be time but rather eternity. If then the present comes to be time only because it moves into the past, how can we say *it is*, when the cause of its being is that it will not be; in fact how can we say truly that time is, except insofar as it tends not to be?[19]

What distinguishes this passage from Derrida's disquisition on "temporalization" is that Augustine invokes the concept of eternity which Derrida steadfastly ignores. The lurking (non)presence of the trace, of *différance* – fissure in being – undermines the possibility of *simplicity*, which is a necessary attribute of Eternity, of God. But this view fails to take into account Derrida's own insights regarding the fallibility of man's knowledge. "There has never been any 'perception,'" Derrida writes, "contrary to what our desire cannot fail to be tempted into believing, the thing it-

---

17 *Ibid.,* p. 53.

18 *Ibid.,* p. 54.

19 *Conf.* XI.14: "Duo ergo illa tempora, praeteritum et futurum, quomodo sunt, quando et praeteritum iam non est et futurum nondum est? Praesens autem si semper esset praesens nec in praeteritum transiret, non iam esset tempus, sed aeternitas. Si ergo praesens, ut tempus sit, ideo fit, quia in praeteritum transit, quomodo et hoc esse dicimus, cui causa ut sit illa est, quia non erit, ut scilicet non vere dicamus tempus esse, nisi quia tendit non esse?"

self always escapes."[20] But what "always escapes" cannot be confidently relegated to nonexistence. Derrida succeeds in refuting the transcendental aspirations of man *qua* man as temporal creature, but he says nothing to disprove an eternity which transcends the temporal limitations which bound us. Indeed if the "thing" always "escapes" us, then there must be a something which escapes. The very notion of being wrong entails something to wrong about.

St. Augustine points out that the inherent fallibility of our perception requires that we try to conceive the basis of true perception on a wholly other mode. Even if we could imagine a mind that knew the entire history of the world, past and future, as well as we might know a familiar psalm, remembering what was sung, anticipating what remained – such a mind would still be incommensurably inferior to God's. Even a mind with a hypothetically infinite memory and foreknowledge would still be bound by time. We must, Augustine urges, think of God's knowledge in completely different terms:

> Your knowledge is far, far more wonderful and far more mysterious. It does not come to you as a well-known psalm to the singer or hearer, whose emotions are changed and senses divided with the expectation of words to come and the memory of those gone by. You are unalterably eternal; that is, the truly eternal creator of minds. Therefore just as you knew *heaven and earth in the beginning* without any change in your knowledge, even so you made *heaven and earth in the beginning* without any expansion of your activity. Let him who understands praise you; let him who understands not praise you.[21]

Derrida successfully shows that logocentric self-identity is a contradiction for a being in the temporal mode such as man, even for such a being with infinite capacities. But as St. Augustine's discussion shows, the same strictures do not apply to God who, *by definition*, wholly transcends this spatio-temporal mode. In fact, Derrida's deconstruction of the pretensions

---

20 *Speech and Phenomena*, pp. 103, 104.
21 *Conf.* XI.31: "Longe tu, longe mirabilius longeque secretius. Neque enim sicut nota cantantis notumve canticum audientis expectatione vocum futurarum et memoria praeteritarum variatur affectus sensusque distenditur, ita tibi aliquid accidit incommutabiliter aeterno, hoc est vere aeterno creatori mentium. Sicut ergo nosti *in principio caelum et terram* sine distentione actionis tuae. Qui intelligit, confiteatur tibi, et qui non intelligit, confiteatur tibi."

of the autonomous, self-identical human subject logically clears the way for an acceptance of the mysterious otherness of the God of Abraham, Isaac, and Jacob. Given the demonstrable fragmentation of our being and identity, our existence in any form, the sense of our precarious personhood slipping out of the grasp of our differential consciousness cries out for some explanation beyond the trace of *différance* – the very slippage itself.

May one speculate that Derrida's indisposition to praise inhibits his understanding of this crucial matter? In deploying a rigorous logic with the aim of undermining logic, Derrida leaves himself a comic exemplar of the Cretan liar paradox: A Cretan said, "All Cretans are liars." From the beginning of his deconstructive project, Derrida has recognized this quandary. In an early essay he writes: "*There is no sense* in doing without the concepts of metaphysics in order to attack metaphysics. We have no language – no syntax and no lexicon – which is alien to this history; we cannot utter a single destructive proposition which has not already slipped into the form, the logic, and the implicit postulations of precisely what it seeks to contest."[22] As E. Michael Jones has observed, Derridean deconstruction, in attacking the hypostatized "intentionalist self" of the Western humanist tradition, merely succeeds in turning language into a covert absolute.[23] This is the ineluctable implication of the notion that *différance* – the metaphysical offspring of the differential structure of the linguistic sign – "irrevocably surpasses onto-theology or philosophy."[24] Robert Magliola maintains that "Derrida's argumentation is *primarily* a critique of *the way we think about* reality and not a judgment of reality."[25] Hence, Magliola concludes, he is not an "absurdist." But even making such an allowance, there is something factitious in Derrida's *exposé* of the metaphoricity of Western philosophy in "White Mythology." "Metaphor is less in the philosophical text . . . than the philosophical text is within metaphor."[26]

For the ultimate ontological project, philosophy's highest truth, as Derrida never ceases to argue, is theological; and theology's center has always been approachable only in terms of a kind of metaphor, analogy. Even as God's essence or nature is identical with his act of existing, St. Thomas

---

22 "Structure, Sign, and Play," *The Structuralist Controversy*, p. 250.
23 "Metaphysics as Tarbaby: Intention, Deconstruction, and Absolutes," *Center Journal,* 1, number 2 (Spring 1982), 29.
24 *Speech and Phenomena,* pp. 103, 104.
25 *Derrida on the Mend,* West Lafayette, IN: Purdue Univ. Press, 1984, p. 18.
26 *Margins of Philosophy,* p. 258.

Aquinas argues, so his knowledge is identical with His act of knowing. Hence man can no more share God's knowledge and reason than he can share God's existence. That is why no individual man can exhaust human nature; there would then be no individual men, since individual beings (except for the Divine Being) are less than their natures: "For if in Peter, man and the act of being a man were not different, it would be impossible to predicate 'man' univocally of Peter and Paul, whose acts of existence are different." Yet this does not mean, St. Thomas continues, that knowledge of God is utterly impossible; that all assertions about Him, based on human metaphorical language, are simply capricious: whatever is "predicated of God and creature" is not merely arbitrary or "equivocal." If there were no real likeness of creature to God, then God's essence would not be the image of the creatures, and He would not know them in knowing Himself." This is as much as to say that God would not be God, and the creatures not His creatures. Likewise, we could gain no inkling of God, could find no "traces" of Him, in nature; and there could be no meaningful distinctions among the arbitrary, equivocal terms that man might apply to God. Therefore, St. Thomas concludes, ". . . it must be said, that the application of the term 'knowledge' to God's knowledge and to ours is neither altogether univocal nor purely equivocal, but according to analogy, which means nothing else but a proportion."[27]

---

27 *Quaestiones Disputatae*, XI.ii.11: "Quidquid autem est in Deo, hoc est suum proprium esse; sicut enim essentia in eo est idem quod esse, ita scientia idem est quod scientum esse in eo; unde, cum esse quod est proprium unius rei nonpossit alteri communicari, impossibile est quod creatura pertingat ad eamdem rationem habendi aliquid quod habetDeus, sicut impossibile est quod esse preveniat. Similiter etiam in nobis esset: si enim in Petro non differret homo et hominem esse, impossibile esset quod homo univoce diceretur de Petro et Paulo, quibus est esse diversum; nec tamen potest dici quod omnio aequivoce praedicetur quidquid de Deo et creatura dicitur, quia si non esset aliqua convenientia creaturae ad Deum secundum rem, sua essentia non esset creaturarum similitudo; et ita cognoscendo essentiam suam non cognosceret creaturas. Similiter etiam nec nos ex rebus creatis in cognitionem Dei pervenire possemus; nec nominum quae aptantur, unum magis de eo dicendum esset quam aliud; quia ex aequivocis non differt quodcumque nomen imponatur, ex quo nulla rei convenientia attenditur.

"Unde dicendum est, quod nec omnio univoce, nec pure aequivoce, nomen scientiae de scientiae Dei et nostra praedicatur; sed secundum analogiam, quod nihil est aliud dictu quam secundum proportionem."

In this passage from *De Veritate*, St. Thomas confronts Derrida's two principal objects: the deconstruction of the autonomous, self-identical human subject; and likewise of absolute, logocentric knowledge of being. St. Thomas specifies the *différance* in human identity; that is, our incompleteness insofar as our existential realization falls short of our essential nature. There is a sense in which what abortionists say about unborn children is true of everyone: we are all only "potentially human." This seems to me simply a more precise formulation of St. Augustine's insight that personal identity is unstable when not supported by grace, an insight most notably realized in his account of Alypius, who found himself unwillingly enthralled by the sight of bloodshed at the gladitorial shows in Carthage. "He was not now the man who had arrived," Augustine writes, "but simply one of the mob to which he had come, a true companion of those who had brought him."[28] This same realization has been noted by a distinguished modern theologian, Hans Urs von Balthasar: "Between that which I actually am or could be or would like or ought to be, and that which I factually live, do, think, judge, or experience just now, there gapes an abyss which I can only bridge by virtue of this advance of hope. I never exist completely in my actions and circumstances."[29] One might suggest that Derrida, in proclaiming the abyss within man's personal self-identity, has merely rediscovered sin. Moreover, although he may regard Christianity as the ultimate logocentric ontotheology, it is not the human logos which is placed at the center. "A Christian never has his unity within himself," von Balthasar continues, "nor does he in any way seek it in himself. He does not collect himself around his own center, but rather wholly elsewhere."[30]

By the same token it is no great scandal, not for the Christian at least, that metaphysical discourse is imperfect and oblique – that "the philosophical text is within metaphor." To know Being – absolute necessary Being as opposed to its contingent, created reflections – is to know God. As Aquinas points out, God's very nature entails that it be impossible for man to make univocal predications regarding his Maker, to capture either his essence or existence in human words. Language is the medium of human knowledge, and both are necessarily limited by the intrinsic limitations of human exis-

---

28 *Conf.* VI.8: "... Et non erat iam ille, qui venerat, sed unus de turba, ad quam venerat, et verus eorum socius, a quibus adductus erat."

29 *Convergences to the Source of Christian Mystery,* trans. E. A. Nelson, San Francisco: Ignatius Press, 1983, p. 14.

30 *Ibid.,* p. 129.

tence. But just because *différance*, the "undecidable trace," haunts our discourse, it cannot therefore be inferred that the same *diffJrance* infiltrates everything about which we speak. That is why our central metaphysical knowledge is neither univocal or equivocal, but analogical: It is incomplete, indirect, if you will, metaphorical. It is not equivocal or, in deconstructionist terms, simply mistaken or meaningless. The very terms "meaningless" and "mistaken," require the concepts of meaning and accuracy even to signify. Likewise, the "signifier" cannot operate without the "signified," even if the latter is always absent and inaccessible. As C. S. Lewis quips, "the *Romance of the Rose* could not, without loss, be rewritten as the *Romance of the Onion*."[31] Now neither the rose nor the onion *is* (or is the same as) the erotic favor of a beautiful lady, but the former provides the better analogy. If Derrida were completely right, if language were altogether equivocal, if the signified/signifier relationship of the sign were completely collapsed, then there would be no way of distinguishing between romantic roses and onions. Where Derrida is right, of course, is in seeing that the rose is not *finally* the lady, the lady is not everything one might have hoped, theology is not faith – much less the beatific vision. In the end, it amounts to saying that Derrida's great discovery is that man is not God.

As Robert Magliola points out, according to Derrida, "Any philosophy of presence can be disproven. The contradictory which unseats the conclusion of a philosophy of presence is also illogical."[32] The law of contradiction can perhaps be contradicted; reason can stumble into its own limits and know that its final certainties are matters of speculation, not evidence. Only faith can sustain the mind above the abyss which opens up before naked human reason, and faith can only be a gift, the work of grace.

It is noteworthy, then, that Derrida and deconstructionists generally are reticent regarding the channels of grace, the sacraments; for the sacraments, especially the Holy Sacrifice of the Mass, are the ultimate affirmation in the face of deconstructive "pure negative reference." In the sacraments of the New Covenant, grace is not merely *signified* or *prefigured*, as in the ceremonies of the Old Covenant; in the New Covenant, grace is contained and conferred: Word, material sign (e.g., bread and wine), and grace all converge in the Presence of the Word. And the sacraments are made possible by

---

31 C.S. Lewis and E.M.W. Tilyard, *The Personal Heresy*, London: Oxford Univ. Press, 1939, p. 97.
32 *Derrida on the Mend*, p. 35. See also p. 45.

the Incarnation, Passion, and Death of the Word, the divine Logos.[33] The Eucharist is especially significant in this regard in that the Church teaches that Jesus Christ, true God and true man, is "really and substantially contained under the appearance of the sensible signs."[34] The doctrine of the Real Presence in the sacrament of the altar of the New Covenant is thus the fulfillment of the Messianic promise – the deconstructive longing for the *deferred* Presence – of the Old Covenant. In this sense, Derrida is true to his heritage of Judaism, which is par excellence the religion of the Book, the deferral of the Presence of the Word.[35] But he might also be seen as the last scion of the Protestant Reformation, which generally displaced the sacraments with an intense emphasis on *writing – sola scriptura*. Derrida would seem to have taken this development as far as it can go: He is a Moses who has broken the Tablets and will not re-ascend the mountain, who offers only more wandering – more *erring* – in the wilderness, with the Promised Land endlessly deferred.

It may seem that I have shown that Derrida has merely reinvented the wheel, and there would certainly be an element of truth in this observation. Yet I am convinced that his work is important, if for no other reason than that he unveils the actual tendency of the secularization of Western philosophy and culture during the past several centuries. In exposing the covert dependency of all "logocentric" metaphysics on the concept of God, he demonstrates the emptiness, indeed the fraudulence, of profane humanisms. He proffers a choice (willingly or not) between the deconstructionist abyss or God, between Derrida or Deity. Perhaps Derrida's role in postmodern intellectual life can best be illustrated by comparing him to a fictional character. In Flannery O'Connor's "A Good Man is Hard to Find," an ordinary Middle American family, driving through rural Georgia, falls into the hands of an escaped murderer, who calls himself the Misfit, and two of his companions. While the two companions are shooting the husband, the wife, and the two children, the Grandmother, a "respectable," and rather shallow,

---

33 Henr. Denzinger et Clem Bannwart, S.J., *Enchiridion Symbolorum Definitionum et Declarationum,* 17th ed., Friburgi Brigoviae: Herder, 1928, #695, #849.

34 *Ibid.,* #874.

35 For Derrida's interest in the Judaic sources of his own thought, see "Edmond Jabès and the Question of the Book" and Violence and Metaphysics: An Essay on the Thought of Emmanuel Levinas," chapters 3 and 4 of *Writing and Difference.*

Christian lady, pleads for her life: "Pray! Jesus, you ought not to shoot a lady, I'll give you all the money I've got!" The Misfit is not interested in the offer of money ("Lady, there never was a body that give the undertaker a tip"), but he is obsessed with Jesus:

> "Jesus was the only One that ever raised the dead," the Misfit continued, "and He shouldn't have done it. He thrown everything off balance. If He did what He said, then it's nothing for you to do but throw away everything and follow Him, and if He didn't, then it's nothing for you to do but enjoy the few minutes you got left the best way you can – by killing somebody or burning down his house or doing some other meanness to him. No pleasure but meanness," he said and his voice had become almost a snarl.

> "Maybe He didn't raise the dead," the old lady mumbled, not knowing what she was saying and feeling so dizzy that she sank down in the ditch with her legs twisted under her.

> "I wasn't there so I can't say He didn't," the Misfit said. "I wisht I had of been there," he said, hitting the ground with his fist. "It ain't right I wasn't there because if I had of been there I would of known. Listen lady," he said in a high voice, "if I had of been there I would of known and I wouldn't be like I am now." His voice seemed about to crack and the grandmother's head cleared for an instant. She saw the man's face twisted close to her own as if he were going to cry and she murmured, "Why you're one of my babies. You're one of my children!" She reached out and touched him on the shoulder. The Misfit sprang back as if a snake had bitten him and shot her three times through the chest. Then he put his gun down on the ground and took off his glasses and began to clean them.

The Grandmother, we are told, "Half sat and half lay in a puddle of blood with her legs crossed under like a child's and her face smiling up at the cloudless sky." Do we deconstruct this term "child" in Derridean fashion? Does the suggestion of spiritual immaturity it conveys undermine the sign of newfound innocence acquired in her sudden but telling acknowledgment of her own sinfulness and kinship with the Misfit? Is she the Devil's mother, or does her confession of parentage restore her childhood hopes? Probably all of these meanings and more are available in the text, but the deconstructive effort to deny the uniqueness of imaginative literature is overwhelmed by the mysterious power of this passage to make meanings coalesce rather than fragment and dissipate. *I* cannot give a sufficient exposition of how the *childish* old woman becomes *childlike*; I can only point to

the grim alternative to her humiliation and death registered in the exchange
that follows between the Misfit and one of his henchmen:

> "She was a talker, wasn't she?" Bobby Lee said, sliding down the ditch
> with a yodel.
>
> "She would of been a good woman," the Misfit said, "if it had been
> somebody there to shoot her every minute of her life."
>
> "Some fun!" Bobby Lee said.
>
> "Shut up, Bobby Lee," the Misfit said. "It's no   real pleasure in
> life."[36]

I shall not claim that the analogy is perfect; they never are. Still, there is
a sense in which Derrida can be compared to the Misfit, we Christians to the
Grandmother. (Liberal commentators, incidentally, have often preferred
the Misfit, seeing in him a socially deprived prophet, to the Grandmother a
Bourgeois hypocrite, so that certainly fits.) I believe that we need a few
Derridas around, to shoot us every minute of our lives. We need the test to
our faith, the reminder that our salvation lies not in the theological equivalent of being a "lady," but rather in faith in Jesus. Perhaps, we can no more
argue with Derrida than with the Misfit; we surely cannot argue with death.
We can, however, hope for the moment of grace, the movement of charity,
which seems to be what the Grandmother experiences at her life's close.
Finally, we can remember that, as the heirs of Western civilization, we must
acknowledge that Derrida, like the Misfit, is "one of our own children."
This will help us to remember that in the alienated, deconstructed,
angst-ridden postmodern world, "It is no real pleasure in life" – unless you
"throw away everything and follow Him."[37]

---

36 *A Good Man Is Hard to Find and Other Stories,* New York: Harcourt Brace
   Jovanovich, 1955, pp. 28–29.
37 I wish to thank my North Carolina State colleagues, Barbara Baines and
   Tom Hester, for their invaluable comments on the earlier draft of this paper.

16.
The Holy and the Good:
Relationship between Religion and Morality in the Thought of Rudolf Otto and Josef Pieper (1986)
John M. Haas

Few things have appeared more pronounced in the Catholic Church in recent years than the process of desacralization, and nowhere has this process been more relentless than in the United States and Western Europe. Priestly garb and religious habits have in some cases almost disappeared. Sanctuaries have sometimes been replaced with eucharistic assembly halls. The awesomely enshrined reserved sacrament, the "living heart of our churches," in the words of Paul VI, has often been removed from the sight of the people.

Accompanying these kinds of changes in the religious manifestations of our faith have been radically profound ones in the moral sphere as well. Catholics at one time recoiled at the very thought of contraception. Abortion was described as unspeakable and abhorrent, as the people of God drew back from the practice with as much dread as they would have drawn back from the profaning of a sacred and holy object. Homosexual acts elicited a horror more associated with the violation of religious taboos than with simple moral disapproval. But moral "reformers" have too often kept pace with their liturgical comrades in today's relentless process of desacralization, and today Catholic moralists can be found discovering ways to excuse anything from racial bigotry to bestiality.[1] In a word, actions which were once considered unthinkable, such as divorcing and remarrying or renouncing one's vows of celibacy, have now lost their startling quality and have be-

---

1 Cf. Timothy E. O'Connell, *Principles for a Catholic Morality,* New York: The Seabury Press, 1978; and Anthony Kosnik, et al., *Human Sexuality,* New York: Paulist Press, 1978.

come almost commonplace. In light of these parallel developments in the religious and moral spheres, the question might be raised whether some kind of correlation exists between them.

Probably one of the most radical expressions of the secularization process in both religion and morality, again suggesting a link between the two, is found in a book by Timothy E. O'Connell entitled *Principles for a Catholic Morality*. In this book on morality O'Connell writes of religion stating that "quite literally . . . salvation is a *human* event."[2] "Christians do not really have 'sacred space' in the theological sense. . . . . We have gathering places for the community Church, nothing more."[3]

The desacralization of religion so evident in the preceding passages is also expressed in O'Connell's secularist ethic.[4] "Christian ethics, like all of the Christian faith," he writes, "is essentially and profoundly human. It is a human task seeking human wisdom about the human conduct of human affairs. . . . Thus, in a certain sense, moral theology is not theology at all. It is moral philosophy pursued by people who are believers."[5]

O'Connell's secular Gospel has no room for the sacred in the lives of persons and so offers an ethic which is not burdened by divine precepts. The "fundamental ethical command imposed on the Christian is . . . 'Be human.'"[6] The Ten Commandments are "a cultic text with some minimal ethical components,"[7] and, as has been indicated cult belongs to another age and another mentality.

What is interesting to note in O'Connell's book is the fact that the shift away from an emphasis on the sacred is accompanied by a shift away from certain Catholic moral teachings which have always been considered exceptionless and unchanging, such as the prohibition against the direct killing of innocent life. Consequently, the question is inevitably raised whether there is some kind of intrinsic relationship between religion and morality, between the holy and the good. This paper can be no more than an initial and limited inquiry into this complex and intriguing question. To address the question, two authors will be discussed who have written of both

---

2   Timothy E. O'Connell, *Principles for a Catholic Morality,* New York: The Seabury Press, 1978, p. 38.

3   *Ibid.,* p. 39

4   *Ibid.,* p. 39

5   *Ibid.,* p. 40.

6   *Ibid.,* p. 39

7   *Ibid.,* p. 129.

the moral and the sacred: Rudolf Otto, a German phenomenologist of religion; and the German Thomistic philosopher Josef Pieper. Each man addressed this question from within his own tradition and consequently each makes his own unique contribution to its resolution. Otto was a Lutheran and, philosophically, an idealist. Pieper was a Catholic and, philosophically, a moderate realist. This paper is an inquiry into the way in which these two thinkers developed the relationship between the sacred or the holy and the good, and their conviction that an openness to both religion and morality is necessary for the fullest flowering of our humanity.

I. Rudolf Otto

Rudolf Otto was born in 1869 and died in 1937. He was professor of systematic theology at Marburg. As a devout Lutheran, he looked to the 16th-century leader of the Protestant revolt for inspiration in the development of his theories on religious experience.

Otto was also strongly influenced by the critical philosophy of Immanuel Kant. Religion for Kant was subordinated to and postulated from morality, a position Otto came to reject. God, freedom, and immortality all had to be posited by the mind and could not be directly known, according to Kant. Religion, therefore, came to be removed from the realm of knowledge – or perhaps the converse could also be said: reason was banished from the realm of religion. This separation of faith and reason has been a tendency in the Protestant religion ever since Luther, in his reaction to scholasticism, showed his deep distrust of reason in the religious sphere by referring to it as "the Devil's whore." Inner subjective experience rather than discursive thought came to be considered as more dependable in the religious sphere in the Lutheran tradition. This is certainly reflected in Otto's thought.

Otto also fell under the influence of the Romantic theologian Friedrich Schleiermacher who taught the centrality of religious experience in order to make religion more accessible to "its cultured despisers." In fact, feeling rather than reason provided for the Romanticist the more dependable grasp of reality.

The task of theology, then, as Otto saw it, was to provide a psychological understanding of concrete experience rather than to provide a dogmatic or systematic exposition of Christian beliefs.

II. The Idea of the Holy

Otto is best known for his book, *The Idea of the Holy, an Inquiry into the Non-Rational Factor in the Idea of the Divine and its Relation to the Rational.* In this book he attempts to articulate the autonomy and uniqueness of religious experience as distinct from both reason and morality. He wants to free religion from the dependence on reason and rationalistic metaphysics which seemed to occur within both scholasticism and Kantianism, even if for different reasons. But, in so doing, his intentions are not antirational. As he says himself, "It will be the task for contemporary Christian teaching . . . to deepen the rational meaning of the Christian conception of God by permeating it with non-rational elements."[8]

In discussing the unique, autonomous experience of the Holy, Otto analyzed it into its various components, showing that it has more primitive and more developed elements. For the most basic, non-rational element in the experience of the Holy, Otto coined the term "numinous." On the subjective side of this numinous experience is "creature-feeling," or the overwhelming sense of one's nothingness in the face of the absolute power of the Holy. The objective side of the numinous feeling is the experience of a *"mysterium"* which is both *"tremendum"* or awe-inspiring and *"fascinans"* or attractive and delightful. Yet the *"mysterium"* itself remains unknown and profoundly mysterious. He writes: "The truly 'mysterious' object is beyond our apprehension and comprehension, not only because our knowledge has certain irremovable limits, but because in it we come upon something 'wholly other,' whose kind and character are incommensurable with our own, and before which we therefore recoil in a wonder that strikes us chill and numb."[9]

The numinous constitutes the most primitive, undeveloped sense of the Holy. The numinous "stands for 'the holy' minus its moral factor and . . . minus its 'rational' aspect altogether."[10] The Holy is not recognized as absolute goodness until the notion has reached the highest stage of its development.

Initially the religious person comes to experience the numinous, not as something good and moral, but simply as a *"mysterium tremendum,"* as something mysterious and peculiarly dreadful. In the face of the *"mysterium tremendum,"* the religious person comes to experience the fear of God which seizes man as something more menacing and overpowering

---

8 Rudolf Otto, *The Idea of the Holy,* New York: Oxford University Press, 1957, p. 108.

9 *Ibid.,* p. 28.

10 *Ibid.,* p. 6

than any created reality. The numinous experience also perceives the "*mysterium*" which confronts it as "*fascinans*," i.e., as profoundly attractive and fascinating. This side of the Holy comes to be expressed in the divine attributes of love, mercy, pity and compassion. In a sense, these attributes, like the wrath of God, are seen to be non-rational in that man receives their benefits without meriting them. They are seen as gratuitous and are expressed in such Christian doctrines as the predestination of the elect.

Still, however, the experience of the Holy is non-moral. When Otto discusses the Holy as a category of value, he points to the experience of two profoundly religious men. When Isaiah is overwhelmed by God's presence in the Temple, he exclaims, "I am a man of unclean lips and dwell among a people of unclean lips." When Peter witnesses God's power in Christ's miraculous deeds, he cries out, "Depart from me, O Lord, for I am a sinful man," However, Otto tells us that we should not regard these exclamations as expressions of moral unworthiness. He writes: "These outbursts of feeling are not simply, and probably not at all, *moral* depreciations, but belong to a quite special category of valuation and appeasement."[11]

These exclamations of depreciation are expressive of the feeling of absolute profaneness in the face of the Holy. The feeling is one of profaneness, not immorality, for "'*qadosh*' or '*sanctus*' is not originally a *moral* category at all."[12]

III. The Connection Between the Holy and the Good

Once Otto has firmly maintained that the Holy is an autonomous, unique, *a priori* category of experience, independent of reason and morality, he proceeds to argue that reason, morality, and the sense of the Holy are all intrinsically linked.

Although the numinous is the expression of the Holy minus its moral quality, a process of moralization and rationalization occurs to bring the Holy to its full development. For example, the experience of the wrath of God eventually comes to be filled with elements derived from the moral reason: it comes to express God's righteousness punishing moral transgression. One of the primitive non-moral expressions of numinous consciousness in the Old Testament is "daemonic dread" which is illustrated by Exodus 4:24, where God meets Moses by the way and tries to kill him.

---

11 *Ibid.*, p. 51.
12 *Ibid.*, p. 52

However, the experience of the numinous does not remain at that level. Otto writes:

> The venerable religion of Moses marks the beginning of a process . . . by which the numinous is throughout rationalized and moralized, i.e., charged with ethical import, until it becomes the "holy" in the fullest sense of the word. . . . This moralizing and rationalizing process does not mean that the numinous itself has been overcome, but merely that its preponderance has been overcome. The numinous is at once the basis upon which and the setting within which the ethical and rational meaning is consummated.[13]

The culmination of this moralizing process in the Old Testament is found in the prophets. But it is in the Gospels that one encounters the "consummation of that process tending to rationalize, moralize, and humanize the idea of God."[14]

Although the moral dimension of holiness reaches its apogee in Jesus, he is not seen merely as a moral teacher. Jesus shows that the "Holy One of Israel" is a "heavenly Father" without losing sight of his holiness. Jesus begins his model prayer with "Our Father . . . holy be your Name." In fact, everyone associated with Jesus comes to share in the numinosity of God. His followers become known as the "holy ones." This title does not mean that the people are morally perfect, as any reading of Paul's letters will show, but that they are "the people who participate in the mystery of the final day."[15]

Although Otto constantly insists on the relationship between reason, morality and numinous experience in the fully developed idea of the Holy, he does not demonstrate it. He says it is merely *felt* as something axiomatic, something whose inner necessity we feel to be self-evident."[16] Consequently, we can see that his final appeal is made to feeling as a cognitive function, and it seems to be here that Otto's analysis fails. Feeling is not cognitive, but rather arises with cognition. Joy, fear, and numinous consciousness arise in response to the cognitive grasp of an object. We must know, possess through knowledge, a desirable object in order to experience joy. We must know a threatening object (through memory or present knowledge) in order to experience fear. And the feeling of numinosity

---

13 *Ibid.*, p. 75.
14 *Ibid.*, p. 82.
15 *Ibid.*, p. 84.
16 *Ibid.*, p. 140.

would arise only as we were confronted by the Holy. There must be an object, a reality, which can be known through the intellect in order to elicit emotion. But, in his idealism, Otto is incapable of moving beyond an analysis of the psychological state of the subject. The *"mysterium tremendum,"* for example, is not something encountered, eliciting dread in the subject, but rather is an expression of a peculiar state of mind in the subject:

> The rational ideas of absoluteness, completion, necessity and substantiality, and no less so those of the good as an objective value, objectively binding and valid, are not to be "evolved" from any sense of sense-perception. . . . Rather, seeking to account for the ideas in question, we are referred away from all sense-experience back to the original and underivable capacity of the mind implanted in the "pure reason" independently of all perception.[17]

IV. Concluding Remarks concerning Otto

Otto's idealist convictions seem to be the principal obstacle to his articulating a link between the numinous and the moral. The most he is able to do is to insist that we *feel* an inner, necessary interpenetration of the two which includes all the complexity of non-rational experiences. The difficulty is insurmountable since we are unable to get outside the self to the object which elicits the feelings of dread, awe, love, and fascination. It is ultimately impossible to know the all-powerful and the all-good. We are left only with the feelings which arise from the encounter.

However, Otto's phenomenological study of religious experience is so perceptive that he cannot help but speak of the Holy as well as the experience of it. The common use of language, his objective scholarship and common sense all seem to conspire to lead him beyond a mere analysis of the psychological state to the reality which gives rise to it. He writes, "The numinous is thus felt as objective and outside the self."[18] He frequently speaks of being confronted by the numinous or the Holy. In fact, he says that religious feeling "in itself has immediate and primary reference to an object outside the self. . . . This is so manifestly borne out by experience that it must be about the first thing to force itself upon the notice of psychologists analyzing the facts of religion."[19]

Otto may take notice of the awareness of an object outside the subject,

---

17 *Ibid.,* p. 112.
18 *Ibid.,* p. 11.
19 *Ibid.,* p. 10.

but he never investigates it. Consequently, he never identifies the link between the Holy and the good.

V. Josef Pieper

Joseph Pieper, born in 1904, was for many years a professor of philosophy at the University of Münster. Although a philosopher, he frequently addressed religious questions from within the Thomistic tradition.

Pieper gave considerable attention to analyses of the sacred,[20] often with insights as penetrating as those of Otto. It was Pieper's conviction that rational reflection on the nature of the human person reveals dimensions to the human personality which not only appear non-rational, in Otto's terminology, but which, as such, help to provide the very basis for a sound rationality open to all of human experience. He writes:

> It is completely natural and human for man not always and exclusively to be practical, to be purposeful – but occasionally to make a *sign* – be it only to light a candle *not* to illuminate a room but to give expression to the festive significance of the moment. . . . It is the deliberate *uselessness* of all this that is important, the element of super-abundance and exuberance, of non-calculation and even of waste. The first portion of wine is not used, it is not drunk, it is squandered, it is shed into the sea or on the floor as a libation in honor of the gods. In the same way, Christendom did *not* build practical meeting rooms, but cathedrals . . .[21]

Pieper argues that there is a sacred reality which transcends reason and upon which reason is grounded. Without this grounding, human reason is left without restraints and begins to assume the posture of the divine, supposing that it can determine and create reality rather than discover it. The sense of the sacred with its non-rational ground becomes lost, and even the most sacred reality known to us, the individual human life, becomes merely a usable and disposable means toward attaining whatever end a man chooses for himself.

One of the greatest intellects the western world ever produced, Thomas Aquinas, never forgot the limited role of reason even though he utilized it as few ever had. Thomas was able to make proper use of reason, according to

---

20 Some of Pieper's writings which concern this theme are *In Tune With the World; Leisure, the Basis of Cultuer; The Silence of St. Thomas, The Realm of the Sacred.*

21 Josef Pieper, "The Realm of the Sacred," *Triumph*, November 1971, p. 22.

Pieper, because he had an abiding awareness of the sacred underlying all those things which were open to his senses and his intellect. Although known for the dispassionate use of his reason, his spiritual sensitivity is evidenced in the beautiful hymns he wrote for the Feast of Corpus Christi. Also a celebrated experience which occurred later in his life is witness to his openness to the Holy. In Pieper's book *The Silence of St. Thomas*, he writes of a profoundly mystical experience which occurred in Thomas' life in 1273 on the Feast of St. Nicholas and which resulted in the end of his writing career. Returning to work after Mass, Thomas encountered an overwhelming experience of the superabundance and power of God's presence. He was so stunned by the experience he put aside the treatise on the Sacrament of Penance he had been writing for the *Summa Theologiae* and never wrote again. When Thomas' friend and companion, Reginald of Piper, asked what had come over him, Thomas could only reply, "I can write no more. All that I have written seems to me nothing but straw . . . compared to what I have seen and what has been revealed to me."[22]

There is in the writings as well as in the life of Thomas ample evidence of what Otto calls the non-rational, numinous element in religious experience. God, for Thomas, remains forever hidden, ultimately unknown to the human mind. Because of His utter transcendence, the "otherness" to which Otto refers, God is never reducible to any of our rational categories or mental concepts. Thomas acknowledges this fact when he writes, "Because we are not capable of knowing what God is but only what He is not, we cannot contemplate how God is but only how He is not."[23] And in the *Questio Disputata de Potentia Dei*, he writes: "This is the ultimate in human knowledge of God: to know that we do not know Him."[24]

The fact that we cannot ultimately know God should always be kept in mind when we engage in theological reflection; it should be kept in mind in order to avoid the constant temptation to reduce God to rational concepts. However, the fact that we cannot know God as He is in Himself does not mean that we cannot know anything about Him. As Thomas tells us, "Although we cannot know the essence of God, nevertheless in [theology] we make use of his effects."[25] Indeed, all we can come to know naturally of God, we know through our experience of the world of sense around us.

---

22 Josef Peiper, *The Silence of St. Thomas* (New York: Pantheon, 1957), p. 39–40.

23 S.T., la, 3, prologue.

24 *Pot. Dei,* 7, 5, ad 14.

It is here that a major difference develops between the idealist approach of Otto and the realist approach followed by Pieper. It will be remembered that Otto insisted that the religious ideas he discussed be "referred away from all sense-experience back to an original and underivable capacity of the mind implanted in the 'pure reason' independently of all perception." Yet Thomas, and following him, Pieper, will come to base all arguments for the existence of God on observable, empirical data and show that a sound contemplation of them will lead one to understand that God exists. Thomas does not recoil from the data of sense experience, but views them as effects of something and in a sense goes *through* them to some understanding of their ultimate cause. In other words, it is only through the senses, through our encounter with the objective world of reality, that we can come to know something of God, however limited that knowledge is.

For all the religious and psychological factors which contributed to the Jewish reluctance to utter the Divine Name, that reluctance did give testimony to a rational truth: God cannot be directly known. Even the most proper name for God, HE WHO IS, cannot capture His essence. So the Jew remains silent. This fact was recognized by Thomas as well:

> ... the existence of God is His essence itself. ... Now our intellect cannot know the essence of God itself in this life, as it is in itself, but whatever mode it applies in determining what it understands about God, it falls short of the mode of what God is in Himself. Therefore the less determinate the names are, and the more universal and absolute they are, the more property they are applied to God. ... Therefore HE WHO IS is the most proper Name of God.[26]

It is only by knowing the limitations of our reason that we can presume to say anything of God. We must always realize that what we do say of Him can be understood only in an analogical not a univocal sense. None of this is to deny the object of our religious experience, but only to say that it is unfathomable. As Pieper points out: "The more intensely we pursue [the] ways of knowledge, the more is revealed to us – of the *darkness*, but also of the *reality* of the mystery."[27] Indeed, the *only* avenue open to that ineffable mystery are the objects of its creative and sustaining power which are held up to our senses, and which can be known through sense experience.

As has been pointed out, Thomas looks to the effects of God's creative

---

25 S.T., la, 13, 11.
26 S.T., la, 13, 11.
27 Pieper, *Silence,* p. 38.

power to know something of God. And it is through an awareness of their being that Being Itself can be known of. Mysticism, therefore, does not mean a turning *away from* the world of sense, but rather a turning toward it. The sacred is always mediated through a physical reality, a tree, a mountain, a hillside, the sound of music, the words of the prophet, the stillness of nature. Through his attention to reality Thomas was always aware of the sacral character of Being. Perhaps it would not be too unscholarly to suggest that Thomas's experience of 1273 was an experience of self-subsisting Being, pure act, whose essence is existence, the source and Creator of all that is.

VI. The Connection Between the Holy and the Good

At this point, our attention should be turned to the objects of man's experience to see if the connection between the Holy and the good may be grounded in reality itself.

It must be remembered that the only being whose existence is necessary is God. Pieper writes: "It is impossible that the substance of any being other than the First Agent be its very act-of-being. . . . It belongs to [God] alone that His substance is nothing other than His act-of-being."[28] As Etienne Gilson points out, reminiscent of Otto, "WHO IS signified: He whose essence is to exist; WHO IS is the proper name of God; consequently, the essence of anything that is not God is not to exist."[29]

Everything, therefore, which can be encountered through the senses must be understood as "*creatura.*" God is the Creator, all else is creature, and utterly dependent on Him.

Pieper maintains that this notion of creation, of all things being essentially dependent on God, is the key to a correct understanding of Thomistic philosophy. The notion of creation, says Pieper, determines and characterizes the interior structure of *nearly all* the basic concepts in St. Thomas's philosophy of Being.

A basic scholastic maxim, "*ens et verum et bonum convertuntur,*" is essential to the thesis that the link between the Holy and the good can be found in reality. Pieper insists that propositions such as "all that exists is good" or "all that exists is true" cannot be understood ". . . unless it be realized that the concepts and theses in question do not refer to a neutral Being that sim-

---

28 C.G. II, 52.
29 Etienne Gilson, *The Christian Philosophy of St. Thomas Aquinas* (New York: Random House, 1956), p. 93.

ply exists, not to an '*ens ut sic*,' not to an indeterminate world of 'objects,' but formally to Being as *creatura*."[30]

Pieper accepts to a degree the proposition common in western thought that "truth" cannot be predicated of what really exists but only of what is thought. He still wants to be able to speak of knowing the truth of reality. Pieper does this by demonstrating that, in the Christian understanding of creation, things exist by virtue of their being products of the creative thought of God's mind. He writes: "The essence of things is that they are creatively thought."[31] Human artifacts, for example, have specific natures because they have been determined by the creative mind. For example, one can speak of the "nature" of a pen because the constructive intellect has invented a pen. Sartre insisted on this insight, saying that there is no nature in things which have not been manufactured. Consequently, he said, it would be impossible to have a human nature since there exists no God to think it creatively.

According to Pieper, however, it is precisely because the world has been creatively thought by God that we can speak of the nature and the truth of things. The real world is able to be known by men because it stands between two knowing intellects. As St. Thomas puts it: "*Res naturalis inter duos intellectus constituta est*."[32] The two subjects are, of course, the divine intellect and the human intellect. The creative knowledge of God gives measure to reality but receives none ("*mensurans non mensuratum*"). Created reality is at once measured by God's knowledge and itself gives measure to the human mind. It possesses intrinsic knowability for the mind ("*mensuratum et mensurans*"). Finally there is human knowledge which is given measure by reality but itself does not give measure, except to artifacts and acts ("*mensuratum non mensurans*"). The reality of things *consists* in their being creatively thought by the Creator. Things, as "*creaturae*," correspond to the archetype of them in the creative mind of God. These things are true for man in so far as his mind "receives its measure" from them, corresponding to their objective reality. Pieper writes: "'True' . . . is an ontological name, a synonym for 'real.' '*Ens et verum convertuntur*.'"[33] Because God gives measure to and bestows essence on things through his creative intellect, they are able to be known by the human intellect. However, even

---

30 Pieper, *Silence*, p. 48.
31 *Ibid.*, p. 51.
32 *Questiones Disputatae de Veritate*, 1, 2.
33 Pieper, *Silence*, p. 58.

created things cannot be completely fathomed. As Thomas says, "The essential grounds of things are unknown to us."[34] Things cannot be known in their essence as the essence is related to God. Consequently, "We do not know substantial forms as they are in themselves."[35] Pieper also quotes Thomas to the effect that "essential differences are unknown to us,"[36] and "created things are darkness in so far as they proceed from nothing."[37]

Even the objects of our sense experience have a mysterious dimension or quality to them. Not only God in His perfect Being has an unutterable Name, *but so do the things which are encountered in the world.* Indeed, through their essential relation as creatures to the Creator, created things not only are unfathomable in themselves but also serve as the means for mediating an awareness of the reality of the totally transcendent and all-powerful Creator to men. It is precisely in the objects of sense experience, then, that the Holy is encountered and arouses in the religiously sensitive soul such overwhelming feelings of dread, awe, and fascination. Something of the numinous, of the "*mysterium tremendum et fascinans,*" is encountered in the objects of reality.

If we locate the object which gives rise to the numinous consciousness in created reality (without, of course, being so foolish as to try to "capture" the Holy there), how do we establish the necessary link between numinous consciousness and the sense of morality? Otto never demonstrated the conjunction of the Holy and the good, but simply insisted that it invariably occurs.[38] Pieper, on the other hand, argued that morality arises from the encounter with objective reality, the same source whence arises the awareness of the sacred and feelings of religious awe.

As has been said, things through their essence express God only in an imperfect manner since things are creatures and the created cannot wholly express the Creator. But they *do* express God for us, even if imperfectly, and are to be viewed as good, for insofar as they exist they do so in relation

---

34 *De Anima,* I, 1, 15.

35 *Questione Disputata de Spiritualibus Creaturis,* II ad 3.

36 *De Veritate,* 4, 1, 15.

37 *De Veritate,* 18, 2 ad 5. Cf., also Gilson, *Christian Philosophy,* pp. 221–22.

38 It is interesting to note that Otto argues that Christianity is the highest religion because it most successfully and completely rationalizes and moralizes the numinous. Islam, a lower religion in Otto's judgment, has not moralized the numinous as effectively as Christianity and is victim to the more irrational elements of the numinous.

to their creative source who is God. It has also been said that their essence cannot be known in their relation to God. Yet even though the essence of things cannot be completely grasped, it is not unknowable. As Pieper says: "Man's intellectual power enables him to penetrate to the essence of things; there can be, therefore, insights and assertions concerning the nature of things which, though not exhaustive, are nevertheless true."[39]

How is it that things can be both inscrutable and knowable to the human intellect? The answer lies, according to Pieper, in the notion of "*creatura*" which pervades the philosophy of Thomas. It is because things are created, because they come forth from the archetype in the creative intellect of God, that they can be known and, at the same time, can remain unfathomable. Because they are rooted in the divine Logos, they partake of His lucid rationality. They can, therefore, be known to the human intellect. But in that they issue forth from the divine, they cannot be known in the ground of their being.

Moreover, in so far as anything exists, it is known as good. "To be good is really the same thing as to exist," Thomas tells us.[40] Being and the true as convertible terms are also convertible with the good. The aspect of self-subsisting Being understood as good would correspond to the "*mysterium fascinans*" of Otto's analysis. It is perceived as appealing, as delectable, as desirable. Indeed everything which exists, which participates in being through the creative act of self-subsisting Being, is good.

The good serves as the motivation for human acts. All things seek the good, seek their full realization, by acting. The human agent acts consciously on behalf of the good understood as the end or "*terminus*" of his action as well as its motivation. Thomas writes: "Every agent acts for an end, since all things seek the good. Now for the agent's action to be suited to the end, it must be adapted and proportionate to it, and this cannot be done save by an intellect that is cognizant both of the end and of its nature as end and again of the proportion between the end and the means . . ."[41]

As one commentator on Aquinas writes, "All human life both in ourselves and in others consists in a search for (objective, ontological) goods outside and beyond ourselves which have been grasped by our minds and accepted by our free wills as worthy of our search."[42] All of our actions are

---

39 Pieper, *Silence,* p. 95.

40 S.T., la, 5, 1.

41 *Pot. Dei,* 1, 5.

42 Augustine Joseph Brennan, *Moral Action in Aristotle and Aquinas* (Sidney:

on behalf of ends perceived as good. This is a metaphysical principle which is obvious upon reflection. The principle is as necessary to explain free, rational action as the principle of contradiction is necessary to explain rational thought.

For the agent to act, his intellect must grasp the end on behalf of which he would act and present it to the will as something desirable. It is the speculative intellect which first grasps simple reality. By knowing reality it comes to know that on behalf of which it would act and in a sense expresses itself *as the practical intellect* when it considers that which is to be done. Pieper is strong in insisting on the unity of the practical and speculative intellects, saying that the "concept of the practical reason necessarily includes and asserts the theoretical reason as well. The 'basic faculty' is the theoretical reason, which 'extends' to become the practical."[43] The practical reason, according to Pieper, is nothing but the theoretical reason regarded under the special function of directing action.

There is, of course, only one faculty of intellect in man. Its task, in terms of human action, is to see that persons act in accord with objective reality, itself understood as the good which it is. In terms of what has already been said, objective reality can be known in its essence although not fully comprehended. This objective reality not only presents itself as numinous under the aspect of religion, but also as good and worthy of acting on behalf of under the aspect of morality. A realist epistemology can lead to an intellectual ethic which can develop into an ethical realism grounded in the objective order of reality.

Not only are material goods encountered and sought through objective reality, such as offspring, a home, adequate wealth, but so are spiritual goods. Love and justice are goods of reality on behalf of which we act. Even these spiritual goods arise from the proper ordering and relationships of the material goods which we encounter. Such realities give measure ("*mensurans*") to the mind which conforms to and in a sense becomes essentially those realities. Pieper writes: "Knowledge of the nature of the good necessarily includes the previous awareness of the essential structure of reality as such."[44]

Yet once the mind receives measure from created reality, it seeks its

---

The Cresta Printing Co.), p. 3.

43 Josef Pieper, *Reality and the Good* (Chicago: Henry Regnery Company, 1967), p. 49.

44 *Ibid.,* p. 68.

greater realization and gives measure or form to the act which it proposes. The agent is free to act on behalf of the good, and the essence of the morally good act is that the agent knowingly and freely acts on behalf of the good. The real always seeks to become more fully that which it is, and therein lies its goodness. Again, to quote Pieper: "The good is nothing else than this goal and end of the movement of being, the realization of the essence. 'Everything has as much of goodness as it has of being.' Perfection and the good mean nothing else than the 'plenitude of being,' '*plenitudo essendi*.'"[45]

It would seem that the sense of both morality and the Holy arise from the same source: created reality in relation to its uncreated ground. Morality seeks the "*plenitudo essendi*" through action and the dread experience of the Holy results whenever this "*plenitudo essendi*" is encountered in its depths. If morality consists in freely acting on behalf of true goods known through a sure grasp of reality, the sense of the Holy consists in an awareness of the essential depths of the same reality.

Are the Holy and the good necessarily linked? They are in so far as they both arise from the same source, created reality in relation to its uncreated ground. Yet there can be good men who have never had an experience of the Holy, and there have been religious men who have not been very moral. King David's awareness of God's transcendent majesty did not prevent him from committing adultery. And certain religions with a keen sense of the numinous have a poorly developed sense of morality. Otto places Islam in this category.

There are contemporary examples of religious awareness coupled with moral underdevelopment. A book by Daniel Maguire deals with morality and includes many beautiful passages extolling the affective beauty and importance of religious experience for the moral life. He argues that moral action is "traceable to what could be called a mystical perception of the inviolable sanctity of human life. . . . This mystical perception undergirds every moral ought and those who are alien to it are alien to moral consciousness."[46] Yet in the book Maguire argues for abortion, suicide, and homosexual liaisons. For some reason, the "mystical perception" Maguire speaks of was incapable of saving him from significant error in the moral sphere. It might be argued that his religious experience was a counterfeit one, but that

---

45 *Ibid.,* p. 69.
46 Daniel Maguire, *The Moral Choice,* Garden City, New York: Doubleday, 1978, p. 81.

would be possibly an unjust accusation and certainly one which could not be substantiated. It can be argued, however, that his moral methodology is inadequate. He is basically an intuitionist, unable to ground his ethics either in the agent or in the objective order of reality. What does him a disservice is not his religious experience, but a philosophy inadequate to the task.

When a realist senses the inviolable sacredness of a human life, he soundly draws the conclusion that it may never under any circumstances be directly violated. He grasps its intrinsic goodness and knows that he may only act on its behalf. To violate it, to act against it, would do violence to what he knows it to be, a good on behalf of which he may or may not act. To act directly against it would be to view it as an evil to be eliminated in order to attain something else viewed as a good, since one always acts on behalf of a good. The reason a Catholic justly recoils from acts of contraception, homosexuality, racism, suicide, or abortion is because he is horrified at the sight of an inviolable and sacred good being violated within those acts.

There is clearly a link between religion and morality, but, in order for it to bear the richest fruit, the religion must be the true one and the morality must be guided by a sound epistemology. The Catholic Church has been divinely guaranteed to possess infallibility in the teaching of religious and moral truth. Two of the greatest aids to her in this task have been as follows: (1) a sacramental liturgical and devotional life capable of arousing the most profound religious experiences and of being the source of the objective assistance of divine grace; and (2) a providentially provided realist epistemology enabling it to show correctly, though inadequately, how we can know the truth which will set us free. The sense of religious awe prevents reason from puffing itself up to idolatrous dimensions, and the realist epistemology prevents the religious experience from degenerating into subjective intuitionism, especially in the area of morality.

Man is not only a rational animal but also a religious one. To deny either of these aspects of his personhood is to make him less than he ought to be. Some people have very limited intellectual capabilities; others a stunted religious sense. But a full flowering of all human potentialities simply makes us more human. One of the tragic concomitants to the growing secularism in the Church is the denial to many in our contemporary society of the opportunity to become fully human. O'Connell upheld the truth when he said the highest moral demand placed on Christians was to be fully human. Unfortunately, his insistence on desacralization evidenced a false anthropology, a lack of understanding of what it means to be fully human. As

Pieper points out, ". . . the teaching and practice of the Church – which from earliest times has persistently maintained the rites of the sacred – are in correspondence with the reality of man. . . . The advocates of desacralization began by denying nature – by denying man's orientation to the sacred."[47]

VII. Conclusion

I believe it has been shown that morality and religion are essentially, i.e., ontologically, linked whether or not both play an equally significant role in any one person's life. I also believe that each can suffer without the influence of the other.

Morality without the influence of religion faces the danger of degenerating to a utilitarian rationalism. With no cognizance of the realm of the sacred there is the danger that the world will lose its sense of awe and mystery. Reality will come to be viewed as totally comprehensible and, therefore, totally manageable. Nothing will any longer excite wonder, provoke humility, demand respect. Pieper writes:

> The danger inherent in this situation is that man might, erroneously, come to regard the world as a whole and the created things with it – above all, man himself – in the same manner in which he regards, correctly, his own artifacts. . . . In other words, man is beginning to consider the whole of creation as completely fathomable, fully accessible to rational comprehension, and, above all, as something which it is permissible to change, transform or even destroy.[48]

The twentieth century has, of course, witnessed "the death of God" and the desacralization of the world. With the elimination of the sacred there disappeared the sense of dread and of wonder and love before anything or anyone. The world became malleable, and capable of being made over in man's own image. Human life became expendable and totalitarian states came to use it as the raw material for their own designs. Without the clear demarcation of sacred and profane, limits and structures and boundaries dissolved and social and private lives descended into chaos. No longer chastened by the overwhelming power of the Holy, reason enthroned itself as divine. No longer placing itself at the service of man, reason subordinated man to its own ends, unrestricted, or, so it thought, by the limits imposed by a divinely created nature and its enduring order.

To lead her people out of the current wilderness, the Church must strin-

---

47 Pieper, *"Realm of the Secret,"* p. 20.
48 Pieper, *Silence,* p. 92.

gently apply a disciplined reason to the mysteries of life and faith, as well as maintain a profound sense of how unfathomable and inexhaustible those mysteries are. It was this juxtaposition of traits in the Catholic Church which Otto could not understand and yet which had traditionally redounded to her glory. Through a rigorous use of reason and a sensitive use of evocative symbols and liturgical gestures, the Church can still call forth from persons the full realization of their potential to be fully human. To enable persons to be fully morally responsive, the Church must guard with care the sacred rites which have been entrusted to her.

It is true, however, that the fear of the Lord is only the beginning of wisdom. Similarly, the awareness of the sacred may be only the beginning of morality. But it is an important beginning and a lasting component. Perhaps nothing could be more important for instilling the beginning of moral wisdom in the people of God than for the priest, through his gestures and attire and bearing, to elicit in the people a sense of stupor and wonder, of awe and admiration, of dread and exaltation in the face of the ineffable presence of God Himself upon the altar and in the tabernacle – the consecrated spaces of the Catholic Church.

17.

Natural Law, the Common Good, and American Politics (1987)

Robert P. George

I.

Liberal political theory has long been concerned with the problem of individual rights and collective interests. Some liberals, most notably J. S. Mill, have taken a utilitarian approach to the problem.[1] Under such an approach, individual rights are themselves ultimately derived from a consideration of collective interests. The argument is that individuals have a right to, say, free speech because overall and in the long run permitting individuals to speak freely redounds to the net benefit of the community (or mankind) as a whole. Restrictions on speech may, of course, offer benefits in the short run, but these are outweighed by the greater benefits likely to accrue as fruits of liberty in the long run.

Most contemporary liberal political philosophers, however, are wary of the utilitarian approach. Their chief concern is that it does not provide a sufficiently secure foundation for individual rights. They worry that many individual rights could be overridden if they were left to stand or fall on the basis of considerations of utility. Claiming to reject utilitarianism, they have developed liberal political theories based on principles of what Mill called "abstract right." The idea here is that basic individual rights are not derived from a consideration of what makes the community better off; on the contrary, such rights exist and should be honored even when their exercise makes the community genuinely worse off.[2]

What alternative account of the moral foundations of individual rights

---

1 See J. S. Mill "On Liberty" in Mary Warnock, editor, *John Stuart Mill, Utilitarianism, On Liberty, Essay on Bentham,* New York: Signet, 1974, p. 136.

2 See Ronald Dworkin, *A Matter of Principle,* Cambridge: Harvard University Press, 1985, p. 350.

is available once the utilitarian account has been rejected? Here a division exists among contemporary liberal political philosophers. Orthodox liberals, e.g., John , Robert Nozick, Ronald Dworkin, and David Richards, argue against the inclusion of "perfectionist" principles in political theory. They maintain that individual rights and other principles of justice must be identified, and political institutions designed, without employing controversial ideas about human nature or conceptions of the human good. In Dworkin's crisp statement, "Political decisions must be, as far as possible, independent of any particular conception of the good life, or of what gives value to life."[3]

The anti-perfectionism of orthodox liberalism has been challenged, however, by a number of contemporary political philosophers who understand themselves to be working broadly within the tradition of liberalism. Vinit Haksar, Joseph Raz, William Galston, and others defend versions of liberalism in which they seek to ground basic human rights in conceptions of human well-being. They eschew value neutrality in the design of political institutions and the identification of principles of justice and individual rights.

In this essay I will criticize a liberal view of individual rights and collective interests and defend an alternative understanding drawn from the tradition of natural law theory. I will focus my critical attention on anti-perfectionist liberalism, and, in particular, on the work of Ronald Dworkin. I maintain that Dworkin's liberalism embodies a distorted understanding both of individual rights and collective interests (or what natural law theorists call the "common good"). Once these distortions are brought to light, the superficial appeal of Dworkin's sharp distinction between the role of courts, as concerned with upholding individual rights, and that of legislatures, as concerned with advancing collective interests, vanishes. So too does the apparent plausibility of Dworkin's argument for an individual "right to moral independence" against governmental regulation of "private" morality.

As Dworkin understands the matter, individual rights constrain the government's pursuit of collective interests. Rights specify things that the government cannot do to a person even when the collective welfare could thereby be advanced.[4] Thus, individual rights and collective interests are viewed as potentially (and, often enough, actually) in conflict. Dworkin en-

---

3 *Ibid.,* p. 191.
4 Dworkin, *Taking Rights Seriously,* Cambridge: Harvard University Press, 1977, p. 198.

dorses what he understands to be the characteristically liberal position that, except in cases of extraordinary emergency, individual rights "trump" collective interests.

Let us first attend to Dworkin's understanding of the realities which, we are told, (ordinarily) trump collective interests. Where do individual rights come from? How are they derived? On these questions Dworkin's anti-perfectionism leaves him ultimately without a satisfactory answer. He holds that the specific political rights to which liberals are committed, e.g., rights to free speech, religious liberty, "privacy," etc., are derived not from considerations of what is truly good for human beings, nor, for that matter, from what other anti-perfectionist liberals have conceived of as general rights to liberty or autonomy, but rather from an abstract right to *equality*, viz., the right to be treated by the government with equal concern and respect.[5]

Whether the specific political rights favored by Dworkin and other liberals can plausibly be derived from this abstract right is questionable. Later on I will attack Dworkin's proposed derivation of one such right, i.e., the right to "privacy" or "moral independence." For now, I simply wish to observe that the abstract right to equality appears to be foundational in Dworkin's theory of political morality – he makes no effort to derive it from more fundamental principles. But this is problematic insofar as the proposition it states appears to be neither a self-evident practical principle nor a necessary truth. Tracing back a chain of practical reasoning from the moral decision to recognize a specific political right, one does not ultimately arrive at a grasp of the self-evident intelligibility of an abstract right to equality which terminates the chain by leaving no relevant questions unanswered. Nor does one contradict oneself in denying the abstract right. The right to equality itself, then, stands in need of a demonstration that would appeal ultimately to self-evident practical principles or necessary truths. Otherwise the assertion that there is such a right states nothing more than a not-so-widely shared intuition.

Let us turn now to Dworkin's view of collective interests. How ought we to conceive of the interests of the community which are, we are told, (ordinarily) trumped when in conflict with individual rights? According to Dworkin, they should be conceived of as the community's general background goals which would, but for the existence of the right, justify governmental interference with the individual's choice and action (e.g., by

5 *Ibid.*, pp. 266–78.

requiring him to do something he might not wish to do, or by impeding or preventing him from doing something he might wish to do). These goals are variously referred to by Dworkin in summary fashion as the "aggregate collective good,"[6] the "general benefit,"[7] the "general interest,"[8] the "collective general interest,"[9] the "public interest,"[10] the "public's welfare,"[11] the "general welfare,"[12] and "general utility."[13] Ought these terms to be taken as implying a utilitarian conception of collective interests? The references to "*aggregate* collective good" and "general utility" notwithstanding, Dworkin has consistently maintained that they *need* not be thus taken.[14] Nevertheless, utilitarian conceptions of collective interests are the only ones Dworkin has ever taken seriously.[15]

It could be argued that this is a result of Dworkin's stated belief that a form of utilitarianism, one he calls "neutral utilitarianism," represents the working conception of collective interests in American politics. He maintains that "it has supplied, for example, the working justification of most of the constraints on our liberty through law that we accept as proper."[16] What is "neutral utilitarianism?" It is the version of utilitarianism that "takes as the goal of politics the fulfillment of as many people's goals for their own lives as possible"[17] and is "neutral between all people *and preferences.*"[18]

---

6 *Ibid.*, p. 91.

7 *Ibid.*, p. 198.

8 *Ibid.*, p. 269; and Dworkin, *Law's Empire,* Cambridge, Harvard University Press, 1986, p. 221.

9 *Law's Empire*, p. 311.

10 *A Matter of Principle*, p. 11.

11 *Ibid.*, p. 387.

12 *Ibid.*, p. 11.

13 *Taking Rights Seriously*, p. 191.

14 See *Ibid.*, pp. 169 and 364–65; *A Matter of Principle*, pp. 370–71; and Dworkin, "A Reply by Ronald Dworkin" in Marshall Cohen, editor, *Ronald Dworkin and Contemporary Jurisprudence,* Totawa: Rowman and Allanheld, 1983, p. 281.

15 At one point Dworkin briefly considers, but then abruptly dismisses, a non-utilitarian conception along the lines of the one I defend *infra*. He labels this conception – which understand collective interests as including the creation and maintenance of "conditions... in which it is most likely that people will in fact choose and lead the lives that are the most valuable lives for them to lead" – "Platonist." While he acknowledges that this conception "does not necessarily justify brainwashing or the other techniques of thought

Now, it does seem to me that American legislators and judges frequently adopt a utilitarian approach to political decision-making. (Consider, e.g., the defense policy of nuclear deterrence or – rhetoric about women's rights aside – the judicially mandated policy of legal abortion.) But Dworkin grossly overstates the case in alleging that a form of utilitarianism which is neutral *among preferences* supplies the working justification for *most* of the laws accepted by Americans as proper. Very many preferences are frustrated by the law not merely because lawmakers consider them to be "outweighed" by competing preferences, but because they judge them to be the sorts of preferences which should in principle be excluded from consideration from the start.[19]

In any event, lawmakers err to the extent that they understand collective interests in *any* utilitarian sense. Twenty years and more of intense philosophical criticism of utilitarianism (and consequentialism generally) has established that the strategy of resolving practical (including political) problems by appeal to a principle of optimizing consequences is utterly hopeless. The constitutive "principle" of utilitarianism cannot *rationally* guide choice and action because it fails to state a coherent proposition. One could choose in such a way as to optimize consequences only if the various forms of good, and the various instantiations of particular forms of good, constitutive of human well-being were commensurable in such a way as to make possible the weighing and comparison of states of affairs required by the utilitarian principle. But, as critics of utilitarianism have conclusively shown, such commensurability is an illusion.[20] Thus, no one can accurately

---

control that we have learned to fear," he excuses himself from further consideration of it on the ground that he "doubt[s] that it appeals to many people." *A Matter of Principle*, pp. 414–15.

16 *Ibid.*, p. 370.

17 *Ibid.*, p. 360.

18 *Ronald Dworkin and Contemporary Jurisprudence*, p. 282 (emphasis supplied).

19 For some examples, see J. M. Finnis, "A Bill of Rights for Britain? The Moral of Contemporary Jurisprudence," The Maccabaen lecture in Jurisprudence, Proceedings of the British Academy, London, Volume LXXI (1985), p. 318; and Vinit Haksar, *Equality, Liberty, and Perfectionism*, Oxford: Clarendon Press, 1979, pp. 260–61.

20 See especially Germain Grisez, "Against Consequentialism," 23 *American Journal of Jurisprudence* 21 (1978); John Finnis, *Fundamentals of Ethics*, Oxford: Oxford University Press, 1983, pp. 86–93; Finnis, Grisez, and

say, for example, that so much friendship is worth so much knowledge; or that this one man's life is worth less (or more) than the lives of these two (or ten, or ten thousand) others.

Beyond this, however, the fact of incommensurability undermines any aggregative conception of collective interests. This means that "collective interests" are, in reality, the interests of *individuals*.[21] There simply are no "collective interests" not reducible to concrete aspects of the well-being of individual members of the collectivity. Does this insinuate the sort of "individualism" characteristic of libertarianism political theories? No. This is because among the concrete interests of every individual human being is living in harmony and friendship with others. Moreover, an appreciation of the values of interpersonal harmony and friendship helps to bring into focus the moral requirement that the benefits and burdens of communal life (including rights and duties) be distributed fairly and with a due regard for the particular needs and abilities of different persons.

Now, Dworkin's practical juxtaposition of individual rights with an aggregative conception of collective interests gives an air of plausibility to his distinction between the role of courts, as concerned with upholding principle, and that of legislatures, as concerned with advancing policy. For Dworkin, "[p]rinciples are propositions that describe rights; policies are propositions that describe goals."[22] To say that rights trump, e.g., the general welfare, is to say that principle should prevail where it conflicts with policy. Courts, according to Dworkin, offer a "forum of principle,"; they are responsible for protecting individual rights. Legislatures, on the other hand, are concerned with matters of policy; they are responsible for advancing collective interests. Under an aggregative conception of collective interests the best policy would be the one that yielded the "most" good – individual

---

Joseph M. Boyle, Jr., *Nuclear Deterrence, Morality and Realism.* Oxford: Clarendon Press, 1987, ch. IX; and Joseph Raz, "Value Incommensurability: Some Preliminaries," *Proceedings of the Aristotelian Society 86* (1985–86), pp. 117–34. Also of interest: Anselm W. Muller, "Radical Subjectivity: Morality versus Utilitarianism and the Virtues," *Mind,* volume xciv (1985), pp. 196–209; and "Morality, Action and Outcome" in Ted Honderich, editor, *Morality and Objectivity,* London: Routledge and Kegan Paul, 1985, pp. 23–28.

21 See Finnis, *Natural Law and Natural Rights,* Oxford: Clarendon Press, 1980, p. 168.

22 *Taking Rights Seriously,* p. 90.

interests and rights notwithstanding. If individual rights nevertheless existed independent of collective interests, it would indeed make sense to provide a political forum with broad powers countervailing to those of legislatures to which individuals could appeal for their protection. The idea of courts as such a forum is by no means unreasonable.

But if we conceive of collective interests in a non-utilitarian, non-aggregative way, the neat contrasts between matters of principle and policy and individual rights and collective interests blur. An appreciation of incommensurability brings to light the profound senses in which legislative responsibilities for policy implicate matters of principle. To advance collective interests (conceived in a non-utilitarian way) is, among other things, to respect the requirements of practical reasoning which structure choice – including legislative choice – in respect of the range of incommensurable aspects of individual and communal human flourishing. These moral requirements may often be expressed in terms of entitlements of individuals not only to particular liberties, but to a great many other opportunities and goods. These entitlements (negative and positive) are the "individual rights" which legislatures must not only respect but protect and advance if they are to fulfill their *policy* responsibilities under a non-aggregative conception of collective interests.

Under a non-aggregative conception of collective interests, no individual's interests may be left out of account by policymakers, nor may any individual's rights be trampled (by legislators, judges, or anyone else), without thereby *damaging* the common welfare. Incommensurability means that it is impossible to say that the state of affairs produced by a violation of individual rights is "better" for the community than the state of affairs which would have obtained had individual rights been respected. Where rights are conceived of as constraints on the pursuit of collective interests, it is assumed that sometimes collective interests actually could be advanced by violating rights (although it would, ordinarily, be wrong to do so). But this could only be true under an aggregative conception of collective interests. And such a conception cannot be justified in light of the problem of incommensurability.

II.

The non-aggregative conception of collective interests I have been sketching out here closely resembles the traditional natural law theory of the common good. While talk of "rights" does not figure prominently in the classical and medieval statements of that theory, its perfectionist concern for human well-being provides ample grounds for the derivation of human rights by its modern exponents. These rights are understood by contemporary natural law theorists not as constraints on the pursuit of the common good, but as constitutive aspects thereof. Thus, for natural law theorists, legislatures are not properly designed or understood as institutions devoted to advancing aggregate good constrained by the power of courts to enforce individual rights. Rather, legislative responsibility for preserving and advancing the common good includes an obligation to honor and protect rights. Courts – even those which do not enjoy the power of judicial review of legislation – share this obligation, albeit in a more or less circumscribed way. But it is certainly not a peculiarly (or even primarily) judicial obligation.

Natural law principles of political morality frequently require the government to refrain from interfering with individual choice and action.[23] Sometimes, the unimpeded individual will choose to act in such a way as to damage not only himself but others as well. This need not imply a view of morality which sacrifices collective interests to individual rights. The goods of individual liberty, autonomy, authenticity, etc. are themselves incommensurable aspects of human well-being. But *this* does not mean that individual choice and action may never be impeded – only that the legitimacy of governmental decisions to interfere with individual choice and action depends upon the consistency of those decisions with the requirements of practical reasoning that structure human choosing in respect of the range of incommensurable human values. Where these requirements exclude governmental interference with individual choice and action, any loss in terms of goods foregone by governmental respect for individual rights is simply not properly understood as a sacrifice of collective interests. Again, regardless of the goods to be gained by a disregard for rights, the incommensurability of goods means that the common good, since it is non-aggregative, simply cannot be advanced by governmental action which infringes rights. Such action *only* damages the common good.

The natural law theory of individual rights and collective interests has the advantage over anti-perfectionist liberalism of providing a rational account of the moral foundations of rights by understanding them as implications of intrinsic human goods and basic moral principles which rationally

---

23 See Finnis, *Natural Law and Natural Rights,* Oxford: Clarendon Press, 1980, p. 168.

guide and structure human choosing in respect of such goods. Its thorough-going rejection of aggregative conceptions of collective interests makes it possible, moreover, to understand rights not as constraints on the pursuit of such interests, but as constitutive aspects of the common good.

Now, what has any of this to do with American politics? Liberalism is not only a political theory; it is a political movement. As a movement, it has an agenda which has been prosecuted vigorously and, on the whole, successfully in the United States. Liberals have achieved many of their goals by effectively capturing the terms of American political debate. These terms typically juxtapose individual rights with collective interests. The "liberal" position is depicted as the one favoring individual rights; the conservative position as the one favoring collective interests.

American conservatism has, by and large, left the liberal understanding of individual rights and collective interests unchallenged. Indeed, in at least some respects, American conservatives seem willing to accept this understanding flat out. In economic matters, for example, conservatives have simply tried to turn the tables on liberals by depicting government regulation as unjustly (and shortsightedly) favoring collective interests over individual rights. Those libertarian-minded conservatives who denounce governmental interference with "capitalist acts between consenting adults" rightly claim to be not so much "conservatives" as "classical liberals." In non-economic matters, e.g., matters of criminal justice, conservatives have made their own play for the rhetorical advantage, juxtaposing "the rights of the criminal" with the "rights of society."

Over the past forty years liberals in the Western democratic nations have campaigned to obtain legal immunities for controversial activities they believe to be matters of individual right. Among the most controversial claims of right they have advanced are those having to do with human sexuality and reproduction. Liberals maintain that these are (for the most part) "private" matters. They must, therefore, be left to individuals to decide for themselves. The government violates individual rights when it bans or unduly restricts abortion, contraception, pornography, and sodomy.

The political strategy American liberals have found most effective has not involved persuading legislators to repeal such legislation; rather, it has involved persuading judges to invalidate it under their power of constitutional judicial review. State laws restricting abortion,[24] contraception,[25] and

---

24 *Roe vs. Wade*, 410 U.S. 113 (1973).

25 *Griswold v. Connecticut*, 381 U.S. 479 (1965); and *Eisenstadt v. Baird*, 405

pornography[26] have been struck down by the federal courts as unconstitutional violations of a putative "right of privacy."[27]

Now, Dworkin has attempted to provide a theoretical justification for something very like the liberal notion of the "right of privacy." He calls it the "right to moral independence."[28] The central premise from which he argues is the abstract right to equality.

In his early work, Dworkin argued that government violates this right whenever it restricts individual liberty on the ground that one citizen's conception of the good life is nobler or superior to another's.[29] This claim, however, came in for stinging criticism. It is far from obvious that a legislative concern for the morality of members of the public is necessarily indicative of contempt for those persons whose preferred conduct is banned or restricted. On the contrary, as John Finnis has argued, morals legislation *"may* manifest, not contempt, but a sense of the equal worth and human dignity of those people, whose conduct is outlawed precisely on the ground that it expresses a serious misconception of, and actually degrades, human worth and dignity, and thus degrades their own personal worth and dignity, along with that of others who may be induced to share in or emulate their degradation."[30]

Some liberals reply to Finnis' argument by denying that conduct typically regulated by morals legislation, e.g., various forms of consensual sexual activity, can ever be inconsistent with human worth and dignity.[31] In their view, there can be nothing morally wrong with such "autonomous" and purely "self-regarding" conduct.[32] Dworkin, however, offers no such

---

U.S. 348 (1972).

26 *Stanley v. Georgia,* 394 U.S. 557 (1969).

27 While the Supreme Court of the United States continues to permit the strict regulation of "obscenity," it has so defined that term as to render only the nastiest forms of pornography "obscene." The Court appears, however, to have drawn the line on "privacy" at homosexual sodomy, recently upholding a Georgia law making sodomy a crime constitutionally valid, at least insofar as applied to homosexual acts. *Bowers v. Hardwick,* 106 S. Ct. 2841 (1986).

28 *A Matter of Principle,* p. 353.

29 *Taking Rights Seriously,* p. 273.

30 Finnis, "Legal Enforcement of 'Duties to Oneself': Kant v. Neo-Kantians," 87 *Columbia Law Review* 433 at p. 437.

31 See e.g., David A. J. Richards, *Sex, Drugs, Death, and the Law,* Totawa: Rowman and Littlefield, 1982, pp. 96–116.

32 Richards understands moral principles as "constraints... that free, rational,

rejoinder. He does not suppose that the right to moral independence exists because "private" choices are never subject to moral standards. Rather, he argues that the right protects the individual from interference with such choices even where he may choose wrongly. Indeed, such choices are, in his view, immune from governmental intrusion as a matter of moral right even where the decision involves conduct which is demeaning, degrading, or destructive.

But where such conduct is involved, there certainly need be nothing inegalitarian in legislative action aimed at preventing it. Such action certainly (but not arbitrarily) prefers some types of *conduct* over others; but it just as certainly need reflect no preference of one *person* over another. It condemns some conduct as unworthy of persons; but it need condemn no person as less worthy than any other. The paternalism involved in a decision to intervene in persons' lives to prevent them from demeaning, degrading, or destroying themselves by their own wrongful choices might very well, as Finnis suggests, be motivated precisely by an appreciation of their equal worth and dignity.[33]

In his more recent work, Dworkin has revised his argument from equality. He still maintains that individuals have a moral right to be free from governmental intrusion in "private" matters, but his argument is more complex. He says that the principle of equality requires that government

> . . . must impose no sacrifice or constraint on any citizen in virtue of an argument that a citizen could not accept without abandoning his sense of equal worth. . . . [But] no self-respecting person who believes that a particular way to live is most valuable for him can accept that this way of life is base or degrading.[34]

But additional complexity fails to afford Dworkin's argument additional cogency. Whether or not the individual whose preferred conduct is proscribed or restricted accepts the argument grounding the proscription or restriction, or even thinks about the matter at all, is irrelevant to whether

---

and equal persons could offer and accept as universally applicable constraints on their *interpersonal* conduct." "Kantian Ethics and the Harm Principle: A Reply to John Finnis," 87 *Columbia Law Review* 457, at 461 (emphasis supplied).

33 See, in addition to the passage quoted *supra* at note 30, *Natural Law and Natural Rights,* pp. 222–23.

34 *A Matter of Principle,* pp. 205–6.

those exercising authority over that conduct are treating that individual with equal concern and respect.

If he happens to think about it and accepts the argument, he in effect agrees that the conduct in question is indeed unworthy of him. He still might find it difficult to conform his behavior to the law; and insofar as he continues to indulge in the unworthy conduct he will likely find it difficult to retain his self-respect. Now, self-respect is a genuine human good; the loss of self-respect is a genuine evil. But in this event damage to the individual's self-respect is not properly attributable to the law, but to his own moral failings. His self-respect will be restored to the extent that he reforms his character and conforms his conduct to the standard required, not only by the law but also by his own revised understanding of the morality of the conduct in question.

But what if he does not accept the argument? In this event there will be no damage to self-respect at all. He will regard the law as backward, stupid, insensitive, unjust. He might express anger towards, and/or sorrow for, those responsible for, or supportive of, the law. He might *feel* as though he is being treated as a second-class citizen for engaging in conduct which he believes to be acceptable or even enriching. He might work for the repeal of the law, and even practice civil disobedience. He cannot, however, reasonably maintain that the law fails to treat him as an equal. To the extent that the law embodies a legislative concern to prevent individuals from demeaning, degrading, or destroying themselves, it treats his welfare as just as important as everyone else's. In seeking to uphold public morals, it favors the moral well-being of each and every member of the public. No one's interest in living a worthy and dignified life is singled out as more or less important.

In a carefully constructed article, Dworkin has attempted to apply his view of individual rights and collective interests to the problem of pornography.[35] Therein he straightforwardly (and accurately) identifies certain significant respects in which the availability of pornography damages collective interests. He says that a decision to recognize a right to use pornography, even in private,

> . . . would sharply limit the ability of individuals consciously and reflectively to influence the conditions of their own and their children's development. It would limit their ability to bring about the cultural structure they think best, a structure in which sexual experience gener-

---

35 "Do We Have a Right to Pornography?" 1 *Oxford Journal of Legal Studies* 177–212 (1981); reprinted in *A Matter of Principle*, pp. 335–72.

ally has dignity and beauty, without which their own and their families' sexual experience are likely to have these qualities in less
degree.[36]

Nevertheless, he argues, such a right exists and should be recognized by
law. Despite the fact that legal restrictions on the availability and use of pornography might very well advance collective interests in such true human
goods as dignity and beauty in human sexual relationships, such legal restrictions would be unjust. They would violate the right to moral independence, and, ultimately, the right to equality, of those individuals wishing to
use pornography.

I have already attacked Dworkin's attempt to derive the putative right
to moral independence from the right to equality. Good faith legislative efforts to combat, e.g., pornography, even where such efforts go awry (as
when valuable non-pornographic materials are prudishly or squeamishly
banned or restricted), imply no denial of the equality of persons. I now want
to conclude my case against Dworkin's view of individual rights and collective interests by challenging him on the specific question of a right to pornography, and demonstrating that anti-pornography legislation need not
violate anyone's rights, nor sacrifice anyone's interests, for the sake of advancing collective interests.

The human interest in dignity and beauty in sexual relationships – and
in the creation and maintenance of a "cultural structure" which supports
these ideals – is a "collective" interest (only) in the sense that it is an interest
shared by each and every individual member of the collectivity. It is a
"common" interest, and a matter of the common good, in the sense that it is
shared by all and may be preserved and advanced by common endeavor.
What is worth noticing is that among those whose interests are preserved
and advanced by anti-pornography legislation are those individuals who
would be inclined to use pornography. Dignity and beauty in sexual relationships (and a supporting cultural structure) are no less goods for them
than for anyone else. To the extent that it serves these (truly common)
goods, anti-pornography legislation preserves and advances, rather than
harms, their interests as well as the interests of everybody else.

This would not be the case, of course, if human interests were ultimately matters of desire – satisfaction. In this event, anti-pornography legislation would represent a favoring of the desires of those who happened to
like dignity and beauty in sexual relationships over those who happened to

36 *A Matter of Principle*, p. 349.

like pornography. A genuine *conflict* of interests would then exist. Collective interests really would be an aggregative matter: Whatever satisfied the most desires (or the desires of most people) would be in the collective interest. Individual rights, if they existed, would constrain the collective pursuit of desire – satisfaction. They would specify immunities which would, in effect, entitle the individual to certain types of desire – satisfaction of his own – even at a cost to the overall desire – satisfaction of the collectivity.

But once we understand interests as having to do with human goods *not* reducible to desire – satisfaction, apparent conflicts of interest of this sort should not trouble us. Anti-pornography legislation, to the extent it is effective, frustrates the desires (or potential desires) of persons inclined to use pornography, but it does so precisely in the interests of, among others, those very individuals. Insofar as it does not treat their interests as in any sense inferior to those of anyone else, it does not fail to treat them with equal concern and respect.

Author's Note: In the fourth sentence of the second paragraph of part II, I suggest that individual liberty and autonomy are basic human goods (i.e., "incommensurable aspects of human well-being"). This suggestion is incorrect. Liberty and autonomy are important *instrumental* goods; they are not, however, *intrinsic* (and, thus, basic) goods. I clarify this point in *Making Men Moral: Civil Liberties and Public Morality* (Oxford: Clarendon Press, forthcoming).

18.

To Be or Not to Be . . . Female (1987)

Joyce A. Little

I.

Since sharing seems today to be one of those things universally recommended, I would like to begin by sharing with you one of my pet peeves. (And I must also confess that I seem to have garnered out of my "lived experience" as an American Catholic an alarming number of this particular type of pet in recent years.)

The one I have in mind has to do with those politicians (of every shade on the political spectrum) who, when confronted with any uncongenial suggestion that something in the way we are living today has gone awry, hasten to assure us that we need not worry because the American people are intelligent and can be trusted to do the right thing. I do not know who first stumbled upon this wonderful rhetorical device, but he must have recognized almost at a glance that it ranks, in terms of human inventiveness, right up there with fire and the wheel.

This avowed trust in the American people kills several birds with one stone. In the first place, it allows us, the people, to bask in the warm rays of our own virtue. Secondly, it allows the politician to present himself as one who recognizes and appreciates our virtue. Thirdly, it manages to suggest that we Americans are a cut above other nations, whose people cannot always be trusted to get things right. And, fourthly and most importantly, it tries and often manages to cut off discussion at the outset, by suggesting that anyone who thinks there is a problem clearly does not trust the American people.

I bring up this particular pet peeve, however, because, annoying as this notion that Americans are somehow exempt from the of things might be in the political realm, it is downright pernicious when it raises its head within the Catholic Church, as we see happening today. I cite only one quite recent example of it. Just a month ago, NBC, in anticipation of John Paul II's second Papal visit to the United States, aired a program entitled "God is Not

Elected," hosted by Maria Schriver.[1] In the opening segment from San Francisco, Fr. George Fitzgerald of Old St. Mary's Cathedral, addressing the differences which American lay Catholics have with the papacy today, said: "I think that part of the reason why you experience the conflict in the American church is you have a very articulate, educated laity, and they're simply saying, `We want to have an active part and an active role in making some determinations about being Catholic.'"

All of this sounds at the least quite benign and at the most quite positive. As an articulate and educated lay person, ought I not bask in the warmth of my own virtue and take great heart that, in this "age of the laity," I am finally coming into my own?

Before rushing to embrace Fr. Fitzgerald's happy appraisal of the American Catholic laity, we ought perhaps first look at some of the articulate and educated laity showcased on this particular program. First, there was Edwina. Characterized as a devout Catholic because she attends Mass thrice weekly and has refused to marry her boyfriend, a divorced man, unless he obtains an annulment from the Church, Edwina admitted that she engages in pre-marital sex with this boyfriend; but she believes herself not culpable and no less a Catholic for doing so. How did she articulate her educated faith? "I know the Vatican is against abortion, I now know the Vatican is against artificial insemination, I know the Vatican is against birth control, but that's about the extent of my knowledge of what the Vatican says or doesn't say."

Then there was Kevin, a sexually active homosexual, a member of Dignity, and a welcome participant in the Mass at Old St. Mary's. He said: "Pronouncements from Rome don't always reflect the lived experience of people in the United States." (Clearly no one has educated Kevin on the Fall and how it tends to affect our "lived experience," even in America.) Since Kevin is presumably one of those articulate and educated parishioners about whom Fr. Fitzgerald waxed so enthusiastically, we may safely assume that Kevin did not have himself in mind when he told us that "a lot more listening needs to happen."

My own personal favorite on the program, however, was Lennie, an Italian Catholic in Los Angeles. Asked how she feels about the Church's teachings, she articulated her educated faith as follows: "There are some doctrines, especially that the pope has come out in the last year or two [sic],

---

1 God in Not Elected. Host: Maria Schriver. NBC News Special. KPRC, Houston, 8/25/87.

that I don't feel good about. The issues . . . brought up recently on homosexuality, birth control, artificial insemination – he's taken many steps backwards [sic] and has alienated a lot of very important, educated Catholic people."

I doubt that anyone, even the pope, could fully appreciate my own lived experience as I listened to her. Here sat I, with my doctorate in theology from a reputable American university, and somehow it had escaped my notice that the pope has spent the last couple of years fabricating doctrines. And why, I asked myself, had my dissertation director at that reputable university, a Jesuit whose knowledge of the faith I much respected, never even so much as intimated to me that popes are not supposed to alienate important, educated Catholics? (I too had read James Hitchcock's *The Pope and the Jesuits*, and I trusted implicitly that, whatever else might be said for or against them, the Jesuits could be counted on to pass along information of this kind.) In fact, my situation was even worse than that. I had actually been laboring for several years under the impression that this pope at least is himself an important and educated Catholic.

Of course, it is easy to poke fun at the alleged education of many American Catholics today, and indeed we must sometimes laugh at it if only to avoid crying. But we must admit that a great many Catholics today no longer have even a Baltimore Catechism knowledge of their faith and, even more tragically, no longer have even that sense of the faith which can often be relied upon to keep us from going astray when all else fails.

And we must also face the fact that these lay Catholics are not entirely culpable for their ignorance. Why is it that Edwina, attending Mass three times a week, knows almost nothing about what the Vatican has to say? Lay Catholics are familiar with the problem. Most of us have our stock of horror stories regarding the imaginative and sometimes even bizarre accounts of the faith to which we have been subjected in recent years. It is no longer even particularly surprising to learn, as we did from Edwina, that the priest counseling her and her boyfriend for marriage has no problem with their practicing birth control – this on the grounds that the pope does not play the game and therefore should not make the rules!

TV Guide, a few months ago, ran a cartoon in which one woman says to another, as both are watching TV, "I am shocked by the things which no longer shock me." I know exactly what that woman means. Only rarely any more do I hear anything which genuinely shocks me, and that fact has begun to disturb me greatly. It no longer surprises me at all, for example, when my students say, as one did recently, that, if it be true that God calls everyone to holiness, she is happy that most people do not enthusiastically embrace the call, because the world would be awfully uninteresting if they did. But it did quite literally shock me to hear Fr. George Fitzgerald say, from the pulpit of Old St. Mary's and on NBC: "If the Church were only to exist for the good, how terribly boring life would be." Let us be grateful that we do not have to hear his homily on heaven. But let us also not be surprised that he happily welcomes into his parish active homosexuals and heterosexuals routinely practicing artificial contraception and that, when he looks out over his congregation, he sees many people whom he personally knows to have undergone abortions. One gathers that his parishioners rarely bore him. If it be true that lay Catholics frequently get the priests they deserve, it is apparently also true that sometimes, at least, a pastor gets the parishioners he deserves.

We the people of God have a right to be educated in our faith, and we are therefore well within our rights to ask why it is that, when we turn to our priests and bishops for the bread we so desperately require, we are so often handed a stone. While many of our clergy manage frequently to avoid answering our questions, we fortunately do have good reason to believe that someday, sooner or later, they will have that same question addressed to them by Someone whom they cannot avoid.

In the meantime, however, we lay people have our own question to answer. It has, in fact, been quite forcefully articulated in a recent novel, *The Thanatos Syndrome*, by Walker Percy.[2] In that novel, we meet Father Smith, a self-admitted failed priest who is, among other things, an alcoholic. But precisely because he can admit his failure, he is an honest man and an honest priest. His parishioners can expect no false flattery from him, no easy assurances that the pope does not appreciate their education and cannot understand their lived experience. Having faced his own sinfulness and guilt, he is indelicate enough to suggest that his parishioners ought to do the same. He is not at all interested in expanding the number of his flock, in welcoming into the parish more members. Oddly enough, and if the truth were known, he seems to think that many already there have somehow inadvertently wandered into the wrong place, and he gives the impression that they ought to think a bit more about whether or not they really want to be

---

2 Walker Percy, The Thanatos Syndrome, New York: Farrar, Straus & Giroux, 1987.

there. We are not surprised when told that he manages to offend everyone.[3]

At the end of the novel, we find ourselves at a Mass celebrating the opening of a hospice for the sick and dying whom our society no longer cares about and indeed has been euthanatizing at a pretty steady rate at a nearby place called Fedville. The chapel is crowded, and the television crews are on hand to cover the big event. Fr. Smith walks in to celebrate the Mass.

Does Fr. Smith smile into the camera and thank everyone for coming? Does he applaud those who are present for being loving and caring people? Does he congratulate them for their sensitivity and compassion? Happily, Fr. Smith is not a recent product of our seminaries and therefore knows how to put the time he has to much better use. He tells them he recognizes their tenderheartedness, but suggests it might be indistinguishable from that tenderheartedness which motivates others to support euthanasia. He tells them he recognizes they experience no guilt in their lives, but, modern psychology notwithstanding, he seems oddly unhappy about their lack of guilt. He claims he cannot see a sinner among them, but that fact clearly brings him no joy. Father Smith is doing there in that chapel, though it is clear that most, if not all, of his audience has lost its grip on what he is doing there.

Father Smith doesn't particularly care whether his parishioners know what he is doing among them or not. But there is one thing he does think they ought to know, one question he does think they ought to be able to answer. He points out that the folks over at Fedville, the doctors and the nurses employed to abort and euthanatize human beings, know what they are doing there. And then he looks out over those gathered in the chapel. "I wonder," he says, "if you know what you are doing here!"[4]

The reader has an advantage over the audience in the chapel, for the reader is privy to Father Smith's earlier conversation with and confession to the narrator. When asked by the narrator why he had become a priest, Father Smith answers, "In the end, one must choose – given the chance." "Choose what?" the narrator asks. "Life or death. What else?"[5] Father Smith, indeed, does know what he is doing in the Catholic Church, but he is not convinced that many of his parishioners can say the same.

While Walker Percy, as a convert to Catholicism, may wonder at just how many lay Catholics in general know what they are doing in this

---

3 Ibid., p. 357.
4 Ibid., p. 358.
5 Ibid., p. 257.

Church, I as a female theologian have to wonder at just how many female Catholics in particular know what they are doing here. This question is a pressing one, for, just as those folks over at Fedville knew what they were doing, so today's feminists, and especially those who remain nominally Catholic, know what they are doing. And what they are doing is, if possible, even more unpleasant than the goings-on over at Fedville. Indeed, Fedville represents only one of many unpleasant projects today's feminists are happy to support. If Walker Percy is correct in saying that to choose to be Catholic is to choose life, and I think he is, it is also and equally true, I believe, that, for women in particular today, to choose to be Catholic is to choose to be female.[6]

II.

Until very recently, it would have sounded strange to say that a woman must choose to be female. After all, women are by nature female and therefore would appear to have no choice at all in the matter. But today we are watching, thanks largely to the feminist movement in general and feminist theology in particular, an enormous irony being played out before our eyes. Women, in the name of women's liberation, are deliberately rejecting those values most explicitly grounded in femaleness. Women, in the name of their own empowerment, are systematically discarding the very strengths which are embodied by the female. And, in so doing, they necessarily find themselves in conflict with the Catholic Church which, virtually alone among today's secular and religious institutions, insists that the real values of the female must be recognized and lived.

No one has pinpointed more accurately the character of the controversy between the Catholic Church and radical feminism than Rosemary Radford Ruether. She has observed:

> One might say that if the Vatican lost its credibility for "infallibility" in matters of morals with the birth-control controversy, it lost its credibility for "infallibility" in matters of faith with the declaration on the admission of women to the priesthood.[7]

---

6   Indeed, one might well argue that, for women in the Church, the choice for life and the choice to be female are simply two sides of the same coin, given the fact that Eve is the "mother of all living" (Gen 3:20) and Mary, as the Mother of God, is mother of all who enter into the new life made available to us in Christ her Son.

7   Rosemary Ruether, "The Roman Catholic Story," in Rosemary Ruether and

Artificial birth control, on the one hand, and a male priesthood, on the other, do indeed define the framework within which the Church would insist that we understand human sexuality, the first by addressing the religious significance of what we do with our sexuality, the second by addressing the religious significance of who we are by virtue of that sexuality.

It is by now well understood that the first of these Church teachings, the ban on artificial contraception, conflicts with the feminist view that women must be freed, as it were, from their biology. Feminist arguments for abortion, of course, proceed very much along these same lines. One feminist, locating herself in a tradition going back to Simone de Beauvoir, tells us, "I am endangered by motherhood. In evacuation from motherhood, I claim my life, body, world, as an end in itself."[8]

What feminists reject here is the identification which Western thought has consistently made between femaleness and materiality. Mother Nature and Mother Earth are but popular expressions of this long-standing identification. Linguistically the identification is equally clear. Karl Stern notes: "Woman, in her being, is deeply committed to *bios*, to nature itself. The words for *mother* and *matter*, for *mater* and *materia* are etymologically related."[9]

Were there no Catholic Church to guide us at this point, the feminist rejection of this identification would be virtually irrefutable. Their case goes something like this. Western thought extending back to Plato and Aristotle has made two assumptions about reality – first, that spirit is superior to matter, and second, that males are to be identified with spirit while females are to be identified with matter. In Plato, this meant that the seductive or destructive characteristics which he attributed to matter are to be attributed to women. In Aristotle, this meant that the inferior characteristics which he attributed to matter (particularly its passivity) are to be attributed to women. Hence women have had to contend with male views of the female which turn women into either seductive temptresses who try (quite often success-

Eleanor McLaughlin (eds), *Women of Spirit*, New York: Simon & Schuster, 1979, p. 380.

8 Jeffner Allen, "Motherhood: The Annihilation of Women" in Marilyn Persall (ed), *Women and Values*, Belmont, CA: Wadworth Publishing Company, 1986, p. 92.

9 Karl Stern, *The Flight from Women*, New York: Farrar, Straus & Giroux, The Noonday Press, 1965, p. 23.

fully) to bring the male down or passive instruments at the service of male activity. One obvious solution presents itself. Women must be freed from these clearly oppressive identifications with materiality. Women must be freed from their biology.

There is a second solution, but it is not at all obvious, and indeed one could argue that, in the absence of the Christian revelation, it might never have occurred to anyone. This second solution is simply the reverse of the first. Instead of rejecting the identification of femaleness with materiality, this solution says we ought to embrace it. But, also and of crucial importance, instead of accepting the notion that spirit is superior to matter, this solution tells us we ought to rethink it or, more accurately, perhaps we ought to think about it for the first time, for, so obvious has it seemed to us that spirit is superior to matter that we have never seriously questioned that assumption at all.

In point of fact, no sense can be made out of the Church's ban on artificial contraception unless we suppose that the human body, human sexuality, human materiality is far more important than we are accustomed to thinking it is. Although Paul VI was the author of the encyclical *Humanae Vitae*, it is John Paul II who has set himself the task of exploring the implications of this teaching. And it is John Paul II who has characterized the results of that exploration as a "theology of the body." The pope is opening before us, as perhaps no one else in the history of our faith has done, a view of creation and salvation in which the striking and singular importance of the human body and human sexuality can at last be appreciated as it never has been before. Indeed, we are beginning to realize that *what we do* with our bodies is in the final analysis indissociable from our maleness and femaleness. And that brings us to Ruether's second problem with Church teaching, the male priesthood.

It is commonplace today among feminists and others to hear it argued that, as long as women cannot be priests, women will feel like second-class citizens in the Church. Indeed, one could easily conclude, listening to media accounts of this controversy, that women who seek equal access to the priesthood are comparable to blacks seeking equal access to better-paying jobs. In fact, however, the actual issue is quite different. Once again, Ruether goes to the heart of the matter:

> Feminist liberation communities necessarily must dismantle clericalism, which is an understanding of leadership as rule that reduces others to subjects to be governed. Clericalism, by definition, disempowers the

people and turns them into "laity" dependent on the clergy. The basic
assumption of clericalism is that the people have no direct access to the
divine. The clergy alone have authorized theological training: they
alone are authorized to preach, to teach, to administer the Church.
They alone possess sacramental power.[10]

The notion that we have "no direct access to the divine" is indeed
indissociable from the notion of priesthood, but it is also indissociable from
the entire Judaeo-Christian tradition. According to that tradition, our access
to God is always mediated, whether by the materiality of creation, or by the
Law and the prophets of the Old Testament, or by the Incarnate Word, or by
the written word of Scripture, or by the public, visible sacraments instituted
by Christ. Indeed, it is quite literally true to say that in Catholicism there is
no purely spiritual realm, for even the Trinitarian God Whom we worship
is, by virtue of the Incarnation, Resurrection, and Ascension of the Son,
eternally united to human nature and human materiality. To remove these
elements of mediation from Catholicism would be to destroy Catholicism.
The feminist critique of the male priesthood, because that critique involves
the rejection of material principles of mediation, constitutes the single most
all-embracing rejection of Catholicism we face today.

Even the Protestant Reformers, despite their rejection of the Church
and many of her sacraments, never went so far as to suppose that we have a
totally unmediated relationship with God. For them, the Bible, if nothing
else, continued to be regarded as an authentic and utterly essential mediation of God's word without which we cannot know Him as He is. But the
feminist "hermeneutics of suspicion," as Elizabeth Schüssler-Fiorenza
among others has characterized it, would take even that away from us, rele-
gating Scripture to the dustbin of patriarchal texts inspired by a culturally
conditioned male chauvinism.

American Catholics today are subject to two powerful streams of
thought, one theological and one philosophical, which operate to undermine our sense of the faith. The first of these, the theological one, is the
Protestant Reformation, with its partial, though substantial, rejection of
Catholic sacramentality. Fr. Walter Ong notes: "The real, deeply felt, but
little understood difficulties of separatists were and are not with [the authority of Fatherhood], but with the mitigated, mediated authority, the symbol

---

10 Rosemary Radford Ruether, *Sexism and God-talk*, Boston: Beacon Press,
   1983, pp. 206–7.

of which must be feminine . . ."[11] These difficulties led the Reformers to reject (1) Church teachings as regards the importance of the Virgin Mary; (2) the Church as female, that is to say, as sacramental and mediational; and (3) human sexuality as sacramental, i.e., marriage as a sacrament. Ong points out: "Almost every characteristic tenet of separatist bodies can be charted in terms of the impulse to insulate religion from the femininely polarized aspects of reality."[12]

Modern Western philosophy, as Karl Stern's *The Flight from Woman* amply illustrates, constitutes a similar rejection of the female. The foundation of this flight is Descartes's methodological doubt, from which contemporary philosophy has been unable to free itself and which feminist theology has made its own under the rubric of hermeneutical suspicion. The Cartesian doubt was and continues to be a flight from materiality.

> For to all of us, the core and meaning of reality was at one time, before all cogitation, the certainty of carnal presence. Descartes, the adult and philosopher, postulates to "doubt sensible things because they have deceived us." . . . The certainty of the flesh which is the foundation of all certainty *had* to be conjured away – because it was here where the terror of pain and abandonment lurked. To the man who was to make an *act of doubt* the basis of all inquiry, doubt had supplanted trust a long time before conceptual thinking...[13]

Such doubt renders meaningless the Incarnation and all that proceeds from it. Stern points out, and this should comes as no surprise to us today: "This wave of the Cartesian tide has left its stain everywhere, even on Christianity – as we witness in certain trends of present-day theology."[14]

American history is, as Herbert Richardson points out, "an effort to `spiritualize' all of reality."[15] Richardson, himself a Protestant, applauds this effort. Indeed, his study on American sexuality, *Nun, Witch, Playmate: The Americanization of Sex*, in which he makes the above observation, is an attempt to demonstrate that human consciousness has throughout history

---

11 Walter J. Ong, *In the Human Grain,* New York: The Macmillan Company; London: Collier-Macmillan Ltd., 1967, p. 190.

12 *Ibid.*, p. 192.

13 Stern, *The Flight from Woman*, p. 100.

14 *Ibid.*, p. 104.

15 Herbert Richardson, *Nun, Witch, Playmate: The Americanization of Sex*, New York/Evanston/San Francisco/London: Harper & Row, 1971, p. x.

moved from an original carnal and biological notion of human sexuality to a progressively spiritualized notion.

This spiritualized view, of course, insists that we see ourselves as "persons" in abstraction from our maleness and femaleness, and relies heavily upon abortion and artificial methods of birth control as the means by which heterosexual relationships achieve their spiritualization. Homosexual relationships, of course, no longer constitute a moral problem, inasmuch as our concern is with persons, not with males and females *per se*. Indeed, one might even argue that homosexual relationships lend themselves more readily to this spiritualizing process, since they require no mediating contraceptive devices to achieve it.

This is the atmosphere in which we live today. And if it has any lesson to teach Catholic women, it is that the feminists are quite wrong in supposing male chauvinism to be our primary enemy. Male chauvinism, in fact, never was the enemy, but only a symptom of the real villain in the piece. For the real villain is today, as it always has been, the uncriticized assumption that only spiritual realities matter (pun intended). No other idea is or ever has been as powerfully entrenched in human thought as this one. It will not be easily dislodged.

The Catholic Church today stands embattled as she has never been embattled before, because the Catholic Church alone among all religions, systems of thought and institutions in the modern world, has the faith, the reason, the will, and the resources to wage and win the war against this false spiritualization of the humanity which the Trinitarian God created in His image, male and and female; whose salvation the Son undertook by becoming flesh; who continues to be present among us in both his Eucharistic Body and his Mystical Body; whose union with that Mystical Body is the "one flesh" union of groom and bride anticipated in Genesis; and whose Resurrection and Ascension, together with His Mother's Assumption, anticipates and realizes the desire of all creation for salvation in a new heaven and a new earth.

Women even more than men have a stake in this war and its outcome, because women, even more than men, have a stake in the material, the biological, and the carnal, and all of the values with which God endowed them before standing back and calling His creation – His very material creation – good.

By the year 2000, it should be obvious to most, if not all, women in the Church that, in the final analysis, we cannot free ourselves from the biological without simultaneously ridding ourselves of the sacramental. It should by then be obvious that to choose to be Catholic is to choose to be female, because only the Catholic Church, by affirming the value of the material and the sacramental, is in a position to affirm the value of all that is most explicitly and properly identified with the female. Indeed, the way things seem to be shaping up now, to be Catholic may well be the only way open to us to be female as we enter the third millennium of our faith.

19.

The Church's Message to Artists and Scientists (1987)

Benedict M. Ashley, O.P.

I.

Recently I revisited the remarkable Rothko Chapel in Houston, a part of the complex centered on the recently opened Menil Museum. When this chapel was first opened by its distinguished Catholic donors John and Dominique de Menil, I happened to be there when the paintings by Mark Rothko were actually being uncrated and installed. I also celebrated what I believe was the first Catholic liturgy in that ecumenical chapel. Seeing it some sixteen years later, I was deeply moved to find that (whether it was the effect of changed lighting or some change in the paint itself or in myself) these almost entirely black panels had begun to glow with a hidden radiance to which I had before been blind.

For me that chapel expresses the spiritual question of our age, no longer modern but "post-modern." Rothko was an artist of deep spiritual sensibility who soon after he completed this work died a violent death, probably but not certainly at his own hands, trapped in the toils of the frauds and exploitations of the art market – in any case a victim of our times, which rewards some artists extravagantly in money yet isolates them in a spiritual void. A Jew uprooted from his heritage, Rothko was inspired in creating this final work by a visit to the remarkable Byzantine Christian chapel of Torticello on a Venetian islet.[1] He wanted to do some thing analogous for our times, on the theme, some say, of the Passion of Christ, ranging from Salvation to Damnation.[2]

---

1 For a biography see Leo Seides, *The Legacy of Mark Rothko,* New York: Rinehart and Winston, 1978; for artistic appreciation see Diane Waldman, *Mark Rothko, 1903–1970: A Retrospective,* New York: Harry N. Abrams, Inc. in collaboration with The Solomon R. Guggenheim Foundation, 1978.

2 Waldman, p. 68; Seldes, p. 63f.

The result is utterly puzzling to many visitors. In a simple octagonal brick building hang fourteen large rectangular panels which appear at first sight to be monochrome black: four single panels on the diagonals of the octagon, one on the entrance wall, and three triptychs on the east, west, and north walls. Gradually, one sees that on some panels the black is set against a very dim red, and that a red or violet wash suffuses the black. As the light changes other atmospheric tones glow in the void.[3]

What is its "meaning"? Although many painters resent such questions, Rothko is quoted as saying, "I am not interested in relations of color or form. . . . I am not an abstractionist," and as declaring that he wanted to express "basic human emotions – tragedy, ecstasy, doom. . . . The people who weep before my pictures are having the same religious experience I had when I painted them. And if you, as you say, are moved by their color relationships, then you miss the point."[4]

Rothko was faced with the fact that "modernism" was an expression of what we can reasonably call "secular humanism," the religion of Man created by the Enlightenment in opposition to a Christianity which seemed to be destroying itself by fratricidal wars. Yet this anti-Christian humanism had a positive content that we find in the neo-classical, realistic, and impressionistic art of the nineteenth century in its glorification of a purely human, empirical, anti-metaphysical world and in the so-called revolutionary expressionist and abstractionist cult of pure creativity. But post-modernism can no longer trust in the human future and is left with an empty aspiration for transcendence. Harold Rosenberg said: "Thus having cancelled or submerged tradition, in modern [read "post-modern"] art the new has reached the point of cancelling itself."[5] Similarly, Michelangelo Antonioni said to Rothko: "We have much in common. I film nothing and you paint nothing."[6]

---

3   For an esthetic analysis of the paintings see Sheldon Nodelman, *Marden, Novros, Rothko: Painting in the Age of Actuality,* Seattle: University of Washington Press for the Institute for the Arts, Rice University, Houston, 1978. Also Dore Ashton, *About Rothko,* New York: Oxford, 1983, pp. 168–85.

4   Waldman, p. 58. Rothko especially loved the works of Fra Angelico, p. 59.

5   Quoted in the introduction by Dore Ashton to Bonnie Clearwater, *Mark Rothko Works on Paper,* New York: Hudson Hills Press, 1984, p. 59.

6   Seldes, p. 64.

Because all the images of the past, including the images of modernity, seem to have undergone a total *kenosis* of meaning, an artist like Rothko, deeply religious by temperament, knew that in our pluralistic post-modern times an ecumenical chapel could only be a place for meditation in a silence which would be receptive of every word, human or divine, because it had no message to convey, but only the question.

II.

Vatican II spoke for the Christian Church of this post-modern silence as follows:

> Although we must be careful to distinguish earthly progress clearly from the increase of the kingdom of Christ, such progress is of vital concern to the kingdom of God, insofar as it can contribute to a better ordering of human society. When we have spread on earth the fruits of our nature and our enterprise – human dignity, brotherly communion, and freedom – according to the command of the Lord and in his Spirit, we will find them once again, cleansed this time from the stain of sin, illuminated and transfigured, when Christ presents to his Father an eternal and universal kingdom "of truth and life, a kingdom of holiness and grace, a kingdom of justice, love and peace." Here on earth the kingdom is present in mystery; when the Lord comes it will enter into its perfection (*Gaudium et Spes* #39).

Vatican II set for Catholic scholars the hard job of trying to discern what in our modern culture is the result of human cooperation with the Creator and therefore to be cultivated for the future, and what is the result of human sin and therefore to be pruned if the future is to be fruitful. This job cannot be executed in a spirit of mere conservatism, as if the *status quo* were simply God's work; nor in a spirit of mere progressivism, as if real progress is guaranteed by following the trends of the time; but only in the spirit of a good physician who looks not only for the symptoms of a patient's disease but also for his "vital signs" that promise a possible recovery if supported by the healing art. I want to speak to you chiefly of what seem to me "vital signs" in the arts and sciences of our time. Hence I must first attempt to diagnose its illness.

What do literary and art critics mean when they speak of "post-modernism?" By "modernism" they mean the movement of radical experimentation that began at the end of the Victorian-Edwardian era with World War I, typified in literature by James Joyce and Ezra Pound, in the plastic arts by Picasso and Henry Moore, in architecture by Frank Lloyd Wright and Ludwig Mies van der Rohe, in music by Stravinski and Schoenberg. It declared itself free of all historic forms and styles and accepted the pluralism and individualism of the twentieth century.

Yet post-modernism, which began with World War II, expresses disillusionment with this whole enterprise. It tends to see these experiments, brilliant as they were, as ultimately dead-ends. Consequently, post-modernism accepts the conclusion of Martin Heidegger that the great human effort to control the world by human science and technology has worked itself out as it was fated to do, and that we must now recover the "Being" we have forgotten, that is, the sense of the transcendent "All" of which we are a part, by a radical new way of thinking, perhaps by the mysticism of the East.

In the sciences in our century, there has been a different development which we might at first suppose is a story of continuous progress. Certainly from the fundamental discoveries of Einstein at the beginning of this century there has been a steady and unprecedented advance in all the natural and life sciences and in their technological application. We seem close to a unified field theory of all basic natural forces and a grasp of molecular biology which will explain all life and its evolution. Cosmology has opened up an astonishing new vision of the universe, perhaps of many parallel universes, each expanding like bubbles from a big-bang into nothing, or disappearing down black-holes.[7] Meanwhile, our technological control of the world advances ever more rapidly. Yet even in the sciences there is a skeptical post-modernistic mood for two reasons. The most obvious reason is that we have become aware that our technology may destroy our environment and ourselves unless it is politically and morally controlled. A deeper reason is that, the more our scientific theories are perfected, the more they seem to show us a world without any purpose or human meaning, a world that can be described mathematically, but whose reality and value slips away from all elucidation. Consequently, scientists, like artists, continue to go about their business, but with the haunting anxiety that all their efforts merely enhance the cosmic absurdity.

---

7 See Heinz R. Pagels, *The Cosmic Code: Quantum Physics as the Language of Nature,* New York: Simon and Schuster, 1982, and the remarkable Gifford Lectures of Sir John C. Eccles, *The Human Mystery,* New York: Springer international, 1979, for the current scientific picture.

What light does theology cast on this historical situation?[8] If we view history in terms of the relation of culture to Christ, we see that our intellectual dilemma did not begin with the modernism of our twentieth century, but with the Enlightenment in the eighteenth. The religious wars between Christians disillusioned most of the intelligentsia of Europe and the Americas with Christianity. At the same time, modern science and its technology, which Christians had begun to develop in the seventeenth century, appeared to these disillusioned intellectuals to provide an alternative to Christianity. There could be, in Kant and Hume's terms, a religion of reason (i.e., science) and a morality without revelation, i.e., without Christianity. This new religion of humanity rather than God, went through a deistic phase and then an agnostic one, and finally produced Marxist atheism. Just as Christianity was faced with Islam in the seventh century, so Christianity has been faced with secular humanism since the eighteenth – a force which now dominates all Western culture.

The term "secular humanism" is being given a bad odor by the fundamentalists, who in fact are much more influenced by it than they imagine, as witness their glorification of our deistic Founding Fathers. However, they are not mistaken in thinking it is the rival of Christianity in our times.[9]

From the outset humanism was internally polarized. The scientific ideal, as its philosophers understood science, required science to be value free. From where then could come a system of human values without which human life is impossible? The answer was found in Romanticism, the other pole to Scientism. Romanticism says that human values are essentially esthetic, a matter of sensibility, feeling, taste, and, therefore, without objective standards. Values are created by human beings, and often come down to, as it was said by G.E. Moore, the guru of the Bloomsbury crowd who typified modernism, "esthetic value and friendship."[10] The doctrine of "human rights" as put forward by most writers today, free of any basis in natu-

---

8 What follows presents a historical hypothesi argued at more length in my *Theologies of the Body: Humanist and Christian*, Braintree, MA: Pope John Center, 1985.

9 Martin Marty has argued that what the fundamentalists call "secular humanism" is really nothing more that the *pluralism* of American society which must remain neutral to religious differences. I think this neglects the basic *uniformity* of the ethical outlook which dominates our education and the public media and from which it is socially risky to dissent publicly.

ral law, amounts simply to "a sense of decency" and crumbles in the face of issues like abortion.

Thus the root of the moral problem of our culture is the notion of science as "value free." Certainly if this simply means "objective," i.e., free from prejudice, the notion has validity. All thinking ought to be objective. But "value free" here means an interpretation of science which requires the elimination of all teleology from nature. If nature is not teleological, there can be no natural moral law, no human purpose or value in nature, including our own human nature which our reason and will must respect.

Moreover, art also must cease to be an "imitation" of nature in the Aristotelian sense, because nature is in the eye of the beholder. It is not a discovery by the artist, but a pure creation, a projection of the artist's own expressive power. Thus the development of modern art toward abstractionism, and of literature toward a realism that is simple reportage of human absurdity, and of formal experiments which make the means more important than the end become perfectly intelligible. The only subject of art becomes art itself. Its meaning is deconstructed so as to be exposed as arbitrary.

I have said theology casts light on our post-modern dilemma, but let me also note that theology itself seems to be suffering from the same dilemma. Many theologians today believe their proper task is to revise classical theology by taking "the turn to the subject" with modern philosophy so that the objective truths of the Gospel become "hermeneutically transformed" into "religious experience" transcendent to empirical reality.[11] Thus theology is being romanticized, estheticized, and further separated from the world with which science deals and which technology manipulates.

But has not the marvelous progress of modern science and technology proved that this "value free" objectivity to be the only way to get ahead in science, whatever the cost? And has not the remarkable emancipation of artistic and literary creativity in our century, including the burst of original

10 Moore's ethical views have been very influential. Yet they were for him very tentative. See the discussion by Frederick Copleston, *A History of Philosophy,* New York: Doubleday-Image Books, 1967, vo. 8, pt. II, pp. 168–74.

11 The Kantian element in Transcendental Thomism is the effort to find an *a priori* element in knowledge, but this negates Aquinas' thorough anti-Platonism, the very basis of his originality as a theologian.

thought in theology, demonstrated the same for the subjective pole of our culture?

III.

What then is sound in modern culture? My answer would be that it is science and the technological power it gives us, but only if science is freed of the false philosophical interpretation given it by humanism, chiefly by Immanuel Kant. *Gaudium et Spes* was the first conciliar document to recognize (although Pius XII had already done so in a less solemn way) that science is the work of the Holy Spirit, not of the devil. God calls us to understand and marvel at his creation, and to use this knowledge to guard and cultivate our garden earth. The great mistake of Christians of the eighteenth century was to permit the humanists and then the Marxists to take science away from the Church, which had laid its basis in the Middle Ages and fostered its modern development in the seventeenth century.

But this science, like every human endeavor in our fallen world, must be redeemed. By redeeming science we redeem creation. We must restore teleology to scientific explanation and thus recover the sense of "nature," i.e., that God has made things to act not simply mechanically (although they use mechanisms) but for intrinsic built-in goals. This does not introduce into science some occult cause, because teleology is not an efficient cause. It merely means to quit ignoring the observable fact that natural causes work in a directed way. Teleology got excluded from science first by mathematicism and then by Kantian philosophy. This exclusion played into the hands of humanism which from the time of deism came to a view of the world as a blank check leaving man totally free to write in his own values.

Once we have rethought the scientific picture of the world and have shown that nature has a purpose; that the world is not ultimately self-explanatory and therefore requires a Creator; and that we as humans are the culmination of the evolutionary process but not ourselves completely explicable by evolution, then the whole ground is cut out from under humanism. Then human culture, including its arts, will be revitalized, because it can draw from the infinite meaningfulness of nature and can be open to the mystery of God, serving as a liturgy in His praise and no longer as a dumb idol.

With this restoration of the central idea of nature and a nature open to God, we can begin to reassimilate all the elements of Christianity that humanism and Marxism have taken from us. Vatican II has taught us that no

Christian strategy is so mistaken as that of attributing everything outside the Christian fold to the devil. It is true, as St. John says (I John 2:16), that all that is in the world and is not of Christ is of the evil one; but the "world" has never been deserted by God, the Holy Spirit has always been at work in it, to redeem it. Consequently, Vatican II taught that the best way to approach other religions is not by pointing out their errors in order to enhance Christian claims, but to point out what is of God in them. We must do the same with humanism and Marxism. If we make clear enough what is good in them, it will become evident that this good has been corrupted by what is evil and can regain its pristine splendor only within the light of the Gospel.

We need to acknowledge that one of the reasons other religions have emerged is because believers in the true religion have failed its own principles. To punish and correct us, God has shared the gifts we have abused with those of other faiths, so as to shame us. Therefore, we should see the rise of humanism and Marxism as punishments on the Church for its failure fully to appreciate human dignity and the gifts of science and technology given us by God. Therefore, as we were humiliated by Islam's great missionary spirit, which Christians neglected because of their internal squabbles; and as Catholics were humiliated by the Protestant zeal for the Scriptures which we had also neglected; so now we are being punished by seeing what humanism has done with science and for human rights, which we failed to do. Our conversion must inspire us to recapture these treasures for Christ.

The first step, I have been arguing, is a better philosophy of science. Many of our best philosophers since Marechal, such as Lonergan and the Transcendental Thomists have accepted the Cartesian and Kantian turn to the subject as the necessary starting point of understanding the modern world in a critical way, and have tried to show that there were roots of this in St. Thomas. Our leading theologians such as Rahner and Schillebeeckx have accepted this.[12] They were not mistaken in seeing that Kant is the key figure, but I believe they made the grave mistake of simply accepting his interpretation of science which empties it of all ontological meaning. Until we have corrected that misstep we will continue to run into a blank wall in our efforts at a true theological *aggiornamento*.

---

12 David Tracy, *Blessed Rage for Order,* New York: Seabury, 1975, and *The Analogical Imagination,* New York: Crossroads, 1981, and Francis Schuessler Fiorenza, *Foundational Theology,* New York: Crossroad, 1984, survey these trends in theology.

In this respect Teilhard de Chardin and the followers of Alfred North Whitehead have been closer to the right road, but in both cases they made the serious and gratuitous mistake of introducing teleology into science by way of panpsychism.

Once we have set science back on the teleological track where it first took off and the cosmos has ceased to appear empty of meaning, as a *second* step we can safely acknowledge many of the insights made by Romantic, idealistic philosophy. It is true that Thomism gave very little attention to human historicity and subjectivity. We have become aware by the dialectic between value-free scientism and the romantic exploration of subjectivity how conditioned every human vision of reality is by the culture, experience, pre-understandings, and special interests of the knower. Consequently, we no longer believe as Aquinas did that most people who disagree with our faith are in bad faith.[13] It becomes possible for orthodox Catholics to accept doctrinal development, the modern notion of Biblical inspiration, and epistemological pluralism, without losing a firm grounding in transcultural and transplural objectivity. Thus the way to true dialogue about our most profound convictions is no longer blocked by our failure to acknowledge the limits of our perspective. It is as if through Vatican II we have heard the Lord's voice saying: "I have left an open door before you which no one can close" (Revelation 3:8).

As a third step, the field of the arts can once again be closely related to the sciences and to ethics. They need no longer be expressions of merely private worlds. This does not imply that the artist will be restricted to a photographic realism which would only express that exaggerated objectivity to which science has condemned itself. Instead, artists will find their inspiration in the inner dynamic natures of creatures as these resonate empathetically with human experience, and they will express these by all the variety of formal techniques employed by modern art. Yet because they will no longer see the natural world as alien to humanity but as revelatory of God's purposes for the whole cosmic community, they will once again be able to find a public language understood by more than an elite. Architecture will be revitalized by its contact with natural forms and the environ-

---

13 Aquinas, S.T., II–II, q. 11, a. 3, defends the death penalty for obstinate heretics, although elsewhere he says that the soldiers who crucified Christ were probably innocent of sin because they supposed they were executing a criminal.

ment. Literature too will no longer be limited to descriptive realism, but will be free to uncover universal ethical values, not by preaching, but by insight into the meaning inherent even in the tragedies and absurdities of human life.

Yet Vatican II warns us that the earthly kingdom which we build contains the Kingdom of Christ only "in mystery" and, until he comes to transform it, it will always remain ambiguous. Consequently, science always will be capable of atheistic misinterpretation, technology of polluting abuse, art of idolatry, literature of lying and pimping. These risks, however, cannot hold back the Catholic from entering into the world and contributing to its life. We need to ask why Catholics have so often lacked creativity in the sciences and the arts, or when they have achieved it have done so only at a sacrifice of the purity of their faith.

I think we must acknowledge that fidelity to the gospel will continue to raise certain obstacles for gifted Catholics who strive to fully realize their scientific and artistic potentialities. As the world creatively rushes toward destruction, Christians remain somewhat peripheral to its main currents. If they were to plunge fully into the stream, they would be lost. Catholic writers, for example, cannot be a part of that sinful world which makes such vivid material for a secularist writer. The result is that Christian creations are often tame and tasteless, lacking the serpentine subtlety and bite of worldly authors. But we should not be ashamed to let the world do what it can, since it has no future.

I would therefore hope that Catholic scholars who wish to be faithful to Christ by fidelity to his Church will not waste their time in nostalgia for the past, nor in bitter denunciations of the errors of the present, but will turn their energies to carrying out the work of Vatican II in a positive way. They will occupy themselves with an analysis of our culture to find in it what is good and true and then will bend every effort to assimilate this to the perennial light of the Gospel which can transform it. This requires a critique both of our culture and of the traditional cultural forms of Christianity, a critique which will enable the Gospel to stand out in its full radiance.

I would particularly point out that the great tensions which are now felt by many between the Vatican Congregations and scholars is not so much the result of a resistance of the Congregation to theological or cultural advance as it is the misunderstanding by scholars of the respective roles of shepherd and scribe. There is a serious ambiguity in some theologians' self-understanding. On the one hand, they claim for themselves the right to be creative, i.e., to criticize old solutions and propose new ones, which is a part of the modern academic notion of what scholarship is all about; and, on the other hand, they retain the old-fashioned notion that theologians share the ecclesial Magisterium of the hierarchy and can therefore serve as a safe guide for the faith and praxis of the laity.[14] That obsolete conception was based on the premise that all theologians are missioned by the Church and are under direct control of the hierarchy. We cannot have it both ways. We must establish clearly in the Church the understanding that the contribution of theologians to the Christian community (unless they accept a mission from the Church and with it an obligation to conform to official teaching) is not direct pastoral leadership but scholarship in the modern sense of exploration without claim to be a direct guide to faith or conscience.

I am optimistic that such a more clear-cut delineation of the respective roles of bishop and theologian will be worked out. What is more fundamental, however, is that theologians and Catholic scholars in general come to see that in the coming century the task will not be to modernize the faith, which already prophesies the final outcome of history, but to assimilate to the faith all the scattered riches of the Spirit, including those of science and art, both for the clear manifestation of what is implicit in the faith and for the transformation of the culture. In a pluralistic global society this means a spirit of genuine ecumenism in its broadcast conception.

John XXIII mocked "the prophets of gloom and doom" when he called for Vatican II. Many today wonder whether they may have been right and the saintly pope wrong. I am convinced, however, that his was the authentic Christian spirit of hope. The upheavals in the Church produced by the Council simply reveal that the Church was not as healthy as it seemed. Every act of God is life-giving, but it also involves a judgment of those who resist it or misread it. Our task is to seek to understand the message of the Council in its deepest and authentic significance and then to help the Church and the world to understand that meaning and how it can be radically implemented given the opportunities of our times. We should not

---

14 Reference is frequently made to Yves Congar's study of the use of the term *Magisterium* in which he showed that in the medieval period it included university theologians, but it should be noted that these professors were subject to episcopal and papal censure, and their custom of condemning positions as heretical (e.g., the condemnations of Luther) is hardly one to be revived in our day.

waste our energies in nostalgia, condemnation, or discouragement, but should employ them in doing well what we believe others are doing badly. What is more useful: a good critique of a bad book or a good book on the same subject?

20.
Four Developments in Modern Physics that Subvert Scientific Materialism (1987)
Stephen M. Barr

I. Introduction

For more than three centuries the advance of scientific knowledge has had a prejudicial effect on religious belief. I believe that this situation is changing, or *can* change if the opportunities that present themselves are seized and exploited. The dominant philosophical world view among most physical scientists (in my experience) is "scientific materialism." What I mean by that term is a system of belief characterized by three denials: a denial of purpose or design in nature; a denial of the centrality of man in nature and a denial that non-physical realities can exist (such as God or the human spirit). In other words, this philosophy is both materialistic and mechanistic. There exists also a strong positivist bias. The proposition that God exists is regarded as impossible to prove or disprove and hence is "operationally" meaningless. Religious belief is thought to have no rational ground and hence is understood in fideistic terms. Usually these views come together with various prejudices about religion and its historical role, and about the Church in particular, which is seen as obscurantist, intolerant, and superstitious. This whole complex of hostile attitudes cannot be overcome easily. (Indeed it may be too much to expect that it will ever be overcome for more than a minority of scientists.) However, the theme of this conference is the 21st century, and I am hopeful that by that time a lot of intellectual (if not sociological) ground can be recaptured.

Why am I hopeful? The reason is that modern physics itself has uncovered various aspects of nature that are in their implications subversive of scientific materialism. I will attempt to explain the substance and significance of four of these developments in this talk.

The body of this talk is, I hope, self-contained. However, I have left the greater part of the detailed explanations and argumentation to a series of appendices which are included at the end of my primary presentation and to which the reader is referred.

II. The Big Bang Theory

It is now believed by scientists on the basis of numerous pieces of strong and convincing evidence that the universe began with a "big bang" about 10 to 15 billion years ago. There is no question that the big bang theory has strongly discomfited many atheists. This has been manifested in various ways. In some quarters there was a prolonged and somewhat irrational attachment to a theory called the steady state theory, according to which the universe was infinitely old, even when the experimental and theoretical indications were heavily on the side of the big bang theory (though before conclusive verification of it). After the fact of a big bang was essentially confirmed, the idea then became popular that this explosion was but the expansive phase of an endlessly "bouncing" universe – again one of infinite age. This notion became popular in spite of the fact that *no* evidence, either theoretical or experimental, existed to support it, and that there were several strong arguments against it. In the first place, such a bouncing universe would require a "closed" rather than an open universe, while the (admittedly preliminary) observational evidence suggests an open universe (though in recent years purely theoretical arguments have made a closed universe more likely). Secondly, no plausible mechanism for such bouncing has been advanced. And, thirdly, even if the universe were bouncing, it is probable that entropy would increase from one bounce to the next. This would imply a finite number of past bounces (probably) and hence a universe of finite age. It is clear from this persistent and obviously strong "theoretical prejudice" that many atheistic scientists feel that a temporal beginning to the universe somehow threatens their cherished beliefs. Why is this?

Let me make very clear at the outset that it is naïve to suppose that the question of the existence of a Creator logically hinges upon whether the age of the universe is finite or infinite. The proofs of God's existence would be no less compelling were the age of the universe infinite, as St. Thomas understood quite clearly.[1] And, conversely, if God's existence could be rationally denied in the case of an infinitely old universe, so could it be with

---

1 St. Thomas Aquinas, *Summa Contra Gentiles,* University of Notre Dame Press, ed. 1975, Bk. II, Ch. 38.

equal consistency in the case of a universe of finite age. Nonetheless, the materialists are right to be discomfited.

The point is that philosophical positions are rarely maintained for strictly logical reasons, but also from a sense of the way things are, the way the world works, what is true to life, or what is fitting. Almost a poetic sense is involved. For example, it was easier to believe that man was central to a divine plan when it was also believed that he dwelled at the geometrical center of the world. Now that man is banished to the periphery of the solar system, on the periphery of a galaxy lost in the inconceivable vastness of the universe, it is easy to fall into thinking that he is insignificant in the cosmic scheme. Logically this does not follow, but psychologically it often does.

Just so, the fact that the universe made a dramatic, sudden and explosive "appearance" out of nothing about 15 billion years ago adds nothing to the logical force of the arguments for a Creator. But to the psychological force, it adds a great deal.

In my view, the deep significance of the big bang theory is that it strikes at the very root of the scientific materialist's notion of causality and explanation. In essence, what this notion amounts to is the idea that the only meaningful and valid kind of explanation is in terms of physical processes. In particular, a set of circumstances is to be explained as the result of a prior set of circumstances evolving according to the laws of physics. In this sense, the "cause" of a situation or event always lies in the past. This has profound implications for arguments for the existence of God as "First Cause" or as "Designer" of the universe. Indeed, we believe that this very contracted notion of causality lies at the root of scientific materialism. We explain why this is so in Part I of Appendix A. In Part II of that Appendix, we discuss the relationship between causality and time in the light of the insights of modern physics on the past-future distinction – the so-called "arrow of time." Here I only wish to say that the big bang theory is disconcerting for the scientific materialist since the big bang cannot be explained in terms of its past since it has no past, and, at least classically (i.e., before quantum effects are taken into account), the big bang is a space-time "singularity" to which the laws of physics do not apply. As long as the universe was believed to be infinitely old the scientific materialist could explain anything in particular – though not everything in general. But if there is a beginning to the universe and hence to time, his chain of efficient causality abruptly ends. The materialist comes to the inexplicable initial conditions in terms of which he tried to explain everything else. Of course, even in an infinitely old universe, he does not really have an explanation for the way the world is. This incompleteness in the materialist's scheme of explanation is somewhat subtle and requires some imagination to grasp in the case of the infinitely old universe. But in the case of the universe of finite age it becomes embarrassingly obvious.

III. The Quest for Beauty and Unity in the Laws of Nature and the Argument from Design

The argument from design for the existence of God is ancient. It can be found at least implicitly in both the Old and New Testaments. A very beautiful statement of it was given as follows by the Latin Apologist Minucius Felix writing circa 235 A.D.:

> If upon entering some home you saw that everything there was well-tended, neat, and decorative, you would believe that some master was in charge of it, and that he himself was much superior to those good things. So too in the home of this world, when you see providence, order and law in the heavens and on the earth, believe there is a Lord and Author of the universe, more beautiful than the stars themselves and the various parts of the whole world.[2]

We have already referred in passing to one of the stumbling blocks of the materialist in accepting this kind of argument, namely, his inability to conceive of a cause external to the physical universe. But the progress of science has thrown up other obstacles as well. The first is raised most sharply by evolution and the mechanism of natural selection. Natural selection shows how, in principle at least, a combination of law and chance can cause complicated structures to emerge. Indeed most scientists believe that all of the amazing variety and intricacy of biological forms can be explained in this way.

The general question is whether structure and order can spontaneously emerge from mere chaos and disorder. The example of evolution – and simpler examples such as the growth of crystals – seem to say yes. However, such an answer is superficial. It is not difficult to see that all such supposed instances of the spontaneous emergence of structure and order actually presuppose that it exists at a deeper level. In particular I would argue (see Ap-

---

2 Minucius Felix, *Octavius;* English translation in *The Faith of the Early Fathers,* William A. Jurgens, Vol. I, p. 108, The Liturgical Press: Collegeville, Minnesota.

pendix D) that *all explanations of structure and order at the level of phenomena presuppose it at the level of law.*

A second issue has to do with the various kinds of order and structure. Some are more suggestive of design than others. To illustrate, suppose we detect signals from some distant part of the galaxy. What would we look for in them to decide if they originated from an intelligent source or were merely manifestations of some inanimate physical processes? A totally chaotic or random signal would not suggest intelligence, but neither would certain kinds of regular patterns. Simple periodic pulses have been observed – they come from pulsars – and have been convincingly explained as being generated by rapidly spinning neutron stars, which act much like natural lighthouse beacons. But suppose a signal were detected which was at once very complex and yet highly structured – something like, say, a Bach fugue? Or suppose it could be deciphered and turned out to be a message – perhaps a formalized mathematical proof? Surely all would draw the obvious conclusion that intelligence had been found.

Ultimately, then, the argument from design leads one to ask: Do the laws of nature themselves exhibit structure? And is that structure of the kind that suggests intelligence? If what we argued above is valid, then the first answer must inevitably be yes. Since scientific explanations always derive structure at one level from structure at a deeper level, then obviously the very deepest level of physical law must exhibit structure of some kind. Physicists have made great progress in uncovering the deepest levels of physical law. In fact, many of them believe that they are very near to a unified mathematical theory of all physical phenomena. And what characterizes these theories? A structure that is at once extremely rich and complex and yet exceedingly unified, symmetric, harmonious and beautiful. It is order, but not trivial order. It is complexity, but not chaos. That is just the sort of thing we do ordinarily associate with intelligent design. As physics has developed in the last century the role of symmetry in nature has been increasingly appreciated by researchers until, indeed, the search for better theories has become dominated almost entirely by considerations of symmetry, simplicity and beauty.

IV. The Anthropic Coincidences and Man's Place in the Cosmos

One of the consequences of the advance of scientific knowledge that has been most prejudicial to religious belief has been the ascendancy of the notion that man is peripheral and insignificant in the cosmos. The Copernican revolution deposed man from the center of the solar system. The discoveries of modern astronomy have shown that the sun itself is a rather ordinary star among the 100 billion in the Milky Way and, indeed, is on the periphery of that galaxy. Furthermore, over 100 billion galaxies are known to exist (and if the universe is open there may be an infinitude of them). Astronomy has also become aware of the vastness of both the age and size of the universe compared to human scales of time and distance. In biology, the Darwinian revolution has had a similar humbling effect. Science in uncovering the hidden workings of nature has revealed an order which seems governed not by a wise and caring "Providence" but by a combination of impersonal laws and blind chance. The universe appears vast, cold, and indifferent to human strivings and sufferings. As the Nobel laureate Steven Weinberg wrote in his popular book *The First Three Minutes*:

> It is almost irresistible for humans to believe that we have some special relation to the universe, that human life is not just a farcical outcome of a chain of accidents . . . but that we were somehow built in from the beginning. . . . It is very hard to realize that [the entire earth] is just a tiny part of an overwhelmingly hostile universe. . . . The more the universe seems comprehensible, the more it also seems pointless.[3]

Man has looked into the structure of the physical world "seeking for a sign" of a Providence that cares or a Purpose somehow related to human purposes. But no Sign has been given to him but the sign of the prophet Jonah. However, this situation too has now changed.

In recent decades physicists and cosmologists have become increasingly interested in what have become known as "anthropic coincidences."[4] These coincidences have been uncovered by asking how, if the *laws* of nature (not the phenomena) had been slightly different, the world would have been changed. If this fundamental constant or that qualitative feature of nature's laws were slightly modified, would intelligent life have been possible and would evolution have been able to occur? The answer seems to be no. There are numerous examples where the actual structure of physical law as

---

3 Steven Weinberg, *The First Three Minutes,* William Collins, Glasgow, 1977, p. 148.

4 See for examples and discussions "The anthropic principle and the structure of the physical world," B. J. Carr, and M. J. Rees, *Nature,* Vol. 278, p. 605 (1979); John D. Barrow and Frank J. Tipler, *The Cosmological Anthropic Principle,* Oxford University Press, 1986; and P. C. W. Davies, *The Accidental Universe,* Cambridge University Press, 1980.

uncovered by scientific investigation and the requirements of a universe where life, especially intelligent life, can evolve seem to coincide. That is why these are called anthropic "coincidences." (See Appendix C for examples of such anthropic coincidences.) The key point is that it does at least *seem*, in the words of Weinberg, that "we were somehow built in from the beginning."

What attitudes can one take toward these coincidences? First, one can try to explain them scientifically. All such attempts involve one or another form of what is called the "anthropic principle." We believe that while some may be explicable in this way, such explanations can never fully succeed. (This is discussed in Appendix D, Section II, C.) Secondly, one may argue that the laws of physics must be as they are in every particular for reasons of self-consistency or because some underlying unifying principle requires it. In that case one cannot do the "gedanken experiment" of adjusting the laws of nature in this or that detail. There is some sense in this objection since, within the framework of particular schemes of "unification," there is often no freedom to contemplate small changes in the theory, which is completely constrained. However, one can contemplate theories that are based on different schemes of unification or that are not "unified" at all. Unless one is prepared to argue (as some are, though quite unsoundly – see Appendix D, Section II, B) that the laws of nature are absolutely necessary and unique, the anthropic coincidences cannot be disposed of thus. Thirdly, one may simply shrug them off as being indeed nothing but coincidences. This possibility is always open. Evidence for anything can always be dismissed as circumstantial by those not disposed to believe it. Finally, one can regard these coincidences as being simply what they appear to be: evidences of design.

The mistake most natural theologians made in the past was to look in the wrong place, i.e., at the level of phenomena rather than at the level of law. Why, in retrospect, would one necessarily have expected that man, if he were central to the order of the cosmos at the level of purpose or value, would also be central to it geometrically? What does it really matter where he is, or how big or small, or whether he is round or square? If we want to know whether we were "built in" from the beginning, we should look at how the universe *is* built – at its laws. Looking at those laws – as we are in a better position to do than those living in the past – we find that the dethronement of man was an act of revolutionary folly, an act far removed from the letter, the spirit and the purpose of the Law.

As we noted, one of the dramatic facts of science that has helped to destroy the notion that man is important in the design of nature is his smallness in comparison to the cosmos. However, even this can be understood in a different, "anthropic" way. According to general relativity, the great size of the universe is necessary for its great longevity. A universe whose maximum extent were, say, the diameter of the solar system would last but a few hours before it collapsed upon itself gravitationally. But if the evolution of stars and planets and eventually life was to occur (processes requiring billions of years), a universe whose maximum extent is at least billions of light years is required. Pascal wrote: ". . . the eternal silence of these infinite spaces frightens me."[5] We see that, if looked at aright, even those infinite spaces and that eternal silence may point to man!

V. The Implications of Quantum Theory

It would be impossible even with much more time and space to do justice to this subject. I will try to give only a summary account, with more details in Appendix E. The philosophical issues that arise from quantum mechanics flow from two aspects of it. First, it is inherently probabilistic. The basic mathematical description of physical systems is in terms of something called the "wavefunction." Wavefunctions tell us probabilities. Secondly, in the traditional understanding of quantum mechanics [as opposed to the so-called Many Worlds Interpretation, see Appendix E], when an "observer" makes a measurement on a "system," the corresponding wavefunction undergoes a sudden and discontinuous change or "collapse" which cannot be analyzed physically within the framework of quantum theory.

Many people who understand and accept the traditional understanding of quantum theory and have thought it through have come to certain conclusions. These may appear to be highly controversial. But they can only be avoided by abandoning quantum mechanics (which indeed might someday become necessary) or by embracing "the Many Worlds Interpretation" of quantum mechanics, which is just as controversial. What are these conclusions? First, the "observer" plays a central role in quantum mechanics. In the traditional understanding there is a radical dichotomy between the "observer" and the "system"; they have a completely different status in the theory. This dichotomy corresponds (in philosophical terms) to the dichotomy between the subject and object of knowledge. Secondly, the wavefunction must be regarded as representing not the system itself but the observer's

---

5 Blaise Pascal, *Pensees*, #206.

state of knowledge of it, because the theory is essentially probabilistic. Probabilities are used when there is incomplete knowledge. Thus, knowledge, and someone who knows (the "observer"), must both enter the theory at a fundamental level. Moreover, it is when a measurement is completed – when the observer knows the result – that the wavefunction collapses. This makes perfect sense if the wavefunction represents his state of knowledge; for when his state of knowledge changes then logically so must the wavefunction. There are other viewpoints but they lead to absurdities (such as solipsism) or paradoxes (such as the "Wigner's friend paradox"). Thirdly, the process (if we can call it that) by which the wavefunction collapses – and hence by which the observer's knowledge increases – is not subject to physical description within the framework of quantum theory.

If one accepts the foregoing, a picture quite inconsistent with simple materialism emerges. Materialism is monistic: Quantum mechanics is not. Materialism reduces *all* mental operations to physical processes. There is no question that much of what we call thinking can be completely understood in physical or cybernetic terms. A human brain certainly performs many operations (such as processing, storage and retrieval of information; motor control; computation; as well as other functions, including many associated with cognition) that are purely mechanical in the sense of being reducible to the operations of a physical system. However, quantum mechanics, as understood by some at least, will not allow us to say that the act of knowing is completely mechanical. Ultimately, the "I" who is the subject of "I know" is not purely physical. And if that is so, there is no reason to deny the same of the "I" in "I will."

VI. Conclusion

I have tried to describe four developments in physics that subvert the world-view I have called scientific materialism. Some people believe that one cannot or should not draw philosophical or theological conclusions from science, that these disciplines deal with different subject matters. But historically, people *have* drawn philosophical conclusions from scientific facts, conclusions hostile to religion in general, and to Christianity in particular. In many cases these conclusions are based on outdated science. The old materialist prejudices are simply not justified anymore (if they ever were) by the state of scientific knowledge. Yet they live on.

I believe that this century will be seen as a climacteric in the relation between religion and science. Science itself has furnished us with new weapons with which to combat the shallow prejudices of an earlier era. The time for rearguard actions is past and the time for a counter offensive is at hand. This is one of the most important tasks for the scholars and intellectuals of the Church in the 21st century and in the years remaining in this century. The perspective on nature of modern science must be appropriated and used as the basis for constructing a more sophisticated and reinvigorated natural theology.

The wheel is coming full circle. Science was born in the Christian West out of a belief that the world has an intelligible structure because it is the work of an intelligent Being; a belief that the world which reflects the glory of its Creator is a place of order, beauty, and law. Materialism has had its apparent victories. But the enterprise which is science has not and will not in the end betray the sources of its original inspiration.

Appendix A
Time and Causality
I. The Scientific Materialist's Notion of Causality

One of the classical proofs of the existence of God is the so-called "cosmological argument." According to this argument, the universe must have a cause. This argument has little or no force for the scientific materialist because he does not know what a cause is. His notion of causality is so restrictive that the possibility of a first cause is ruled out *a priori*, and, indeed, becomes totally incomprehensible.

To assign a cause for a thing is to explain it, and, corresponding to the variety of ways we have of explaining things, one can speak of a variety of types of causes. Indeed, the medieval schoolmen (following Aristotle) spoke of "efficient," "material," "formal," and even "meritorious" causes. Some of these kinds of causes can even lie in the future of their effects. For example, a student might say he is studying *because* there is an exam tomorrow. Or someone might say that water flows downhill to reach the sea. These kinds of "final" causes are clearly connected with the notion of "purpose."

Since Newton's time, physics has had no essential use for final causes. Historians of science tell us that with the overthrow of Aristotelian physics teleology has been progressively banished from science. The Newtonian physicist could claim that, given complete information about the state of the world at a time (t_1) and knowledge of the laws of physics, he could *in principle* exactly calculate, or predict, the state of the world at a later time (t_2). To make this prediction he need not know anything about what happens *after* t₂. The past completely determines the future. Thus for the physicist the complete and sufficient "explanation" or cause of the present state of things lies in the past state of things, together with the laws of physics. For this reason, it seems an evident principle to most physicists that *a "cause" must precede its "effects" in time*. Indeed, this *is* true of what I would call physical causes. It does not follow, however, as the scientific materialist believes, that physical causes are the only type of causes, or that this principle need apply to causality in general.

The devastating consequences that this notion of causality must have on religious belief should be clear. There can be no cosmological argument for God's existence. If God is to be the cause of the universe, according to this view, He must precede the universe *in time*. If the universe is infinitely old, this is obviously impossible. What is less obvious but equally true is that even if the universe has a finite age (as appears to be the case), God cannot precede it in time. This can be demonstrated in two ways. In the first place, as modern cosmology and general relativity teach, it makes no sense to refer to a time before the initial moment of the universe – a point brilliantly grasped already in the 5th century by St. Augustine. Secondly, God cannot be located in time any more than in space, since temporal relationships like spatial ones obtain only among things or events in the created world (see Appendix B).

Not only the cosmological argument suffers, but the argument from design and the whole idea of purpose in nature. For the idea of purpose is connected with final causes. Yet final causality is taboo to the scientific materialist.

Central to scientific materialism is this restricted notion of causality. It is my contention, however, that modern physics undermines this faulty notion in two ways. The first way has to do with the notion of the past-future distinction, or, as it is sometimes called, "the arrow of time." This is not completely understood by physics at the present day; however, enough *is* understood to see through certain naïve fallacies. In my view, a careful consideration of the physical origin of the arrow of time reveals that the notion of *causal priority* underlies the notion of *temporal priority*, rather than the other way around. This is not in any way to deny the physicist's "principle of causality" as applied to physical cause and effect. But it is to assert that temporal priority forms no part of the definition or *general* notion of cause, but rather derives from it.

II. The "Arrow of Time" and What We Can Learn from It

We have argued that a critical postulate of the scientific materialist's philosophy is that *a cause must always precede its effect in time.* This is not regarded as merely an empirical statement but as an absolute metaphysical principle which would apply to any kind of cause and in any kind of world. It is, then, essential to the idea of cause, and can be used as a criterion for recognizing causes.

For this viewpoint to be correct, *it must always be possible to decide whether A comes "before" B in time, that is, to distinguish "past" and "future" in some absolute sense, without prior reference to causal relationships,* or else we would be involved in a circular definition. We shall see whether this is true.

To distinguish past and future appears to be very easy. Most people think of time as something that has an inherent movement in one direction like a river. Events float along on this river and we can see whether they are upstream or downstream without paying any attention to what they are or how they influence each other. However, to a physicist, these notions are naïve. It is true that one can set up time coordinates and locate events in time without much reference to what they are. But the difference between "past" and "future" is not so easy in theory (as distinct from practice). Time itself, from the physicist's point of view, does not "flow" or move. Events, rather, have an ordering in time. The psychological feeling of a motion of time comes from the causal and informational structure of physical processes: We can only get information about or remember the past; we can only affect the future. This, in turn, is the result of the fact that the physical processes by which information is transmitted and stored, decisions formulated, and actions carried out involve something called "thermodynamic irreversibility." The main point is that time in and of itself has no "flow." The space-time manifold itself seems to be quite symmetric between past and future. And the laws of physics appear to be essentially symmetric under "time reversal symmetry." Why then can we not reverse certain processes? Why does water never flow uphill? Why do spilt milk and broken glasses never reassemble themselves? This has to do with the fact that certain *processes* have intrinsic orientations. The apparent "flow" of time has to do with the relative orientations in time of our mental processes and the processes we observe, rather than some intrinsic velocity of time itself. And the orientations of processes are ultimately *causal* orientations. We remember only the past because only events in the past or "information" from those events can cause impressions in our organs of sense and memory. Our activity is future directed because we can only cause events in the future. It is the causal structure of our world that underlies the notion of past and future not the other way around. Cause and effect relationships have to be recognizable if the past and future are to be distinguished. The notion of cause is a part of the definition of past and future.

We explain the confusing in terms of the clear and simple, the apparently unrelated or disordered in terms of the intelligible pattern. This aspect which causes have that leads us to regard them as explaining their effects has nothing inherently to do with time. For want of a better word I will call it "coherence" or "orderliness." This concept has an analogue in physics that can be made precise. It is called entropy, or rather "low entropy." Entropy (or "disorder") increases as we go from the physical efficient cause to its effects. This precise physical concept of entropy is only applicable when we are analyzing a physical process *as* a physical process. There are processes which may occur in and through physical mechanisms which we would never analyze in terms of the motions of atoms and fields, as, for example, economic, political, or sociological processes. That is why, in identifying causes in a more general context than the purely physical, I would argue that some less easily defined and quantified notion, which has its analogue in physical entropy, is involved. We can consider the same processes from different points of view and give different *kinds* of explanations of the same things.

In our universe, entropy – on the average – is increasing everywhere, and at every time and in all physical systems *in the same direction in time*. This is what gives rise to what is very misleadingly called "the arrow of time." This is why we never see milk unspill, watches unsmash, water flow uphill, or people grow younger. This is why the causal arrows of our cognitive processes are lined up in the same direction as those of the physical processes we observe, and therefore why time seems to "flow." But *why* this is is a profound mystery of physics at present. It seems that in some sense the universe had *very* low entropy initially. This is not at all understood. Thus the future directedness of physical processes in our universe is not somehow a metaphysical necessity; but it may easily appear so because we naturally take it for granted. It has become part of our intuition.

We conclude from all this that causal priority is a more fundamental notion than temporal priority, and really underlies it. It may be helpful to give an example where temporal priority is clearly not involved in the notion of cause. In even the materialist's favorite kind of explanation physical law is invoked. The apple fell on Newton's head *because* he was sitting under it *and because* of the law of gravity. But the law of gravity is not something that can be located in time. It is immanent in the structure of the process. It is indeed a cause of the apple's falling, what would be called in Scholastic philosophy a "formal cause"; and it obviously does not have to precede in time that of which it is the cause.

Cause, then, is "bound up" with time but only for those causes that operate through physical processes. (Even then, causes only precede effects in time if they are efficient causes.) But the notion of God as Cause does not involve the idea that He creates the universe through a physical process. Rather He is to be thought of as an infinite Mind whose creative act occurs not in time but timelessly and eternally.

Appendix B
The Augustinian and Scholastic View of Creation and Time

The conception most believers have of the act of Creation is that it was an event in time. Their conception of God's "eternity" is that it is infinite duration in time. God existed for an infinite time "before" the creation of the universe and will continue to exist for an infinite time "after" it comes to an end. From the viewpoint of modern physics, such a conception makes little or no sense. Time, like space, is something physical. Indeed, it cannot be thought of as something apart from space. Spacetime is a set of relations between events in the physical world. It is influenced physically by those events. Spacetime can be curved, can oscillate, and can even carry energy in these oscillations. At the big bang, time began. It is meaningless to discuss time "before" the first moment of the universe, because the first moment of the universe was the first moment of time.

Not only modern physics but also theology has told us many of these things since the time of St. Augustine, who realized that time is an aspect of the created world: "There can be no time without creation."[6] Indeed, he realized that time is itself created: "Or what times could there be . . . not made by you [God]?"[7] Remarkably, he even grasped that there was no time "before" the universe: "You made that very time and no time could pass by before you made those times. But if there was no time before heaven and

---

6 St. Augustine, *Confessions*, Bk. 11, Ch. 30. (I quote from The Image Books edition. [Transl. John K. Ryan, Doubleday, 1960]).
7 *Ibid.*, Bk. 11, Ch. 13.

earth, why do they ask what you did 'then'? There was no 'then,' where there was no time."[8]

Nor can the idea of a God existing for infinite time be maintained theologically. Since space and time are a feature of the universe they do not pertain to God. He cannot be localized in time anymore than in space. He is extended neither in time nor space. Indeed God, as the medieval scholastics emphasized, is utterly "simple," without parts, or extent.[9] There are no real distinctions in God. One cannot distinguish properly one part of God from another, or one act of God from another. One cannot even distinguish God Himself from His acts; there is only one Act of God to which He is Himself identical.[10] God is pure Act.[11] This Act is an eternal act of love, knowledge, will, understanding, and creation. So God is an utterly simple One in Whom there is no change[12] and, therefore, in Whom there is no time.[13] He lives in "the sublimity of an ever-present eternity."[14] Now one *can* say that God causes the many events of the universe to unfold in time, but the causation does not unfold in time, and the cause is not many but one. Just as many things can be grasped in a single act of understanding[15] so many things are created by a single act.[16]

The creative "Word" which God spoke in Genesis is not therefore to be understood as a Word spoken in time; it is a Word which proceeds from

---

8 *Ibid.* See also St. Thomas Aquinas, *Summa Contra Gentiles*, Bk. II, Ch. 35, p. 6.
9 This indeed was a conception that did not originate with the Scholastics. St. Irenaeus of Lyons in *Adversus Haereses*, written between 180 and 199 A.D., writes "For far removed is the Father of all from those things which operate in us, the affections and the passions. He is simple, composed of no parts, without structure,..." English translation from *The Faith of the Fathers*, (see William Paley, "Natural Theology,"contained in *The Works of William Paley,* Oxford: Clarendon Press, 1938, Vol. IV, p. 87). (See also St. Thomas Aquinas, *Summa Contra Gentiles*, Bk. I, Ch. 18).
10 St. Thomas Aquinas, Summa *Contra Gentiles*, Bk. I, Chs. 21, 45, and 73. (Also, Chs. 75 and 76).
11 *Ibid.,* Bk. I, Ch. 16, p. 7, and Bk. I, Ch. 28, p. 6.
12 "I am the Lord, and I change not," *Malachi 3:6.*
13 *Summa Contra Gentiles*, Bk. I, Ch. 15, p. 3.
14 St. Augustine, *Confessions*, Bk. 11, Ch. 13; St. Thomas Aquinas, *Summa Contra Gentiles*, Bk. I, Ch. 66, p. 7.
15 *Summa Contra Gentiles*, Bk. I, Ch. 55, p. 2–3
16 *Ibid.*, Bk. I, Ch. 77, p. 4.

Him eternally, timelessly, even though its effects may enjoy among themselves temporal (and spatial) relationships.

God, then, as the Cause of all things, precedes them, indeed, in a causal sense but not in a temporal sense. As St. Augustine said: "It is not in time that you precede time."[17] Moreover, God as Cause does not need to precede the world in time since He does not create the world through some physical process. Rather, this creative act is the eternal Act of an infinite Mind. This notion of God may be difficult to grasp, especially for those who are used to conceive of mind in purely materialistic terms. I recommend to those for whom all philosophical writings that predate modern physics are opaque Bernard J. F. Lonergan's *Insight, A Study of Human Understanding*.[18]

Appendix C
Anthropic Coincidences

The existence of an "anthropic coincidence" is usually established by a certain kind of contra-factual argument. One contemplates what the universe would be like if some single quantitative or qualitative feature of the laws of nature were different than it is.

An objection to this kind of argument is that if the laws of nature form a unified system it may be inconsistent to contemplate one feature being different without the whole structure being different. Indeed, some physicists anticipate that the true "unified theory" will turn out to have no "free parameters" and to have a structure completely determined by some basic principles or symmetries. In this case no arbitrariness would remain in the laws of nature. Of course, this objection only has force if one can argue that the unified system of laws that govern the physical universe is somehow logically necessary and absolutely unique. But this cannot be the case. There are an infinity of self-consistent theories any one of which could be the law of a possible universe. Admittedly, "most" of these would lead to somewhat boring or trivial universes. But, unless one is willing to involve some variation of "the Anthropic Principle" (see Appendix D), that is beside the point. The laws of nature are *not* somehow logically necessary. That is why physics is an experimental science rather than a branch of mathematics.

A second objection is that one may overlook some less obvious consequences of an altered physical law that may somehow compensate for the

---

17 St. Augustine, *Confessions*, Bk. 11, Ch. 13.

18 Bernard J. F. Lonergan, S.J., *Insight, A Study of Human Understanding*, Longmans, Green and Co. Ltd., London, 1958.

negative consequences (for evolution) that one considered. Or it may be that a plurality of very different paths of biological evolution are possible, and that were the laws of nature different another, totally unsuspected path would open up at the same time that the actual path followed on our own planet was closed off. It is hard absolutely to rule out such possibilities, but they would require a certain kind of conspiracy in favor of life that is rather far-fetched. While the anthropic coincidence arguments may be lacking somewhat in demonstrative force they certainly suggest that the probability that life – especially sentient life – can evolve depends very sensitively on the precise details of the laws of nature. If this is so, the existence of life is as much an evidence for design as ever it was if one transposes the argument from the level of phenomena to the level of law.

We will now present a few examples of anthropic coincidences. For more on the subject, see the works cited in note 4 of the main text.

(1) Water

All life on earth is based on water. It seems unlikely that any other compound could replace water in this role. (Ammonia has sometimes been suggested.) This is because water has a set of very special – almost unique – properties.

> Water is actually one of the strangest substances known to science. This may seem a rather odd thing to say about a substance as familiar, but it is surely true. Its specific heat, its surface tension, and most of its other physical properties have values anomalously higher or lower than those of any other known material. The fact that its solid phase is less dense than its liquid phase (ice floats) is virtually a unique property. . . . These strange properties make water a uniquely useful liquid and the basis for living things. Indeed, it is difficult to conceive a form of life which can spontaneously evolve from non-self-replicating collections of atoms to the complexity of living cells and yet is not based in an essential way on water.[19]

(2) Nucleon Masses

Neutrons (n) are slightly heavier than protons (p). Were it the other way around most protons would have decayed into neutrons in the early period of the universe. There would be little hydrogen (except deuterium) today

---

19 J. D. Barrow and Frank J. Tipler, *The Cosmological Anthropic Principle*, Oxford University Press, 1986, p. 524 (see also note 4 above)

and hence hydrogen-burning stars like the sun would not exist. Even more disastrous, there would be essentially no water.

(3) The Nuclear Force

Probably, the strength of the nuclear force that holds nuclei together has to be very close to its actual value for life to have been able to evolve.[20] If slightly weaker, deuterium would not exist and the build up of the heavier elements in stars inhibited. If slightly stronger, protons would have fused into ^{2}He and no ordinary hydrogen to speak of would exist.

(4) Nucleosynthesis

The heavy elements required for life were synthesized mostly in stars. There is a barrier to the synthesis of elements heavier than Be due to the famous mass gaps at mass 5 and 8. The gap at 8 is bridged only due to a very delicate process known as the "three alpha process." However, the three alpha process would not proceed at a high enough rate were it not greatly enhanced by the existence of a "resonance" in the ^{12}C spectrum at just the right energy. Were it not for this very strategically placed stepping stone, again, life would not exist.[21]

(5) The Large and Small Numbers

Certain important ratios of constants of nature have astonishingly small numerical values. An important example is the ratio of the "cosmological constant" to the Planck energy density. This is known to vanish to at least 120 decimal places. Were it larger than that the universe would have collapsed shortly after the big bang. That the universe has persisted for over 10 billion years is sometimes called the "oldness problem"[22] and is connected to the "cosmological constant problem."[23]

---

20 See B. J. Carr and M. J. Rees, "The anthropic principle and the structure of the physical world," *Nature,* Vol. 278, p. 605 (1979); (see also note 4 above).

21 See J. D. Barrow and Frank J. Tipler, *The Cosmological Principle*, pp. 252–53.

22 This is also related to the so-called "flatness problem." See the paper by Alan Guth published in *Inner Space/Outer Space, The Interface Between Cosmology and Particle Physics,* University of Chicago Press, 1986, p. 287.

23 See, for example, S. Bludman and M. Ruderman, *Phys. Rev. Lett. 38* (1977), or A. Zee, in *High Energy Physics, In Honor of P.A.M. Dirac's 80th Birthday,* Mintz and Perlmutter, Plenum.

Another important ratio is that of the proton mass to the Planck mass (or unification scale). The exceeding smallness of this ratio is sometimes called the "gauge hierarchy problem."[24] In grand unified theories ("GUTs") this ratio has to be less than about 10^{-14} if protons and neutrons are to have lasted from the time they were formed in the big bang to the present day. But aside from this, the size and lifetimes of stars depend on this ratio. Every change of a factor of ten in this ratio would change the lifetime of stars like the sun by a factor of one hundredth.

In any event, it is clear that very small and very large numbers are required if life is to evolve. Evolution takes a long time: The ratio of astrophysical to chemical time scales has to be enormous. One needs many particles: a human body contains about 10^{29} of them. One probably needs many stars and planets to have even one "successful" planet in evolutionary terms. The kinds of numbers that enter into the equations of most mathematically elegant theories tend to be (like 2, e, B, etc.) "of order one."

(6) The Dimensions of Space and Time

Even the dimensionality of space and time have "anthropic significance."[25] Moreover, it is not somehow a matter of logical necessity that there are one time and three space dimensions. (Indeed, theories with more space dimensions are currently fashionable.) If the number of space dimensions were less than three one could not have complicated circuitry: "Wires" would cross. Probably complex brains would be impossible. With more than three space dimensions (and leaving the general form of the laws of gravity and electromagnetism unaffected) certain disasters would occur. Atoms would be unstable, with electrons falling into the nucleus. Planetary orbits would be unstable due to perturbations, and temperatures on planetary surfaces would vary drastically over time.

The number of time dimensions is even more critical. Were there none or more than one, obviously, the whole causal structure of the world would be radically different. It is hard to imagine what biology could be like at all.

(7) The Arrow of Time

This has been discussed at length in Appendix A. This too can be regarded as the greatest of all fine-tuning problems.[26] It would appear that the

---

24 Edad Gilderner, *Phys. Rev.* D14, 1667 (1976).
25 See ref. 19, Ch. 4. 8.
26 See R. Penrose, "Singularities and Time-Asymmetry," chapter 12 of

total entropy of the (observable) universe started out something like 10^{120} times smaller than it could have been. The "orderliness" of the big bang was incredibly high.

(8) The Fine Structure Constant

The fine structure constant, alpha, determines the strength of the electromagnetic force. It is believed to be small due to the great ratio between the "weak" and "Planck" scales (the so-called "gauge hierarchy"). In some sense, then this is already understood in terms of grand unification. But what if alpha had been close to one instead of approximately equal to 1/137? All but very small nuclei would be unstable due to spontaneous fission. Only a few stable elements would exist and the possibilities for chemistry and biology would be severely limited. Again, almost certainly, no life would be possible.

(9) Qualitative Features of the Laws of Nature

Up to this point we have been talking quantitatively. But what about the gross qualitative features of the laws of nature? How can we account for the fact that there is an electromagnetic interaction and hence light and atoms.[27] Why is nature quantum mechanical instead of classical? In a classical world matter would be unstable and have continuously variable properties. There would be no periodic table, and chemistry as we know it would be impossible. What about the particles like quarks and leptons of which we are made? The so-called standard model would be equally consistent without them. The list could be indefinitely extended.

Appendix D
The Argument from Design
I. An Objection to the Argument

The main "scientific" objection to the argument from design is that or-

---

General Relativity, An Einstein Centenary Survey, ed. S. W. Hawking and W. Israel, Cambridge University Press, 1979, p. 630.

27 Some ideas for explaining the existence of light along the lines of the approaches of Appendix D Part II are to be found in H. B. Nielson, "Did God have to fine-tune the laws of nature to create light?" *Particle Physics 1980,* ed. By I. Andric I. Dadic, & N. Zovko. Proceedings of the 3rd Adriatic Summer Meeting on Particle Physics, Dubrovnik, Yugoslavia. North-Holland Publishers, Amsterdam, 1981. See note 28.

der can emerge spontaneously from chaos through the operation of physical laws. For example, if a glass of water is left outside on a day when the temperature is below 0°C, it will freeze. The water molecules, which were very chaotic in their movements, will settle down to a highly ordered crystalline structure. Dramatic examples exist in nature of configurations that look like the work of human engineers but are purely the result of natural forces. The theory of evolution by natural selection dealt one of the greatest blows to the argument from design. For natural selection is certainly a mechanism which can explain the evolution of complex biological forms from simpler ones. All of these examples show that indeed "blind" forces *can* lead to the emergence of highly ordered structures.

The response to this objection is simple. The "blind" forces *themselves* exhibit structure and symmetry! Consider the freezing of water or the formation of any kind of crystal. First, it is important to point out that the regularity of crystalline structures would not emerge were space itself not symmetric. Space is, at least on small scales, "rotationally invariant" and "translationally invariant" (that is, each point is equivalent to any other). Secondly, it is crucial that all water molecules have identical properties. These two underlying symmetries, as well as others that are responsible for the orderly structures of crystals, can in turn be traced further back to symmetries in the fundamental laws of nature. In particular, they can be traced to the "lorentz" and "general coordinate" invariance of the laws of gravity (and indeed of the other laws) and the quantum principle of the indistinguishability of particles (which itself flows from the principles of quantum field theory). To take another example, why is the earth's orbit nearly circular, and why are planets and stars nearly spherical? Again, these shapes emerge through blind physical processes. But these particular shapes would not have arisen except for the rotational invariance of the laws that govern those processes.

To turn to the major example, biological evolution may indeed happen according to "blind" physical laws, but not all physical laws would lead to evolution. This is something we discussed at length under the rubric of "anthropic coincidences." How many of all the conceivable systems of physical law would admit the possibility of self-reproducing structures like DNA? Surely, very few. Moreover, evolution is driven by a competition for scarce resources. What would a "resource" be except in the overall context of the First and Second Laws of Thermodynamics? ("Resources" are usually *energy* resources, which brings in the First Law: energy conservation.

The need to replenish resources would seem to be connected to the Second Law.) But the First and Second Laws are not absolute metaphysical principles but aspects of the particular laws that govern our universe.

To summarize, structure, whether it is of objects (like crystals or DNA) or processes (like evolution) or organisms, requires and presupposes structure at the level of laws. Sometimes, admittedly, it is possible to explain the structure of the laws in some dynamical way. For example, in "Kaluza Klein" theories, one tries to explain the "gauge symmetries" of the laws from the shapes of extra space dimensions. However, these shapes are themselves a consequence of the symmetries of an underlying theory. One *cannot* escape from order.

II. Three Ways to Escape Design

There are various ideas that are probably motivated, at least in part, by a desire to escape the argument from design. All involve an attempt to eliminate in some way the *arbitrariness* of the world we see or of its laws. (For "arbitrariness" suggests, as the etymology of the word implies, "will"). I will describe these under the headings "Triviality and Chaos," "Uniqueness," and "The Statistical Ensemble and the Anthropic Principle."

(A) Triviality and Chaos

We have argued that structure can only emerge "spontaneously" from prior structure, and that the very rich phenomena of our world must and do come from a very "non-trivial" structure in the basic laws of nature. Some physicists[28] have tried to derive the known laws of nature from a chaotic or random starting point. However, no one has succeeded in deriving laws from complete chaos. Obviously they cannot because to "derive" anything requires a *rule of derivation*, and then the starting point is not chaos but a rule. Though these ideas may have some limited success and utility in

---

28 Such a program has been pursued by H. B. Nielson and by J. Iliopoulos. Their ideas could also be regarded as an attempt to eliminate the arbitrariness of initial conditions as in "Attitude 3" discussed in sec. II B 1 of Appendix D, or a version of the "Statistical Ensemble" approaches discussed in sec. II C of Appendix D. Indeed these various approaches are akin to one another. For details of the Nielson and Iliopoulos ideas, see H. B. Nielson and N. Brene, *Nucl. Phys.* B224 (1983), p. 396, and references cited in ref. 5 of that article.

avoiding the fine-tuning of initial conditions, they are doomed from the start.

More interesting is the possibility that very rich structure at the level of phenomena can come from very simple structure, even almost trivial structure, at the level of laws. That is, the world is to be reduced – not to chaos – but to triviality.

There is a fascinating mathematical game invented by the mathematician J. H. Conway[29] called the "game of life." It is an instance of a class of mathematical structures called "cellular automata" which have been much studied in recent years. What makes the life-game interesting to some people is that a system obeying a very simple set of rules can exhibit very complicated behavior, including processes reminiscent of reproduction. Indeed, it can be shown that the life-game cellular automaton can act like a "universal computer." Such games do teach us one thing, viz., that simple rules acting on a large number of objects can generate complex results. However, such games are far from showing that structure can be derived from what is truly trivial.

We actually know something about the basic "rules" of nature, and they are certainly *not* trivial. A final refuge of the trivializers could be that the laws of physics as we now know them might themselves be merely "phenomenological laws" that emerge from an even deeper level where the laws are much more trivial. Even if this were true, it would remain the case that these supposedly trivial ur-laws would have to be remarkably special. (If they were truly trivial and not very special, we would not have to wait for the long and laborious process of scientific investigation to reach its goal. We could just hit on them by guesswork with very little trouble and show that they lead to a world like our own. I think this is patently absurd.) But if such laws were very special, then we are back to design.

(B) Uniqueness

A more popular notion among physicists is that the laws of physics are in some sense unique.[30] In fact some thinking has gone beyond this to the

---

29 Conway, J. H., unpublished (1970). Discussed by M. Gardner in "Mathematical Games," *Scientific American 224* (1971), Feb., p. 112; Mar., p. 106; Apr., p. 114; 226 (1972), Jan., p. 104. See discussions by S. Wolfram, "Statistical Mech. Of Cellular Automata," *Rev. Mod. Phys. 55,* (1983), p. 637 and references cited therein.

30 This is discussed in A. Zee, *Fearful Symmetry,* Macmillan, 1986, pp.

idea that the *universe* is the only uniquely possible one. This larger claim would involve showing three things: that the laws are the uniquely possible ones; that the "initial conditions" or, more generally, the boundary conditions are uniquely fixed; and that these laws and initial conditions uniquely determine everything, i.e., that physics is deterministic. Let us deal with the last two points first:

1. Initial Conditions. There is an interesting paper by the relativist J. Hartle on the subject of initial conditions.[31] He discussed four possible "attitudes" toward them:

Attitude 1: "That's the way it is." In other words, many initial conditions are possible. The actual ones are arbitrary to be taken as given and not to be explained by physics.

Attitude 2: "The boundary conditions which determine the universe are not initial conditions but present conditions and in particular the fact that we exist. This idea is related to the set of ideas called the anthropic principle." This either involves the notion of a design which had man in view or, as Hartle says, some version of the "anthropic principle."

Attitude 3: "Initial conditions are not needed; dynamics does it all." What is meant here is that the dynamics are such that, whatever the initial conditions, the outcome is qualitatively the same. That is, cosmology is insensitive to initial conditions. Normally, this is not so. In fact, in standard cosmology the initial conditions must be very special to lead to the type of world we see. A very promising idea for eliminating much of this sensitivity to or unnatural "fine-tuning" of initial conditions goes by the name of "inflation" or "inflationary cosmology." However, only certain kinds of theory lead to acceptable inflation. In fact, no fully satisfactory model exists. So that the price of eliminating the specialness of the initial conditions may be the specialness of the theory.

Attitude 4: "There is a law of physics specifying the initial conditions." This is the only real way to eliminate entirely the arbitrariness of initial con-

---

281–283. He quotes Einstein as saying "What I'm really interested in is whether God could have made the world in a different say; that is, whether the necessity of logical simplicity leaves any freedom at all." (Of course, the "necessity" referred to is not a necessity.)

31 J. Hartle, "Initial Conditions," published in *Inner Space/Outer Space, The Interface Between Cosmology and Particle Physics,* University of Chicago Press, 1986, p. 467.

ditions. The same remark applies here: Only special theories would have this feature. So far this is only a hope.

2. Indeterminacy. To eliminate the indeterminacy of quantum mechanics one must either modify quantum mechanics, which is very difficult, or one must adopt the so-called "Many Worlds Interpretation" of quantum mechanics (See Appendix E). This is one reason for the popularity in some quarters of the Many Worlds Interpretation.

3. Uniqueness of Laws. Even if the arbitrariness of the initial conditions and of quantum indeterminacy can be eliminated, one remains with the central issue of the laws themselves. There are some definite reasons why the notion of unique laws has been advanced. In the first place, as the known laws of physics have become more "unified," certain features that seemed arbitrary were found to be dictated by the requirements of unification. For example, if "grand unification" is correct, the strengths of the strong, weak, and electromagnetic interactions, otherwise arbitrary, must have a definite relationship to each other. Moreover, it is now appreciated that certain theories have *no* free adjustable parameters because they are so constrained by a unifying symmetry, and yet have a rich structure. One example is QCD, the theory of strong interactions (if we neglect quark masses); another is the class of superstring theories, now popular as a candidate for a complete theory of physics. A second reason is that if we make certain realistic requirements of a theory it is sometimes found that there are few ways of satisfying them.

Is it possible that somehow the laws of physics are the uniquely possible ones and thus somehow necessary? The answer is obviously *no*. One can write down many perfectly self-consistent sets of laws that could be the laws of physics for some possible universe. Most of these universes would be devoid of life and utterly boring. To take an extreme case, I could imagine a universe with one "degree of freedom" governed by, say, the pendulum equation! Uniqueness only begins to make sense when one requires the theory to satisfy certain conditions. For example, if we specify that it must be a unitary, , quantum field theory including gravity, the possibilities become very limited. But these requirements are necessarily *themselves* of an arbitrary nature. Without requirements, there is an infinity of possibilities. Similarly, the possible requirements that could be imposed are infinite. One requirement that some have discussed is that life – specifically intelligent life – could evolve. Either this leads us back to design or it leads to some version of the "anthropic principle." But uniqueness as a separate possibility cannot work.

(C) Statistical Ensembles and the "Anthropic Principle"

This idea is best explained by an analogy. Suppose (as is probably the case) that the conditions on the surface of the earth are just right to support life (temperature, chemical abundances, surface gravity, etc.). If the earth were the only planet in the universe, this would appear as a coincidence – an "anthropic coincidence" – and perhaps an evidence of design. But suppose (as is the case) that there is a vast and perhaps infinite number of planets on which the conditions vary over a whole range of possibilities. Then given any particular conditions (such as those required to support life), there is bound to be at least one planet that fulfills them. The "coincidence" evaporates.

One might hope to explain at least the "anthropic coincidences" we discussed in this way. This type of explanation is referred to as the "anthropic principle," which comes in various forms.[32] More ambitiously, one might hope to eliminate all "arbitrariness." This would require that the universe we observe is but one of a vast statistical population or "ensemble" of actually existing "universes." This might come about in one of two ways: Either (a) the laws of this universe are such as to give rise to a large or infinite number of different sectors, mutually unobservable, where very different conditions or phenomena occur; or (b) one has an ensemble of universes which have nothing to do with each other.

The first kind of ensemble actually arises in two types of theory we have already discussed. In the "Many Worlds Interpretation" of quantum mechanics, the universe has many "branches" that are constantly subdividing as all quantum "probabilities" are realized. In certain versions of "inflationary cosmology," the universe contains many regions which are so far apart that they are outside of each others' "horizons." Such ensembles could be used to explain some "initial conditions problems" and even certain of the anthropic coincidences. However, as such ensembles of "branches" or "regions" of the universe only arise in certain special types of theory, that cannot fully eliminate "arbitrariness," the "anthropic coincidences," or the argument from design. Again, it is at the level of *law* that arbitrariness must be eliminated.

To really be able to destroy the argument from design and explain the

---

32 See note 4.

anthropic coincidences, the ensemble must be of the second kind and include many different universes *with different laws.* Indeed it must include *all possible universes with any self-consistent laws or even without laws,* for any limitation on the membership of the ensemble is inherently arbitrary. The "statistical ensemble" attack on design only works in this extreme case, which essentially amounts *to eliminating the distinction between the possible and the actual or real,* since all possibilities are realized. In that case to "exist" is just to be "self-consistent" and the cosmological argument is destroyed as well. Unfortunately or fortunately, this whole approach is self-destructive. For, if *all* possibilities are represented in the ensemble and we use the statistical reasoning which characterizes these arguments, we would have to conclude that there is essentially a zero probability that the laws of physics will continue to be obeyed tomorrow or 5 seconds from now! Indeed, there are universes in the ensemble where they will be, but for each one of those there is an infinity where they will not! And, indeed, for each universe which exhibits the regularity we call law, there are an infinity that do not or where that regularity is sporadic. The whole framework of explaining things by laws disintegrates once anything can (and does) happen. A further difficulty is that when dealing with an uncountable infinity of possibilities, as we are, to talk about "probability" requires what is called a "measure" of probability. One has to decide what is equiprobable. But there is an infinity of completely arbitrary ways of doing this. Only in the framework of some all embracing theory that describes the whole ensemble and provides a "measure" for it, as in the first type of ensemble, can we really talk about probabilities. But then we are back in the soup. How are the special features of that theory to be accounted for?

Appendix E
The Implications of Quantum Theory

This is a much controverted[33] and confused subject. I will present here my own view, which can be supported both by solid arguments and by the authority of weighty figures in the field. First, I will clear up some terminological confusion.

People often talk about various "interpretations" of quantum mechan-

---

33 For a semipopular introduction to the issues surrounding quantum mechanics see P. C. W. Davies and J. R. Brown, *The Ghost in the Atom,* Cambridge University Pres, 1986. For a lucid but technical account see E. P. Wigner, *Symmetries and Reflections,* Ox Bow Press, 1979, Ch. 12, 13, 14.

ics (Q.M.). There are really only two: the traditional interpretation (T.I.) and the "Many Worlds Interpretation" (M.W.I.) The formalism of Q.M. is mathematically unambiguous, there is only *one theory* of Q.M., universally agreed upon. And, until 1957, when the M.W.I. was proposed by Everett, one could say that there was also only one "interpretation" of Q.M. (Peierls,[34] who regards the M.W.I. as a semantic confusion, still says that there is only one "interpretation." Hence, he regards the word "interpretation" as mischievous and misleading). Sometimes one hears people talk about the so-called "Copenhagen interpretation" of Q.M. It is a term with no agreed upon meaning. Some people mean a set of beliefs held by Niels Bohr, including all sorts of subjectivistic metaphysical baggage. Others mean no more than the T.I. In any case, it is a term best avoided. Wigner, since he presumably did not want to use this misleading term to describe the T.I., chose to call it in his writings the "orthodox interpretation."[35] Before 1957, I think this would have been appropriate. Now that it has a competitor in the M.W.I., I have chosen a more neutral term. Of course, Q.M. may be incomplete. Our discussions are all based upon the (dangerous) assumption that the principles of Q.M. are true, since they have stood for the last sixty years.

In Q.M. one talks about "the system," "the observer," and "the wavefunction" (w.f.) of the system. As Wigner says (following von Neumann), the wavefunction of the system changes "in two ways."[36] Between measurements made on the system, the w.f. evolves *in an absolutely deterministic way* according to the laws of Q.M., namely the so-called "time-dependent Schrödinger equation." The element of chance enters when "the observer" makes a measurement or observation of the system. The w.f. (usually) does not predict definitely the result of this observation; rather, the w.f. contains various "components" corresponding to the various possible outcomes. The magnitudes (squared) of these components allow the observer to predict the relative probabilities of these outcomes. After the measurement is completed, however, the outcome is certain. Only one component of the w.f. represents the true state of affairs, although *which* one could not have been predicted even in principle beforehand. The w.f. thus "collapses," as is said. How it collapses is random and not determined by any equation or law. The component corresponding to the actual result is set

---

34 See P. C. W. Davies and J. R. Brown, ref. 33, p. 71.
35 See E. P. Wigner, ref. 33.
36 See E. P. Wigner, ref. 33.

to one, and the others are set to zero. Most of the controversy and all of the significant questions raised by Q.M. revolve around the issues of *what* the w.f. represents, *when* and *how* it collapses, and *who* "the observer" is whose observation collapses it.

There is a famous "paradox" that brings these issues into focus called the "Schrödinger's cat paradox." What it essentially involves is a "system" which includes a cat (albeit it does not have to be a cat). An experiment is devised whose possible outcome includes situations in which the cat has been killed by the experiment and in which the cat has been spared. Until the observer comes along and makes his observation of the result, the w.f. according to Q.M. must have components corresponding to both of those possibilities. Only at the moment of the observation does the w.f. collapse, unpredictably, to a live cat or a dead cat. (This is even more paradoxical than at first appears, since in most cases in Q.M. components of the w.f. representing apparently exclusive possibilities can "interfere" with each other.)

If we adopt an obvious and natural viewpoint, namely, that *the wavefunction is a description of the system*, we will get into trouble. (By the system here, I mean the system as it exists in reality apart from anyone's knowledge of it.) In the Schrödinger's cat experiment, since prior to the observation the components representing a live cat and a dead cat were equally a part of the w.f., they must equally have been a part of reality. The cat would appear to be in a state of suspended animation! This is disconcerting because a living being is involved, it is less so for, say, an electron. (That such paradoxical things actually happen for electrons can be demonstrated experimentally, since one can actually set up situations where the aforementioned interference occurs.) A more telling version[37] of this paradox goes by the name "the Wigner's friend paradox." Instead of a cat, a human (Wigner's friend) is involved, and not his life or death but his state of knowledge is at issue. The punchline comes when Wigner makes his observation by means of asking his friend a yes or no question about what he has seen and receiving a reply. According to Q.M., *if* Wigner can describe the contents of the mind of his friend using a w.f., then, until Wigner receives his answer, the state of mind of his friend is not decided. It also is in a state of suspended animation.

There are two ways to avoid these troubles. The first is the M.W.I. According to this, the w.f. *never* collapses even when an observation is made.

---

37 Ibid., pp. 176 and 179.

The components of the w.f. representing the various conditions of the cat (alive or dead) all correspond to equally real "branches" of the world's history. Before the observation, the observer knows the same things in each branch, but afterwards his knowledge is different in the different branches. In some, he "knows" the cat is alive, in others he "knows" the cat is dead! In fact, the world is continually splitting up into branches with every quantum transition, and we each have an infinity of life histories and fates, all equally real. Of course such a viewpoint is not open to an orthodox Christian. (The M.W.I. is also impossible to subject to any empirical test since the "branches" are "non-interfering.") We will briefly return to the M.W.I. later.

The second way out of trouble is to abandon the "obvious and natural viewpoint" underlined above, namely, that the wavefunction describes the system itself. Rather one must say that *it describes the observer's state of knowledge of the system.* This is not at all to deny the reality of the system; it is not to say anything about the system! It is only to make a statement about what the wavefunction is. If we cling to the idea that the w.f. describes the system itself – the reality of the situation – then one must say that Wigner's friend's mind in reality had no definite thoughts until Wigner got an answer to his question. That is, Wigner's consciousness is given a special status higher than that of his friend. One is led inexorably to some variety of solipsism or subjectivism. Moreover, if the w.f. is interpreted as being the objective state of the system, one runs into the problem of *which* observer is "the observer" who collapses "*the* wavefunction."

On the view of the w.f. as the observer's *knowledge* of the system, many difficulties evaporate. It is not the cat (or Wigner's friend's mind) that is in "suspended animation" but the observer's judgment that is suspended. Corresponding to each "observer" of a system there is a w.f. That is, a w.f. is not just associated with an object, a system, but with a particular subject, an observer. Who then is "the observer" who collapses "the wavefunction"? Obviously, it is the observer whose state of knowledge is represented by that wavefunction! How then is the collapse of the w.f. to be understood? If the w.f. represents a state of knowledge, then when that state of knowledge changes (as it does when an observation is made), the w.f. must naturally also change as suddenly. This is common sense.

There are four questions that are usually thought to be embarrassing to the T.I. (1) What is the dividing line between the system and the observer? (2) When in the complex process of performing a measurement does the w.f. actually collapse? (3) Who is "the observer"? Must is be a human? and (4) How does the w.f. collapse?

The answer to the first question is that there is some arbitrariness in drawing the line. The observer could, if he were interested is describing physically the measurement process itself, define the system to include not only the thing being measured but also the measurement apparatus and even the observer's own interaction with these devices, his sensory organs, nervous system, etc. The observer can never be totally swallowed up by the system, however, and completely included in the physical description. Unless he remains distinct from the system, there will never be an observation, the w.f. will never collapse, and the description will be completely deterministic (as in the M.W.I.) rather than probabilistic. Thus there is an irremovable boundary between the system and observer. This corresponds to Western philosophy's metaphysics where the subject and object of knowledge are sharply distinguished. (And has little resemblance – *pace* Capra and Zukav – to Eastern mystical ideas which tend to deny the reality of this distinction.)

The answer of Wigner (note 35) and Peierls[38] (note 33) to the second question is that the measurement process is only complete when the result enters the "consciousness" or "knowledge" of the observer. Wigner tends to use the word "consciousness" and insists that only a "conscious" being – as opposed to an inanimate device – can collapse the wavefunction. Certainly, if the device can be described by the laws of Q.M. (the time-dependent Schrödinger equation), it cannot collapse the w.f. since those equations are deterministic and the collapse is random. But Wigner's point of view has been assailed by those who ask where one is to draw the line in the animal kingdom between "conscious" and "non-conscious." We would all agree on humans as conscious, but what about chimpanzees, cats, frogs, insects, worms, bacteria? In my view, since the w.f. represents state of knowledge, any organism that can be said to "know" that which is contained in wavefunctions can be an "observer" in the sense of Q.M. Its state of knowledge of a system will be represented by a w.f.; and when that knowledge changes, the corresponding w.f. will collapse. Is a chimpanzee able to know in this sense? I do not know, since I do not know what goes on in a chimpanzee's mind. This answers the third question.

The fourth question is answered as we suggested above. Since the w.f.

38 R. Peierls, *Symposium on the Foundations of Modern Physics,* ed. By P. Lahti and P. Mitteltaedt, World Scientific Publishing co., 1985, pp. 187–96.

represents a state of knowledge, it "collapses" when that state of knowledge changes. As we have noted, this collapse, being non-deterministic, is not describable via the laws of Q.M. Thus we must conclude that the "process" or better "act" by which the observer's state of knowledge changes is not completely describable in physical terms.

One might worry, as some have, that the T.I. necessarily involves abandoning the notion of objective reality. I do not believe it does. One can show that the observations or knowledge of various observers (as long as they do not make mistakes in their measurements) must agree when compared with each other. This in my view suffices to show that we do not have a subjectivist theory here. One might ask whether one can speak of the true and objective state of a physical system apart from any observer's knowledge and measurements of it. I do not know, but certainly such a thing could not be the object of any human science that depended on measurement and observation! Since it is an element of such a science, it need not overly worry us that the w.f. does not provide us with such a description.

In any event, if one is to avoid solipsism within the framework of the T.I. of Q.M. (as opposed to the M.W.I.), one is led to the three conclusions of the text.

The difference between the M.W.I.[39] and the T.I. is that in the former the w.f. never collapses; it just keeps on ramifying. Thus the observer has no fundamental role. It is a view which gladdens the materialist but should arouse the hostility of the positivist. Since these are often the same person, there is not much enthusiasm for the M.W.I.

(There is a fallacious argument for the M.W.I. from quantum cosmology.[40] It is said that if one considers the w.f. of the whole physical universe, there can be no observer external to the system and hence such a w.f. will never collapse. In practice, of course, quantum cosmologists study w.f.'s which describe the universe as a whole but not in every detail. They use variables which average over little lumps in the matter distributions like you and me. Moreover, even if one contemplates a wavefunction that involves *every* physical degree of freedom in the universe, it begs the question to suppose that it describes also the minds of all observers. Therefore *logically* we are external to the system described, though we are *geometrically* internal to it.)

---

39 P. C. W. Davies and J. R. Brown, ref. 33, pp. 34–38 gives an account of the
   Many Worlds Interpretation.
40 *Ibid.*, pp. 89–90.

Actually, the observer in the T.I. could perversely refuse to collapse the w.f. but continue to carry around all of the components that correspond to results he did not obtain in his measurement. The real difference between T.I. and the M.W.I., then, and the only real room for "interpretation" in quantum mechanics, is whether one regards all those other "branches" of the world – the "paths not taken" – as being as *real* as the one experienced by the observer. This cannot be settled by experiment, only on the basis of "reasonableness." The T.I. asks us to believe in the reality of our own minds as more than complicated physical systems, as being capable of "knowledge" which is not merely a chemical process. This is not asking much since if it is not true, then what we "believe" about the world is just a question of chemistry anyway and not very interesting. As Wigner (note 35) points out, moreover, we have more direct empirical grounds for believing in our own minds than in anything else. The Many Worlds Interpretation asks us to believe in a staggering number of "branches" of the world of which we can have no empirical evidence whatever.

21.
The Renewal of the Church: Toward the 21st Century (1987)
Thomas Weinandy, OFM

To identify the central issues confronting the world and the Church at the end of the second millennium, I have decided to take my cue from Pope John Paul II. In reading the pope's encyclicals and his weekly audiences and addresses, I have been struck by his numerous references to the approaching Millennial Jubilee. Significantly, John Paul's three major encyclicals on the Trinity – *Redemptor Hominis, Dives in Misericordia*, and *Dominum et Vivificantem*, as well as his encyclical on Mary, *Mater Redemptoris* – are set within the context of the approaching year 2000 Jubilee. I have concluded that it would be helpful to examine these encyclicals to see how John Paul speaks of the year 2000 in light of the Church's and the world's needs.

I. Redemptor Hominis

"The Redeemer of man, Jesus Christ, is the center of the universe and of human history" (#1). Pope John Paul II, in this opening sentence from his first encyclical, proclaimed that Jesus, as the incarnate Son of God, must be acknowledged as the pre-eminent person in creation and in human history. As John Paul began his pontificate, this truth acquired even greater significance for him because God had entrusted to him the Chair of Peter at a time "already very close to the year 2000" (#1). He conceded that it is difficult to know "what mark that year will leave on the face of human history," but "for the Church, the People of God . . . it will be the year of a great Jubilee" (#1).

We uncover here, at the very outset of John Paul's pontificate, the heart of his strategy for the renewal of the Church and of his solicitude toward the world as the year 2000 nears: the centrality and primacy of Jesus and the salvation he brings. The Incarnation marked the high point of God's plan.

"God entered the history of humanity and, as a man, became an actor in that history . . ." (#1).

Evaluating Vatican II and the previous pontificates of this century, John Paul asked himself: "In what manner should we continue? What should we do, in order that this new advent of the Church connected with the approaching end of the second millennium may bring us closer" to our Father (#7)? There is only one answer: "Our spirit is set in one direction, the only direction for our intellect, will, and heart, towards Christ our Redeemer, towards Christ, the Redeemer of man. We wish to look towards Him, because there is salvation in no one else but Him, the Son of God . . ." (#7). The foremost task of the Church at this juncture in human history is to ensure "that each person may be able to find Christ . . ." (#13).

With the approach of the third millennium, the world and the Church need Jesus and his salvation more than ever. John Paul insists that this present century is "groaning in travail"; that it is increasingly "subjected to futility." The environmental crisis, numerous and ever-increasing armed conflicts, the threat of nuclear war, social and economic injustice, the disintegration of the marriage and family life, and the contempt for human life (even of the unborn) make this abundantly clear.

Cognizant of this frightful situation, the pope heralded Jesus as the Liberator from this bondage to evil: "Christ, the new Adam, in the very revelation of the mystery of the Father and of his love, *fully reveals man to himself* and brings to light his most high calling." The pope contended that Christ is "himself the perfect man who has restored in the children of Adam that likeness to God which had been disfigured ever since the first sin" (#8). Jesus, through the Incarnation, has raised humanity to a new dignity by uniting himself to each person. Only in Christ can we be restored to our rightful rank as reflections of God's image. Only in Christ can we be recreated and made new. Thus, only in Christ can the world find an answer to the present threat of self-annihilation begotten by the wages of sin.

From this perspective, the pope made a concluding reference to the year 2000. Here he spoke not of a time of jubilation, but of an hour for intense prayer in the face of immense problems and difficulties; a moment that could be decisive both for the Church and the world for better or worse:

> Faced with these tasks that appear along the ways for the Church . . . we feel all the more our need for a profound link with Christ. . . . We feel not only the need but even a categorical imperative for great intense and growing prayer by all the Church. Only prayer can prevent all

these great succeeding tasks and difficulties from becoming a source of crisis and make them instead the occasion and, as it were, the foundation for ever more mature achievements on the People of God's march toward the Promised Land in this state of history approaching the end of the second millennium.

He concluded by asking us to join with Mary's intercession for "humanity's new advent" (#22).

II. Dives in Misericordia

If we say that John Paul's second encyclical is just the next installment of his trinitarian trilogy, treating of God the Father, we would be missing its full significance. Yes, it does discuss the Father, but more specifically and importantly, it speaks of the Father's mercy. It is this specific attitude which the pope believes the world most needs to experience at this critical time.

The Father's mercy is poured out most abundantly through his Son, Jesus. "It became *visible in Christ and through Christ*, through his actions and his words, and finally through his death on the cross and his resurrection . . . [Jesus] *makes it incarnate* and personifies it. *He himself, in a certain sense, is mercy*" (#2). The supreme act of mercy is the cross of Jesus. He reconciled us to the Father, making peace through the blood of the cross. He put to death our sinful nature so that we might become the very holiness of God.

Looking at the world, the pope asked whether the fears and tensions within contemporary culture and society have become "less disquieting" since first addressed by the Second Vatican Council:

> It seems not. On the contrary, the tensions and threats that in the Council document seem only to be outlined . . . have revealed themselves more clearly in the space of these years; they have in a different way confirmed that danger, and do not permit us to cherish the illusions of the past (#10).

He then enumerated the evils, physical and moral, that confront mankind today. Despite the dilemmas that face the world and the Church, human beings have become oblivious and insensitive to God's mercy and, in turn, have hardened themselves against showing mercy to others. Resentment, bitterness, anger, hatred and unforgiveness have gripped and enslaved the entire world. To the pope's mind, humanity is desperate for the mercy of God made manifest through his Son, Jesus Christ. Without this mercy there is no hope. Human strategies and designs for resolving the problems of the world are not suited to the task at hand. Only Jesus is capable of destroying the sin and evil that imperils humanity. Only the power of his cross and the Spirit can free human beings from their callous and obstinate hearts and their darkened minds.

John Paul II concluded this encyclical with an impassioned call for prayer. "Everything that I have said in the present document on mercy should therefore *be continually transformed into an ardent prayer*: into a cry that implores mercy according to the needs of man in the modern world" (#15). Having stated with great intensity the crisis confronting the modern world, he insisted:

[The mystery of Christ] obliges me to have recourse to that mercy and to beg for it at this difficult, critical phase of the history of the Church and of the world, as we approach the end of the second millennium. In the name of Jesus Christ crucified and risen, in the spirit of his messianic mission . . . *we raise our voices and pray* that the Love which is in the Father may once again be revealed at this stage of history, and that, through the work of the Son and Holy Spirit, it may be shown to be present in our modern world and to be more powerful than evil: more powerful than sin and death (#15).

III. Dominum et Vivificantem

More than in any previous encyclical, the pope sets *Dominum Vivificantem* within the context of the approaching 21st century. This emphasis highlights the perilous condition of this present age. Part II of the encyclical, which is its heart, focuses exclusively on the Spirit's mission of convicting people of sin and manifesting the saving and healing work of Christ crucified. Part III applies this work of the Spirit to today's circumstances. John Paul judged that with the close of this second millennium the Church must be even more committed to "the mission of proclaiming the Spirit" (#1).

The first task of the Holy Spirit is to bring to light our sinful nature and the iniquity which flows from it. This work is crucial today. John Paul believes that Pope Pius XII was absolutely correct when he declared that "the sin of the century is the loss of the sense of sin . . ." (#47).

This accent on sin is not one of pessimism, cynicism, or despair. Rather, the pope realizes that sin is our worst enemy. It undermines and destroys the integrity of humanity and fosters hate and animosity both within the Church and the world. Until the Spirit convicts us of sin and leads us to repentance and a change of heart, the plight of the present age will not be abated.

Moreover, only the Spirit convicts us of the righteousness of Jesus and moves us to faith in him. Jesus promised that he would send us another Counselor, who would lead us to the fullness of truth. Thus, it is the Holy Spirit who bears witness to Jesus, who is the truth. John Paul declared that *"the witness of the Spirit* inspires, guarantees and convalidates the faithful transmission of this revelation . . ." (#5). He performs his work in the hearts and minds of men and women by bringing them to faith in Jesus. "Here the Spirit is to be man's supreme guide and the light of the human spirit" (#6). This faith will make us righteous in the Righteous One – Jesus Christ. In Christ, we become new creations: Our lives can actually change.

The convincing of the Spirit "becomes at the same time a convincing *concerning the remission of sins,* in the power of the Spirit . . . the gift of the certainty of redemption" (#31). This conviction of sin leads to the cross by which our fallen natures are put to death. Through the cross we become new creations in the Spirit (#44). "It is in the power of this crucifixion that he [Jesus] says to them [the apostles]: 'Receive the Holy Spirit.' . . . . There is no sending of the Holy Spirit (after original sin) without the Cross and the Resurrection . . ." (#24).

The third and final section of the encyclical is an application of the Spirit's work to our millennial age. The coming of Jesus into the world marked the "fullness of time" and "the *great Jubilee* at the close of the second Millennium . . ." celebrates both the birth of Jesus and its actualization "by the power of the Holy Spirit" (#50). This Spirit who accomplished the act of Incarnation is the same Spirit who prepares us for the coming Jubilee: "The Church cannot *prepare* for the Jubilee in any other way than *in the Holy Spirit.*" Only the Spirit can impart to the Church the saving mystery of Christ in this "new phase of man's history on earth: the year 2000 from the birth of Christ" (#51).

As in the previous encyclicals, the pope addressed the critical times in which we live. The real battle is between the flesh and spirit. In our day, the pope asserted, this dispute is more fiercely fought than ever before and "reaches its clearest expression in *materialism . . .*" (#56). This materialism, this exclusive focusing on man and his sensual passions and egotistical drives to the exclusion of God, has given rise to the great evils of our age – from nuclear war to abortion:

> Unfortunately, this is only a partial and incomplete sketch of the *picture of death* being composed in *our age,* as we come ever closer to the end of the second Millennium of the Christian era. Does there not rise

up a new and more or less conscious plea to the life-giving Spirit from the dark shade of materialistic civilization, and especially from those increasing *signs of death* in the sociological and historical picture in which that civilization has been constructed? (#57).

Despite the urgency of our present age, the pope is not without hope: "Yes, we groan but in an expectation filled with unflagging hope, because it is precisely this human being that God has drawn near to, God who is Spirit" (#57). The pope is clear that even though this is a perilous age, there is a power far stronger than sin and evil. The Church fervently clings to and boldly proclaims the gospel as it anticipates the third millennium: "The great Jubilee of the year 2000 thus contains a message of liberation by the power of the Spirit, who alone can help individuals and communities to free themselves from the old and new determinisms, by guiding them with the 'law of the Spirit, which gives life in Christ Jesus' . . ." (#60).

John Paul concluded by pointing out that in celebrating the Jubilee we are anticipating the Second Coming. This is ultimately the event for which the Church and the world are preparing and will celebrate for all eternity. The pope asked that we pray: "Come, Lord Jesus!" This prayer not only anticipates Jesus' second coming and the consummation of the world, but at the same time *"this prayer is directed towards a precise moment of history* which highlights the 'fullness of time' marked by the year 2000. The Church wishes *to prepare* for this Jubilee *in the Holy Spirit*, just as the Virgin of Nazareth – in whom the Word was made flesh – was prepared by the Holy Spirit" (#66).

IV. Redemptoris Mater

John Paul's fourth encyclical goes beyond being just a treatise on Mary. It proceeds logically (as the above quotation suggests) from his trinitarian encyclicals, not only in treating Mary's intimate association with the Trinity's work of redemption, but also in pointing to her as the exemplar of the Church's proper response to it. Thus, this encyclical is a call to action, an invitation to respond to the gospel in faith as Mary did, a summons to renewal and holiness of life patterned after Mary, and a cry to prepare, as she did, for Jesus' coming as we approach the 2000th anniversary of his birth. This insistence on action culminated in John Paul's proclamation of the Marian Year. This year was to be a concrete preparation, in union with Mary, for the approaching Jubilee Year. It was to be a year of intercession and renewal.

Thus Mary is seen as the most faithful respondent to the gospel message as proclaimed in the previous encyclicals. As such, she leads us to a restoration of faith that will not only rejuvenate the faltering Church, but bring salvation to the wary world. "With good reason, then, we Christians who know that the providential plan of the Most Holy Trinity is *the central reality of Revelation and of faith* feel the need to emphasize the unique presence of the Mother of Christ in history, especially during these last years leading up to the year 2000" (#3).

The pope wants us to reflect on Mary as she exemplifies the perfect pilgrim of faith: "*The pilgrimage of faith indicates the interior history*, that is, the story of souls. But it is also the story of all human beings . . ." (#6). As the Church prepares to celebrate the Jubilee year, she looks to Mary who fervently prepared for the coming of her son 2000 years ago:

> Thus by means of this Marian Year *the Church is called* not only to remember everything in her past that testifies to the special maternal cooperation of the Mother of God in the work of salvation in Christ the Lord, but also, on her own part, *to prepare* for the future the paths of this cooperation. For the end of the Second Christian Millennium opens up as a new prospect (#49).

Not surprisingly, in this Marian encyclical John Paul spoke more extensively about ecumenism, especially between the East and the West, than in the previous encyclicals. Recognizing that Mary is the mother of Jesus, the common life of every Christian denomination, and that she is the exemplar of every Christian's faith, the pope used this occasion to stress that this millennial age is ardently calling the churches to a unity of faith. Division weakens the renewal efforts of every church and likewise gives scandal to non-believers. As Christians grow in unity, their task to revitalize themselves and the world becomes easier and more vigorous:

> The journey of the Church, especially in our own time, is marked by the sign of ecumenism: Christians are seeking ways to restore that unity which Christ implored from the Father. . . . The unity of Christ's disciples, therefore, is a great sign given in order to kindle faith in the world, while their division constitutes a scandal (#29).

Both the encyclical and in the call to faith during this Marian Year, we see again the pontiff's concerns as we near the year 2000. The Church calls out to Mary at this time to "assist your people who have fallen, yet strive to rise again." In light of our fallen nature and its potential of sin the pope wants us to unite us to Mary so that – like her – we might be purified of sin, and commit ourselves to her son, Jesus. He would have us join our prayers with Mary for the transformation of our own hearts, the restoration of Christian unity, and the conversion of the entire world. This Marian year is primarily a call to repentance and faith, for only through these will the Church, the churches, and the world come to experience the truth expressed in these encyclicals: the mercy of the Father, the redemption of Jesus and the forgiveness and new life in the Spirit. Only in this way can we be truly prepared to joyfully celebrate the Jubilee Year.

V. What Have We Learned?

What have we learned from examining these four papal encyclicals? First, the critical nature of this millennial era is quite apparent. John Paul views it in almost apocalyptic proportions. The world is so entangled in evil and sin that its very life is threatened. Nor is the Church immune from this deadly affliction of confusion, rebellion, and spiritual depression. The world and the Church are confronted with options: The world may be converted to the gospel of Jesus Christ, curing it of the cancerous sin that imperils it, or it can continue on its deadly path to disaster; the Church can renew itself through reconversion to Jesus Christ and become a leaven of life for the world, or it can continue in its weakened condition, thereby contributing to the world's deplorable state. The Church is the future's physician. A renewed Church will be a source of life; a desolate Church will contribute to the world's demise.

Any renewal movement in the Church today must perceive this menacing situation as well as the role which the Church must play to correct it. Individuals and groups within the Church who fail or refuse to acknowledge the precarious nature of our age will be useless. Indeed, such thinking will only contribute to an already unstable condition. Naïve prophets of facile optimism are largely responsible for much of the malaise that exists.

Secondly, John Paul II is deeply convinced that the only cure capable of reviving the Church and, in turn, the world is the Gospel. It alone has the power to excise the sin that has infected the Church and the world and to resurrect men and women to a new and vibrant life. According to the pope, the heart of this gospel consists of the following: (1) The Holy Spirit convicting us of sin, and leading us to repentance; (2) the experience of the mercy of the Father guiding us to faith in Jesus as Savior and Lord; (3) the recognition that only through the death of Jesus have Satan, sin, and death been conquered, and only through Christ's resurrection can we become new creations in the Spirit, anticipating eternal life. To the world, and even to many in the Church, this remedy appears both unrealistic and mindless. The world considers the gospel impotent in the face of concrete and practical problems. To many in the Church, the gospel is ethereal, pietistic rhetoric. Yet, nothing else but this gospel is the forceful and anguished message of the encyclicals.

Notice that the pope's solution is not some human program or scheme. It does not involve an elaborate system of conferences, workshops, and seminars. The heart of the Church's renewal and of the world's hope is simply the gospel. This alone is what God has given. It is enough. We need nothing else.

Thus, if they are to be credible to a skeptical Church and an unbelieving world, any movements of renewal which are worthy of the name must embody within them vigorous life of the gospel. They must recognize and existentially experience the mercy and love of the Father made manifest in Jesus. This divine mercy must awaken them to their own sinful state and bring them to repentance, faith, and new life in Christ.

Thirdly, any renewal movement which is a true work of the Spirit must embrace as its central mission the proclamation of the same gospel by which its members are renewed. This ought to be accomplished in a way that those who become members of the movement, as well as those to whom it ministers, experience the transforming power and life of the gospel – the call to repentance, mature faith in Jesus, and holiness of life.

I have emphasized the lived witness of people, for unless a personal transformation has actually occurred, there is no renewal. John Paul is calling for precisely this type of event within the Church and anticipating this kind of evidence. Only the lived Gospel can renew the Church and, in turn, the world. The Marian Year, he believes, can contribute to this perceptible expression of faith life through a recommitment to the gospel after the example and through the intercession of Mary.

VI. Movements of Renewal: The Charismatic Renewal

The Cursillo Movement, the Focolare Movement, Comunione e Liberazione, and Opus Dei all bear witness in distinctive ways and in various degrees to the renewal of the gospel in many people's lives. There are probably others. But I believe these are some of the larger movements that are in accord with John Paul's vision for a renewed Church and world. I have purposely left out such movements as Marriage Encounter, Engaged

Encounter, and social action groups, since their primary focus is not the gospel itself, even though they arise out of gospel concerns.

Because it uniquely qualifies as a work of the Spirit in this critical Millennial Age, I would like to treat one movement of renewal more extensively. That movement is the Charismatic Renewal. Along with Comunione e Liberazione and Opus Dei, John Paul has appointed a representative of the Charismatic Renewal to attend the Synod on the Laity.

The Charismatic Renewal's relationship with the Holy Spirit is obvious. Those in the Renewal point out that Pope John XXIII, in anticipation of Vatican II, prayed for a "new Pentecost." The Renewal's roots, however, are found in Pope Leo XIII's 1897 encyclical on the Holy Spirit, *Divinum Illud Munus*, and in the outbreak of the Pentecostal movement shortly thereafter, within Protestantism. However, the force of Pentecostalism's full potential was only perceived on a denominational and global scale when it emerged within the Catholic Church in the mid-1960's. From a faith perspective, it could be argued that the Holy Spirit for over a century has been preparing the entire Christian Church and the world for the 2000 year Jubilee celebration.

The World Christian Encyclopedia: A Comparative Study of Churches and Religious in the Modern World A.D. 1900–2000, edited by David B. Barrett (published in 1982), states that globally Pentecostalism is the fastest growing movement of the century. At its continued rate of growth, it will have affected more people by the year 2000 (the Jubilee Year) than any other Christian movement of the century. One of its unique features is that it has impacted all Christian denominations. Thus, more than any other renewal movement within the Church, and within Christianity at large, the Charismatic Renewal is, by nature, ecumenical. In his book, *One Lord, One Spirit, One Body*, (Word Among Us Press, Washington, D.C., 1987), Fr. Peter Hocken argues that the ecumenical nature of the Charismatic Renewal is one of its real graces. Without underestimating the real divisions between the various denominations or diluting the truths of the gospel, the Spirit – through the Renewal – has fostered an ecumenism that is founded upon a renewed and vibrant faith in Jesus Christ and his gospel. This is in keeping with John Paul's own parameters and understanding.

The considerable growth of Pentecostal/charismatic Christianity is evident not only in Europe and North America, but also in Latin America where it is profoundly altering the present religious environment. Its growth in Africa has been slow, partly due to its checkered history among Catholics, but its expansion among the indigenous black Christian churches is extensive. There are vibrant charismatic and Pentecostal groups in Communist countries, even in Russia. Their strength and dynamism are attested to by the fear and persecution they have evoked from Communist authorities. Even in China we are discovering that Christianity is not only more alive than previously expected, but that the Pentecostal movement has been notably responsible for its preservation and vitality. This phenomenal growth within Christianity is not presented as the legitimization of the Renewal, but it does call for an appropriate hearing.

Participants in the Renewal are, as a group, acutely aware that the Church is suffering spiritually and is in need of reconversion or revitalization. This awareness stems from the Holy Spirit convicting them of their own desperate state (prior to their renewal) as well as their on-going weaknesses. They recognize that their former faith was dead or at best nominal; prior to their "conversion," their lives were out of order and enslaved by habitual sin. This personal awareness of sin has heightened their consciousness of the pervasive sin that is destroying the lives of others, of the lethargy and apathy within the Church, and of the world's complete rebellion against God.

This heightened awareness of sin and the need for a renewed life of faith compels charismatics to bear witness to the transforming power of the gospel of Jesus Christ. The Spirit can bring people to repentance, heal them of sin, and establish a new life with God in Christ. They have seen this in their own lives.

Herein is the basis for misunderstanding and friction between those within the Renewal and those outside it. The charge is sometimes leveled that charismatics are elitists, who insist, at least implicitly, that all become as they are. Since the Renewal encompasses very large numbers of people, not all of whom are prudent, sophisticated, and articulate (not to mention sinless), what is said and done is often not pure, but mixed and even inaccurate. What must be acknowledged, however, is that, despite the negative elements, charismatics are aware that the faith life of many people in the Church is inadequate and anemic. Those who accuse them of elitism are sometimes the very ones who are self-satisfied and complacent. Moreover, what members of the Renewal want for others is not unique or separatist, but rather the full life of the gospel, something that is available to all through the Holy Spirit. (This is not to imply that charismatics possess a fully mature faith or are sinless. By no means. What it does mean is that charismatics realize that the gospel can change people's lives.)

Those within the Renewal testify to the Father's mercy. They are profoundly aware that they were and are sinners, whose only hope is in the mercy of God. They recognize, more clearly and personally than most Christians, that without the mercy of God manifested in Christ, they – and the whole human race – deserve nothing less than eternal damnation.

Thus, people within the Charismatic Renewal have a deep appreciation of Jesus and what he has done. They recognize, as the pope has underscored, that the Spirit has renewed and nourished their faith in Jesus. Through the experience of Baptism in the Spirit, they have received an interior and personal revelation of Jesus as the Son of God; that on the cross he alone saved them from sin and death; and that he now is the resurrected Lord of the universe who deserves all honor and praise. Their personal and enthusiastic commitment to Jesus accompanied by their vocal praise and worship of him is often considered the distinguishing mark of the Renewal. But this must be seen as a work of the Spirit. No one can believe and proclaim that Jesus is truly Savior and Lord except by the Holy Spirit.

The enthusiasm of charismatics gives rise to a second common criticism, that of religious fanaticism or emotionalism. Admittedly, there is usually some foundation for every criticism: Some charismatics can be overly emotional. Nonetheless, allowing for the immaturity of some, one can still ask: Should not Christians be single minded for Jesus? Should we not devote our minds, hearts, and emotions to him? Does he not deserve our praise, yes, even exuberant vocal praise, just as much or more than the current movie or rock star, or the home team sport's hero? Society tolerates and even encourages enthusiastic endorsement of the newest cars, clothes, music, and trends. On the other hand, it ridicules religious fervor as irrational and fanatical. The Church itself has too often adopted this attitude. Vocally and enthusiastically to praise and worship Jesus, to center one's whole life on him, to live differently from what is perceived as "normal" is often considered as "overdoing it." To criticize the Renewal for religious fanaticism and emotionalism is often more a comment on the sad state of the Church and the world than a valid reproach.

Because of this transforming experience of the Spirit, charismatics want to evangelize and are empowered and compelled to do so. When they have personally experienced the life changing power of the gospel, they feel impelled to share it with others. They can attest with conviction to the reality of the gospel and its transforming power. Their own lives become the source of their gospel proclamation. Until people are actually transformed by the gospel, it is impossible for them to proclaim it. A true test of the Church's state and of the life of its people is to examine whether and to what extent it is evangelistic. An inability or unwillingness to share one's faith indicates a weak and immature belief.

At the center of the Renewal's promise and vigor is the Holy Spirit. Those involved in the Renewal testify that it was the Spirit who first convicted them of sin, exposed the disorder in their lives, and brought them to repentance. They realize that the Spirit has brought them to new or renewed faith in Jesus, through which their lives have been healed and restored. The exercise of the charismatic gifts – the most distinguishing and visible signs of Renewal – is actually a manifestation of the Spirit's interior achievement.

If what I have said is true, why is it that many ecclesiastics and academics have not taken the Charismatic Renewal more seriously? The fear of elitism, emotionalism, and fanaticism, which I have already mentioned are partially responsible. But there are also a few other reasons.

One is that academics find it difficult to "get a handle on it." Unlike other movements of renewal, the Charismatic Renewal has no human author; it is entirely a spontaneous and sovereign work of the Spirit. No man or woman decided that the Church and the world needed what we find in the Renewal: Baptism in the Spirit and the spiritual gifts. Undeniably there are leaders within the Renewal, but the Renewal was as much a surprise to them as to others. Their understanding of the Spirit's work grew *from* their experience and not *prior* to it.

For this reason, there is no book or treatise outlining the founder's intentions, purposes, and spirit. This is in contrast to Focolare or Opus Dei where one has easy access to the founder's ideas and goals. This lack of a preconceived and written plan and program complicates analysis and criticism of the Renewal. To discern the validity of the Renewal is more, then, than an academic affair; it requires an examination of the lives of real people. Moreover, what one is attempting to analyze is the work of God: his supernatural intervention in time and space as it touches the lives of men and women today.

Moreover, because the Renewal has no set program other than the basic gospel message, it is perplexing, especially for Americans. We are a society and culture of methods, programs, and systems. If the Renewal had "a program" with specific blueprints and goals for each week, month, and year, complete with instruction books, spread sheets, discussion questions for small groups, etc., its credibility would probably improve noticeably among pastors and teachers. The fact that the Renewal has simply to do with preaching and the appropriation of the gospel, somehow works against it. The suspicion is that there must be a plan, a program, some secret scheme if the gospel is to work. So weak is our faith that, unlike the pope, we do not believe that the gospel can stand on its own and change people's lives. Yet this alone is what Jesus has given us for our salvation. Someone may ask: What about the Life in the Spirit Seminars? Actually, the seminars are just a systematic way of presenting the gospel. They are successful only if the gospel is presented in a clear and convincing manner, and if those participating yield themselves to the work of the Spirit in faith.

Furthermore, because the Renewal is primarily composed of ordinary Christians, scholars can, to a greater or lesser degree, stand aloof and even hold it in contempt. Indeed, one of their dominant criticisms is that of fundamentalism. This charge is leveled both against the Renewal's understanding of the gospel and its approach to Scripture. This fundamentalism is conceived and nourished, they believe, in the credulous minds of the uneducated.

Again, this charge has a trace of validity. In today's world, anyone who possesses no formal training and little historical sense of how the Bible has been traditionally read and understood will tend to interpret it literally. Reading the newspaper is the paradigm for all reading. Despite this, a number of points can be made. First, the fact that some charismatics have misinterpreted the Bible is in itself evidence that it is, at least, being read. Better that the Bible be read and occasionally misinterpreted than never read at all. Moreover, the misinterpretations among Catholics usually are not as flagrant nor as frequent as one is led to believe. Secondly, no group of conventional Catholics spend more time and effort reading and studying the Bible than those in the Renewal. Catholic charismatics, on the whole, are attempting to conquer their ignorance. Any Christian book store owner will verify that Catholic charismatics are by far the most numerous patrons of Christian literature, especially Biblical studies. The fact that the Renewal has given rise to the two largest Catholic scripturally oriented periodicals: *God's Word Today* (89,000) and *The Word Among Us* (80,000),[1] also demon-

---

1   By 1992, the circulation of *The Word Among Us* has climbed to 208,000, and

strates that the Renewal has done more for critical Biblical scholarship than any other movement. Thirdly, the charge of fundamentalism is frequently made not by men and women of real faith but by those who manifest the spirit of secularism. Accordingly, anyone who affirms anything supernatural is considered a naïve fundamentalist who interprets Scripture in an uncritical literalist fashion.

Another area of concern focuses on the fear of some ecclesiastical authorities that the Renewal weakens people's commitment to the Catholic Church and that other Pentecostal denominations attract and steal Catholics away from the Church, especially the young. Unfortunately, some people have joined Pentecostal denominations. This fear of defection from Catholicism is especially prevalent within the Hispanic Catholic community. The way to attack this problem is not to attack the Renewal or even the Pentecostal denominations, but to recognize that these people are hungry for spiritual renewal. The Church has the obligation to provide it, and the Church herself must accept the blame for many of the defections.

Lastly, one of the unrecognized reasons that the Renewal is not taken seriously by some pastors and academics is their own spiritual poverty. Whether we are of the theological right or left, our sinfulness can blind us to the Spirit's work. The sinful patterns that enslave us – anger, suspicion, resentment, greed, arrogance, lust, and ambition – deaden and distort our spiritual perception. Our lack of prayer, or its barren routineness, contributes to our failure to see the Spirit's work today or judging it to be of little consequence.

VII. The Call to Sanctity

As the Church nears the end of the second millennium, it does so with the realization that a great task is set before it, viz., that it must renew itself and then the world. John Paul II unquestionably recognizes that preaching and appropriating the gospel is the answer. The Spirit is actively present within the Church today. The Charismatic Renewal is one of the primary ways the Spirit is using to foster renewal in all Christian denominations. At the core of this Renewal is the gospel alone, the very thing John Paul is so anxious for the Church and the world to seize upon. We must look then, not to some great plan, some new seminar, program, or scheme, but to the constant daily preaching of the gospel, the bringing of people to conversion.

was being published monthly in English, Spanish, Japanese, Portuguese, and Polish (Author's Note).

This is the real answer for renewal of the Church and the salvation of the world as the third millennium rushes upon us. It is not easily accomplished for it primarily demands the labor of holy men and women. No program, conference, or seminar alone can lead people to holiness, only those who are themselves holy can do so. In the end what the Church must foster and what the world needs most is saints.

This call to sanctity falls most heavily upon us who are pastors and teachers. We can proclaim the gospel and lead people to Jesus only if we ourselves are living that gospel and actually know Jesus. Thus, like our saintly ancestors, we too must pray every day, despite our hectic schedules and routines. This is John Paul's ardent summons in each encyclical. Prayer is our most potent weapon against sin and evil. It is the source and fount of the Spirit's holiness. We are also called to daily repentance and a living faith in the presence and power of Jesus. Scripture and the Eucharist will nourish our hearts and minds. The Father's will must be our food. Finally, we are commissioned to evangelize our communities, our families, our students, and even our colleagues.

In so doing we will not only be preparing ourselves for the Jubilee Year 2000, we will also be contributing to the jubilation of the whole Body of Christ. The Spirit's ultimate design is to nourish all of God's people, to form the entire community of faith. He does this by conforming the mind of the Church and the minds of all believers to the mind of Christ. As the Spirit accomplishes his task, what will become most central to the Church will be Jesus himself, not the various agendas of assorted theological and political constituencies. Jesus established the Church, not for its own sake, but for himself, to give him glory, to do his will, to serve his purposes. This is the vision that John Paul holds out to us at the dawn of the third millennium, a vision where all men and women are bound together by their faith in and love for Jesus. They desire him alone and wish solely to build his Kingdom. A Church suffused with the Spirit and conformed to the mind of Christ is our only hope.

22.
Principles of Catholic Scholarship (1988)
Patrick Lee

There are two fundamental objections to the very idea of a Catholic scholar that are often voiced or felt by those outside Catholicism, and sometimes by those inside as well. First, Catholic scholars are often accused of being intolerant. Second, Catholic scholars are often accused of "toeing a party line," that is, of being obscurantist. These are also objections to the Catholic faith itself. The idea that the Catholic faith leads to intolerance and obscurantism undoubtedly prevents many people from looking further into the Catholic religion. In this talk I will take up these two objections. My purpose is not to show in the first place that the act of Catholic faith is a reasonable act, but to answer certain objections to the position that the Catholic faith, and specifically, Catholic scholarship, are reasonable.

Even though Alexander Solzhenitsyn is not a Catholic, the reaction which he elicited by his famous speech at Harvard ten years ago in 1978 typifies the kind of reaction that outsiders to the Catholic Church often have to the Catholic faith and to Catholic scholarship. In that speech, as you recall, Solzhenitsyn criticized the affluent West for being too materialistic and lacking firm convictions or principles. *The New York Times*, reporting the event, replied that it thought Solzhenitsyn was "dangerous" and a "zealot," because, "he believes himself to be in possession of the Truth."

The objection, in other words, is that thinking that one possesses truth must lead to intolerance. The objection assumes, it seems to me, that one cannot possess truth. Presumably, the objector is not dangerous because, whatever positions he takes, he is ready to categorize them as "points of view," rather than as being *actually true* – the latter is a dangerous concept.

Well, *is* the Catholic scholar necessarily intolerant of other persons who disagree with him or her? To *tolerate* something is to allow something that one thinks is bad or mistaken to exist in peace. Applied to convictions and opinions, what that means is that one refrains from using force to bring it about that others agree with one's own convictions. Clearly, there have been Catholics who were intolerant. But, also, there is nothing in the Catholic faith which necessarily leads to intolerance. If one thinks one possesses an important truth, one need not use force in trying to communicate it to others. In fact, one of the truths one might hold is that one ought not to use force in that way. And, again in fact, it is a teaching of the Catholic faith that one ought not to try to coerce another to believe; and it is also a teaching of Vatican Council II that we ought not, acting as members of a political society, forbid people from expressing false religious views simply because they are false.

So, the Catholic faith need not lead to intolerance. Still, one might think that holding the position that truth varies from culture to culture or even from person to person, i.e., a relativist position, would be more conducive to the virtue of tolerance. But this also seems not to be the case. In fact, I think that, ironically, it is the denial of objective truth that inevitably leads to intolerance. In denying objective truth, the relativist denies that there is a structure independent of his own thinking, and that there are values independent of his own choosing. That is, relativism implies something like a metaphysical position or an ontology. The implied ontology will be something like what Jean-Paul Sartre made explicit in his famous early work, *Being and Nothingness*: Reality is amorphous, and meaning and value are creations of each subject, and are thus relative to each subject. But, as Sartre also made clear, the existence of other people – other subjects who are the creators of meaning and value perhaps contradictory to my meaning and value system – presents something of a problem.

Now, if these people agree to play the relativist game – i.e., if they agree to restrict their claims only to their own subjective perspectives, then the basic inconsistency of relativism can be successfully ignored. If we all play the relativist game, if we adopt a relativist social contract, then it can still seem that reality is simply a product of my own thinking and valuing, even if other people's thinking and valuing is quite different from mine. But the objectivist threatens to spoil the whole game. For, by disagreeing as he or she does, the objectivist becomes an element of reality that resists the meaning and values the relativist attempts to impose on it. Now, suddenly, the relativist is forced to disagree fundamentally with someone; he is forced to say that someone is radically wrong. If the relativist is not careful, or if the situation persists, the relativist spell might be broken. The relativist may realize that he is asserting the relativist position itself to be objectively true – that he is asserting that it is true for all times and places that no one can make a statement that is true for all times and places! Therefore, the relativist cannot help feeling, not just that the objectivist is mistaken, but that the objectivist is somehow acting improperly, that the objectivist is, if truth be told, not playing by the rules of the game.

In other words, to put it perhaps too summarily, I think the relativist project is quite different from the objectivist project. The relativist game can only be played by relativists, and the very existence of non-relativists threatens to end the game. The existence of non-relativists threatens to make impossible the relativist subterfuges, subterfuges which serve definite purposes which the relativists apparently value very highly. And so relativism, by the nature of the case, leads to actual hostility toward, and fear of, those who disagree with relativism. So, not only does being a Catholic scholar not necessarily lead to intolerance; it is the other way around; one ought not to embrace relativism as a means to increase the virtue of tolerance, for relativism in fact leads to intolerance.

The second accusation often raised against Catholic scholars is that of narrow-mindedness. Here the objection is that the Catholic scholar must, as it were, toe the party line, and that this means that he or she is not open to various arguments, and is opposed to unbridled inquiry – i.e., that the Catholic scholar is, in certain key areas, opposed to inquiry and arguments. The objector, as the reference to "the party line" indicates, often wishes to compare the Catholic Church to the Communist Party: Just as a Communist suppresses inquiry and argument in order to further the revolution, so the Catholic scholar is simply out to advance his or her cause, to beef up the argumentative case for Catholicism, and to ignore or suppress any unfavorable evidence.

The first point to make in reply to this objection is that, yes, both today and in the recent past (say, the last forty years), regrettably it *has* often been true that Catholic scholars have subordinated respect for inquiry and evidence to their cause. But this subordination is a falling short of what one is called to by the Catholic faith, and by one's vocation to be a Catholic scholar. A good or consistent Catholic scholar will be quite different from a Communist ideologue, who must serve the party line, while the Catholic scholar is called to serve truth. But it is important not only to answer the objection but to get straight in our own minds what belongs to the nature of our vocation, to spell out what that difference is.

The primary difference is between those things to which the Communist on the one hand, and the Catholic on the other hand, are committed. The

Communist is committed, ultimately, to the establishment of a quite definite political and economic structure; i.e., his goal is a limited or definite
state of affairs – the world classless communist society. This limited objective is *the* criterion for distinguishing good actions from bad actions, permissible from impermissible pursuits. And so everything else, including
honesty, becomes subordinate to that definite goal.

For the Catholic, on the other hand, the ultimate goal is the eternal kingdom, which is quite different from a limited economic and political structure. The kingdom of God includes, first of all, a mysterious, experimental
union with God. But it also includes all other human goods: human fellowship, our moral accomplishments, our human bodily life, and, what is most
important here, possession of truth. Moreover, although the completed eternal kingdom will only be present at the end of this world, after God's
recreative work, it is already present in mystery. This world is not simply a
means in relation to the ultimate end or goal, but a bringing about or participation in all of the components of the eternal kingdom (for these points, see
Gaudium et Spes, #19, #34, and #39). Now, Catholic faith is the acceptance
of God's offer of fellowship; it is the acceptance of God's proposal of a
common life. Included in this act of faith, if it is living faith, is a commitment to do one's own part in building up that common life. This means that
our commitment of faith *includes* a commitment to the human good of possession of truth, a good that we begin to realize here and now, and not just at
some time in the future.

So, the answer to the objection is that a Catholic need not be guilty of
narrow-mindedness or obscurantism, since the commitment of faith includes a commitment to truth. A Catholic cannot consistently suppress truth
or argument or inquiry as a means by which to realize his or her objective,
since part of the goal he or she should be dedicated to precisely is the truth
or argument one might be tempted to suppress. And so if the Catholic is acting consistently, he or she will not be obscurantist, that is, will not suppress
argument or inquiry or evidence for the sake of promoting his or her case.

But there is a more subtle version of the accusation that being a Catholic scholar involves repeating a party line, and this version is quite often today offered by Catholic theologians themselves instead of by non-
Catholics. This objection has to do specifically with teachings in the Church
which are not necessarily part of the faith.

I will not here go into the basis of the distinction, but suffice it to say that it is Catholic teaching that there are three types of teaching in the Church. First, there are doctrines that have been infallibly proposed because they have been formally defined either by the college of bishops united under the pope or by the pope himself. Second, there can be doctrines that have been infallibly proposed by the ordinary Magisterium. That is, there can be teaching on faith or morals that have not been formally defined, but have been proclaimed by the bishops dispersed throughout the world, in agreement with the pope, in such a way that they too must be held definitively. But the objection we are now considering concerns teaching that belongs to a third category.

In this third category are the various doctrines that have *not* been infallibly proposed, although they *have* been taught as doctrines to be held definitively and with certainty. The reason they have not been infallibly proposed is simply that not all of the bishops throughout the world have taught on the issue or not all of the bishops agree. (So, we are not talking about a doctrine that is proposed tentatively, or that has been quietly dropped, or something that is only proposed as a disciplinary matter.) Now, a Catholic scholar, with some rare exceptions, still owes assent to such teaching – not the assent of divine faith, but religious assent.

Now here, the objection is sometimes raised, one cannot deny that Catholic scholars are being told to suppress argument and evidence, and merely to defend what appears to be a party line. For, if the teaching has not been proposed infallibly, so the objection might run, then it could be mistaken. But if a Catholic scholar is, nevertheless, required to assent to that teaching, then Catholic scholars are required to believe what may be false. Here, if not elsewhere, the objector might press, the Catholic scholar is subordinating his or her concern for truth to a concern for unity or public order.

Of course, this objection or something close to it is often raised by Catholic scholars themselves. The question about what are the reasonable or permissible limits of dissent from teaching by leaders of the Church, I need hardly add, has been a hotly debated topic. My question here is as follows: Is the obligation of a Catholic scholar to give religious assent to noninfallibly proposed teachings by popes and bishops one that is reasonable, or does it, on the contrary, involve a violation of intellectual integrity? Of course, to answer this question, I will have to indicate what I think are the obligations of Catholic scholars in this area, as derived from a reasonable reading of *Lumen Gentium* #25. My question, then, is not simply what

it is that Catholic scholars are required to do or permitted to do but whether
what is required of them by the teaching of the Church is a *reasonable* act,
indeed, a morally permissible act.

According to the Church the faithful, including Catholic scholars, are
to give "religious assent" to the authoritative teachings of bishops, especially those of the pope.

> Bishops, teaching in communion with the Roman Pontiff, are to be re-
> spected by all as witnesses to divine and Catholic truth. In matters of
> faith and morals, the bishops speak in the name of Christ and the faith-
> ful are to accept their teaching and adhere to it with a religious assent of
> soul. This religious submission of will and intellect must be given in a
> unique way to the authoritative teaching of the Roman Pontiff, even
> when he does not speak *ex cathedra* (*Lumen Gentium* #25; translation).

Clearly, whatever else this document means, it does *not* mean that a
Catholic scholar can take the attitude that he will assent to a papal teaching
only if he is persuaded by the arguments for it. Also, it does not mean
merely that one begins one's inquiry with a presumption in favor of the papal teaching: More than that is clearly asserted here. What it *does* say is that,
at least generally, a Catholic must submit his intellect and will to the papal
teaching, which can only mean that the Catholic should trust the papal
teaching more than his or her own intellect and will. That is, a Catholic must
be ready to assent to teaching on faith or morals even in cases where his or
her own inquiry would suggest an opposite answer. If a Catholic does not
have such a readiness, at least to some extent, then the pope and the bishops
are simply not being related to as teaching authorities.

Before returning to the objection that this teaching demands or leads to
obscurantism, I would like to clarify the question by setting aside a common
but confused, and I think question-begging, way of posing it. The way the
question is often asked is: What should I do if my conscience tells me to act
in one way and the pope tells me to act in another? Or: What should I do if
my conscience conflicts with Church teaching? Do I follow the pope or my
conscience?

This way of posing the question is very misleading. What we mean by
"conscience" is simply our best judgment about a moral action, *after* we
have taken into consideration all of the relevant factors. So, literally speaking, if my *conscience* tells me that I should act contrary to Church teaching,
then I have already considered the papal teaching and for some motive or
reason set it aside. The real question is not, what should I do if I find my

conscience disagreeing with the pope, but whether it is reasonable for me to get to that point to begin with.

The way to formulate the question without a begging of the issue is as follows: Suppose I examine a question on faith or morals on my own, and simply on the basis of what I can figure out, before or independently of taking into account the fact that the pope teaches thus or so, and the answer seems to me to be opposite from what in fact the pope does teach? In such a case, when on the basis of what I can figure out, the answer seems to be one thing, and, meanwhile, the pope teaches the opposite, what is the most reasonable thing for me to do? Notice, my question now is not what does the Church say that I should do, but what does a sincere respect for truth and commitment to the work of Jesus and the Church require that I should do?

I am supposing here the following regarding the evidence for the judgment opposite to that of the papal teaching: (1) it is not so clear as to compel my judgment and (2) it does not consist in a stronger authority drawn from faith itself (say, a clear teaching of Scripture or a teaching of a previous pope or ecumenical council). If one arrived at either one of these positions, then I think one would no longer have an obligation to assent. And, as I understand it, this position is consistent with the meaning of *Lumen Gentium* #25. Nevertheless, these exceptions would, by the nature of the case, be very rare.

So, I study the question. My own study leads me to one answer, and the pope teaches the opposite as certain. The question is: which is it more *reasonable* for me to follow: my own reasoning or the authority of the leader of the Church?

There are three considerations which make it more reasonable for me to follow the judgment of the leader of the Church, rather than my own reasoning abilities. First, the leaders of the Church in some way have divine assistance in the exercise of their office. Admittedly, how this works is not entirely clear and needs further examination. Yet the fact that the pope is the successor of St. Peter, and the bishops are successors of apostles, is sufficient to tilt the scale, as it were, in favor of a papal or episcopal teaching.

Secondly in the kinds of questions that become controversial, there will often be an additional reason to distrust my own inquiry, since I will often have a particular interest in the matter. If the issue is a moral question and the answer will have a great impact on how easy or difficult my life will be, then I should welcome a less biased judge in the matter, and correspondingly trust my own judgment less.

Thirdly, matters of faith and morals are never purely academic matters. These questions always concern our Christian way of life; they concern the saving truth which has been handed on to us from Christ. Moreover, we have an obligation and a responsibility to communicate this saving truth to others, and to build up the family of God which is initiated by acceptance of this truth. Now, to accomplish this work effectively, unity is required. Significant disagreements about what is required by the Christian way of life make it difficult for the Church to act as one. In short, unity about what is required by the Christian way of life is needed for common action. And so it *is* reasonable, provided that following this judgment is not irrational for other reasons, to follow the judgment of the pope or bishops.

It is important to note, in regard to this point, however, that the value of unity just by itself is not what makes it reasonable to follow the judgment of the pope or bishop. If that were the case, that is, if that were the *only* reason offered for following the authority's judgment, then it seems to me that the submission to Church authority *would* be analogous to holding to a party line. But other considerations already make it at least a reasonable thing to prefer the pope's or bishops' judgment to my own. This consideration, it seems to me, changes what would otherwise be just a reasonable option into the thing that I really ought to do.

Two analogies will illustrate the situation here. Suppose I have written a paper and asked a friend of mine who is a very experienced writer and the editor of a reliable scholarly journal, to read it and to test for mistakes, both substantive and stylistic. And suppose my friend suggests that one of my favorite paragraphs just is not clear at all, and that it should be rewritten, even though, when I read it, it still seems clear to me. Clearly, in the large majority of cases, it would be more reasonable for me to follow the judgment of my friend the editor than my own judgment, especially since I am not an unbiased judge of what I have written. Certainly, no one would accuse me of undue servility if I chose to follow the editor's judgment rather than what seems to me to be the case just looking at it on my own. And I think a similar conclusion must be drawn with respect to following the judgment of the leaders of the Church.

Again, suppose the gas company sends a crew of workers out to an old vacant lot to dig up and repair the underground gas lines. Working from old maps, they must make several measurements and calculations in order to determine exactly where the gas lines are. And it is important for their safety that they make the right measurements and calculations. Suppose I am a member of the crew, and, having observed the measurements, I make the mathematical calculations and conclude that the gas line is in a certain spot. But the foreman, using his company-issued electronic calculator, also calculates on the basis of the measurements, and concludes that the gas line is in a different spot. Now, it seems clear that it would be more reasonable for me to place more trust in the judgment of the foreman than in my own calculations. Even though the foreman is not infallible, his calculations are a more reliable guide than my own. And the reasonable thing for me to do is to follow the more reliable guide. Similarly, the teaching of the pope on faith and morals, even when it is not *ex cathedra* and therefore infallible, is still the best guide one has in the circumstances.

Moreover, in our example, the crew of workers must be united for the sake of their common action. They can scarcely do their job well if different members are digging in different places. Similarly, unity of judgment about matters of faith is needed for common action by the Church. Finally, it is worth noting that the gas company is quite reasonable and is only requiring that its employees be reasonable when it insists that the crew follow the calculations of the foreman, since he has the electronic calculator and unity is necessary for their work. The analogy is not exact, but, similarly, it is quite reasonable for the Church to insist that those who teach in her schools, for example, follow the more reliable guide of the teaching of the leaders of the Church.

There are several cases, then, in which the most reasonable thing for me to do is to follow someone else's judgment rather than what would seem to me to be the case independently. And among those cases are my judgments concerning faith and morals, even on matters on which there is not a teaching that has been infallibly proposed (either by a definition or by a universal teaching of the bishops in communion with the pope). Concern for truth itself, along with concern for the unity of the Church – but not concern for unity independently of concern for truth – rationally justify a Catholic scholar's submission to Church authority even on teachings not infallibly proposed. Such submission is reasonable and therefore is not an instance of obscurantism.

23.

Human Life and the Primacy of Contemplation (1989)

Alice Ramos

I. The Crisis of Contemporary Man

In 1935, Edmund Husserl spoke of the crisis of the European sciences as a crisis of the European man himself. According to Husserl, Western man's inability to live up to his philosophical destiny has brought him to a crisis point, in which he finds himself literally sick. Man's sick body can be cured by the science of medicine, but for his sick soul, there is no science of the spirit. The humanistic sciences which deal with man's spirit have become blinded by naturalism and objectivism. Man's life is "not to be taken in a physiological sense but rather as signifying *purposeful living*, manifesting spiritual creativity."[1] The fact is, according to Husserl, that man's life, his very spirit, is being studied according to the methods of natural science, with the effect that nature and spirit are considered equal realities, and with the ensuing danger that the spirit is naturalized. A new mode of thought is necessary if Western man is to survive the crisis in which he finds himself. As Husserl puts it: "The crisis of European existence can end in only one of two ways: in the ruin of a Europe alienated from its rational sense of life, fallen into a barbarian hatred of spirit; or in the rebirth of Europe from the spirit of philosophy, through a heroism of reason that will definitively overcome naturalism."[2] Modern reason has failed; rationalism has collapsed due to its absorption in naturalism. Because our age wants to believe only in facts, in "realities," and because its strongest reality is science, what our age most needs then is philosophical science.[3] Rather than witness the demise

---

1 Edmund Husserl, "Philosophy and the Crisis of European Man," in *Phenomenology and the Crisis of Man,* trans. by Quentin Lauer, New York: Harper & Row, 1965, p. 150. Italics mine.

2 *Ibid.,* p. 192.

3 Husserl, "Philosophy as Rigorous Science," in edition cited, p. 145.

of Europe, Husserl launches a challenge for the renewal of Europe in the spirit of the universal science, that is, philosophy. The philosophical ideal which Husserl proposes, that thirst for knowledge and the truth inherent in the theoretical attitude in ancient Greece, is founded, of course, in the very constitution of man. Man's life is consciously teleological because he is a rational being, and his *telos* lies in the infinite – in the contemplation of the truth – for which reason man's intelligence is operatively infinite and his will is guided by moral norms.

We might say that Husserl's vision of the crisis of Europe is prophetic and indicative, to a great extent, of the crisis befalling man at the present time. It is noteworthy that exactly fifty years after Husserl had lectured on the crisis of philosophy and European man at the University of Prague, in 1985, a group of leading figures in Western thought were gathered at the Palace of Castelgandolfo presenting their opinions on the crisis of man to a sole and silent spectator: Pope John Paul II. Among the protagonists of this event was Leszek Kolakowski who, in his paper titled "The Philosophy of Modernity," referred to one of the topics of present scientific discussions: the destructive effects of secularization in Western civilization with "the apparent progressive evaporation of our religious heritage and the sad spectacle of a world without God": "a world that has forgotten God has forgotten the distinction between good and evil, has converted human life into something without meaning and has drowned it in nihilism."[4] From a philosophical perspective, Kolakowski, like Husserl, noted that the essence of modernity is rationalization. Kolakowski refers to Max Weber who understands rationalization as a process of "disenchantment" of the world, a process which in the Occidental world has led to the separation of the positive sciences from metaphysics, to an autonomous art separated from the imitation of nature, and to a morality and jurisprudence based on their own principles. It is precisely this "disenchantment" of nature which leads to a destruction of the religious image of the world and to its substitution by a profane culture.[5] Husserl's prophecy with respect to the crisis of man, to the real possibility of his falling into a "barbarian hatred of the spirit" has been fulfilled in the process of secularization, in man's attempt to deny that radical relatedness which constitutes his very being as a creature. Kolakowski's

---

4 In *Nuestro Tiempo,* Pamplona: EUNSA, October 1985, p. 112.

5 Alejandro Llano, *"Elementos para un balance de la modernidad,"* non-published lecture given at the University of Navarre in Spain, November 1985, p. 3.

consideration of the irreligious character of the world is rooted, in fact, in man's alienation from that rational sense of his life – to use Husserl's words – or, from a life that has objective meaning.

As Kolakowski rightly notes in his paper, Descartes was probably the first one responsible for a philosophical current that has gradually led to a massive secularization. In Cartesian and in subsequent rationalist philosophy, nature is stripped of its very being, of its finality, only to be explained as a great mechanism, whose functioning can be modified without any limits, in accordance with the interests of man's reason. Nature is to be dominated rather than respected and perfected, for no longer does man recognize the teleological character of nature, the inclinations proper to it. Man, therefore, imposes finalities on nature and as such dominates it. His superiority is expressed not in terms of his higher nature, but in terms of his endowment with reason – a reason which is no longer the faculty for the contemplation of nature but rather the capacity for dominion of a passive matter, deprived of its principle of operations. Now, when nature is, so to speak, denaturalized, the secularization of the world and inevitably, that of man also, is sure to follow. For as has been said, "The critique of the *anthropomorphism of nature* leads to the *naturalism of anthropos*, to conceiving man as a sophisticated piece of matter."[6] This reduction of man leads undoubtedly to the domination and manipulation of man himself. Certainly, this is one of the paradoxes of modern thought: He who is given primacy because of his reason eventually finds himself, like nature, denaturalized.

When reason liberates itself, as it were, from the natural, we are led to the great ideal of modern rationalism, that is, autonomy. In Kantian practical philosophy, for example, the action of reason proposes the ideal of a pure will, endowed with absolute autonomy, which prescribes its own laws. Man considers himself independent from the physical world and even from the political community; he freely disposes of nature, liberating himself from its exigencies and thus imposing on it the sovereignty of the interests of his reason.[7]

II. Dominion of Nature v. Self-Dominion

This active dominion on the part of man, as producer of nature and also of man himself, cannot be overly emphasized, since it is that with which we are continually confronted, especially where issues of man's life and death

6 *Ibid.,* p. 5.
7 *Ibid.,* pp. 9–11.

are concerned. Contemporary man tends to transfer the means proper to the domination of nature to himself, because as we have seen, the denaturalization of nature leads to the naturalism of man. If the actions of man become disconnected from his nature, then the moral licitude of the technological means available to him will not be questioned. When man strips himself of his very nature, then his actions are no longer perfective of himself; his goal becomes not self-protection or self-mastery – a goal indispensable to him as a human person – but rather self-realization, self-fulfillment, as if he were no more than a needy being, whose every desire had to be fulfilled.

More than twenty years ago, the encyclical *Humanae Vitae* recognized the problem with the application of the methods for the domination of nature to the domination of man himself: "Man has made stupendous progress in the domination and rational organization of the forces of nature, such that he tends to extend this domination to his own total being: to the body, to physical life, to social life and even to the laws which regulate the transmission of life . . ."[8] In his comments on this encyclical, Pope John Paul II notes: "This extension of the sphere of the means of 'the domination . . . of the forces of nature' threatens the person, for whom the method of 'self-mastery' is and remains specific. The mastery of self, in fact, corresponds to the fundamental constitution of the person: it is indeed a 'natural' method. On the contrary, the resort to 'artificial means' destroys the constitutive dimension of the person; it deprives man of the subjectivity proper to him and makes him an object of manipulation."[9] So, in proclaiming his independence, his autonomy with respect to a teleologically oriented nature, man becomes subject to arbitrariness and in effect, to the irrational. When *homo faber* substitutes for *homo sapiens*, when action takes precedence over contemplation – an action understood as the effectuation or production of the interests or ends of man's practical reason or of his will, rather than action as *praxis* that is teleologically constituted because it is proper to a given nature, then man may find himself subject to the interests or ends of his own or other men's will or sentiments, as we see in contemporary issues concerning man's life. If man himself can be dominated, as nature is through scientific and technological developments, then he easily becomes an object, a thing to be used or discarded. We have only to think of such is-

---

8 Pope Paul VI, *Humanae Vitae,* Boston: St. Paul Editions, 1968, p. 4.

9 Pope John Paul II, *Reflections on Humanae Vitae,* Boston: St. Paul Editions, 1984, p. 30

sues as contraception, abortion, *in vitro* fertilization, surrogate motherhood, genetic manipulations, and the like, where the utilitarian norm, rather than the personalist norm, prevails. The person becomes a means for the other's pleasure; the consideration of the person as an end, as a being willed for himself or herself is not taken into account; man becomes a product of technology; he is made, rather than begotten.[10] We might say that the rationalist ideal of autonomy whereby man declared his independence and became his own lawgiver has only led to the enchainment of man, that is, to the reduction of his life to self-gratification, or, as in the cases of abortion and euthanasia, to the dependence of man's life on the arbitrary decisions of other men. When the nature of man is no longer in question, when he is no longer the recipient of a nature from a higher instance than himself, then it becomes difficult, if not impossible, to speak of man's objective rights and duties.

What we have here is the opposition between the realist teleology of nature and the rationalist teleology of human reason. If nature does not have an internal, dynamic and, consequently, teleological order, then nature is not intelligible, it is not meaningful; the intelligibility and meaning of nature will thus be referred to the interests or ends of man's reason, his will, or his emotions, so that nature, or man himself, becomes no more than a product or construct of man. If, however, we hold to the teleological character of nature, then meaning is present and man's attitude will be different; it will be an attitude of admiration, of gradual intellectual penetration into the nature of each thing, into the reason for its being, so that man can respect it and let it be what it is. To hold a realist teleology of nature is, in effect, to maintain that the nature of each being is its own principle of its activities, operations which are oriented toward an end which is constitutive of that very nature. It can, therefore, be said that all beings have as their end those operations which are proper to them. If I insist on the teleological dimension of nature – on its operative character which is finalized – it is because the different levels of life are characterized by different operations, by different capacities for action. Action, in the strictest sense, as in the Aristotelian *praxis*, refers to man's well-lived life, to his own perfectioning. To live thus is to act according to the end proper to man's nature. And the end of man's

---

10 Rev. Ronald Lawler, O.F.M. Cap., Joseph M. Boyle, Jr., and William E. May, *Catholic Sexual Ethics,* Huntington, Indiana: Our Sunday Visitor, Inc., 1985, p. 175.

actions, of his life, is contemplation. Man's actions are thus aimed at beholding and possessing the truth.

Now, when referring to contraception, the present pope speaks of self-mastery as the "natural" method, proper to the person's very constitution; he is thus emphasizing that the person possesses himself and can dominate himself. Self-possession is thus necessary for self-mastery, for self-determination, in fact, for freedom. And he adds that only in so far as man possesses himself can he give himself to the other.[11] The gift of self as it is realized in the conjugal act is not merely a corporeal union; the body is expressive of the person, of femininity or masculinity. "The conjugal act 'signifies' not only love, but also potential fecundity, and for this reason cannot be deprived of its full and adequate significance by artificial interventions. In the conjugal act it is not licit to separate artificially the unitive significance from the procreative significance, because they both pertain to the intimate truth of the conjugal act. Consequently, in this case the conjugal act, *deprived of its interior truth*, by being artificially deprived of its procreative capacity, *ceases* also *to be an act of love*."[12] Love unites persons, and in the conjugal act, when recourse is made to artificial birth control, that union is then not open to life; the truth of the act is thus not realized. "If this truth is not present, we cannot speak of the truth of self-mastery, nor of the truth of the reciprocal gift and of the reciprocal acceptance of self on the part of the person."[13] What John Paul II insists upon is that the body expresses more than just sexual reactivity, that it expresses the person in his or her masculinity or femininity, and thus in his or her fecundity.[14] To deny this is to deny the language of the body, its signifying character, and the truth of the person. And to act in this way constitutes a separation from man's end; the denial of the truth in man's acts cannot therefore lead to his possession of the truth.

In this regard, a contemporary philosophical anthropologist notes that if the person is fecundity-endowed with the creative capacity of giving himself freely, then to exist in a denial of that fecundity is to exist in the denial of being a person. The same anthropologist quotes Plato's definition of love as the desire to engender in beauty according to the body and the soul. If the person exists denying his fecundity, it is because of the absence of beauty,

---

11 Pope John Paul II, *Reflections on Humanae Vitae*, pp. 32–33.
12 *Ibid.*, p. 33. Italics mine.
13 *Ibid.*, p. 34.
14 *Ibid.*, p. 32.

which in Plato, is actually the absence of the divinity.[15] This, to my mind, is indicative of what Kolakowski calls "the sad spectacle of a world without God" (see note 4).

When the conjugal act is deprived of its full significance, of its interior truth, then the persons themselves are not perfected, since they act contrary to the truth. Now, in speaking of "responsible parenthood," *Humanae Vitae*, as well as John Paul II's comments on this encyclical, emphasize the knowledge and respect which should be had for the biological laws inscribed in the person's very being, the dominion which reason and will have to exercise over the passions, and the decision by which responsible parenthood is exercised. The practice of regulating birth by natural means demands a struggle in self-dominion. And "the observance of periodic continence is the form of self-mastery, whereby is manifested 'the purity of the married couples.'"[16] John Paul II points out that purity is life according to the spirit; to practice purity is to read the language of the body and to observe the laws of nature, to respect nature.[17] It is to adopt an attitude and to practice a behavior in conformity with man's rational nature, for to live virtuously demands the application of man's intelligence and free will and thus constitutes moral living – life in accordance with man's nature, with what he is, with the truth of his being. The difficulties involved in this right moral behavior require the presence of love, a love which John Paul II defines as "strength," that is, a capacity of the human spirit, which is of a theological and moral character. Love is "the strength that is given to man to participate in the love with which God Himself loves in the mystery of the creation and of the redemption." It is love "which takes delight in the truth."[18] This love, together with chastity which expresses self-mastery, is an intelligent love and such a love is free, unlike the love of concupiscence.[19] This rational love permits the married couple to read the language of the body, so as to realize and safeguard the interior truth of the conjugal act and thus bring about

---

15 Jacinto Choza, "Persona y Fecundidad," in *La Supresion del Pudor*, Pamplona: EUNSA, 1980, pp. 112–13.

16 Pope John Paul II, *Reflections on Humanae Vitae*, p. 37.

17 *Ibid.*, pp. 39–40.

18 *Ibid.*, p. 55.

19 Robert Spaemann, "Lo Natural y lo Racional," in book of same title trans. by D. Innerarity & J. Olmo, Madrid: Rialp, 1989, pp. 116–17. Cf. Kenneth L. Schmitz, *The Gift: Creation*, Milwaukee: Marquette University Press, 1982, pp. 84–86.

the good and perfect themselves. Only thus can the person's life be a true gift of self, and the person be recognized as a being willed for himself and not be reduced to a means.

III. The "Hermeneutics of the Gift"

For the person to give himself, he must understand that his life, that his very being is a gift. No contemporary thinker has done more to further this understanding of human life than Pope John Paul II. And together with this notion of the gift, frequent references are made to the fact that "the glory of God is the living man," and there is also added, "yet man's life is the vision of God."[20] To live in the spirit of giving is to exercise intelligent love; it is to see as God sees and thus to participate in His vision of creation. It is, in effect, to live the ideal of contemplation, rather than the modernist ideal of spontaneous action.

In his theology of the body, which is grounded in a metaphysics of the truth of created being, John Paul II develops what he terms an "adequate anthropology" in order to establish the fundamental truth about man. When it is said that man has been created in the image of God, reference is made to man's spiritual operations, through which he most properly mirrors God. The pope refers not only to this aspect, but also to the fact that in man's very body is found the image of God; man, in his *dual* dimension of male and female, bears from the very "beginning" the divine image imprinted on his body; he states: "Man and woman constitute, as it were, two different ways of the human 'being a body' in the unity of the image."[21] Now, in order to better understand and interpret how man is related to the Creator, John Paul II develops a "hermeneutics of the gift"; the dimension of the gift is at the very heart of creation. When God creates, by calling into existence from nothingness, He creates not out of need, but because of love. So, when God beholds what He has created, He sees that it is good: Only love gives a beginning to the good and delights in the good. Creation, therefore, in its most radical and fundamental meaning, is a gift, a giving in which the gift comes into being precisely from nothingness. The concept of giving does not refer here to nothingness, but rather indicates the one who gives and the one who receives the gift, and also refers to the relationship that is established be-

---

20 Pope John Paul II, *Dominum et Vivificantem*, Boston: St. Paul Editions, 1986, p. 119.

21 Pope John Paul II, *Original Unity of Man and Woman*, Boston: St. Paul Editions, 1981, p. 101.

tween them.[22] This relationship emerges at the very moment of the creation of man: "God created man in his own image, in the image of God he created him" (Genesis 1:27). The very term "image" indicates a relation. Within the whole account of the origins of the world, the creation of man is the culminating point: Everything that is made before man is made *for man*. The only creature that is willed for its own sake is man, everything else is ordered to and for man. "Creation is a gift, because there appears in it man who, as the 'image of God,' is capable of understanding the very meaning of gift in the call from nothingness to existence. And he is capable of answering the Creator with the language of this understanding."[23] Man appears then in creation as the one who received the world as a gift, and it can also be added that the world received man as a gift.[24] For the perfection of the universe, there was need of intellectual beings, who would respond to the Creator with the language of the gift, acting as intelligent and free beings, and returning, giving back, in a sense, all that they had received to the Creator. But the real culminating point in the whole account of Genesis, according to John Paul II, is the receiving of the other as a gift: Man-male receives the female as a gift.

An analysis of the beginning of man shows how man is conscious of being alone through his very body: He is a body among other bodies, but he is separated from these bodies in that he is a person, for the body of man expresses who he is. Man is an intellectual being who knows that no other being is similar to him; his knowledge of who he is is deduced from the knowledge of what he is not. In addition, man experiences that he is a free being, capable of determining himself: that "living being" who is man is also liable to non-existence. Man is, therefore, distinct from other beings: Having been created in the image of God, man is related to God, and he is alone in this. The distinction and relatedness of man accounts for the transcendence peculiar to the person; only a being like himself can complement him. Consequently, it can be said that man is alone not only because he is unlike other beings around him, but especially because there is no other being like him. So, the woman is created like him, on the basis of the same humanity; the male and the female are both physically and personally complementary. They have the same human nature, and yet are two distinct corporeal and personal ways of being. With the help of the woman, man as

22 *Ibid.*, pp. 103–4.
23 *Ibid.*, p. 104.
24 *Ibid.*

male recognizes his own humanity. We have here the existence of the person for the person; from the very beginning of man, he is made to live in communion with the other.

Now, man's awareness of himself, of his own humanity, is carried out through a perception of the world which is brought about directly by means of the body: man discovers his humanity through an "exterior" perception, which is expressed by means of physical nakedness. To this "exterior" perception corresponds the interior participation in the vision of the Creator Himself: When God created everything, He saw that it was all good. The male and the female participate in this vision, for which reason their nakedness could not originally be a source of shame. It is precisely because they share in God's vision of the world that they can be a gift one for the other. All that is created is *given* through love, and it is this love, as was previously stated, which gives rise to the good. The naked body, in its masculinity and femininity, seen then as good, as a gift, brings about that communion of persons, whereby each becomes a gift for the other. In being called to existence, man is actually being called to give; for this reason, we may say that man discovers himself only in a sincere giving of himself.[25]

As John Paul observes, the nuptial meaning of the body – that gift of self – is followed by an experience which impedes the person from giving himself freely. Once shame is experienced, the vision of the other is distorted because it no longer participates in the original vision of the mystery of creation. The man and the woman cease to enjoy the whole truth concerning the creation of man, that is, that man is the only creature willed for his own sake and that he finds himself only in self-giving.

Prior to the introduction of sin in the world, the man and the woman were able to give themselves precisely because they were free from shame, because they were masters of themselves, that is, in control of themselves. It is, though, in effect, this freedom which makes possible the nuptial meaning of the body. The human body reveals a value which surpasses the physical level of sexuality: The other, in his naked body, is accepted as willed for himself, as a person loved, meant to enter into relationship with the other, as the very image of God. In the state of original innocence, shame had no place, for the man-male accepted the other as a gift, as a result of God's creative love. Man's original innocence, in which he was able to correspond to the language of the gift, was founded in his participation in God's own inte-

---

25 *Ibid.,* p. 115.

rior life, in His very holiness.[26] The man and the woman, in their reciprocal gift of each other, in the state of the grace of original innocence, became a sign of the mystery of divine life, which is the mystery of truth and love.[27]

Man not only has his source in holiness, but is also created for holiness, for the gift of his person, and it is this giving of the person which characterizes the very life of the Divine Persons. From the beginning of man, from the state of original innocence, it can be deduced that man in his entire being – both body and soul – is called to live.

On the other hand, the loss of original innocence – the state of sin – stripped man of participation in the gift; man is alienated from that creative love which had given rise to the gift. He thus loses the original certainty which was born in the human body itself of being the image of God. The body ceases here to draw upon the power of the spirit, and it is precisely this power of the spirit which raised man to the level of image of God. The body then becomes a center of resistance to the spirit and threatens the very unity of the man-person.[28] There arises an interior imbalance in man, which is manifested through immanent shame. Man is ashamed of his body because of lust, which is a new way of looking at the other. No longer does man participate in God's vision, in His knowledge of things, which is to see that all is good; man looks at the woman in a different way, a look which no longer corresponds to the original vision of the world, to its original truth. There is here no freedom in giving, since concupiscence reduces man's self-control. If man does not possess self-mastery, then he cannot give himself freely. The body becomes, therefore, an object of lust, an object to be appropriated. We have then the loss of the nuptial meaning of the body.

Man is, nonetheless, called to the truth and to love, for such is his beginning; he is called to self-control, to the mastery of his instincts, for his origin is the peaceful gaze of God's creative love. The Creator "has written in the heart of both (the male and the female) the gift of communion, that is, the mysterious reality of His image and likeness."[29] The heart is, in effect, called to be pure, and for John Paul II, as we have already noted, to live purity means to live a life according to the Spirit. It means to free oneself from selfishness so as to free oneself for a sincere giving of self. However, John

---

26 *Ibid.,* p. 123.

27 *Ibid.,* pp. 143–44.

28 Pope John Paul II, *Blessed Are The Pure of Heart,* Boston: St. Paul Editions, 1983, pp. 50–51.

29 *Ibid.,* p. 195.

Paul II does not advocate a return to the state of original innocence, for the truth about historical man is that he also sinned and was redeemed. Redemption is also redemption of the body. According to the Pauline doctrine of the body, it is not merely the human spirit which accounts for the dignity of the human body, but more importantly the indwelling of the Holy Spirit in the soul and body of man. "The fruit of the redemption is, in fact, the Holy Spirit, who dwells in man and in his body as a temple. In this Gift, which sanctifies every man, the Christian receives himself again as a gift from God. And this new, double gift is binding."[30] Man's body is therefore, as it were, not his own. "The redemption of the body involves the institution, in Christ and through Christ, of a new measure of the holiness of the body."[31] Man is "the subject of holiness,"[32] initiated from and destined for holiness. In order thus to become aware of the value of his body, freed through redemption from the bonds of sin, man, his very heart, must open itself to purity, that is, to life according to the Spirit. What we see here, in effect, is a new understanding of man's life.

Finally, if we introduce the eschatological dimension of the redemption of the body, the fact that the body itself will resurrect, we enter into the very fullness of humanity. In the resurrection of the body, there is, we might say, a spiritualization of the body; the body is glorious, it cannot die; it is incorruptible, perfect; for the resurrection there is a new submission of the body to the Spirit; there is a divinization of humanity, for man, in his body and soul, is united to the vision of God. Man will experience there the perfection of communion, and as a result, the perfection of his own subjectivity. God gives Himself, and man gives himself fully. In this full participation in the life of God, man discovers himself. He has been called to communion of persons, and he can only know himself fully in this way.[33] This call constitutes an essential truth about man. We see then that man's life, from its beginning to its end, is meant to be lived in the gift of self, in communion of persons, in the vision of God, which is the contemplative mode proper to man, in the contemplation of Truth and Love.[34]

---

30 *Ibid.*, p. 244.

31 *Ibid.*, p. 245

32 *Ibid.*, p. 252.

33 Pope John Paul II, *The Theology of Marriage and Celibacy*, Boston: St. Paul Editions, 1986, pp. 41–43.

34 This communion of persons is made manifest in marriage and procreation. The emphasis here is on the duality of man, but since man is also "alone"

As is evident, the interpretation given here of man's life is radically different from that "barbarian hatred of the spirit" which characterizes much of contemporary society. Life according to reason, according to the Spirit, is what is most appropriate for man; such a life affirms the primacy of contemplation, for which man's life is meant.[35]

---

before God, there also are cases in which man and woman will choose virginity, celibacy. They then become a sign of the truth of man, of Christ. Through this continence, which is understood for the sake of the kingdom, man fulfills himself by becoming a "true gift to others."

35 For a more complete study of the third part of this paper, see my article, "Foundations for a Christian Anthropology, " in *Anthropotes,* V/2 (1989), pp. 225–57.

24.

A Historical Perspective on Evangelization in the United States (1990)

Rev. Marvin R. O'Connell

Jonathan Swift, you may recall, was the dean of St. Patrick's, the Anglican cathedral in Dublin, at the beginning of the eighteenth century. He was a waspish man, by all accounts, one who did not suffer fools or Tories gladly, and many a politician and ecclesiastic – largely a distinction without a difference in his time as, unhappily, in ours – felt the sharp edge of his tongue or his pen. His strong literary suit was satire, in an age of great satirists, and he would no doubt have been chagrined had he lived long enough to have witnessed one of his most acidic treatises, *Gulliver's Travels*, be considered merely a fairy tale for children. Swift, almost alone among the Irish Protestant ascendancy of penal times, earned the respect and affection of the masses of persecuted Irish Catholics, for whom he had the courage to act as advocate, not only in his writings but in his personal protestations at Dublin Castle and even at the court of St. James's itself. One of the books he wrote in this continuing battle against bigotry and cruelty was a satire called *A Modest Proposal for the Preventing the Children of Poor People from Being a Burden to their Parents or the Country*, in which he argued that the solution for the hunger and deprivation endured by the people of Ireland was the fattening and consequent eating of Irish babies.

An outrageous suggestion, to be sure, even from a satirist. But let me put before you an outrageous suggestion of my own, a modest proposal of my own. And let me say from the start that, unlike Swift, I do not mean to advance it in a satirical way. My modest proposal is that we American Catholics return to our ghetto. To the extent that the Catholic left – by which I mean that clique of prelates who presently dominate the National Conference of Catholic Bishops; the partisan bureaucracy of the United States Catholic Conference; the ideologues who have captured our once respectable learned societies and journals; the bland and fearful technocrats who govern most of our colleges and universities – to the extent, I say, that the Catholic left would pay the slightest attention to such a proposal made at a gathering like this one – doubtful in the extreme – the reaction would be one of mock horror or, from the slightly more intelligent, a smug "I told you so." The latter assessment would be elaborated – to the limited degree, of course, that Bishop X, Professor Y, or President Zed were capable of sustained argument, a dubious proposition in itself – something akin to this: You people wonder why we have marginalized you, why we pay no attention to you, why we label you "fundamentalists" and thus equate you with the likes of Jim Bakker and Jimmy Swaggert, why we keep you away from the decision-making process at every level, why we ignore your books and, yes, make fun of your conferences. You wonder why. Well, the reason is clear: You have a ghetto-mentality, you are not open, you are too ultramontane, you are insensitive, you are inflexible, you cannot adjust to the temper of the modern mind, you doubtless need counseling, preferably by an ex-priest or by a nun who wears an unfashionable mu-mu and too much eye-shadow.

Since this is the kind of reaction my modest proposal would no doubt receive from the ecclesiastical powers-that-be, it is incumbent upon me to explain what I mean with great care. Let me try to do so by pointing to, in a highly schematic form, the historical roots we share with those who tyrannize over us, in order to suggest that a return to the ghetto may be the only realistic course open to the American Catholic community. While Shakespeare posited seven ages of man, I would posit five ages of the Catholic Church in the United States: the age of survival, of expansion, of assimilation, of consolidation, and, finally, in our own day, of survival once again. Everything, they say, that goes around, comes around. I intend no original dissertation here, nothing more pretentious than a survey of our shared past and of the modes of evangelization dictated by the varying imperatives of that past.

The first age, I say, was the age of survival, begun with Lord Baltimore's colony in Maryland, where, it was hoped, Catholics might find toleration for their religion which was brutally denied them in England. In exchange they offered toleration to others, only to discover – as Mary Queen of Scots had discovered when she tried to find a *modus vivendi* with John Knox – that British hatred of popery was too deep and pervasive to admit of any form of accommodation: As soon as Protestant numbers in Maryland made it feasible, Catholics there were deprived of all civil rights, as was already the case in the other colonies. The old faith, however, though it cannot be said to have flourished along the Maryland shore, did manage to survive there, adapting to its own needs the social model of the Catholics living under the penal laws in England.

A handful of wealthy families, like the Carrolls and the Spaldings, imitated their English counterparts – the Talbots, the Vauxes, the Petres – by sealing themselves and their tenants off from the rest of society, depending – much as the Amish do today – on their ability to sustain themselves in economic independence, and cultivating a variety of Catholic practice as understated and unobtrusive as possible.

This latter characteristic should by no means be considered blameworthy in these "Old Catholics" of America, as we might label them; they lived, after all, on the sword's edge, never entirely safe from overt persecution. But it must be observed also that these Marylanders, like their cousins in England, had never been allowed to experience the fruit of that great moral, intellectual, and spiritual revival of Catholicism we call the Counter Reformation. They knew nothing of the Oratory or of Saint-Sulpice, nothing of the Spanish mystics or of the revival of Thomism, nothing of Vincent de Paul and the Sisters of Charity, or of Pascal, or of Alphonsus Liguori, or of Daniel Papebroch. English-speaking Catholics, on either side of the Atlantic, remained a proscribed and endangered minority, heroic indeed, but also narrow, introspective, circumscribed by the realization that only the regard of their countrymen for the sacredness of private-property – a spiritual principle Albion held dearer than any other – saved them from obliteration.

In the kind of situation that prevailed among Maryland Catholics, cultural in-breeding was as inevitable as intermarriage. Their community assumed the character of its dominant families, who came to regard themselves, also inevitably, as the measure of all things Catholic. Their brave and steadfast adherence to the faith has surely earned them our plaudits, though their aristocratic hubris quickly rendered them irrelevant once other than English immigrants had arrived in any numbers. Yet the hubris, sometimes absurdly, lingered: One of their descendants was John Lancaster Spalding – note the middle name – the celebrated first bishop of Peoria, who always maintained that he was by blood a Plantagenet, sprung in a direct line from King Henry II.

The able Jesuits, who were the younger sons of the Catholic squires and who, after a spell of education in Italy or France, came back to Maryland to minister to them, were in essence domestic chaplains. Among them was John Carroll, cousin of that Charles Carroll of Carrollton who signed the

Declaration of Independence. But while John was still in Europe the Society of Jesus was suppressed, and so he returned to Maryland a secular priest and, after the revolution, was selected first bishop and then archbishop of Baltimore. Given the social realities governing the tiny Catholic minority, in the new United States – scarcely 25,000 souls, less than one percent of the population – the appointment to this post of a scion of the Maryland squirearchy was surely sensible. So it was that Carroll became the father of the American episcopate and, more immediately, the presider over the beginnings of the age of American Catholic expansion.

You may think "presider" a rather bland word, and so it is, but I use it purposely. Nothing in John Carroll's antecedents or training led him to adopt the ways of a fiery missionary. Nor was he ever such. Indeed, he had enough trouble simply holding together the little pockets of Catholics strung along the Atlantic seaboard. But neither Carroll's temperament nor his Enlightenment proclivities weigh much in the balance when compared to his status as a successor of the apostles present on these shores. As St. Ignatius of Antioch had testified 1,700 years earlier, the Church is where the bishop is; and so, from the moment when John Carroll fixed the miter on his head, the Church stood in the United States of America as proud and as complete as the Church did anywhere in the world.

The expansion of Catholicism over which Carroll first presided was very modest and, no doubt, of a kind not always in tune with his aristocratic sensibilities. Native converts were few – Elizabeth Seton and Rose Hawthorne did not set any particular precedents. But nevertheless the numbers of Catholics grew steadily, if not spectacularly, by reason of immigration. The new land, blessed with its remarkable constitution and its bill of rights, bright with the promise of economic opportunity, attracted peoples dissatisfied with the European old world, including Catholics who, thanks to the first amendment, had no hostile establishment to fear any more. Prejudice they had indeed to endure, for many generations yet to come. But prejudice, however distasteful and ignoble, is a far cry from tar-and-feathers or a knock on the door in the middle of the night.

The expansion of the nation *ipso facto* involved the expansion of Catholicism. The purchase of Louisiana and Florida, and, later, the conquest of the Spanish southwest and California, brought into the American Catholic community the venerable churches of St. Augustine and New Orleans, St. Louis and Santa Fe and Los Angeles, and with them a zestful and healthy new Latin flavor. And meanwhile, as the march of manifest destiny brought ever-increasing crowds of settlers across the Appalachians into the rich valleys of the Ohio and the Tennessee and finally to the banks of the Mississippi itself, the Catholics came with them: English and French at first, then, more and more, the Irish and Germans.

To be sure, many of the immigrants stayed in the great eastern cities, presenting to the new bishoprics established there immense institutional challenges. But many more pushed into Ohio and Kentucky and Michigan, and in those frontier places the difficulties were, if anything, more formidable. A late esteemed colleague of mine wrote a book about all this which he called, *Cathedrals in the Wilderness*. An apt title indeed, for long after John Carroll had departed the scene his episcopal successors labored in an America he had never dreamed of; and long after the rather effete Maryland Catholicism had been swept aside by the tide of events, its rough, bustling, lower-class, egalitarian successor – from Boston to Erie, from Mobile to Cincinnati to Detroit – had taken its place.

The Civil War is the great watershed in our national history, and that cataclysmic and searing experience marks also the divide between my age of expansion and age of assimilation. The division, however, was by no means a rigid one, for the expansion of Catholicism, despite the Yankee bigotry exhibited in the brief but vicious nativism of the Know-nothing movement, continued apace with the huge increase, after the war, of immigration. Nor was there any significant abatement for the next fifty years. Hordes of indigent Irish, fleeing the ravages of the Great Famine, were followed by Italians, Poles, more Germans, Hungarians, Czechs, Croatians. By 1889, a century after John Carroll had begun his episcopate, there were 8,000,000 Catholics in the United States, sixty bishops, thousands of churches and schools, hospitals, and foundling homes.

During these tumultuous decades evangelization, broadly understood, meant, first of all, providing an ecclesial home for these mostly poor and uneducated masses, speaking a babel of tongues and clinging to the various customs they had brought with them from the old country. An ecclesial home: that is, a building, however humble and simple, where the eternal sacrifice of calvary might be fittingly celebrated; a schoolroom, however cramped and even wretched, where an immigrant child might learn about his faith without being ridiculed and proselytized by the still dominant Protestant culture.

It has become fashionable in our own day for the fastidious descendants of those immigrants to deride the so-called brick-and-mortar preoccupa-

tions of those days. But such negative criticism betrays remarkable ignorance as well as a good deal of snobbishness. Perhaps the greatest boast of
the American church during the age of assimilation is precisely its achievement, won at terrible cost, of providing for itself a physical structure: a
place to go to Mass, a place to go to school, a place, not too far away, where
the sisters would take care of you if you were sick or old or achingly alone.
It can never be said too often: ours is an incarnational religion. We are neither Docetists nor Quakers nor Christian scientists nor any other species of
spiritualists. We depend, humanly speaking, upon the predictable cycle of
feast and fast; we partake in the ordinary rhythms of human life; we divinize
– if I may put it so – the rites of passage; we incorporate into our worship all
human moods and all human emotions, just as our most sacred rituals rest
upon the use of simple physical things – a flagon of water, a jug of oil, a
crust of bread. We repudiate with equal vigor foolish Pelagian optimism
and the monstrous conceit of Lutheran and Calvinist predestination.

So it is with sacred space: we cannot do without places, places that are
ours. The historical record is very clear: at the time of the Reformation,
when for a while it seemed that the new Protestant evangel would sweep everything before it, the Catholic faith survived only where the traditional
structure survived, however deformed that structure may have been by the
abuses of the time. In Poland and Bavaria and Hungary Catholicism successfully rebounded from the early Protestant assaults, because in those
countries the structure of parish and convent and school was maintained; in
England and Holland, by contrast, Catholicism suffocated and died during
the sixteenth century, because the persecutors succeeded in depriving it of
its sacred space.

Three hundred years later, during the nineteenth century, that lesson
apparently had been forgotten in the European Catholic heartland, as it
passed through profound demographic changes. Indeed, the old continent,
in the grips of a population explosion, was experiencing something parallel
to the influx of alien peoples into the United States, and that was the vast
shift of the populace from the countryside to the teeming concentrations of
people in the new industrial centers. The lamentable failure of the Catholic
hierarchies to provide physical facilities for these men and women, and
their children, who had left their village church and its embracing culture
behind them, was by no means the least important reason the European
working classes were lost to the church, and remain lost to this day.

American Catholic leadership did not make this mistake, for which we must be eternally grateful. But this passion, largely realized, of immigrant Catholics in the United States to provide themselves with a solid, palpable, permanent ecclesial home brought with it another, very poignant, aspiration. Polish and Irish and Italian Catholics wanted themselves and their institutions to belong to the larger American society, and – perhaps even more important to them – to be *recognized* as belonging. For some of them – notably Archbishop John Ireland of St. Paul and his allies in the so-called Americanist party – this desire became almost an obsession. They pointed to the admirable American political and economic institutions which gave poor Catholics a chance to practice their religion unhindered, even as they enjoyed the opportunity to make a decent living. Contrast our situation, they argued cogently, with that of our co-religionists in the old countries of Europe, where almost universally the salvific work of the church was inhibited by hostile governments, where Catholic schools were shut down and religious orders disbanded and, in Germany, bishops imprisoned, where even the pope was cabined up inside the leonine walls, a self-proclaimed "prisoner of the Vatican."

No such enormities occurred in the land of the free and the home of the brave, where, besides, civic virtues like sobriety, self-reliance, tolerance, industriousness, and delayed gratification were duly honored and rewarded. Indeed, so impressed were the more advanced Catholic Americanists that they proposed the ecclesial structure arrived at in the United States as the model to be adopted by the universal church.

Thus did the age of expansion evolve into the age of assimilation. There were difficulties, to be sure, not least the lingering distaste for and suspicion of popery within the overall still nominal Protestant society. Nor could one always assert unequivocal approval of America during the aptly nicknamed "Gilded Age," during the time of the "Robber Barons" and of the Trusts, during the time of seemingly endless industrial violence in the cities and similar outbreaks in frustration across the countryside, as well as the signs of a crude and aggressive imperialism marked by the irrational determination to go to war with Spain.

Witnesses as they were to these events, it is to the credit of the most enthusiastic Americanists that they qualified their call for assimilation into the American community by insisting upon a very important condition. "It is true," John Ireland proclaimed in a famous speech delivered in Baltimore in 1888, "the choicest field which providence offers in the world today to the occupancy of the Church is this republic, and she welcomes with delight the signs of the times that indicate a glorious future for her beneath the starry banner. But " – and here we must pay special attention – " it is true also that the surest safeguards for her own life and prosperity the [American] republic will find in the teachings of the Catholic Church, and the more America acknowledges those teachings the more durable will [those] institutions be made."

A large measure of the assimilation of immigrant Catholics into American culture was, of course, made inevitable by the simple passage of time. Prelates like Ireland and Michael Augustine Corrigan of New York quarreled indecorously for a generation over the *pace* of that amalgamation, but the process went relentlessly forward without, in the end, being much affected by their feuding. The children of the immigrants spoke English and played baseball and joined labor unions, and not a few of them sailed off with "Black Jack" Pershing to fight in France in 1917. Then, after the war, restrictive legislation reduced the flow of immigration from Europe to a trickle. The age of consolidation for American Catholics had come.

I speak now of an era in which I myself grew up and which, therefore, I may be tempted to romanticize as "the good old days." This is a temptation that must be stoutly resisted, all the more so because historical memory is so easily confused with nostalgia. But certain generalizations, I think can be safely made without the intrusion of any sentimentality. The five decades or so between the first world war and the Second Council of the Vatican witnessed to a degree the realization of the hopes of the Americanists. Catholics assumed an ever more comfortable place in American life, and clearly came to be accepted as partners in the national scheme of things. Not equal partners, to be sure; not in the board rooms of the great corporations, nor in the smart country clubs, nor in the academic establishment – remember the shrewd aphorism that "anti-Catholicism is the anti-Semitism of the intellectuals"! – nor in the arena of national politics, of which the presidential campaign of 1928 remains a sour symbol. Nevertheless, Catholics, a solid twenty percent of the population (and much higher than that outside the deep south and inside the big cities) exercised a real influence within the larger American society, influence felt particularly within the labor movement, in urban youth work, and in mildly leftish programs of social amelioration. If the whole truth be told, the aching desire of Catholics for acceptance was often expressed in trivial ways, like Notre Dame football or the success of Catholic film stars – I remember how my sixth grade teacher, Sister Kathleen, was bursting with pride as she told us how a very young

Gregory Peck, by reason of his knowledge of some obscure rubrical details, had won the role of the priest in the movie version of A. J. Cronin's *The Keys of the Kingdom.* "Give that man," Sister Kathleen quoted the producer as saying "give that man a collar, a cassock, and a contract."

What strikes me as particularly remarkable about that period of Catholic consolidation was the perhaps grudging but nevertheless genuine and widespread admiration for the Catholic community's adherence to certain ethical standards – especially sexual and familial ones – which other Americans, most of them by then cut off from any seriously dogmatic religion, vaguely regretted to see slipping away. There was as well in the public consciousness enormous respect for the priesthood and the religious life, and particularly for the various Catholic sisterhoods. The sacrifices cheerfully borne by the teaching and nursing nuns – and by their cloistered sisters as well – were no doubt only partially understood by non-Catholic Americans – and indeed the popular depiction of these women, by the likes of Ingrid Bergman and Loretta Young, was often embarrassingly mawkish – yet admiration for them was universal, so much so that the savage attacks and the snide caricatures directed against the nuns of the last generation – a staple now of stage, screen, and nightclub comedy – shocks an old fogie like me as little else can.

One characteristic of this age of consolidation, as I have dubbed it, appears to me to explain its ethos and, perhaps, much of its success. The Americanists' dream of the integration of Catholics into secular society was fulfilled only partially. American habits of daily life, American ideals, American civic and economic values: all these Catholics embraced as ardently as any other group. Indeed, when America went to war, Catholics rallied to the grand old flag perhaps even more ardently than others. Even so, the Catholic community, taking advantage of the genius of the American dream, continued in many respects to stand aloof from the majority, continued to insist on making its contribution to American life, not by merging into some common secular consensus, but by asserting, freely and responsibly, its own uniqueness. Let me, for lack of a more satisfactory term, label this, analogously, a kind of federalism. Catholics of my vintage vigorously denied that their differences from the secular mainstream – moral and ideological differences of the greatest moment – denied that such differences somehow made them less American. Quite to the contrary. What is America, they asked more than rhetorically, if not a vast concourse of peoples, sprung from every race and clime, and representing divergent points of view, who have entered a constitutional compact to live in harmony and mutual respect with each other? Federalism is an American ideal, they might have argued, that goes beyond the merely political arrangement between the states and the central government. *Vivent les différences*!

This conviction took on its most concrete expression in one issue, or perhaps I should say in one institution: the Catholic school. Catholics of the age of consolidation stubbornly defended the principle that the Church should be directly involved in the education of their children. In doing so they were following the mandate laid down in 1888 by the fathers of the third plenary council of Baltimore, who decreed that every parish must have its own school. This ideal proved, of course, physically impossible of complete fulfillment, but the ideal remained in place, and by the eve of the Second Council of the Vatican there were millions of children enrolled in parochial grammar and secondary schools, as well as an elaborate catechetical apparatus to service those who, for whatever reason, could not attend them. Add to this remarkable system more than five hundred Catholic colleges and universities, and you have some quantitative measure of what a cohesive and idealistic Catholic community could achieve.

But here was a matter upon which the otherwise tolerant secular majority took continuing umbrage. It may have been because, of all its accomplishments, the American citizenry was proudest, understandably so, of the establishment of a system of free, compulsory, universal, non-sectarian education. The existence of a lively rival to the romanticized little red school house seemed to most Americans to be a kind of reproach, and it certainly was an irritant. So, unlike every other developed nation, the United States has consistently refused to offer support for the confessional schools to be found within its borders – which has meant, with few exceptions, Catholic schools. On this crucial question, however much accommodation there may have been on other, less sensitive fronts, the twain between the secular majority and the Catholic minority did not meet. Consolidation and federalism for American Catholics involved the maintenance, at enormous sacrifice, of their own schools. And their pride rightly paralleled that taken by their secular neighbors in the public schools: never in the 2,000-year history of the Church has any group of Catholics anywhere created anything approaching the educational system American Catholics built and supported during the age of consolidation.

And it is all gone now, whistling down the wind, or practically so. Even the most affluent parishes have difficulty keeping a school open now, and, except for a handful, Catholic colleges and universities, as they scramble to become as comprehensively mediocre as most of their secular counterparts, have ceased to stand for anything distinctive. We American Catholics have arrived at the fifth age in our collective history, another age of survival. We who are proud to call ourselves Catholics scholars naturally focus our attention upon the collapse of our institutions of learning, and, to tell the truth, upon the very shriveling up of learning itself within our community. Can anything be more deplorable than the state of the science of theology in this American place and time, when, for example, Matthew Fox and his coven of witches are taken seriously? Can anyone estimate the long-term damage being done at this very moment by the pop-psychologists and pop-sociologists – the real savants of this dreary age – who edit our journals, control our seminaries and novitiates, and teach our children that "values," undefined and indeed undefinable, are to be preferred to virtues?

But it is not only within the limited parameters of the intellectual life that we find plentiful evidence of decay. Let me cite some instances quite at random.

The liturgical renewal, which held such promise on the eve of the council, has degenerated in many places into idiosyncracy and irrelevance and, sometimes, into a vulgarity bordering on blasphemy. All too often people who simply want to pray the mass are afflicted with the silly self-aggrandizing of the preening priest, for whom eye-contact with the front pew is more important than the meaning of the memorial of Christ's passion that he is celebrating. Preaching, which was not very good before, is even worse now due to that same kind of self-indulgence and, of course, due also to the woeful level of training offered by most seminaries.

The scandal of the Catholic divorce mills continues unabated. An officer of an archdiocesan tribunal told me not long ago that he and his colleagues are now convinced that no marriage is valid and binding, because nobody is mature enough to make a permanent commitment. I dare say his opinion was shaped to some degree by the fact that he was in the process of deserting his wife of thirty-six years, the mother of his six children (themselves all married in Catholic ceremonies, presumably invalidly), because he had finally found true love in the person of Patty, a woman twenty-five years his junior, whom he was – you guessed it – "counseling" due to her own troubled marriage. When confronted recently by a five-year-old granddaughter who asked, "Why do you make mommy and grandma cry?," he replied, "Honey, God sent Patty to me, to make up for all the unhappiness I've had in my life." Now I need hardly say that lust in old men is hardly a novelty; witness Susannah and the elders, as recorded in the book of Daniel. What does seem to me to be novel in this instance – but what has become unhappily commonplace in our second age of survival – is that people who no longer want to abide by the Catholic moral code or to accept Catholic dogmatic teaching are not content to go their way and do their thing. Instead they seek, indeed they demand, your approval and mine, and the sanction of the Church. The same unsavory sanctimoniousness of course marks the conduct of many men who have defected from the priesthood.

The failure of our leadership to face straightforwardly the issue of feminism, and specifically the question of women's ordination, presents us with a crisis of another kind. To give him credit, the archbishop of Milwaukee has put his sensitive political finger on the central problem: the relation between decision-making within the church and the sacrament of orders. It is a question of power. But by that very fact it is also a question of hormones. It remains, however much our anointed leaders wish it were otherwise, a question of sexuality. Blurring that reality serves no purpose. Nor does blaming the present pope, as so many American bishops do in hopes that the militant feminists will leave them, the bishops, alone. Another archbishop has said publicly that no resolution of the problem of women's ordination – by which of course he means surrender to the agenda of the most extreme feminists – will be possible during the present pontificate. By this he implies that no benighted Pole could be expected to accede to women's legitimate claims but that in the future a more enlightened occupant of the throne of St. Peter will put things right. He might as well have said, *Après moi, le déluge*!

Why could he not say that Jesus chose only males as the vehicles for the transmission of his revelation to the world, not simply as a matter of the acculturation, long since passed away, of the first century, but because of the physiological and emotional differences between the sexes of which we have more than sufficient experience and which in any case have been revealed to us in the Scriptures. Let us not beat about the bush; sexual equality, as affirmed in the most ancient revelation God has deigned to give us, does not mean sexual identity. One cannot blithely accept the first chapter of Genesis and ignore the third chapter. Nor can anyone of even minimal intelligence fail to see that the functional difference between the active and the passive, between physical assertion on the one hand and acceptance on the other in the most intimate of human relationships, is bound to have social and indeed political consequences.

Perhaps the prelate I cite did not say all this because he is too delicate. Or – the evidence is rather stronger on this side – perhaps he is too ignorant. For he *did* say that a useful compromise might be to ordain women as deacons, which proposal displays a breathtaking ignorance of the developed theology of holy orders. Indeed, I am convinced that our radical problem *is* intellectual. Granted, knowledge is not a virtue. Granted, that the recent bizarre events in Atlanta and at Covenant House in New York are not without precedent. But surely one might argue, for example, that the depressingly widespread incidence of homosexuality within the priesthood, and the dreadful instances of pederasty, are attributable, to some degree at least, to the ambiguity of recent Catholic teaching on sex. I do not mean the magisterial teaching, of course; I do mean the sort of mush, now so prevalent in our diocesan press, that insists upon honoring "alternate lifestyles," and that seems more concerned to demonstrate compassion for the victims of AIDS than to instruct young Catholics on how to avoid contracting AIDS.

It seems to me we have entered a period of sharp decline. Even the numbers are disheartening. We have now upwards of 300 bishops, at least a hundred more than we need. And how many of them have recently ventured into the highways and by-ways, or hoisted themselves onto the rooftops, to proclaim, "Repent! The Kingdom of God is at hand"? We have bloated bureaucracies, growing all the time and sucking up our diminishing resources, at the national and diocesan and even parochial levels. The only numbers that have fallen, and they precipitously, are those of practicing Catholics. You may recall that last spring, when the archdiocese of Chicago closed nearly fifty parishes for financial reasons, there were many protests and even one appeal to the Vatican. To justify its action the archdiocese released some statistics, the most arresting of which had to do with mass attendance and therefore contributions: of the 2.4 million nominal Catholics living in the archdiocese of Chicago, about 600,000 go to mass on a given Sunday. Twenty-five percent, or about the same as Italy, much less than Alsace or Brittany, light years less than in Poland or Ireland or in the young Churches of Africa and Asia.

And so I recommend, as the evangelization proper to these unhappy times, a return to the ghetto, by which I mean something quite precise. I think we need to recapture a sense of ourselves, who we are, how we differ from the consumerist world around us, what it is in contemporary American society that we admire and what we despise. We need to find again that spirit of community and fellowship that we have lost. Those of us dedicated to the intellectual life have, it seems to me, a special call: through our often lonely and unappreciated scholarly endeavors we need to rediscover that Catholic tradition which has nourished our forebears across three centuries in America and, more than that – hardly a wink in the long history of the Church – across nearly two millennia and which, once we have found it, has to be shared with our brothers and sisters in Christ. The road will be long and narrow and rutted, the sign posts few, the hazards many. To reach the goal we shall need something of the stubborn loyalty to the faith of the old Maryland Catholics; something also of the missionary zeal that gloriously lit up the years of our expansion here in this new land; and something of the wisdom of our immediate ancestors who looked sharply at America, loved it for its goodness, and heartily worked to make it even better.

Toward the end of his long life, the chronicles tell us, Dean Swift grew more and more whimsical and capricious, morbidly suspicious and crotchety. He was struck down, finally, by paralysis, and it became necessary to appoint guardians of his person and estate. Learned physicians debated over the causes of the dementia which afflicted him just before he died and which caused, as they put it, "the automatic utterance of words ungoverned by intention." Yet, despite all his frailties, despite even this curiously unchecked rush of speech, the same doctors testified that their patient "never talked nonsense or said a foolish thing."

May the same be said of me, and of my modest proposal.

25.
Life Issues in a Pluralistic Culture (1991)
Janet E. Smith

I.

What a piece of work is a man, how noble in reason, how infinite in faculties, in form and moving how express and admirable, in action how like an angel, in apprehension how like a god: the beauty of the world, the paragon of animals; and yet to me, what is this quintessence of dust? Man delights not me; nor woman neither . . . (Hamlet, II, ii, 310–19)

The modern age too little shares Hamlet's admiration for man and too much his disdain for man. We, like Hamlet, seem depressed and lost and unable to delight in the wonders of this world, perhaps because we, too, fail to embrace our duties and to act as we ought. Whatever the reason, the modern age seems not to experience awe at the thought of human powers and human nature. We take some pride in man's technological advances but these hardly balance our experience of and fear of man's inhumanity to man. Our century in particular has given us reason to think that man is "the paragon of animals" only insofar as he surpasses all other animals in his cruelty and bloodthirstiness. The millions dead because of holocausts, wars, and of famines that could be averted have brought us to have a dismal evaluation of human nature, an assessment confirmed by daily reportings of individuals who randomly commit horrific brutalities.

The rot in the state of Denmark, rather than serving to galvanize Hamlet into action, cast him into a state of doubt and depression. Our age exhibits the same signs; the offenses against life in this century have not served to increase our respect for life or our zeal to protect life. Rather, we have sunk into a state of lethargy and indifference, and as in the state of Denmark, the pile of corpses only gets higher. Indeed, abortion and euthanasia provide the quintessential evidence that we have lost our reverence for life. Some ethicists – highly respected and published by the most prestigious presses – now argue that some forms of animal life have greater value than the lives of some humans suffering various debilitating conditions. In the name of respecting life, researchers and physicians seem to be salivating over the prospect of using fetal tissue to treat a variety of diseases.

There is a paradox or contradiction at the very heart of our approach to human life. We go to great lengths to preserve human life and to diminish human suffering, yet at the same time we increasingly treat human life in such a cavalier and utilitarian fashion that one wonders why we continue to make herculean efforts to improve the human lot. One suspects that it is more a desire to advance and test our own technological prowess or just mere sentiment that leads us to dig small children out of wells and to spend hundreds of thousands of dollars to keep tiny neonates alive. A residue of the grand and noble vision of man that informed Hamlet's musings lingers, but it is rapidly disappearing.

In respect to the "life issues," the pluralism of our culture is not a benign multiculturalism; it is not just a matter of "my people" wearing its national costumes and doing its national dances, or a question of whose heroes we are going to celebrate, or whose novels and histories we are going to read. It is not a matter of protecting such fundamental rights as the free practice of religion; nor is it a matter of fundamental fairness such as public funding for private schools. Pluralism in this case goes to the very heart of existence; it strikes at the *most* fundamental of all rights, the right to life. Pluralism in the life issues means that some people approve of the taking of innocent human life, and some people do not; some approve of the making of babies in laboratories and others do not; some people approve of the killing of the dying and infirm and others do not. These values are not just pluralistic but contradictory. This is not a pluralism that is tolerable. We no longer share a common vision of man and of life from which we can then construct a social system protecting man's fundamental rights. Having lost the vision of man that Hamlet articulates, we have also lost the values derived from this vision.

There are many reasons, often interrelated, why we in the modern world succumb so easily to the temptation to destroy human life, especially the unborn, weak, and dying. Here, hoping to be as comprehensive as possible, but knowing that some reasons likely have been missed, I shall list some fifteen of the reasons why our society is losing the will to do what it ought to do in protecting human life. In the final portion of the paper, special attention will be paid to one of these items, that of feminism, since it is a particularly powerful element in our society.

First, the secular world has completely lost any sense that there is a life beyond this one. Many Christians, too, have an extremely diminished – if any – sense of our ordination to another life. This leads to distortions that cause us to devalue life. For instance, we come to think that what happiness we shall ever experience, we must experience in this life. Confusing happiness with pleasure, we have lost sight of an understanding of happiness that links it with the virtuous life, with the pursuit of what is good and noble. Few believe that they will be rewarded in the next life for the good that they have done in this. Thus, we labor to ensure that our lives are filled with pleasure and we seek to avoid all pain. We largely live in accord with a utilitarian ethic that leads us to maximize pleasure and minimize pain, even at the expense of the lives of others. Thus, both women and men are not prepared to shoulder the responsibilities of parenthood because these impinge upon the goals they have for their own lives; they also feel justified in taking the lives of the unborn. Those who are dying see no reason to endure the pain and suffering of their condition.

Second, we have lost the understanding that self-sacrifice has a value and that it can be ennobling. Being so concerned to ensure our own happiness, we have lost the sense of the noble gesture through which we make some great sacrifice for something of great importance and worth. It used to be thought that women would lay down their lives for their children (may Gianna Beretta Molla's cause prevail!), but now women routinely kill the children within their wombs. They are thought to be stupid to think of making a sacrifice for another; they are thought to be enlightened and responsible when they have an abortion so that they might not inconvenience themselves. We think it unreasonable to ask children to make sacrifices for their dying parents and do not object when they hasten them towards euthanasia. The neglect of many in the Church to preach the heroic lives of the saints has left the young without the exemplars they need.

Thirdly, the secular world certainly has no appreciation for suffering, but Christians, as well, have lost the love of the cross. Again, if we had a sense of the reality of the afterlife, we might better be able to embrace our crosses. Christianity has become a religion that in practice often seeks to *eliminate* all pain rather than to teach us how to live with and embrace pain and sometimes even to seek the pain that is an inevitable part of a life well-lived. One of the primary (though not only) reasons for the appeal of euthanasia is that no one likes to suffer and few know how to offer their sufferings up and to unite them with those of Christ. The failure to preach penance and fasting may contribute to this phenomenon; we have not learned to endure hardship.

Fourth, the sense of sin has nearly disappeared. The modern age has a "victim" mentality; we feel that we have suffered or been discriminated against and thus should be excused for whatever wrong we might do. We have no sense that we are ultimately accountable for our actions, no fear of impending punishment. Guilt and fear are unacceptable motivating factors in the modern age and most of those who represent the Church have abandoned mention of judgment day. They think mention of sin is to "lay a guilt trip" on others and prefer to motivate by love rather than by fear, a laudable goal in many ways but not one without its dangers. A gospel of repentance and redemption is rarely preached, for, if we are not sinners, we do not need to be saved. As victims, what we need is consolation and assistance.

Fifth, there is widespread belief that there are no objective truths, that there are no moral absolutes binding on all. We believe one opinion is as good as another, one value as good as another. All morality, all law, is the imposition of someone's morality on someone else. As Justice Clarence Thomas' Supreme Court hearings manifested, we have lost entirely an understanding of and appreciation for the concept of natural law. We think all law is man-made and arbitrary. Indeed, in defense of abortion, one feminist said that she refused to be subject to "anachronistic laws of nature."

This refusal to recognize the demands of objective reality dovetails with our fifth point. We think that any constraint, even the constraint of objective reality, is an infringement upon our freedom; and this is our sixth point. As recent encyclicals repeatedly note, our age has a corrupt sense of freedom; the freedom to choose seems to be valued above all other goods. We have no sense at all of the need for freedom from sin or for the fact that freedom brings with it immense responsibility. We make some reluctant concessions for the sake of the public peace but basically we want to do what we want, when we want, and even think the state exists in large part to ensure us the possibility of fulfilling all our wants. It is almost a Nietzschean view of man that dominates, a view that we are answerable only to our own passions and that reason should be employed to help satisfy the passions rather than to control and guide the passions.

Women want to be free to choose and value that freedom over the objective fact that what they are choosing is to kill their babies. Those who would practice euthanasia justify it by claiming that the patient would not choose to continue life in certain circumstances. The morality of the act of euthanasia seems to rest simply in the question: "What does the patient wish?" not in the question: "What is the moral action here?" Euthanasia, assisted suicide, and suicide are, thus, rapidly gaining strength as legitimate choices.

This mistaken view of freedom has also crippled our ability to outlaw such practices as pornography and to put limits on obscenity in the media and the entertainment world. Obscenity simply serves further to diminish our sense of the value of human life – we peddle pictures showing human beings in postures and acts that we find offensive for animals.

Seventh, there is great confusion about the meaning and purpose of sexuality and what constitutes responsible sexuality. Sexual intercourse is no longer understood to have a *telos*, an end, or purpose. To speak of the "purpose" of sexual intercourse and to suggest that we are obliged to live in accord with that purpose; this is language that is virtually incomprehensible in this age. The nearly universal use of contraception has almost completely obliterated the notion that sexual intercourse has a procreative purpose. Sex is considered to be wholly a pleasure-giving activity with no deeper meaning. Since couples think sex is simply to be used for pleasure (not the same as union), they feel perfectly comfortable about having sexual intercourse even when they are completely unprepared to have babies. Pregnancy is then perceived as an accident for which they are not accountable.

Indeed, the loss of a teleological view of nature has tremendously undermined all of sexual ethics. Many kinds of deviant sexual activity are considered acceptable since they are various forms of seeking pleasure. Again, contraception is clearly a major contributing factor to this mentality, since it robs sexual intercourse of its procreative meaning. The real seamless garment is one that connects contraception, abortion, adultery, homosexuality, divorce, sexual abuse, and as related evils, alcoholism, drug abuse, homelessness, and the like. These are often the consequences of deviant sexual practices and dysfunctional families. Few have been taught that contraception is a great evil; fewer have been taught why it is. Indeed, it is ironic that most Catholics know that the Church teaches that contraception is immoral, not from anything they have heard at Church, but from the reportings by a hostile media of the speeches of Pope John Paul II and of the reactions of dissenting theologians.

Eighth, there is a great confusion about sexual identity. Feminism rejects motherhood as an invention of an androcentric patriarchy designed to keep women in submission. Pregnancy and babies are seen as obstacles to women's self-fulfillment rather than as means for self-fulfillment. Feminists no longer value the innate feminine abilities for nurturing and self-sacrifice. Men, too, are mocked and considered condescending if they seek to act upon their protective instincts. Fatherhood is no longer seen as a lofty calling for men, but a kind of subservience to a conventional lifestyle. The value of the father as an authority has disappeared; it is assumed that he could only exercise this role in a domineering and selfish way. Clearly, a culture with such views of motherhood and fatherhood is predictably very comfortable with abortion; women are not expected to nurture; men are not expected to protect.

Ninth, the breakdown in family life contributes greatly to the anti-life mentality. Families are the school of love and those who are not schooled to love in the family have a difficult time expressing and experiencing love. It is easy to mistake sexual attraction for love. Many unwanted pregnancies that end in abortion are the result of unloved young women seeking love. Much of the clamor for euthanasia is a result of a lack of love for the sick and elderly. They feel like they are burdens that cannot be endured; they feel they put too many demands on their loved ones (if they have them) – or on the hospital staff – emotionally, physically, financially. They feel they are doing others a service and maintaining their own dignity if they seek an early demise.

Tenth, the breakdown in the family and certain liberal philosophies have led to an excessive individualism. We no longer feel we are defined as members of a human community, such as the family or state, which we must serve and to which we must subordinate our own wishes. Rather, we strive to actualize our selves with little cognizance of how our actions impact upon others. If unborn babies or the dying get in the way of our actualizing ourselves, we find them altogether dispensable.

Eleventh, there is little sense that God is the Lord of Life or that Man is made in the image and likeness of God. We do not view life as a gift to be returned in some way, but as a happenstance that we can use at our own discretion. If life becomes burdensome, we believe we have the right to kill or to die to avoid burdens. Human life seems little more than animal life; when animals are inconvenient to us, we eliminate them. We have little ability to reason why we should not treat humans in the same way. Again, some philosophers are eloquent in their defense of animal rights and think that some animal life is more worthy of protection than some human life, since animals at some stages of their existence have greater powers than human fetuses.

Twelfth, there is an often justifiable distrust of the medical profession and a sense that doctors are too enamored of technology. We suspect that they will put people on machines needlessly and then will not be able to discern when it would be moral to remove them. Technological prowess makes doctors inclined to seek to prolong life at all costs. Our society is so torn between wanting to hasten the demise of the dying and wanting to pursue procedures that unnecessarily prolong the dying process, that few, not even the leaders of the Church, know how to make the proper distinctions between what is ordinary and necessary care and what is extraordinary and unnecessary.

Thirteenth, moderns believe, it seems erroneously, that the earth is overpopulated and that anything that reduces the number of humans on the face of the earth is good; thus there again need not be any resistance to abortion and euthanasia. Few seem to draw the proper conclusions from the fact that the places on the earth that are the most burdensome on the world's resources are relatively sparsely populated; generally their rate of reproduction is not even at replacement level. These countries are highly industrialized, materialistic, and wasteful in the extreme. The disparity between what it takes to support a small middle-class family in the developed world and what it takes to support large families in third world countries almost defies belief. Why do we not then conclude that it is materialism, greed, and wastefulness that are the problem, not the number of people?

Fourteenth, we have lost an appreciation of the power of grace. We feel we cannot face our own difficulties nor expect others to face theirs. We do not think that people can change their ways; thus abortion becomes an answer to unwanted pregnancy – we have little hope that a woman with an unwanted pregnancy can face her troubles and overcome them. We have little sense that the suffering that accompanies the process of dying can be a grace insofar as it leads us to reconcile ourselves with each other and with God.

Fifteenth, and finally, inertia is not on the side of life; we have become accustomed to abortion, and the practice of euthanasia more and more seems inevitable. The status quo is now with those who find life cheap and who fight any restriction on "choice." The current generation are "survivors" of abortion. But as with Hamlet, this fact tends not to energize the younger generation to defend life, but to render them depressed and confused. Anecdotal evidence reports that they hold even their own lives to be of little value. When asked if they think their mother should have aborted them if her pregnancy had posed a significant burden, young people generally answer in the affirmative. Apparently, their mother's willingness to bear them does not obscure the fact that they were all potential members of the class of the unwanted.

II.

Now I would like to take a moment to focus on one of the items on the above list, and that is feminism. Feminism is a particularly virulent strain of the virus that is loose in our land. Most women, even those who reject nearly all of the items on the agenda of the official feminist organizations, call themselves feminists. In doing so, they believe they are primarily committing themselves to the claim that women are equal to men intellectually and spiritually, that women deserve access to all professions and should not be discriminated against on the basis of sex, and that women have historically been unfairly excluded from the public sphere. They define themselves over against some group whom they view as Neanderthal; they attribute to their putative opponents the belief that women are subhuman and exist only to perform demeaning and servile jobs. Generally those who refuse the appellation of feminist do so not because they think women are inferior to men but because they cannot ally themselves with abortion, divorce, lesbianism, witchcraft, and marxism. These are prominent items at feminist conventions, they are also the subject of much feminist scholarship, and they are what many feminist politicians work for politically. Moreover, those who oppose feminism generally do so because they believe feminism works against the values of motherhood. Some feminists have deplored the description of women as "nurturing," since this suggests to them a subservient role, one foisted upon them by an androcentric, patriarchal society. Indeed, it is easy to find in feminist literature statements that are altogether hostile to motherhood and to traditional descriptions of a woman's role.

Yet, what is also true, and encouraging, is that it is becoming increasingly possible to find in feminist literature statements that affirm the female interest in the sources of life and in the mothering and nurturing role. Logically one would expect that acceptance of these principles would lead feminists to reject such life-destroying acts as abortion, to eschew such alienating acts as *in vitro* fertilization, and to have some hesitancy in supporting euthanasia. However, they have not yet come to recognize the conflict between some of the values that they say they hold and some of the ethical and political items on their agenda. I think it incumbent upon those of us fighting for the value of innocent human life, that we laud them for these admirable principles they do hold, and also relentlessly point out to them the conflict with these principles and their advocacy of life-destroying acts. Here I would like to cite and comment on passages from a few essays appearing in a collection entitled, *Feminist Theology: A Reader*,[1] for the authors fairly frequently express values that logically should move feminists away from abortion advocacy towards an alliance with the pro-life movement.

Feminists on occasion speak of women as having a special interest in the transmission and preservation of life. Beverly Wildung Harrison speaks of women in this fashion: "Women have been the doers of life-sustaining things, the 'copers,' those who have understood that the reception of the gift of life is no inert thing, that to receive this gift is to be engaged in its tending, constantly."[2] She also states, "My basic thesis [is] that a Christian moral theology must be answerable to what women have learned by struggling to lay hold of the gift of life, to receive it, to live deeply into it, to pass it on..."[3] In spite of this strong affirmation that women are the special guardians of life, Harrison herself remains pro-abortion.

Although many feminists have rejected the notion that women are to be characterized as nurturers, Harrison should not be counted among them. She maintains, "Women's lives literally have been shaped by the power not only to bear human life at the biological level but to nurture life, which is a social and cultural power. Though our culture has come to disvalue women's role, and with it to disvalue nurturance, genuine nurturance is a formidable power. Insofar as it has taken place in human history, it has been largely through women's action. For better or worse, women have had to face the reality that we have the power not only to create personal bonds between people but, more basically, to build up and deepen *personhood itself*. And to build up 'the Person' is also to deepen relationship, that is, to bring

---

1 *Feminist Theology: A Reader* ed. By Ann Loades, Westminster; John Knox Press, 1990.
2 "The Power of Anger in the Work of Love: Christian Ethics for Women and Other Strangers," *Ibid.*, p. 201.
3 *Ibid.*, p. 200.

forth community."[4] Although Harrison seems to value nurturance here primarily as a source of power, it is significant that she recognizes that women have a special role in nurturing and that this is essential to valuing the dignity of the person and to building community.

Feminists for the most part have promoted the values of autonomous individualism in their quest to be recognized as full persons and they generally believe that it is best for women to seek to be fully self-sufficient and dependent upon no man. Yet, community is becoming of increasing importance to feminists and they are beginning to extol women's special capacities for communication and the building of relationships. Again, Harrison states, "I believe that our world is on the verge of self-destruction and death because the society as a whole has so deeply neglected that which is most human and most valuable and the most basic of all the works of life – the work of human communication, of caring and nurturance, of tending the personal bonds of community. This activity has been seen as women's work and discounted as too mundane and undramatic, too distracting from the serious business of world rule."[5]

Feminism has also been noted for its rejection of the domestic and mundane; feminism has been greatly responsible for propelling women out of the home and into the workplace, in promoting the notion that it is salary and prestige that most accurately reflect the value of one's work. It is well known that feminists largely feel themselves pitted against women who are content to concentrate their energies exclusively on matters of the home. Yet there are encouraging signs that feminists are willing to reclaim the home as a special female province. One feminist theologian, Nicola Slee, bemoans the paucity of parables and stories about women in the New Testament, yet rightly finds the feminine presence extolled implicitly in the parables of celebration and feasting in the New Testament:

> The banquet image is, of course, a symbol of the eschatological Kingdom deeply embedded in the Old Testament and the intertestamental literature. But again, it does speak to women whose lives are very much bound up with the rituals of feeding and feasting, which take on special significance at the celebration of births, marriages, anniversaries and achievements, and at the more sombre times of death and departure, but can also have a treasured place in the rhythm of daily life.[6]

---

4 *Ibid.*, p. 203.
5 *Ibid.*, p. 203–4.
6 "Parables and Women's Experience," *Ibid.*, p. 43.

Further on she observes:

> This space for sharing and the kindling into celebration of the simple necessities of life is a quality of living which women may be able to affirm in a special way because of its place in our family and social lives. The banquet parables call us to create this space of celebration, with room for all, in our families, our various social groupings and, most of all, in the Eucharistic community of the Church, where so often the table seems so bare, the occasion so devoid of festivity, the community so impoverished of love.[7]

Slee is right to observe that women have a special interest in the celebratory moments of life, precisely because they are celebrations of *life* and love. The capacity for welcoming hospitality that is a woman's gift, should never be denied the child in her womb or the parents who have nourished her.

The alliance of the feminist movement with the ecological movement should also help to move feminists in the direction of the protection of life. Sallie McFague, a feminist advocate for the protection of the environment, uses a promising image when she makes this plea: "We should become mothers and fathers to our world, extending those natural instincts we all have, whether or not we have children of our bodies (or adopted children), to what Jonathan Schell calls 'universal parenthood.'"[8] McFague's primary purpose is to extend this universal instinct to be a parent to other species but she does insist that there is a deep parental instinct within all of us and describes it in this way: "The will deep within all of us which could be called the parental instinct, the will not to save ourselves but to bring others into existence. Most broadly, whether or not one is a biological or adoptive parent, the parental instinct says to others, 'It is good that you exist!' even if this involves a diminishment and in some cases, the demise of the self."[9] Some of McFague's remarks seem to suggest that she would be an advocate of euthanasia since she might construe voluntary euthanasia as a product of the willingness to sacrifice one's own life for others. It is not possible to discern McFague's position on abortion from her article although there is disquieting praise of a specialist in world population control; moreover, the omission of abortion as an offense against life is telling in its own way. Still

---

7 *Ibid.,* p. 44.
8 "The Ethic of God as Mother, Lover and Friend," *Ibid.,* p. 258.
9 *Ibid.*

it is difficult to see how she could be pro-abortion in light of her description of the parental instinct.

Now there is much in these feminist articles that is highly objectionable, as theology, as philosophy, as credible observations about the realities of existence. Nonetheless there are glimmers of an ethic that might lead some feminists to reexamine their whole acceptance of the anti-life ethic of our times. We need to begin to draw out the values of feminism that are compatible with a life ethic and hope that the intellectual virtue of consistency might lead feminists to direct women to place their life-serving, nurturing instincts at the service of those for whom they are most directly responsible, the unborn. And then that the true feminine capacity for cultivating relationship might lead us to build communities where the terminally ill, the elderly, and the dying feel so loved and cared for that their deaths become not a nightmarish experience of difficult decision-making over technological resources, but a time of peaceful preparation for death.

As we have noted above, feminism is only one of the obstacles in the path of promoting the value of life in our society. Despite the heroism and effectiveness of most of the pro-life movement in fighting abortion and euthanasia, I believe it is not facing imminent success, not because of any weakness in effort on its part but because of the nature of the task that faces it. The task before us, the task of changing the fundamental values of society, is enormous. Those who have access to the young in particular need to work strenuously to combat the attitudes I have detailed above, for until we share Hamlet's wonder at "what a piece of work is a man," the pile of corpses will just grow and grow.

26.
How the Catholic Church Serves the Common Good (1991)
J. Brian Benestad

Many Americans are expressing dissatisfaction or even strong opposition to the Catholic Church's engagement in the debates on public issues, especially abortion. People say that the Catholic Church is violating the legally-mandated separation of Church and State. A few others simply wonder why the Church spends so much time on public policy when there are pressing problems within the Church that need sustained attention.

The First Amendment to the Constitution clearly allows individuals, associations, and churches to address any public issue. The constitutional guarantee of religious liberty allows both the clergy and the laity to have religiously motivated reasons for taking a particular policy position. The Church, of course, may also for religious reasons freely establish schools, hospitals, and various kinds of social services.

The charge that the Catholic bishops violate the time-honored American principle of separation between Church and State by speaking out on the affairs of the polity is not supported by a serious argument. The appeal to the separation principle functions as a substitute for substantive engagement of the issues; in short, it is a rhetorical ploy. People opposed to the bishops' policy positions should give their reasons, and not try to make use of a procedural device in order to silence the Church's voice.

It is becoming more evident, however, that large numbers of highly educated men and women do not welcome the bishops' voice in the public arena. These people are persuaded that a liberal state can survive quite well without public recognition of religion and traditional morality. They believe that the bishops' input, at best, contributes nothing substantial to the well-being of the liberal state. Their worst fear is that the bishops are more likely to be an obstacle to greater liberation from traditional morality, e.g., the Church's teaching on sexual morality and on the use of material goods.

The secular critique of the bishops may soon bear the label of "politically correct," if it has not already achieved that status. While Catholics may correctly regard this secular critique as insubstantial and biased, there is a serious criticism of the bishops' mode of addressing public issues based on theological considerations. Fr. Avery Dulles, S.J., outlines a number of theological reasons why the bishops should exercise restraint in proposing "detailed answers in controverted areas." For example, devising policy proposals takes a lot of time and energy. Dulles asks: "Is it justified for [bishops] to go so far afield when many ecclesiastical matters, for which the bishops have inescapable responsibility, are crying out for greater attention? The impression is given that the bishops are more at ease in criticizing the performance of secular governments than in shouldering their own responsibilities in the Church."[1] Ironically, *The New York Times* made exactly the same point last November in a news-analysis piece on the annual bishops' meeting in Washington (1990).

Dulles continues: "When the bishops devote so much attention to worldly affairs, they can unwittingly give the impression that what is truly important in their eyes is not the faith or holiness that leads to everlasting life, but rather the structuring of human society to make the world more habitable."[2] Talk of justice and peace – narrowly understood as a seamless garment of policy positions on the major issues of domestic and foreign policy – seems to predominate nearly everywhere. Comparable attention is not directed either to a seamless garment of Catholic teaching on faith and morals, or to the non-policy aspects of justice and peace, especially the virtues of faith, prudence, and fortitude. There is a widespread sense that the Church no longer takes sufficient pains to teach all aspects of Catholicism, especially the truths that go against the grain of American culture. Over the past twenty-five years the bishops themselves have used their national association (The National Conference of Catholic Bishops) to address political affairs more than Church matters. Surely, there is an imbalance here.

Dulles also points out that the bishops must allow and even encourage dissent from their debatable political opinions. "The spirit of criticism and dissent thus unleashed can scarcely be prevented from spreading to strictly religious matters in which the bishops have unquestionable authority in the Church."[3] The laity, Dulles implies, will have great difficulty drawing a line

1 Avery Dulles, *The Reshaping of Catholicism: Current Challenges in the Theology of the Church*, 176, New York, Doubleday, 1988.
2 *Ibid.*, 176.

between proper and improper dissent from episcopal teaching. In other words, lay people may come to regard some authoritative Catholic teachings in the same light as ordinary political opinions.

The response to the theological critique of the bishops' mode of political activity should not, however, be a call for the Church to withdraw from the public arena. Rather, the hierarchical Church should be encouraged to have an even deeper impact on American culture and public policy, but to do so as Church – not as an ordinary lobby, nor in such a way as to create false impressions.

The main purpose of this paper is to explain what guidance Leo XIII's *Rerum Novarum* and John Paul II's *Centesimus Annus* offer to the Church in her work to promote the common good. In order to put my remarks in context, I will briefly summarize Vatican Council II's understanding of the Church's mission, with a focus on the role of the laity in the world. With its limited scope, this paper does not pretend to offer an exhaustive treatment of the subject. Nevertheless, by means of these two social encyclicals, it aims to direct attention to certain themes that are not adequately grasped by American Catholics, both clergy and lay.

I. The Church's Mission: Salvation and the Renewal of the Temporal Order

The Church's mission, according to Vatican II's *Lumen Gentium,* is "to proclaim and spread among all peoples the Kingdom of Christ and of God and to be on earth, the initial budding forth of that kingdom" (*LG* #5). The Decree on the Apostolate of the Laity says the mission of the Church is two-fold: By spreading the kingdom of Christ everywhere on earth to make all men and women partakers in salvific redemption and through those who accept salvation to order all things to Christ (*Apostolicam Actuositatem* #2). The Church is "an instrument for the redemption of all" (*LG* #9). In short, the ultimate end of the Church is the salvation of human beings "which is to be achieved by faith in Christ and by his grace" (*AA* #6), and fully attained only in the after life (*GS* #40). Avery Dulles points out that all the internal ministries of the Church "are directed to the sanctification of the faithful and to the glory thereby given to God" (*Sacrosanctum Concilium* #10).[4]

The specific mission that Christ entrusted to his Church, according to *Gaudium et Spes*, "is not in the political, economic, or social order. The pur-

---

3 *Ibid.,* 178.
4 *Ibid.,* 143.

pose which he set before her is a religious one" (*GS* #42). That mission is salvation through sanctification. Nevertheless, the Church's religious mission "entails duties in the temporal sphere." Men and women having received the message of salvation have the duty to imbue all temporal things with a Christian spirit. "Out of the Church's religious mission," says *Gaudium et Spes*, "comes a function, a light, and an energy that can serve to structure and consolidate the human community according to divine law" (*GS* #42). "The mission of the Church in its full range," Dulles concludes, "may therefore be said to include not only the directly religious apostolate but also the penetration of the temporal sphere with the spirit of the Gospel" (*AA* #5).[5] At first glance it may seem that Vatican II is saying that the Church does and does not have a proper mission in the political, social, and economic order. Dulles explains the apparent contradiction:

> To preach faith in Christ and to administer the sacraments are . . . proper to the Church. The Church was established precisely in order that these activities might be performed. But to erect a just and prosperous society is not . . . the proper business of the Church. To contribute to such a society is, however, a responsibility of Christians insofar as they are citizens of the earthly community. Unless they live up to civic obligations, they will be guilty in the sight of God. All Christians, whether clergy or laity, have duties as members of the human community, but to penetrate secular professions and organizations with the spirit of the gospel is preeminently the responsibility of the laity (*GS* #43; *AA* #7).[6]

The so-called apostolate of the Church is quite logically a function of the Church's mission.

> The apostolate of the Church . . . and of each of its members, aims primarily at announcing to the world by word and action the message of Christ and communicating to it the grace of Christ. The principal means of bringing this about is the ministry of the word and of the sacraments (*AA* #6).

While the clergy have as their proper task this apostolate of evangelization and sanctification, the laity also have an important role to play in this work. In addition, the laity also exercise the apostolate "when they endeavor to have the Gospel spirit permeate and improve the temporal order, going about it in a way that bears clear witness to Christ and helps forward the sal-

5 *Ibid.*, 147.
6 *Ibid.*, 148.

vation of men" (*AA* #2). In other words, the laity act as leaven in the world in every aspect of their lives.

The duty of the laity to renew the temporal order flows from the Church's mission "in its full range," to use the expression of Avery Dulles. While the Church has no proper mission in the political, economic, and social order, it is the work of the entire Church to make men and women capable of rightly constructing the order of temporal things and of ordering all things to God through Christ. It is specifically the work of pastors to set forth moral principles as guidelines for the renewal of the temporal order in Christ and to provide spiritual help to the laity. It is the distinctive task of lay people to renew the temporal order. Guided by the gospel and the mind of the Church, and prompted by love, lay people act on their *own* responsibility and use their *own* particular competence to seek the justice of God's kingdom in all things – e.g., through family life and other mediating structures or voluntary associations, and through business, the trades, the professions, the institutions of the political community, international relations, etc.

This task of renewing the temporal order is both difficult to execute *and* even to conceive. Vatican II explains:

> Under the influence of original sin people have fallen into very many errors about the true God, human nature and the principles of morality. As a consequence human conduct and institutions became corrupted, the human person itself held in contempt. Again in our own days not a few, putting an immoderate trust in the conquests of science and technology, turn off into a kind of idolatry of the temporal, they become the slaves of it rather than the masters (*AA* #7).

Because of ignorance caused by sin, lack of education as well as the simple human inability to grasp complex concepts and situations, lay people often have a more or less limited understanding of what the renewal of the temporal order entails. What can be done to foster the stability of marriages, to raise exit requirements from public schools, to insure the education of the underclass in the nation's cities, to improve general education in the universities? What initiatives will help produce a consensus on the purpose of medicine among health-care professionals? Can anything be done to persuade lawyers and their clients not to press frivolous, immoral lawsuits?

Even when lay people achieve the requisite clarity for their work of renewal, they must still contend with their own weaknesses, as well as opposition from others, caused by ignorance or by disordered passions such as immoderate love of pleasure, gain, honor, and power; or, fear of toil, and laziness.

Despite the obstacles posed by ignorance and weakness, individual lay persons, dedicated to the pursuit of holiness, will find ways to bring more order, harmony, and justice to family and social life, to the conduct of the trades, business and the professions, to political life. Even when large-scale problems resist resolution, individual men and women can still be good husbands and wives, fathers and mothers, good doctors and plumbers, dedicated volunteers and active citizens, etc.

In working for any kind of political and social reform, lay people would do well to keep in mind the prudent advice Thomas More gives in his *Utopia*:

> . . . Suggestions ought not to be made or advice proffered which you are sure will never be taken. . . . If erroneous beliefs cannot be plucked out root and all, if you cannot heal long established evils to your satisfaction, you must not therefore desert the state and abandon the ship in a storm, because you cannot check the winds. Nor should you force upon people strange and unaccustomed discourses which you know will have no weight with them in their opposite beliefs. But you should try and strive obliquely to settle everything as best you may, and what you cannot turn to good, you should make as little evil as possible. For it is not possible for everything to be good unless all men are good, and I do not expect that that will come about for many years.[7]

More's stress on moderate expectations for reform is not at all cynical resignation to the status quo, but rather an invitation to reach for the possible with enthusiasm and serenity. Aiming too high could lead to the kind of revolutionary zeal that thrives on anger and hatred. The would-be reformers must be careful not to let anger at opponents devour their souls. Impatience with the way things are can lead to the sadness and despair of Goethe's Faust who, after renouncing hope and faith, exclaims "and cursed above all be patience." Commenting on the line, the theologian Romano Guardini wrote:

> [Faust] is the ever-immature who never sees reality or accepts it as it is. Always he flies above it in his fancy. Always he is in a state of protest against his destiny, whereas the maturity of man begins with his accep-

---

7 St. Thomas More, *Utopia*, translated by Peter K. Marshall, New York: Washington Square Press, 1969, pp. 34–35.

tance of what is, of reality. Only this gives him the power to change and to re-shape it.[8]

Because of the ever-present temptation to give up when confronted with ignorance and sin, Guardini urges us to make this prayer:

> Lord, have patience with me, and give me patience so that the possibil-
> ities granted to me may, in the short span of my lifetime, those brief
> years, grow and bear fruit.[9]

We will now turn to *Rerum Novarum* and *Centesimus Annus* for commentary on the proposition that the Church serves the common good by accomplishing her mission. These encyclicals also show how the laity promote the renewal of the temporal order through mediating structures and through government.

II. Rerum Novarum

In 1891, Leo XIII formally expressed the Church's solution to the penurious condition of workers in his famous encyclical *Rerum Novarum*. Leo urged the acceptance of four general proposals: the protection of the right to private property, reliance on religion and the Church to teach virtue, reliance on the state to assume responsibility for the common good, and co-operation among employers and associations for the material and spiritual well-being of workers and their families.[10] Through these four proposals Leo XIII attempted to prove that the common good of a nation requires the protection of rights and the practice of virtue by citizens, families, political leaders, bishops, and priests. It belongs to the state to protect rights, especially the "sacred" right to private property, to foster virtue in various ways and to secure both liberty and a reasonable amount of property for all.

Anyone steeped in the theological and political thought of Augustine and Aquinas will be somewhat startled to find Leo XIII begin his encyclical with a defense of the right to private property. Leo's ringing endorsement of a natural and sacred right to property was a response to socialists who were proposing the abolition of private possessions in favor of state administration of all goods. Leo XIII and the socialists were in agreement on the problem – the penurious condition of the working class. Leo, however, believed

---

8 Romano, Guardini, *The Virtues,* p. 32, Chicago, Henry Regnery, 1963.

9 *Ibid.,* 36.

10 *Two Basic Social Encyclicals: Rerum Novarum and Quadragesimo Anno,*
   Latin text with English translation (1943).

that the socialist solution would ultimately harm workers by causing disorder in society, "a harsh and odious enslavement of citizens," and a low economic standard of living for all. As an explanation of this last point Leo writes: "If incentives to ingenuity and skill in individual persons were to be abolished, the very fountains of wealth would necessarily dry up and the equality conjured up by the socialist imagination would, in reality, be nothing but uniform wretchedness and meanness for one and all, without distinction."[11] What is more, the socialist remedy is "openly in conflict with justice, inasmuch as nature confers on man the right to possess things privately as his own."[12] Leo affirms a true and perfect right for a worker "to demand his wage" and "to spend it as he wishes." A worker may also exercise full control over any land he may buy with his wages. Workers, says Leo, need the freedom to dispose of their own wages and land in order to have "the hope and the opportunity of increasing their property and securing advantages for themselves."[13] Leo XIII clearly implies that society must rely on the self-interest of individuals to procure the necessities of life.

According to Leo XIII, the foundation of the right to private property is the law of nature and also divine law, which forbids us from even desiring what belongs to another. Civil laws have protected this right – even by force – and the practice of all ages points to "private possession as something best adopted to man's nature and to peaceful and tranquil living together."[14] The official Italian version of *Rerum Novarum* actually locates the existence of rights in the Gospel ("*Ecco l'ideale dei diritti e doveri contenuto nel vangelo* [sic]."[15]: "Behold the ideal of rights and duties contained in the gospel" [sic]). The Latin text actually reads *Christiana philosophia* (Christian Philosophy) and not "gospel."[16]

Both natural law and divine law, according to Leo XIII, teach that the individual qua individual has a right to property. Leo emphasizes this point by affirming that rights "have much greater validity when viewed as fitted into and connected with the obligations of human beings in family life."[17]

---

11 *Rerum Novarum*, #22.
12 *Ibid.*, #10.
13 *Ibid.*, #9.
14 *Ibid.*, #17.
15 *L'Enciclica, Rerum Novarum: Testo Autentico E Redazioni Preparatorie Dai Documenti Originali*, ed. G. Antonazzi, 218 (1957).
16 *Rerum Novarum*, #39.
17 *Ibid.*, #18.

Leo clearly implies that rights have validity even apart from the obligations people have toward one another. In my judgment, this is a startling innovation in Catholic social teaching. From the perspective of Aquinas and Augustine, it would make no sense to understand rights apart from ordination toward duties or obligations.

Leo XIII's initial position on the right to private property bears a striking resemblance to the teaching of John Locke, who is justly regarded as one of the fathers of capitalism. Leo sounds Lockean, especially in affirming that an individual may dispose of his wages and land as he wishes (*"uti velit"*)[18] and by holding that individual rights are well grounded and solid apart from any connection to individual duties. Leo does offer a corrective to his initial Lockean position on the use of property by affirming that a father of a family has a duty to provide for his offspring: "It is a most sacred law of nature that the father of a family see that his offspring are provided with all the necessities of life . . ."[19]

Leo XIII's grounding of the right to private property in natural law and divine law is also foreign to the Catholic tradition. There is simply no statement about the right to property in the natural law teaching of Thomas Aquinas. Thomas Aquinas never argued that anyone had a natural right to property much less "a sacred right." He did say that "the division of possessions is not according to natural right, but rather arose from human agreement. . . . Hence, the ownership of possessions is not contrary to natural right but an addition thereto devised by human reason."[20] Aquinas defended private ownership not as a right but simply as an efficient means of promoting industry, order and peace.[21] (It is important to note that Aquinas's reference to natural right is not at all a synonym for natural rights or human rights. The latter concepts refer to the subjective claims of the individual against other individuals and governmental power, while natural right refers to moral principles that have validity apart from the claims and opinions of individuals. Aquinas, in fact, never spoke of natural or human rights. The concepts of universal natural rights only emerged in the seventeenth century in the writings of Thomas Hobbes.)[22]

---

18 *Ibid.,* #9.

19 *Ibid.,* #20.

20 St. Thomas, *Summa Theologica,* II, II, q. 66, a. 2.

21 *Ibid.*

22 Leo Strauss, *Natural Right and History,* Chicago: University of Chicago Press, 1953, p. 166–202.

Leo quotes from Deuteronomy 5:21 to prove that divine law undergirds the right to property. That text reads: "Thou shall not covet thy neighbor's wife, nor his house, nor his field, nor his maid-servant, nor his ox, nor his ass, nor anything that is his." Rather than affirm an individual right to property, the text affirms the duty of all not to desire the property or wife of another. If the duty is observed, the people will enjoy the possession of their property without disturbance.

The first section of *Rerum Novarum* is, of course, not the whole story of Leo XIII's view of property. In subsequent sections Leo puts forth the traditional Catholic teaching on property as expressed by Thomas Aquinas. Citing Thomas Aquinas he writes: ". . . Man ought not regard external goods as his own but as common so that, in fact, a person should readily share them when he sees others in need." Wherefore, the apostle says: "Charge the rich of this world . . . to give readily to others."[23] According to Leo, then, there really is no absolute right to dispose of wages, land, and personal property as one wishes (*uti velit*). Rather, Christians have an obligation to use their property and talents for their own good and the good of others.

> . . . Whoever has received from the bounty of God a greater share of goods, whether corporeal and external, or of the soul, has received them for this purpose, namely, that he employ them for his own perfection, and likewise, as a servant of Divine Providence, for the benefit of others.[24]

In the section on the role of the State, Leo XIII clearly says that duties owed to God take precedence over rights belonging to human beings. In this Leonine perspective it makes no sense to speak of individual rights to property apart from obligations to love God, self, and neighbor.

Rerum Novarum teaches that nothing in life is more important than virtue. Those examining the example given by Jesus, says Leo, cannot fail to understand these truths: "The true dignity and excellence of human beings consist in moral living, that is in virtue; virtue is the common inheritance of man, attainable equally by the humblest and the mightiest, by the rich and poor; and the reward of eternal happiness will follow upon virtue and merit alone, regardless of the person in whom they may be found."[25] *Rerum*

---

23 *Rerum Novarum*, #36.
24 *Ibid.*
25 *Ibid.*, #37.

Novarum also teaches that the attainment of the common good – including the material relief of the working class – can only be attained if people practice virtue at home, in the marketplace, and in positions of political and civic leadership. "Wherefore, if human society is to be healed, only a return to Christian life and practices will heal it."[26] (*"Revocatio vitae institutorumque Christianorum"*; *"il ritorno alla vita e ai costumi Christiani"*):

> . . . Since religion alone, as we said in the beginning, can remove the evil root and branch, let all reflect upon this. First and foremost, Christian morals must be re-established, without which even the weapons of prudence [*arma prudentiae*], which are considered especially effective, will be of no avail to secure well-being.[27]

To understand why virtue is necessary for the common good it is necessary to understand what virtue is. Leo XIII, of course, does not present a systematic comprehensive treatment of virtue in *Rerum Novarum*. He surely presupposes that his readers will rely upon their knowledge of authoritative Catholic tradition to understand his full intent. Leo, nevertheless, does give indications.

Throughout the centuries, the great Christian theologians have clearly shown that virtue moderates passions for wealth, pleasure, honor, glory, power; overcomes sloth or acedia, envy, pride, anger, and brooding resentment over injuries. Leo XIII lays stress on the role of Christian morals in restraining "the twin plagues of life – excessive desire for wealth and thirst for pleasure – which too often make men wretched amidst the very abundance of riches . . ."[28] These vices lead people both to dissipate their own material goods and to be unjust toward their neighbor by doing harm and by failing to do good. People overly intent on wealth and pleasure will not be attentive to ways they might serve their neighbor.

Another important theme in theological writing on virtue is bearing the pains and injustices of life. Patient endurance is the most prominent theme in St. Ambrose's *De Officiis*. Leo XIII lays stress on bearing with equanimity natural and social inequity "the evil consequences of sin," and unavoidable poverty.[29] Leo tries to mitigate the offensiveness of inequality by pointing out that people are unequal by nature with respect to talents, skill,

26 *Ibid.,* #41.
27 *Ibid.,* #82.
28 *Ibid.,* #42.
29 *Ibid.,* #26, 27, 37.

health, etc., and that any community "requires varied aptitudes and diverse services." In other words, without differences among men and women and truly superior talents in some individuals, the common good of a nation cannot be achieved. Leo's observations on sin are based on the premise that "the best course is to view human affairs as they are . . ."[30] All people will inevitably suffer the consequences of their own sins as well as the sins of others. Leo is not preaching any kind of fatalism. In fact, he exhorts people to seek virtue in their lives and beseeches civic and political leaders as well as all citizens to fight injustices and every other kind of evil. Finally, he subscribes to the belief that fortune has a lot to with whether one ends up poor in life. He attempts to console the poor by arguing that they may still seek and acquire the most important good in life, viz., virtue. He urges the poor not to grow bitter because of their lot in life but to look to the example of Jesus Christ "who for the salvation of men, being rich, became poor. . . ."[31]

In discussing eternal life Leo adds a few more significant reflections on suffering. He clearly implies that everyone, whether rich or poor, will suffer various pains in this life:

> Jesus Christ by His "plentiful redemption" has by no means taken away the various tribulations with which mortal life is interwoven, but has so clearly transformed them into incentives to virtue and sources of merit . . .[32]

He even adds that every mortal must carry his cross in order to attain salvation. However, Jesus Christ, says Leo, "has wonderfully lightened the burden of suffering and labor, and not only by his example but also by his grace and by holding before us the hope of eternal reward."[33]

Ordered passions and patient endurance are necessary if virtue is to overcome conflict and bring about concord among the various classes in society. Leo is convinced that the performance of duties by employers and employees will bring together and unite the various members of society. For example, a sense of duty inclines employees to do their work well and not to injure employers or the larger society while seeking their interests. Conscientious employers treat their workers with respect and fulfill their most important duty, to pay a just wage. In short, if employers and employ-

---

30 *Ibid.,* #27.
31 *Ibid.,* #37.
32 *Ibid.,* #33.
33 *Ibid.,*

ees "obey Church teachings, not merely friendship but brotherly love will also bind them to each other."[34]

The virtues of justice and charity incline people to take initiatives in order to meet the needs of others. The Church, says Leo, "ameliorates the conditions of the worker through her numerous and efficient institutions,"[35] and attempts "to have the thought and energy of all classes of society united to this end, that the interests of the workers be protected as fully as possible."[36] While Leo urges his readers to rely on divine help to solve social problems, he also exhorts every concerned party to make use of any appropriate means within human power. As already mentioned in the discussion on property, virtue leads a person to use wealth and talents as a means to love God and neighbor.

Leo does not give an exhaustive account of how one comes to understand and practice virtue, but he still gives a few indications. For Leo the Church plays an important role in educating the mind and forming the will. He says that priests should not cease "to impress upon men of all ranks examples of Christian living drawn from the Gospel."[37] They should also "aim both to preserve in themselves and to arouse in others . . . the mistress and queen of the virtues, charity."[38] The Church receives divine assistance in her work to educate the laity to a life of virtue from "the instruments" given to her by Jesus Christ. (This must be a reference to sacramental grace.) With divine help people can overcome selfishness and love both God and neighbor. In Leo's perspective, divine grace generating virtue in the laity is necessary for the solution of political and social problems.

Leo's treatment of the State gives indications of how governmental leaders practice virtue in their position and how laws enforce a certain measure of virtue, especially by preventing people from doing harm to one another. Through laws and institutions a correctly founded State seeks both private and public well-being. To secure these goals, wise political leaders must see to it that States have the following:

> Wholesome morality, properly ordered family life, protection of religion and justice, moderate imposition and equitable distribution of

---

34 *Ibid.,* #38.
35 *Ibid.,* #25.
36 *Ibid.*
37 *Ibid.,* #83.
38 *Ibid.,* #40.

public burdens, progressive development of industry and trade, thriving agriculture, and by all other things of this nature.[39]

Still other factors contributing to the private and public welfare are, of course, peace and good order, punishment for crime, strong citizens capable of supporting and protecting the State, the availability of work, a moral and healthy atmosphere in one's place of work. In any case where the elements of a flourishing State are threatened "the power and authority of the law, but of course within certain limits, manifestly ought to be employed."[40] Leo specifies limits to the reach of law because "it is proper that the individual and the family should be permitted to retain their freedom of action, so far as this is possible without jeopardizing the common good and without injuring anyone."[41]

Since the use of material goods is an element of a well-constituted State and necessary for the practice of virtue, the state must make sure that there is an adequate supply and a just distribution of material goods. It is the State's responsibility to protect all citizens "maintaining inviolate that justice especially which is called *distributive*."[42] For example, the State must see to it that workers have adequate housing, clothing, and security. "In protecting the rights of private individuals however, special consideration must be given to the weak and the poor."[43] The rich, argues Leo, have less need of governmental protection.

Other duties of the State are as follows: Restrain those who stir up disorder and incite workers to violence; anticipate and prevent the evil of strikes by removing early the causes of discontent through "the authority of the law"; limit the hours of work so that people will not be crushed in spirit or body; shield women and especially children from physical labor beyond their capacity; intervene, if necessary, to make sure that wages are sufficient to support a thrifty worker and his family.[44]

Leo lays particular stress on the State's duty to use the law both to protect the "sacred right" of property and to foster ownership of property among the largest possible number of citizens. From the protection of the right to property by the State will flow the following benefits: a more equi-

39 *Ibid.*, #48.
40 *Ibid.*, #53.
41 *Ibid.*, #52.
42 *Ibid.*, #49.
43 *Ibid.*, #54.
44 *Ibid.*, #53.

table distribution of goods, a greater abundance of national wealth and as a consequence a strong incentive to remain in the country of one's birth.[45] Leo explains that the opportunity to possess private property will stir workers to be more productive, thus, making a significant contribution to national wealth. Greater productivity stimulated by state-created opportunities will at length remove the difference between extreme wealth and extreme poverty with the result that "one class will become neighbor to the other."[46] Leo clearly suggests that great harmony among citizens depends on greater equality in property holdings.

Not only does Leo lay great stress on the State guarantee of the right to property, but he also holds that the power of the State should protect "first of all, the goods of [the workers'] soul (*bona animi*).[47] This is because the ultimate purpose of life is to perfect the life of the soul "through knowledge of truth and love of good."[48] When Leo explicitly discusses the State responsibility toward the "*bona animi*," he does not give enough concrete examples to explain his meaning. He does seem to imply that the State has to insure "necessary cessation from toil and work on Sundays and Holy Days of Obligation." Leo clearly implies that the State directly protects goods of the soul by its action to promote morality, properly ordered family life, religion and justice.[49]

Not only the Church and government can make a significant contribution to the resolution of the social question but also employers and workers themselves. In other words, individuals can form various kinds of associations in order to promote the well-being of various groups, especially those who cannot help themselves. The pope first praises associations for giving mutual aid, i.e., those caring for children, adolescents and the aged and those providing for the families of workers who die prematurely or become incapacitated through sickness or accidents.

Leo ascribes the most importance to associations of workers, either alone or of workers with employers. The purpose of these workers' associations should be to procure for individual members "an increase in the goods of body, of soul, and of prosperity."[50] Their principal goal, says Leo XIII,

---

45 *Ibid.*, #66.
46 *Ibid.*
47 *Ibid.*, #57.
48 *Ibid.*
49 *Ibid.*, #48.
50 *Ibid.*, #76.

should, of course, be moral and religious perfection. To accomplish this goal Leo suggests that associations provide opportunity for religious instruction so that workers may understand clearly their duties to God, neighbor, and self. For example, workers must be taught that the sacraments "are the divine means for purifying the soul from the stains of sin and for attaining sanctity."[51]

Among the most important services to be provided by workers associations are as follows:

> That the workers at no time be without sufficient work, and that the monies paid into the treasury of the association furnish the means of assisting individual members in need, not only during sudden and unforeseen changes in industry, but also wherever anyone is stricken by sicknesses, old age, or by misfortune.[52]

So, even though Leo stresses the spiritual role of workers associations, he expects them to deliver adequate financial help to needy members.

Leo thinks that the existence of associations is very important for the well-being of society. In fact as "man is permitted by his right of nature to form associations, the State does not have the authority to forbid them."[53] The State may, of course, regulate or even oppose associations if their objectives are clearly at variance "with good morals, with justice, or with the welfare of the State."[54] The pope's position on associations follows from the well established principle that man is a social animal.

> Just as man is drawn by his natural propensity into civil union and association, so also he seeks with his fellow citizens to form other societies, admittedly small and not perfect, but societies none the less.[55]

Without associations, including the commonwealth, people could not provide for their physical needs nor develop their intellectual and spiritual lives.

Despite the problems posed by tensions with *Rerum Novarum* it is an extraordinary document that still sheds light on the role of the Church in the world, especially because of its teaching on virtue, the State's role in protecting rights and promoting the goods of the soul, and the important tasks

---

51 *Ibid.*, #47.
52 *Ibid.*, #79.
53 *Ibid.*, #72.
54 *Ibid.*
55 *Ibid.*, #70.

of individuals and voluntary associations. This last point anticipates Pius XI's emphasis on subsidiarity as an essential element of any political order (*Quadragesimo Anno*, 1931).

III. Centesimus Annus

Very recently, John Paul II issued his encyclical *Centesimus Annus* on the one hundredth anniversary of *Rerum Novarum*. The pope reaffirmed the orientation of *Rerum Novarum* by endorsing Leo XIII's four general proposals with respect to private property, the Church, the State, and voluntary associations. John Paul II's latest contribution to the development of papal social teaching is not so much the endorsement of the free economy or the correction of the market by public intervention; for John Paul II's endorsement of a free economy is qualified: "It would appear that on the level of industrial nations and of international relations, *the free market* is the most efficient instrument for utilizing resources and responding to needs." His endorsement of State intervention to guide the market and correct abuses is familiar Catholic teaching. In my mind, what is really striking about *Centesimus Annus* is the reaffirmation and development of *Rerum Novarum's* teaching on virtue as well as the further clarification of Catholic teaching on the relation between rights and virtue.

When the Church accomplishes her mission – which is, of course, to evangelize – she not only contributes to the salvation of all, but also makes her best contribution to the renewal of the temporal order. In John Paul II's words "there can be *no genuine solution of the 'social question' apart from the Gospel . . .*"[56] Evangelization, says John Paul II "must include among its essential elements a proclamation of the Church's social doctrine." "The guiding principle . . . of the Church's social doctrine," affirms John Paul II, "*is a correct view of the human person . . .*"[57] From an accurate knowledge of the human person there necessarily follows "a correct picture of society." In proclaiming her social doctrine, the Church clearly is aiming at promoting the common good of society, but she is also directing men and women, says John Paul II "on the path of salvation."[58]

John Paul II logically draws two conclusions regarding the Church's contribution to society. First, the Church makes a specific and decisive contribution to true culture "by preaching the truth about the creation of the

---

56 Pope John Paul II, *Centesimus Annus,* #15.
57 *Ibid.,* #13.
58 *Ibid.,* #54.

world . . . and by preaching the truth about the Redemption . . ."[59] Second, the Church's "contribution to the political order is precisely her vision of the dignity of the human person revealed in all its fullness in the mystery of the Incarnate Word."[60]

John Paul's vision of the human person and society in *Centesimus Annus* is not easily summarized. I will attempt to bring out the pope's angle on the person by explaining his concept of obedience to truth and his many and varied references to virtue, and also his defense of human rights.

The human person is bound to obey the truth about God and man. Created in the image and likeness of God he or she is free but under an obligation to live in accordance with God's will. In other words, the human person "must . . . respect the natural and moral structure with which he has been endowed."[61] Since redemption frees people from sin and thereby forges bonds of unity, they have the ability and obligation to love all of humanity.

Freedom not bound to the truth ends up "submitting itself to the vilest of passions, to the point of self-destruction."[62] Examples of disordered passions having personal and social consequences readily come to mind, viz., inordinate love of pleasure, gain, honor, glory, as well as anger, hatred, envy, sloth and pride.

John Paul locates "the origin of all the evils to which *Rerum Novarum* wished to respond" in an understanding and exercise of freedom which, "in the area of economic and social activity, cuts itself off from the truth about man."[63] Personal and social evils are bound to occur when the grounds for choice are not truth, goodness and communion with others. Freedom without truth becomes self love, says John Paul, "self love carried to the point of contempt for God and neighbor, a self-love which leads to an unbridled affirmation of self-interest and which refuses to be limited by any demand of justice."[64] This Augustinian-sounding sentence means that without a sense of obligation to truth, human beings will necessarily have no scruples about unabashedly pursuing their interests, and seeking power without regard for what is right or even the rights of others. Thus, without a bond between freedom and truth there is "no sure principle of guaranteeing just relations be-

---

59 *Ibid.*, #51.
60 *Ibid.*, #47.
61 *Ibid.*, #38.
62 *Ibid.*, #4.
63 *Ibid.*
64 *Ibid.*, #17.

tween people"[65] and there is no firm ground for the duty to respect rights, the leading moral principle of liberal democracies.[66]

Without virtue there is disorder in the soul and deficient justice within nations and between nations. "Authentic democracy," says John Paul II, "is possible only in a state ruled by law, and on the basis of a correct conception of the human person."[67] If democratic citizens do not practice virtue, "a democracy . . . easily turns into open or thinly disguised totalitarianism."[68]

John Paul does not attempt to explain all aspects of virtue but focuses on the ordination of virtue toward the common good. The pope describes solidarity as "one of the fundamental principles of the Christian view of social and political organizations."[69] In *Solicitudo Rei Socialis* he defines the Christian virtue of solidarity as "a firm and persevering determination to commit oneself to the common good . . ."[70]

In the present encyclical, *Centesimus Annus*, he identifies solidarity with "friendship," "social charity," and the "civilization of love," concepts used respectively by Pope Leo XIII, Pius XI, and Paul VI.[71] People practice the virtue of solidarity in many different ways. For example, they do not regard their property as simply their own but recognize that material possessions are in some way "common to all."[72] They are inclined to put their property and talents at the service of others. Solidarity also leads people to do their work conscientiously for the sake of others. In other words, they turn out a quality product or service as a contribution to the common good. Talented people use their initiative and entrepreneurial ability to establish useful businesses. Solidarity also inclines people to dismantle "structures of sin" established by inordinate desire for power and profit. Solidarity, of course, leads citizens to work for just public policy.

Still another example of solidarity is work to help the poor acquire expertise in order to survive *and* to be in a position to make a contribution to the common good. The poor do not live by bread alone. The preferential option for the poor, then, must include serious attention to education, family

---

65 *Ibid.,* #44.
66 *Ibid.,* #17.
67 *Ibid.,* #46.
68 *Ibid.*
69 *Ibid.,* #10.
70 *Solicitudo Rei Socialis,* #38.
71 *Centesimus Annus,* #10.
72 *Ibid.,* #30.

life, job training, in addition to protection from crime and state-provided aid for the unemployed.

John Paul II underlines his point regarding the importance of living the virtue of solidarity by offering a new slant on the concept of alienation.

> A man is alienated if he refuses to transcend himself and to live the experience of self-giving and of the formation of an authentic human community oriented toward his final destiny, which is God. A society is alienated if its forms of social organization, production and consumption make it more difficult to offer this gift of self and to establish this solidarity between people.[73]

Production and consumption should not hinder the spiritual, moral, and intellectual development of the human person. Rather, John Paul II says, "it is . . . necessary to create life styles in which the quest for truth, beauty, goodness and communion with others for the sake of common growth are the factors which determine consumer choices, savings and investments."[74]

Solidarity is the kind of overarching virtue in John Paul's thought that depends on the work of other virtues. For example, to practice the virtue of solidarity, a person needs control over his appetites for pleasure, money, power and prestige. He or she must have the patience to bear up in the face of difficulties. In other words, citizens need temperance and fortitude, not to mention prudence and justice.

John Paul II brings out clearly that the attempt to live a virtuous life demands a lifelong struggle. He writes, ". . . as long as time lasts the struggle between good and evil continues even in the human heart itself."[75] In other words, there is no absolutely firm hold on a virtuous character. There will always be temptation and room for improvement.

The successful struggle against evil by the practice of virtue not only requires constant human effort but willingness to receive God's gift of grace. John Paul II explains:

> Therefore, in order that the demands of justice be met, and attempts to achieve this good may succeed, what is needed is the *gift of grace, a gift* which comes from God. Grace in cooperation with human freedom constitutes the mysterious presence of God in history which is Providence.[76]

---

73 *Ibid.*, #41.
74 *Ibid.*, #36.
75 *Ibid.*, #25.
76 *Ibid.*, #59.

This stress on the necessity of grace to live a virtuous life reinforces John Paul II's point that the Church makes her best contribution to society by fulfilling her God given mission.

The failure of citizens to overcome their vices has profound consequences for the life of society according to John Paul II. The pope goes so far as to say that the two world wars would not have been possible "without the terrible burden of hatred and resentment which had been built up as a result of so many injustices both on the international level and within individual states."[77] A bright future for Eastern Europe, he adds, depends on overcoming the ill will and hatred that accumulated during the Communist domination of Eastern Europe. Communist Eastern Europe needs not only economic reform but "moral reconstruction" both in order to avoid a resurgence of hatred and to promote "basic virtues of economic life, such as truthfulness, trustworthiness, and hard work,"[78] which were denigrated under communism.

Finally, John Paul II is aware that education to virtue requires decisive input from the family and a favorable environment created by the culture of a nation – in addition to the work of the Church. It is in *"the family"* that people receive their "first formative ideas about truth and goodness and [learn] what it means to love and to be loved, and thus what it actually means to be a person."[79]

While obedience to truth or the practice of virtue are the most important aspects of a person's dignity, the protection of human rights gives a person the freedom to fulfill his or her duties. "In a certain sense," John Paul writes, "the source and synthesis of their rights is religious freedom, understood as the right to live in the truth of one's faith and in conformity with one's transcendent dignity as a person."[80] John Paul gives a list of other rights requiring protection by democratic government: the right to life; the right to live in a united, loving family; the right to educate one's mind; the right to earn a living through work; the right to found a family and rear children through the responsible exercise of one's sexuality. It is, of course, hard to see how some of these rights could be guaranteed by law. For example, the only guarantee for growing up in a loving, united family is parents with the requisite character traits and convictions.

---

77 *Ibid.*, #17.
78 *Ibid.*, #27.
79 *Ibid.*, #39.
80 *Ibid.*, #47.

Other rights deserving protection according to John Paul are as follows: the right to private property, the right to form associations, the right to a just wage and decent working conditions, the right to procure what is necessary to live, the rights of the human conscience which is bound only by natural and revealed truth, the rights of a whole people to subsistence and progress. Securing the protection of these rights requires not only appropriate constitutional guarantees, federal and state laws, but also individuals and mediating structures guided by a sense of justice.

Appendix

Other Practical Implications of Catholic Social Thought for the Church's Service of the Common Good

1)The Church must keep in mind that government, voluntary associations, individuals, and the Church all make a contribution to the common good.

2)What the Church does to promote its own internal renewal benefits the political and social order.

3)Consequently, in order to promote the common good – not to mention salvation – the Church must continue to improve the following:

a)Liberal education for candidates to the priesthood and religious life, especially philosophical education as mentioned in the Final Report of the 1985 Synod.

b)The religious education of children and young people in Catholic schools and CCD programs.

c)Marriage preparation and ministry to families.

d)Religious instruction from the pulpit.

e)Liberal education in Catholic colleges and universities.

f)Education of the nation's underclass from grades K through 12 in Catholic schools.

g)Education of the laity to take up all tasks pertaining to the attainment of the common good, e.g., work and involvement in the formation of policy.

h)Actual widespread involvement of the laity in volunteer work and the formation of policy at all levels of government.

i)Work to establish a tradition of learning among Catholics.

4)In addressing the American public the Church makes a significant contribution to the renewal of liberal democracy by focusing on the following themes:

a)The elements of the common good in a liberal democracy, especially virtue, education, family life, the role of law in building character, the importance of conscientious work, ethics in the professions and trades.

b)The reasons why the nation should restrict abortion and not legalize euthanasia.

c)The problems of the underclass, e.g., safety, education, family life, drugs.

d)Public morality of generosity and chastity.

e)The overemphasis on rights.

f)The crisis in the legal profession manifested by the plethora of unjust lawsuits.

g)The argument that religion and the Church benefit contemporary culture and liberal democracy by teaching and works of mercy.

Themes Of Catholic Social Thought Needing Clarification

1.What the State can do to promote moral standards and dispose citizens to the practice of virtue through law.

2.The meaning of virtue and its connection to the common good.

3.a)The relation between rights and virtue.

27.

Opening the Mystery of Christ in the Scriptures: Considerations of Approach for Preaching the Scriptures (1992)

Sister Joan Gormley, S.S.M.W.

The purpose of the present paper is to address the problem of the movement from the written word of the Scripture to the spoken word of preaching and teaching. This will be done in two principal stages. First, we will consider the nature of preaching and some specific challenges which arise for it on the contemporary scene. Then we will suggest an approach to Scripture which corresponds to its reality as the inspired word of God, whose meaning is found in Christ and whose purpose is fulfillment of the divine plan for salvation and sanctification of humankind, measuring the approaches of historical criticism and patristic exegesis by the criterion of adequacy for opening the inspired word of God. Finally, by way of conclusion, we will give an example of traditional patristic exegesis with its concern for the literal and spiritual dimensions of the sacred text.

I. The Nature of Preaching and Contemporary Challenges

In a sermon addressed to pastors, St. Augustine raises the question of how to deal with those in the congregation who are not just weak, but sick from evil desires and attachment to sin, and thus unable to make any move in their Christian lives. Augustine's advice is to act like the friends of the paralytic who, unable to get to Jesus through the door, removed the tiles from the roof and lowered the paralyzed man before Jesus (Mark 2:1–12). The pastor should lower the paralyzed members of his flock down before Jesus by opening to them the Scriptures: ". . . for the true understanding of Scripture is hidden. Reveal therefore what is hidden and thus you will open the roof and lower the paralytic to the feet of Christ."[1] Augustine gives here

---

1 St. Augustine, Sermon 46, 13 in *The Liturgy of the Hours according to the*

a wonderful summation of the nature of the Church's preaching and teaching of God's word: It brings the listeners to the saving encounter with Christ, who has the power to free from sin and the paralysis accompanying it.

Through preaching, the written words of the Bible are transposed into the living voice of the minister of the word, a pattern consonant with God's way of revealing himself through the living testimony of chosen messengers – prophets, apostles, their successors, priests, catechists, teachers. The movement from written to spoken word enables a more immediate encounter of God with his people and of Christ with his Church, since face-to-face meeting is always more personal than encounter with a book.[2] Also, in preaching or teaching, the scriptural words are opened up and interpreted so that they might illuminate the lives of those who hear them, bringing them into the company of the witnesses who met Jesus during his ministry. The dynamic of the transmission of the gospel is ever the same as that described in the opening verses of the First Letter of John, likewise used to open *Dei Verbum*, the Vatican II Constitution on Divine Revelation: "We declare to you what was from the beginning, what we have heard, what we have seen with our eyes, what we have looked at and touched with our hands . . . so that you may have fellowship with us; and truly our fellowship is with the Father and with his Son Jesus Christ" (I John 1:1–3).[3]

The preaching and teaching of the word of God, especially of the Word Incarnate, was seen by the apostles and evangelists to be a work of salvation; one might say a matter of life and death. Their purposes in their apostolic preaching were, as St. Paul makes abundantly clear in numerous passages in his letters, radically different from professional rhetoricians of their day. The apostles of Jesus Christ did not speak in order to please or en-

---

Roman Rite, Vol. IV, (New York: Catholic Book Publishing Co., 1975), p. 286.

2 St. Jerome, commenting on Galatians 4:9, says that the reason Paul longs to see the Galatians face to face is because of the greater power of the spoken word. See Jerome, *In Galatas,* in *Oeuvres complètes de* Jérôme, Paris: Louis Vives, 1884, pp. 308–9. Cardinal Bea, in his commentary on *Dei Verbum* speaks of a "certain deficiency" permitted by God in the written word which makes necessary the spoken (Augustin Cardinal Bea, The Word of God and Mankind (Chicago: Franciscan Herald Press, 1967, p. 155).

3 Scriptural quotations are taken from *The Holy Bible: New Revised Standard Version* New York: Oxford University Press, 1989.

tertain their listeners but to transmit the word of God and to preach salvation through the Cross and Resurrection of Christ (I Corinthians 2:1–5; Galatians 4:19–20; etc.). From Paul's testimony, we hear that the preached word was powerful. The Thessalonians received it, not as a human word, but as the word of God, backed up by the convincing power of the Spirit and bearing fruit in the lives of faith, love, and hope which were manifest to all who saw them (I Thessalonians 1:2–10). The apostle recalls the Galatians to the cross of Christ which was displayed before them in his preaching and accompanied by the activity of the Spirit and miracles (Galatians 3:1–5). Repeatedly in his letters, Paul encourages those he had evangelized to recall the event of his preaching of Christ among them as their own personal meeting with God's power in Christ and to recall the powerful effects of the proclamation of Christ: the overcoming of sin and death; the living of new life in Christ. The very structure of the Pauline letters indicates that Paul expects to see effects of his preaching: he announces the gospel of Christ and then exhorts the Christians to live in accord with it.

Turning from apostolic times to our own day, we might wonder if the word of God has lost its power or whether we have lost access to that power, both for preaching and teaching the word and for receiving it. For those who preach the gospel and those who listen to the preaching, come from the same culture where faith is severely weakened and separated from life. Many, including some who attend Sunday Mass and who are involved in the transmission of the faith to others, neither know nor live their faith,[4] in spite of the fact that they think they do. It would seem that, at least to some extent, we witness the fulfillment of the words of Amos prophesying a coming famine for the word of the Lord: "The time is surely coming, says the

---

4 Angel Cardenal Suquía, *"Discurso Inaugural,"* XVI *Asamblea Plenaria de la Conferencia Episcopal Española,* (Madrid: Orinoco, 1992). The archbishop of Madrid and president of the Spanish Episcopal Conference speaks of the advanced dechristianization of Europe in words which no doubt have their application in the U.S. Besides manifest deficiencies in preaching and catechesis, there is the problem of the "post-modern Christian" who does not even understand the terminology of the Christian faith – though he thinks he does – and does not see life in terms of faith. Cardinal Suquía speaks of a separation of faith and life so profound that there is no substantial difference between the way the contemporary Christian views life and the perspective of a pagan. This underscores the need for a new evangelization, able to touch the heart of the modern person.

Lord God, when I will send a famine on the land; not a famine of bread, or a thirst for water, but of hearing the words of the Lord. They [the people] shall wander from sea to sea, and from north to east; they shall run to and fro, seeking the word of the Lord but they shall not find it" (Amos 8:11–12).

Ministers of the word – and here we use the term in the broader sense of *Dei Verbum* (#23, #25) where it refers primarily to the priest who preaches the liturgical homily, but also to teachers and catechists who transmit the word of God to others – might rightly claim that much of the material which is provided them for understanding Scripture, is not entirely helpful. Certainly scholarly exegesis often confuses and obscures instead of clarifying and illuminating. It is not just that scholars tend toward abstraction from ordinary life, but that help for preaching is sought in methods, linked from birth to the anti-Christian cultural project we know as the Enlightenment,[5] that, is to the same dominant culture which is largely responsible for the weakening of faith described above.

If it is true that, in spite of a plethora of books on Scripture and on the formation of study groups and the like, many Christians experience a deprivation of the nourishment and sustenance for life found only in God's word, we can expect that they will, as the prophecy of Amos says, "run here and there" looking for substitutes. Witness for example, the interest in self-help books, which now occupy extensive space in bookstores, including Catholic bookstores; interest in creation spirituality, participation in fundamentalist Bible study groups. Those charged with preaching the gospel, for their part, come to terms with the difficulties of opening the Scriptures in a variety of ways. Some use "canned" homilies from one of the many available homily services; some, with little attention to matters of faith, pass on the results of historical criticism of the Bible;[6] others reduce the homily or in-

---

5 Msgr. Francisco Javier Martínez, "*Studia Semitica Novi Testamenti: Presentación" Jesucristo: su persona y su obra* by Cesar A. Franco Martínez, *Collección Studia Semitica Novi Testamenti* I Madrid: Fundación San Justino, 1992), pp. 9–18.

6 The problem we are describing is exacerbated immensely if the one proclaiming the gospel has lost faith in the word of God proclaimed in the Church. In this paper, we are not speaking specifically of those alienated from the Church. However, an interesting example of such can be found in David Friedrich Strauss, author of *Das Leben Jesu*, published in English as *The Life of Jesus Critically Examined*, (Philadelphia: Fortress Press, 1972). In his introduction, the editor, Peter Hodgson, describes the problem of

struction to the level of conventional wisdom, of gospel values or principles.[7] Still others suggest the replacement of scriptural homilies with ones
based on dogma or catechesis; they recommend thematic sermons which
give the Church's teaching on pertinent issues such as abortion or contraception. All of these solutions are attempts to deal with what can only be
called a crisis in preaching. While it is true that such a crisis is part of a
much larger phenomenon, we can nonetheless concentrate our attention on
this one important dimension of the problem of faith in the contemporary
world. For, as Paul exclaims in Romans, the proclamation of the minister of
the gospel is irreplaceable for engendering faith: "How are they to believe
in one of whom they have never heard? And how are they to hear without
someone to proclaim him? . . . Faith comes through what is heard, and what
is heard comes through the word of Christ" (Romans 10:14–17).

II. Finding a Method in accord with Scripture as Inspired

The most basic theological principle for the interpretation of Scripture,
to which every preacher and teacher must have constant recourse, is that it is
the inspired word of God and thus the work of both divine and human authors.[8]

To illuminate the mystery of the divine and human origin of Scripture,
Vatican II invoked the parallel between the inspiration of Scripture and the
Incarnation of the Eternal Son of God: "For the words of God, expressed in
human language, have been made like human discourse, just as the Word of
the Eternal Father, when He took to Himself the flesh of human weakness,
was made like men" (*DV* #15). This parallel shows the importance attached
in the tradition to the human, as well as to the divine aspects of Scripture.

conscience which arose for Strauss in his office as pastor, charged with
preaching the Scriptures to "ordinary Christians" who believed things which
he no longer did (p. xxi). It is not surprising that Strauss is considered an
"alienated theologian" and "first of the modern 'unhappy lovers' of
Christian theology" (p. xv).

7   For examples, at times humorous, see Donald G. Miller, *The Way to Biblical
    Preaching* (New York: Abingdon Press, 1958).

8   Pope John Paul II, addressing the plenary session of the Pontifical Biblical
    Commission, called for an exegesis which is theological as well as historical
    ("Exegesis is a Theological Discipline," *L'Osservatore Romano*, April 22,
    1991). On the necessity of choosing a method, adequate to the reality being
    studied, see Luigi Giussani, *The Religious Sense*, (San Francisco: Ignatius
    Press, 1990), pp. 7–17.

Just as the tradition refuses insistently any denial of the humanity of Christ, or any denial of his bodily presence in the Eucharist, or any denial of the visible aspect of the Church, so it insists on the primary and basic importance of the human word of Scripture (*Dei Verbum* #11). In approaching the Scriptures, therefore, it is necessary, for preachers and teachers, as well as for exegetes and scholars, to search for the intended meaning of the human author, understood as the literal meaning of the text. Because the human words of Scripture, through which God's word comes to us, were not written in our own time and space, our approach to the scriptures must necessarily include various aspects of historical inquiry: study of languages, literary genres, political and cultural traditions, figures of speech (*Dei Verbum* #12). Even those who do not engage directly in such work must respect the historical character of the Bible, not imposing meaning coming from our own historical and cultural situation, but seeking the meaning intended by the sacred author. For it is precisely *within* the human words which God assumed and made his own – not beyond them – that the meaning which God wishes to communicate for our salvation is to be found (*Dei Verbum* #11). With a view to underscoring the essential importance of the literal meaning, Luis Alonso-Schökel paraphrases the question about love of God and neighbor found in I John 4:20: If anyone does not understand the human author who is speaking, how can he understand the ineffable God?[9] Also without careful attention to the word of the human author, the danger is that the so-called spiritual meanings will be little more than flights of fancy – the substitution of a human word for God's word.[10]

But, in giving norms for interpretation of Scripture, *Dei Verbum* does not stop with the call for attention to the meaning intended by the human author but calls also for attention to three theological norms: the unity of the Scriptures, the living tradition of the Church, and the analogy of faith or harmony existing among elements of the faith. The basis for addition of these theological norms was expressed in a patristic formula found many times in Origen and St. Jerome: Theological norms are to be applied be-

---

9 Luis Alonso-Schökel et. Al., Commentarios a la constitución Dei Verbum (Madrid: Biblioteca de autores cristianos, 1969).
10 For warnings against imposition of meaning on Scripture, see Leo XIII, *Providentissimus Deus*, and Pius XII, *Divino Afflante Spiritu*, #27.

cause "Sacred Scripture must be read and interpreted in the same Spirit[11] in which it was written."[12]

Thus, it is impossible for anyone, whether scholar or minister of the word, to arrive at the full understanding of the mystery of the inspired words by human effort alone and without the aid of the Holy Spirit who inspired the words. Writer, reader, and interpreter of Scripture, though distant in time and space, are all united by being moved by the one Holy Spirit and by sharing one faith. The Spirit in which the Scriptures were written is the Spirit of Christ, the mystery handed on in the Church. Apart from Christ and His Church, there is no possibility of reading and interpreting the Scriptures "in the same Spirit in which they were written" or of penetrating to the divine mystery mediated by the human words.

As we have seen, Vatican Council II approved, encouraged, and even mandated critical historical inquiry to determine the literal meaning of the text, a work for which understanding in the Spirit is not a replacement. (In fact, the Church has had countless examples of saints and Fathers who were critical scholars. Preeminent among them for the study of the Bible were Origen and St. Jerome, both of whom were convinced of the presence of the mystery of Christ in the words of the Bible and both of whom devoted themselves to the critical study of scripture using all the means at their disposal).[13] At present, preachers and teachers of God's word have available many resources gathered over the last two centuries which illuminate the

---

11 We translate here according to the Latin text which reads: "*Sed, cum Sacra Scriptura eodem Spiritu quo scripta est etiam legenda et interpretanda sit....*" The NCWC translation, published by the Daughters of St. Paul, does not capitalize the first letter of Wilfrid Harrington's translation omits the phrase "in the same Spirit," reading instead that Scripture must be read and interpreted "with its divine authorship in mind" (*Vatican Council II: The Conciliar and Post-Conciliar Documents*, ed. by Austin Flannery, O.P. (Northport, NY: Costello Publishing Company, 1975), p. 758.

12 Ignace de la Potterie, "Interpretation of Holy Scripture in the Spirit in Which it was Written (*Dei Verbum*12c)" in *Vatican II: Assessment and Perspectives Twenty-Five Years After*, Vol. I, ed. by René Latourelle (New York: Paulist Press, 1988), pp. 220–65.

13 On the prodigious work of Origen, see Jean Daniélou, *Origen*, (New York: Sheed and Ward, 1955), pp. 131–73 and Hans Urs von Balthasar, *Origen: Spirit and Fire; a Thematic Anthology of his Writings*, Washington, D.C.: CUA Press, 1984), pp. 1–3. For the critical work of Jerome, see Yvon Bodin, *St. Jerome et l'église*, Paris: Beauchesne, 1966, pp. 27ff. and *passim*.

Bible and its historical context. However, such methods, valuable and irreplaceable as they are, cannot give access to the full meaning of the inspired word, but can only prepare the way.

In fact, it is necessary for the interpreter, especially one who is involved in the Church's ministry of preaching and teaching, to be aware of those presuppositions and premises of contemporary historical criticism, which are alien, and can even be directly opposed, to Christian faith. Many conclusions of exegetical study have been seriously marred through imposition of philosophical and ideological presuppositions:[14] the Hegelian dialectic, Darwinian evolutionism, Heideggerian existentialism have all had their day as controlling the exegetical endeavor. Closer to our own time, we have seen the influence of feminist and liberation ideologies on the work of exegesis. Yet another difficulty is the tendency of form criticism to go beyond the limits of their method, creating reconstructions of the primitive Church to which they attribute greater certainty than evidence allows.[15] Finally, faith in what the Scriptures say has been regarded by proponents of historical criticism as an obstacle to understanding of the Scripture.

Thus, while the historical critical method can help in the understanding of the Bible, it also can prevent the interpreter from entering into its deeper meaning. It is faith expressing itself in prayer which prevents the preacher from being like those interpreters of the Bible, described by Origen, who sit by the wells which are the Scripture without ever taking a drink (*Hom. Gen.* 7, 6).

To penetrate to the full meaning of the Scriptures, one must take as presupposition and first premise the truth and efficacy of the mystery of Christ and our salvation in him which lies at the very center of Scripture.[16] The

---

14 Some erroneous premises of form criticism are listed in the instruction of the Pontifical Biblical Commission, Sancta Mater Ecclesia, April 21, 1964.

15 Joseph Cardinal Ratzinger, "Biblical Interpretation in Crisis: On the Question of the Foundations and Approaches of Exegesis Today," New York: Jan. 27, 1988.

16 Martínez, Jesucristo, pp. 11–12. Msgr. Martínez, in his essay introducing the new series of exegetical studies being published by the Fundación San Justino, establishes as starting point the Christian Faith as expressed in the New Testament and the Church's tradition, with faith in Jesus of Nazareth as Son of God as its center. This faith does not necessitate the renunciation of reason or history, but to the contrary, to face any and all historical problems with complete openness and confidence in the truth of the Christian claim.

deeper truth of the Scripture can be found only if one recognizes the "vast sea of mysteries" – to use the expression of Origen – which the inspired word contains. Such was the view of Scripture held in patristic exegesis. Pastors and teachers in the Church can find in the exegesis of the Fathers, direction for their own interpretation and transmission of the word of God in Scripture.

It must be admitted that in having recourse to the Fathers, we go against the fashion. Since the advent of historical criticism in the eighteenth century, and indeed until recently, patristic exegesis has fallen into disuse, not to say opprobrium, even within the Church. The norms for theological interpretation given in *Dei Verbum* #12 appear, however, to point the way to a return to the spirit, if not the modes, of patristic exegesis.[17] For many, this suggestion conjures up images of abandonment of historical criticism and return to allegorical interpretation, though such is not the necessary consequence.

Perhaps the best known data about patristic interpretation is the schema of four levels of meaning of the Scriptures, which perdured into the medieval period: the literal meaning (always considered to be of basic importance); the allegorical meaning, which was really the Christological meaning since the text was read in light of the mystery of Christ; the moral meaning, in which the biblical text was applied to the life in this world; and the mystical or eschatological meaning which sought meaning from the text with regard to the Christian's destiny to the fullness of contemplative union with God. Though the levels of interpretation are often regarded as naïve, archaic, and as exaggerating the spiritual meaning to the detriment of the literal meaning, we can perhaps find in them, if not a method in the strict sense of that term, at least a direction for an approach to interpretation and proclamation of Scripture which moves the hearts of those who hear and, at the same time, takes account of the humanity and divinity of the inspired word.

In the first place, the literal meaning of Scripture was regarded by the

---

17 This is suggested in an article on Dei Verbum #12 by Ignace de la Potterie, S.J., "Reading Holy Scripture 'in the Spirit': Is the Patristic Way of Reading the Bible Still Possible Today? *Communio*, 13 (1986), pp. 308–25. Denis Farkasfalvy makes a similar suggestion in an article in the same issue of *Communio*, "A Post-Critical Method of Biblical Interpretation," 288–307. The author points to the success of patristic exegesis in stimulating theological reflection and in preserving unrelenting interest in the human person, thus supporting spiritual life and holiness in the Church.

Fathers as of primary importance. Witness the labors of such exegetes as Origen (in spite of the fact that he was an Alexandrian) and Jerome to discern that meaning, as was mentioned above. Since God has assumed the body of the human word to use it for his salvific purposes, it cannot be laid aside or bypassed.

But that human word is not the whole meaning of God's revelation in Scripture; it is not the heart of the matter but rather the outside of the word; the leaves of the tree, not the root, to use the words of Jerome. The mystery at the heart of the words of the Scripture and preaching on the Scripture, is the Word Incarnate, Jesus Christ. For this reason, Jerome can say, in words picked up by *Dei Verbum* #25 that ignorance of the Scriptures is ignorance of Christ. The revelation of the Old Testament, both in words and deeds, is "deliberately oriented" to the coming of Christ and bears hidden within it the mystery of Christ (*Dei Verbum* #15). The same Christ is manifested in the New Testament. This is done, as Augustine made clear in his sermon to the pastors mentioned above, primarily by opening the hidden meaning of the Scriptures, which is Christ, present and active as during his ministry and in the superlative redemptive act of his death for us, ready to heal and forgive, to enter into intimate relationship and sharing with us the very life of God.

As the Fathers understood well, the mystery of Christ opens into the mystery of our salvation. The meeting with Christ through the Church's preaching is a way of looking upon his face, an action which Paul says transforms us from glory to glory (II Corinthians 3:18). As Paul before them, so the Fathers of the Church expected that the Christian once evangelized and baptized into Christ, would make progress in becoming like Christ. In a famous example (*Hom. Num.* 27), Origen shows the stages of the Christian life. What is especially interesting is that, as the Christian advances in the moral and mystical life, he advances toward a deeper penetration of Scripture. The reverse is also true: As a Christian progresses toward a deeper understanding of Scripture, he or she makes progress in the moral and mystical life. Patristic exegesis in general looked to Scripture for the so-called moral and mystical meanings. Just as the partial revelation of God's action in the Old Testament points toward the fullness of revelation in Christ, so too does the inaugurated but as yet incomplete transformation in Christ, visible in the moral life of the Christian in his journey through this life, point toward the fullness of participation in his glory in the future.

Contemporary preachers of the gospel can profit much from considering the strong pastoral interest of the Fathers. They did not preach on abstractions such as gospel values or principles, but announced the Lord Jesus Christ and then called for conformity to him in all of life. And not only did they call for such conformity, but they pointed the way to it, so that the preached word of God could truly be a lamp to the feet and a light for the way. One of the greatest deficiencies in preaching today may well be that little clear direction, based on God's word, is given for the real life of the people. It is small wonder that they do not consider the gospel as a power for salvation and small wonder that they forget about the call to sanctification of life. Always the one communicating God's word must display Christ before the people and then point the way in life which is demanded by that meeting and intimate bond with him.

III. Conclusion: An Example of Patristic Understanding

By way of conclusion, an example of patristic understanding might be in order. In his magnificent poem, "The Pearl," St. Ephrem the Syrian contemplates the richness of the Christian mystery. As he turns the pearl over in his hand, he sees various faces in succession. The pearl is a "body" full of light which suggests to Ephrem other bodily realities in which divinity is present: Mary with Christ in her womb; the Church full of Christ; Christ full of divinity. Though never losing contact with the concrete reality of the pearl, Ephrem penetrates it with his gaze educated by faith, and finds therein the riches of the Christian mystery.[18]

> One day, my brothers,
> I picked up a pearl. I saw within it mysteries. . . .
>   It became a fountain
> And from it I drank of the mysteries of the Son. . . .
> I set it, my brothers, in the palm of my hand
> that I might observe it. I was about to look at it
> on one side, but it had faces on all sides. . . .
>   In its clarity I saw the Clear One
> who is not clouded. In its purity,
> a great mystery: the body of Our Lord. . . .
> It became Mary, for I saw there
> His pure conception. It became the Church
> with the Son therein. . . .[19]

---

18 Francisco Javier Martínez, "*Los himnos 'sobre la perla' de San Efrén de Nisibe (de fide, LXXXI–LXXXV),*" *Salmanticensis* 38 (1991) p. 8.

19 These excerpts from Ephrem's poem "The Pearl" are taken from an

St. Ephrem wrote at a time when Greek rationalism was intruding into the Church's life under the guise of Arianism, a reductive rereading of Christianity which would leave it emptied of transcendence and diluted into a rationalism serving the then dominant culture. Through his poetry, Ephrem showed the appropriate attitude in approaching God's word of revelation – that of wonder, adoration, and openness before the incomparable beauty of the mystery of God revealed in Christ.[20]

The word of God in Scripture is like Ephrem's pearl. It reveals mysteries upon mysteries, all of them radiant and full of meaning for us. The mission of the preacher and teacher of the gospel, as that of the Church as a whole, is to show to all the face of Christ and the way to arrive at the fullness of union with him. When the Fathers refused to stop at the outermost level of the Scriptures, they were following the way taken by the Risen Lord when he opened the Old Testament Scriptures to the disciples on the way to Emmaus (Luke 24:13–27). He showed them that the Scriptures had to do with himself and that the mystery of his death and resurrection were hidden in them. The disciples, up to then disheartened and disappointed by the death of Jesus, were left not only with new understanding but with hearts burning. The preacher and teacher in the Church today must continue in our time, as the Fathers of the Church did in theirs, Christ's work of opening the Scriptures. Then his presence will be manifest and those who hear will see in him the way to walk through life and to face the vision of eternity.

---

unpublished manuscript by Edward G. Mathews, Jr., St. Ephrem,"
"Mandrase on Faith," 81–85; "Hymns on the Pearl," 1–11.
20 Martínez, "*Los himnos*," p. 9.

28.

Catechetics and the Governance of the Church: *The Catechism of the Catholic Church* (1992)

His Eminence John Cardinal O'Connor

I.

I begin with a Hasidic Tale, told by Elie Wiesel in his book, *Gates of the Forest*:

> When the great Rabbi Israel Baal Shem-Tov saw misfortune threatening the Jews it was his custom to go into a certain part of the forest to meditate. There he would light a fire, say a special prayer, and the miracle would be accomplished and the misfortune averted.

> Later, when his disciple, the celebrated Magid of Mazeritch, had occasion, for the same reason, to intercede with heaven, he would go to the same place in the forest and say: "Master of the Universe, listen! I do not know how to light a fire, but I am still able to say the prayer." And again the miracle would be accomplished.

> Still later, Rabbi Moshe-Lieb of Sassov, in order to save his people once more, would go into the forest and say: "I do not know how to light the fire; I do not know the prayer, but I know the place and this must be sufficient." It was sufficient and the miracle was accomplished.

> Then it fell to Rabbi Israel of Rizhin to overcome misfortune. Sitting in his armchair, his head in his hands, he spoke to God: "I cannot even find the place in the forest. All I can do is to tell the story, and this must be sufficient." And it was sufficient.

If we are to be *realistic*, not *pessimistic*, we must admit that we are dealing today with a Church in which millions of its members can hardly even tell the story. In his fine address to you yesterday, Father Alfred McBride cited a poll taken in January 1992, on Catholics' understanding of the Eucharist. The poll found that only 30% of those surveyed believed that in the Eucharist they receive the Body and Blood of Jesus Christ, under the appearance of bread and wine.

Of course we really do not have to quantify it statistically. We know of the critical need. And we would be dishonest if we pretended we do not know.

I have been asked to address the topic "Catechetics and the Governance of the Church," with emphasis on the new *Catechism of the Catholic Church*.

If there is any doubt as to the teaching role of the bishop, Vatican Council II itself spells it out for us.

> . . . through the Holy Spirit who has been given to them, bishops have been made true and authentic teachers of the faith. . . . The bishops should present Christian doctrine in a manner adapted to the needs of the times. . . . They should also guard that doctrine, teaching the faithful to defend and spread it. . . . They should also strive to use the various means at hand today for making Christian doctrine known: namely . . . preaching and catechetical instruction which always hold pride of place, then the presentation of this doctrine in schools, academies, conferences, and meetings of every kind . . . (Decree on Bishops *Christus Dominus*, #3, #13).

I would like to speak first, but only in a cursory way, of only a few of the many serious philosophical and psychological impediments to the teaching *effectiveness* of bishops. One impediment to effective episcopal teaching relates to Vatican II. While there was preparation by various commissions *prior* to the deliberations of Vatican II, there was virtually no *post*-Vatican-II preparation of the Church at large to receive, understand, and rationally implement the conciliar documents. We are still trying to recover from the chaos of misunderstanding and the distortions caused by this.

Well-intended liturgical experiments permitted to run wild naturalized the supernatural, and even more, *de*sacralized the sacred for large numbers of young people (*lex orandi est lex credendi*). The vacuum in understanding of the faith left by failure to prepare the people for the documents of the Council was too often filled by false prophets with false interpretations of the Council, and particularly with ambiguous ecclesiologies.

A second major impediment to episcopal teaching, I believe, developed out of the manner of preparing for, the extensive delay in the promulgation of, and the variety of interpretations given to Pope Paul VI's *Humanae*

Vitae. I believe that circumstances surrounding the publication of *Humanae Vitae* seriously eroded the credibility of Church teaching. I am not for a moment questioning the validity of *Humanae Vitae*. I *am* saying that when Catholics learned – and it took them no time at all – that they could shop around among confessors for opinions on birth control, they soon decided that they really did not have to confess the matter at all. In my judgment, we have not yet recovered from this confusion.

Another, and not unrelated impediment to effective episcopal teaching is the ambiguity about the authority of local ordinaries relative to local Catholic colleges and universities which may permit distortions of Church teaching to go unchallenged. Poor selection, training or supervision of campus ministers can result in further depriving Catholic college students of orthodox guidance. Years of confusion and diversity in catechetical instructional materials has left an entire generation in a state of ambiguity.

For example – and in large measure, I believe, because of the ambiguity and confusion – the powerful abortion lobby has been able to target the Catholic Church and has poured its tremendous financial resources into furthering the contraceptive mentality that exists in our nation. A bizarre coalition of abortion advocates and homosexual activists who vehemently oppose Church teaching has attacked churches and has even desecrated the Blessed Sacrament. As distressing as these activities are, the climate of sympathy that they have generated is, in a sense, even more distressing in terms of trying to teach what the Church teaches. Instead of their proponents having to justify abortion and homosexual activity, the Church is put in a position of having to respond to charges of "lack of compassion," "discrimination," "imposing its belief on others," and so on – charges that come even from Catholics, and not only lay Catholics. Witness the furious attack on the Congregation for the Doctrine of the Faith by certain Catholic writers in response to the Church's recent paper on homosexuality and the law.

It is not difficult to be intimidated by the forceful emphasis given today to freedom of conscience. You must follow your conscience, of course. The Vatican Council said you must follow your conscience. I quote from the Vatican Council's frequently quoted Declaration on Religious Freedom:

> In all his activity a man is bound to follow his conscience faithfully in order that he may come to know God for whom he was created. It follows that he is not to be forced to act in a manner contrary to his conscience (#3).

The Vatican Council did not stop there, however, though some would have you believe it stopped there. The Council goes on to say what is less frequently quoted:

> In the depths of his conscience, man detects a law which he does not impose upon himself, but which holds him to obedience. Always summoning him to love good and avoid evil, the voice of this law can when necessary speak to his heart more specifically: do this, shun that. For man has in his heart a law written by God. To obey it is the very dignity of man; according to it he will be judged (Pastoral Constitution on the Church in the Modern World, *Gaudium et Spes*, #16).

Or again:

> Conscience frequently errs from invincible ignorance without losing its dignity. The same cannot be said of a man who cares but little for truth and goodness, or of a conscience which by degrees grows practically sightless as a result of habitual sin (*Lumen Gentium* #19).

This is what St. Paul was talking about in his famous first chapter to the people of Rome, when Rome had become so almost incredibly decadent and corrupt. He says: "And hence men are given over to various shameful practices with men; women with women" (Romans 1:26–27). People just shut everything except their own self interests. This is what happens when our consciences become darkened, when they become ridden with the cancer of the world.

A very brief and almost simplistic glance at three intertwined cultural forces can further help us appreciate why it is difficult to teach the faith in all its purity in the United States. These forces are: (1) the moral philosophies that are at the heart of the American experience; (2) the American emphasis on group dynamics and process; and (3) American pluralism.

As regards moral philosophy, for purposes of simplicity, I suspect we could agree that four moral philosophies have gone into shaping our culture: pragmatism, utilitarianism, social evolutionism, and the natural moral law.

While a number of the American Founding Fathers were deists or pure rationalists, their thinking was nonetheless influenced significantly by the natural moral law, even though as modified for them by John Locke. Catholicism is pre-eminently attuned to the basic principles of the American Republic, as articulated by the Founding Fathers, in large measure, I believe, because of its affinity with natural moral law. I suggest that Catholic moral teaching has been accepted or rejected in almost direct proportion to the acceptance or rejection of natural moral law in the formulation of public policy and on the part of college and university educators.

In place of the natural moral law, Supreme Court Justice Oliver Wendell Holmes substituted the philosophy of *pragmatism*: The good is whatever *works*, or is expedient. It was pragmatism that, in my judgment, opened the door to moral relativism in American life. Jeremy Bentham's *utilitarianism* took an American form by way of "the greatest happiness of the greatest number," a rationale which takes advantage of the political philosophy that the majority rules. It is an easy step from there to the concept that majority rule determines what is *morally* good for everyone. The thrust is to reject moral absolutes or teaching about intrinsic good and evil. Doctrine becomes irrelevant.

One of the most powerful proponents of *social evolutionism* was President Theodore Roosevelt, with his hearty but destructive emphasis on "rugged individualism." "The survival of the fittest" became the canon of all social morality. No American philosophy has been more antagonistic to the belief that all men are created equal, or to our belief in the worth, the dignity, and the sacredness of every human person as made in the Image of God.

With regard to the American emphasis on group dynamics and process, encounter groups and sensitivity sessions have deluged America, and the country has become caught up in *dialogue* – a dialogue frequently unrelated to the exchange of information or the communication of truths. *Dialogue* has been used simply as a *process* intended to achieve *consensus*. Dialogue has been successful or unsuccessful only to the degree in which consensus has occurred or failed to occur. Substance became irrelevant. The medium became the message.

I suggest that the development in which metaphysical propositions came to be considered meaningless played a major role in the emergence of consensus theology, in which ontological truth plays little role. Wittgenstein and Schlicht, of the *Wiener Kreis*, the Vienna Circle, must be laughing in their graves – if, metaphysically they *are* in graves and not merely operationally deceased! I suggest further that, as seminaries stopped teaching philosophy, and particularly metaphysics, theology lost the language of substance and of absolutes. Theological speculation became a search for consensus, which in turn was found in *praxis*, the theological equivalent of *process*. The formation of conscience became almost a lost art, as did the practice of confession for huge numbers, since the entire notion of *sin* had meanwhile become, at best, speculative.

Pluralism is another critical factor with respect to the effectiveness of episcopal teaching. Every American bishop, including myself, by the way, would fight to preserve the American pluralistic political system, safeguarded in part by constitutional checks and balances, and by a very strong commitment to the principle of "one person, one vote."

Even political pluralism has been undergoing changes, however, and unhappily in a direction feared by some of the Founding Fathers, that is, leaning toward the "tyranny of the minority." Combined with the politically valid principle of "one person, one vote," political pluralism, particularly in this deviant form of the tyranny of the minority, offers an alluring rationalization for a unique and pervasive form of the theology of dissent. Magisterial teaching becomes no more authoritative than the opinion of any single individual; my vote is as good as yours. The contemporary response to a Magisterium that ever attempts to "impose" Church teaching is to organize into a vociferous minority, co-opt the media, and then charge the Magisterium – even the Holy Father! – with the most heinous of crimes in the American lexicon: discrimination!

I wish I could spend more time talking about "choice" under the rubric of pluralism. "Choice" has become *the* prevailing virtue, over and above life itself. Life is now secondary. "I *choose*. I am an American, I have the right to choose and no one can tell me anything different. I *choose* to have an abortion. I *choose* to have this retarded child destroyed within two days after birth – and you know that two Nobel Prize winners have both advocated that parents should have at least three days after birth to *choose* whether or not a child should live. And it may well be, in time, that I *choose* to pull the plug on my mother or father, as we move closer and closer to euthanasia and to assisted suicide in fact, if not in law, in our steady creation of a consistent ethic of death.

In Dostoevsky's novel *The Possessed*, Kirilov says, "I shall kill myself in order to assert my insubordination, my new and dreadful liberty." This is where we are today. This is what we are now caught up in, I believe, in the United States today.

There is a passage from another one of Dostoevsky's works, *Crime and*

Punishment. Raskolnikov is the "hero"; he is the murderer. In the passage that I am going to cite, he is asked to clarify his position, which suggests that:

> There are certain persons who have the right to commit breaches of morality and crimes. All men are divided into ordinary and extraordinary. Ordinary men have to live in submission, have no right to transgress the law because, don't you see, they are ordinary. But extraordinary men have a right to commit any crime and to transgress the law in any way just because they are extraordinary.

Then he goes on to say that it would have been perfectly justifiable for Isaac Newton to have killed hundreds and hundreds of people if that had been necessary to have his theory of gravitation become public. He says that it was certainly justifiable for Napoleon to kill as many people as he wanted to kill because of his own greatness; he was greater than any of those that he killed. Raskolnikov then talks about the woman that he had killed, an old woman:

> A hundred thousand good deeds could be done and helped on that old woman's money, which will be buried in a monastery. Hundreds, thousands perhaps, might be set on the right path. Dozens of families saved from destitution, from ruin, from vice – and all with her money. So I said to myself, kill her, take her money, and with the help of it, devote yourself to the service of humanity and to the good of all. What do you think? Would not one tiny crime be wiped out by thousands of good deeds? For one life thousands would be saved from corruption and decay. One death and a hundred lives in exchange. It is simple arithmetic. Besides, what value has the life of that sickly, stupid, ill-natured old woman in a balance of existence? No more than the life of a louse, of a black beetle; less in fact, because the old woman is doing harm wearing out the lives of others.

II.

As I stated at the outset, I do not intend these remarks to be pessimistic, but rather *realistic*. Too many wonderful people have poured out too many years of their lives as catechists for me to imply even remotely that it has all been "sounding brass or a tinkling cymbal." Lives have been turned around, souls opened to oceans of graces through the dedication, the skill, and the personal sanctity of priests, religious, lay teachers, and parents as they go about sharing the Good News. But we have had problems.

In 1984, the Archdiocese of New York agreed to hold a Synod. It took us four years to do the preparatory work – including surveys, study of the documents of Vatican II, and intensive prayer – and ultimately some 235 people – lay persons, religious, priests, and bishops, of every race, and every religious background – met for the 18th Synod of the Archdiocese of New York.

Not surprisingly, *the plea for clear, unambiguous presentation of the word of God topped and pervaded the list of priorities proposed to me for action.* The Synod – as extraordinary and representative a cross section of this complex archdiocese as has ever been achieved – left absolutely no doubt about this. The people want the word of God; they want it presented in clear preaching, not in speculations or opinions on what the Church actually teaches. The people want the word of God expressed in reverent, devotional liturgy. The people want Catholic schools to teach the word of God by way of Catholic doctrine. The people want programs of religious education that make the word of God intelligible, at every level of maturity, and taught in such fashion as to inspire true devotion and advance sound moral behavior.

The classroom or out-of-school religion teacher must be an extension of the bishop – literally taking the place of the bishop as teacher. That is an awesome responsibility and a sacred trust, and it means that the teacher must be faithful to what the Church truly teaches – not personal opinion or speculation – as the bishop himself must be.

Now, finally, to the question of putting the new *Catechism of the Catholic Church* to work. This is obviously going to be a monumental task. In his Apostolic Exhortation *"Catechesi Tradendae,"* our Holy Father says:

> Catechesis is intrinsically linked with the whole of liturgical and sacramental activity, for it is in the sacraments, especially in the Eucharist, that Christ Jesus works in fullness for the transformation of human beings.

Naturally, our Holy Father includes the homily within the context of liturgical and sacramental activity. I quote from paragraph #48:

> Respecting the specific nature and proper cadence of this setting, the homily takes up again the journey of faith put forward by catechesis, and brings it to its natural fulfillment. Accordingly, one can say that catechetical teaching too finds its source and its   fulfillment in the Eucharist, within the whole cycle of the liturgical year. Preaching, centered upon the Bible texts, must then in its own way make it possible to familiarize the faithful with the whole of the mysteries of the faith and with the norms of Christian living.

Fortunately, the structure of the *Catechism* lends itself beautifully to the Holy Father's admonitions. The *Catechism* is broken down into the following proportions: .9% Prologue; 36.3% on the Creed; 21.8% on the Sacraments; 30.3% on the Commandments; 10.8% on Prayer, particularly the "Our Father."

Why, then, do I say the task is monumental? Again, I note that 36.3% of the *Catechism of the Catholic Church* concerns itself with the Creed, the Profession of Faith. Let me read to you the profession of faith that I am told by an eye and ear witness was used by the principal celebrant, president of a very well-known and highly expensive Catholic college, in the Mass of the Holy Spirit opening the school year, after a woman chaplain had read the gospel and preached the homily. The celebrant began: "Let us proclaim together our common faith using this creed from a base community in El Salvador." The "creed" in question then reads:

> We believe in God,
> who created us free and walks with us in the struggle for liberation.
> We believe in Jesus Christ,
> crucified again in the suffering of the poor, the suffering which calls out to the conscience of people and nations, the suffering which ends in resurrection.
> We believe in the power of the Spirit,
> capable of inspiring the same compassion which has led our best brothers and sisters to martyrdom.
> We believe in the Church called forth by Jesus and the Holy Spirit.
> We believe that when we gather, Jesus is with us, Mary our Mother, is at our side, a sign of faithfulness to our God.
> We believe in the Christian Community where we proclaim our ideals, through which we practice our Christian faith.
> We believe in building a Church where we pray and reflect on our reality and share in the prophetic, priestly, and pastoral mission of Jesus. In this way we make the Kingdom of God present on earth.
> We believe in unity in the midst of differences.
> We believe that we need to love one another, to correct one another compassionately, to forgive each other's errors and weaknesses.
> We believe that we need to help one another recognize our limitations, to support each other in the faith.
> We believe that the poor, the sick, the illiterate, the tortured and persecuted, are closest to the Gospel of Jesus. Through them, Christ challenges us to work for justice and peace. Their cause is our cause.
> We believe that Christ is also present in those who are slaves to their passions and vices, to lies and injustice, to power and money.

> We commit ourselves to never give up hope in the possibility of our
> conversion, of the possibility that we will truly respond to the Gospel
> and live to build the Kingdom.
>   AMEN!

This is certainly one kind of obstacle to the *Catechism of the Catholic
Church*. For another thing, I refer to a draft of a paper by Archbishop Eric
D'Arcy of Hobart, Tasmania, entitled "The *Catechism of the Catholic
Church* and Cardinal Newman." Noting that the *Catechism* itself is not
meant for the classroom, he reminds us that actual classroom catechisms
must be produced for all the different countries and cultures where the
Church lives and teaches. He says:

> This is an exhilarating prospect. It offers faith-educationists their
> greatest opportunity in four hundred years. Nevertheless it bristles
> with difficulties, and in the English-speaking First World these are par-
> ticularly acute. One of these cuts deeper than all the others: many of
> our most dedicated faith-educationists do not believe the *Catechism of
> the Catholic Church* to be a providential initiative at all. They simply
> do not believe in a faith-education which is systematically doctrinal
> and systematically addressed to the cognitive powers – intellect, rea-
> son, imagination, and memory.

Let us reflect only on these two obstacles. The first reverts to what I
said about huge numbers of people no longer even able to tell the story.
When the elite attend well-known Catholic colleges – those whose parents
in most cases are paying far more than they can afford to send them to them
– and the very opening liturgy ignores liturgical precepts and replaces the
fundamental summary and expression of our faith, the Creed, by a childish
exercise in a pale version of liberation theology, where are our future Catholic leaders going to learn what the Church teaches? To say they already
know by the time they get to college is to defy the kind of data presented
yesterday by Father Alfred McBride, data that Catholic high school teachers all over the country could substantiate with hair-raising stories of their
own, and that any priest who has heard confessions in the past ten years
could verify in spades. If the opening liturgy in the college cited here is in
any way illustrative, one must ask: If this is happening in the green wood,
what of the dry?

Several of the papers that I read on catechetics in preparing this address
use the term "faith illiteracy" or a similar term. Does the problem go even
deeper than "faith illiteracy"?

In the paper of Archbishop D'Arcy that I mentioned, he cites Cardinal Newman's reverence for (and now I am quoting Newman):

> [T]hat true religious zeal which leads theologians to keep the sacred Ark of the Covenant in every letter of its dogma, as a tremendous deposit for which they are responsible. In this curious skeptical world, such sensitiveness is the only human means by which the treasure of faith can be kept inviolate.

Has the Ark of the Covenant itself been lost? Or as William Butler Yeats would ask, "Has the center given way?" Has our Catholic culture itself been so relativized and secularized that the term "Catholic" is virtually devoid of meaning? Would the description of the Christian life in the second-century Letter to Diognetus fit today's world? Should it?

> Christians are indistinguishable from other men either by nationality, language, or customs. They do not inhabit separate cities of their own, or speak a strange dialect, or follow some outlandish way of life. . . . With regard to dress, food, and manner of life in general, they follow the customs of whatever city they happen to be living in. . . . And yet there is something extraordinary about their lives. They live in their own countries as though they were only passing through. They play their full role as citizens, but labor under all the disabilities of aliens. Any country can be their homeland, but for them their homeland, wherever it may be, is a foreign country. Like others they marry and have children, but they do not expose them. They share their meals, but not their wives. They live in the flesh, but they are not governed by the desires of the flesh. They pass their days upon earth, but they are citizens of heaven. Obedient to the laws, they yet live on a level that transcends the law.

It seems to me that it would be irresponsible for us to pretend that our task is simply to introduce the new *Catechism of the Catholic Church* in reasonably intelligible language to those of our Catholic people who consciously hunger and thirst for its teaching. What of that great number of Catholics who do not even know of the existence of the *Catechism* and are not at all conscious of either being hungry or thirsty for its teachings?

In his extraordinary pastoral, "Priests Among Men," Cardinal Suhard, Archbishop of Paris, wrote more than forty years ago:

> [The priest] must not remain deaf to Isaias' entreaty: "Cry, cease not, lift up thy voice like a trumpet, and show my people their wicked doings, and the house of Jacob their sins" (Isaiah 58:1). Whether it is wel-

comed or not he has to bring his fellow human beings the eternal and ever efficacious word of God. His voice must not be timid nor is he to make concessions nor tone his message down as do those who plead human causes.

One of the priest's first services to the world is to tell it the truth. Amidst the streams of propaganda which rival each other for adherents, the priest's voice must cry out boldly and sternly so as to "bear witness to truth and to light" (John 18:37; 15:26–27; 1:7).

The revolt which the priest must advocate is the insurrection of consciences, the order which he comes to disturb is the apparent calm which covers up disorders and hatreds. . . . So it can be said without contradiction that his way of bringing about order is to start a ferment. His way of obeying the laws of men is to appeal unceasingly to the law of God.

In my judgment, the great revolution in teaching will come and the great revelation in learning too, when the truth is preached clearly from pulpits, unambiguously in classrooms and textbooks and newspapers and magazines and on radio and television programs. The revolution will come when the truth is expressed reverently in every eucharistic liturgy, in which the crucifixion and death and resurrection of Christ are permitted to be *experienced*, rather than *concealed* beneath the ego and the ideology of celebrants, who sometimes might as well be casting dice over the garments of the crucified Christ. Then the production of our catechisms rooted in the *Catechism of the Catholic Church* will truly be what Archbishop D'Arcy calls "an exhilarating prospect."

This brings me to Archbishop D'Arcy's point that many of our most dedicated "faith-educationists" simply do not believe in a faith education which is "systematically doctrinal and systematically addressed to the cognitive powers – intellect, reason, imagination, memory." He says that they would take up this work out of "Catholic solidarity and loyalty, but without much interior conviction." I think this to be, though a problem, a far lesser problem, and one with the happy capacity of resolving itself. If our educators at every level, in and out of classrooms, are willing "out of Catholic solidarity and loyalty" to *learn* the *Catechism of the Catholic Church*, to recognize the prayer and reflection and study that produced it and the motivation behind it, I suspect that many of them will be convinced of its validity and its utility even prior to experiencing its effectiveness in the hearts and minds of those they teach. Once they do engage the Catechism in the actual teaching process, I suspect that they will be astonished and delighted by its effect on the hearers; so that in time, that which they attempted out of "Catholic solidarity and loyalty" will win their "interior conviction" as well. Then, not only will Catholics be *able* to tell the story; they *will* tell it, and jubilantly. There is a delightful Hasidic tale passed on by Martin Buber which describes the power of such "inner conviction."

> My grandfather was paralyzed. Once he was asked to tell a story about his teacher and he told how the Holy Baal Shem Tov used to jump and dance when he was praying. My grandfather stood up while he was telling the story and the story carried him away so much that he had to jump and dance to show how the master had done it. From that moment, he was healed.

It seems to me to be the bishop's responsibility to be steadfast in his insistence that every catechist indeed *study* the *Catechism of the Catholic Church*, that all instructional materials henceforth be true to it, and that extensive educational and training programs to be carried out throughout the diocese to ensure the competency of all catechists in the use of the new *Catechism* and in the catechetical materials derived from it.

Thanks to the vision of my predecessor, Cardinal Cooke, and of his right hand, Monsignor Michael Wrenn, we are fortunate in the Archdiocese of New York to have an Archdiocesan Catechetical Institute authorized to award masters' degrees in religious studies. We have in place, as well, regional catechetical congresses which annually attract very large numbers of our catechists. Further, since our detailed catechetical guidelines are created at Archdiocesan level and must be approved by the Ordinary before publication and distribution, we already have a built-in system that will at least facilitate start-up efforts. Indeed, many months ago, I discussed with the fine director of the Archdiocesan Catechetical Office, Sister Joan Curtin, S.N.D., the implementation of the *Catechism of the Catholic Church* and requested that she develop an implementing procedure. She has been faithfully engaged in doing so.

There will be further integration of the *Catechism* into the various spiritual development and spiritual leadership programs already extant in the Archdiocese. The *Catechism* itself will be distributed massively. I will not bore you with the details of programmatic implementation, but this is already planned and is very extensive.

But what Ordinary would not feel encouraged when the director of the Archdiocesan Catechetical Office, submitting such an extensive plan for implementation after months of thought and prayer, would write: "Personally, I feel this is really a new moment of grace for all of us in the Church. I am privileged to be part of it." And what Ordinary would not have a much easier time in implementing the new *Catechism* who has the services of such an old hand as Monsignor George Kelly, and a newer but highly professional and dedicated hand as Monsignor Michael Wrenn, both here present?

I opened with an Hasidic tale. Let me close with one:

> Rabbi Hananiah ben Teradyon was one of the Ten Martyrs of the Faith in Roman times. . . . In those days to teach the Torah or to study it meant capital punishment. Rabbi Hananiah decided to teach the Torah, not clandestinely but in the marketplace. Naturally, he was arrested. The Romans sentenced him to be burned. They wrapped him in the Torah, in the scrolls, and lit the fire.

> And then comes a very beautiful passage in the Talmud, one that we recite every Yom Kippur. As he was burning, his disciples said, "Rabbi, tell us, what do you see?" His answer became a classic: "What do I see? The parchments are burning – but the letters remain alive. The letters are indestructible."

29.
The Scriptural Foundations of Natural Family Planning (1993)
Rev. Paul Quay, S.J.

The natural reaction to the title of this talk might well be: "There aren't any." There are no discussions, pro or con, in the Bible about what we designate as NFP. Yet, I think, some genuine scriptural foundations exist for this. The Scriptures do not have to address a topic directly in order to cast the light of God's revelation upon that topic. The Bible offers great clarity on the wrongness of the contraceptive pill, without any of its human authors ever having had any least notion of such a pill.

Of the many aspects we might consider I will focus on three: the biological data upon which NFP is based; their natural symbolism; and the supernatural realities that the Scripture shows us symbolized in their turn by these natural symbols. I will not address directly the moral questions concerning NFP since these are easily enough decided when viewed in the light of the basic symbolism. I know that there are conflicts among good Catholics concerning the moral use of NFP, but I think that these derive mostly from different practical judgments as to its effects in various situations. The problems seem to be generated more by the circumstances than by the intrinsic morality of the planning of the couple's sexual activity.

I would stress from the start that the entire symbolic structure, both natural and supernatural, is given by God. The particular way in which we respond to this structure is our own doing. As rational and faith-filled people, we seek to ascertain what are the right and wrong, better or poorer, ways of responding. But concentration on the human response should not distract us from the fundamentals that God has built into our being. I will also argue that the natural structures of fertility themselves fulfill in good measure what NFP achieves, constituting to some degree a natural NFP. *do we natural twice?* that God has built into man. Like all things in our fallen world, what is natural does not always suffice; and artificial elements – in this case, the deliberate timing of sexual intercourse so as to attain or to avoid conception – are needed in addition.

Let me summarize the framework within which I shall be speaking: God is the sole source of all things. Hence, all things are like God, there being nothing else for them to be like. In particular, man was created in the Image of God which is Christ Jesus, and in the Likeness of God which is the Holy Spirit. Hence all of man – body, soul, activity – are meant by their very nature and intrinsic structure to show forth the mysteries of God. Sexuality in all its aspects is presented to us in Scripture as central to what God wishes us to understand of His relation with His people.

Hence the norm governing all sexual activity is this: Those sexual activities which, by their natural structure and symbolism, symbolize one or other aspect of the union between Christ and His Church are good; those activities which are not possible symbols of any aspect of Christ's union with His Church are immoral uses of one's sexual powers.

Since I would argue that this is a perfectly general principle, it should apply to those less obvious aspects of sexuality that are involved in NFP. Hence, our question: What is the symbolism, natural and supernatural, of the patterns of human fertility, infertility, and sterility? Does NFP fit well into this symbolism, if so, how?

In the first part of this talk, I will indicate what the Bible says about the natural and the supernatural symbolisms of the temporal patterns of fertility: in children, in adults, in old age. In the second part, I will try to develop the scriptural understanding of our only recently acquired knowledge of genetics and of gametic union in fertilization.

I. Patterns of Fertility

Children are infertile, even though they can feel some degree of sexual pleasure. If some sort of coitus is forced upon them, they remain incapable of either fertility or conjugal love; genital pleasure is isolated from the meanings of genitality. Only with approaching adulthood do children become fertile. This infertility of the child, seen in contrast with the fertility that goes with adulthood, shows that procreation is for adults only. Likewise, the slow maturation of the child, unique among mammals in the shape and slowness of the growth curve, points to the abiding need for adult care. The existence of some twelve to fourteen years of childhood points directly to the family, however it be structured. Bringing children to full physical adulthood and to normal socialization takes still longer, calling for stability of the family unit. All these things, only people who are truly adult can provide.

Now, the Scriptures are clear enough that this long infertile childhood is the chosen symbol of Israel's early relations with the Lord. Already in Hosea (11:1–4), God recalls how He brought His son out of Egypt and taught him to walk. But then He rebukes Israel for behaving, already adult, like an infant that will not come out of the womb (13:13). Deuteronomy (32:5–6, 18–20) and many a short passage in Isaiah again rebuke His people for being untrue to their high dignity as the Lord's children. The whole long chapter 16 in Ezekiel portrays the growing up of Israel. So too and most importantly, St. Paul takes up this theme and gives it strong doctrinal content in Galatians 3:23 – 4:7. But the Scriptures make clear also that the Church is the New Israel, intended to grow within each culture, readying it for adulthood in Christ so that it too can bring forth children to the Lord.

Once he has reached puberty, a young man's fertility is continuous. Though desire may fluctuate or even psychic impotence occur, his seed remains steadily powerful. Usually he can contribute it at will. Ordinarily, too, he remains fertile throughout his life, undergoing no equivalent to menopause, though spontaneous arousals generally decline sharply in frequency during his 50s.

The young woman's fertility is cyclic during the years when she possesses it. Only once in a lunar month or thereabouts does her body release an ovum that can be fertilized. Simply from the point of view of time, infertility is the rule. In addition to the limitations on fertility set by her monthly cycle, a long period of infertility is induced by pregnancy. This continues for some three or four weeks after childbirth, and much longer if she nurses her child at her breasts regularly and often.[1] Finally, with menopause, a woman ceases to ovulate and becomes sterile for the rest of her life.

What, then, is the natural meaning and symbolism of these seasons and periods of fertility? As in other aspects of sexuality, the primary level of

---

1 Breast feeding alone, with no other action to decrease fertility, is sufficient to space children at intervals of four to five years, though such large intervals are rare due to their dependence on a pattern of very frequent feeding. Cf., Peter W. Howie, "Synopsis of Research on Breast feeding and Fertility," in : *Breastfeeding and Natural Family Planning,* M. Shivanandan (ed.), Bethesda (MD): KM Associates (1986), pp. 7–22; and also: R. V. Short, "Breast Feeding," *Scientific American 250,* 35 (1984, #4, April).

meaning seems little more than a redescription of the facts at the level of the human perception and understanding of them.

Most obvious, yet most important, is the fact that human fertility in its integral sense belongs only to a couple and is realized only through coitus. The natural meaning of coitus is sexual union. It bespeaks a union, of souls as well as of bodies, that can be found only in marital love. Inasmuch as it is sexual, it bespeaks a total openness and desire for children.[2] The fact that fertility properly belongs to the couple, not to either individual alone, symbolizes that the child is to come into the world from the hidden depths of mutual love, originating in human love and delight.[3] Human reproduction calls for genuinely human and adult intercourse between a man and a woman who are united not only in body but in heart and mind, and consecrated for the generation and upbringing of children.

Another element in the meaning of the cycles stands out if we consider what would happen were a woman continuously fertile. Then nearly every act of coitus would result in pregnancy. Hence, if coitus occurred more often than every nine months, both the woman's own life and those of the infants in her womb would be in jeopardy. Integral fertility, then, is not to be identified with the simple possibility of conception but with the possibility of "advantageous conception." That is, nature establishes through the rhythm of the cycles conditions for conception that reduce the absolute number of conceptions precisely in order to render those that do occur more likely to continue healthily while preserving the health and physical strength of the mother; also, to guarantee a suitable spacing of the siblings.[4] Thus, fertility, even biologically, in its fundamental meaning is both positively and negatively at the service of the family.

The same purpose is visible in the prolonged post-partum infertility of the nursing mother. Not only does nursing assist in restoring to the womb its tone and proper strength before another child is conceived, but this special infertility also protects the mother from the physical drain of having to

---

2 Cf. Paul Quay, S.J., *Christian Meaning of Human Sexuality*, San Francisco: Ignatius Press (1982), chap. 3, for details of the argument merely indicated here.

3 Wisdom 7: 2.

4 The spacing between siblings has its own importance for their psychological growth as well as for their physical health. Cf. Herbert Ratner, M. D., "Child Spacing," *Child and Family 8*, 290–291 (1969); 9, 2–3; 99–101 (1970).

nurse one or more children while carrying others in her womb.[5]

To learn how revelation makes use of the natural meaning of cyclic fertility to signify symbolically something of the supernatural mysteries, look first at how the Bible deals with the larger cycles of nature. Setting the tone for all that follows in Scripture is the passage in which God establishes His covenant with Noah (Gen 8:22):

> While the earth remains, seedtime and harvest, cold and heat, summer and winter, day and night, shall not cease. . . . I set My bow in the clouds and it shall be a sign of the covenant between Me and the earth (9:13).

The context is one of beneficence: of God's reconciliation with sinful man and His promise no more to destroy the world because of man's perversity. Here God consecrates the cycles of nature as abiding goods, excellent for man and the other creatures, confirming that the cycles of sun and moon, begun on the fourth day of creation (Gen 1:14–19), are good with a goodness given them by God at their creation. The less regular but more frequent glory when rain yields to sunlight becomes the commemorative sign of this peace between God and man, of the universal covenant writ in nature.

The cycles of the world are good, established ultimately for man's good,[6] precisely as a firm framework, on which man can rely in his labors.[7] So God corrected the more sophisticated pagans' misunderstandings: They often saw the cycles of nature as wheels of fate, ineluctable and, ultimately, without intrinsic sense or meaning, not far at times from Nietzsche's eternal and idiot recurrences. But His people saw them in truth, as abiding signs of God's fidelity and His tolerance for the sinful people who so defiled His image in themselves.

In the Noachic covenant the natural meaning of the menstrual cycle,

---

5 Consider the problems that arise when the mother entrusts someone else with the task of nursing; cf. Howie, op. cit., pp. 18–19. He Tells of Lady Traquair, wife of the 4th Earl of Traquair, who bore him 17 children, one every 10 or 11 months, apart from one gap due to illness, and who lived to be 88 years of age. The secret of such fertility, however, lay in her use of a wet-nurse for all her children. Cf. also note 2 above. Note, too, that since the situation is not improved by replacing the wet-nurse by a bottle, a consistent approach to NFP will require a rethinking of American dependence on the bottle.

6 Cf. Acts 14:15–17. Recall too that even the Sabbath was made for man.

7 Cf. Psalms 104(103):19–23.

though not mentioned as such, seems clearly indicated in God's command to be fruitful and multiply and fill the earth.[8] It also, like the rainbow and the cycle of the seasons, is an ever recurring promise of God's favor and willingness that the race of men, in spite of sin, be propagated and prosper.[9]

Supernaturally, human fertility symbolizes – though in no way imaging – divine fertility in two ways. The permanence of male fertility symbolizes the divine fertility *ad intra* in the eternal processions of Son and Spirit. Female fertility, as cyclic, symbolizes the divinely given and maintained fertility of the Church. It is the Holy Spirit, who animates her, who is the Breath that bears in power the word of God that is preached to all nations. Like both man and woman, He abides always. Yet, as Jesus told us, "like the wind that goes round and round and on its circuits returns (Eccles 1:6), the Spirit breathes as He wills, no one knowing whence or whither (Jn 3:8). Yet, like the cycle of our own breathing, He maintains life and draws man ever again towards peace with God who is faithful.

The same dialectic is seen in all the gifts God has given His Church. What abides is committed in custody to the priests (e.g., the Scriptures, the Sacraments, the Mass). But by their continual adaptation to all the Church's children, sometimes fruitful, sometimes not, the woman's fertility is indicated.

But there are also the times of nurturing those newly born, when the Church is infertile, not conceiving still newer children for the Father, showing scant interest in missionary effort until those already hers have begun to mature.[10] Before long, the basic conflict between the Gospel and any human culture begins to manifest itself and a movement of quiet deepening and enrichment of the Church and her newly born begins.

Infertility is not to be identified with sterility. The times of infertility are not a sort of temporary sterility, betokening death, but of burgeoning life and growth. The infertile portion of the cycle is but the quiet period of the development and healthy ripening of a new ovum. Infertility is natural in the strongest sense of the word and, indeed, is required if fertility itself is to

---

8 Genesis 8:17 for animals; 9:17 for men.
9 Genesis 4:1–2, 17; 5:1–3; 9:1–7.
10 Needless to say, this in no way conflicts with the insight that one of the best ways for a young church to mature in faith is to become interested in the missions at an adult level. But a precocious activity is unavailing or even damaging, since conducted by those too spiritually immature to understand what it is that the Lord truly desires of them.

be of full value to the species. The inner vitality of the infertile periods can be seen in the analogous cycle of the seasons of the year,[11] which also show times of manifest fertility and others, equally necessary and life-giving, that are infertile but not sterile.

The continuous, rhythmic, but rarely completely regular alternation of the couple between fertility and infertility would seem to symbolize, at a minimum, man's oneness with the natural world, whose lord he is as God's steward, and his sharing of its cyclic rhythms in himself. But in particular, it symbolizes that the wintry and least promising seasons of our lives still have good grounds for hope in the hidden growth of a fertility that leads to new life.

The various nature-religions witness to this understanding, with their myths and mysteries centered on the death and resurrection of their deities of fertility, on whose sexual activity all fruitfulness of field, flock, and family depended. The symbolism here is so strong that these religions have discovered in myth and symbol what Christians know as fact in the death and resurrection, for the sake of His bride the Church, of the Son of God made man.

The cycles of solar year and lunar month were prominent in Israelite liturgy. This was not due to any special religious significance belonging to these periods as such. Rather, given these cycles, Israel was required to acknowledge God's gifts given in and through them, in having once again the wherewithal to sow and, through His blessing, to have crops to harvest or increase of flocks and herds. The Lord's rebuke is sharp (Jer 5:23–24) for His people's wickedness in not recognizing that He is the giver of the cycles of fertility to their land, and that their sins have subverted this natural order.

More prominent in these cycles than the seasonal feasts or thanksgiving for the harvest are the anniversaries: the Passover, the Day of Atonement, the Feast of Tabernacles, and such later festivals as Purim and Dedication. All these are commemorations, in the circle of months and years, of the great historical interventions of the Lord in the life of Israel for the salvation of His people. Indeed, even the feast of the first fruits of the harvest (Ex 23:14–17) was converted in time to a commemoration of the first entry into the land flowing with milk and honey, which the Lord had sworn to give their fathers (Deut 26). The cycles themselves are but frameworks.

But God has created a new order of the world through the fertility of

---

11 As but one example, see John and Nancy Ball, *Joy in Human Sexuality,* Colegeville (MN): Liturgical Press (1975), pp. 52ff.

one woman from whose womb was born our Savior. His redemptive actions are commemorated in their human concreteness in the cycles of the Church's year. A woman's ovulatory cycle symbolizes, therefore, not merely the goodness of God's world but His gift to His Bride of saving fertility, as recalled in the Church's liturgical cycle, running annually through the seasons of grace.[12]

As in ancient Israel, the years and months are not intrinsically religious. They but provide the cyclic framework for ever again recalling and giving thanks for God's great deeds for His people. These deeds are not brought back to mind in their historical sequence and spacing but as linked to the cycles of months and seasons of the year or even, as with jubilees and holy years, to the passage of the years within the centuries and millennia. The links are those of metaphoric association. For example, Easter comes in springtime when all nature can join with the Church bursting out into new life as she gives birth through baptism to those prepared and growing within her, nurtured by her instruction in faith during her months of pregnancy.

The whole Christian life of devotion, though its particular forms are conventional and man-made constructions, lives with such rhythms. For, a life rooted in basic and natural rhythms does not spontaneously choose to act arrhythmically. Mass on the Lord's Day, novenas and retreats, Forty Hours and the Rosary either have a breathing rhythm in themselves or occur only at a breathing frequency during the year.

The cycles of the Church's fertility show also that times of imperceptible spiritual growth need not be times of sterility. Most of us have much need to be often reminded of this lesson in the area of the spiritual, where we so easily become disheartened because we do not perceive a better progress, for ourselves or for the Church suffering from the sins of her members. Hence, too, the proper nurturing of her children alone makes possible a suitable evangelization of those outside.

What then of the onset of sterility at menopause? After menopause, a woman's pleasure in coitus, as well as her husband's, can well remain as intense as ever. For some women, at least, the pleasure becomes greater as the often quite unconscious fears of another conception are definitively allayed.

---

12 "Quando autem, dilectissimi, oportunius ad remedia divina decurrimus, quam cum ipsa nobis sacramenta redemptionis nostrae temporum lege referuntur?" CCL 138: *Sancti Leonis Magni Romani Pontificis Tractatus Septem et Nonaginta,* ed. A. Chevasse, Turnhout: Brepois (1973), "Tractatus XLII," #3, p. 254.

Satisfying sexual activity remains possible, in any case, for many years more for men and women both.

This continuation of sexual desire and power of enjoyment into old age, long outlasting fertility, symbolizes clearly that personal union is a good that may be sought through coitus indefinitely, even when children cannot be. There is a first element here of a loosening (not a separation) of love and union from the procreation of children.

Indeed, as physical beauty fades and as the possibility of having children ceases, as the home empties out and as physical strength and ability to work diminish slowly, the couple – but especially the wife – feel increased need of reassurance, of confirmation that each is loved by the other, even though less and less remains of the charms that first attracted them to each other. Hence, the significance of the coitus' remaining well beyond all these diminishments.

Scripture lays considerable emphasis on the sterility of many great women from Sarah to Elizabeth. Though sterile, each was to be regarded as at least the equal of her husband's other wives and concubines, to be loved and cherished by her husband even more than were she fertile. God gave offspring to each for her trust in Him, precisely through her husband's continued cherishing of her. Though often cut off by a double sterility, that of bodily defect as well as of old age, from giving new lives to Israel, yet they were not cut off from maintaining the life already given to Israel by its religion and, in some weaker sense, its culture.

Even before menopause, however, human sexual desire is not closely linked to fertility. In this, man differs from all subhuman animals. In these, fertility makes itself manifest by means of the special smells, sights, and sounds of estrus-all the physical signs that the female is in heat. The cycles of fertility are automatic and automatically responded to by the animals. For, estrus is not only the external sign of fertility but normally the sole inducement to copulation. When the female is in heat, the males respond with sexual interest and arousal; when she is not, the males show no desire to copulate. Sexual desire is the clear sign of fertility.

Though there are some remnants of the estrus cycle in man, they are sufficiently dim and obscure that rarely if ever is a woman able to know her fertile days solely through the strength of her desire. Still less is her husband able.[13] Moreover, desire can as easily be roused in either partner in times of

---

13 Some men, it seems, can tell by smell when their wife is fertile, and find it harder to abstain from intercourse in NFP because of her "fertile scent" –

infertility as in the fertile times. Most pathological infertilities do not ordinarily show themselves in any lack of sexual desire.

Though both sexes experience fluctuations in sexual appetite, no universal pattern seems to be discernible in either sex. In any case, whatever variations in the intensity of sexual desire that are rooted in the cycles of the body are largely masked or obscured by the much stronger psychic variations due to the individuals' emotional reaction to the varied circumstances of their lives. Man and woman are drawn spontaneously to sexual intercourse at almost any time when external and psychological circumstances are favorable. There is no need to depend on "being in heat" to trigger their sexual activity.[14]

On the other hand, there is some evidence that, as with the young people among the Muria, a total avoidance of commitment can produce psychic infertility.[15] Likewise, the presence of great fear, anxiety, or deep sorrow seems to work against fertility. Apparently, too, at times deep love and affection can augment fertility.

Thus, there is in man a considerable decoupling between sexual desire and fertility and there can be no expectation that every act of coitus should result in conception.[16] The existence of a fertility cycle that is not coupled in any obvious way to the desire for sexual intercourse not only does not guar-

---

Prof. T. N. Moore, lecture at St. Margaret's Hospital, Sydney, Australia, July 1973.

14 At least this is true in our fallen condition. Some people speak as if we, men especially, were in rut permanently. And indeed, if chastity is not taught and learned, something close to that seems to become the ordinary condition of our race. But, by the grace of Christ, the truly natural condition of man, including perfect chastity according to his state, is restored. What might have been true before the Fall seems unclear, though I see nothing in the lives of Jesus or Mary that would indicate in them anything resembling estrus; if anything, one should describe the state of integrity as a still greater freedom from such compulsions (Quay, *Christian Meaning*, 100–103).

15 George Maloof, "The Psychology of Fertility Awareness and Natural Family Planning," *Marriage and Family Newsletter 8*, 2–6 (Oct.-Dec. 1977), p. 4 and note 3, concerning the exceedingly low pregnancy rate among the sexually hyperactive youth of the Muria people in India.

16 This is not a discussion of whether coitus should be limited in such a fashion as never to take place except when conception is likely – a moral question that we shall consider later. Here the topic is simply the meaning of the cyclicity for the couple at the psychic level.

antee actual fertility; it signifies that conception is not always in order, that it is not always to be desired – since one cannot truly desire what is not possible. Hence, one may argue to a certain priority of mutual love (defined by the natural and supernatural symbolism of sexuality) over procreation. Thus, too, the emphasis on procreation in Genesis 1 is balanced in chapter 2, where the reason given for the woman's creation is not the bearing of children but to be a companion and helpmate for man.

This double aspect to a man's love for his wife, whether she be fertile at the moment or not, symbolizes Christ's love for His Church, which never fails, whether she is bearing new children for the Father then or nursing those she has borne or even, through the sins of her members, grown old and sterile among a particular people.

Note that this is not to argue in any way that it might be licit to separate procreation from personal union, seeking one while blocking the other. It is not. Nonetheless, it is important in any discussion of the moral arguments concerning NFP to know whether there are adequate grounds for coitus even should fertility be absent.

An obvious question at this point is: What is it in man that replaces estrus? – for Scripture is clear that he is to increase and multiply. Set free from estrus, is he delivered into servitude to his own desires, with chance alone determining whether a child is conceived? Since many in our country today seem to be in just that situation, it is important to be clear about this replacement.

The more completely estrus dominates sexual behavior in the subhuman world, the more clearly mating is linked to the death of the copulating pair as a sort of escape from death, not of the pair but, through them, of the species. To the extent that coitus is unbound from the death of the pair, ceasing to be the goal of the entire life of each individual, to the same extent estrus subsides as the sole control of coitus. What comes in to supplement its action is increased awareness of and interaction with the surrounding world and a corresponding complexity of drives and instincts other than those connected to survival to adulthood and mating.

For rational beings, words replace estrus as the dominant influence in bringing about coitus. Coitus itself is rightly understood only insofar as it is made the word of love. Love, as distinct from passion, as the *free* choice to give oneself to another, is characterized chiefly by words. So it has been with the Father, giving Himself to His Son, His Word, and through Him to the Spirit. So it has been when God, who in many and various ways spoke of old to our fathers, in these last days has spoken to us by His Son (Heb 1:1–2).

And how did Christ express His love most intensely and most strikingly for the Church? And how does He wish her to express hers for Him? The Word came to speak the words of God to men, to preach, and teach the way of salvation. Still more, He came as God's own Word become flesh. As a human word, if it is to be understood as part of a message, must sound and then fall to silence and disappear, so too for Christ. Once uttered into this world, He sounded in time during His life and then fell into the silence of death through His sacrifice of Himself on the Cross in order for His meaning to be made manifest to us in His resurrection and enthronement.

As it is the word of love that actuates the merely potential fertility of the couple, so it is the words spoken by the Word, active through the power of the Spirit, that makes the Church fertile in act. For the Church herself lives by words. Words are needed to bring about each sacrament. Words are the normal medium of her prayer, law, teaching and, above all, her worship in and through that sacrifice of His into which she is incorporated constantly by the words of the priest. For it is not sufficient to speak of the Church, who is our mother. Christ's presence to His people requires the fatherhood of the priests.[17] It is they who preach the word, as did the apostles. It is they who receive the children, born of the Church who, like Mary, conceives virginally in response to God's words given power through the Spirit.

II. Gametic Union

Sexuality as such, wherever it is found, exists primarily for the sake of offspring. If there were no need for offspring, there would be no sexuality. Yet, as seen, there is a decoupling between fertility and sexual desire which illumines the complex relation between spousal love and children. There is, however, another decoupling to consider, that between sexual union and fertilization. Biologically speaking, all aspects of sexuality exist only for the sake of the union of the gametes (germ cells) and the nurturing of the conceptus. Yet, strangely, coitus during a fertile time is insufficient for gametic union and conception.

---

17 Cf. Henri de Lubac's strking phrase: "The motherhood of the Church, the privileged expression of which is the fatherhood of her spiritual leaders...," In *The Motherhood of the Church,* tr. S. Englund, San Francisco: Ignatius Press (1982), p. 113. Cf. also all of Chapter 5: "Fatherhood of the Clergy," and 6: *"Ecclesia de Trinitate."*

The gametes, formed by and in the bodies of adults, depend on these bodies for the environment that enables them to live. Yet the germ cells, as long as they remain in a hospitable environment, are independent organisms. Each lives with a life of its own, not with the life of the person within whose body it has been formed. Though a couple's germ cells cannot unite without the cooperation of the couple, the gametes act independently of their knowledge and will; and fusion of the gametes occurs some time after coitus, brought about by whatever the biological attraction is that draws the spermatozoa to seek out and penetrate the ovum.

The conceptus (zygote, embryo, fetus) likewise is wholly dependent upon his mother's body for his own sustenance and protection, indeed for seemingly everything if he is to continue to live and grow. Despite the fact that each parent provides a single germ cell, which contributes a numerically equal, genetic component to the constitution of this organism, there is a great difference in size and structure between male and female germ cells. The receptive ovum, vastly larger than the fertilizing sperm, is built not only for genetics but for nurture and conservation. Even at the gametic level, it is made clear that, once constituted, everything else the child needs of a material nature for its growth and development is supplied by the mother: food, elimination of waste, warmth, physical protection, suitable environment, etc. Yet, the conceptus is an organism that is radically distinct from the mother in whose womb it lives. It can, in principle, be separated from her completely and still survive wherever it proves possible to substitute for her nurturing activities artificially.

The newborn, too, is profoundly dependent upon others for its life and physical and intellectual development. It becomes *part* of a family, a clan, a tribe, a people. From them it must learn a language and a culture – or like a wolf-child it will be unable ever to think at all, or at best, only on a level hardly distinguishable from the animals. Yet, this new human being has his own destiny as an individual, under God's grace, whatever the destiny of the others whom it may have to resist, oppose, even fight. Further, his own participation in society will invariably change the language and the culture, modifying them for children yet unborn.

In sum, at every level of human life one can speak of normal growth and development of an individual only insofar as he exists both in radical dependence and radical independence of others – the ancient dialectical relation between the individual and the community. Only by total self-gift to others can the individual develop fully his potentialities; only by living in proper independence of others will he have character enough to be able to give anything.

Even at the pre-personal level of the gametes, the symbolism is writ large: Each individual whether gamete or person, lives well only insofar as it is in continuous transition from a state of nearly total dependency to a state of nearly total independence, which latter brings it into a new dependency at a higher level. And at all intermediate stages, too, this same dialectical duality occurs that makes further growth essential. What is new today is that for the first time we are able to see clearly this entire dialectic symbolized at the hitherto unsuspected level of the pre-personal life of the gametes.

The Scriptures show the full range of this dialectic as it is manifested in the interaction of the individual and the people to which he belongs. There is a general awareness, as well, of the dialectic as it is found in the infant, even before his birth, still living in the womb.[18] So Jeremiah was called, even before he was conceived, in a uniquely personal way (Jer 1:5) yet compacted of maternal blood and paternal seed (Wis 7:2). St. Paul speaks in like fashion of Him "who had set me apart before I was born and had called me through His grace" (Gal 1:15). There is a somewhat dimmer appreciation of the transmission of genetic traits and the independence of conception from coitus.

This symbolism reaches its supernatural term in the baptismal incorporation of each individual into the Church. There is a "natural" difference of natures simultaneously active: e.g., the supernatural life seems, like the bodily lives of the couple with respect to the germ cells, only accidental (in the Aristotelian sense) to the independent beings – unconverted "natural" men – whose whole reality, however, has been derived from it. It is in the Church, too, that the strongest dialectic relation exists between the independence and freedom of her members and their total dependence upon her for salvation.

If, then, a child is conceived, we should be able to see more clearly than prior generations that he has not been produced, even unconsciously, by his parents. Neither has he been brought about technically by their will as an

---

18 Cf. e.g. Psalms 139:13–16; Wisdom 7:1–6; and Job 10:8–12. How compatible these passages and such others as Jeremiah 1:3–4 are with a later Jewish notion that life begins only with the first breath taken at birth is not immediately clear. Cf. Wisdom 8:19–20 for what seems still another approach.

object that they have made and that is, therefore, owned by them.[19] His actualization, biologically speaking, was not their doing but resulted from the
independent activity of the gametes. Coitus permitted the gametes to unite
in accord with their own natures; but it did not actualize their union. The entire process of fertilization says symbolically that the child is not the property of his parents. Indeed, the whole freedom of the children of God is here
symbolized. Each person belongs ultimately to God alone, not to parents,
still less to the state or to society or to the people.

One evil of *in vitro* fertilization (IVF) lies in its rejection and attempted
denial of this fact.[20] But if IVF ignores and tramples on one pole of this dialectic – treating the germ cells (and, implicitly, the child that results) as if
parts of the parents or as if subject to their control – contraception treats the
gametes as some sort of foreign bodies, alien to each of the couple (or as a
bit of property to be disposed of at will).

The meaning of the marital act is not, therefore, contingent upon an actual fusion of germ cells.[21] Provided that the couple has not intrinsically altered the nature of their act through contraceptive intervention of poisoning
or blockage, the act continues to symbolize the fullness of spousal love even
should fusion not follow. The intrinsic meaning of coitus, therefore, includes children in a different and less direct way than it includes love and
personal union between the spouses. The act *means* marriage, the union between the spouses themselves at all levels of their being. It does not *mean*
actual union of gametes but only the putative possibility of their union. To
state it a little differently, the self which each spouse gives to the other contains his or her fertility, such as it is, strong or weak, healthy or impaired or
nonexistent. So, each spouse's fertility, such as it is, must be included with-

19 Cf. William E. May, "The Laboratory Generation of Human Life-I,"
   Fellowship of Catholic Scholars Newsletter 9, pp. 7–8 (#3, June 1986).
20 IVF reflects symbolically a clear technological will to "make" a child,
   regardless of what happens to the marital union in the context of which it
   takes place; regardless of what happens to the zygote "if things don't work
   out"; regardless of the implied claim of ownership and consequent
   expectations laid upon the child that has been so "made"; and, above all,
   regardless of the radically altered understanding of what it is to be human
   that is implicit in the "making" process. Cf. Joseph M. Boyle, Jr., "The
   Laboratory Generation of Human Life-II," *op. cit.,* pp. 8–9.
21 Conversely, the fact that the fusion of gametes can take place on occasion
   through masturbatory genital contacts does nothing to change the evil nature
   of these modes of "togetherness."

out reserve in the gift of self that constitutes each act of coitus. But this gift must often fail to bring about conception.

In the couple's procreative act, an adoptive aspect can be discerned. For, the parents are called upon freely to accept a child who, though from them, is not theirs but God's only (Ezek 16:20–21; 23:37). Though begotten and borne by them from what seems their own substance, each child is yet genetically different from each parent and hence, to some degree a stranger to his parents at birth. His siblings, though form the same lineage, differ also from each other over a range from genetic identity to complete dissimilarity.

Though a child's every physical trait and his entire genetic endowment comes from his parents, half from his father and half from his mother, yet whenever the union of the germ cells results in a healthy zygote, a new genetic type is formed, hitherto nonexistent.[22] That this particular new genetic type is formed rather than some other of the incredible number theoretically possible, is determined by factors that lie wholly beyond the knowledge and control of the couple. This differentiation has brought about the extraordinary variety of individuals within any one species, rarely duplicating genetically any individuals yet on earth. Sexual reproduction continually stirs up and activates the genetic pool for the conception of ever new types of individuals capable of new adjustments to the changes in the world around them.

Yet such genetic combination and recombination can only indicate the infinite number of aspects of the human nature that is Christ's, as these are endlessly conceived and brought to birth by the Church. For the fact is, each person is, in a far stronger sense than the genetic one, wholly new. For just as we are begotten and conceived of parents who, in one aspect, must adopt us, so the First Letter of John speaks of the divine adoption of sons as a being begotten by God the Father. But always we are adopted so that we might

---

22 In principle, though utterly improbable in fact, there could be parents of such genetic structure that a child might have exactly the same set of genes as one or other parent. (It would, of course, still be the case that half the genes would come from one parent and half from the other.) This is in strong contrast to the relation between siblings, whose genetic structures though occasionally identical as in the case of identical twins, usually range over a quasi-infinity of combinations, and may even share no genes at all (if one speaks only of those freely varying traits that do not alter the basic life-processes).

make visible in the world the endless variety of ways our older Brother can be imaged.

This adoptive quality points also to the awesome freedom God has given to His children. Here I am speaking not of the natural freedom of the will but that freedom that comes from charity, by which Christians (hence, the Church) freely receive and love whomever God gives, whatever their own preferences or missionary efforts may have been. They may have labored long for certain conversions – and none result. They may have felt little attraction for others – and yet they are born to the Church in great numbers.

As many couples know who have longed for children, their generative powers must be "well-disposed" in some way that thus far escapes human awareness and control. Hidden and mysterious is the activity of gametes that, for reasons no one knows, sometimes results in conception, sometimes not. As seen above, the fertility cycles also are hidden. Even should a woman's fertility be perceived, it remains inaccessible to direct regulation or control by the couple, despite its sensitivity to the woman's emotions.

Though the temporal patterns of her fertility can be detected, with sufficient skill and attention on the part of the woman, and though this detection is sufficient to render NFP as effective as "the pill" for the avoidance of conception, yet certitude is not possible, whatever one's choice of means.[23] There are *no* signs that are sufficient if one's concern is with the union of the gametes. Not only the intrinsic viability and biogenetic match between ovum and sperm but their time of survival within the particular woman in a particular cycle is unknown and, save on some sort of average, unknowable.

This hiddenness of the gametes is the sign that makes us aware most concretely of the mystery of every human conception, a mystery some of whose aspects can be delineated but which is not given over in fullness to man's understanding. Further, as most male infertility shows, the activity of the gametes escapes human control as well as understanding. The generation of man is ultimately God's doing, not man's. The perennial mystery of

---

23 Even surgical excision of large sections of the Fallopian tubes and other modes of sterilization have turned out not to prevent all conception, though greatly increasing the likelihood that such conceptions as do take place will be ectopic or defective. Though NFP is highly effective for avoidance of children, it is much less so when used for the sake of conception, helpful though it often is in this case too. In any event, it is not possible to see each act of coitus as directly tied to conception.

human existence remains: What is the connection between the free human person and the biochemical determinisms of the gametes? More importantly for our present purposes, however, it is evident that, even were we to find a description of conception solely in biochemical terms, the natural symbolism would not be altered by the biology of fertility except for greater specification and clarity.

What the Scripture sees symbolized by the hiddenness of fertility is that conception is not of human doing but divine. Well aware that a man's seed must act within a woman to beget a child, the patriarchs and all Israel after them saw conception as effected by divine power, however dependent on human action. We today, for all our increased biological knowledge, must acknowledge the same.

Recall the account of the giving of the promise to Abraham, that through carnal union with sterile Sarah, he should have an heir in whom all the world would be blessed. The generation of Isaac resulted from ordinary coitus between himself and Sarah. Yet this conception was God's miraculous doing.[24] But God acts in the darkness of every human conception. "You [the Lord] formed my inward parts. You knit me together in my mother's womb. . . . You know me right well. My frame was not hidden from You when I was being made in secret, intricately wrought in the depths of the earth. Your eyes beheld my unformed substance" (Ps. 139:13–16). Or, as Job said: "Your hands fashioned and made me. . . . Remember that you have made me of clay. . . . Did you not pour me out like milk and curdle me like cheese? You clothed me with skin and flesh, and knit me together with bones and sinews. You have granted me life and steadfast love" (Job 10:8–12). But it is He also who causes sterility, who closed, for example all the wombs in the household of Abimelech,[25] and who alternately opened and shut the wombs of Leah and Rachel.[26]

Almost all religions recognize the hidden mystery and respond to it by acknowledging the divine activity. The awe that the nature religions felt be-

---

24 Genesis 15–18 & 21: 1–7. Cf. Hebrews 11:11. Cf. also the analogous case of the conceptions of Samson, Samuel, and in the New Testament, of John the Baptist.

25 Cf. Genesis 20:17–18.

26 Cf. Genesis 29:31–32; 30:1–2, 14–24. God's intervention is not needed for the conception of animals. His action reported in Genesis 30:31–43 is confined to over-riding ordinary genetics in favor of Jacob's plans and prosperity.

fore the mysteries of conception was not misplaced, though it was wrongly directed to nonexistent deities.

The freedom of the gametes from human control would seem to be a clear indication that man is not to consider his own sexual activities, *a fortiori*, his fertility, as the all-consuming aspect of his life. The same thing is true with regards to the cycles, of course. But clearly there is a decoupling here: Man is not morally coerced into having children, into having intercourse, in fact, at every moment that he wishes or feels the urge or desire to do so. Nor is he restrained from it when he does not desire it. What this does do is open out in still another way the symbolic aspect of sexual union that is mutual love. There is something that counts far more than either physical or psychic desire, and that is the free choice of two people to love each other mutually, to give themselves to each other in whatever way is suitable at the moment – that gift, being sometimes physical through coitus, sometimes physical through other means, sometimes being simply psychological through their own presence, one to another, above all through their ability to speak to one another of their love. Love must have primacy over direct sexual desire. In human beings reason, enlightened by faith, alone is meant to govern human activity in its overall thrust towards union with other people, whether marital union or social union of any sort. Indeed it governs our relations with God Himself.

Do we need all the children we can have? Clearly the Church insists that all the children we have should be brought to Christ, insofar as we have anything to say about it. We must bring all men to Christ, all men to heaven. God "desires all men to be saved and come to the knowledge of the truth" (1 Tim 2:4). "Our citizenship is in heaven" (Phil 3:20). But no number has been given. The Lord has told us nothing about that. In Revelation, myriads of myriads, i.e., hundreds of millions, stand before Him, praising Him. We have our hundreds of millions. But if our citizenship is in heaven, we must do all we can to bring every child that is conceived to Christ. Yet He has told us some things about how many children we might bring into the world.

In the Old Testament, natural fertility was a great blessing from the Lord. I am sure you all know passage after passage which makes it very clear that a couple should have children and that they are the greatest blessing God can give a couple. "Your wife will be like a fruitful vine within your house; your children will be like olive shoots around the table. Lo, thus shall the man be blessed who fears the Lord."[27] Children are God's blessing

---

27 Psalms 128:3–4.

on the individual and the family and the entire people (Deut 28:11; Ps 127:3).

According to the Law, a woman, after she had her period, had to be cleansed. Then, after she was purified, the couple could come together again. Herbert Ratner has told me that this time of renewed intercourse is, for the average woman, the time of maximum fertility. In other words, there has been roughly a two-week period when, according to the Law, they cannot have intercourse. Now they come together. Their appetite for each other is stronger, and at this time the woman is maximally fertile – clearly something that aims at large fecundity.

As I mentioned at the beginning, the natural structures of fertility themselves fulfill in good measure what NFP achieves, constituting to some degree a natural NFP built into man. If one reads the genealogical materials in scripture with some attention, one notices that there are not many large families except in the households of kings. Given their understanding of fertility and nursing, it seems clear that, barring special circumstances, even without NFP, a couple is not likely to be overwhelmed by children, remembering too the incidence of miscarriages and other fatalities.

What does that symbolize supernaturally? It means God wanted His people to survive, to grow, to flourish, eventually to become those who would carry the Good News to all the world. It took a long time to train them, to lead them to the point where the Messiah could come. Nonetheless, that fertility was aimed at the coming of the Messiah. And so maximal fertility among the Jews was precisely a witness to their hope for the coming Messiah.

The Old Testament symbolism of fertility has its counterpart in the New Testament in conversion and baptism – the rebirth from above. Christ wants all men to be re-born. We are not members of His people by nature any longer. We are made members of His Body, we become His people, through faith and baptism. This was St. Paul's great message constantly: Carnal descent is not enough. One is truly incorporated into the people of God only by faith. And he argued that if you really looked back hard at your history and understood it, you would see this truth even in the Old Testament from the time of Abraham on, who believed in God and this was reckoned to him as righteousness. From that point onward, you only truly belonged to God's people if you were someone reborn by faith. Consequently, for the Church of the Gentiles, maximal fertility is no longer a witness to the coming of the Messiah. Quite the contrary, the Christ has come.

Since He has come, there is no need to have the maximum number of children possible to maintain the people so that out of the family of David the Christ should come.

Furthermore, in the Old Testament we find that fertility was something that, while every good Jewish woman desired it enormously, many of the heroines of the Old Testament were not fertile – indeed they were not only not fertile, they were sterile. Sarah, Hannah, the mother of Samson – there's a long list of them. God in His providence chose here and there these sterile woman for his own purposes to become fertile, to have children. We see that as late as Zachary and Elizabeth – Elizabeth was sterile and yet she was to give birth to John the Baptist, the precursor of Our Lord.

This unpredictable, random scattering of sterility in the midst of a nation that sought fertility above all else, clearly symbolizes the hard sayings in St. Paul about the freedom of God in His gifts of His grace to His Church. The Church does not flourish all over the world instantly. In any given nation to which she comes, the seed is planted by missionaries; sometimes it takes root, other times it simply vanishes. You remember Cyril and Methodius, the apostles of the Slavic nations. Before they went to the Slavs, at least the ones that we call Slavs today, they went off to the area to the north of the Caspian Sea, to try to convert the Khazars. They had no success at all. They preached, a few were baptized. The Church died out almost at once. A few years later, some Jewish missionaries arrived, and the Khazars all became Jews – as far as I know, the largest single conversion to Judaism in history. But they were not yet ready for the Christ. God's grace works when and as it wishes. There are seasons for each nation, each culture, each people in the Lord. Those that were sterile, like Sarah, St. Paul tells us, become fertile, and so it is that the Jerusalem in heaven which is our mother, unlike the Jerusalem on earth, is constantly being replenished but in a manner which no man knows, except Christ Himself.

Turning then to NFP, in all its forms coitus itself is left basically unchanged in its structure, and therefore in its intelligibility and consequently in its symbolic meaning, both natural and supernatural. Now, in God alone there is no limitation to fertility; God begets eternally and "without alteration or shadow of turning" (Jas 1:17)[28] a Son in all respects His equal and who, with the Son, breathes forth the Spirit of their mutual love. But limits to fertility are connatural to every creature. And because we are human be-

---

28 The Greek word *trope* has as its primary meaning a turning point in a cycle, such as the solstices.

ings, conscious planning may be called for in some circumstances. But I think the ideal is to accept all the children that God gives us *when our planning is as open as possible to children*. In other words, we plan to have children, as long as God gives them to us unless some serious reason argues against this. For it can happen that a couple is forced to say: "Here is a great good which is proper to our marriage, which we cannot achieve if we have another child now, or a grave evil that would arise if we do not defer." Since nothing in the symbolic structure of the couple's intercourse is altered, the scriptural symbolisms sketched here provide, I think, all the warrant needed.

30.
America's Catholic Institutions and the New Evangelization (1994)
Gerard V. Bradley

My question is how the Catholic identity of Catholic hospitals, schools, and social services might be "renewed," or "renewed" enough, so that they effectively contribute to the "New Evangelization." The question is very large; indeed, the entirety of next year's Fellowship convention is devoted to (just) the question of Catholic universities. I therefore trust you will forgive me for narrowing the focus of my remarks here. I propose to do two things: first, to describe and criticize as disastrous the prevailing approach to the question of "renewing" (and maintaining) the Catholic identity of these Catholic institutions; and, second, to describe and briefly defend the indispensable core of any sound approach to both Catholic identity *and* the new evangelization: fidelity to the Church's moral teaching. As the Holy Father made so powerfully clear in his encyclical *Veritatis Splendor*, when we preach the Gospel, we preach the good news of salvation through Jesus, and that it is "precisely on the path of the moral life that the way of salvation is open to all" (*VS* 3). Not only must the converted walk in the way of the Lord to inherit eternal life, but moral truth is the path to salvation for those who, through no fault of their own, have not embraced the faith.

What *is* the "prevailing" approach to the "renewal" of Catholic institutions? We can thank Fordham University for supplying a detailed and (we have no reason to doubt) accurate report on how the people whose actions would constitute "renewal" – the heads of Catholic universities, hospitals, social services, as well as the American Bishops – propose to go about it. In 1991 and as part of its 150th birthday celebration, Fordham undertook an exhaustive study[1] of its own Catholic identity which turned into a broader

---

1 C. Fahey, M. Lewis, Editors, *The Future of Catholic Institutional Ministries: A Continuing Conversation* (Fordham, 1992) [hereafter *Fordham*"].

pulse-taking. Fordham sent out a total of 720 lengthy questionnaires, including one to every bishop in the United States, asking about the present state and likely future course of Catholic higher education, hospitals, and social services. (Surveyed in 1990, many of the questions referred to the year 2015.) 151 bishops responded, as did 191 leaders of the Catholic institutions, and 48 "other" non-episcopal respondents.

The study's managers broke down the 390 responses by category of respondent. Thus we can compare the bishops' opinions to those of the institutional actors. The findings I wish to highlight initially were hardly surprising.[2] The bishops were much more likely than the others to say that a particular immoral action – abortion, sterilization – was incompatible with Catholic identity. Four out of five of the bishops thought that a health facility could not do tubal ligations and still be Catholic, for example, while only one in five of health care professionals thought so. The higher education respondents disagreed sharply with the bishops about the compatibility with Catholic identity of granting tenure to pro-choice, gay, and adulterous professors. Seven higher education respondents would deny tenure to a professor living with someone other than his or her spouse; about 82 – a slight majority of – bishops would.

More generally, half of the bishops thought that the Vatican should *not* exercise greater control over teaching and research at Catholic universities (30% thought the Vatican should and 20% were uncertain); not one of the 105 higher educational respondents (including many priests) was uncertain: *Two* thought the Vatican should, and 103 thought the Vatican should *not*.

The bishops held a much more positive general view – though, again, they hardly spoke with one voice – of episcopal involvement in the ministries than those in the ministry held. Social service agencies were reasonably close to the bishops on this, likely because the local ordinary already has more practical and legal influence upon the Diocesan Catholic Charities than he does upon nearby universities and hospitals.

Thus far we have the outline of the "*standard picture*" of Catholic identity and Catholic institutions – a snapshot of the struggle over implementing Pope John Paul II's Apostolic Constitution on universities *Ex Corde Ecclesiae*, to cite one example. The "standard picture" is, basically, this: Some bishops seem confused, and a couple have been derailed entirely. But most are sound; the episcopacy on the whole is far sounder on Catholic

---

2   The raw data to which I refer throughout this essay may be found on B. at pp. 36–22 of *Fordham*.

identity than are the institutional actors themselves. Greater episcopal involvement – and ultimately Vatican direction – are the mainstays of any solution to the problem of diminishing Catholic identity.

But there is going to be a fight: The institutions are dead square against
"outside" intervention by the local ordinary; they are even more opposed to
Vatican direction. But that opposition does not affect the bishop's duty to
monitor Catholic identity. As officials of the Church they must prevent enti-
ties that are no longer Catholic from misrepresenting themselves as Catholic (*See VS* 116). Because the Bishops (or many of them) do not relish
confrontation, and few are inclined to the kind of trench warfare that recapture of, say, Catholic universities would entail, they tend not to act decisively. The solution is to get bishops to simply be bishops, that is, pastors.
We at the Fellowship of Catholic Scholars are, I suppose, in the business of
helping bishops to be bishops.

I *endorse* this "standard picture."

Wait a second. Did I not say just minutes ago that I would criticize as
"disastrous" the prevailing view? Indeed I did. The "standard picture" is
true as far as it goes, but it does not go very far. It is a superficial account of
Catholic institutional ministries. The "standard picture" holds that the problem is that bishops do not act decisively, though by and large they know
what to do. The deeper, more complex "prevailing view" throws the latter
assumption into doubt.

Again, the Fordham findings direct our investigation. They present a
very curious mix of pessimism and optimism. With the exception of questions about Catholic Social Services, the respondents across categories
agreed that *both* the number of Catholic institutions *and* the Catholicity of
the survivors would decrease by the year 2015.[3] It could hardly be clearer
that the respondents as a whole expect a dramatic decline of de facto autonomy: They agree that workers will be non-Catholic and need "special formation" for these Catholic ministries; that government control (especially
in conjunction with public funding) will increase, and that this will pose
more and more "dilemmas"; they agree that these ministries can serve
non-Catholic clients and still be Catholic, but also that greater "empowerment" of the consumer is likely to raise more of a "challenge" to Catholic

---

3 The Catholic Social Services story, reported at *Fordham*, 66–67, is very hard
   to summarize. There was support for the view that there will be *more* CSS
   agencies in 2015. But only about one-quarter of the respondents disagreed
   that they would be more Catholic than today.

identity. One would expect that leaders of these institutions – with neither Catholic staff nor Catholic clients, funded predominantly by secular sources and subject to ever greater accountability to the wider secular public through law, and eschewing a tighter relationship to the Church – would be writing solemn eulogies to their *past* Catholic character.

Not so. *This* question was posed to all respondents about each of the institutional ministries: "If strategies are adopted, this ministry will be able to retain its Catholic identity in the next 25 years." Agreement among respondents in each category was between 80 and 96 percent. That such "strategies" are presently "available" attracted a near-majority (or more) in each category of respondents. To be precise, the Bishops were very close to higher ed. respondents (55.0 to 46.7) on available strategies for higher ed; optimistic but still well behind health care (59.6 to 78.5) and Social Services (65.6 to 85.7).

Well then, what *are* those strategies? Are the bishops going to be bishops? Are these institutions going to confess fidelity to the Magisterium? Are we going to remake the culture, so that a genuinely Catholic apostolate in health care, social service, and higher education is sustainable?

Scan the Fordham report from front to back and you will find *nothing* resembling a "strategy" – a set of policies which, if implemented, would bring into reality a Catholic identity – and scarcely a trace of one.

What is going on here? Granted, even the more optimistic findings – like the 78.5% in health care who opined that strategies are available – do not imply a genuine consensus. Four out of five may have a strategy in mind, but each may have a different strategy in mind. Recall, though, that *no* (not one!) strategy was specified. That in turn suggests (but does not imply) some dissensus on what constitutes "Catholic identity"; the apparent "agreement" masks a radical dissensus on what "Catholic identity" means. *In either of these cases, there is no "prevailing view" at all.* But, in the event, there was striking agreement on a "Catholic identity." *It* is my Exhibit A, the central finding of the survey. *It* is the "prevailing view." Rounding off the numbers a little, three quarters of those responding thought that a "mixed" scenario is somewhere between the "sectarian" and "secular" models, each of which attracted marginal support from the respondents.

Here, in full, is the "mixed scenario":

> This future would envision continuity with the current practice. Catholic institutional ministries will be marked by close association with of-

ficial Church bodies but perform public functions in a pluralistic society. They would live with the ambiguities arising from having a rootedness in both the secular and the sacred and would continue to live with considerable tension arising from different and sometimes conflicting expectancies on the part of the various stakeholders.[4]

Note well: This is, and was well advertised in the questionnaire as, the "mixed scenario" for *Catholic institutional ministries*. We can better understand this mixture by considering the rejected "sectarian scenario": "Only those activities would be known as Catholic institutional ministries which would be marked by Church juridical control, an evangelical culture, a sacramental character and dependence on Church support."[5] Granted, this is hard to entirely affirm. (Question: Was it designed to be an unacceptable choice?) The most obvious sense of "Church support" is, I think, a financial contribution that no one supposes is going to be forthcoming. "Juridical control" is also ambiguous; does it mean ownership by the Ordinary? By a majority of religious on the Board of Trustees? Who knows? But "sectarian" most obviously means fidelity to the Magisterium, and that sectarian so rendered is more Catholic than the "mixed" scenario is undeniable. Did the bishops (at least) prefer it?

Clearly not. The three-quarter approval rating was not broken down by category of respondent. The editors did not literally say how many of 151 episcopal respondents thought the "mixed" scenario should prevail. But the Fordham publication reports that on these questions, there "was no discernible difference among respondents by reason of their particular status."[6] Thus, only about 20 (of 151) Bishops thought the sectarian scenario should prevail; roughly 120 thought the mixed scenario "should."

Fordham held a follow-up conference in April, 1991, on Catholic institutional ministries. The speakers included the President of Fordham, the President of the Catholic Health Association, the Executive Director of Catholic Charities, USA, and Joseph Cardinal Bernardin. Theirs was the task of commenting on the survey results. Most interestingly, Cardinal Bernardin "fully agree[d]" with the "mixed" scenario.[7] He elaborated that scenario by using the imagery of "tectonic plates" – sectarian and secular –

---

4 *Fordham* at 36.
5 *Id.* at 35.
6 *Id.* at 75.
7 *Id.* at 75.

in "tension with one another," and opined that "shifts in the plates cause tremors which create anxiety and are, at times, seen as threats."[8]

The conference papers as a group seem to hold that the "mixed model" is about what *Gaudium et Spes* requires: Nothing human is foreign to the Church. The Council, according to Cardinal Bernardin, invited Catholics to "dialogue" with the world. He said that Catholic educators, health care personnel, and social service providers work along the fault line of this dialogue. "[T]hey are in a privileged position to learn from the world and to share that knowledge and insight with the rest of the community of faith. At the same time, they have the opportunity, and the responsibility, to speak the truth in love and to share the values of our Catholic tradition with others."[9] But theirs was not, according to Cardinal Bernardin, an entirely enviable lot. He likened the daily experience of these administrators to an encounter with "ambiguity, chaos, mess."[10]

I should add that Cardinal Bernardin stated that there is, in theory, a point at which Catholic identity calls a halt to dialogue. Bend, but do not break. My question is: How would one know when that point is reached? In the "mixed" scenario, Catholic identity has no bottom; it results from interaction of two principles – "sectarian" and "secular" – neither of which, itself, is thought to be sound. In this construal, Catholic identity rests on no irreducible content of actions. An institution could, in principle, do anything and still be Catholic.

"Catholic identity," on at least this look at the survey in light of the follow-up papers, is a set of virtues: The open, caring, dedicated, tolerant, accepting institution is the Catholic institution. With this gloss, the one I think institutional administrators will favor, the "Church" (i.e. the bishops and the Vatican) articulates "principles" which function not as genuine norms but as ideals, deviation from which is regrettable (perhaps) but hardly grave matter – matter which would raise the question of institutional martyrdom. The institution listens to this exhortation, while, into the other ear, the secular world sings its seductive song, inviting (pressuring) the Catholic hospital, school, and social service agency to further compromise its ideals. The institution is, in other words, between the Garden and the Wilderness, or, as Cardinal Bernardin put it, it has one foot in the Church and the other in the secular world.[11]

---

8 *Id.* at 76.
9 *Id.* at 77.
10 *Id.* at 78.

But institutions do not have feet. They do not have souls. They do not do anything, save by the actions of doctors, professors, deans, counselors, nurses. They have feet. But their feet are attached to one person, and person act as integrated wholes. If there is more to the "mixed" scenario than the call to openness, and dialogue, it is that there is an autonomous morality of Catholic institutions that is very tenuously related to the moral teaching of, say, *Veritatis Splendor*.

Consider Cardinal Bernardin's rejection of the "sectarian" scenario. He said that there simply is no turning back the clock, and that we should not want to.[12] He dismissed the sectarian scenario as (in his words) tied to "isolat[ing] ourselves from the pluralistic society in which we live . . ."[13] (Does Mother Teresa, whose ministry is Catholic in the richest sense of the word, "isolate" herself from Indian society? Perhaps we should ask Msgr. Kelly if, in his view, Cardinal Spellman did not live in the real world?) Cardinal Bernardin would not have us "impose our views"[14] on a pluralistic society. What could it mean to "impose" *our* views on "society"? If "our views" of, say, abortion, are true – if abortion *is* a grave injustice – in what important sense are they "ours"? What *other* basis for society's views – say, the law's view – of abortion is there supposed to be, other than the truth of the matter about abortion? The real question, in any event, is whether Catholic views are to be "imposed upon" Catholic institutional ministries.

The "mixed" scenario supposes that in the Catholic tradition of moral reflection there is – as in most contemporary secular political theories – a sharp divide between the "public" or "social" morality of institutional, especially governmental affairs, and some "private" sectarian morality governing the conduct of individuals. It is a first cousin of Mario Cuomo's "I am personally opposed to abortion, but would not impose my Catholic convictions about abortion on a pluralistic society."

But Catholic moral reflection is not so divided. The same basic norms govern all human choices. There is no separate "public morality" in the Catholic tradition. The backbone of *all* Catholic moral teaching – the exceptionless negative moral norms like those against intentionally killing the innocent – is also the backbone of what even those exercising public authority must do. As Pope John Paul II wrote in *Veritatis Splendor*: "These

11 *Id.* at 76.
12 *Id.* at 77.
13 *Id.* at 77.
14 *Id.*

norms in fact represent the unshakable foundation and solid guarantee of a just and peaceful human coexistence, and hence of genuine democracy, which can come into being and develop only on the basis of the equality of all its members, who possess common rights and duties. *When it is a matter of the moral norms prohibiting intrinsic evil, there are no privileges or exception for anyone*" (*VS* 9; emphasis in original). Those who deny this teaching give up the human person's inviolable rights, without which there can be no decent society.

Someone might object along these lines, as sketched out by Cardinal Bernardin. He would divide the pastoral labor between the Church and the institutional operators. The former would offer "principles"; the latter would "concrete[ly]" apply them. People of good faith, the Cardinal added, may reasonably differ on "concrete application."[15] Maybe, in some senses. Yet it seems to me the relevant term for the former is "norm"; in any event, "principles" include the modes of voluntariness – formal and material cooperation – as well as the norms against giving scandal and requiring clear and consistent witness. Cardinal Bernardin does not mention these considerations, which must be at the heart of every Catholic's moral deliberation. What he does say raises serious questions about whether he appreciates the wide scope and large number of "concrete" moral judgments that a bishop can, and should, authoritatively make about action of Catholic institutions.

Other things being equal,[16] a Catholic institution's material cooperation in immoral activities is much more likely to be scandalous than an individual Catholic's: The institution claims to be distinguished from other institutions performing the same service by being Catholic (in the Fordham study, as Catholic institutional ministries). Its acts will reasonably be taken by non-Catholics and Catholics alike as the Church's own acts. Since institutional acts are expressed in the form of complex, settled policies, contractual arrangements, and ethical directives, they will be presumed deliberate and free, and not the product of ignorance or weakness.

Am I being too glib about the value of Catholic institutions? Am I too quick to discount the great goods served by, say, Catholic hospitals, even one which, in order to get along, refer interested patients to a contraception counseling center, with which the Catholic hospital maintains a contract to handle such referrals? I do not think so. We should carefully consider what it is that distinguished a Catholic hospital, school, or counseling center.

---

15 *Id.* at 84.

16 The next few pages reflect fruitful conversations with Germain Grisez.

That an institution delivers health care or a professional education or a bachelor's degree is not what makes it Catholic, no matter how well it does those things. What distinguishes a Catholic institution in its provision of some service or good in ways that witness to the faith. Thus, health care as such, even if delivered by dedicated persons in accord with sound professional norms, is not an "apostolate." It is not an institutional "ministry." Catholics may commit themselves to health care as an apostolate – in which case they commit themselves to providing health care without compromising the faith. A Catholic institution's cooperation in wrongdoing inevitably undermines it s capacity to provide credible witness, and thus makes it ineligible to serve as a medium of evangelization. Indeed, the question of "Catholic identity" probably arises only in times of crisis: How much is *enough* so that we can continue to call ourselves Catholic? That is, "Catholic identity" is likely to emerge as a distinct and important question after it is too late to preserve it, short of dramatic measures. Institutions are hardly prone to dramatic overhauls.

I suspect that many dedicated people in Catholic hospitals and universities would disagree with me. They might be struggling to retain what, until very recently, were basic professional standards. They just want to be doctors, like Marcus Welby, or to be lawyers like Atticus Finch – dedicated people of integrity. These folks are, perhaps heroically, resisting the dehumanizing pressures exerted by market forces, increasing specialization, technological dominance. For dedicated Catholic educators, one's plate may be full just trying to provide a simple liberal education, to acquaint the average student with the rudiments of the Western tradition.

I would grant for discussion purposes that Catholic institutions might be better than most of their secular counterparts by these standards. But that is not enough to constitute "Catholic identity"; indeed, on the terms of this counterargument, "Catholic identity" would be what until recently was the *secular* standard of good practice.

I submit that any sound approach to Catholic institutions and the new evangelization must focus on what the Fordham respondents studiously neglect and what their rhetoric obscures: what any clear-headed and conscientious Catholic may do, and must not do. As the Holy Father said in *Veritatis Splendor*: "No one can escape from the fundamental question: *What must I do? How do I distinguish good from evil?*" (*VS* 2, emphasis in original). You may run from these questions, but you cannot hide from them, even in Catholic institutions.

Focusing on what to *do* will take us deep into the heart of the "renewal" of Catholic institutions and the new evangelization. It will, however, result in the "renewal" of precious few institutions; It will in all likelihood lead to the extinction of the vast majority of them. Catholic institutions are very likely to face in the next few years choices which entail, for faithful Catholic actors, institutional martyrdom. The "scenarios," if you like, boil down to these two: Genuinely renew, and thus witness to the truth for as long as one can do so, accepting that institutional martyrdom is likely to be in store. The alternative is to be as Catholic as possible in this mixed-up world, but *be*, most of all. Better a Catholic presence, if a muted one, than none at all. This scenario, I am convinced, cannot be chosen, however, for it will lead people into mortal sin. Let me explain.

It is very likely that clear-headed and conscientious Catholics will soon (if they do not already) find it morally impossible to sustain Catholic hospitals. They will have to accept the martyrdom of these institutions. Many Catholic health care professionals may well find it impossible to work in their fields at all. Market forces, national health care legislation, and demands by patients may contribute to the Catholic gynecologist's conclusion that he cannot avoid all formal and unfair material complicity in contraception. If so, the Catholic gynecologist has no real choice but to cease ordinary practice. He may then concentrate on research into NFP, on training engaged and married couples in its upright, effective use, in caring for homeless pregnant women and delivering their babies, on medical mission (if consistent with his other responsibilities in life, and if the United Nations does not succeed in making the practice of medicine all over the globe the same moral minefield it is in the United States). No doubt this faithfulness to the moral truth will be costly; teaching NFP will be much less remunerative and prestigious than working in a major metropolitan medical center.

Public authority has the wherewithal and, it is more and more apparent, the will to make most Catholic institutions extinct. How so? Catholic Social Services is in the adoption business, which means that it is part of the process by which the legal relation of father, mother, child is established and protected. Put simply, you are not adopted until the state says you are. Any informal (i.e. extralegal, underground) adoption placement might work for a while. But it would always be open to disruption by natural parents (whose rights were never legally terminated), to scrutiny by medical personnel who would question any claimed authority to consent to a minor's medical treatment where the consenting adult has no legally recognized relationship to the minor. Without valid consent, the medics will not treat. For without valid consent, their "treatment" is a battery. So, one continues in the adoption business on conditions set by the state.

Are we so far from the date when every adoption agency will have to agree to place children in "families" regardless of the "parents" sexual orientation? That such a couple simply cannot be married – true as it is – will be dismissed as a "sectarian" viewpoint to be entertained privately, with no warrant in the public square. (Question: Does Cardinal Bernardin's Fordham talk unwittingly contribute to this dismissal?) So, too, will protests that the parents are unsuitable moral exemplars. The way things are going, one will be a fighter pilot, the other an Episcopal priest. Both will be women. When this day comes (as it will, I think, within a decade) the local ordinary will have to decide whether any Catholic institutional ministry can place a child with unrepentant homosexual parents. If not, CSS is out of the adoption business.

Catholic colleges and universities possess greater survival potential. The law's grip on colleges is looser than it is on other institutions, looser even than its grip on Catholic primary and secondary schools, which must be certified by public authorities as qualified to satisfy the compulsory school attendance laws. But even small Catholic colleges have to have faculties, and the autonomy necessary to staff such places with, as *Ex corde Ecclesiae* requires, a predominant number of faithful Catholics, will (I think) be increasingly hard to come by.

It is true that federal employment discrimination laws which prohibit discrimination in hiring, compensation and other terms and conditions of employment, contain certain exemptions for religious schools.[17] But those exemptions are often misunderstood to be much more liberal – in the sense of granting autonomy – than they really are. Since it is likely that sexual orientation will soon be added to the list of forbidden grounds for discrimination, that the exemption allows discrimination on grounds only of the employ*ee*'s religion[18] – not on all grounds suggested by the employ*er*'s religion – becomes all important.

Imagine this scenario: A small Catholic college in the near future expresses an interest in hiring a freshly minted Ph.D. in theology from, say, Notre Dame. The courtship goes well, but once the candidate reveals that he

---

17 Commonly referred to as Title VII [of the Civil Rights Act of 1964, as amended]; the proper citation is 42 U.S.C. §2000, et seq.
18 See U.S.C. §2000 c–1(a), and §2000 e–2(e)(2).

is gay, the process is ended. Clearly, that is why the Catholic college loses interest. The person eventually hired possesses inferior academic credentials. The disappointed gay candidate sues, alleging a Title VII violation. The Catholic college can hardly deny – because it is the case – that if the candidate were not gay he would have been hired. But, the plaintiff insists, he *is* Catholic. To prevail on the available exemption (that is, to avoid having to hire the candidate) the college's attorneys will have to show that being gay is incompatible with being a faithful Roman Catholic. Think of all the "expert" witnesses that the plaintiff could line up today for the negative of that proposition!

Consider another case. Substitute "divorced and remarried" for "gay" in the above example. How many such persons are Eucharistic ministers? Teach in parish grade schools? Serve on the faculties of universities, the Catholicity of which no ordinary has questioned?

It is true that even if legislation and other government action would force such choices upon Catholic institutions, these schemes may be stymied – and Catholic institutions protected – by constitutional guarantees of freedom of religion. There is reason to think from the already decided cases that some security for Catholic institutions may be reasonably expected. But my considered opinion is that, on the whole, constitutional guarantees will not long postpone the day of reckoning. The constitutional doctrines are more unsound than sound; in any event, they are largely verbal formulae through which judges' presuppositions about religion, public life, and human flourishing pass unimpeded. Those presuppositions are and will continue to be hostile to Catholicism. They are especially hostile to "autonomy" for Catholic institutions which, as the judge is liable to see it, are governed not by reason but rooted in dogma, and which do grave harm to persons, notably including gay couples or women seeking "reproductive health." Simply put, the judiciary of the near future will make law out of prepossessions very similar to those ascendant at the Cairo Conference, on the New York Times editorial board, and in the U.S. Surgeon General's office. And, if I am only mostly right about this – if I am only a mediocre prophet – them my main point is secured. Catholic institutions will soon be facing the two choices I offered a moment ago.

I suppose a final objection is that I am being too scrupulous, that in light of the great good done by Catholic hospitals or by CSS, toleration of some evil is both inevitable and acceptable. My response is that, if by "toleration" is meant only material cooperation that is not scandalous or otherwise immoral, I agree: To insist on a purity of witness that does not tolerate that kind of evil *is* too scrupulous. That is not what I am talking about. I am talking about immoral choices and scandal. I fear that the dedication to Catholic institutions as such has wrought a muddling of the distinction between genuine toleration and immoral complicity. The muddling cannot be tolerated. It is dangerous.

Why? False institutional witness about one moral truth (say, that contraception is always wrong) can no more be "tolerated" in the service of a greater good, than mortal sins in one area of a Catholic's life (say, in the marital bedroom) are "tolerable" because compensated for by a lot of good works at, say, the office. The false witness is intolerable for precisely *that* reason: It will lead persons into immoral choices concerning grave matters, and for those who do so reflectively and freely, into mortal sin, and the loss of eternal happiness.

31.
Church Tradition and the Catholic University (1995)
Rev. Robert Sokolowski

There are a number of things that are obviously required for a Catholic university to remain and to flourish as a Catholic institution. It must have a sufficient number of faculty and students who share the Catholic faith and an even greater number who are dedicated to the university's mission; it must implement its mission in its curriculum and public activities; it must be attentive to the spiritual welfare of its students, faculty, and staff; and its administrators must be devoted to its Catholic identity. These requirements, which are mentioned in Pope John Paul II's Apostolic Constitution on universities *Ex Corde Ecclesiae*, are well recognized and have been discussed in other talks at this meeting of the Fellowship of Catholic Scholars. I wish to make two other points concerning the identity of Catholic universities, one dealing with the internal workings of the university and one dealing with the Church. I think that both these issues are important for the current controversy about how Catholic universities can maintain their heritage and avoid becoming simply secular institutions, as many of the Protestant universities and colleges in our country have become.

I.

My first point, touching on the internal structure of the university, is somewhat practical and empirical. It deals with the politics and the sociology of the faculty, with the way faculty members work out issues of university governance and policy, and also with the influence that some faculty members have on others.

My thesis is that those faculty members who teach theology and the disciplines that are closely related to theology have a particularly strategic role to play in working out a successful harmony between the university and the Church and between reason and faith. In particular, they have an important and specific role to play in maintaining the Catholic character of a university. Their role consists in showing to the rest of the faculty how the belief and the authoritative teachings of the Church can have a place within the academic world. These faculty members are in a position to show other scholars that the Church and its authoritative teaching can be a source of truth, one that can be recognized and reflected upon in a scholarly way. To show this in theory and in practice is to get at the core of the identity of a Catholic university.

For a Catholic university to be successful as Catholic, the faculty at large must be enthusiastic about the contributions their work can make to the intellectual cultivation of Christian religious belief. They have to see this contribution as a good, something to which they can dedicate their energies. They also have to see the cultivation of the Catholic intellectual heritage as compatible with their scholarly disciplines and scholarly activities; that is, they must be able to see how their specifically intellectual work can contribute to the Christian heritage, and also how their academic work can be inspired by Christian faith and nourished by it. As professionals, they have to see that the two ventures of being academics and being involved in a Catholic enterprise are not only compatible but mutually reinforcing. The opinion that faith and reason can help one another must be a widespread conviction among the faculty if a university is to remain Catholic.

But there is a problem in making such an opinion widely accepted in a contemporary university. The secular sciences and academic fields as they are now constituted claim to be independent of any authority external to their disciplines. They claim that their ways of thinking begin within each discipline itself, with principles, methods, and sources of that discipline, independent of any authority outside it. This claim rests on a conviction concerning the nature of human reason: Reason is seen as self-authorizing and autonomous, as generating its own principles and not accepting anything on authority, as setting itself up as the beginning and the judge of thinking. In this perspective, accepting things on faith has a tinge of gullibility and uncritical submission, of what Kant called heteronomy, which he saw as the deepest betrayal of reason.

Very many people in academic life, very many faculty and students, spontaneously accept this Enlightenment understanding of reason and the university. This understanding is behind the concept of academic freedom demanded in the university and it is embodied in most of the slogans of academic life. Such an understanding of reason, academic freedom, and authority is implied in the commonplaces, the *topoi*, the premises that can be taken for granted in public speeches and public discussions about academic matters. For most academics, reason and its freedom seem to be at odds with authority and with the acceptance of authority. The teaching authority of the Church, therefore, is looked on with a mixture of suspicion and anxiety when it claims to be a factor internal to the academic discipline of theology.

In Catholic institutions the theologians stand at a crucial point in this apparent conflict between reason and faith. In this regard, what the theologians do is of great importance politically and socially within the university. If they say that their own academic discipline has as its object the living belief and tradition of Christianity as interpreted by the teaching Church, they can play an especially important role in showing that reason and faith are compatible; they can play an important role in helping other faculty members to see this compatibility. They can not only argue for but also illustrate a more adequate understanding of the relationship between scholarly reason and the authority that preserves the truth for us.

No one else can do this in the way that the theologians can. If people in some other discipline, such as history or politics or philosophy, try to argue for the compatibility between Church teaching and reason, it will seem that they are trying to impose a constraint on someone else, on the theologians. The actual influence of these other scholars will be weaker no matter how good their arguments may be; their influence will be weaker rhetorically and dialectically because of who they are, because they are not the ones most affected by the point they are making. However, when the theologians make this point, their word has greater weight, because they are regarded as the experts in this matter and because the issue of authority affects them most of all.

If, on the other hand, the theologians try to maintain the more rationalistic or Enlightenment notion of academic freedom, the faculty at large will tend to believe and support them and will tend to see conflicts between academic reason and ecclesiastical authority. This is in fact how the dynamics of faculty politics works.

Looking at the matter rather formally, teachers of theology and their related disciplines can follow two different paths in respect to Church authority and academic inquiry:

1. They can recognize the teaching Church as an authoritative source

within the discipline of theology. If they do so, they will greatly help the rest of the faculty see the possibility of integrating their scholarly, intellectual efforts with the faith of the Church.

2. They can accept the rationalist understanding of science and academic freedom and try to apply it to their own discipline of theology. They may see the authority of the Church as external to their discipline, and in times of controversy they may call upon the faculty to help them protect their theology from such "outside" influences. Given the widespread acceptance of the Enlightenment understanding of academic freedom, very many if not most of the faculty will tend to support them. To put it concretely, if the teachers of theology call out, "We are under assault; come and help us in our academic distress," the faculty will generally respond, "We must help the beleaguered theologians."

The theological faculty can move even farther in this direction. They may warn the rest of the faculty that the teaching Church will interfere not only in theology but in other disciplines as well. This is a common rhetorical device, often used in the head of controversies dealing with academic freedom. The teachers of theology and its related fields will try to marshal faculty support by frightening the rest of the faculty into supporting them. Here, the claim will be, "If this Church intervention comes to pass, you too will be vulnerable," and the faculty will tend to reply, "We must help them, for we are in danger ourselves."

Obviously, if the second of these paths is followed, the university will come to a standstill in its development of the Catholic intellectual life. Over time, its identity as a Catholic institution will be diluted. The school's identity will be weakened at its academic core.

The first path, on the other hand, the one that acknowledges the respective authorities of both the scholars and the Magisterium, will be productive and illuminating. It will promote theological development and will serve the Church. It will, furthermore, also make an important contribution to academic life generally, even outside the domain of religious studies. It will do so by locating academic intelligence and research within a wider human context. It will show that truth is achievable outside the academy and its specialized scientific disciplines, and it will show by example how academic thinking can respect the intelligence of cultural and moral traditions, even while making their own contribution to them. The example of theological thinking can thus help bring about a better integration of the specialized disciplines, even the natural sciences, into the wider realm of human life.

Thus, the proper integration of academic and religious truth can play a strategic role in contemporary culture, and the teachers of theology are at a pivotal position in this issue. They can help overcome the Enlightenment prejudice, which is itself now under severe attack by the irrationality of deconstruction. A proper understanding of faith and reason will not only help preserve the Catholic identity of colleges and universities, but also provide a better resolution for the crisis in which the humanities and sciences now find themselves.

II.

I now come to my second major point, which deals not with academic matters directly but with the Church and its teaching and practice. I submit that in current controversies about the university and the magisterium, the Church has put itself and its own authority at a disadvantage because of the comprehensive revision of the liturgy that was carried out after the Second Vatican Council. The impression was made, even though it may not have been intended, that the Church was distancing itself from its inherited liturgy, and this impression has had an important impact on the relationship between the academic scholar and the teaching Church.

In making the following remarks I will be speaking about the psychological and social impressions that have been made in the past twenty-five years. I am not saying that the Church had no right to change the liturgy, nor that the new order of the liturgy is illegitimate in any way, nor even that the Church should not have changed its liturgy. I am saying that the way the academic world looks at Church authority has been influenced by changes in the Church's liturgy.

Let us recall that the liturgy is truly the one thing needful in the life of the Church. The liturgy is not a mere accessory to the Church's work; it is the point of contact between the believer and God, the place where the Church lives its life to the highest degree. It is the moment when the Church is most itself. The liturgy is not just an instrument in the life of the Church; it is the life of the Church fully and sacramentally expressed.

Some twenty-five years ago, the Church restructured its liturgy in a way that it had never done before. The manner in which the liturgical changes were made was unprecedented. It reflected a specifically modern impulse to make things new. We must recognize how distinctive this action was. Nevertheless, the restructuring is now a matter of fact and history, a choice that was made in the life of the Church. No one can cancel what has been done, but the urgent question does arise: Where do we go from here?

What trajectory do we follow? As we move on, do we recede still farther from the old rite of the liturgy, or do we attempt to emphasize, visibly and palpably, the continuity between the old rite and the new? We stand at an important intersection in the life of the Church, and our next steps will be of critical significance. Furthermore, as we take these next steps, whose authority will guide us?

To develop this issue, and to show its relevance to the Catholic university, I wish to examine the nature of Church authority.

The authority of a bishop is that of a shepherd. His pastoral rule is based not primarily on laws or the will of the people but on the tradition that has been inherited. It is not just that the tradition provides the Church with the episcopal office; rather, the inherited tradition of liturgy and doctrine is what the bishop is supposed to preserve. The shepherd is given custody of something that he must protect and hand on. The pastor rules the flock, but he does so as the custodian of the liturgical and doctrinal life of the Church, which provides the measure for his rule. This liturgical and doctrinal life has developed in an organic way, and the authority of the bishop is there to preserve the living whole that he has inherited.

There are two passages in St. Paul's first letter to the Corinthians that bring out this dependence of pastoral authority on tradition. In chapter 15 St. Paul teaches the Corinthians about the resurrection of Christ, and he introduces this exercise of his teaching office by saying, "I handed on to you as of first importance what I also received" (I Cor 15:3). In chapter 11 he makes authoritative decisions about the eucharistic liturgy and he introduces these remarks by saying, "I received from the Lord what I also handed on to you" (I Cor 11:23). St. Paul's pastoral authority is based on the need to preserve and transmit what was handed on to him.

Likewise, the strength of episcopal and papal authority rests on the duty to preserve and transmit the tradition the Church has received. The tradition is what the bishops and pope appeal to when they exercise their authority; they can decide certain things and can say and do certain things because they are handing on what they have received. Their authority is both measured and justified by the inherited tradition. This dependence of their authority on what they are to preserve is true not only theologically but also psychologically, sociologically, and rhetorically. People more easily recognize the authority of the pastor when he appeals to the tradition he has to maintain. The inherited tradition is the staff on which pastoral authority rests.

The changes introduced into the liturgy after the Second Vatican Council were an attempt to protect, preserve, nourish, and apply the liturgical life of the Church for the good of souls. But the changes were very comprehensive and they were done very suddenly. They were not incremental. They were beneficial in many ways, but they also caused some serious difficulties, which ought to be faced.

One difficulty was that some people got the impression that the hierarchy claimed the authority to redesign the liturgy, not just to hand on what they received. Instead of being seen as preserving and cultivating what was received, the Church was perceived by some to be reconstructing it. The shepherding authority of the hierarchy seemed to be changed into another kind of authority, that of the executive. Indeed, subsequent demands that Church officials change the inherited discipline of clerical celibacy and the restriction of ordination to men show that many people think that the pope and the bishops can make changes "at the stroke of a pen." If the Church could change the liturgy as much as it did, why can it not change many other things as well? The liturgy seemed to become something that is *established* primarily by law and decree, rather than being a living tradition of the whole Church that is *protected* by laws and decrees.

At first glance, one might suppose that such a shift in the meaning of authority, from shepherd to executive, would serve to make the hierarchy more powerful. The bishops and pope seem charged not only to shepherd what they receive, but also to reconfigure it according to what they deem necessary and appropriate. The liturgy and the life of the Church seem to be even more under their control. But in fact, this apparent shift in the meaning of authority has weakened the authority of the bishops, and for two different reasons.

First, the authority of the hierarchy became subordinate to that of the historians and experts of the liturgy. When the bishops are seen as shepherds, when the point of episcopal authority is to preserve what has been inherited, the measure of what is to be done is ready at hand and visible to everyone: it is the liturgy that had evolved organically over time as a result of countless decisions and adaptations made by countless individuals, under the guidance of the Holy Spirit. You do not need to be an expert to know what it is: It is there in front of everybody in the way the Church lives its life. The Church must still distinguish between essentials and accidentals, and must apply the tradition to current situations, but what is to be preserved is there for everyone to see.

However, if a major redesign of the liturgy is to take place, what can serve as the measure for the change? You cannot use what you have in front of you as a guide; by definition, the thing you have in front of you needs to be reconfigured. You have to get to something more essential. Given the historicist temper of our day, the logical place to look for a norm and measure became the liturgy as it was supposed to be at the beginning, in the early Church. This earliest form will be the measure for what we ought to have now. And who knows what this earliest form was like? Not the hierarchy, certainly, but the experts, the scholars who know the languages and the sources relevant to this matter and who form hypotheses about it. Because of the project of liturgical revision, the hierarchy seems forced to yield some of its authority to those who are expert in the liturgy and its history. The pastoral authority to preserve what has been received is given over in part to those who know the hidden original form of what has been received.

In fact, in the Church controversies of the past two decades, the popular image of the biblical scholar or the liturgical historian has become the image of the person who gets at the truth of the liturgy, in contrast with the "prejudices" of those who adhere to the received tradition. To illustrate this, I would like to appeal to an offhand remark made by Martin Stannard in his biography of Evelyn Waugh. Waugh, as everyone knows, was devoted to the old liturgy and tried to prevent major changes in it. His biographer does not sympathize with his stand, at one point even calling it "logically absurd" (*Evelyn Waugh, The Later Years 1939–1966* [New York: W. W. Norton, 1992], p. 463). During his exposition and critique of Waugh's ideas on the liturgy, Stannard makes the following remark: "Scholars had already scraped away the encrustations of ceremony which had grown slowly since the second century" (p. 462).

This brief remark contains a whole philosophy. Since the second century, for nineteen hundred years, we have had encrustation of ceremony, not a living liturgy, not an organic tradition. Since the second century alien elements had intruded on and distorted the life of the Church. Furthermore, it is the scholars who can "scrape away the encrustations" and get at the pristine form, the original, the "true" liturgy that should be restored. This casual remark is an excellent example of the challenge to the authority of the shepherd of tradition. It implies that what we have inherited, rather than being what we must hand on, first needs to be redrafted in view of what existed before encrustations began to grow. This, then, is one way in which the authority of the teaching Church has been weakened because of the changes that have been introduced in the liturgy.

The second way in which it has been weakened comes from another direction. If the historical and scholarly challenge to the Church comes from those who are experts about the past, another kind of challenge comes from those who claim to be experts about the present. These are the pressure groups in the Church, those who claim to know what the present age demands, who say they know what changes are appropriate for modern man. Right now the most conspicuous claims are being made on behalf of feminist groups, but other voices have been raised on behalf of the young, the intellectuals, various social classes or ethnic groups, people who have different moral opinions, or modern forms of political life. Once again, the hierarchy becomes vulnerable to such claims once it decides to restructure the liturgy, because groups such as these claim to know how the liturgy ought to be adapted to the modern world.

Thus, the authority of the shepherd is dealt a two-pronged attack when its custodial character is diluted and it is less directly measured by what it has received. Experts about the past claim special knowledge of what is inherited, while the experts about the present claim special knowledge of what is needed here and now. Such challenges arise because of the thoroughgoing revision of the Church's liturgical life.

To bring this problem into sharper focus, I suggest that we consider an analogous situation and look at the liturgy of the Orthodox Church in Russia. That church is now free, after having suffered seventy years of severe oppression. The KGB did horrible things to the Russian church, but whatever it did to that Church, it never changed the liturgy. The liturgy that was preserved under persecution and that is now openly practiced is simply the inherited liturgy. It has not been updated and its encrustations have not been scraped away. Would this Orthodox liturgy speak more effectively to modern man, in Russia or anywhere else, if it had been updated? What impact would it now have if it had been redesigned during the past twenty-five years? Should we in the West encourage the Russian church, now that it is free, to modernize its liturgy as quickly as it can?

Again, I am not saying that the Roman liturgy should not have been modified, nor do I wish to deny the benefits of the new rite, but I am asking where we should go from here. I am also saying that whatever is done next will have an extremely important effect on the authority of the Church. The next steps will be crucial, because if the Church revises its liturgy even more to suit the temper of the times, it will ratify the risky aspects of the choice it made some twenty-five years ago. It is of great importance for the Church to heal the apparent breach between the old liturgy and the new, and do everything possible to make it clear to everyone that its *Novus Ordo* is not something radically different from what it has received. In this regard, it does seem to have been unwise for the Church to have prohibited the old rite of the liturgy for about fifteen years after the new rite was introduced.

What do these remarks about the liturgy have to do with academic freedom and the nature of the Catholic university? I think they help explain why many academic scholars think that their work is parallel with rather than subordinated to the pastoral and teaching authority of the Church. Scholarly work and expertise seem to have been given an authority to determine the new shape of the liturgy and, by implication, the teaching of the Church. Scholars are the experts in the original forms of liturgy and doctrine, and if revisions are going to take place, it is the scholars who seem to be in the best position to determine what the changes should be. Church authority is displaced and the Church inevitably becomes more vulnerable to pressure groups and their demands. Even the papacy is presented as though it were something of an intruder on the domain of liturgy and theology, and the pope is described not as an authoritative figure but as a man who is trying to impose his personal conservative viewpoint.

Our present situation would be very different if the authority of the Church were seen to be primarily the authority to preserve and hand on the visible tradition that has been inherited. If the bishops seem to be under siege in regard to liturgical practice and Church teaching, it is because the basis and measure for their authority to rule, the inherited tradition that they are to hand on, seems to have been yielded by them and taken by others. The tangible and evident authority based on tradition gives way to an authority based on reason and academic expertise, and the culture of the Enlightenment makes great inroads into the life of the Church.

III.

I have finished the two major points I wanted to make in my talk, one dealing with the faculty of a Catholic university and the other dealing with the authority of the teaching Church. In closing, I wish to make two distinctions.

The first is taken from a book by Yves Simon entitled, *A General The-*

ory of Authority (Notre Dame: University of Notre Dame Press, 1962). In that work Simon makes a distinction that is of great help in discussions about academic freedom. Some people claim that we ought to submit Church doctrine and practice to the give and take of academic debate, to controversy and refutation, to the marketplace of ideas. Such free inquiry works well in the sciences. If Church doctrines are true, will they not be vindicated in such debates? Will the truth not be able to take care of itself? In response to such a claim, Simon would say that the marketplace of ideas may serve very well to determine the truth of what he calls "positive" statements, claims that are empirical and easy to communicate, the kind that Enrico Fermi called "sharp statements." But there are other kinds of assertions, which Simon calls "transcendent" statements, and these cannot be expected to survive in such give-and-take. Such statements are not easy to communicate and to decide. They cannot take care of themselves in the marketplace of ideas; they need an authoritative institution to protect them. I think that Simon's distinction between positive and transcendent statements show why the Church cannot be a debating society or an academy but must be the place where the deepest truths about God, the world, and the human condition are authoritatively preserved.

Furthermore, the fact that Church teachings and other transcendent truths are not decidable in the marketplace of ideas does not make them into a second-best sort of truth; they are not less rigorous and less verifiable than the truths reached by academic scholarship and experiment; rather, they are deeper truths and require a different kind of communication and verification. They involve the engagement of an entire life and the protection of an authoritative teacher, not just a scholarly method.

A second distinction I wish to bring to mind is that between academic freedom and freedom of speech. These two things are very often confused, even by judges in law courts, let alone commentators in the media. Academic freedom is not simply one form of the right of free speech, but the right of a scholar to be guided by the methods, principles, and sources of his discipline, and to be free of pressures that might force him to say things in his professional work that are not warranted by his discipline. Academic freedom is supported to protect a scholarly discipline, not the right of a citizen to speak freely. In regard to Church teaching, academic freedom is not the right of a scholar to say what he thinks the Church ought to be teaching; rather, it is the right to reflect, in a scholarly way, on what the Church teaches, on the inherited deposit of faith.

Our discussions at this conference have been about preserving the identity of Catholic institutions of higher education. Will these institutions remain Catholic, or will they become secular? There is ample evidence for the danger of secularization, and I would like to comment on what is at stake here.

If this secularizing comes to pass, our current generation will see an enormous alienation of Church resources, the loss to the Church of its institutions of higher education, both small and large, both colleges and universities. This loss would be momentous and would call to mind the losses suffered by the Church during the Reformation in England and the great secularizations in Europe. It would greatly weaken the Church's ability to educate her people and influence contemporary culture. The educational inheritance of the Church in America, the institutions that were built up over the past two centuries by the sacrifices of the laity, religious, and clergy, may well be handed over to the secular culture to be used for its own educational purposes, in the service of its own values. No persecutions will have brought this about; if it does occur, it will have been done freely. It will have happened quickly, within one or two generations, but great historical changes can happen in a short span of time, and such change once done cannot be undone. What had been built up over many generations can be given away in one.

Moreover, this alienation, if it occurs, will have taken place right at the moment when the culture to which our institutions were given was entering into spiritual disarray. We will have been misled by voices that told us that what we as Catholics had achieved was not good enough. We were encouraged to make our colleges and universities into a gift to the nation, right at the moment when what the nation really needed was not our institutions but the education that our institutions were providing. To draw an analogy from the Old Testament, if this donation of our institutions to the secular world should come to pass, it will be like an inverted exodus, an exodus run in reverse. Whereas the Israelites despoiled the Egyptians, escaped from slavery, and entered into freedom, we will have trudged back into Egypt, handed over our institutions, and asked others what we should do with ourselves. None of us knows how God will judge those who allow this to happen, but history certainly will not be kind to them.